CHAMBERS

SUPER-MINI
BOOK OF
FACTS

CHAMBERS

SUPER-MINI BOOK OF FACTS

edited by
Trevor Anderson

CHAMBERS

CHAMBERS

An imprint of Chambers Harrap Publishers Ltd
7 Hopetoun Crescent
Edinburgh EH7 4AY

© Chambers Harrap Publishers Ltd 1999, 2001

This edition first published Chambers 1999
New edition 2001

British Library Cataloguing in Publication Data for this book
is available from the British Library

ISBN 0-550-13004-7

The editor would like to thank Melanie Parry and Helen Bleck
for their contributions to this book.

This book contains information assembled for Chambers *Book
of Facts* (1998), extensively revised and updated.

Typeset in Great Britain by Chambers Harrap Publishers Ltd
Printed and bound in Malaysia by SNP SPrint (M) Sdn Bhd

CONTENTS

History

—————————— Thought and Belief ——————————

ALPHABETICAL CONTENTS

ABBREVIATIONS

AD	Anno Domini	in	inch(es)
admin	administration	Ital	Italian
BC	Before Christ	Jap	Japanese
c	century	K	Kelvin
c.	circa	kg	kilogram(s)
C	Celsius (Centigrade)	kJ	kilojoules
		l	litre(s)
Chin	Chinese	L	Lake
CIS	Commonwealth of Independent States	Lat	Latin
		lb	pound(s)
		m	metre(s)
cm	centimetre(s)	mi	mile(s)
Co	County	mm	millimetre(s)
cont.	continued	Mt	Mount(ain)
cu	cubic	Mts	Mountains
cwt	hundredweight	N	north(ern)
e	estimate	no.	number
E	east(ern)	oz	ounce(s)
eg	for example	p(p)	page(s)
Eng	English	pop	population
F	Fahrenheit	pt	pint(s)
fl oz	fluid ounce(s)	R	River
fl	flourished (floruit)	Russ	Russian
		S	south(ern)
Fr	French	sec	second(s)
ft	foot (feet)	Span	Spanish
g	gram(s)	sq	square
gal	gallons	St	Saint
Ger	German	Sta	Santa
Gr	Greek	Ste	Sainte
h	hour(s)	Swed	Swedish
ha	hectare(s)	TV	television
Hung	Hungarian	UT	Unified Team
I(s)	Island(s)	W	west(ern)
ie	that is (id est)	yd	yard(s)

SPACE

Planetary data

Planet	Distance from Sun (million km) Maximum	Minimum	Planet year	Planet day (equatorial)	Diameter (equatorial) km
Mercury	69.4	46.8	88 d	58 d 16 h	4 878
Venus	109.0	107.6	224.7 d	243 d	12 104
Earth	152.6	147.4	365.256 d	23 h 56 m	12 756
Mars	249.2	207.3	687 d	24 h 37 m 23 s	6 794
Jupiter	817.4	741.6	11.86 y	9 h 50 m 30 s	142 800
Saturn	1 512	1 346	29.46 y	10 h 14 m	120 536
Uranus	3 011	2 740	84.01 y	16–28 h[1]	51 118
Neptune	4 543	4 466	164.79 y	18–20 h[1]	49 492
Pluto	7 364	4 461	247.7 y	6 d 9 h	2 300

y: earth years d: earth days h: hours m: minutes s: seconds km: kilometres

[1] Different latitudes rotate at different speeds.

Sun data

Physical characteristics of the Sun

Diameter	1 392 530 km
Volume	1.414×10^{18} km^3
Mass	1.9891×10^{30} kg

Density (water = 1)

Mean density of entire Sun	1.410 g cm^{-3}
Interior (centre of Sun)	150 g cm^{-3}
Surface (photosphere)	10^{-3} g cm^{-3}
Chromosphere	10^{-6} g cm^{-3}
Low corona	1.7×10^{-16} g cm^{-3}

Temperature

Interior (centre)	15 000 000 K
Surface (photosphere)	6 050 K
Sunspot umbra (typical)	4 240 K
Penumbra (typical)	5 680 K
Chromosphere	4 300 to 50 000 K
Corona	800 000 to 5 000 000 K

Rotation (as seen from Earth)

Of solar equator	26.8 days
At solar latitude 30°	28.2 days
At solar latitude 60°	30.8 days
At solar latitude 75°	31.8 days

Chemical composition of photosphere

Element	% weight
Hydrogen	73.46
Helium	24.85
Oxygen	0.77
Carbon	0.29
Iron	0.16
Neon	0.12
Nitrogen	0.09
Silicon	0.07
Magnesium	0.05
Sulphur	0.04
Other	0.10

Solar system

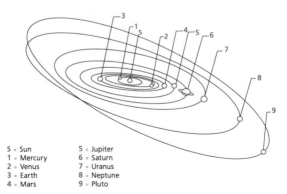

S = Sun	5 = Jupiter
1 = Mercury	6 = Saturn
2 = Venus	7 = Uranus
3 = Earth	8 = Neptune
4 = Mars	9 = Pluto

Total and annular solar eclipses 1991–2020

The eclipse begins in the first country named. In an annular eclipse, part of the Sun remains visible.

Date	Type of eclipse	Visibility path
15 Jan 1991	Annular	S Pacific, New Zealand, S Australia
11 Jul 1991	Total	Mid-Pacific, C and S America
4–5 Jan 1992	Annular	N American coast, Mid-Pacific
30 Jun 1992	Total	S American coast, S Atlantic
10 May 1994	Annular	Mid-Pacific, N America, N Africa
3 Nov 1994	Total	Indian Ocean, S Atlantic, S America, Mid-Pacific
29 Apr 1995	Annular	S Pacific, S America
24 Oct 1995	Total	Middle East, S Asia, S Pacific
9 Mar 1997	Total	C and N Asia, Arctic
26 Feb 1998	Total	Mid-Pacific, C America, N Atlantic
22 Aug 1998	Annular	Indonesia, S Pacific, Indian Ocean
16 Feb 1999	Annular	Indian Ocean, Australia
11 Aug 1999	Total	N Atlantic, N Europe, Middle East, N India
21 Jun 2001	Total	S Atlantic, S Africa, Madagascar
14 Dec 2001	Annular	Pacific, C America
10 Jun 2002	Annular	Indonesia, Pacific, Mexico
4 Dec 2002	Total	S Africa, Indian Ocean, Australia
31 May 2003	Annular	Iceland, Greenland
23 Nov 2003	Total	Antarctic
8 Apr 2005	Annular/Total	Pacific, Panama, Venezuela
3 Oct 2005	Annular	Atlantic, Spain, Libya, Indian Ocean
29 Mar 2006	Total	Atlantic, Libya, Turkey, Russia
22 Sep 2006	Annular	Guyana, Atlantic, Indian Ocean
7 Feb 2008	Annular	Antarctic
1 Aug 2008	Total	Arctic, Siberia, China
26 Jan 2009	Annular	S Atlantic, Indian Ocean, Borneo
22 Jul 2009	Total	India, China, Pacific
15 Jan 2010	Annular	Africa, Indian Ocean, China
11 Jul 2010	Total	Pacific, S Chile
20–21 May 2012	Annular	China, N Pacific, N America
13 Nov 2012	Total	N Australia, Pacific
9–10 May 2013	Annular	Australia, Pacific
3 Nov 2013	Total	Atlantic, C Africa, Ethiopia
20 Mar 2015	Total	N Atlantic, Arctic
9 Mar 2016	Total	Indonesia, Pacific
1 Sep 2016	Annular	Atlantic, Africa, Madagascar, Indian Ocean
26 Feb 2017	Annular	Pacific, S America, Atlantic, Africa
21 Aug 2017	Total	Pacific, N America, Atlantic
2 Jul 2019	Total	Pacific, S America
26 Dec 2019	Annular	Middle East, Sri Lanka, Indonesia, Pacific
21 Jun 2020	Annular	Africa, Middle East, China, Pacific
12 Dec 2020	Total	Pacific, S America, Atlantic

Lunar eclipses 1991–2020

Date	Type of eclipse	Time of mid-eclipse UT[1]	Where visible
21 Dec 1991	Partial	10.34	Pacific, N America (W Coast), Japan, Australia
15 Jun 1992	Partial	04.58	N, C and S America, W Africa
9–10 Dec 1992	Total	23.45	Africa, Europe, Middle East, part of S America
4 Jun 1993	Total	13.02	Pacific, Australia, SE Asia
29 Nov 1993	Total	06.26	N and S America
25 May 1994	Partial	03.32	C and S America, part of N America, W Africa
15 Apr 1995	Partial	12.19	Pacific, Australia, SE Asia
4 Apr 1996	Total	00.11	Africa, SE Europe, S America
27 Sep 1996	Total	02.55	C and S America, part of N America, W Africa
24 Mar 1997	Partial	04.41	C and S America, part of N America, W Africa
16 Sep 1997	Total	18.47	S Africa, E Africa, Australia
28 Jul 1999	Partial	11.34	Pacific, Australia, SE Asia
21 Jan 2000	Total	04.45	N America, S America, SW Europe, W Africa
16 Jul 2000	Total	13.57	Pacific, Australia, SE Asia
9 Jan 2001	Total	20.22	Europe, Asia, Africa
5 Jul 2001	Partial	14.57	Asia, Australia, Pacific
16 May 2003	Total	03.41	Americas, Europe, Africa
9 Nov 2003	Total	01.20	Americas, Europe, Africa, W Asia
4 May 2004	Total	20.32	Europe, Africa, Asia
28 Oct 2004	Total	03.05	Americas, Europe, Africa
17 Oct 2005	Partial	12.05	E Asia, Pacific, N America
7 Sep 2006	Partial	18.53	Australia, Asia, E Africa
3 Mar 2007	Total	23.22	Europe, Asia, Africa
28 Aug 2007	Total	10.39	Australia, Pacific, part of N America
21 Feb 2008	Total	03.27	Americas, Europe, Africa
16 Aug 2008	Partial	21.12	Europe, Africa, W Asia
31 Dec 2009	Partial	19.23	Asia, Africa, Europe
26 Jun 2010	Partial	11.39	Pacific Rim
21 Dec 2010	Total	08.17	N and S America
15 Jun 2011	Total	20.12	Asia, Africa, Europe
10 Dec 2011	Total	14.32	Pacific, Australia, E Asia
4 Jun 2012	Partial	11.03	Pacific, Australasia
25 Apr 2013	Partial	20.09	Asia, Africa, Europe
14 Apr 2014	Total	07.47	N and S America
8 Oct 2014	Total	10.54	Pacific, Australia, W Americas
4 Apr 2015	Partial	12.01	Pacific, Australasia
28 Sep 2015	Total	02.47	Africa, Europe, Americas
7 Aug 2017	Partial	18.21	Asia, Africa, Australia
31 Jan 2018	Total	13.30	Pacific, Australia, Asia
27 Jul 2018	Total	20.22	Asia, Africa, part of Europe
21 Jan 2019	Total	05.12	Americas, part of Europe
16 Jul 2019	Partial	21.31	Asia, Africa, Europe

[1] Universal Time, equivalent to Greenwich Mean Time (GMT).

The lunar 'seas'

Latin name	English name	Latin name	English name
Lacus Mortis	Lake of Death	Mare Serenitatis	Sea of Serenity
Lacus Somniorum	Lake of Dreams	Mare Smythii	Smyth's Sea
Mare Australe	Southern Sea	Mare Spumans	Foaming Sea
Mare Crisium	Sea of Crises	Mare Tranquillitatis	Sea of Tranquility
Mare Fecunditatis	Sea of Fertility	Mare Undarum	Sea of Waves
Mare Frigoris	Sea of Cold	Mare Vaporum	Sea of Vapours
Mare Humboldtianum	Humboldt's Sea	Oceanus Procellarum	Ocean of Storms
Mare Humorum	Sea of Moisture	Palus Epidemiarum	Marsh of Epidemics
Mare Imbrium	Sea of Showers	Palus Nebularum	Marsh of Mists
Mare Ingenii	Sea of Geniuses	Palus Putredinis	Marsh of Decay
Mare Marginis	Marginal Sea	Palus Somnii	Marsh of Sleep
Mare Moscoviense	Moscow Sea	Sinus Aestuum	Bay of Heats
Mare Nectaris	Sea of Nectar	Sinus Iridum	Bay of Rainbows
Mare Nubium	Sea of Clouds	Sinus Medii	Central Bay
Mare Orientale	Eastern Sea	Sinus Roris	Bay of Dew

The constellations

Latin name	English name	Latin name	English name
Andromeda	Andromeda	Coma Berenices	Berenice's Hair
Antlia	Air Pump	Corona Australis	Southern Crown
Apus	Bird of Paradise	Corona Borealis	Northern Crown
Aquarius	Water Bearer	Corvus	Crow
Aquila	Eagle	Crater	Cup
Ara	Altar	Crux	Southern Cross
Aries	Ram	Cygnus	Swan
Auriga	Charioteer	Delphinus	Dolphin
Boötes	Herdsman	Dorado	Swordfish
Caelum	Chisel	Draco	Dragon
Camelopardalis	Giraffe	Equuleus	Little Horse
Cancer	Crab	Eridanus	River Eridanus
Canes Venatici	Hunting Dogs	Fornax	Furnace
Canis Major	Great Dog	Gemini	Twins
Canis Minor	Little Dog	Grus	Crane
Capricornus	Sea Goat	Hercules	Hercules
Carina	Keel	Horologium	Clock
Cassiopeia	Cassiopeia	Hydra	Sea Serpent
Centaurus	Centaur	Hydrus	Water Snake
Cepheus	Cepheus	Indus	Indian
Cetus	Whale	Lacerta	Lizard
Chamaeleon	Chameleon	Leo	Lion
Circinus	Compasses	Leo Minor	Little Lion
Columba	Dove	Lepus	Hare

Latin name	English name	Latin name	English name
Libra	Scales	Pyxis	Mariner's Compass
Lupus	Wolf	Reticulum	Net
Lynx	Lynx	Sagitta	Arrow
Lyra	Harp	Sagittarius	Archer
Mensa	Table	Scorpius	Scorpion
Microscopium	Microscope	Sculptor	Sculptor
Monoceros	Unicorn	Scutum	Shield
Musca	Fly	Serpens	Serpent
Norma	Level	Sextans	Sextant
Octans	Octant	Taurus	Bull
Ophiuchus	Serpent Bearer	Telescopium	Telescope
Orion	Orion	Triangulum	Triangle
Pavo	Peacock	Triangulum Australe	Southern Triangle
Pegasus	Winged Horse	Tucana	Toucan
Perseus	Perseus	Ursa Major	Great Bear
Phoenix	Phoenix	Ursa Minor	Little Bear
Pictor	Easel	Vela	Sails
Pisces	Fishes	Virgo	Virgin
Piscis Austrinus	Southern Fish	Volans	Flying Fish
Puppis	Ship's Stern	Vulpecula	Fox

The 20 brightest stars

The apparent brightness of a star is represented by a number called its magnitude. The larger the number, the fainter the star. The faintest stars visible to the naked eye are slightly fainter than magnitude 6. Only about 6 000 of the billions of stars in the sky are visible to the naked eye.

Star name	Distance (light years)	Apparent magnitude	Absolute magnitude
Sirius A	8.6	-1.46	+1.4
Canopus	98	-0.72	-8.5
Arcturus	36	-0.06	-0.3
Alpha Centauri A	4.3	-0.01	+4.4
Vega	26.5	+0.04	+0.5
Capella	45	+0.05	-0.7
Rigel	900	+0.14	-6.8
Procyon A	11.2	+0.37	+2.6
Betelgeuse	520	+0.41	-5.5
Achernar	118	+0.51	-1.0
Beta Centauri	490	+0.63	-5.1
Altair	16.5	+0.77	+2.2
Aldebaran	68	+0.86	-0.2
Spica	220	+0.91	-3.6
Antares	520	+0.92	-4.5
Pollux	35	+1.16	+0.8

Star name	Distance (light years)	Apparent magnitude	Absolute magnitude
Fomalhaut	22.6	+1.19	+2.0
Deneb	1 500	+1.26	-6.9
Beta Crucis	490	+1.28	-4.6
Alpha Crucis	120	+0.83	-4.0

The 20 nearest stars

Star name	Distance (light years)	Apparent magnitude	Absolute magnitude
Proxima Centauri	4.3	+11.05	+15.5
Alpha Centauri A	4.3	-0.01	+4.4
Alpha Centauri B	4.3	+1.33	+5.7
Barnard's Star	5.9	+9.54	+13.3
Wolf 359	7.6	+13.53	+16.7
Lalande 21185	8.1	+7.50	+10.5
Sirius A	8.6	-1.46	+1.4
Sirius B	8.6	+8.68	+11.6
Luyten 726-8A	8.9	+12.45	+15.3
UV 726-8B	8.9	+12.95	+15.3
Ross 154	9.4	+10.60	+13.3
Ross 248	10.3	+12.29	+14.8
Epsilon Eridani	10.8	+3.73	+6.1
Ross 128	10.8	+11.10	+13.5
Luyten 789-6	10.8	+12.18	+14.6
61 Cygni A	11.1	+5.22	+7.6
61 Cygni B	11.1	+6.03	+8.4
Epsilon Indi	11.2	+4.68	+7.0
Procyon A	11.2	+0.37	+2.7
Procyon B	11.2	+10.70	+13.0

Significant space missions

Mission	Nation/ Agency	Launch date	Event description
Sputnik 1	USSR	4 Oct 57	Earth satellite
Sputnik 2	USSR	3 Nov 57	Dog Laika
Explorer 1	USA	1 Feb 58	Discovered radiation belt (Van Allen)
Luna 1	USSR	2 Jan 59	Escaped Earth gravity
Vanguard 2	USA	17 Feb 59	Earth photo
Luna 2	USSR	12 Sep 59	Lunar impact
Luna 3	USSR	4 Oct 59	Lunar photo (far side)
TIROS 1	USA	1 Apr 60	Weather satellite
Transit 1B	USA	13 Apr 60	Navigation satellite
ECHO 1	USA	12 Aug 60	Communications satellite
Sputnik 5	USSR	19 Aug 60	Two dogs recovered alive

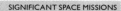

Mission	Nation/ Agency	Launch date	Event description
Vostok 1	USSR	12 Apr 61	Manned orbital flight
Mariner 2	USA	26 Aug 62	Venus flyby
Vostok 6	USSR	16 Jun 63	Woman in orbit
Ranger VII	USA	28 Jul 64	Close-up television pictures of the Moon
Mariner 4	USA	28 Nov 64	Mars flyby pictures
Early Bird	USA	6 Apr 65	Commercial geostationary communications satellite
Venera 3	USSR	16 Nov 65	Venus impact
A-1 Asterix	France	26 Nov 65	French launched satellite
Gemini 7	USA	4 Dec 65	Manned rendezvous
Gemini 6	USA	15 Dec 65	Manned rendezvous
Luna 9	USSR	31 Jan 66	Lunar soft landing
Gemini 8	USA	16 Mar 66	Manned docking
Luna 10	USSR	31 Mar 66	Lunar orbiter
Surveyor 1	USA	30 May 66	US soft landing on Moon
Lunar Orbiter 1	USA	10 Aug 66	US lunar orbiter
Cosmos 186/188	USSR	22–28 Oct 67	Automatic docking
WRESAT	Australia	29 Nov 67	Australian launched satellite
Zond 5	USSR	14 Sep 68	Animals around the Moon
Apollo VIII	USA	21 Dec 68	Manned lunar orbit
Soyuz 4	USSR	14 Jan 69	Transfer of crews
Soyuz 5	USSR	15 Jan 69	Transfer of crews
Apollo XI	USA	16 Jul 69	Manned lunar landing
Oshumi	Japan	11 Feb 70	Japanese launched satellite
Long March	China	24 Apr 70	Chinese launched satellite
Venera 7	USSR	17 Aug 70	Venus soft landing
Luna 16	USSR	12 Sep 70	Unmanned sample return
Luna 17	USSR	10 Nov 70	Unmanned Moon rover
Mars 2	USSR	19 May 71	Mars orbit
Mars 3	USSR	28 May 71	Mars soft landing, no data returned
Mariner 9	USA	30 May 71	Mars orbit
Prospero	UK	28 Oct 71	UK launched satellite
Pioneer 10	USA	3 Mar 72	Jupiter flyby; Crossed Pluto orbit; Escaped solar system
Pioneer 11	USA	6 Apr 73	Jupiter flyby; Saturn flyby
Mariner 10	USA	3 Nov 73	Venus flyby; Three Mercury flybys
Venera 9	USSR	8 Jun 75	Venus orbit
Apollo/Soyuz	USA/USSR	15 Jul 75	Manned international co-operative mission
Viking 1	USA	20 Aug 75	Spacecraft operations on Mars surface
Voyager 2	USA	20 Aug 77	Jupiter flyby; Saturn flyby; Uranus flyby; Neptune flyby
Voyager 1	USA	5 Sep 77	Jupiter flyby; Saturn flyby

Mission	Nation/Agency	Launch date	Event description
ISEE-C	USA	12 Aug 78	Comet intercept
Ariane/CAT	ESA	24 Dec 79	European launcher
Rohini	India	18 Jul 80	Indian launched satellite
STS-1 (Columbia)	USA	12 Apr 81	Space shuttle flight
STS-2 (Columbia)	USA	12 Nov 81	Launch vehicle re-use
SoyuzT9	USSR	27 Jun 83	Construction in space
STS-51A (Discovery)	USA	8 Nov 84	Satellite retrieval
Vega 1	USSR	15 Dec 84	Halley flyby
Giotto	ESA	2 Jul 85	Close-up of comet Halley
SoyuzT15	USSR	13 Mar 86	Ferry between space stations
SoyuzTM4/6	USSR	21 Dec 87	Year-long flight
Phobos 2	USSR	12 Jan 88	Phobos rendezvous
Buran	USSR	15 Nov 88	Unmanned space shuttle
Muses-A	Japan	24 Jan 90	Moon orbiter
HST	USA/ESA	24 Apr 90	Large space telescope
SoyuzTM11	USSR	2 Dec 90	Paying passenger flight
Galileo	USA	18 Oct 89	Close-up photographs of an asteroid
STS-47 (Endeavour)	USA	12 Sep 92	50th Space shuttle flight
Pegsat	USA	5 Apr 90	First airborne launch
Lacrosse 2	USA	8 Mar 91	Radar surveillance
Almaz 1	Russia	30 Mar 91	Survey mapping
CGRO	USA	5 Apr 91	Gamma-ray astronomy
Topex/Poseidon	ESA	10 Aug 92	Geodetic mapping
Clementine	USA	25 Jan 94	Lunar/asteroid exploration
P. 91 (STEP 2)	USA	19 May 94	Explosion scatters space debris
ISO	ESA	17 Nov 95	Infrared space observatory
SOHO	USA	2 Dec 95	Monitoring solar activity
NEAR	USA	17 Feb 96	Asteroid rendezvous
MGS	USA	7 Nov 96	Mars global survey
MPF	USA	4 Dec 96	Mars Pathfinder explored surface
Haruka	Japan	12 Feb 97	Radio astronomy
Iridium	USA	5 May 97	Communication constellation
Cassini/Huygens	USA	15 Oct 97	Saturn/Titan study in 2004
Lunar Prospector	USA	7 Jan 98	Lunar surface investigation
Deep Space 1	USA	24 Oct 98	Ion propulsion spacecraft
STS 95	USA	29 Oct 98	John Glenn's return to space
Zarya	USA/Russia/ESA/Canada/Japan	20 Nov 98	First launch in International Space Station assembly
MCO	USA	11 Dec 98	Mars climate survey
MPL	USA	30 Jan 99	Mars surface investigation
Stardust	USA	7 Feb 99	Capture and analysis of comet particles
Shenzhou	China	22 Nov 99	China launches manned spacecraft

EARTH

There are no universally agreed estimates of the natural phenomena given in this section. Surveys make use of different criteria for identifying natural boundaries, and use different techniques of measurement. The sizes of continents, oceans, seas, deserts, and rivers are particularly subject to variation.

Vital statistics

Age	4 500 000 000 years (accurate to within a very small percentage of possible error)
Area	509 600 000 sq km / 197 000 000 sq mi
Mass	5976×10^{27} grams
Land surface	148 000 000 sq km / 57 000 000 sq mi (c.29% of total area)
Water surface	361 600 000 sq km / 140 000 000 sq mi (c.71% of total area)
Circumference of equator	40 076km / 24 902mi
Circumference of meridian	40 000km / 24 860mi

Continents

Name	Area sq km	Area sq mi	
Africa	30 293 000	11 696 000	(20.2%)
Antarctica	13 975 000	5 396 000	(9.3%)
Asia	44 493 000	17 179 000	(29.6%)
Europe[1]	10 245 000	3 956 000	(6.8%)
North America	24 454 000	9 442 000	(16.3%)
Oceania	8 945 000	3 454 000	(6.0%)
South America	17 838 000	6 887 000	(11.9%)

[1] Including the former western USSR.

Oceans

Name	Area sq km	Area sq mi		Greatest depth	m	ft
Arctic	13 986 000	5 400 000	(3%)	Eurasia Basin	5 122	16 804
Atlantic	82 217 000	31 700 000	(24%)	Puerto Rico Trench	8 648	28 372
Indian	73 426 000	28 350 000	(20%)	Java Trench	7 725	25 344
Pacific	181 300 000	70 000 000	(46%)	Mariana Trench	11 040	36 220

Largest seas

Name/Location	Area[1]	
	sq km	sq mi
Coral Sea	4 791 000	1 850 000
Arabian Sea	3 863 000	1 492 000
S China (Nan) Sea	3 685 000	1 423 000
Mediterranean Sea	2 516 000	971 000
Bering Sea	2 304 000	890 000
Bay of Bengal	2 172 000	839 000
Sea of Okhotsk	1 590 000	614 000
Gulf of Mexico	1 543 000	596 000
Gulf of Guinea	1 533 000	592 000
Barents Sea	1 405 000	542 000
Norwegian Sea	1 383 000	534 000
Gulf of Alaska	1 327 000	512 000
Hudson Bay	1 232 000	476 000
Greenland Sea	1 205 000	465 000
Arafura Sea	1 037 000	400 000
Philippine Sea	1 036 000	400 000
Sea of Japan	978 000	378 000
E Siberian Sea	901 000	348 000
Kara Sea	883 000	341 000
E China Sea	664 000	256 000
Andaman Sea	565 000	218 000
North Sea	520 000	201 000
Black Sea	508 000	196 000
Red Sea	453 000	175 000
Baltic Sea	414 000	160 000
Arabian Gulf	239 000	92 000
St Lawrence Gulf	238 000	92 000

Oceans are excluded.

[1] Areas are rounded to the nearest 1 000 sq km/sq mi.

Largest islands

Name	Area[1]	
	sq km	sq mi
Australia	7 692 300	2 970 000
Greenland	2 175 600	840 000
New Guinea	790 000	305 000
Borneo	737 000	285 000
Madagascar	587 000	226 600
Baffin	507 000	195 800

Area[1]

Name	sq km	sq mi
Sumatra	425 000	164 100
Honshu (Hondo)	228 000	88 000
Great Britain	219 000	84 600
Victoria, Canada	217 300	83 900
Ellesmere, Canada	196 000	75 700
Celebes	174 000	67 200
South I, New Zealand	151 000	58 300
Java	129 000	49 800
North I, New Zealand	114 000	44 000
Cuba	110 900	42 800
Newfoundland	109 000	42 100
Luzon	105 000	40 500
Iceland	103 000	39 800
Mindanao	94 600	36 500
Novaya Zemlya (two islands)	90 600	35 000
Ireland	84 100	32 500
Hokkaido	78 500	30 300
Hispaniola	77 200	29 800
Sakhalin	75 100	29 000
Tierra del Fuego	71 200	27 500

[1] Areas are rounded to the nearest 100 sq km/sq mi.

Major island groups

Name	Country	Sea/Ocean	Constituent islands
Aeolian	Italy	Mediterranean	Stromboli, Lipari, Vulcano, Salina
Åland	Finland	Gulf of Bothnia	Ahvenanmaa, Eckero, Lemland, Lump-arland, Vardo
Aleutian	USA	Pacific	Andreanof, Adak, Atka, Fox, Umnak, Unalaska, Unimak, Near, Attu, Rat, Kiska, Amchitka
Alexander	Canada	Pacific	Baranof, Prince of Wales
Antilles, Greater	—	Caribbean	Cuba, Jamaica, Haiti and the Dominican Republic, Puerto Rico
Antilles, Lesser	—	Caribbean	Windward, Leeward, Netherlands Antilles
Andaman	India	Bay of Bengal	over 300 islands including N Andaman, S Andaman, Middle Andaman, Little Andaman
Azores	Portugal	Atlantic	nine main islands: Flores, Corvo, Terceira, Graciosa, São Jorge, Faial, Pico, Santa Maria, Formigar, São Miguel

Name	Country	Sea/Ocean	Constituent islands
Bahamas, The	The Bahamas	Atlantic	700 islands including Great Abaco, Acklins, Andros, Berry, Cat, Cay, Crooked, Exuma, Grand Bahama, Inagua, Long, Mayaguana, New Providence, Ragged
Balearic	Spain	Mediterranean	Ibiza, Majorca, Menorca, Formentera, Cabrera
Bay	Honduras	Caribbean	Utila, Roatan, Guanja
Bismarck Archipelago	Papua New Guinea	Pacific	c.200 islands including New Britain, New Ireland, Admiralty, Lavonga, New Hanover
Bissagos	Guinea-Bissau	Atlantic	15 islands including Orango, Formosa, Caravela, Roxa
Canadian Arctic Archipelago	Canada	Arctic	main islands: Baffin, Victoria, Queen Elizabeth, Banks
Canary	Spain	Atlantic	Tenerife, Gomera, Las Palmas, Hierro, Lanzarote, Fuerteventura, Gran Canaria
Cape Verde	Cape Verde	Atlantic	10 islands divided into 1. Barlavento (windward) group: Santo Antão, São Vicente, Santa Luzia, São Nicolau, Boa Vista, Sal and 2. Sotavento (leeward) group: São Tiago, Maio Fogo, Brava
Caroline	USA	Pacific	c.680 islands including Yop, Ponape, Truk, Kusac, Palau
Chagos	UK	Indian	Diego Garcia, Peros, Banhos, Salomon
Channel	UK	English	Jersey, Guernsey, Alderney, Sark
Chonos Archipelago	Chile	Pacific	main islands: Chaffers, Benjamin, James, Melchior, Victoria, Luz
Commander	Russia	Bering Sea	main islands: Bering, Medny
Comoros	Comoros (excluding French Mayotte)	Mozambique Channel	Grand Comore, Anjouan, Mohéli, Mayotte
Cook	New Zealand	Pacific	main islands: Rarotonga, Palmerston, Mangaia
Cyclades	Greece	Aegean	c.220 islands including Andros, Mikonos, Milos, Naxos, Paros, Kithnos, Sérifos, Tinos, Siros
Denmark	Denmark	Baltic	main islands: Zealand, Fyn, Lolland, Falster, Bornholm
Desolation	France	Indian	Kerguélen, Grande Terre, and 300 islets
Dodecanese	Greece	Aegean	12 islands including Kásos, Kárpathos, Rhodes, Sámos, Khalki, Tilos, Simi, Astipalaia, Kós, Kálimnos, Léros, Pátmos

Name	Country	Sea/Ocean	Constituent islands
Ellice	Tuvalu	Pacific	main islands: Funafuti, Nukefetau, Nukulailai, Nanmea
Falkland	UK	Atlantic	over 200 islands including W Falkland, E Falkland, S Georgia, S Sandwich
Faroe	Denmark	Atlantic	22 islands including Stromo, Ostero
Fiji	Fiji	Pacific	main islands: Viti Levu, Vanua Levu
Frisian, East	Germany and Denmark	North Sea	main islands: Borkum, Juist, Norderney, Langeoog, Spiekeroog, Wangerooge
Frisian, North	Germany and Denmark	North Sea	main islands: (German) Sylt, Föhr, Nordstrand, Pellworm, Amrum; (Danish) Rømø, Fanø, Mandø
Frisian, West	Netherlands	North Sea	main islands: Texel, Vlieland, Terschelling, Ameland, Schiermonnikoog
Galapagos	Ecuador	Pacific	main islands: San Cristóbal, Santa Cruz, Isabela, Floreana, Santiago, Fernandina
Gilbert	Kiribati	Pacific	main islands: Tarawa, Makin, Abaiang, Abemama, Tabiteuea, Nonouti, Beru
Gotland	Sweden	Baltic	main islands: Gotland, Fårö, Karlsö
Greenland	Denmark	N Atlantic/Arctic	main islands: Greenland, Disko
Hawaiian	USA	Pacific	8 main islands: Hawaii, Oahu, Maui, Lanai, Kauai, Molokai, Kahoolawe, Niihau
Hebrides, Inner	UK	Atlantic	main islands: Skye, Eigg, Coll, Tiree, Mull, Iona, Staffa, Jura, Islay
Hebrides, Outer	UK	Atlantic	Lewis, Harris, N and S Uist, Benbecula, Barra
Indonesia	Indonesia	Pacific	13 677 islets and islands including Java, Sumatra, Kalimantau, Celebes, Lesser Sundas, Moluccas, Irian Jaya
Ionian	Greece	Aegean	Kerkira, Kefalliniá, Zakinthos, Levkas
Japan	Japan	Pacific	main islands: Hokkaido, Honshu, Shikoku, Kyushu, Ryuku
Juan Fernandez	Chile	Pacific	Más á Tierra, Más Afuera, Santa Clara
Kuril	Russia	Pacific	56 islands including Shumsu, Iturup, Urup, Paramushir, Onekotan, Shiaskhotan, Shikotanto, Kunashir, Shimushir
Laccadive	India	Arabian Sea	27 islands including Amindivi, Laccadive, Minicoy, Androth, Kavaratti
Line	Kiribati	Pacific	main islands: Christmas, Fanning, Washington
Lofoten	Norway	Norwegian Sea	main islands: Hinnøy, Austvågøy, Vestvågøy, Moskenes
Madeira	Portugal	Atlantic	Madeira, Ilha do Porto Santo, Ilhas Desertas, Ilhas Selvagens

Name	Country	Sea/Ocean	Constituent islands
Malay Archipelago	Indonesia, Malaysia, Philippines	Pacific/Indian	main islands: Borneo, Celebes, Java, Luzon, Mindanao, New Guinea, Sumatra
Maldives	Maldives	Indian	19 clusters, main island: Male
Malta	Malta	Mediterranean	main islands: Malta, Gozo, Comino
Mariana	Mariana Islands	Pacific	14 islands including Saipan, Tinian, Rota, Pagan, Guguan
Marquesas	France	Pacific	10 islands including Nukultiva, Ua Pu, Ua Huka, Hiva Oa, Tahuata, Fatu Hiva, Eïao, Hatutu
Marshall	Marshall Islands	Pacific	main islands: Bikini, Wotha, Kwajalein, Eniwetok, Maiura, Jalut, Rogelap
Mascarenes	—	Indian	main islands: Réunion, Mauritius, Rodrigues
Melanesia	—	Pacific	main groups of islands: Solomon Islands, Bismarck Archipelago, New Caledonia, Papua New Guinea, Fiji, Vanuatu
Micronesia	—	Pacific	main groups of islands: Caroline, Gilberts, Marianas, Marshalls, Guam, Kiribati, Nauru
New Hebrides	Vanuatu	Pacific	main islands: Espíritu Santo, Malekula, Efate, Ambrim, Eromanga, Tanna, Epi, Pentecost, Aurora
New Siberian	Russia	Arctic	main islands: Kotelny, Faddeyevski
Newfoundland	Canada	Atlantic	Prince Edward, Anticosti
Nicobar	India	Bay of Bengal	main islands: Great Nicobar, Camorta with Nancowry, Car Nicobar, Teressa, Little Nicobar
Northern Land	Russia	Arctic	main islands: Komsomolets, Bolshevik, October Revolution
Novaya Zemlya	Russia	Arctic	2 main islands: North, South
Orkney	UK	North Sea	main islands: Mainland, South Ronaldsay, Sanday, Westray, Hoy, Stronsay, Shapinsay, Rousay
Pelagian	Italy	Mediterranean	Lampedusa, Linosa, Lampione
Philippines	Philippines	Pacific	over 7 100 islands and islets including Luzon, Mindanao, Samar, Palawan, Mindoro, Panay, Negros, Cebu, Leyte, Masbate, Bohol
Polynesia	—	Pacific	main groups of islands: New Zealand, French Polynesia, Phoenix Islands, Hawaii, Line, Cook Islands, Pitcairn, Tokelau, Tonga, Society, Easter, Samoa, Kiribati, Ellice
Queen Charlotte	Canada	Pacific	150 islands including Prince Rupert, Graham, Moresby, Louise, Lyell, Kunghit

Name	Country	Sea/Ocean	Constituent islands
São Tomé and Príncipe	São Tomé and Príncipe	Atlantic	main islands: São Tomé, Príncipe
Scilly	UK	English Channel	c.150 islands including St Mary's, St Martin's, Tresco, St Agnes, Bryher
Seychelles	Seychelles	Indian	115 islands including Praslin, La Digue, Silhouette, Mahé, Bird
Shetland	UK	North Sea	100 islands including Mainland, Unst, Yell, Whalsay, West Burra
Society	France	Pacific	island groups: Windward, Leeward; main island: Tahiti
Solomon	Solomon Islands	Pacific	main islands: Choiseul, Guadalcanal, Malaita, New Georgia, San Cristóbal, Santa Isabel
South Orkney	UK	Atlantic	main islands: Coronation, Signy, Laurie, Inaccessible
South Shetland	UK	Atlantic	main islands: King George, Elephant, Clarence, Gibbs, Nelson, Livingstone, Greenwich, Snow, Deception, Smith
Sri Lanka	Sri Lanka	Indian	main islands: Sri Lanka, Mannar
Taiwan	Taiwan	China Sea / Pacific	main islands: Taiwan, Lan Hsü, Lü Tao, Quemoy, the Pescadores
Tasmania	Australia	Tasman Sea	main islands: Tasmania, King, Flinders, Bruny
Tierra del Fuego	Argentina / Chile	Pacific	main islands: Tierra del Fuego, Isla de los Estados, Hoste, Navarino, Wallaston, Diego Ramírez, Desolación, Santa Inés, Clarence, Dawson
Tres Marías	Mexico	Pacific	María Madre, María Magdalena, María Cleofás, San Juanito
Tristan da Cunha	UK	Atlantic	5 islands including Tristan da Cunha, Gough, Inaccessible
Tuamotu Archipelago	France	Pacific	c.80 islands including Makatea, Fakarava, Rangiroa, Anaa, Hao, Reao, Gambiev, Duke of Gloucester
Vesterålen	Norway	Norwegian Sea	main islands: Hinnøy, Langøya, Andøya, Hadseløy
Virgin	USA	Caribbean	over 50 islands including St Croix, St Thomas, St John
Virgin	UK	Caribbean	main islands: Tortola, Virgin Gorda, Anegada, Jost Van Dyke
Zanzibar	Tanzania	Indian	main islands: Zanzibar, Tumbatu, Kwale
Zemlya Frantsa-Iosifa	Russia	Arctic	c.167 islands including Graham Bell, Wilczekland, Georgeland, Hooker, Zemlya Aleksandry, Ostrov Rudol'fa

Largest lakes

Name/Location	Area[1]	
	sq km	sq mi
Caspian Sea, Iran/Russia/ Turkmenistan/Kazakhstan/ Azerbaijan	371 000	143 240[2]
Superior, USA/Canada	82 260	31 760[3]
Aral Sea, Uzbekistan/ Kazakhstan	64 500	24 900[2]
Victoria, E Africa	62 940	24 300
Huron, USA/Canada	59 580	23 000[3]
Michigan, USA	58 020	22 400
Tanganyika, E Africa	32 000	12 360
Baikal, Russia	31 500	12 160
Great Bear, Canada	31 330	12 100
Great Slave, Canada	28 570	11 030
Erie, USA/Canada	25 710	9 930[3]
Winnipeg, Canada	24 390	9 420
Malawi/Nyasa, E Africa	22 490	8 680
Balkhash, Kazakhstan	17 000–22 000	6 560–8 490[2]
Ontario, Canada	19 270	7 440[3]
Ladoga, Russia	18 130	7 000
Chad, W Africa	10 000–26 000	3 860–10 040
Maracaibo, Venezuela	13 010	5 020[4]
Patos, Brazil	10 140	3 920[4]
Onega, Russia	9 800	3 780
Rudolf, E Africa	9 100	3 510
Eyre, Australia	8 800	3 400[4]
Titicaca, Peru	8 300	3 200

The Caspian and Aral Seas, being entirely surrounded by land, are classified as lakes.

[1] Areas are rounded to the nearest 10 sq km/sq mi.
[2] Salt lakes.
[3] Average of areas given by Canada and USA.
[4] Salt lagoons.

Highest mountains

Name	Height[1]		Location
	m	ft	
Everest	8 850	29 030	China-Nepal
K2	8 610	28 250	Kashmir-Jammu
Kangchenjunga	8 590	28 170	India-Nepal
Lhotse	8 500	27 890	China-Nepal
Kangchenjunga S Peak	8 470	27 800	India-Nepal
Makalu I	8 470	27 800	China-Nepal
Kangchenjunga W Peak	8 420	27 620	India-Nepal
Lhotse E Peak	8 380	27 500	China-Nepal
Dhaulagiri	8 170	26 810	Nepal
Cho Oyu	8 150	26 750	China-Nepal
Manaslu	8 130	26 660	Nepal
Nanga Parbat	8 130	26 660	Kashmir-Jammu
Annapurna I	8 080	26 500	Nepal
Gasherbrum I	8 070	26 470	Kashmir-Jammu
Broad Peak I	8 050	26 400	Kashmir-Jammu
Gasherbrum II	8 030	26 360	Kashmir-Jammu
Gosainthan	8 010	26 290	China
Broad Peak Central	8 000	26 250	Kashmir-Jammu
Gasherbrum III	7 950	26 090	Kashmir-Jammu
Annapurna II	7 940	26 040	Nepal
Nanda Devi	7 820	25 660	India
Rakaposhi	7 790	25 560	Kashmir
Kamet	7 760	25 450	India
Ulugh Muztagh	7 720	25 340	Tibet
Tirich Mir	7 690	25 230	Pakistan
MuzTag Ata	7 550	24 760	China
Communism Peak	7 490	24 590	Tajikistan
Pobedy Peak	7 440	24 410	China-Kyrgyzstan
Aconcagua	6 960	22 830	Argentina
Ojos del Salado	6 910	22 660	Argentina-Chile

[1] Heights are given to the nearest 10 m / ft.

Largest deserts

Name/Location	Area[1] sq km	sq mi
Sahara, N Africa	8 600 000	3 320 000
Arabian, SW Asia	2 330 000	900 000
Gobi, Mongolia and NE China	1 166 000	450 000
Patagonian, Argentina	673 000	260 000
Great Victoria, SW Australia	647 000	250 000
Great Basin, SW USA	492 000	190 000
Chihuahuan, Mexico	450 000	174 000
Great Sandy, NW Australia	400 000	154 000
Sonoran, SW USA	310 000	120 000
Kyzyl Kum, Kazakhstan	300 000	116 000
Takla Makan, N China	270 000	104 000
Kalahari, SW Africa	260 000	100 000
Kara Kum, Turkmenistan	260 000	100 000
Kavir, Iran	260 000	100 000
Syrian, Saudi Arabia / Jordan / Syria / Iraq	260 000	100 000
Nubian, Sudan	260 000	100 000
Thar, India / Pakistan	200 000	77 000
Ust'-Urt, Kazakhstan	160 000	62 000
Bet-Pak-Dala, S Kazakhstan	155 000	60 000
Simpson, C Australia	145 000	56 000
Dzungaria, China	142 000	55 000
Atacama, Chile	140 000	54 000
Namib, SE Africa	134 000	52 000
Sturt, SE Australia	130 000	50 000
Bolson de Mapimi, Mexico	130 000	50 000
Ordos, China	130 000	50 000
Alashan, China	116 000	45 000

[1] Desert areas are very approximate, because clear physical boundaries may not occur.

Longest rivers

Name	Outflow	Length[1] km	mi
Nile-Kagera-Ruvuvu-Ruvusu-Luvironza	Mediterranean Sea (Egypt)	6 690	4 160
Amazon-Ucayali-Tambo-Ene-Apurimac	Atlantic Ocean (Brazil)	6 570	4 080
Mississippi-Missouri-Jefferson-Beaverhead-Red Rock	Gulf of Mexico (USA)	6 020	3 740
Chang Jiang (Yangtze)	E China Sea (China)	5 980	3 720
Yenisey-Angara-Selenga-Ider	Kara Sea (Russia)	5 870	3 650
Amur-Argun-Kerulen	Tartar Strait (Russia)	5 780	3 590
Ob-Irtysh	Gulf of Ob, Kara Sea (Russia)	5 410	3 360
Plata-Parana-Grande	Atlantic Ocean (Argentina-Uruguay)	4 880	3 030
Huang He (Yellow)	Yellow Sea (China)	4 840	3 010
Congo-Lualaba	S Atlantic Ocean (Angola-Congo, Democratic Republic of)	4 630	2 880
Lena	Laptev Sea (Russia)	4 400	2 730
Mackenzie-Slave-Peace-Finlay	Beaufort Sea (Canada)	4 240	2 630
Mekong	S China Sea (Vietnam)	4 180	2 600
Niger	Gulf of Guinea (Nigeria)	4 100	2 550

[1] Lengths are given to the nearest 10km/mi, and include the river plus tributaries comprising the longest watercourse.

Highest waterfalls

Name	Height[1] m	ft
Angel (upper fall), Venezuela	807	2 648
Itatinga, Brazil	628	2 060
Cuquenán, Guyana-Venezuela	610	2 001
Ormeli, Norway	563	1 847
Tysse, Norway	533	1 749
Pilao, Brazil	524	1 719
Ribbon, USA	491	1 611
Vestre Mardola, Norway	468	1 535
Kaieteur, Guyana	457	1 500
Cleve-Garth, New Zealand	450	1 476

[1] Height denotes individual leaps.

Deepest caves

| | Depth | |
Name/Location	m	ft
Jean Bernard, France	1 494	4 902
Snezhnaya, Caucasus	1 340	4 396
Puertas de Illamina, Spain	1 338	4 390
Pierre-Saint-Martin, France	1 321	4 334
Sistema Huautla, Mexico	1 240	4 068
Berger, France	1 198	3 930
Vqerdi, Spain	1 195	3 921
Dachstein-Mammuthöhle, Austria	1 174	3 852
Zitu, Spain	1 139	3 737
Badalona, Spain	1 130	3 707
Batmanhöhle, Austria	1 105	3 625
Schneeloch, Austria	1 101	3 612
G E S Malaga, Spain	1 070	3 510
Lamprechstofen, Austria	1 024	3 360

Major volcanoes

| | Height | | Last eruption |
Name	m	ft	(year)
Aconcagua (Argentina)	6 959	22 831	extinct
Ararat (Turkey)	5 137	16 853	extinct
Awu (Sangihe Is, Indonesia)	1 327	4 355	1992
Bezymianny (Russia)	2 800	9 186	1997
Coseguina (Nicaragua)	847	2 779	1835
Cotopaxi (Ecuador)	5 897	19 347	1975
El Chichón (Mexico)	1 350	4 430	1982
Erebus (Antarctica)	4 023	13 200	1995
Etna (Italy)	3 239	10 625	1994
Fuji (Japan)	3 776	12 388	1707
Galunggung (Java)	2 181	7 155	1984
Hekla (Iceland)	1 500	4 920	1991
Helgafell (Iceland)	215	706	1973
Hudson (Chile)	1 750	5 742	1991
Jorullo (Mexico)	1 330	4 255	1774
Katmai (Alaska)	2 047	6 715	1974
Kilauea (Hawaii)	1 250	4 100	1995
Kilimanjaro (Tanzania)	5 928	19 450	extinct
Klyuchevskoy (Russia)	4 850	15 910	1997
Krakatoa (Sumatra)	818	2 685	1995
Laki (Iceland)	500	1 642	1996
Lamington (Papua New Guinea)	1 781	5 844	1956

Name	Height m	ft	Last eruption (year)
La Soufrière (St Vincent)	1 234	4 048	1997
Lassen Peak (USA)	3 186	10 453	1921
Mauna Loa (Hawaii)	4 171	13 685	1987
Mayon (Philippines)	2 464	8 084	1993
Nyamuragira (Congo, Democratic Republic of)	3 056	10 026	1995
Paricutín (Mexico)	3 188	10 460	1952
Pelée, Mont (Martinique)	1 397	4 584	1932
Pinatubo, Mt (Philippines)	1 759	5 770	1995
Popocatèpetl (Mexico)	5 483	17 990	1998
Rainier, Mt (USA)	4 394	14 416	1882
Ruapehu (New Zealand)	2 797	9 175	1996
St Helens, Mt (USA)	2 549	8 364	1991
Santoríni/Thíra (Greece)	566	1 857	1950
Soufrière Hills (Montserrat)	914	3 000	1997
Stromboli (Italy)	931	3 055	1996
Surtsey (Iceland)	174	570	1967
Taal (Philippines)	1 448	4 752	1988
Tambora (Sumbawa, Indonesia)	2 868	9 410	1880
Tarawera (New Zealand)	1 149	3 770	1973
Unzen (Japan)	1 360	4 461	1996
Vesuvius (Italy)	1 289	4 230	1944
Vulcano (Italy)	503	1 650	1890

Major earthquakes

All magnitudes on the Richter scale. The energy released by earthquakes is measured on the logarithmic Richter scale. Thus

2	Barely perceptible;	5	Rather strong;	7+	Very strong

Location	Year	Magnitude	Deaths
Nantou Province (Taiwan)	1999	7.6	2 400+
Izmit (NW Turkey)	1999	7.4	17 000+
Armenia (Colombia)	1999	6.0	1 100+
Badakhshan Province (Afghanistan)	1998	7.1	5 000+
Rustaq (Afghanistan)	1998	6.1	4 000+
Qayen (E Iran)	1997	7.1	2 400
Ardabil (NW Iran)	1997	5.5	965+
Biak I (Indonesia)	1996	7.9	108
Lijiang, Yunan Province (China)	1996	7.0	304
Manzanillo (Mexico)	1995	7.6	66
S Mexico	1995	7.3	—
Neftegorsk, Sakhalin I (E Russia)	1995	7.5	2 000
Kobe (Japan)	1995	7.2	6 300

Location	Year	Magnitude	Deaths
Hokkaido I (Japan) and Kuril Is (Russia) (undersea)	1994	8.2	16+
Bolivia (617km underground)	1994	8.2	5
Paez River Valley (SW Colombia)	1994	6.8	269
Java (Indonesia)	1994	7.7	200
Sumatra I (Indonesia)	1994	7.2	215
Los Angeles, California (USA)	1994	6.8	61
Maharashtra State (India)	1993	6.5	22 000
Guam (Mariana Is)	1993	8.1	—
Okushiri and Hokkaido Is (N Japan)	1993	7.8	185
Papua New Guinea	1993	6.8	60
Maumere, Flores I (Indonesia)	1992	7.5	1 232
Cairo (Egypt)	1992	5.9	552
Erzincan (Turkey)	1992	6.8	500
Nusa Tenggara Is (Indonesia)	1992	6.8	2 500
Uttar Pradesh (India)	1991	6.1	1 000
Georgia	1991	7.2	100
Afghanistan	1991	6.8	1 000
Pakistan	1991	6.8	300
Cabanatuan City (Philippines)	1990	7.7	1 653
NW Iran	1990	7.5	40 000
San Francisco (USA)	1989	6.9	100
Armenia	1988	7.0	25 000
SW China	1988	7.6	1 000
Nepal / India	1988	6.9	900
Mexico City (Mexico)	1985	8.1	7 200
N Yemen	1982	6.0	2 800
S Italy	1980	7.2	4 500
El Asnam (Algeria)	1980	7.3	5 000
NE Iran	1978	7.7	25 000
Tangshan (China)	1976	8.2	242 000
Guatemala City (Guatemala)	1976	7.5	22 778
Kashmir (India)	1974	6.3	5 200
Managua (Nicaragua)	1972	6.2	5 000
S Iran	1972	6.9	5 000
Chimbote (Peru)	1970	7.7	66 000
NE Iran	1968	7.4	11 600
Anchorage (USA)	1964	8.5	131
NW Iran	1962	7.1	12 000
Agadir (Morocco)	1960	5.8	12 000
Erzincan (Turkey)	1939	7.9	23 000
Chillan (Chile)	1939	7.8	30 000
Quetta (India)	1935	7.5	60 000
Gansu (China)	1932	7.6	70 000
Nan-shan (China)	1927	8.3	200 000
Kwanto (Japan)	1923	8.3	143 000

Location	Year	Magnitude	Deaths
Gansu (China)	1920	8.6	180 000
Avezzano (Italy)	1915	7.5	30 000
Messina (Italy)	1908	7.5	120 000
Valparaiso (Chile)	1906	8.6	20 000
San Francisco (USA)	1906	8.3	500
Ecuador/Colombia	1868	*	70 000
Calabria (Italy)	1783	*	50 000
Lisbon (Portugal)	1755	*	70 000
Calcutta (India)	1737	*	300 000
Hokkaido (Japan)	1730	*	137 000
Catania (Italy)	1693	*	60 000
Caucasia (Caucasus)	1667	*	80 000
Shensi (China)	1556	*	830 000
Chihli (China)	1290	*	100 000
Silicia (Asia Minor)	1268	*	60 000
Corinth (Greece)	856	*	45 000
Antioch (Turkey)	526	*	250 000

*Magnitude not available

Earthquake severity measurement

Mercalli and Richter scales

Mercalli	Description	Richter
1	detected only by seismographs	<3
2	feeble	3–3.4
	just noticeable by some people	
3	slight	3.5–4
	similiar to passing of heavy lorries	
4	moderate	4.1–4.4
	rocking of loose objects	
5	quite strong	4.5–4.8
	felt by most people even when sleeping	
6	strong	4.9–5.4
	trees rock and some structural damage is caused	
7	very strong	5.5–6
	walls crack	
8	destructive	6.1–6.5
	weak buildings collapse	
9	ruinous	6.6–7
	houses collapse and ground pipes crack	
10	disastrous	7.1–7.3
	landslides occur, ground cracks and buildings collapse	
11	very disastrous	7.4–8.1
	few buildings remain standing	
12	catastrophic	>8.1
	ground rises and falls in waves	

Geological time scale

Eon	Era	Period	Epoch	Million years before present
Phanerozoic	Cenozoic	Quaternary	Holocene	0.01–
			Pleistocene	2–0.01
		Tertiary	Pliocene	7–2
			Miocene	25–7
			Oligocene	38–25
			Eocene	54–38
			Palaeocene	65–54
	Mesozoic	Cretaceous		140–65
		Jurassic		210–140
		Triassic	Late	
			Middle	250–210
			Early	
	Palaeozoic	Permian	Late	290–250
			Early	
		Carboniferous	Pennsylvanian	360–290
			Mississippian	
		Devonian		410–360
		Silurian		440–410
		Ordovician		505–440
		Cambrian		580–505
Precambrian	Proterozoic			2 500–580
	Archaean			4 500–2 500

CLIMATE AND ENVIRONMENT

Climatic zones

The earth may be divided into zones, approximating to zones of latitude, such that each zone possesses a distinct type of climate.

The principal zones are:

□ Tropical One zone of wet climate near the equator (either constantly wet or monsocnal with wet and dry seasons, tropical savannah with dry winters); the average temperature is not below 18°C;
  Amazon forest
  Malaysia
  S Vietnam
  India
  Africa
  Congo Basin
  Indonesia
  S E Asia
  Australia

□ Subtropical Two zones of steppe and desert climate (transition through semi-arid to arid);
  Sahara
  Central Asia
  Mexico
  Australia
  Kalahari

□ Mediterranean Zones of rainy climate with mild winters; coolest month above 0°C but below 18°C;
  California
  S Africa
  S Europe
  parts of Chile
  SW Australia

□ Temperate Rainy climate (includes areas of temperate woodland, mountain forests, and plains with no dry season;

influenced by seas — rainfall all year, small temperate changes); average temperature between 3°C and 18°C;
  Most of Europe
  Eastern Asia
  NW/NE USA
  New Zealand
  Southern Chile

□ Boreal Climate with a great range of temperature in the northern hemisphere (in some areas the most humid month is in summer and there is ten times more precipitation than the driest part of winter. In other areas the most humid month is in winter and there is ten times more precipitation than in the driest part of summer); in the coldest period temperatures do not exceed 3°C and in the hottest do not go below 10°C;
  Prairies of USA
  parts of S Africa
  parts of Russia
  parts of Australia

□ Polar caps Snowy climate (tundra and ice-cap) with little or no precipitation. There is permafrost in the tundra and vegetation includes lichen and moss all year, and grass in the summer; the highest annual temperature in the polar region is below 0°C and in the tundra the average temperature is 10°C;
  Arctic regions of Russia and N America
  Antarctica

Great ice ages

Precambrian era	Early Proterozoic
Precambrian era	Upper Proterozoic
Palaeozoic era	Upper Carboniferous
Cenozoic era	Pleistocene[1]
	(Last 4 periods of glaciation)
	Günz (Nebraskan or Jerseyan) 520 000–490 000 years ago
	Mindel (Kansan) 430 000–370 000 years ago
	Riss (Illinoian) 130 000–100 000 years ago
	Würm (Wisconsin and Iowan) 40 000–18 000 years ago

[1] The Pleistocene epoch is synonymous with 'The Ice Age'.

Meteorological extremes

The hottest place is Dallol, Ethiopia, at 34.4°C/93.9°F (annual mean temperature).

The highest recorded temperature in the shade is 58°C/136.4°F, at al'Aziziyah, Libya, on 13 September 1922.

The coldest place is Pole of Cold, Antarctica, at -57.8°C/-72°F (annual mean temperature).

The driest place is the Atacama desert near Calama, Chile, where no rainfall was recorded in over 400 years to 1972.

The most rain to fall in 24 hours was 1 870mm/74 in, which fell on Cilaos, Réunion, in the Indian Ocean, on 15–16 March 1952.

The wettest place is Tutunendo, Colombia, where the rainfall is 11 770mm/464 in (annual average).

The greatest amount of snow to fall in 12 months was 31 102mm/1 225 in, at Paradise, Mt Rainier, in Washington, USA, in 1971–2.

The most rainy days in a year are the c.350 experienced on Mt Waialeale, Kauai, Hawaii, USA.

The least sunshine occurs at the North and South Poles, where the Sun does not rise for 182 days of winter.

The greatest amount of sunshine occurs in the eastern Sahara: more than 4 300 hours a year (97% of daylight hours).

The highest recorded surface wind speed is 371kph/231mph, at Mt Washington, New Hampshire, USA, on 12 April 1934.

Map of shipping forecast areas

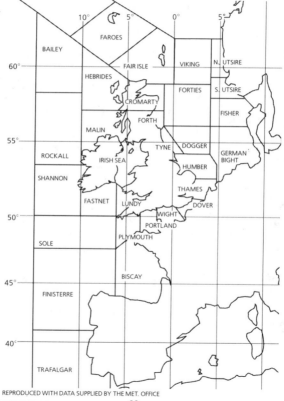

Acid rain

A term generally used for polluted rainfall associated with the burning of fossil fuels.
It is implicated in damage to forests and the stonework of buildings, and increases the acid
content of soils and lakes, harming crops and fish.

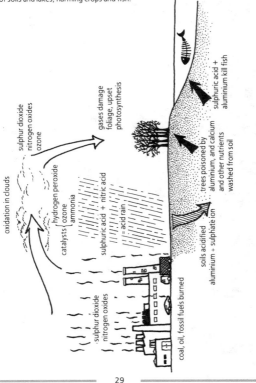

sulphur dioxide
nitrogen oxides
ozone

gases damage
foliage, upset
photosynthesis

oxidation in clouds

catalysts { hydrogen peroxide
ozone
ammonia

sulphuric acid + nitric acid
= acid rain

trees poisoned by
aluminium, and calcium
and other nutrients
washed from soil

sulphuric acid +
aluminium kill fish

sulphur dioxide
nitrogen oxides

soils acidified
aluminium + sulphate ion

coal, oil, fossil fuels burned

World Heritage sites

This list is up-to-date to December 1998. It comprises the 552 sites in 113 countries selected by UNESCO as being of such outstanding natural, environmental or cultural importance that they merit exceptional international efforts to make them more widely known and to save them from damage and destruction.

□ Albania

Butrinti

□ Algeria

Algiers (Casbah)

Al Qal'a of Beni Hammad

Djémila (Roman ruins)

M'Zab Valley

Tassili N'Ajjer

Timgad (Roman ruins)

Tipasa (archaeological site)

□ Argentina

Iguazú National Park

Jesuit Missions of the Guaranis (shared with Brazil)

Los Glaciares National Park

□ Armenia

Haghpat Monastery

□ Australia

Central Eastern Australian Rainforest

Fraser I

Great Barrier Reef

Heard and McDonald Is

Kakadu National Park

Lord Howe Is

Macquarie I

Queensland (wet tropics)

Riversleigh/Naracoorte (mammal fossil sites)

Shark Bay

Tasmanian Wilderness

Uluru-Kata Tjuta National Park

Willandra Lakes region

□ Austria

Hallstatt-Dachstein Salzkammergut cultural landscape

Salzburg (historic city centre)

Schönbrunn palace and gardens

□ Bangladesh

Bagerhat (historic mosque city)

Paharpur (ruins of the Buddhist Vihara)

Sundarbans (mangrove forest)

□ Belarus

Belovezhskaya Pushcha/Bialowieza Forest (shared with Poland)

□ Belize

Barrier Reef Reserve System

□ Benin

Dahomey (royal palaces)

□ Bolivia

Jesuit Missions of the Chiquitos

Potosi (mining town)

Sucre (historic city)

□ Brazil

Bom Jesus do Congonhas (sanctuary)

Brasilia

Iguaçu National Park

Jesuit Missions of the Guaranis (shared with Argentina)

Olinda (historic centre)

Ouro Preto (historic town)

Salvador da Bahia (historic centre)

São Luis (historic centre)

Serra da Capivara National Park

□ Bulgaria

Boyana Church

Ivanovo rock-hewn churches

Kazanlak (Thracian tomb)

Madara Rider

Nessebar (old city)

Pirin National Park

Rila Monastery

Srebarna Nature Reserve

Sveshtari (Thracian tomb)

□ Cambodia

Angkor

□ Cameroon

Dja Faunal Reserve

❑ Canada
Anthony I
Canadian Rocky Mountain Parks
Dinosaur Provincial Park
Gros Morne National Park
Head-Smashed-In Buffalo Jump complex
L'Anse aux Meadows Historic Park
Lunenburg (old city)
Nahanni National Park
Quebec (historic area)
Tatshenshini-Alsek, Kluane National Park,
Wrangell St Elias National Park and Reserve,
and Glacier Bay National Park (shared with
USA)
Waterton Glacier International Peace Park
(shared with USA)
Wood Buffalo National Park
❑ Central African Republic
Manovo-Gounda St Floris National Park
❑ Chile
Rapa Nui National Park (Easter I)
❑ China
Beijing (Imperial Palace of the Ming and
Qing dynasties)
Chengde (mountain resort and outlying
temples)
Mt Emei scenic area including Leshan giant
Buddha scenic area
Great Wall
Huanglong area
Mt Huangshan
Jiuzhaigou Valley area
Lhasa (Potala Palace)
Lijiang (old town)
Lushan National Park
Mausoleum of the first Qin emperor
Mogao caves
Mt Taishan
Ping Yao (ancient city)
Qufu (temple and cemetery of Confucius
and the K'ung family mansion)
Suzhou (classical gardens)
Wudang mountains (ancient building
complex)
Wulingyuan area
Zhoukoudian (Peking Man site)

❑ Colombia
Cartagena (port, fortress and monuments)
Los Katios National Park
San Agustín Archaeological Park
Santa Cruz de Mompox (historic centre)
Tierradentro National Archaeological Park
❑ Congo, Democratic Republic of (Zaïre)
Garamba National Park
Kahuzi-Biega National Park
Okapi Faunal Reserve
Salonga National Park
Virunga National Park
❑ Costa Rica
Cocos I National Park
La Amistad National Park (shared with
Panama)
❑ Côte d'Ivoire
Comoé National Park
Mt Nimba Nature Reserve (shared with
Guinea)
Taï National Park
❑ Croatia
Dubrovnik (old city)
Plitvice Lakes National Park
Porec (episcopal complex of the Euphrasian
basilica in the historic centre)
Split (historic centre with Diocletian's
Palace)
Trogir (historic city)
❑ Cuba
Old Havana and its fortifications
Santiago de Cuba, San Pedro de la Roca
Castle
Trinidad and the Valley de los Ingenios
❑ Cyprus
Paphos (archaeological site)
Troödos region (painted churches)
❑ Czech Republic
Cesky Krumlov (historic centre)
Kutna Hora (historic centre) with Church of
St Barbara and the Cathedral of Our Lady at
Sedlec
Lednice-Valtice cultural landscape
Prague (historic centre)
Telc (historic centre)

Zelena Hora (pilgrimage church of St John of Nepomuk)

□ Denmark
Jelling (mounds, runic stones and church)
Roskilde Cathedral

□ Dominica
Morne Trois Pitons National Park

□ Dominican Republic
Santo Domingo

□ Ecuador
Galapagos Is National Park
Quito (old city)
Sangay National Park

□ Egypt
Abu Mena (Christian ruins)
Abu Simbel to Philae (Nubian monuments)
Cairo (Islamic sector)
Memphis and its Necropolis with the Pyramid fields
Thebes and its Necropolis

□ El Salvador
Joya de Cerén (archaeological site)

□ Estonia
Tallinn (historic centre, old town)

□ Ethiopia
Aksum (archaeological site)
Awash Lower Valley
Fasil Ghebbi and Gondar monuments
Lalibela rock-hewn churches
Omo Lower Valley
Simien National Park
Tiya (carved steles)

□ Finland
Old Rauma
Petäjävesi (old church)
Suomenlinna (fortress)
Verla groundwood and board mill

□ France
Amiens Cathedral
Arc-et-Senans (Royal saltworks)
Arles (Roman and Romanesque monuments)
Avignon (historic centre)
Bourges Cathedral
Canal du Midi

Carcassonne (historic fortified city)
Chambord (château and estate)
Chartres Cathedral
Corsica (Cape Girolata, Cape Porto, Scandola Natural Reserve and the Piana Calanches)
Fontainebleau (palace and park)
Fontenay (Cistercian abbey)
Mont St Michel and its bay
Nancy (Place Stanislas, Place de la Carrière and Place d'Alliance)
Orange (Roman theatre and triumphal arch)
Paris (banks of the Seine)
Pont du Gard (Roman aqueduct)
Pyrenees, Mt Perdu landscape (shared with Spain)
Reims (Cathedral of Notre-Dame, St Remy Abbey and Palace of Tau)
St Savin-sur-Gartempe (church)
Strasbourg (Grande Île)
Versailles (palace and park)
Vézelay (basilica and hill)
Vézère (decorated caves)

□ Georgia
Bagrati Cathedral and Gelati Monastery
Mtskheta (historic church ensemble)
Upper Svaneti

□ Germany
Aachen Cathedral
Bamberg
Bauhaus and its sites in Weimar and Dessau
Brühl (Augustusburg and Falkenlust castles)
Cologne Cathedral
Eisleben and Wittenberg, the Luther memorials
Hildesheim (St Mary's Cathedral and St Michael's Church)
Lorsch (abbey and Altenmünster)
Lübeck (Hanseatic city)
Maulbronn (monastery)
Messel Pit (fossil site)
Potsdam and Berlin palaces and parks
Quedlinburg (collegiate church, castle and old town)
Rammelsberg mines and historic town of Goslar
Speyer Cathedral

Trier (Roman monuments, cathedral and
  Liebfrauen church)
Völklingen ironworks
Wies (pilgrimage church)
Würzburg Residence

□ Ghana
Ashante traditional buildings
Forts and castles of Ghana

□ Greece
Athens (Acropolis)
Bassae (temple of Apollo Epicurius)
Daphni, Hossios Luckas and Nea Moni of
  Chios monasteries
Delos
Delphi (archaeological site)
Epidaurus (archaeological site)
Meteora
Mt Athos
Mystras
Olympia (archaeological site)
Rhodes (medieval city)
Samos (Pythagoreion and Heraion)
Thessalonika (Paleochristian and Byzantine
  monuments)
Vergina (archaeological site)

□ Guatemala
Antigua Guatemala
Quirigua (archaeological site and ruins)
Tikal National Park

□ Guinea
Mt Nimba Nature Reserve (shared with
  Côte d'Ivoire)

□ Haiti
Citadel, Sans-Souci Palace and Ramiers
  National Historic Park

□ Honduras
Maya ruins of Copan
Río Plátano Biosphere Reserve

□ Hungary
Aggtelek caves and the Slovak Karst
  (shared with Slovakia)
Budapest (banks of the Danube and the
  Buda Castle quarter)
Hollókő (traditional village)
Pannonhalma, Millenary Benedictine Abbey
  and its natural environment

□ India
Agra Fort
Ajanta caves
Elephanta caves
Ellora caves
Fatehpur Sikri (Moghul city)
Goa (churches and convents)
Hampi (monuments)
Humayun's Tomb
Kaziranga National Park
Keoladeo National Park
Khajuraho (monuments)
Konarak (Sun Temple)
Mahabalipuram (monuments)
Manas Wildlife Sanctuary
Nanda Devi National Park
Pattadakal (monuments)
Qutb Minar
Sanchi Buddhist monuments
Sundarbans National Park
Taj Mahal
Thanjavur (Brihadisvara Temple)

□ Indonesia
Borobudur Temple compounds
Komodo National Park
Prambanan Temple compounds
Sangiran (early man site)
Ujung Kulon National Park

□ Iran
Esfahan (Meidan Emam)
Persepolis
Tchogha Zanbil Ziggurat and complex

□ Iraq
Hatra

□ Ireland
Skellig Michael
Valley of the Boyne

□ Israel
Jerusalem (old city and its walls)

□ Italy
Agrigento (archaeological area)
Alberobello (the trulli)
Amalfi (the coast)
Barumini, Sardinia (the nuraghi)
Casale (Villa Romana)

Caserta (18th-c palace, park, aqueduct of Vanvitelli and the San Leucio complex)
Castel del Monte
Crespi d'Adda
Ferrara (Renaissance city)
Florence (historic centre)
I Sassi di Matera
Modena (cathedral, Torre Civica and Piazza Grande)
Naples (historic centre)
Padua (botanical garden)
Pienza (historic city centre)
Pisa (Piazza del Duomo)
Pompeii, with Herculaneum and Torre Annunziata archaeological areas
Portovenere, Cinque Terre and the islands of Palmaria, Tino and Tinetto
Ravenna, early Christian monuments and mosaics
Rome (historic centre)
San Gimignano (historic centre)
Santa Maria delle Grazie with *The Last Supper* by Leonardo da Vinci
Siena (historic centre)
Turin (royal houses of Savoy)
Valcamonica (rock drawings)
Venice and its lagoon
Vicenza (city and Palladian villas of the Veneto)
❏ Japan
Ancient Kyoto (Kyoto, Uji and Otsu cities)
Himeji-jo
Hiroshima Peace Memorial (Genbaku Dome)
Horyu-ji area (Buddhist monuments)
Itsukushima Shinto shrine
Shirakami-Sanchi
Shirakawa-go and Gokayama (historic villages)
Yakushima
❏ Jordan
Petra
Quseir Amra
❏ Kenya
Mt Kenya (national park and natural forest)
Sibiloi and Central I national parks

❏ Korea, Republic of (South Korea)
Ch'angdokkung Palace complex
Chongmyo Shrine
Haeinsa Temple including woodblocks of the Tripitaka Koreana
Hwasong Fortress
Sokkuram Grotto
❏ Laos
Luang Prabang
❏ Latvia
Riga (historic centre)
❏ Lebanon
Anjar (archaeological site)
Baalbek
Byblos
Tyre (archaeological site)
❏ Libya
Cyrene (archaeological site)
Ghadamès (old town)
Leptis Magna (archaeological site)
Sabratha (archaeological site)
Tadrart Acacus (rock art sites)
❏ Lithuania
Vilnius (historic centre)
❏ Luxembourg
City of Luxembourg, old quarters and fortifications
❏ Macedonia
Ohrid and its lake
❏ Madagascar
Tsingy Bemaraha Nature Reserve
❏ Malawi
Lake Malawi National Park
❏ Mali
Cliffs of Bandiagara (land of the Dogons)
Djenné (old towns)
Timbuktu
❏ Malta
Hal Saflieni Hypogeum
Megalithic temples
Valetta (old city)
❏ Mauritania
Ancient ksour of Ouadane, Chinguetti, Tichitt and Oualata
Banc d'Arguin National Park

❑ Mexico
Chichen Itza (pre-Hispanic city)
El Tajin (pre-Hispanic city)
El Vizcaino Whale Sanctuary
Guadalajara (hospicio Cabañas)
Guanajuato (historic town) and adjacent mines
Mexico City (historic centre and Xochimilco)
Morelia (historic centre)
Oaxaca (historic zone) and Monte Alban (archaeological site)
Palenque (pre-Hispanic city and national park)
Popocatepetl (16th-c monasteries on the slopes)
Puebla (historic centre)
Queretaro historic monuments zone
Sian Ka'an (Biosphere reserve)
Sierra de San Francisco (rock paintings)
Teotihuacán (pre-Hispanic city)
Uxmal (pre-Hispanic town)
Zacatecas (historic centre)

❑ Morocco
Aït-Ben-Haddou (fortified village)
Fez (Medina)
Marrakesh (Medina)
Meknes (historic city)
Tétouan (Medina)
Volubilis (archaeological site)

❑ Mozambique
Island of Mozambique

❑ Nepal
Chitwan National Park
Kathmandu Valley
Lumbini (birthplace of Lord Buddha)
Sagarmatha National Park

❑ The Netherlands
Amsterdam defence line
Kinderdijk-Elshout (mill network)
Schokland and its surroundings
Willemstad (historic area, inner city and harbour)

❑ New Zealand
Te Wahipounamu
Tongariro National Park

❑ Niger
Air and Téneré (nature reserves)
'W' National Park

❑ Norway
Alta (rock drawings)
Bergen (Bryggen area)
Røros (mining town)
Urnes Stave Church

❑ Oman
Arabian Oryx Sanctuary
Bahla Fort
Bat, Al-Khutm and Al-Ayn (archaeological sites)

❑ Pakistan
Lahore (fort and Shalamar gardens)
Mohenjo Daro (archaeological site)
Rohtas Fort
Takht-i-Bahi Buddhist ruins
Taxila (archaeological remains)
Thatta (historical monuments)

❑ Panama
Darien National Park
La Amistad National Park (shared with Costa Rica)
Panama (historic district, with Salón Bolívar)
Portobelo and San Lorenzo fortifications

❑ Paraguay
Jesuit Missions

❑ Peru
Chan Chan (archaeological site)
Chavin (archaeological site)
Cuzco (old city)
Huascarán National Park
Lima (historic centre)
Machu Picchu (historic sanctuary)
Manu National Park
Nasca and Pampas de Jumana (lines and geoglyphs)
Rio Abiseo National Park

❑ Philippines
Baroque churches of the Philippines
Rice terraces of the Philippine Cordilleras
Tubbataha Reef Marine Park

❑ Poland
Auschwitz concentration camp

Belovezhskaya Pushcha / Bialowieza Forest (shared with Belarus)
Cracow (historic centre)
Malbork (castle of the Teutonic order)
Torun (medieval town)
Warsaw (historic centre)
Wieliczka saltmines
Zamosc (old city)

❏ Portugal
Alcobaça (monastery)
Angra do Heroismo (Azores)
Batalha (monastery)
Belém (tower) and Monastery of the Hieronymites
Evora (historic centre)
Oporto (historic centre)
Sintra (cultural landscape)
Tomar (Convent of Christ)

❏ Romania
Biertan
Danube Delta
Horezu Monastery
Painted churches of northern Moldavia

❏ Russian Federation
Kamchatka volcanic region
Kizhi Pogost
Kolomenskoye (Church of the Ascension)
L Baikal
Moscow (Kremlin and Red Square)
Novgorod (historic monuments)
St Petersburg (historic centre)
Sergiev Posad
Solovetsky Is
Virgin Komi forests
Vladimir and Suzdal monuments

❏ Senegal
Djoudj Bird Sanctuary
Gorée I
Niokolo-Koba National Park

❏ Seychelles
Aldabra Atoll
Vallée de Mai Nature Reserve

❏ Slovakia
Aggtelek caves and the Slovak Karst (shared with Hungary)
Banska Stiavnica

Spissky Hrad
Vlkolinec

❏ Slovenia
Skocjan caves

❏ Spain
Altamira Cave
Avila (old town) with its Extra-Muros churches
Barcelona (Parque and Palacio Güell, Casa Milá, Palau de la Musica Catalana and Hospital de Sant Pau)
Burgos Cathedral
Caceres (old town)
Córdoba (historic centre)
Cuenca (historic walled town)
Doñana National Park
El Escurial (monastery and site)
Garajonay National Park (Canary Is)
Granada (Alhambra, Generalife and Albayzin)
Kingdom of Asturias (its churches)
Las Médulas
Mérida
Poblet Monastery
Pyrenees, Mt Perdu landscape (shared with France)
Salamanca (old city)
San Millán Yuso and Suso monasteries
Santa Maria de Guadalupe (royal monastery)
Santiago de Compostela (old town and route)
Segovia (old town and its aqueduct)
Seville (cathedral, Alcazar and Archivo de Indias)
Teruel (Mudejar architecture)
Toledo (historic city)
Valencia, 'La Lonja de la Seda'

❏ Sri Lanka
Anuradhapura (sacred city)
Dambulla (Golden Rock Temple)
Galle (old town and its fortifications)
Kandy (sacred city)
Polonnaruwa (ancient city)
Sigiriya (ancient city)
Sinharaja Forest Reserve

❑ Sweden
Birka and Hovgården
Drottningholm Palace
Engelsberg ironworks
Gammelstad (church town)
Laponian area
Skogskyrkogården
Tanum (rock carvings)
Visby (Hanseatic town)

❑ Switzerland
Berne (old city)
Müstair (Benedictine convent)
St Gall (convent)

❑ Syria
Aleppo (old city)
Bosra (ancient city)
Damascus (old city)
Palmyra (archaeological site)

❑ Tanzania
Kilimanjaro National Park
Kilwa Kisiwani and Songa Mnara
  ruins
Ngorongoro area
Selous Game Reserve
Serengeti National Park

❑ Thailand
Ayutthaya (historic city) and associated
  towns
Ban Chiang (archaeological site)
Sukhothai (historic city) and associated
  towns
Thungyai-Huai Kha Khaeng (wildlife
  sanctuaries)

❑ Tunisia
Carthage (archaeological site)
Dougga / Thugga
El Djem (amphitheatre)
Ichkeul National Park
Kairouan
Kerkuane (Punic town and necropolis)
Sousse (Medina)
Tunis (Medina)

❑ Turkey
Divrigi (Great Mosque and hospital)
Göreme National Park and rock sites of
  Cappadocia

Hattusha (Hittite city)
Hierapolis-Pamukkale
Istanbul (historic areas)
Nemrut Dag (archaeological site)
Safranbolu (old city)
Xanthos-Letoon

❑ Uganda
Bwindi Impenetrable National Park
Rwenzori Mountains National Park

❑ Ukraine
St Sophia and Lavra of Kiev-Pechersk

❑ UK
Bath
Blenheim Palace
Canterbury Cathedral, St Augustine's
  Abbey and St Martin's Church
Durham (castle and cathedral)
Edinburgh (old town and new town)
Giant's Causeway and its coast
Gough Island Wildlife Reserve (South
  Atlantic Ocean)
Greenwich (maritime buildings and
  park)
Gwynedd (castles and towns of King
  Edward I)
Hadrian's Wall
Henderson I (Pacific Ocean)
Ironbridge Gorge
St Kilda I
Stonehenge, Avebury and related
  megalithic sites
Studley Royal Park and the ruins of
  Fountains Abbey
Tower of London
Westminster (palace and abbey) and St
  Margaret's Church

❑ USA
Cahokia Mounds site
Carlsbad Caverns National Park
Chaco Culture National Historical Park
Everglades National Park
Grand Canyon National Park
Great Smoky Mountains National Park
Hawaii Volcanoes National Park

Independence Hall, Philadelphia
Mammoth Cave National Park
Mesa Verde National Park
Monticello and the University of Virginia in
 Charlottesville
Olympic National Park
Pueblo de Taos
Puerto Rico (La Fortaleza and San Juan
 historic site)
Redwood National Park
Statue of Liberty
Tatshenshini-Alsek, Kluane National Park,
 Wrangell St Elias National Park and Reserve,
 and Glacier Bay National Park (shared with
 Canada)
Waterton Glacier International Peace Park
 (shared with Canada)
Yellowstone National Park
Yosemite National Park
❑ Uruguay
Colonia del Sacramento (historic quarter)
❑ Uzbekistan
Bukhara
Itchan Kala (historic city)
❑ Vatican City
Vatican City

❑ Venezuela
Canaima National Park
Coro and its port
❑ Vietnam
Ha Long Bay
Hué (complex of monuments)
❑ Yemen
Sana'a (old city)
Shibam (old walled city)
Zabid (historic town)
❑ Yugoslavia
Durmitor National Park
Kotor and its gulf
Stari Ras and Sopocani Monastery
Studenica Monastery
❑ Zambia
Victoria Falls / Mosi-oa-Tunya (shared with
 Zimbabwe)
❑ Zimbabwe
Khami ruins
Great Zimbabwe National Monument
Mana Pools, National Park and Sapi and
 Chewore safari areas
Victoria Falls / Mosi-oa-Tunya (shared with
 Zambia)

Tropical rainforest (Rate of destruction)

The destruction of the world's rainforests has taken place largely as a result of economic pressures for more agricultural land and products. This destruction has led to a huge increase in the amount of carbon dioxide being released into the atmosphere. It also causes the degradation and erosion of top-soil, increasing the risk of rivers silting up and flooding. Rainforests are home to half the world's plant and animal species, many of which are now in imminent danger of extinction. The following data are 1997 FAO estimates for 87 tropical countries, taken from *State of the World's Forests 1997* published by the Food and Agriculture Organization of the United Nations.

Region	Forest area 1995 (1 000 ha) [1]	Annual forest loss 1990–5 (1 000 ha)	Annual rate of destruction (%)
Africa			
West Sahelian Africa	39 827	295	0.7
East Sahelian Africa	57 542	420	0.7
West Moist Africa	46 324	492	1
Central Africa	204 677	1 201	0.6
Tropical Southern Africa	141 311	1 158	0.8
Insular East Africa	15 220	131	0.8
Total Tropical Africa	*504 901*	*3 695*	*0.7*
Asia			
South Asia	77 137	141	0.2
Continental Southeast Asia	70 163	1 164	1.6
Insular Southeast Asia	132 466	1 750	1.3
Total Tropical Asia	*279 766*	*3 055*	*1.1*
North and Central America			
Central America and Mexico	75 018	959	1.2
Caribbean	4 425	78	1.7
Total Tropical North and Central America	*79 443*	*1 037*	*1.3*
South America	827 946	4 655	0.6
Oceania	41 903	151	0.4
TOTAL	1 733 959	12 593	0.7

[1] One hectare (ha) = 10 000 sq m. To convert ha to sq km, divide by 100; to convert ha to sq mi, multiply by 0.003861.

Tropical rainforest distribution

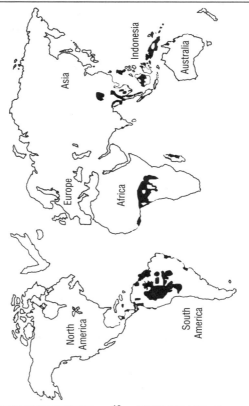

TIME

The seasons

N Hemisphere	Duration
Spring	From vernal equinox (c.21 Mar) to summer solstice (c.21 Jun)
Summer	From summer solstice (c.21 Jun) to autumnal equinox (c.23 Sep)
Autumn	From autumnal equinox (c.23 Sep) to winter solstice (c.21 Dec)
Winter	From winter solstice (c.21 Dec) to vernal equinox (c.21 Mar)

S Hemisphere	Duration
Autumn	From autumnal equinox (c.21 Mar) to winter solstice (c.21 Jun)
Winter	From winter solstice (c.21 Jun) to spring equinox (c.23 Sep)
Spring	From spring equinox (c.23 Sep) to summer solstice (c.21 Dec)
Summer	From summer solstice (c.21 Dec) to autumnal equinox (c.21 Mar)

Months (Associations of gems and flowers)

In many Western countries, the months are traditionally associated with gemstones and flowers. There is considerable variation between countries. The following combinations are widely recognized in North America and the UK.

Month	Gemstone	Flower
January	Garnet	Carnation, Snowdrop
February	Amethyst	Primrose, Violet
March	Aquamarine, Bloodstone	Jonquil, Violet
April	Diamond	Daisy, Sweet Pea
May	Emerald	Hawthorn, Lily of the Valley
June	Alexandrite, Moonstone, Pearl	Honeysuckle, Rose
July	Ruby	Larkspur, Water Lily
August	Peridot, Sardonyx	Gladiolus, Poppy
September	Sapphire	Aster, Morning Glory
October	Opal, Tourmaline	Calendula, Cosmos
November	Topaz	Chrysanthemum
December	Turquoise, Zircon	Holly, Narcissus, Poinsettia

International time differences

The time zones of the world are conventionally measured from longitude 0° at Greenwich Observatory (Greenwich Mean Time, GMT).

Each 15° of longitude east of this point is one hour ahead of GMT (eg when it is 2pm in London it is 3pm or later in time zones to the east). Hours ahead of GMT are shown by a plus sign, eg +3, +4/8.

Each 15° west of this point is one hour behind GMT (eg 2pm in London would be 1pm or earlier in time zones to the west). Hours behind GMT are shown by a minus sign, eg -3, -4/8.

Some countries adopt time zones that vary from standard time. Also, during the summer, several countries adopt Daylight Saving Time (or Summer Time), which is one hour ahead of the times shown below.

Afghanistan	$+4\frac{1}{2}$	Cape Verde	-1	Gambia, The	0
Albania	+1	Central African		Georgia	+4
Algeria	+1	Republic	+1	Germany	+1
Andorra	+1	Chad	+1	Ghana	0
Angola	+1	Chile	-4	Gibraltar	+1
Antigua and		China	+8	Greece	+2
Barbuda	-4	Colombia	-5	Greenland	-3
Argentina	-3	Comoros	+3	Grenada	-4
Armenia	+4	Congo	+1	Guatemala	-6
Australia	$+8/10\frac{1}{2}$	Congo, Democratic		Guinea	0
Austria	+1	Republic of	+1/2	Guinea-Bissau	0
Azerbaijan	+3	Costa Rica	-6	Guyana	-4
Bahamas, The	-5	Côte d'Ivoire	0	Haiti	-5
Bahrain	+3	Croatia	+1	Honduras	-6
Bangladesh	+6	Cuba	-5	Hong Kong	+8
Barbados	-4	Cyprus	+2	Hungary	+1
Belarus	+2	Czech Republic	+1	Iceland	0
Belgium	+1	Denmark	+1	India	$+5\frac{1}{2}$
Belize	-6	Djibouti	+3	Indonesia	+7/9
Benin	+1	Dominica	-4	Iran	$+3\frac{1}{2}$
Bermuda	-4	Dominican Republic	-4	Iraq	+3
Bhutan	+6	Ecuador	-5	Ireland	0
Bolivia	-4	Egypt	+2	Israel	+2
Bosnia-Herzegovina	+1	El Salvador	-6	Italy	+1
Botswana	+2	Equatorial Guinea	+1	Jamaica	-5
Brazil	-2/5	Eritrea	+3	Japan	+9
Brunei	+8	Estonia	+2	Jordan	+2
Bulgaria	+2	Ethiopia	+3	Kazakhstan	+4/6
Burkina Faso	0	Falkland Is	-4	Kenya	+3
Burundi	+2	Fiji	+12	Kiribati	+12
Cambodia	+7	Finland	+2	Korea, Democratic	
Cameroon	+1	France	+1	People's Republic of	
Canada	$-3\frac{1}{2}/8$	Gabon	+1	(North Korea)	+9

42

Korea, Republic of (South Korea)	+9	New Zealand	+12	South Africa	+2	
Kuwait	+3	Nicaragua	-6	Spain	+1	
Kyrgyzstan	+5	Niger	+1	Sri Lanka	$+5\frac{1}{2}$	
Laos	+7	Nigeria	+1	Sudan, The	+2	
Latvia	+2	Norway	+1	Suriname	-3	
Lebanon	+2	Oman	+4	Swaziland	+2	
Lesotho	+2	Pakistan	+5	Sweden	+1	
Liberia	0	Panama	-5	Switzerland	+1	
Libya	+1	Papua New		Syria	+2	
Liechtenstein	+1	Guinea	+10	Taiwan	+8	
Lithuania	+2	Paraguay	-4	Tajikistan	+5	
Luxembourg	+1	Peru	-5	Tanzania	+3	
Macedonia	+1	Philippines	+8	Thailand	+7	
Madagascar	+3	Poland	+1	Togo	0	
Malawi	+2	Portugal	0	Tonga	+13	
Malaysia	+8	Qatar	+3	Trinidad and		
Maldives	+5	Romania	+2	Tobago	-4	
Mali	0	Russia	+2/12	Tunisia	+1	
Malta	+1	Rwanda	+2	Turkey	+2	
Marshall Is	+12	St Kitts and Nevis	-4	Turkmenistan	+5	
Mauritania	0	St Lucia	-4	Tuvalu	+12	
Mauritius	+4	St Vincent and the		Uganda	+3	
Mexico	-6/8	Grenadines	-4	Ukraine	+2	
Micronesia, Federated		Samoa	-11	United Arab Emirates	+4	
States of	+10/11	San Marino	+1	UK	0	
Moldova	+2	São Tomé and		Uruguay	-3	
Monaco	+1	Príncipe	0	USA	-5/10	
Mongolia	+8	Saudi Arabia	+3	Uzbekistan	+5	
Morocco	0	Senegal	0	Vanuatu	+11	
Mozambique	+2	Seychelles	+4	Venezuela	-4	
Myanmar (Burma)	$+6\frac{1}{2}$	Sierra Leone	0	Vietnam	+7	
Namibia	+1	Singapore	+8	Yemen	+3	
Nauru	+12	Slovakia	+1	Yugoslavia, Federal		
Nepal	$+5\frac{3}{4}$	Slovenia	+1	Republic of	+1	
Netherlands, The	+1	Solomon Is	+11	Zambia	+2	
		Somalia	+3	Zimbabwe	+2	

International time zones

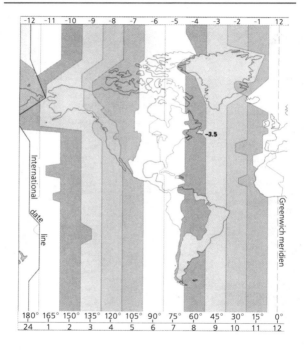

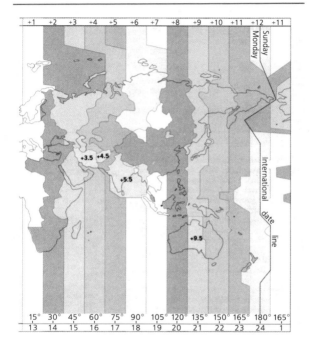

Chinese animal years and times 1972–2007

Chinese	English	Years			Time of day (hours)
Shu	Rat	1972	1984	1996	2300–0100
Niu	Ox	1973	1985	1997	0100–0300
Hu	Tiger	1974	1986	1998	0300–0500
Tu	Hare	1975	1987	1999	0500–0700
Long	Dragon	1976	1988	2000	0700–0900
She	Serpent	1977	1989	2001	0900–1100
Ma	Horse	1978	1990	2002	1100–1300
Yang	Sheep	1979	1991	2003	1300–1500
Hou	Monkey	1980	1992	2004	1500–1700
Ji	Cock	1981	1993	2005	1700–1900
Gou	Dog	1982	1994	2006	1900–2100
Zhu	Boar	1983	1995	2007	2100–2300

Year equivalents

–Jewish [1] (AM)

5756	(25 Sep 1995 –13 Sep 1996)	5769	(30 Sep 2008 –18 Sep 2009)
5757	(14 Sep 1996 –1 Oct 1997)	5770	(19 Sep 2009 –8 Sep 2010)
5758	(2 Oct 1997 –20 Sep 1998)	5771	(9 Sep 2010 –28 Sep 2011)
5759	(21 Sep 1998 –10 Sep 1999)	5772	(29 Sep 2011 –16 Sep 2012)
5760	(11 Sep 1999 –29 Sep 2000)	5773	(17 Sep 2012 –4 Sep 2013)
5761	(30 Sep 2000 –17 Sep 2001)	5774	(5 Sep 2013 –24 Sep 2014)
5762	(18 Sep 2001 –6 Sep 2002)	5775	(25 Sep 2014 –13 Sep 2015)
5763	(7 Sep 2002 –26 Sep 2003)	5776	(14 Sep 2015 –2 Oct 2016)
5764	(27 Sep 2003 –15 Sep 2004)	5777	(3 Oct 2016 –20 Sep 2017)
5765	(16 Sep 2004 –3 Oct 2005)	5778	(21 Sep 2017 –9 Sep 2018)
5766	(4 Oct 2005 –22 Sep 2006)	5779	(10 Sep 2018 –29 Sep 2019)
5767	(23 Sep 2006 –12 Sep 2007)	5780	(30 Sep 2019 –18 Sep 2020)
5768	(13 Sep 2007 –29 Sep 2008)		

–Islamic [2] (H)

1416	(31 May 1995 –18 May 1996)	1429	(10 Jan 2008 –28 Dec 2008)
1417	(19 May 1996 –8 May 1997)	1430	(29 Dec 2008 –17 Dec 2009)
1418	(9 May 1997 –27 Apr 1998)	1431	(18 Dec 2009 –6 Dec 2010)
1419	(28 Apr 1998 –16 Apr 1999)	1432	(7 Dec 2010 –26 Nov 2011)
1420	(17 Apr 1999 –5 Apr 2000)	1433	(27 Nov 2011 –14 Nov 2012)
1421	(6 Apr 2000 –25 Mar 2001)	1434	(15 Nov 2012 –4 Nov 2013)
1422	(26 Mar 2001 –14 Mar 2002)	1435	(5 Nov 2013 –24 Oct 2014)
1423	(15 Mar 2002 –3 Mar 2003)	1436	(25 Oct 2014 –13 Oct 2015)
1424	(4 Mar 2003 –21 Feb 2004)	1437	(14 Oct 2015 –1 Oct 2016)
1425	(22 Feb 2004 –9 Feb 2005)	1438	(2 Oct 2016 –21 Sep 2017)
1426	(10 Feb 2005 –30 Jan 2006)	1439	(22 Sep 2017 –10 Sep 2018)
1427	(31 Jan 2006 –20 Jan 2007)	1440	(11 Sep 2018 –31 Aug 2019)
1428	(21 Jan 2007 –9 Jan 2008)	1441	(1 Sep 2019 –19 Aug 2020)

— Hindu[3] (SE) —

1917	(22 Mar 1995–20 Mar 1996)	1930	(21 Mar 2008–21 Mar 2009)
1918	(21 Mar 1996–21 Mar 1997)	1931	(22 Mar 2009–21 Mar 2010)
1919	(22 Mar 1997–21 Mar 1998)	1932	(22 Mar 2010–21 Mar 2011)
1920	(22 Mar 1998–21 Mar 1999)	1933	(22 Mar 2011–20 Mar 2012)
1921	(22 Mar 1999–20 Mar 2000)	1934	(21 Mar 2012–21 Mar 2013)
1922	(21 Mar 2000–21 Mar 2001)	1935	(22 Mar 2013–21 Mar 2014)
1923	(22 Mar 2001–21 Mar 2002)	1936	(22 Mar 2014–21 Mar 2015)
1924	(22 Mar 2002–21 Mar 2003)	1937	(22 Mar 2015–20 Mar 2016)
1925	(22 Mar 2003–20 Mar 2004)	1938	(21 Mar 2016–21 Mar 2017)
1926	(21 Mar 2004–21 Mar 2005)	1939	(22 Mar 2017–21 Mar 2018)
1927	(22 Mar 2005–21 Mar 2006)	1940	(22 Mar 2018–21 Mar 2019)
1928	(22 Mar 2006–21 Mar 2007)	1941	(22 Mar 2019–20 Mar 2020)
1929	(22 Mar 2007–20 Mar 2008)		

Gregorian equivalents are given in parentheses and are AD (= Anno Domini, also called CE, Common Era).

[1] Calculated from 3761BC (= Before Christ, also called BCE, Before Common Era), said to be the year of the creation of the world. AM = Anno Mundi.

[2] Calculated from AD622, the year in which the Prophet went from Mecca to Medina. H = Hegira.

[3] Calculated from AD78, the beginning of the Saka era (SE), used alongside Gregorian dates in Government of India publications since 22 Mar 1957.

Month equivalents

Gregorian equivalents to other calendars are given in parentheses; the figures refer to the number of solar days in each month.

— Gregorian —

(Basis: Sun)
January (31)
February (28 or 29)
March (31)
April (30)
May (31)
June (30)
July (31)
August (31)
September (30)
October (31)
November (30)
December (31)

— Jewish —

(Basis: Moon)
Tishri (Sep – Oct) (30)
Heshvan (Oct – Nov) (29 or 30)
Kislev (Nov – Dec) (29 or 30)
Tevet (Dec – Jan) (29)
Shevat (Jan – Feb) (30)
Adar (Feb – Mar) (29 or 30)
Adar Sheni (*leap years only*)
Nisan (Mar – Apr) (30)
Iyar (Apr – May) (29)
Sivan (May – Jun) (30)
Tammuz (Jun – Jul) (29)
Av (Jul – Aug) (30)
Elul (Aug – Sep) (29)

—Islamic—

(Basis: Moon)
Muharram (Sep – Oct) (30)
Safar (Oct – Nov) (29)
Rabi I (Nov – Dec) (30)
Rabi II (Dec – Jan) (29)
Jumada I (Jan – Feb) (30)
Jumada II (Feb – Mar) (29)
Rajab (Mar – Apr) (30)
Shaban (Apr – May) (29)
Ramadan (May – Jun) (30)
Shawwal (Jun – Jul) (29)
Dhu al-Qadah (Jul – Aug) (30)
Dhu al-Hijjah (Aug – Sep) (29 or 30)

—Hindu—

(Basis: Moon)
Chaitra (Mar – Apr) (29 or 30)
Vaisakha (Apr – May) (29 or 30)
Jyaistha (May – Jun) (29 or 30)
Asadha (Jun – Jul) (29 or 30)
Dvitiya Asadha (*certain leap years*)
Sravana (Jul – Aug) (29 or 30)
Dvitiya Sravana (*certain leap years*)
Bhadrapada (Aug – Sep) (29 or 30)
Asvina (Sep – Oct) (29 or 30)
Karttika (Oct – Nov) (29 or 30)
Margasirsa (Nov – Dec) (29 or 30)
Pausa (Dec – Jan) (29 or 30)
Magha (Jan – Feb) (29 or 30)
Phalguna (Feb – Mar) (29 or 30)

National holidays

The first part of each listing gives the holidays that occur on fixed dates (though it should be noted that holidays often vary according to local circumstances and the day of the week on which they fall). Most dates are accompanied by an indication of the purpose of the day, eg Independence = Independence Day; dates which have no gloss are either fixed dates within the Christian calendar (for which see below) or bank holidays.

The second part of the listing gives holidays that vary, usually depending on religious factors. The most common of these are given in abbreviated form (see list below).

A number in brackets such as (Independence) (2) refers to the number of days devoted to the holiday.

The listings do not include holidays that affect only certain parts of a country, half-day holidays, or Sundays.

The following abbreviations are used for variable religious feast-days:

A	Ascension Thursday
Ad	Id-ul-Adha (also found with other spellings — especially Eid-ul-Adha; various names relating to this occasion are used in different countries, such as Tabaski, Id el-Kebir, Hari Raja Haji)
Ar	Arafa
As	Ashora (found with various spellings)
C	Carnival (immediately before Christian Lent, unless specified)
CC	Corpus Christi
D	Diwali, Deepavali
EM	Easter Monday
ER	End of Ramadan (known generally as Id / Eid-ul-Fitr, but various names relating to this occasion are used in different countries, such as Karite, Hari Raja Puasa)
ES	Easter Sunday
GF	Good Friday

HS   Holy Saturday
HT   Holy Thursday
NY   New Year
PB   Prophet's Birthday (known generally as Maul-id-al-Nabi in various forms and spellings)
R   First day of Ramadan
WM   Whit Monday

The following fixed dates are shown without gloss:

Jan 1   New Year's Day
Jan 6   Epiphany
May 1   Labour Day (often known by a different name, such as Workers' Day)
Aug 15 Assumption of Our Lady
Nov 1   All Saints' Day
Nov 2   All Souls' Day
Dec 8   Immaculate Conception
Dec 24 Christmas Eve
Dec 25 Christmas Day
Dec 26 Boxing Day/St Stephen's Day
Dec 31 New Year's Eve

Afghanistan Apr 27 (Sawr Revolution), May 1, Aug 19 (Independence); Ad (3), Ar, As, ER (3), NY (Hindu), PB, R

Albania Jan 1, 11 (Republic), May 1, Nov 28 (Independence), 29 (Liberation)

Algeria Jan 1, May 1, Jun 19 (Righting), Jul 5 (Independence), Nov 1 (Revolution); Ad, As, ER, NY (Muslim), PB

Andorra Jan 1, 6, Mar 19 (St Joseph), May 1, Jun 24 (St John), Aug 15, Sep 8 (Our Lady of Meritxell), Nov 1, 4 (St Charles), Dec 8, 25, 26; A, C, CC, EM, GF, WM

Angola Jan 1, Feb 4 (Commencement of the Armed Struggle), May 1, Sep 17 (National Hero), Nov 11 (Independence), Dec 10 (MPLA Foundation), 25 (Family)

Antigua and Barbuda Jan 1, May 1, Jul (CARICOM), Nov 1 (Independence), Dec 25, 26; C (2), EM, GF, WM

Argentina Jan 1, May 1, 25 (National), Jun 10 (Malvinas Islands Memorial), 20 (Flag), Jul 9 (Independence), Aug 17 (Death of General San Martin), Oct 12 (Columbus), Dec 8, 25, 31; GF, HT

Armenia Jan 1, 6 (Armenian Christmas), Apr 24 (Day of Remembrance of the Victims of the Genocide), May 28 (Declaration of the First Armenian Republic, 1918), Dec 7 (Day of Remembrance of the Victims of the Earthquake); EM, ES, GF, HS; Sep Holiday

Australia Jan 1, Apr 25 (Anzac), Dec 25, 26 (*except South Australia*); Australia (Jan), EM, GF, HS; *additional days vary between states*

Austria Jan 1, 6, May 1, Aug 15, Oct 26 (National), Nov 1, Dec 8, 24, 25, 26; A, CC, EM, WM

Azerbaijan Jan 1, 20 (Sorrow), 8 Mar (Women), May 28 (Republic), Oct 9 (Armed Services), 18 (Statehood), Nov 17 (National Survival), Dec 31 (Day of Azerbaijani Solidarity Worldwide); Ad

Bahamas, The Jan 1, Jul 10 (Independence), Dec 25, 26; EM, GF, WM; Labour (Jun), Emancipation (Aug), Discovery (Oct)

Bahrain Jan 1, Dec 16 (National); Ad (3), As (2), ER (3), NY (Muslim), PB

Bangladesh Feb 21 (Shaheed), Mar 26 (Independence), May 1, Jul 1, Nov 7 (National Revolution), Dec 16 (Victory), 25, 31; Ad (3), ER (3), NY (Bengali), NY (Muslim), PB, Shab-e-Barat (Apr), Buddah Purnima (Apr/May), Shab-I-Qadr (May), Jumat-ul-Wida (May), Durga Puza (Oct)

Barbados Jan 1, Nov 30 (Independence), Dec 25, 26; EM, GF, WM, Kadooment (Aug), May Holiday, United Nations (Oct)

Belarus Jan 1, 7 (Russian Orthodox Christmas), Mar 8 (Women), May 1, 9 (Victory), Jul 27 (Independence), Nov 2 (Dsiady/Day of Commemoration), Dec 25; GF, HS, ES, EM, Russian Orthodox Easter (2)

Belgium Jan 1, May 1, Jul 21 (National), Aug 15, Nov 1, 11 (Armistice), Dec 25; A, EM, WM; May, Aug, Nov Bank Holidays; Regional Holiday (Jul in N, Sep in S)

Belize Jan 1, Mar 9 (Baron Bliss), May 1, 24 (Commonwealth), Sep 10 (National), 21 (Independence), Oct 12 (Columbus), Nov 19 (Garifuna Settlement), Dec 25, 26; EM, GF, HS

Benin Jan 1, 16 (Martyrs), Apr 1 (Youth), May 1, Oct 26 (Armed Forces), Nov 30 (National), Dec 25, 31 (Feed Yourself); Ad, ER

Bhutan May 2 (Birthday of Jigme Dorji Wangchuk), Jun 2 (Coronation of Fourth Hereditary King), Jul 21 (First Sermon of Lord Buddha, Death of Jigme Dorji Wangchuk), Nov 11–13 (Birthday of HM Jigme Singye Wangchuk), Dec 17 (National)

Bolivia Jan 1, May 1, Aug 6 (Independence), Nov 1, Dec 25; C (2), CC, GF

Bosnia-Herzegovina Jan 9 (Republic), Mar 1 (Independence), May 1, Nov 25 (Republic)

Botswana Jan 1, 2, Sep 30 (Botswana), Dec 25, 26; A, EM, GF, HS, President's Day (Jul); Jul, Oct Public Holidays

Brazil Jan 1, Apr 21 (Independence Hero Tiradentes), May 1, Sep 7 (Independence), Oct 12, Nov 2 (Memorial), 15 (Proclamation of the Republic), Dec 25; C (2), CC, GF, HS, HT

Brunei Jan 1, Feb 23 (National), May 31 (Royal Brunei Malay Regiment), Jul 15 (Sultan's Birthday), Dec 25; Ad, ER (2), GF, NY (Chinese), NY (Muslim), PB, R, Meraj (Mar – Apr), Revelation of the Koran (May)

Bulgaria Jan 1, May 1 (2), 24 (Slav Literature, Bulgarian Education and Culture), Sep 9 (National), Nov 7 (October Revolution)

Burkina Faso Jan 1, 3 (1966 Revolution), May 1, Aug 4, 15, Nov 1, Dec 25; A, Ad, EM, ER, PB, WM

Burma ► Myanmar

Burundi Jan 1, May 1, Jul 1 (Independence), Aug 15, Sep 18 (Victory of Uprona), Nov 1, Dec 25; A

Cambodia Jan 9 (National), Apr 17 (Victory over American Imperialism), May 1, 20 (Day of Hatred), Sep 22 (Feast of the Ancestors); Cambodian New Year (Apr)

Cameroon Jan 1, Feb 11 (Youth), May 1, 20 (National), Aug 15, Dec 25; A, Ad, ER, GF

Canada Jan 1, Jul 1 (Canada) (*except Newfoundland*), Nov 11 (Remembrance) Dec 25, 26; EM, GF, Labour (Sep), Thanksgiving (Oct), Victoria (May); *additional days vary between states*

Cape Verde Jan 1, 20 (National Heroes), Mar 8 (Women), May 1, Jun 1 (Children), Sep 12 (National), Dec 24, 25; GF

Central African Republic Jan 1, Mar 29 (Death of President Boganda), May 1, Jun 1 (Mothers), Aug 13 (Independence), 15, Sep 1 (Arrival of the Military Committee for National Recovery), Nov 1, Dec 1 (Republic), 25; A, EM, WM

Chad Jan 1, May 1, 25 (Liberation of Africa), Jun 7 (Liberation), Aug 11 (Independence), Nov 1, 28 (Republic), Dec 25; Ad, EM, ER, PB

Chile Jan 1, May 1, 21 (Battle of Iquique), Jun 29 (Sts Peter and Paul), Aug 15, Sep 11 (National Liberation), 18 (Independence), 19 (Armed Forces), Oct 12 (Day of the Race), Nov 1, Dec 8, 25, 31; GF, HS

China Jan 1, May 1, Oct 1 (National) (2); Spring Festival (4) (Jan/Feb)

Colombia Jan 1, 6, May 1, Jun 29 (Sts Peter and Paul), Jul 20 (Independence), Aug 7 (National), 15, Oct 12 (Columbus), Nov 1, 15 (Independence of Cartagena), Dec 8, 25, 30, 31; A, CC, GF, HT, St Joseph (Mar), Sacred Heart (Jun)

Comoros May 9 (Islamic New Year), 18 (Ashoura), Jul 6 (Independence), 18 (Mouloud/Prophet's Birthday), Nov 17 (President Abdallah's Assassination), 28 (Leilat al-Meiraj/Ascension of the Prophet); Ad, ER, R

Congo Jan 1, Mar 18 (Day of the Supreme Sacrifice), May 1, Jul 31 (Revolution), Aug 13–15 (The Three Glorious Days), Nov 1 (Day of the Dead), Dec 25 (Children), 31 (Foundation of the Party and People's Republic)

Congo, Democratic Republic of (Zaïre) Jan 1, 4 (Martyrs of Independence), May 1, 20 (Mouvement Populaire de la Révolution), Jun 24 (Anniversary of Currency, Promulgation of the 1967 Constitution, and Day of the Fishermen), 30 (Independence), Dec 25

Costa Rica Jan 1, Mar 19 (St Joseph), Apr 11 (National Heroes), May 1, Jun 29 (Sts Peter and Paul), Jul 25 (Annexation of Guanacaste), Aug 2 (Our Lady of the Angels), 15 (Mothers), Sep 15 (Independence), Oct 12 (Day of the Race), Dec 8, 25; CC, GF, HS, HT

Côte d'Ivoire Jan 1, May 1, Aug 15, Nov 1, Dec 7 (Independence), 24, 25, 31; A, Ad, EM, ER, GF, WM

Croatia Jan 1, 6, May 1, 30 (Republic), Jun 22, Aug 5 (Assumption), 15 (Assumption), Nov 1, Dec 25, 26; EM, GF

Cuba Jan 1 (Day of Liberation), May 1, Jul 25 (National Rebellion) (2), Oct 10 (Beginning of the Independence Wars)

Cyprus Jan 1, 6, Mar 25 (Greek Independence), May 1, Oct 28 (Greek National), 29 (Turkish National), Dec 25, 26; Ad, EM, ER, GF, HS, PB

Czech Republic Jan 1, 2, May 1, Jul 5 (Sts Cyril and Methodius), 6 (Martyrdom of Jan Hus), Oct 28 (Independence), Dec 24, 25, 26; EM

Denmark Jan 1, Jun 5 (Constitution), Dec 24, 25, 26; A, EM, GF, HT, WM, General Prayer (Apr/May)

Djibouti Jan 1, May 1, Jun 27 (Independence) (2), Dec 25; Ad (2), ER (2), NY (Muslim), PB, Al-Isra Wal-Mira'age (Mar–Apr)

Dominica Jan 1, May 1, Nov 3 (Independence), 4 (Community Service), Dec 25, 26; C (2), EM, GF, WM, August Monday

Dominican Republic Jan 1, 6, 21 (Our Lady of Altagracia), 26 (Duarte), Feb 27 (Independence), May 1, Aug 16 (Restoration of the Republic), Sep 24 (Our Lady of Mercy), Dec 25; CC, GF

Ecuador Jan 1, May 1, 24 (Independence Battle), Jun 30, Jul 24 (Bolivar), Aug 10 (Independence), Oct 9 (Independence of Guayaquil), 12 (Columbus), Nov 2, 3 (Independence of Cuenca), Dec 6 (Foundation of Quito), 25, 31; C (2), GF, HT

Egypt Jan 7 (Eastern Orthodox Christmas), Apr 25 (Sinai Liberation), May 1, Jun 18 (Evacuation), Jul 1, 23 (Revolution Anniversary), Oct 6 (Armed Forces); Ad (2), Ar, ER (2), NY (Muslim), PB, Palm Sunday and Easter Sunday (Eastern Orthodox), Sham El-Nessim (Apr – May)

Eire ▶ Ireland, Republic of

El Salvador Jan 1, May 1, Jun 29, 30, Sep 15 (Independence), Oct 12 (Columbus), Nov 2, 5 (First Cry of Independence), Dec 24, 25, 30, 31; GF, HT, Ash Wednesday, San Salvador (4)

England and Wales Jan 1, Dec 25, 26; EM, GF, Early May, Late May and Summer (Aug) Bank Holidays

Equatorial Guinea Jan 1, May 1, Jun 5 (President's Birthday), Aug 3 (Armed Forces), Oct 12 (Independence), Dec 10 (Human Rights), 25; CC, GF, Constitution (Aug)

Eritrea Jan 1, 6, May 24 (Independence), Jun 20 (Martyrs'), Sep 1 (Beginning of the Armed Struggle), Dec 25; ER, Ad

Estonia Jan 1, Feb 24 (Independence), May 1 (Spring), Jun 23 (Victory/Anniversary of the Battle of Vönnu), 24 (St John), Dec 25, 26; GF, HS, ES, EM, Whit Sunday

Ethiopia Jan 7 (Ethiopian Christmas), 19 (Ethiopian Epiphany), Mar 2 (Victory of Adwa), Apr 6 (Patriots), May 1, Sep 12 (Revolution), 27 (Finding of the True Cross); Ad, ER, NY (Ethiopian, Sep), PB, Ethiopian Good Friday and Easter

Fiji Jan 1, Oct 12 (Fiji), Dec 25, 26; D, EM, GF, HS, PB, August Bank Holiday, Queen's Birthday (Jun), Prince Charles's Birthday (Nov)

Finland Jan 1, May 1, Oct 31 (All Saints Observance), Nov 1, Dec 6 (Independence), 24, 25, 26, 31; A, EM, GF, Midsummer Eve and Day (Jun), Twelfthtide (Jan), Whitsuntide (May – Jun)

France Jan 1, May 1, 8 (Armistice), Jul 14 (Bastille), Aug 14 (Assumption Eve), 15, Oct 31 (All Saints' Eve), Nov 1, 11 (Armistice), Dec 24, 25, 31; A, EM, GF, HS, WM, Ascension Eve, Whit Holiday Eve, Law of 20 Dec 1906, Law of 23 Dec 1904

Gabon Jan 1, Mar 12 (Anniversary of Renewal), May 1, Aug 17 (Independence), Nov 1, Dec 25; Ad, EM, ER, WM

Gambia, The Jan 1, Feb 18 (Independence), May 1, Aug 15 (St Mary), Dec 25; Ad, As, ER (2), GF, PB

Georgia Jan 6 (Eastern Orthodox Christmas), May 26 (Independence), Dec 31; GF, HS, ES, EM

Germany Jan 1, May 1, Jun 17 (National), Oct 3 (Unity), Dec 24, 25, 26; A, EM, GF, WM, Day of Penance (Nov)

Ghana Jan 1, Mar 6 (Independence), May 1, Jun 4 (June 4 Revolution), Jul 1 (Republic), Dec 25, 26, 31 (Revolution); EM, GF, HS

Greece Jan 1, 6, Mar 25 (National), May 1, Aug 15, Oct 28 (National), Dec 25, 26; GF, EM, WM, Monday in Lent

Grenada Jan 1–2, Feb 7 (Independence), May 1, Aug 3–4 (Emancipation), Oct 25 (Thanksgiving), Dec 25, 26; CC, EM, GF, WM

Guatemala Jan 1, May 1, Jun 30 (Army), Jul 1, Sep 15 (Independence), Oct 12 (Day of the Race), 20 (1944 Revolution), Nov 1, Dec 24, 25, 31; GF, HS, HT

Guinea Jan 1, Apr 3 (Second Republic), May 1, Aug 15, Oct 2 (Independence), Nov 1 (Army), Dec 25; Ad, EM, ER, PB

Guinea-Bissau Jan 1, 20 (National Heroes), Feb 8 (BNG Anniversary and Monetary Reform), Mar 8 (Women), May 1, Aug 3 (Martyrs of Colonialism), Sep 12 (National), 24 (Establishment of the Republic), Nov 14 (Readjustment), Dec 25

Guyana Jan 1, Feb 23 (Republic), May 1, Aug 1 (Freedom), Dec 25, 26; Ad, D, EM, GF, PB, Phagwah (Mar), Caribbean (Jul)

Haiti Jan 1 (Independence), 2 (Ancestry), Apr 14 (Americas), May 1, Aug 15, Oct 17 (Dessalines), 24 (United Nations), Nov 1, 2, 18 (Vertières), Dec 5 (Discovery), 25; A, C, CC, GF

Honduras Jan 1, Apr 14 (Pan American), May 1, Sep 15 (Independence), Oct 3 (Francisco Morazán's Birthday), 12 (America's Discovery), 21 (Armed Forces), Dec 25, 31; GF, HT

Hungary Jan 1, Apr 4 (Liberation), May 1, Aug 20 (Constitution), Nov 7 (October Socialist Revolution), Dec 25, 26; EM

Iceland Jan 1, May 1, Jun 17 (Independence), Dec 25, 26; A, EM, GF, HT, WM, First Day of Summer, August Holiday Monday

India Jan 1 (some states), 26 (Republic), May 1 (some states), Jun 30, Aug 15 (Independence), Oct 2 (Mahatma Ghandi's Birthday), Dec 25, 31; NY (Parsi, Aug, some states)

Indonesia Jan 1, Aug 17 (Independence), Dec 25; A, Ad, ER (2), GF, NY (Icaka, Mar), NY (Muslim), PB, Ascension of the Prophet (Mar/Apr), Waisak (May)

Iran Feb 11 (Revolution), Mar 20 (Oil), 21 (Now Rooz) (4), Apr 1 (Islamic Republic), 2 (13th of Farvardin), Jun 5 (15th Khordad Uprising); Ad, As, ER, PB, Prophet's Mission (Apr), Birth of the Twelfth Imam (Apr/May), Martyrdom of Imam Ali (May), Death of Imam Jaffar Sadegh (Jun/Jul), Birth of Imam Reza (Jul), Id-E-Ghadir (Aug), Death of the Prophet and Martyrdom of Imam Hassan (Oct/Nov)

Iraq Jan 1, 6 (Army), Feb 8 (8th February Revolution), Mar 21 (Spring), May 1, Jul 14 (14th July Revolution), 17 (17th July Revolution); Ad (4), As, ER (3), NY (Muslim), PB

Ireland Jan 1, Mar 17 (St Patrick), Dec 25, 26; EM, GF, June Holiday, August Holiday, October Holiday, Christmas Holiday

Ireland, Northern ► Northern Ireland

Israel Jan 1, May 14 (Independence); NY (Jewish, Sep/Oct), Purim (Mar), First Day of Passover (Apr), Last Day of Passover (Apr), Pentecost (Jun), Fast of Av (Aug), Day of Atonement (Oct), Feast of Tabernacles (Oct) (2)

Italy Jan 1, 6, Apr 25 (Liberation), May 1, Aug 14 (Mid-August Holiday) (2), Nov 1, Dec 8, 25, 26; EM

Jamaica Jan 1, May 23 (Labour), Aug 5 (Independence), Oct 20 (National Heroes), Dec 25, 26; Ash Wednesday, EM, GF

Japan Jan 1, 2, 3, 15 (Adults), Feb 11 (National Founding), Mar 21 (Vernal Equinox), Apr 29 (Emperor's Birthday), May 3 (Constitution Memorial), 5 (Children), Sep 15 (Respect for the

Aged), 23 (Autumn Equinox), Oct 10 (Health-Sports), Nov 3 (Culture), 23 (Labour Thanksgiving)

Jordan Jan 1, May 1, 25 (Independence), Jun 10 (Great Arab Revolt and Army), Aug 11 (Accession of King Hussein), Nov 14 (King Hussein's Birthday), Dec 25; Ad (4), R, ER (4), NY (Muslim), PB

Kazakhstan Jan 1, Mar 8 (Women), 22 (Nauryz Meyrami/Kazakh New Year), May 1, 9 (Victory), Aug 30 (Constitution), Oct 25 (State Sovereignty), Dec 16 (Independence), 31

Kenya Jan 1, May 1, Jun 1 (Madaraka), Oct 20 (Kenyatta), Dec 12 (Kenyatta), 25, 26; EM, GF, ER (3)

Kiribati Jan 1, Jul 12 (Independence) (3), Dec 25, 26; GF, HS, EM, Youth (Aug)

Korea, Democratic People's Republic of (North Korea) Jan 1, Feb 16 (Kim Jong Il's Birthday) (2), Mar 8 (Women), Apr 15 (Kim-Il Sung's Birthday), May 1 (May Day), Aug 15 (Liberation), Sep 9 (Independence), Oct 10 (Foundation of the Korean Workers' Party), Dec 27 (Constitution)

Korea, Republic of (South Korea) Jan 1–3, Mar 1 (Independence Movement), 10 (Labour), Apr 5 (Arbor), May 5 (Children), Jun 6 (Memorial), Jul 17 (Constitution), Aug 15 (Liberation), Oct 1 (Armed Forces), 3 (National Foundation), 9 (Korean Alphabet), Dec 25; NY (Chinese, Jan/Feb), Lord Buddha's Birthday (May), Moon Festival (Sep/Oct)

Kuwait Jan 1, Feb 25 (National) (3); Ad (3), ER (3), NY (Muslim), PB, Ascension of the Prophet (Mar/Apr), Standing on Mt Arafat (Aug)

Kyrgyzstan Jan 1, 7 (Russian Orthodox Christmas), Feb 9 (Orozo Ait), Mar 8 (Women), 21 (Nooruz/Lunar New Year), Apr 18 (Kurban Ait), May 1, 9 (Victory), Aug 31 (Independence)

Laos Jan 24 (Army), May 1, Dec 2 (National); Lao New Year/Water Festival (3) (Mid-April)

Latvia Jan 1, May 1, Jun 23 (St John), 24 (Midsummer Festival), Nov 18 (National/Proclamation of the Republic), Dec 24, 25, 26; GF

Lebanon Jan 1, Feb 9 (St Maron), May 1, Aug 15, Nov 1, 22 (Independence), Dec 25; Ad (3), As, EM, GF, ER (3), NY (Muslim), PB

Lesotho Jan 1, Mar 12 (Moshoeshoe's Day), 21 (National Tree Planting), May 2 (King's Birthday), Oct 4 (Independence), Dec 25, 26; A, EM, GF, Family (Jul), National Sports (Oct)

Liberia Jan 1, Feb 11 (Armed Forces), Mar 15 (J J Roberts), Apr 12 (Redemption), May 14 (National Unification), Jul 26 (Independence), Aug 24 (National Flag), Nov 29 (President Tubman's Birthday), Dec 25; Decoration (Mar), National Fast and Prayer (Apr), Thanksgiving (Nov)

Libya Mar 2 (Declaration of Establishment of Authority of People), 8 (National), 28 (Evacuation of British Troops), Jun 11 (Evacuation of US Troops), Jul 23 (National), Sep 1 (National), Oct 7 (Evacuation of Italian Fascists); Ad (4), ER (3), PB

Liechtenstein Jan 1, 6, Feb 2 (Candlemas), Mar 19 (St Joseph), May 1, Aug 15, Nov 1, Dec 8, 24, 25, 26, 31; A, C, CE, EM, WM

Lithuania Jan 1, Feb 16 (Independence), May 1, Jun 14 (Mourning and Hope), Jul 6 (Anniversary of the Coronation of Grand Duke Mindaugas), Nov 1, Dec 25, 26; GF, EM; Mothers Day (May)

Luxembourg Jan 1, May 1, Jun 23 (National), Aug 15, Nov 1, 2, Dec 25, 26, 31; A, EM, WM, Shrove Monday

Macedonia Jan 1, 2, May 1 (2); Aug, Oct Bank Holidays

Madagascar Jan 1, Mar 29 (Memorial), May 1, Jun 26 (Independence), Aug 15, Nov 1, Dec 25, 30 (National); A, EM, GF, WM

Malawi Jan 1, Mar 3 (Martyrs), May 14 (Kamuzu), Jul 6 (Republic), Oct 17 (Mothers), Dec 22 (Tree Planting), 25, 26; EM, GF, HS

Malaysia Jan 1 (*some states*), May 1, Jun 3 (Head of State's Birthday), Aug 31 (National), Dec 25; Ad, D (*most states*), ER (2), NY (Chinese, Jan/Feb, *most states*), NY (Muslim), PB, Wesak (*most states*); *several local festivals*

Maldives Jan 1, Jul 26 (Independence) (2), Nov 11 (Republic) (2); Ad (4), ER (3), NY (Muslim), PB, R (2), Huravee (Feb), Martyrs (Apr), National (Oct/Nov) (2)

Mali Jan 1, 20 (Army), May 1, 25 (Africa), Sep 22 (National), Nov 19 (Liberation), Dec 25; Ad, ER, PB, Prophet's Baptism (Nov)

Malta Jan 1, Mar 31 (National), May 1, Aug 15, Dec 13 (Republic), 25; GF

Marshall Islands Jan 1, Mar 1 (Memorial and Nuclear Victims' Day), May 1 (Constitution Day), Jul 4 (Fisherman's Day), Sep 1 (Worker's Day), 30 (Customs Day), Oct 21 (Compact Day), Nov 17 (President's Day), Dec 4 (Thanksgiving Day), 25

Mauritania Jan 1, May 1, 25 (Africa), Jul 10 (Armed Forces), Nov 28 (Independence); Ad, ER, NY (Muslim), PB

Mauritius Jan 1, 2, Mar 12 (Independence), May 1, Nov 1, Dec 25; Ad, D, ER, PB, Chinese Spring Festival (Jan/Feb)

Mexico Jan 1, Feb 5 (Constitution), Mar 21 (Birthday of Benito Juárez), May 1, 5 (Puebla Battle), Sep 1 (Presidential Report), 16 (Independence), Oct 12 (Columbus), Nov 2, 20 (Mexican Revolution), Dec 12 (Our Lady of Guadaloupe), 25, 31; HT, GF

Micronesia, Federated States of Jan 1, 11 (Constitution Day, Kosrae), Mar 1 (Yap Day, Yap), 31 (Culture Day, Pohnpei), May 10 (Proclamation of the Federated States of Micronesia), Sep 11 (Pohnpei Liberation Day, Pohnpei), 23 (Charter Day, Chuuk), Oct 24 (United Nations Day), Nov 4 (National Day), 8 (Constitution Day, Pohnpei), Thanksgiving (last Thurs in Nov, Kosrae), Dec 24 (Constitution Day, Yap), 25; GF (Pohnpei only)

Moldova Jan 1, 7 (Moldovan Christmas) (2), Mar 8 (Women), May 1, 9 (Victory and Commemoration), Aug 27 (Independence), 31 (Limba Noastra/National Language); GF, EM; Mertsishor/Spring Festival (1st week in Mar)

Monaco Jan 1, 27 (St Devote), May 1, 8 (Armistice, 1945), Jul 14 (National), Aug 15, Sep 3 (Liberation), Nov 1, 11 (Armistice, 1918), 19 (Prince of Monaco), Dec 8, 25; EM, WM

Mongolia Jan 1, 2, Mar 8 (Women), May 1, Jul 10 (People's Revolution) (3), Nov 7 (October Revolution)

Morocco Jan 1, Mar 3 (Throne), May 1, 23 (Fête Nationale), Jul 9 (Youth), Aug 14 (Qued-ed-Dahab), Nov 6 (Al-Massira), 18 (Independence); Ad (2), ER (2), NY (Muslim), PB

Mozambique Jan 1, Feb 3 (Heroes), Apr 7 (Mozambican Women), May 1, Jun 25 (Independence), Sep 7 (Victory), 25 (Armed Forces), Dec 25

Myanmar (Burma) Jan 4 (Independence), Feb 12 (Union), Mar 2 (Peasants), 27 (Resistance), Apr 1, May 1, Jul 19 (Martyrs), Oct 1, Dec 25; NY (Burmese), Thingyan (Apr) (4), End of Buddhist Lent (Oct), Full Moon days

Namibia Jan 1, Mar 21 (Independence), May 1, 4 (Casinga), May 25 (Africa/Anniversary of the OAU's Foundation), Aug 26 (Heroes), Dec 10 (Human Rights), Dec 25, 26; GF, HS, ES, EM, A

Nauru Jan 1, 31 (Independence), May 17 (Constitution), Jul 1 (Takeover), Oct 27 (Angam), Dec 25, 26; GF, EM (2)

Nepal Jan 11 (King Prithvi Memorial), Feb 19 (Late King Tribhuvan Memorial and Democracy), Nov 8 (Queen's Birthday), Dec 16 (King Mahendra Memorial and Constitution), 29 (King's Birthday); NY (Sinhala/Tamil, Apr), Maha Shivarata (Feb/Mar)

Netherlands Jan 1, Apr 30 (Queen's Birthday), May 5 (Liberation), Dec 25, 26; A, EM, GF, WM

New Zealand Jan 1, 2, Feb 6 (Waitangi), Apr 25 (Anzac), Dec 25, 26; EM, GF, Queen's Birthday (Jun), Labour (Oct)

Nicaragua Jan 1, May 1, Jul 19 (Sandinista Revolution), Sep 14 (Battle of San Jacinto), 15 (Independence), Dec 8, 25; GF, HT

Niger Jan 1, Apr 15 (Assumption of Power by Supreme Military Council), May 1, Aug 3 (Independence), Dec 18 (National), 25; Ad, ER, PB

Nigeria Jan 1, May 1, Oct 1 (National), Dec 25, 26; Ad (2), EM, ER (2), GF, PB

Northern Ireland Jan 1, Mar 17 (St Patrick, *not general*), Dec 25, 26, 29; GF, EM, Early May, Late May, July Bank Holiday, Summer Bank Holiday (Aug)

Norway Jan 1, May 1, 17 (Constitution), Dec 25, 26; A, EM, GF, HT, WM

Oman Nov 18 (National) (2), Dec 31; Ad (5), ER (4), NY (Muslim), PB, Lailat al-Miraj (Mar/Apr)

Pakistan Mar 23 (Pakistan), May 1, Jul 1, Aug 14 (Independence), Sep 6 (Defence of Pakistan), 11 (Death of Quaid-e-Azam), Nov 9 (Iqbal), Dec 25 (Christmas/Birthday of Quaid-e-Azam), 31; Ad (3), As (2), ER (3), PB, R

Panama Jan 1, 9 (National Mourning), May 1, Oct 11 (Revolution), 12 (Dia de la Hispanidad), Nov 3 (Independence from Colombia), 4 (Flag), 28 (Independence from Spain), Dec 8 (Mothers), 25; C (2), GF

Papua New Guinea Jan 1, Aug 15 (National Constitution), Sep 16 (Independence), Dec 25, 26; EM, GF, HS, Queen's Birthday (Jun), Remembrance (Jul)

Paraguay Jan 1, Feb 3 (St Blás), Mar 1 (Heroes), May 1, 14 (National Flag), 15 (Independence), Jun 12 (Peace with Bolivia), Aug 15, 25 (Constitution), Sep 29 (Battle of Boqueron), Oct 12 (Day of the Race), Nov 1, Dec 8, 25, 31; CC, GF, HT

Peru Jan 1, May 1, Jun 29 (Sts Peter and Paul), 30, Jul 28 (Independence) (2), Aug 30 (St Rose of Lima), Oct 8 (Combat of Angamos), Nov 1, Dec 8, 25, 31; GF, HT

Philippines Jan 1, May 1, Jun 12 (Independence), Jul 4 (Philippine–American Friendship), Nov 1, 30 (National Heroes), Dec 25, 30 (Rizal), 31; GF, HT

Poland Jan 1, May 1, Jul 22 (National Liberation), Nov 1, Dec 25, 26; CC, EM

Portugal Jan 1, Apr 25 (Liberty), May 1, Jun 10 (Portugal), Aug 15, Oct 5 (Republic), Nov 1, Dec 1 (Independence Restoration), Dec 8, 24, 25; C, CC, GF

Qatar Sep 3 (Independence), Dec 31; Ad (4), ER (4)

Romania Jan 1, 2, May 1 (2), Aug 23 (National)

Russia Jan 1, 7 (Russian Orthodox Christmas) (2), Mar 8 (Women), Apr 2 (Unity of the Peoples), May 1 (Spring and Labour) (2), 9 (Victory in Europe), Jun 12 (Russian Independence), Aug 22 (Anniversary of 1991 Restoration and National Flag Day), 31 (Language), Nov 7 (October Revolution); Spring Festival (1st week in Mar), Russian Orthodox Easter (Apr)

Rwanda Jan 1, 28 (Democracy), May 1, Jul 1 (Independence), 5 (Peace), Aug 1 (Harvest), 15, Sep 25 (Referendum), Oct 26 (Armed Forces), Nov 1, Dec 25; A, EM, WM

St Kitts and Nevis Jan 1, Sep 19 (Independence), Dec 25, 26, 31; EM, GF, WM, Labour (May), Queen's Birthday (Jun), August Monday

St Lucia Jan 1, 2, Feb 22 (Independence), May 1, Dec 13 (St Lucia), Dec 25, 26; C, CC, EM, GF, WM, Emancipation (Aug), Thanksgiving (Oct)

St Vincent and the Grenadines Jan 1, 22 (Discovery), Oct 27 (Independence), Dec 25, 26; C (Jul), EM, GF, WM, Labour (May), Caricom (Jul), Emancipation (Aug)

Samoa Jan 1, 2, Apr 25 (Anzac), Jun 1 (Independence) (3), Oct 12 (Lotu-o-Tamai), Dec 25, 26; EM, GF, HS

San Marino Jan 1, 6, Feb 5 (Liberation and St Agatha), Mar 25 (Arengo), Apr 1 (Captains Regents' Ceremony), May 1, Jul 28 (Fall of Fascism), Aug 15, Sep 3 (San Marino and Republic), Oct 1 (Investiture of the New Captains Regent), Nov 1, 2 (Commemoration of the Dead), Dec 8, 25, 26

São Tomé and Príncipe Jan 1, Feb 3 (Liberty Heroes), May 1, Jul 12 (National Independence), Sep 6 (Armed Forces), 30 (Agricultural Reform), Dec 21 (Power of the People), 25 (Family)

Saudi Arabia Sep 23 (National); Ad (7), ER (4)

Scotland Jan 1, 2, Dec 25, 26; GF, Early May, Late May and Summer (Aug) Bank Holidays

Senegal Jan 1, Feb 1 (Senegambia), Apr 4 (National), May 1, Aug 15, Nov 1, Dec 25; Ad, EM, ER, NY (Muslim), PB, WM

Seychelles Jan 1, 2, May 1, Jun 5 (Liberation), 29 (Independence), Aug 15, Nov 1, Dec 8, 25; CC, GF, HS

Sierra Leone Jan 1, Apr 19 (Republic), Dec 25, 26; Ad, EM, ER, GF, PB

Singapore Jan 1, May 1, Aug 9 (National), Dec 25; Ad, D, ER, GF, NY (Chinese, Jan/Feb) (2), Vesak

Slovakia Jan 1 (New Year and Independence), 6, May 1, 8 (Liberation of the Republic), Jul 5 (Sts Cyril and Methodius), Aug 19 (Slovak National Uprising), Sep 1 (Constitution of the Slovak Republic), 15 (Our Lady of the Seven Sorrows), Dec 24, 25; GF, EM

Slovenia Jan 1, 2, Feb 8 (Prešeren Day), Apr 27 (Day of Uprising Against Occupation), May 1 (2), Jun 25 (National Day), Aug 15, Oct 31 (Reformation Day), Nov 1, Dec 25, 26; EM, ES

Solomon Islands Jan 1, Jul 7 (Independence), Dec 25, 26; EM, GF, HS, WM, Queen's Birthday (Jun)

Somalia Jan 1, May 1, Jun 26 (Independence), Jul 1 (Union), Oct 21 (Revolution) (2); Ad (2), ER (2), PB

South Africa Jan 1, Apr 6 (Founders), May 31 (Republic), Oct 10 (Kruger), Dec 16 (Vow), 25, 26; A, GF, Family (Mar/Apr)

Spain Jan 1, 6, Mar 19 (*most areas*), May 1, Aug 15, Oct 12 (Hispanity), Nov 1, Dec 6 (Constitution), 8, 25; CC, GF, HS, HT

Sri Lanka Jan 14 (Tamil Thai Pongal), Feb 4 (Independence), May 1, 22 (National Heroes), Jun 30, Dec 25, 31; Ad, D, ER, GF, NY (Sinhala/Tamil, Apr), PB, Maha Sivarathri (Feb/Mar), Full Moon (*monthly*)

Sudan, The Jan 1 (Independence), Mar 3 (Unity), Apr 6 (Revolution), Dec 25; Ad (5), ER (5), NY (Muslim), PB, Sham al-Naseem (Apr/May)

Suriname Jan 1, Feb 25 (Revolution), May 1, Jul 1 (Freedom), Nov 25 (Independence), Dec 25, 26; EM, ER, GF, Holi (Mar)

Swaziland Jan 1, Apr 25 (National Flag), Jul 22 (King's Birthday), Sep 6 (Independence), Oct 24 (United Nations), Dec 25, 26; A, EM, GF, Commonwealth (Mar)

Sweden Jan 1, 6, May 1, Nov 1, Dec 24, 25, 26, 31; A, EM, GF, WM, Midsummer Eve and Day (Jun)

Switzerland Jan 1, Aug 1 (National), Aug 15 (*many cantons*), Nov 1 (*many cantons*), Dec 24, 25, 26; A, CC (*many cantons*), EM, GF, WM; *several local holidays*

Syria Jan 1, Mar 8 (Revolution), Apr 17 (Evacuation), May 1, 6 (Martyrs), Jul 23 (Egyptian Revolution), Sep 1 (Libyan Unity), Oct 6 (Liberation), Dec 25; Ad (3), ER (4), ES, NY (Muslim), PB

Taiwan Jan 1, 2, 3, Mar 29 (Youth), Apr 5 (Ching Ming), Jul 1, Sep 28 (Birthday of Confucius), Oct 10 (National), 25 (Taiwan Restoration), 31 (Birthday of Chiang Kai-Shek), Nov 12 (Birthday of Dr Sun Yat Sen), Dec 25 (Constitution); NY (Chinese, Jan/Feb) (3), Dragon Boat Festival (Jun), Mid-Autumn Festival (Sep/Oct)

Tajikistan Jan 1, Mar 8 (Women), 21 (Navrus), May 9 (Victory), Sep 9 (Independence), Oct 14 (Formation of the Tajik Republic); ER

Tanzania Jan 1, 12 (Zanzibar Revolution), Feb 5 (Chama Cha Mapinduzi and Arusha Declaration), May 1, Jul 7 (Saba Saba Peasants), Dec 9 (Independence/Republic), 25; Ad, EM, ER (2), GF, PB

Thailand Jan 1, Apr 6 (Chakri), 13 (Songkran), May 1, 5 (Coronation), Jul 1 (Mid-Year), Aug 12 (Queen's Birthday), Oct 23 (King Chulalongkorn), Dec 5 (King's Birthday), 10 (Constitution), 31; ER, Makha Bucha (Feb), Visakha Bucha (May), Buddhist Lent (Jul)

Togo Jan 1, 13 (Liberation), 24 (Economic Liberation), Apr 24 (Victory), 27 (National), May 1, Aug 15, Nov 1, Dec 25; A, Ad, ER

Tonga Jan 1, Apr 25 (Anzac), May 5 (Birthday of Crown Prince Tupouto'a), Jun 4 (Emancipation), Jul 4 (Birthday and Coronation of King Taufa'ahau Tupou IV), Nov 4 (Constitution), Dec 4 (King Tupou I), 25, 26; EM, GF

Trinidad and Tobago Jan 1, Jun 19 (Labour), Aug 1 (Discovery), 31 (Independence), Sep 24 (Republic), Dec 25, 26; CC, EM, GF, WM

Tunisia Jan 1, 18 (Revolution), Mar 20 (Independence), Apr 9 (Martyrs), May 1, Jun 1 (Victory), 2 (Youth), Jul 25 (Republic), Aug 3 (President's Birthday), 13 (Women), Sep 3 (3 Sep 1934), Oct 15 (Evacuation); Ad (2), ER (2), NY (Muslim), PB

Turkey Jan 1, Apr 23 (National Sovereignty and Children), May 19 (Youth and Sports), Aug 30 (Victory), Oct 29 (Republic); Ad (4), ER (3)

Turkmenistan Jan 1, 12 (Remembrance/Anniversary of the Battle of Geok-Tepe), Feb 19 (Birthday of Turkem President Sapurmurat Turkmenbashi), Mar 8 (Women), May 9 (Victory); Navrus Bayram (Feb), Gurban Bayram (Apr), Day of Revival and Unity (May), Independence (Oct)

Tuvalu Jan 2, Mar 3 (Commonwealth), Jun 14 (Queen's Official Birthday), Aug 14 (Children), Oct 1 (Tuvalu/Independence) (2), Nov 14 (Prince of Wales's Birthday), Dec 25, 26; EM, ES, GF, HS

Uganda Jan 1, Apr 1 (Liberation), May 1, Oct 9 (Independence), Dec 25, 26; EM, ER, GF, HS

UK ► England and Wales; Northern Ireland; Scotland

Ukraine Jan 1, 7 (Eastern Orthodox Christmas) (2), Mar 8 (Women), May 1, 2, 9 (Victory), Aug 24 (Independence) (3), Nov 7 (Revolution) (2); EM, GF, HT

United Arab Emirates Jan 1, Aug 6 (Accession of Ruler), Dec 2 (National) (2); Ad (3), ER (4), NY (Muslim), PB, Lailat al-Miraj (Mar/Apr)

Uruguay Jan 1, Apr 19 (Landing of the 33 Orientales), May 1, 18 (Las Piedras Battle), Jun 19 (Artigas), Jul 18 (Constitution), Aug 25 (Independence), Oct 12 (Columbus), Nov 2, Dec 25; C (2), GF, HT, Mon – Wed of Holy Week

USA Jan 1, Jan 21 (Martin Luther King's Birthday) (*not all states*), Jul 4 (Independence), Nov 11 (Veterans), Dec 25; Washington's Birthday (3rd Mon in Feb), Memorial (last Mon in May), Labor (1st Mon in Sep), Discoverers' (2nd Mon in Oct), Thanksgiving (last Thurs in Nov); *much local variation*

Uzbekistan Jan 1, 2, Mar 8 (Women), 21 (Navrus), Sep 1 (Independence), Dec 8 (Constitution)

Vanuatu Jan 1, Mar 5 (Chiefs), May 1, Jul 30 (Independence), Aug 15, Dec 25, 26; A, EM, GF, Constitution (Oct), Unity (Nov)

Venezuela Jan 1, 6, Mar 19 (St Joseph), Apr 19 (Constitution), May 1, Jun 24 (Battle of Carabobo), 29 (Sts Peter and Paul), Jul 5 (Independence), 24 (Bolivar), Aug 15, Oct 12 (Columbus), Nov 1, Dec 8, 25; A, C (2), CC, GF, HT

Vietnam Jan 1, May 1, Sep 2 (Independence)

Western Samoa ► Samoa

Yemen Jan 1, Mar 8 (Women), May 1, 22 (National), Jun 22 (Corrective Move), Sep 26 (Revolution, *N area*), Oct 14 (Revolution), Nov 30 (Independence); Ad (3), ER (2), NY (Muslim), PB

Yugoslavia, Federal Republic of Jan 1, 2, 7 (Eastern Orthodox Christmas), Apr 27 (Constitution Day), May 1, 2, 9 (Victory Day), Dec 29 (Day of the Republic) (2)

Zaïre ► Congo, Democratic Republic of

Zambia Jan 1, May 1, 25 (Africa Freedom), Oct 24 (Independence), Dec 25; GF, HS, Youth (Mar), Heroes (Jul), Unity (Jul), Farmers (Aug)

Zimbabwe Jan 1, Apr 18 (Independence), 19 (Defence Forces), May 1, 25 (Africa), Aug 11 (Heroes) (2), Dec 25, 26; EM, G

NATURAL HISTORY

Cereals

English name	Species	Area of origin
barley	*Hordeum vulgare*	Middle East
maize (or corn, sweet corn, Indian corn)	*Zea mays*	C America
millet, common	*Panicum miliaceum*	tropics, warm temperate regions
millet, foxtail (or Italian millet)	*Setaria italica*	as common millet
millet, bulrush	*Pennisetum americanum*	as common millet
oats	*Avena sativa*	Mediterranean basin
rice	*Oryza sativa*	Asia
rye	*Secale cereale*	Mediterranean, SW Asia
sorghum (or Kaffir corn)	*Sorghum bicolor*	Africa, Asia
wheat	Genus *Triticum*, 20 species	Mediterranean, W Asia

Edible fruits (Temperate and mediterranean)

English name	Species	Colour	Area of origin
apple	*Malus pumila*	green, yellow, red	temperate regions
apricot	*Prunus armeniaca*	yellow, orange	Asia
bilberry	*Vaccinium myrtillus*	blue, black	Europe, N Asia
blackberry (or bramble)	*Rubus fruticosus*	purple, black	N hemisphere
blackcurrant	*Ribes nigrum*	black	Europe, Asia, Africa
blueberry	*Vaccinium corymbosum*	blue, purple, black	America, Europe
Cape gooseberry ► physalis			
cherry (sour)	*Prunus cerasus*	red	temperate regions
cherry (sweet)	*Prunus avium*	purple, red	temperate regions
clementine	*Citrus reticulata*	orange	W Mediterranean
cranberry	*Vaccinium oxycoccus*	red	N America
damson	*Prunus institia*	purple	temperate regions
date	*Phoenix dactylifera*	yellow, red, brown	Persian Gulf
date-plum ► persimmon			
fig	*Ficus carica*	white, black, purple, green	W Asia
gooseberry	*Ribes grossularia*	green, red	Europe

English name	Species	Colour	Area of origin
grape	Vitis vinifera	green, purple, black	Asia
grapefruit	Citrus × paradisi	yellow	W Indies
greengage	Prunus domestica	green	temperate regions
kiwi fruit	Actinidia chinensis	brown skin, green flesh	China
kumquat	Fortunella margarita	orange	China
lemon	Citrus limon	yellow	India, S Asia
lime	Citrus aurantifolia	green	SE Asia
loganberry	Rubus loganobaccus	red	America
loquat	Eriobotrya japonica	yellow	China, Japan
lychee	Litchi chinensis	reddish-brown skin, white flesh	China
mandarin (or tangerine)	Citrus reticulata	orange	China
medlar	Mespilus germanica	russet brown	SE Europe, Asia
melon	Cucumis melo	green, yellow	Egypt
minneola ► tangelo			
mulberry	Morus nigra	purple, red	W Asia
nectarine	Prunus persica nectarina	orange, red	China
orange	Citrus sinensis	orange	China
peach	Prunus persica	yellow, red	China
pear	Pyrus communis	yellow	Middle East, E Europe
persimmon (or date-plum)	Diospyros kaki	yellow, orange	E Asia
physalis (or Cape gooseberry)	Physalis alkekengi	yellow	S America
plum	Prunus domestica	red, yellow, purple, orange	temperate regions
pomegranate	Punica granatum	red, yellow	Persia
pomelo	Citrus maxima	yellow	Malaysia
quince	Cydonia oblonga	golden	Iran
raspberry	Rubus idaeus	red, crimson	N hemisphere
redcurrant	Ribes rubrum	red	Europe, Asia, Africa
rhubarb	Rheum rhaponticum	red, green, pink	Asia
satsuma	Citrus reticulata	orange	Japan
strawberry	Fragaria ananassa	red	Europe, Asia
tangelo (or mineola, or ugli)	Citrus × tangelo	orange, yellow	N America
tangerine ► mandarin			
ugli ► tangelo			
watermelon	Citrullus vulgaris	green, yellow	Africa
white currant	Ribes rubrum cv.	white	W Europe

Edible fruits (Tropical)

English name	Species	Colour	Area of origin
acerola	*Malpighia glabra*	yellow, red	America
avocado	*Persea americana*	green, purple	C America
banana	*Musa acuminata*	yellow	India, S Asia
breadfruit	*Artocarpus altilis*	greenish brown, yellow	Malaysia
carambola	*Averrhoa carambola*	yellow, green	S China
cherimoya	*Annona cherimola*	green skin, white flesh	Peru
guava	*Psidium guajava*	green, yellow	S America
mango	*Mangifera indica*	green, yellow, orange, red, purple	S Asia
papaya (or pawpaw)	*Carica papaya*	green, yellow, orange	tropics
passion fruit	*Passiflora edulis*	purple, yellow, brown	S America
pineapple	*Ananas comosus*	green, yellow	S America
sapodilla plum	*Manilkara zapota*	brown	C America
soursop	*Annona muricata*	green	America
tamarind	*Tamarindus indica*	brown	Africa, S Asia

Herbs

Herbs may be used for medicinal, cosmetic or culinary purposes. Any part of those marked * may be poisonous when ingested.

English name	Species	Part of plant used	Area of origin
aconite* (or monkshood or winter aconite)	*Aconitum napellus*	tuber	Europe, NW Asia
agrimony	*Agrimonia eupatoria*	flowers	Europe
alecost (or costmary)	*Balsimata major*	leaves, flowers	E Mediterranean
aloe	*Aloe vera*	leaves	Africa
aniseed	*Pimpinella anisum*	fruits (seed heads)	Asia
basil	*Ocimum basilicum*	leaves, flowering shoots	Middle East
borage	*Borago officinalis*	leaves, flowers	Mediterranean
celandine	*Chelidonium majus*	buds	Europe
celery	*Apium graveolens*	roots, stems, leaves	Europe
chamomile	*Anthemis nobilis*	flowers	Europe, Asia
chervil	*Anthriscus cerefolium*	leaves	Europe, Asia
chicory	*Cichorium intybus*	leaves, roots	Europe
chives	*Allium schoenoprasum*	leaves	Europe, America
coriander	*Coriandrum sativum*	leaves, fruit	N Africa, W Asia
dandelion	*Taraxacum officinalis*	leaves, roots	Europe
deadly nightshade*	*Atropa belladonna*	root	Europe, Asia

English name	Species	Part of plant used	Area of origin
dill	Anethum graveolens	leaves, fruits (seeds)	S Europe
elderberry	Sambucus nigra	flowers, fruits	Europe
epazote	Chenopodium ambrosioides	leaves	C and S America
fennel, Florentine	Foeniculum vulgare var. azoricum	leaves, stems, fruits (seeds)	Mediterranean
feverfew	Tanacetum parthenium	leaves, flowers	SE Europe, W Asia
foxglove*	Digitalis purpurea	leaves	Europe
garlic	Allium sativum	bulbs	Asia
gentian	Gentiana lutea	rhizomes, roots	Europe
ginseng	Panax pseudo-ginseng	roots	China
guaiacum	Guaiacum officinale	leaves	Caribbean
heartsease (or wild pansy)	Viola tricolor	flowers	Europe
hemlock*	Conium maculatum	all parts	Europe
hemp (or ganja or cannabis or marijuana)	Cannabis sativa	leaves, flowers	Asia
henbane	Hyoscyamus niger	leaves, fruit (seeds)	Europe, W Asia, N Africa
henna	Lawsonia inermis	leaves	Asia, Africa
horseradish	Armoracia rusticana	roots, flowering shoots, leaves	SE Europe, W Asia
hyssop	Hyssopus officinalis	leaves, flowers	S Europe
juniper	Juniperus communis	fruits (berries)	Mediterranean
lavender	Lavandula vera	flowers, stems	Mediterranean
leek	Allium porrum	stem, leaves	Europe
lemon	Citrus limon	fruits	Asia
lemon balm	Melissa officinalis	leaves	S Europe
lily of the valley	Convallaria majalis	leaves, flowers	Europe, N America
lime	Tilia cordata	flowers	Europe
liquorice	Glycyrrhiza glabra	roots	Europe
lovage	Levisticum officinale	leaves, shoots, stems, roots	W Asia
mandrake	Mandragora officinarum	roots	Himalayas, SE Europe, W Asia
marjoram	Origanum majorana	leaves, shoots, stems	Africa, Mediterranean, Asia
marsh mallow	Althaea officinalis	leaves, roots	Europe, Asia
maté	Ilex paraguariensis	leaves	S America
milfoil ► yarrow			
monkshood ► aconite			
mugwort	Artemesia vulgaris	leaves	Europe, Asia
myrrh	Commiphora myrrha	resin	Middle East, Africa

English name	Species	Part of plant used	Area of origin
myrtle	*Myrtus communis*	leaves, flower heads, fruits (berries)	Asia, Mediterranean
nasturtium	*Tropaeolom majus*	leaves, flowers, fruits	Peru
onion	*Allium cepa*	bulbs	Asia
oregano	*Origanum vulgare*	leaves, shoots, stems	Mediterranean
parsley	*Petroselinum crispum*	leaves, stems	Mediterranean
peony	*Paeonia officinalis*	roots, seeds	Europe, Asia, N America
peppermint	*Mentha × piperita*	leaves	Europe
poppy*, opium	*Papaver somniferum*	fruits, seeds	Asia
purslane	*Portulaca oleracea*	leaves	Asia
rosemary	*Rosmarinus officinalis*	leaves	Mediterranean
rue	*Ruta graveolens*	leaves, stems, flowers	Mediterranean
saffron	*Crocus sativus*	flowers	Asia
sage	*Salvia officinalis*	leaves	N Mediterranean
sorrel	*Rumex acetosa*	leaves	Europe
spearmint	*Mentha spicata*	leaves	Europe
tansy	*Tanacetum vulgare*	leaves, flowers	Asia
tarragon, French	*Artemesia dracunculus*	leaves, stems	Asia, E Europe
thyme	*Thymus vulgaris*	leaves, stems, flowers	Mediterranean
valerian	*Valeriana officinalis*	rhizomes, roots	Europe, Asia
vervain	*Verbena officinalis*	leaves, flowers	Europe, Asia, N Africa
watercress	*Nasturtium officinale*	leaves, shoots, stems	Europe, Asia
witch hazel	*Hamamelis virginiana*	leaves, shoots, bark	N America, E Asia
wormwood	*Artemesia absinthium*	leaves, flowering shoots	Europe
yarrow (or milfoil)	*Achillea millefolium*	flower heads, leaves	Europe, W Asia

Spices

English name	Species	Part of plant used	Area of origin
allspice	*Pimenta dioica*	fruits	America, W Indies
annatto	*Bixa orellana*	seeds	S America, W Indies
asafoetida	*Ferula assa-foetida*	sap	W Asia
bay	*Laurus nobilis*	leaves	Mediterranean, Asia
caper	*Capparis spinosa*	flower buds	Europe
caraway	*Carum carvi*	seeds	Europe, Asia
cardamom	*Elettaria cardamomum*	seeds	SE Asia
cayenne	*Capsicum annuum*	fruit pods	America, Africa

English name	Species	Part of plant used	Area of origin
chilli pepper	*Capsicum frutescens*	fruit pods	America
cinnamon	*Cinnamomum zeylanicum*	bark	India
cloves	*Syzygium aromaticum*	buds	Moluccas
cocoa	*Theobroma cacoa*	seeds (beans)	S America
coconut	*Cocus nucifera*	fruits	Polynesia
coriander	*Coriandrum sativum*	fruits	S Europe
cumin	*Cuminum cyminum*	fruits (seed heads)	Mediterranean
curry leaf	*Murraya koenigii*	leaves	India
fennel	*Foeniculum vulgare*	fruits	S Europe
fenugreek	*Trigonella foenum-graecum*	seeds	India, S Europe
horseradish	*Armoracia rusticana*	roots	E Europe
ginger	*Zingiber officinale*	rhizomes	SE Asia
mace	*Myristica fragrans*	seeds	Moluccas
mustard, black	*Brassica nigra*	seeds	Europe, Africa, Asia, America
mustard, white	*Sinapis alba*	seeds	Europe, Asia
nutmeg	*Myristica fragrans*	seeds	Moluccas
paprika	*Capsicum annuum*	fruit pods	S America
pepper	*Piper nigrum*	seeds	India
sandalwood	*Santalum album*	heartwood, roots	India, Indonesia, Australia
sassafras	*Sassafras albidum*	root bark	N America
sesame	*Sesamum indicum*	seeds	tropics
soya	*Glycine max*	fruit (beans)	China
tamarind	*Tamarindus indica*	fruits	Africa, S Asia
turmeric	*Curcuma longa*	rhizomes	SE Asia
vanilla	*Vanilla planifolia*	fruit pods	C America

Vegetables

English name	Species	Part eaten	Area of origin
artichoke, Chinese	*Stachys affinis*	tuber	China
artichoke, globe	*Cynara scolymus*	buds	Mediterranean
artichoke, Jerusalem	*Helianthus tuberosus*	tuber	N America
asparagus	*Asparagus officinalis*	young shoots	Europe, Asia
aubergine (or eggplant)	*Solanum melongena*	fruit	Asia, Africa
avocado	*Persea americana*	fruit	C America
bean sprout	*Vigna radiata*	shoots	China
bean, blackeyed	*Vigna unguiculata*	seeds	India, Iran
bean, borlotti (or Boston bean or pinto bean)	*Phaseolus vulgaris*	seeds	America
bean, broad	*Vicia faba*	seeds and pods	Africa, Europe
bean, flageolet	*Phaseolus vulgaris*	seeds	America
bean, French	*Phaseolus vulgaris*	pods	America

English name	Species	Part eaten	Area of origin
bean, haricot	*Phaseolus vulgaris*	seeds	America
bean, kidney	*Phaseolus vulgaris*	seeds	America
bean, runner	*Phaseolus coccineus*	pods	America
bean, soya	*Glycine max*	seeds	E Asia
beetroot	*Beta vulgaris*	root	Mediterranean
broccoli	*Brassica oleracea*	buds and leaves	Europe
Brussels sprout	*Brassica oleracea* (Gemmifera)	buds	N Europe
cabbage	*Brassica oleracea*	leaves	Europe, W Asia
cardoon	*Cynara cardunculus*	inner stalks and flower heads	Mediterranean
carrot	*Daucus carota*	root	Asia
cauliflower	*Brassica oleracea* (Botrytis)	flower buds	Middle East
celeriac	*Apium graveolens* var. *rapaceum*	root	Mediterranean
celery	*Apium graveolens* var. *dulce*	stalks	Europe, N Africa, America
chayote (or chocho)	*Sechium edule*	fruit	America
chick-pea	*Cicer arietinum*	seeds	W Asia
chicory	*Cichorium intybus*	leaves	Europe, W Asia
chinese leaf	*Brassica pekinensis*	leaf stalks	E Asia, China
chives	*Allium schoenoprasum*	leaves	Europe, N America
courgette (or zucchini)	*Cucurbita pepo*	fruit	S America, Africa
cucumber	*Cucumus sativus*	fruit	S Asia
eggplant ► aubergine			
endive	*Cichorium endivia*	leaves	S Europe, E Indies, Africa
fennel, Florentine	*Foeniculum vulgare* var. *azoricum*	leaf stalks	Europe
kohlrabi	*Brassica oleracea* (Gongylodes)	stems	Europe
laver	*Porphyra leucosticta*, *P. umbilicalis*	leaves and stems	Europe
leek	*Allium porrum*	leaves and stems	Europe, N Africa
lentil	*Lens culinaris*	seeds	S Asia
lettuce	*Lactuca sativa*	leaves	Middle East
marrow	*Cucurbita pepo*	fruit	America
mooli	*Raphanus sativus*	root	E Africa
mushroom	*Agaricus campestris*	fruiting body	worldwide
okra	*Abelmoschus esculentus*	pods and seeds	Africa
onion	*Allium cepa*	bulb	C Asia
parsnip	*Pastinaca sativa*	root	Europe

English name	Species	Part eaten	Area of origin
pea	*Pisum sativum*	pods and seeds	Asia, Europe
pepper	*Capsicum annuum*	fruit	S America
potato	*Solanum tuberosum*	tuber	S America
pumpkin	*Cucurbita pepo*	fruit	S America
radish	*Raphanus sativus*	root	China, Japan
salsify	*Tragopogon porrifolius*	root	S Europe
sorrel	*Rumex acetosa*	leaves	Europe
spinach	*Spinacea oleracea*	leaves	Asia
squash, summer	*Cucurbita pepo*	fruit	America
squash, winter	*Cucurbita maxima*	fruit	America
swede	*Brassica napus* (Napobrassica)	root	Europe
sweet potato	*Ipomoea batatas*	tuber	C America
swiss chard	*Beta vulgaris* subsp. *cicla*	leaves and stems	Europe
tomato	*Lycopersicon esculentum*	fruit	S America
turnip	*Brassica rapa*	root	Middle East
watercress	*Nasturtium officinale*	leaves and stems	Europe, Asia
yam	Genus *Dioscorea* 60 species	tuber	tropics

zucchini ► courgette

Flowers (Bulbs, corms, rhizomes and tubers)

English name	Genus/Family	Colour	Area of origin
acidanthera	*Acidanthera*	white	NE Africa
African lily (or lily of the Nile)	*Agapanthus*	white, purple	S Africa
agapanthus	*Agapanthus*	blue, white	S Africa
allium	*Allium*	blue, lilac, white, rose	Asia, Europe
amaryllis (or belladonna lily)	*Amaryllis*	rose-pink	S Africa, tropical America
anemone	*Anemone*	white, lilac, blue	Mediterranean, Asia, Europe
belladonna lily ► amaryllis			
bluebell	*Hyacinthoides*	blue	Europe
camassia	*Camassia*	white, cream, blue, purple	N America
chionodoxa (or glory of the snow)	*Chionodoxa*	blue, white, pink	Greece, Turkey
crinum	*Crinum*	rose-pink, white	S Africa
crocosmia	*Crocosmia*	orange	S Africa
crocus	*Crocus*	purple, rose, yellow, pink, orange	Mediterranean, Asia, Africa
crown imperial	*Fritillaria*	orange	N India

English name	Genus/Family	Colour	Area of origin
curtonus	*Curtonus*	orange	S Africa
cyclamen	*Cyclamen*	white, pink, red	Asia, Mediterranean
daffodil (or narcissus)	*Narcissus*	white, yellow, orange	Mediterranean, Europe
dog's tooth violet ▶ erythronium			
erythronium (or dog's tooth violet)	*Erythronium*	purple, pink, white, yellow	Europe, Asia
fritillaria	*Fritillaria*	red, yellow	Europe, Asia, N America
galtonia	*Galtonia*	white	S Africa
gladiolus	*Gladiolus*	purple, yellow	Europe, Asia, NE Africa
glory of the snow ▶ chionodoxa			
harebell	*Campanula*	blue	N temperate regions
hippeastrum	*Hippeastrum*	pink, white, red	tropical America
hyacinth	*Hyacinthus*	blue, white, red	S Europe, Asia
hyacinth, grape	*Muscari*	blue	Europe, Mediterranean
hyacinth, wild	*Scilla*	blue, purple, pink, white	Asia, S Europe
iris	*Iris*	purple, white, yellow	N temperate regions
Ithuriel's spear	*Brodiaea*	white, pink, blue	N America
lapeirousia	*Lapeirousia*	red	S Africa
lily	*Lilium*	white, pink, crimson, yellow, orange, red	China, Europe, America
lily of the Nile ▶ African lily			
lily of the valley	*Convallaria*	white	Europe, Asia, America
naked ladies	*Colchicum*	white, pink, purple	Asia, Europe
nerine	*Nerine*	pink, salmon	S Africa
ornithogalum	*Ornithogalum*	white, yellow	S Africa
peacock (or tiger flower)	*Tigridia*	white, orange, red, yellow	Asia
rouge, giant	*Tigridia*	white, yellow, red, lilac	Mexico
snake's head	*Fritillaria*	purple, white	Europe
snowdrop	*Galanthus*	white	Europe
snowflake	*Leucojum*	white, green	S Europe
solfaterre	*Crocosmia × crocosmiflora*	orange, red	S Africa
Solomon's seal	*Polygonatum*	white	Europe, Asia
squill	*Scilla*	blue, purple	Europe, Asia, S Africa
sternbergia	*Sternbergia*	yellow	Europe
striped squill	*Puschkinia*	bluish-white	Asia
tiger flower ▶ peacock			
tiger lily	*Lilium*	orange	Asia
tulip	*Tulipa*	orange, red, pink, white, crimson, lilac	Europe, Asia
wand flower	*Dierama*	white, pink, mauve, purple	S Africa
winter aconite	*Eranthis*	yellow	Greece, Turkey

Flowers (Herbaceous)

English name	Genus/Family	Colour	Area of origin
acanthus	Acanthus	white, rose, purple	Europe
African violet	Saintpaulia	violet, white, pink	Africa
alum root	Heuchera	rose, pink, red	N America
alyssum	Alyssum	white, yellow, pink	S Europe
anchusa	Anchusa	blue	Asia, S Europe
anemone	Hepatica	white, red-pink, blue	Europe, Caucasus
asphodel	Asphodelus	white, yellow	S Europe
aster	Aster	white, blue, purple, pink	Europe, Asia, N America
astilbe	Astilbe	white, pink, red	Asia
aubrietia	Aubrieta	purple	SE Europe
begonia	Begonia	pink	S America, the Pacific
bellflower	Campanula	blue, white	N temperate regions
bergamot	Monarda	white, pink, red, purple	N America
bistort	Polygonum	rose-pink	Japan, Himalayas
bleeding heart	Dicentra	pink, white, red	China, Japan, N America
bugbane	Cimicifuga	white	N America, Japan
busy lizzie	Impatiens	crimson, pink, white	tropics
buttercup	Ranunculus	yellow	temperate regions
carnation	Dianthus	white, pink, red	temperate regions
catmint	Nepeta	blue, mauve	Europe, Asia
celandine, giant	Ranunculus	white, copper-orange	Europe
Christmas rose	Helleborus	white, pink	Europe
chrysanthemum	Chrysanthemum	yellow, white	China
cinquefoil	Potentilla	orange, red, yellow	Europe, Asia
columbine (or granny's bonnet)	Aquilegia	purple, dark blue, pink, yellow	Europe
Cupid's dart	Catananche	blue, white	Europe
dahlia	Dahlia	red, yellow, white	Mexico
daisy	Bellis	white, yellow, pink	Europe
delphinium	Delphinium	white, mauve, pink, blue	Europe, N America
echinacea	Echinacea	rose-red, purple	N America
edelweiss	Leontopodium	yellow, white	Europe, Asia
evening primrose	Oenothera	yellow	N America
everlasting flower (or immortelle)	Helichrysum bracteatum	yellow	Australia
everlasting flower, pearly	Anaphalis	white	N America, Himalayas
fleabane	Erigeron	white, pink, blue, violet	Australia
forget-me-not	Myosotis	blue	Europe
foxglove	Digitalis	white, yellow, pink, red	Europe, Asia
fraxinella	Dictamnus	white, mauve	Europe, Asia
gentian	Gentiana	blue, yellow, white, red	temperate regions

English name	Genus/Family	Colour	Area of origin
geranium	*Pelargonium*	scarlet, pink, white	temperate regions, subtropics
geum	*Geum*	orange, red, yellow	S Europe, N America
goat's beard	*Aruncus*	white	N Europe
golden rod	*Solidago*	yellow	Europe
granny's bonnet ► columbine			
gypsophila	*Gypsophila*	white, pink	Europe, Asia
Hattie's pincushion (or the melancholy gentleman)	*Astrantia*	white, pink	Europe
heliopsis	*Heliopsis*	orange-yellow	N America
hellebore	*Helleborus*	plum-purple, white	Asia, Greece
herb Christopher	*Actaea*	white	N America
hollyhock	*Alcaea*	white, yellow, pink, red, maroon	Europe, China
hosta	*Hosta*	violet, white	China, Japan
immortelle ► everlasting flower			
kaffir lily	*Schizostylis*	red, pink	S Africa
kirengeshoma	*Kirengeshoma*	yellow	Japan
liatris	*Liatris*	heather-purple	N America
lobelia	*Lobelia*	white, red, blue, purple	Africa, N America, Australia
loosestrife	*Lysimachia*	rose-pink, purple	Europe
lotus	*Lotus*	yellow, pink, white	Asia, America
lupin	*Lupinus*	blue, yellow, pink, red	N America
marigold, African (or French marigold)	*Tagetes*	yellow, orange	Mexico
marigold, pot	*Calendula*	orange, apricot, cream	unknown
meadow rue	*Thalictrum*	yellow-white	Europe, Asia
mullein	*Verbascum*	yellow, white, pink, purple	Europe, Asia
nasturtium	*Tropaeolum*	yellow, red, orange	S America, Mexico
orchid	*Orchidaea*	red, purple, white, violet, green, brown, yellow, pink	tropics
ox-eye	*Buphthalmum*	yellow	Europe
pansy	*Viola*	white, yellow	temperate regions
peony	*Paeonia*	white, yellow, pink, red	Asia, Europe
Peruvian lily	*Alstroemeria*	cream, pink, yellow, orange, red	S America
petunia	*Petunia*	blue, violet, purple, white, pink	S America
phlox	*Phlox*	blue, white, purple, red	America
poppy	*Papaver*	red, orange, white, yellow, lilac	N temperate regions
primrose	*Primula*	yellow	N temperate regions

English name	Genus/Family	Colour	Area of origin
primula	*Primula*	white, pink, yellow, blue, purple	N temperate regions
red-hot poker	*Kniiphofia*	white, yellow, orange, red	S Africa
salvia	*Salvia*	red, yellow, blue	S America, Europe, Asia
sea holly	*Eryngium*	blue, green-grey, white	Europe, S America
sidalcea	*Sidalcea*	lilac, pink, rose	N America
snapdragon	*Antirrhinum*	white, yellow, pink, red, maroon	Europe, Asia, S America
speedwell	*Veronica*	blue, white	Europe, Asia
spiderwort	*Tradescantia*	white, blue, pink, red, purple	N America
stokesia	*Stokesia*	white, blue, purple	N America
sunflower	*Helianthus*	yellow	N America
sweet pea	*Lathyrus*	purple, pink, white, red	Mediterranean
sweet william	*Dianthus*	white, pink, red, purple	S Europe
thistle, globe	*Echinops*	blue, white-grey	Europe, Asia
thistle, Scotch (or cotton thistle)	*Onopordum*	purple	Europe
violet	*Viola*	mauve, blue	N temperate regions
water chestnut	*Trapa*	white, lilac	Asia
water lily	*Nymphaea*	white, blue, red, yellow	worldwide
wolfsbane	*Aconitum*	blue, white, rose, yellow	Europe, Asia
yarrow	*Achillea*	white, cream	Europe, W Asia

Flowers (Shrubs)

English name	Genus/Family	Colour	Area of origin
abelia	*Abelia*	white, rose-purple	Asia, China, Mexico
abutilon	*Abutilon*	lavender-blue	S America
acacia (or mimosa or wattle)	*Acacia*	yellow	Australia, tropical Africa, tropical America
almond, dwarf	*Prunus*	white, crimson, rose-pink	Asia, Europe
ampelopsis	*Ampelopsis*	green (blue-black fruit)	Far East
anthyllis	*Anthyllis*	yellow	Europe
azalea	*Rhododendron*	pink, purple, white, yellow, crimson	N hemisphere
berberis	*Berberis*	yellow, orange	Asia, America, Europe
bottle brush	*Callistemon*	red	Australia
bougainvillea	*Bougainvillea*	lilac, pink, purple, red, orange, white	S America
broom	*Cytisus*	yellow	Europe
buckthorn	*Rhamnus*	red, black	N hemisphere
buddleia	*Buddleja*	purple, yellow, white	China, S America

English name	Genus/Family	Colour	Area of origin
cactus	Cactaceae	red, purple, orange, yellow, white	America
calico bush (or mountain laurel)	Kalmia	white, pink	China
camellia	Camellia	white, pink, red	Asia
caryopteris	Caryopteris	blue, violet	Asia
ceanothus	Ceanothus	pink, blue, purple	N America
ceratostigma	Ceratostigma	purple-blue	China
Chinese lantern	Physalis	orange, red	Japan
cistus	Cistus	white, pink	Europe
clematis	Clematis	white, purple, violet, blue, pink, yellow	N temperate regions
clerodendrum	Clerodendrum	white, purple-red	China
colquhounia	Colquhounia	scarlet, yellow	Himalayas
cornelian cherry	Cornus	yellow	Europe
coronilla	Coronilla	yellow	S Europe
corylopsis	Corylopsis	yellow	China, Japan
cotoneaster	Cotoneaster	white (red fruit)	Asia
currant, flowering	Ribes	red, white, pink	N America
desfontainia	Desfontainia	scarlet-gold	S America
deutzia	Deutzia	white, pink	Asia
diplera	Diplera	pale pink	China
dogwood	Cornus	white	Europe, SW Asia
embothrium	Embothrium	scarlet	S America
escallonia	Escallonia	white, pink	S America
euchryphia	Euchryphia	white	Chile, Australasia
euryops	Euryops	yellow	S Africa
fabiana	Fabiana	white, mauve	S America
firethorn	Pyracantha	white (red, orange, yellow fruits)	China
forsythia	Forsythia	yellow	China
frangipani	Plumeria	white, pink, yellow	tropical America
fuchsia	Fuchsia	red, pink, white	C and S America, New Zealand
gardenia	Gardenia	white	tropics
garland flower	Daphne	pink, crimson, white, purple	Europe, Asia
garrya	Garrya	green	California and Oregon
gorse (or furze or whin)	Ulex	yellow	Europe, Britain
hawthorn	Crataegus	white (orange-red berries)	N America, Europe, N Africa
heath, winter-flowering	Erica	white, pink, red	Africa, Europe
heather	Calluna	pink, purple, white	Europe, W Asia
hebe	Hebe	blue-white	New Zealand

English name	Genus/Family	Colour	Area of origin
helichrysum	*Helichrysum*	yellow	Australia, S Africa
hibiscus	*Hibiscus*	pink, mauve, purple, white, red	China, India
honeysuckle	*Lonicera*	white, yellow, pink, red	temperate regions
hydrangea	*Hydrangea*	white, pink, blue	Asia, America
hyssop	*Hyssopus*	bluish-purple	S Europe, W Asia
indigofera	*Indigofera*	rose-purple	Himalayas
ipomoea (or morning glory)	*Ipomoea*	white, red, blue	tropical America
japonica	*Chaenomeles*	white, pink, orange, red, yellow	N Asia
jasmine	*Jasminum*	white, yellow, red	Asia
Jerusalem sage	*Phlomis*	yellow	Europe
kerria	*Kerria*	yellow	China
kolkwitzia	*Kolkwitzia*	pink	China
laburnum	*Laburnum*	yellow	Europe, Asia
lavender	*Lavandula*	purple	Europe
leptospermum	*Leptospermum*	red, white	Australasia
lespedeza	*Lespedeza*	rose-purple	China, Japan
leycesteria	*Leycesteria*	claret	Himalayas
lilac (or syringa)	*Syringa*	purple, pink, white	Balkans
lion's tail	*Leonotis*	red	S Africa
magnolia	*Magnolia*	yellow, white, rose, purple	China, Japan
mahonia	*Mahonia*	yellow	Japan
malus	*Malus*	white, pink, red	N America, Asia
menziesa	*Menziesa*	wine-red	Japan
mimosa ▶ acacia			
mimulus	*Mimulus*	cream, orange, red	N America
mock orange	*Philadelphus*	white	Europe, Asia, N America
moltkia	*Moltkia*	voilet-blue	Greece
morning glory ▶ ipomoea			
mother-of-pearl	*Symphoricarpus*	pink, white, red fruit	N America
mountain ash ▶ rowan			
myrtle	*Myrtus*	pink, white	Europe
oleander	*Nerium*	white, pink, purple, red	Mediterranean
olearia	*Olearia*	white, yellow	New Zealand
oleaster	*Elaeagnus*	yellow	Europe, Asia, N America
osmanthus	*Osmanthus*	white	China
pearl bush	*Exochorda*	white	China
peony	*Paeonia*	pink, red, white, yellow	Europe, Asia, N America
pieris	*Pieris*	white	China
poinsettia	*Euphorbia*	scarlet	Mexico

English name	Genus/Family	Colour	Area of origin
potentilla	*Potentilla*	yellow, red, orange	Asia
rhododendron	*Rhododendron*	red, purple, pink, white	S Asia
rhus	*Rhus*	foliage grey, purple, red	Europe, N America
ribbon woods	*Hoheria*	white	New Zealand
robinia	*Robinia*	rose-pink	N America
rock rose (or sun rose)	*Helianthemum*	white, yellow, pink, orange, red	Europe
rose	*Rosa*	pink, red, white, cream, yellow	N temperate regions
rosemary	*Rosmarinus*	violet	Europe, Asia
rowan (or mountain ash)	*Sorbus*	white (red, yellow berries)	Europe, Asia
sage, common	*Salvia*	green, white, yellow, reddish purple	S Europe
St John's wort	*Hypericum*	yellow	Europe, Asia
sea buckthorn	*Hippophae*	silver, orange	SW Europe
senecio	*Senecio*	yellow	New Zealand
skimmia	*Skimmia*	white	Japan, China
snowberry	*Symphoricarpos*	pink, white	N America
spiraea	*Spiraea*	white, pink, crimson	China, Japan
stachyurus	*Stachyurus*	pale yellow	China
staphylea	*Staphylea*	rose-pink	Europe, Asia
sun rose ▸ rock rose			
syringa ▸ lilac			
tamarisk	*Tamarix*	pink, white	Europe
thyme	*Thymus*	purple, white, pink	Europe
veronica	*Veronica*	white, pink, lilac, purple	New Zealand
viburnum	*Viburnum*	white, pink	Europe, Asia, Africa
Virginia creeper	*Parthenocissus*	foliage orange, red (blue-black fruits)	N America
wattle ▸ acacia			
weigela	*Weigela*	pink, red	N China
winter sweet	*Chimonanthus*	yellow	China
wisteria	*Wisteria*	mauve, white, pink	China, Japan
witch hazel	*Hamamelis*	red, yellow	China, Japan

Fungi

English name	Species	Colour	Edibility
base toadstool (or ugly toadstool)	*Lactarius necator*	green, brown	poisonous
beautiful clavaria	*Ramaria formosa*	yellow, ochre, red, purple	poisonous
beefsteak fungus	*Fistulina hepatica*	red	edible

English name	Species	Colour	Edibility
blusher	Amanita fubescens	red, brown	poisonous (raw) or edible (cooked)
brain mushroom	Gyromitra esculenta	chestnut, dark brown	poisonous
buckler agaric	Entoloma clypeatum	grey, brown	edible
Caesar's mushroom	Amanita Caesarea	red, yellow	edible
chanterelle	Cantharellus cibarius	yellow, ochre	excellent
clean mycena	Mycena pura	purple	poisonous
clouded agaric	Lepista nebularis	grey, brown	poisonous
common earthball	Scleroderma aurantium	ochre, yellow, brown	poisonous
common grisette	Amanita vaginita	grey, yellow	edible
common morel	Morchella esculenta	light brown, black	edible
common puffball	Lycoperdon perlatum	white, cream, brown	edible
common stinkhorn	Phallus impudicus	white, green	edible
death cap, common	Amanita phalloides	grey, green, yellow, brown	deadly
deceiver, common	Laccaria laccata	purple, pink, orange	edible
destroying angel	Amanita virosa	white, brown	deadly
dingy agaric	Tricholoma portentosum	grey, black, yellow, lilac	edible
dryad's saddle	Polyporus squamosus	yellow, brown	edible
fairies bonnets	Coprinus disseminatus	grey, purple	worthless
fairy ring champignon	Marasmius oreades	beige, ochre, red, brown	edible
field mushroom	Agaricus campestris	white, brown	excellent
firwood agaric	Tricholoma auratum	green, yellow, brown	edible
fly agaric	Amanita muscaria	red, orange, white	poisonous
garlic marosmius	Marosmius scorodonius	red, brown	edible
gypsy mushroom	Rozites caperata	yellow, ochre	edible
hedgehog mushroom	Hydnum repandum	white, beige, yellow	edible
honey fungus	Armillaria mellea	honey, brown, red	inedible
horn of plenty (or trumpet of the dead)	Craterellus cornucopiodes	brown, black	very good
horse mushroom	Agaricus arvensis	white, yellow, ochre	very good
Jew's ear fungus	Auricularia auricula judae	yellow, brown	worthless
larch boletus	Suillus grevillei	yellow	edible
liberty cap (or 'magic mushroom')	Psilocybe semilanceata	brown	poisonous
lurid boletus	Boletus luridus	olive, brown, yellow	poisonous (raw) or edible (cooked)
morel	Morchella esculenta	brown, black	edible
naked mushroom	Lepista nuda	purple, brown	edible

English name	Species	Colour	Edibility
old man of the woods	Strobilomyces floccopus	brown, black	edible
orange-peel fungus	Aleuria aurantia	orange, red	edible
oyster mushroom	Pleurotus ostreatus	brown, black, grey, blue, purple	edible
panther cap (or false blusher)	Amanita pantherina	brown, ochre, grey, white	poisonous
parasol mushroom	Macrolepiota procera	beige, ochre, brown	excellent
penny-bun fungus	Boletus edulis	chestnut brown	excellent
périgord truffle	Tuber melanosporum	black, red-brown	excellent
Piedmont truffle	Tuber magnatum	white	edible
purple blewit	Tricholomopsis rutilans	yellow, red	edible
saffron milk cap	Lactarius delicioses	orange, red	poisonous (raw) or edible (cooked)
St George's mushroom	Calocybe gambosa	white, cream	edible
Satan's boletus	Boletus satanus	grey	poisonous (raw) or edible (cooked)
scarlet-stemmed boletus	Boletus calopus	grey, brown	poisonous
shaggy ink cap (or lawyer's wig)	Coprinus comatus	white, ochre	edible
sickener (or emetic russala)	Russula emetica	pink, red	poisonous
stinkhorn	Phallus impudicus	olive, green	inedible
stinking russula	Russula foetens	ochre, brown	poisonous
stout agaric	Amanita spissa	grey, brown	edible
strong scented garlic	Tricholoma saponaceum	grey, green, brown	poisonous
sulphur tuft (or clustered woodlover)	Hypholoma fasciculare	yellow, red, brown	poisonous
summer truffle	Tuber aestivum	dark brown	very good
white truffle	Tuber magnatum	cream, pale brown	excellent
winter fungus (or velvet shank)	Flammulina velutipes	yellow, brown, ochre	edible
wood agaric	Collybia dryophila	yellow, brown, rust	edible
wood mushroom	Agaricus sylvaticus	grey, red, brown	edible
woolly milk-cap (or griping toadstool)	Lactarius torminosus	pink, brown	poisonous
yellow stainer	Agaricus xanthodermus	white, yellow, grey	poisonous
yellow-brown boletus (or slippery jack)	Suillus luteus	yellow, brown	edible

Trees (Europe and N America)

English name	Species	Deciduous/ Evergreen	Area of origin
alder, common	*Alnus glutinosa*	deciduous	Europe
almond	*Prunus dulcis*	deciduous	W Asia, N Africa
apple	*Malus pumila*	deciduous	Europe, W Africa
apple, crab	*Malus sylvestris*	deciduous	Europe, Asia
ash, common	*Fraxinus exzcelsior*	deciduous	Europe
aspen	*Populus tremula*	deciduous	Europe
bean tree, Red Indian	*Catalpa bignonioides*	deciduous	America, E Asia
beech, common	*Fagus sylvatica*	deciduous	Europe
beech, copper	*Fagus purpurea* ('Atropunicea')	deciduous	Europe
beech, roble	*Nothofagus obliqua*	deciduous	S America
birch, silver	*Betula pendula*	deciduous	Europe, America, Asia
box	*Buxus sempervirens*	evergreen	Europe, N Africa
Brazil nut	*Bertholletia excelsa*	evergreen	S America
camellia, deciduous	*Stewartia pseudo-camellia*	deciduous	Asia
castor-oil tree, prickly	*Eleutherococcus pictus*	deciduous	tropics
cedar of Lebanon	*Cedrus libani*	evergreen	Asia
cedar, smooth Tasmanian	*Athrotaxis cupressoides*	evergreen	Australia
cedar, white	*Thuja occidentalis*	evergreen	America
cherry, morello (or sour cherry)	*Prunus cerasus*	deciduous	Europe, Asia
cherry, wild (or gean)	*Prunus avium*	deciduous	Europe
chestnut, horse	*Aesculus hippocastanum*	deciduous	Asia, SW Europe
chestnut, sweet (or Spanish chestnut)	*Castanea sativa*	deciduous	Europe, Africa, Asia
cypress, Lawson	*Chamaecyparis lawsoniana*	evergreen	America
deodar	*Cedrus deodara*	evergreen	Asia
dogwood, common	*Cornus sanguinea*	deciduous	Europe
elm, Dutch	*Ulmus × hollandica*	deciduous	Europe
elm, English	*Ulmus procera*	deciduous	Europe
elm, wych	*Ulmus glabra*	deciduous	Europe
fig	*Ficus carica*	evergreen	Asia
fir, Douglas	*Pseudotsuga menziesii*	evergreen	America
fir, red	*Abies magnifica*	evergreen	America
ginkgo	*Ginkgo biloba*	deciduous	Asia
grapefruit	*Citrus × paradisi*	evergreen	Asia
gum, blue	*Eucalyptus globulus*	evergreen	Australia

English name	Species	Deciduous/ Evergreen	Area of origin
gum, cider	*Eucalyptus gunnii*	evergreen	Australia
gum, snow	*Eucalyptus panciflora*	evergreen	Australia
gutta-percha tree	*Eucommia ulmoides*	deciduous	China
hawthorn	*Crataegus monogyna*	deciduous	Europe
hazel, common	*Corylus avellana*	deciduous	Europe, W Asia, N Africa
hemlock, Western	*Tsuga heterophylla*	evergreen	America
holly	*Ilex aquifolium*	evergreen	Europe, N Africa, W Asia
hornbeam	*Carpinus betulus*	deciduous	Europe, Asia
Joshua-tree	*Yucca brevifolia*	evergreen	America
Judas-tree	*Cercis siliquastrum*	deciduous	S Europe, Asia
juniper, common	*Juniperus communis*	evergreen	Europe, Asia
laburnum, common	*Laburnum anagyroides*	deciduous	Europe
larch, European	*Larix decidua*	deciduous	Europe
larch, golden	*Pseudolarix kaempferi*	deciduous	E Asia
leatherwood	*Eucryphia lucida*	evergreen	Australia
lemon	*Citrus limon*	evergreen	Asia
lime	*Citrus aurantiifolia*	evergreen	Asia
lime, small-leafed	*Tilia cordata*	deciduous	Europe
locust tree	*Robinia pseudoacacia*	deciduous	America
magnolia (or white laurel)	*Magnolia virginiana*	evergreen	America
maple, field (or common maple)	*Acer campestre*	deciduous	Europe
maple, sugar	*Acer saccharum*	deciduous	America
medlar	*Mespilus germanica*	deciduous	Europe
mimosa	*Acacia dealbata*	deciduous	Australia, Europe
mockernut	*Carya tomentosa*	deciduous	America
monkey puzzle	*Araucaria araucana*	evergreen	S America
mountain ash ► rowan			
mulberry, common	*Morus nigra*	deciduous	Asia
mulberry, white	*Morus alba*	deciduous	Asia
myrtle, orange bark	*Myrtus apiculata*	evergreen	S America
nutmeg, California	*Torreya californica*	evergreen	America
oak, California live	*Quercus agrifolia*	deciduous	America
oak, cork	*Quercus suber*	evergreen	S Europe, N Africa
oak, English (or common oak)	*Quercus robur*	deciduous	Europe, Asia, Africa
oak, red	*Quercus rubra*	deciduous	America
olive	*Olea europaea*	evergreen	S Europe
orange, sweet	*Citrus sinensis*	evergreen	Asia
pagoda-tree	*Sophora japonica*	deciduous	China, Japan
pear	*Pyrus communis*	deciduous	Europe, W Asia

English name	Species	Deciduous/ Evergreen	Area of origin
pine, Austrian	*Pinus nigra* subsp. *nigra*	evergreen	Europe, Asia
pine, Corsican	*Pinus nigra* subsp. *laricio*	evergreen	Europe
pine, Monterey	*Pinus radiata*	evergreen	America
pine, Scots	*Pinus sylvestris*	evergreen	Europe
plane, London	*Platanus × hispanica*	deciduous	Europe
plane, Oriental	*Platanus orientalis*	deciduous	SE Europe, Asia
plum	*Prunus domestica*	deciduous	Europe, Asia
poplar, balsam	*Populus balsamifera*	deciduous	America, Asia
poplar, black	*Populus nigra*	deciduous	Europe, Asia
poplar, Lombardy	*Populus nigra* 'Italica'	deciduous	Europe
poplar, white	*Populus alba*	deciduous	Europe
quince	*Cydonia oblonga*	deciduous	Asia
raoul	*Nothofagus procera*	deciduous	S America
rowan (or mountain ash)	*Sorbus aucuparia*	deciduous	Europe
sassafras, American	*Sassafras albidum*	deciduous	America
service tree, true	*Sorbus domestica*	deciduous	Europe
silver fir, common	*Abies alba*	evergreen	Europe
spruce, Norway	*Picea abies*	evergreen	Europe
spruce, sitka	*Picea sitchensis*	evergreen	America, Europe
strawberry tree	*Arbutus unedo*	evergreen	Europe
sycamore ('plane')	*Acer pseudoplatanus*	deciduous	Europe, W Asia
tamarack	*Larix laricina*	deciduous	N America
tree of heaven	*Ailanthus altissima*	deciduous	China
tulip-tree	*Liriodendron tulipfera*	deciduous	America
walnut, black	*Juglans nigra*	deciduous	America
walnut, common	*Juglans regia*	deciduous	Europe, Asia
whitebeam	*Sorbus aria*	deciduous	Europe
willow, pussy (or goat willow or sallow willow)	*Salix caprea*	deciduous	Europe, Asia
willow, weeping	*Salix babylonica*	deciduous	Asia
willow, white	*Salix alba*	deciduous	Europe
yew, common	*Taxus baccata*	evergreen	N temperate regions

Trees (Tropical)

Name	Species	Deciduous/ Evergreen	Area of origin
African tulip tree	*Spathodea campanulata*	evergreen	Africa
almond, tropical	*Terminalia catappa*	deciduous	Asia
angel's trumpet	*Brugmansia × candida*	deciduous	S America
autograph tree	*Clusia rosea*	evergreen	Asia
avocado	*Persea americana*	evergreen	America
bamboo	*Schizostachyum glauchifolium*	deciduous	America
banana	*Musa × paradisiaca*	plant dies after fruiting	Asia
banyan	*Ficus benghalensis*	evergreen	Asia
baobab (or dead rat's tree)	*Adansonia digitata*	deciduous	Africa
beach heliotrope	*Argusia argentea*	evergreen	S America
bo tree	*Ficus religiosa*	deciduous	Asia
bombax	*Bombax ceiba*	deciduous	Asia
bottle brush	*Callistemon citrinus*	evergreen	Australia
breadfruit	*Artocarpus altilis*	evergreen	Asia
brownea	*Brownea macrophylla*	evergreen	C America
calabash	*Crescentia cujete*	evergreen	America
candlenut	*Aleurites moluccana*	evergreen	Asia
cannonball	*Courouptia guianensis*	evergreen	S America
chinaberry (or bead tree)	*Melia azedarach*	deciduous	Asia
Christmas-berry	*Schinus terebinthifolius*	evergreen	America
coconut palm	*Cocus nucifera*	evergreen	Asia
coffee tree	*Coffea liberica*	evergreen	Africa
Cook pine	*Araucaria columnaris*	evergreen	America
coral tree	*Erythrina coralloides*	deciduous	C America
coral shower	*Cassia grandis*	deciduous	Asia
cotton, wild	*Cochlospermum vitifolium*	deciduous	C and S America
crape myrtle	*Lagerstroemia indica*	deciduous	Asia
date palm	*Phoenix dactylifera*	evergreen	Asia and Africa
dragon-tree	*Dracaena draco*	evergreen	Canary Is
durian	*Durio zibethinus*	evergreen	Asia
ebony	*Diospyros ebenum*	evergreen	Asia
elephant's ear	*Enterolobium cyclocarpum*	deciduous	S America
flame-tree	*Delonix regia*	deciduous	Madagascar
gold tree	*Cybistax donnell-smithii*	deciduous	Asia

Name	Species	Deciduous/ Evergreen	Area of origin
golden rain	*Koelreuteria paniculata*	deciduous	Asia
golden shower	*Cassia fistula*	deciduous	Asia
guava	*Psidium guajava*	evergreen	S America
ironwood (or casuarina)	*Casuarina equisetifolia*	deciduous	Australia and Asia
jacaranda	*Jacaranda mimosifolia*	deciduous	S America
jackfruit (or jack)	*Artocarpus heterophyllus*	evergreen	Asia
kapok tree	*Ceiba pentandra*	deciduous	Old and New World tropics
koa	*Acacia koa*	evergreen	Hawaii
lipstick tree	*Bixa orellanna*	evergreen	America
lychee	*Litchi chinensis*	evergreen	China
macadamia nut	*Macadamia integrifolia*	evergreen	Australia
mahogany	*Swietenia mahogoni*	evergreen	S America
mango	*Mangifera indica*	evergreen	Asia
mesquite	*Prosopis pallida*	evergreen	America
monkeypod (or rain-tree)	*Albizia saman*	evergreen	S America
Norfolk Island pine	*Araucaria heterophylla*	evergreen	Norfolk I
octopus tree	*Schefflera actinophylla*	evergreen	Australia
ohi'a lehua	*Metrosideros collina*	evergreen	Hawaii
pandanus (or screw pine)	*Pandanus tectorius*	evergreen	Oceania
paperbark tree	*Melaleuca quinquenervia*	evergreen	Australia
powderpuff	*Calliandra haematocephala*	evergreen	S America
royal palm	*Roystonea regia*	evergreen	Cuba
sandalwood	*Santalum album*	deciduous	Asia
sand-box tree	*Hura crepitans*	deciduous	Americas
sausage tree	*Kigelia pinnata*	evergreen	Africa
scrambled egg tree	*Cassia glauca*	evergreen	Americas
Surinam cherry	*Eugenia uniflora*	evergreen	S America
teak tree	*Tectona grandis*	evergreen	Asia
tiger's claw	*Erythrina variegata*	deciduous	Asia
yellow oleander	*Thevetia peruviana*	evergreen	W Indies

Fish (Record holders)

Fastest	Over short distances, the sailfish can reach a speed of 110kph/68mph; however marlins are the fastest over longer distances, and can reach a burst speed of 68–80kph/40–50mph.
Largest	The whale shark (*Rhincodon typus*) is said to reach over 18m/59ft, with the largest on record being 12.65m/41ft 6in, weighing an estimated 21.5 tonnes.
Smallest	The dwarf pygmy goby (*Pandaka pygmaea*), found in the streams and rivers of Luzon in the Philippines, measures 7.5–9.9mm and weighs 4–5mg.
Smallest in British waters	Guillet's goby (*Lebetus guilleti*) reaches a maximum length of 24mm.
Most widespread	The distribution of the bristlemouths of genus *Cyclothone* is worldwide excluding the Arctic.
Most restricted	The devil's hole pupfish (*Cyprinodon diabolis*) inhabits only a small area of water above a rock shelf in a spring-fed pool in Ash Meadows, Nevada, USA.
Deepest dweller	In 1970 a brotulid *Bassogigas profundissimus* was recovered from a depth of 8 299m/27 230ft, making it the deepest living vertebrate.
Largest fish ever caught on a rod	In 1959 a great white shark measuring 5.13m/16ft 10in and weighing 1 208kg/2 664 lb was caught off S Australia.
Largest freshwater fish found in Britain and Ireland	Reportedly, in 1815 a pike (*Esox lucius*) was taken from the River Shannon in Ireland weighing 41.7kg/92 lb; however there is evidence of a pike weighing 32.7kg/72 lb having been caught on Loch Ken, Scotland, in 1774.
Largest saltwater fish caught by anglers in the UK	In 1933 a tunny weighing 385.989kg/851 lb was caught near Whitby, Yorkshire.
Longest-lived species	Some specimens of the sturgeon are thought to be over 80 years old.
Shortest-lived species	Tooth carp of the suborder *Cyprinodontidae* live for only 8 months in the wild.
Greatest distance covered by a migrating fish	A bluefin tuna was tagged in 1958 off California and caught in 1963 in Japan; it had covered a distance of 9 335km/5 800mi.

Birds (Record holders)

Highest flier	Ruppell's griffon, a vulture, has been measured at 11 275m (about 7mi) above sea level.
Furthest migrator	The arctic tern travels up to 36 000km/22 400mi each year, flying from the Arctic to the Antarctic and back again.
Fastest flier	The peregrine falcon can dive through the air at speeds up to 185kph/115mph. The fastest bird in level flight is the eider duck, which can reach about 80kph/50mph.
Fastest animal on two legs	The ostrich can maintain a speed of 50kph/31mph for 15 minutes or more, and it may reach 65–70kph/40–43mph in short bursts, eg when escaping from predators.
Smallest	The bee hummingbird of Cuba is under 6cm/2.4in long and weighs 3g/0.1oz.
Greatest wingspan	The wandering albatross can reach 3.65m/12ft.
Heaviest flying bird	The great bustard and the kori bustard both weigh up to 18kg/40 lb, with swans not far behind at about 16kg/35 lb.
Deepest diver	The emperor penguin can reach a depth of 265m/870ft. The great northern diver or loon can dive to about 80m/262ft — deeper than any other flying bird.
Most abundant	Africa's red-billed quelea is the most numerous wild bird, with an estimated population of about 1 500 million. The domestic chicken is the most abundant of all birds, numbering over 4 000 million.
Most feathers	The greatest number of feathers counted on a bird was 25 216, on a swan.

Mammals (Record holders)

Largest	The blue whale, up to 30m/98ft long and weighing up to 150 tonnes, is the largest known mammal. The largest existing land mammal is the male African elephant, standing up to 3.3m/11ft at the shoulder and weighing up to 7 tonnes.
Tallest	The giraffe stands up to 5.5m/18ft high.
Smallest	The pygmy white-toothed shrew, also called the Etruscan shrew, has a body about 5cm/2in long and weighs up to 2.5g/0.1oz. Some bats weigh even less.
Fastest on land	The cheetah can reach 100kph/62mph, but only in short bursts. The pronghorn can maintain speeds of 50kph/31mph for several kilometres.
Most prolific breeder	A North American meadow mouse produced 17 litters in a single year (4–9 babies per litter).
Most widespread	Humans are the most widely distributed of mammals, closely followed by the house mouse, which has accompanied humans to all parts of the world.

Mammals

Mammals are the group of animals to which humans belong. They are characterized by the presence of mammary glands in the female which produce milk on which the young can be nourished. They are divided into monotremes or egg-laying mammals; marsupials in which the young are born at an early stage of development and then grow outside the mother's womb, often in a pouch; placental mammals in which the young are nourished in the womb by the mother's blood and are born at a late stage of development. A crucial aspect of mammals is the fact that their hair and skin glands allow them to regulate their temperatures from within, ie they are endothermic (warm-blooded). This confers on them a greater adaptability to more varied environments than that of reptiles. There are over 4 000 species of mammals, most of which are terrestrial, the exceptions being species of bat which have developed the ability to fly, and the whale which leads an aquatic existence.

Name	Size (cm) [1]	Distribution	Special features
❑ **Monotremes**			
echidna, long-beaked	45–90	New Guinea	prominent beak
echidna, short-beaked	30–45	Australia, Tasmania and New Guinea	fur covered in protective spines
platypus	45–60	E Australia and Tasmania	duck-like snout
❑ **Marsupials**			
bandicoot	15–56	Australia and New Guinea	highest reproductive rate of all marsupials
kangaroo	to 165	Australia and New Guinea	bounding motion and prominent female pouch
kangaroo, rat	28.4–30	Australia and New Guinea	rabbit-sized version of its larger namesake
koala	78	E Australia	diet consists of eucalyptus leaves; intensive management has significantly revived population numbers
mole, marsupial	13–15	Australia	specializes in burrowing
oppossum	7–55	C and S America	known for its dreadful smell
possum, brushtail	34–70	Australia, New Guinea, Solomon Is and New Zealand	most commonly encountered of all Australian mammals
wallaby ► kangaroo			
wombat	70–115	SE Australia and Tasmania	poor eyesight; keen senses of smell and hearing
❑ **Placental mammals**			
aardvark	105–130	Africa S of the Sahara	tubular snout
anteater	16–22	C and S America	elongated snout
antelope, dwarf	45–55	Africa	female larger than male

Name	Size (cm) [1]	Distribution	Special features
armadillo	12.5–100	southern N America, C and S America	protective suit of armour
ass	200–210	Africa and Asia	renowned as a beast of burden
baboon and mandrill	56–80	Africa	able to walk over long distances
badger	50–100	Africa, Europe, Asia and N America	black and white markings on European species
bat	15–200 (wingspan)	worldwide except for the Arctic and Antarctic	only vertebrate, apart from birds, capable of sustained flight
bear, black	130–180	N America	more adaptable than grizzly bear
bear, grizzly (or brown bear)	200–280	NW America and former USSR	large in size (up to half a ton)
beaver	80–120	N America, Asia and Europe	constructs dams and lodges in water
beaver, mountain	30–41	Pacific Coast of Canada and USA	land-dwelling and burrowing animal
bison, American	to 380	N America	now exists only in parks and refuges
bison, European	to 290	former USSR	extinct in the wild in 1919, but now re-established in parts of the former USSR
boar	58–210	Europe, Africa and Asia	intelligent and highly adaptable
buffalo, wild water	240–280	SE Asia	adept at moving through its muddy habitat
bush baby	12–32	Africa and S Asia	highly agile; arboreal
bushbuck	110–145	Africa S of the Sahara	dark brown or chestnut coat with white markings
camel	190–230 (height of hump)	Mongolia	two humps
capybara	106–134	S America	largest living rodent
cat	20–400	worldwide	acute sense of vision and smell
cattle	180–200	worldwide	long-horned and polled or hornless breeds
chamois	125–135	Europe and Asia	adapted to alpine and subalpine conditions
cheetah	112–135	Africa	fastest of all land animals
chimpanzee	70–85	W and C Africa	most intelligent of the great apes
chinchilla	25	S America	hunted for food and fur
civet	33–84	Africa and Asia	cat-like carnivore
colugo	33–42	SE Asia	stretched membrane allows it to glide from tree to tree
coyote	70–97	N America	unique howling sound
coypu	50	S America	highly aquatic rodent

Name	Size (cm) [1]	Distribution	Special features
deer	41–152	N and S America, Europe and Asia	male uses antlers to attack other males during the rutting period
dingo	150	Australasia	descendant of the wolf
dog	20–75	worldwide	first animal to be domesticated
dolphin	120–400	worldwide	highly developed social organization and communication systems
dolphin, river	210–260	SE Asia and S America	highly sensitive system of echo location
dormouse	6–19	Europe, Africa, Turkey, Asia and Japan	nocturnal rodent; hibernates during winter
dromedary	190–230 (height of hump)	SW Asia, N Africa and Australia	camel with one hump
duiker	55–72	Africa S of the Sahara	dives into cover when disturbed
eland	250–350	Africa	spiral-horned antelope
elephant, African	600–750	Africa S of the Sahara	largest living mammal
fox	24–100	N and S America, Europe, Asia and Africa	noted for its cunning and intelligence
gazelle	122–166	Africa	birth peaks coincide with abundance of feeding vegetation during spring
gerbil	6–7.5	Africa and Asia	wide field of vision; low frequency hearing
gerenuk	140–160	Africa	graceful and delicate
gibbon	45–65	SE Asia	swings among trees using arms
giraffe	380–470	Africa S of the Sahara	mottled coat and long neck
gnu	194–209	Africa	massive head and mane
goat, mountain	to 175	N America	ponderous rock climber
goat, wild	130–140	S Europe, Middle East and Asia	subspecies includes domestic goat
gopher	12–22.5	N America	highly adapted burrower
gorilla	150–170	C Africa	largest living primate
guinea pig	28	S America	tailless rodent
hamster	5.3–10.2	Europe, Middle East, former USSR and China	aggressive towards own species in the wild
hare	40–76	N and S America, Africa, Europe, Asia and Arctic	well-developed ability to run from predators
hare, Patagonian	45	S America	strictly monogamous
hartebeest	195–200	Africa	long face, sloping back
hedgehog	10–15	Europe, Asia and Africa	protective spined back
hippopotamus	150–345	Africa	barrel-shaped; short stumpy legs

Name	Size (cm) [1]	Distribution	Special features
horse	200–210	worldwide in domesticated form; Asia, N and S America and Australia in the wild	historically useful as a beast of burden and means of transport
hyena	85–140	Africa and Asia	scavenger and hunter
ibex	85–143	C Europe, Asia and Africa	large horns; saved from extinction in C Europe
impala	128–142	Africa	fawn and mahogany coat
jackal	65–106	Africa, SE Europe and Asia	unfair reputation as cowardly scavenger
jaguar	112–185	C and S America	only cat in the Americas
jerboa	4–26	N Africa, Turkey, Middle East and C Asia	moves by hopping and jumping with long hind legs
lemming	10–11	N America and Eurasia	Norway lemming is noted for its mass migration
lemur	12–70	Madagascar	mainly nocturnal and arboreal
lemur, flying ► colugo			
leopard	100–190	Africa and Asia	nocturnal hunters
lion	260–330	Africa	most socially organized of the cat family
llama	230–400	S America	S American beast of burden
lynx	67–110	Europe and N America	well adapted to snow
macaque	38–70	Asia and N Africa	heavily built; partly terrestrial
marmoset	17.5–40	S America	squirrel-like monkey
marten	30–75	N America, Europe and Asia	one species, the fisher, unique for its ability to penetrate the quilled defences of the porcupine
mole	2.4–7.5	Europe, Asia and N America	almost exclusively subterranean existence
mongoose	24–58	Africa, S Asia and SW Europe	often seen in the tripod position, ie standing up on hind legs and tail
monkey, capuchin	25–63	S America	lives in social groupings
mouse ► rat			
narwhal	400–500	former USSR, N America and Greenland	distinctive single tusk in the male can reach up to 300cm
okapi	190–200	C Africa	mixture of giraffe and zebra
orang-utan	150	forests of N Sumatra and Borneo	sparse covering of long red-brown hair
otter	40–123	N and S America, Europe, Asia and Africa	only truly amphibious member of weasel family
panda, giant	130–150	China	rare; poor breeder

Name	Size (cm)[1]	Distribution	Special features
polar bear	250–300	N polar regions	large white coat
porcupine (New World)	30–86	N and S America	arboreal; excellent climber
porcupine (Old World)	37–47	Africa and Asia	heavily quilled and spiny body
porpoise	120–150	N temperate zone, W Indo-Pacific, temperate and sub-antarctic waters of S America and Auckland Is	large range of sounds for the purpose of echo location
puma	105–196	N and S America	wide-ranging hunter
rabbit, European	38–58	Europe, Africa, Australia, New Zealand and S America	burrowing creature; opportunistic animal in widespread environment
racoon	55	N, S and C America	black masked face
rat (New World)	5–8	N and S America	highly adaptable
rat (Old World)	4.5–8.2	Europe, Asia, Africa and Australia	highly adaptable
reedbuck	110–176	Africa	distinctive whistling sounds; leaping movements
rhinoceros	250–400	Africa and tropical Asia	horn grows from snout
seal	117–490	mainly polar, subpolar and temperate seas	graceful swimmer and diver
sheep, American bighorn	168–186	N America	large horns and body similar to an ibex
sheep, barbary	155–165	N Africa	large head and horns up to 84cm in length
sheep, blue	91 (shoulder height)	Asia	blue coat; curved horns
shrew	3.5–4.8	Europe, Asia, Africa, N America and northern S America	generally poor eyesight, compensated for by acute senses of smell and hearing
shrew, elephant-	10.4–29.4	Africa	long pointed snout
skunk	40–68	N and S America	evil-smelling defence mechanism
sloth, three-toed	56–60	S America	smaller version of the two-toed sloth
sloth, two-toed	58–70	S America	arboreal; nocturnal; slow
springbuck	96–115	S Africa	migrates in herds of tens of thousands

Name	Size (cm)[1]	Distribution	Special features
springhare	36–43	S Africa	burrowing creature; like a miniature kangaroo
squirrel	6.6–10	N and S America, Europe, Africa and Asia	includes arboreal, burrowing and flying species
tapir	180–250	C and S America and SE Asia	nocturnal mammal with distinctive snout
tarsier	11–14	islands of SE Asia	ability to rotate neck
tiger	220–310	India, Manchuria, China and Indonesia	solitary hunter; stalks for prey
vole	10–11	N America, Europe, Asia and the Arctic	population fluctuates in regular patterns or cycles
walrus	250–320	Arctic seas	thick folds of skin; twin tusks
waterbuck	177–235	Africa	shaggy coat and heavy gait
weasel	15–55	Arctic, N and S America, Europe, Asia and Africa	certain species have been exploited for their fur, eg mink, ermine
whale, beaked	400–1 280	worldwide	dolphin-like beak
whale, blue	to 3 000	Arctic and subtropics	largest animal that has ever lived
whale, grey	1 190–1 520	N Pacific	long migration to breed, from the Arctic to the subtropics
whale, humpback	1 600	worldwide	highly acrobatic; wide range of sounds
whale, killer	900–1 000	worldwide in cool coastal waters	toothed; dorsal fin narrow and vertical
whale, long-finned pilot	600	temperate waters of the N Atlantic	best known for mysterious mass strandings on beaches
whale, sperm	to 2 070	widespread in temperate and tropical waters	largest of the toothed whales; prodigious deep sea diver
whale, white	300–500	N Russia, N America and Greenland	white skin; wide range of bodily, facial and vocal expressions
wild cat	50–80	Europe, India and Africa	domestic cat may be descended from the African wild cat
wolf, grey	100–150	N America, Europe, Asia and Middle East	noted for hunting in packs
wolverine	to 83	Arctic and subarctic regions	heavily built; long dark coat of fur
zebra	215–230	Africa	black and white stripes

[1] To convert cm to inches, multiply by 0.3937; generally, size denotes length from head to tip of tail.

Birds

Birds are warm-blooded, egg-laying, and, in the case of adults, feathered vertebrates of the class Aves; there are approximately 8 600 species classified into 29 Orders and 181 Families. Birds are constructed for flight. The body is streamlined to reduce air resistance, the fore-limbs are modified as feathered wings, and the skeletal structure, heart and wing muscles, centre of gravity, and lung capacity are all designed for the act of flying. Two exceptions to this are the ratites or flightless birds which have become too large to be capable of sustained flight, eg the ostrich, kiwi and emu, and the penguin which has evolved into a highly aquatic creature. Birds are thought to have evolved from reptiles, their closest living relative being the crocodile.

Name	Size (cm)[1]	Distribution	Special features
◻ Flightless birds			
cassowary	150	Australia and New Guinea	claws can be lethal
emu	160–190	Australia	highly mobile, nomadic population
kiwi	35–55	New Zealand	smallest of the Ratitae order; nocturnal
ostrich	275	dry areas of Africa	fastest animal on two legs
rhea	100–150	grasslands of S America	lives in flocks
tinamou	15–49	C and S America	able to sustain flight over short distances
◻ Birds of prey			
buzzard	80	worldwide except Australasia and Malaysia	perches often; kills prey on ground
condor	60–100	the Americas	Andean condor has largest wingspan of any living bird (up to 300cm)
eagle, bald	80–100	N America	white plumage on head and neck
eagle, golden	80–100	N hemisphere	kills with talons
eagle, harpy	90	C America to Argentina	world's largest eagle
eagle, sea	70–120	coastline worldwide	breeds on sea cliffs
falcon	15–60	worldwide	remarkable powers of flight and sight
harrier	50	worldwide	hunts using regular search pattern
kite	52–58	worldwide	most varied group of hawks
osprey	55–58	worldwide	feet adapted to catching fish
owl	12–73	worldwide	acute sight and hearing
owl, barn	30–45	worldwide	feathered legs
secretary bird	100	Africa	walks up to 30km/20mi per day
sparrow-hawk	to 27 (male), to 38 (female)	Eurasia, NW Africa, C and S America	long tail, small round wings

Name	Size (cm) [1]	Distribution	Special features
vulture (New World)	60–100	the Americas	lives in colonies
vulture (Old World)	150–270 (wingspan)	worldwide except the Americas	no sense of smell
☐ Songbirds			
accentor	14–18	Palaearctic	complex social organization
bird of paradise	12.5–100	New Guinea, Moluccas and Eastern Australia	brilliantly ornate plumage
bowerbird	25–37	Australia and New Guinea	male builds bowers to attract female
bulbul	13–23	Africa, Madagascar, S Asia and the Philippines	beautiful singing voice
bunting	15–20	worldwide	large family including species of sparrow, finch and cardinals
butcherbird	26–58	Australia, New Guinea and New Zealand	highly aggressive; known as 'bushman's clock'
chaffinch	11–19	Europe, N and S America, Africa and Asia	strong bill; melodious singing voice
cowbird	17–54	N and S America	gaping movements of the bill
crow	20–66	worldwide, except New Zealand	complex social systems
dipper	17–20	Europe, S Asia and western regions of N and S America	strong legs and toes allow mobility to walk under water
drongo	18–38	S Asia and Africa	pugnacious
flowerpecker	8–20	SE Asia and Australasia	short tongue specially adapted for feeding on nectar
flycatcher (Old World)	9–27	worldwide except N and S America	tropical species brightly coloured
flycatcher, silky	to 14	N and S America	feeds on the wing
honeycreeper, Hawaiian	10–20	Hawaiian Is	varying bills between species
honeyeater	10–32	Australasia, Pacific Is, Hawaii and S Africa	brush tongue adapted for nectar feeding
lark	11–19	worldwide	ground-dwelling; elaborate singing displays
leafbird	12–24	S Asia	forest dwellers; ability to mimic sounds of other birds
magpie-lark	19–50	Australasia and New Guinea	adapted to urban environment
mockingbird	20–33	N and S America	great ability to mimic sounds
nuthatch	14–20	worldwide except S America and New Zealand	European species can break open nuts

Name	Size (cm) [1]	Distribution	Special features
oriole	18–30	Europe, Asia, Philippines, Malaysia, New Guinea and Australia	melodious singing voice
palmchat	18	Hispaniola and W Indies	communal nesting with individual compartments for each nesting pair
robin	13	worldwide except New Zealand	territorial; uses song to deter intruders
shrike	15–35	Africa, N America, Asia and New Guinea	sharply hooked bill
shrike, cuckoo-	14–40	Africa, S Asia	peculiar courtship display
shrike, vanga-	12–30	Madagascar	some endangered species
sparrow	10–20	African tropics in origin, now worldwide	some species noted for urban adaptability
starling	16–45	Europe, Asia and Africa	nests in colonies
sunbird	8–16	Africa, SE Asia and Australasia	bright plumage
swallow	12–23	worldwide	strong and agile flight
thrush	12–26	worldwide	loud and varied singing voice
tit	11–14	N America, Europe, Asia and Africa	nests in holes
tree-creeper	12–15	N hemisphere and S Africa	forages on trees for food
tree-creeper, Australian	15	Australia and New Guinea	forages for food on tree-trunks
vireo	10–17	N and S America	thick and slightly hooked bill
wagtail	14–17	worldwide, although rare in Australia	spectacular song in flight
warbler, American	10–16	N and S America	well developed and often complex songs
wattle-bird	25–53	New Zealand	fleshy fold of skin at base of bill
waxbill	9–13.5	Africa, SE Asia and Australasia	several species drink by sucking
waxwing	18	W hemisphere	wax-like, red tips on secondary flight feathers
white-eye	12	Africa, SE Asia and Australasia	ring of tiny white feathers around the eyes
wood-swallow	15–20	tropical Asia and Australasia	tends to huddle together in small groups in trees
wren	8–15	N and S America, Europe and Asia	nests play ceremonial role in courtship

□ Waterfowl

diver ► loon			
duck	wide range	worldwide	gregarious; migratory

Name	Size (cm)[1]	Distribution	Special features
flamingo	90 – 180	tropics, N America, S Europe	red/pink colour of plumage caused by diet
goose	wide range	N hemisphere	migratory
great northern diver ► loon			
grebe	22 – 60	worldwide	highly aquatic
hammerhead	56	Africa S of the Sahara, Madagascar and S Arabia	elaborate nest with entrance tunnel and internal chamber
heron	30 – 140	worldwide	mainly a wading bird
ibis	50 – 100	warmer regions of all continents	includes species of spoonbill
loon (or diver)	66 – 95	high latitudes of the N hemisphere, migrating to temperate zones	highly territorial and aggressive
screamer	69 – 90	warmer parts of S America	trumpet-like alarm call
shoebill	120	E Africa	large head on a short neck
stork	60 – 120	S America, Asia, Africa and Australia	long bill and long neck
swan	100 – 160	worldwide, freshwater, sheltered shores and estuaries	very long neck

□ Shorebirds

auk	16 – 76	cold waters of the N hemisphere	includes varieties of puffin and guillemot
avocet	29 – 48	worldwide, except high latitudes	particularly graceful walk
courser	15 – 25	Africa, S Europe, Asia and Australia	inhabits dry flat savanna, grassland and river shores
curlew, stone-	36 – 52	Africa, Europe, Asia, Australia and parts of S America	leg joints give alternative name of thickknee
gull	31 – 76	worldwide, scarce in the tropics	elaborate communication system
jacana	17 – 53	tropics	ability to walk on floating vegetation gives alternative name of lily trotter
oystercatcher	40 – 45	tropical and temperate coastlines, except tropical Africa and S Asia	powerful bill for breaking shells; do not eat oysters
phalarope	19 – 25	high latitudes of the N hemisphere	wading bird; also regularly swims
plover	15 – 40	worldwide	swift runner; strong flier

Name	Size (cm)[1]	Distribution	Special features
plover, crab	38	coasts of E Africa, India, Persian Gulf, Sri Lanka and Madagascar	single species with mainly white and black plumage
sandpiper	12–60	worldwide	spectacular flight patterns
seedsnipe	17–28	W coast of S America	named after its diet
sheathbill	35–43	sub-Antarctic and E coast of S America	communal and quarrelsome scavenger
skimmer	37–51	tropics and subtropics of N and S America, Africa and S Asia	uniquely shaped bill aids capture of prey in shallow waters
skua	43–61	mainly high latitudes of the N hemisphere	chases other seabirds until they disgorge their food
snipe, painted	19–24	S America, Africa, S Asia and Australia	spectacular female plumage
stilt ► avocet			
□ Seabirds			
albatross	70–140	S hemisphere	noted for its size and power of flight
cormorant (or shag)	50–100	worldwide	marine equivalent of falcons
darter	80–100	tropical, subtropical, temperate regions	distinctive swimming action
frigatebird	70–110	tropical oceans	enormous wings; forces other birds to disgorge their food
fulmar	to 60	N and S oceans	comes to land only to breed
gannet	to 90	worldwide	complex behaviour during mating
guillemot	38–42	N hemisphere	egg shape adapted to cliffside dwelling
pelican	140–180	tropics and subtropics	known for its long bill
penguin	40–115	S hemisphere	flightless; wings modified as flippers; highly social
petrel, diving-	16–25	S hemisphere	great resemblance to the auk
petrel, storm-	12–25	high latitudes of N and S hemispheres	considerable powers of migration
puffin	28–32	N hemisphere	nests in burrows in very large colonies
shag ► cormorant			
shearwater	28–91	subantarctic and subtropical zones	many species known for long migrations
tropicbird	25–45	tropical seas	elongated central tail feathers
□ Arboreal birds			
barbet	9–32	tropics, except Australasia	nests in rotten timber or sand banks
bee-eater	15–38	Africa, Asia and Australia	colourful plumage

Name	Size (cm) [1]	Distribution	Special features
cuckoo	15–90	worldwide	some species lay eggs in the nests of other birds
cuckoo-roller	38–43	Madagascar and Comoros Is	diminishing population
honeyguide	10–20	Africa and S Asia	eats the wax of honeycombs
hoopoe	31	Africa, SE Asia and S Europe	distinctive 'hoo hoo' call
hornbill	38–126	tropics of Africa and Australasia	long heavy bill
jacamar	13–30	tropical America	long slender bill
kingfisher	10–46	worldwide	colourful plumage
motmot	20–50	tropical America	distinctive long tail feathers
mousebird	30–35	Africa S of the Sahara	crest and long tail
parrot	10–100	mainly tropics of S hemisphere	mainly sedentary; unmelodic voice
pigeon	17–90	worldwide, except high latitudes	distinctive cooing sound
puffbird	14–32	tropical America	stout puffy appearance
roller	27–38	Africa, Europe, Asia, Australia	courtship display of diving from great heights in a rolling motion
sandgrouse	25–48	Africa, S Europe and S Asia	mainly terrestrial
tody	10–12	Greater Antilles	captures insects from the underside of leaves and twigs
toucan	34–66	S America	bright plumage and immense bill
trogon	25–35	tropics, except Australasia	colourful plumage
turaco	35–76	Africa S of the Sahara	loud and resounding call
woodhoopoe	21–43	Africa S of the Sahara	long graduated tail; strongly hooked bill
woodpecker	10–58	worldwide, except Australasia and Antarctica	excavates wood and tree bark for food

▢ Aerial feeders

Name	Size (cm)	Distribution	Special features
frogmouth	23–53	SE Asia and Australasia	distinctively shaped bill
hummingbird	6–22	N and S America	wings hum when hovering
nightjar	19–29	worldwide	nocturnal
nightjar, owlet-	23–44	Australasia	perches in upright owl-like way
oilbird	53	tropical S America	only nocturnal fruit-eating bird
potoo	23–51	tropical C and S America	nocturnal; also known as 'tree-nighthawk'
swift	10–25	worldwide	spends most of life flying
swift, crested	17–33	SE Asia and New Guinea	prominent crest on head

Name	Size (cm)[1]	Distribution	Special features
❑ Passerines[2]			
antbird	8–36	parts of S America and W Indies	some species follow armies of ants to prey
bellbird	9–45	C and S America	long metallic sounding call
broadbill	13–28	tropical Africa and Asia, and the Philippines	colourful broad bill
false sunbird	15	Madagascar	bright blue and emerald wattle develops around the male's eyes during breeding season
flycatcher (New World)	9–27	N and S America	feeds on the wing
flycatcher, tyrant	5–14	N and S America, W Indies and Galapagos Is	spectacular aerial courtship display
gnateater	14	parts of S America	long thin legs; short tail
lyrebird	80–90	SE Australia	extravagant tail resembles a Greek lyre
manakin	9–15	C and S America	highly elaborate courtship display
ovenbird	to 25	S America	one species builds substantial nests like mud-ovens
pitta	15–28	Africa, SE Asia and Australasia	long legs; short tail; colourful plumage
plantcutter	18–19	western S America	bill is adapted for feeding on fruit and plants
scrub-bird	16–21	E and SW Australia	small terrestrial bird; long graduated tail
tapaculo	8–25	S and C America	moveable flap covers the nostril
woodcreeper	20–37	S America and W Indies	stiff tail feathers used as support in climbing trees
wren, New Zealand	8–10	New Zealand	thought to have colonized the islands in the Tertiary Period[3]
❑ Game-birds and cranes			
bustard	37–132	Africa, S Europe, Asia and Australia	frequently pauses for observation while walking
coot	14–51	worldwide	loud nocturnal vocal strains
crane	80–150	worldwide, except S America and Antarctica	long legs
currasow	75–112	southern N America and S America	agility in running along branches before taking flight
finfoot	30–62	tropics of America, Africa and SE Asia	long slender neck
grouse	30–90	N hemisphere	many species threatened by hunting

Name	Size (cm) [1]	Distribution	Special features
guinea fowl	45–60	Africa	virtually unfeathered head and neck
hoatzin	60	tropical S America	musky odour; top heavy
kagu	56	New Caledonia	sole species; forest dwelling
limpkin	60–70	C and S America	sole species; wailing voice
mesite	25–27	Madagascar	highly terrestrial; sedentary
pheasant	40–235	worldwide	elaborate courtship display
plains wanderer	16	SE Australia	male incubates the eggs and raises the young
quail, button	11–19	Africa, S Asia and Australia	secretive; terrestrial
seriema	75–90	S America	heavily feathered head and crest
sunbittern	46	forest swamps of C and S America	complex markings
trumpeter	43–53	tropical S America	trumpeting call of warning or alarm
turkey	90–110	N America	male exhibits distinctive strutting displays during breeding

[1] To convert cm to inches, multiply by 0.3937.

[2] Any bird of the worldwide order *Passeriformes* ('perching birds'), which comprises more than half the living species of birds; landbirds.

[3] See Geological time scale p25.

Amphibians and Reptiles

Amphibians are a class of cold-blooded vertebrates including frogs, toads, newts and salamanders. There are approximately 4 000 species. They have a moist, thin skin without scales, and the adults live partly or entirely on land, but can usually only survive in damp habitats. They return to water to lay their eggs, which hatch to form fish-like larvae or tadpoles that breathe by means of gills, but gradually develop lungs as they approach adulthood.

Reptiles are egg-laying vertebrates of the class Reptilia, having evolved from primitive amphibians; there are 6 547 species divided into Squamata (lizards and snakes), Chelonia (tortoises and turtles), Crocodylia (crocodiles and alligators) and Rhynococephalia (the tuatara).

Most reptiles live on the land, breathe with lungs, and have horny or plated skins. Reptiles require the rays of the sun to maintain their body temperature, ie they are cold-blooded or ectothermic. This confines them to warm, tropical and subtropical regions, but does allow some species to exist in particularly hot desert environments in which mammals and birds would find it impossible to sustain life.

Extinct species of reptile include the dinosaur and pterodactyl.

Name	Size (cm) [1]	Distribution	Special features
□ Amphibians			
common spadefoot	to 8	C Europe	toad with a pale-coloured tubercle (the spade) on its hind foot
frog, arrow poison	0.85–1.24	C and S America	smallest known amphibian; skin highly poisonous
frog, common	to 10	Europe except Mediterranean region and most of Iberia	most widespread European frog
frog, edible	to 12	S and C Europe	often heavily spotted; whitish vocal sacs
frog, goliath	to 81.5	Africa	world's largest frog
frog, leopard	5–13	N America	usually has light-edged dark spots on body
frog, marsh	to 15	SW and E Europe and SE England	extremely aquatic
frog, painted	to 7	Iberia and SW France	usually smooth and yellow-brown, grey or reddish with dark spots
frog, parsley	to 5	W Europe	slender bodied, with a whitish underside
hellbender	to 63	America	salamander with wrinkled folds of flesh on body
mudpuppy	18–43	N America	salamander with bright red external gills

Name	Size (cm)[1]	Distribution	Special features
natterjack	to 10	SW and C Europe	toad with bright yellow stripe along its back
newt, alpine	to 12	C Europe	dark mottled back and a uniformly orange belly and bluish spotted sides
newt, Bosca's	7–10	Iberian peninsula	similar to smooth newt without a dorsal crest
newt, marbled	to 15	Iberia and W France	bright yellow or orange stripe on velvety green and black mottled back
newt, palmate	to 9	W Europe	palmate (webbed feet); short filament at end of breeding male's tail
newt, smooth	to 11	Europe	breeding male develops a wavy crest
newt, warty (great crested newt)	to 17	Europe except Iberia and Ireland	bright red, orange or yellow spotted belly and warty skin
salamander, alpine	to 15	C Europe	large glands on back of head
salamander, fire	to 25	C and S Europe	large glands on sides of head contain venomous secretion
salamander, giant Chinese	114 (average)	China	world's largest amphibian
salamander, goldstriped	15–16	Iberian peninsula	thin with shiny skin
salamander, spectacled	to 11	W Italy	only European salamander with four toes on hind feet
toad, common	to 15	Europe except N Scandinavia, Ireland and some Mediterranean islands	largest European toad; usually brownish or greyish with warty skin
toad, green	to 10	E Europe	distinctive colouring: grey or greenish with darker marbled markings
toad, marine	to 23.8	S America	world's largest toad
toad, midwife	to 5	W Europe	male carries strings of eggs wrapped around hind legs
toad, surinam	to 20	S America	female incubates eggs on her back
toad, yellow-bellied	to 5	C and S Europe	usually bright yellow or orange, black-blotched belly
treefrog, common	to 5	C and S Europe	usually bright green; often found in trees high above ground
▫ Reptiles			
alligator	200–550	southern America, C and S America and E China	although rare, attacks can cause human fatalities; endangered species apart from American alligator

Name	Size (cm)[1]	Distribution	Special features
anguid	6–30	N and S America, Europe, Asia and NW Africa	bony-plated scales reach round its underside giving a rigid appearance
boa	200–400	western N America, S America, Africa, Madagascar, Asia, Fiji, Solomon Is and New Guinea	famous constricting snake, includes species of anaconda
chameleon	2–28	Africa outwith the Sahara, Madagascar, Middle East, S Spain, S Arabian peninsula, Sri Lanka, Crete, India and Pakistan	noted for its ability to change colour and blend with its environment
crocodile	150–750	pantropical and some temperate regions of Africa	distinguished from the alligator by the visible fourth tooth in the lower jaw; several species endangered
gecko	1.5–24	N and S America, Africa, S Europe, Asia and Australia	noted for its vocalization and ability to climb; sheds its tail for defence
iguana	to 200	C and S America, Madagascar, Fiji and Tonga	terrestrial and tree-dwelling lizard; able to survive in exceptionally high temperatures
lizard, beaded	33–45	SW America, W Mexico to Guatemala	possesses a mildly venomous bite
lizard, blind	12–16.5	SE Asia	eyes concealed within the skin
lizard, Bornean earless	to 20	Borneo	no external ear opening; partly aquatic
lizard, chisel-tooth	4–35	Africa, Asia and Australia	distinctive teeth; family includes the flying dragon
lizard, girdle-tailed	5–27.5	Africa S of the Sahara, Madagascar	terrestrial; active by day; adapted to arid environments
lizard, monitor	12–150	Africa, S Asia, Indo-Australian archipelago, Philippines, New Guinea and Australia	consumes its prey whole; includes the Komodo dragon, the largest living lizard, which is capable of killing pigs and small deer
lizard, night	3.5–12	C America	most species active by night
lizard, snake	6.5–31	New Guinea and Australia	snake-like appearance; broad but highly extensible tongue
lizard, wall and sand	4–22	Europe, Africa, Asia and Indo-Australian archipelago	lives in open and sandy environments; terrestrial; active by day

Name	Size (cm)[1]	Distribution	Special features
lizard, worm	15–35	subtropical regions of N and S America, Africa, Middle East, Asia and Europe	worm-like, burrowing reptile; some species have the rare ability to move backwards and forwards
pipesnake	to 100	S America, SE Asia	tail has brilliantly coloured red underside; feeds on other snakes
python	100–1 000	tropical and subtropical Africa, SE Asia, Australia, Mexico and C America	capable of killing humans, especially children, by constriction
skink	2.8–35	tropical and temperate regions	terrestrial, tree-dwelling or burrowing species, including highly adept swimmers
snake, dawn blind	11–30	C and S America	short tail, indistinct head, one or two teeth in the lower jaw
snake, front fanged	38–560	worldwide in warm regions	highly venomous family with short fangs
snake, harmless	13–350	worldwide	most species unable to produce venomous saliva
snake, shieldtail	20–50	S India and Sri Lanka	tail forms a rough cylindrical shield
snake, thread	15–90	C and S America, Africa and Asia	small and exceptionally slender burrowing snake
snake, typical blind	15–90	C and S America, Africa S of the Sahara, SE Europe, S Asia, Taiwan and Australia	burrowing snake with tiny concealed eyes and no teeth on lower jaw
tortoise	10–140	S Europe, Africa, Asia, C and S America	includes smallest species of turtle, the speckled cape tortoise (10cm) and one of the longest-lived turtles, the spur-thighed tortoise
tuatara	45–61	islands off New Zealand	third eye in the top of its head
turtle, Afro-American side-necked	12–90	S America, Africa, Madagascar, Seychelles and Mauritius	seabed-dweller that rarely requires to come to the surface
turtle, American mud and musk	11–27	N and S America	lives mostly in freshwater; glands produce evil smelling secretion
turtle, Austro-American side-necked	14–48	S America, Australia and New Guinea	includes the peculiar looking matamata, the most adept of the ambush-feeders at the gape and suck technique of capturing prey

Name	Size (cm) [1]	Distribution	Special features
turtle, big-headed	20	SE Asia	large head which cannot be retracted
turtle, Central American river	to 65	Vera Cruz, Mexico, Honduras	freshwater creature with well-developed shell
turtle, Mexican musk	to 38	Mexico to Honduras	freshwater creature dwelling in marshes and swamps
turtle, pig-nosed softshell	55 or over	New Guinea and N Australia	specialized swimmer; plateless skin and fleshy, pig-like snout
turtle, pond and river	11.4–80	N and C America, S Europe, N Africa, Asia and Argentina	family ranges from tiny bog turtle (11.4cm) to the largest of the river turtles, the Malaysian giant turtle
turtle, sea	75–213	pantropical, and some subtropical and temperate regions	rapid movement through water contrasts with slow movements on land
turtle, snapping	47–66	N and C America	large-headed aggressive sea-bed dweller
turtle, softshell	30–115	N America, Africa, Asia and Indo-Australian archipelago	leathered plateless skin; noted for its prominent pointed snout
viper	25–365	N and S America, Africa, Europe and Asia	venomous family of snakes, including the rattlesnake and the sidewinder
whiptail and racerunner	37–45	N and S Asia	eaten by South American Indians; used in traditional medicines
xenosaur	10–15	Mexico, Guatemala and S China	terrestrial, sedentary and secretive

[1] To convert cm to inches, multiply by 0.3937.

Fish

Name	Size (cm) [1]	Range and habitat	Special features
albacore	to 130	tropical, warm temperate	food and sport fish
anchovy	9–12	temperate	important food fish
angler fish	5–8	tropical, temperate	large jaws
barracuda	30–240	tropical, warm temperate	carnivorous; large teeth
blenny	20–49	temperate, tropical	devoid of scales
bonito	to 90	temperate, warm	food fish; sport fish
bream	41–80	temperate (N Europe)	deep-bodied; food fish
brill	to 70	temperate	flatfish; food fish
butterfly fish	to 15	tropical	brightly coloured
carp	51–61	temperate	important food fish
catfish	90–135	temperate (N America)	important food fish

Name	Size (cm) [1]	Range and habitat	Special features
chub	30–60	temperate (Europe)	popular sport fish
cod	to 120	temperate, N hemisphere	common cod important food fish
conger eel	274	temperate	upper jaw longer than lower
dab	20–40	temperate (Europe)	flatfish; food fish
dace	15–30	temperate (Europe, former USSR)	sport fish
damsel fish	5–15	tropical, temperate	brightly coloured
devil ray ► manta ray			
dogfish	60–100	temperate (Europe)	food fish (sold as rock salmon)
dolphin fish	to 200	tropical, warm temperate	prized sport fish; food fish
dory	30–60	temperate	deep-bodied; food fish
eagle ray	to 200	tropical, temperate	fins form 'wings'; young born live
eel	to 50 (male), to 100 (female)	temperate	elongated cylindrical body; important food fish
electric eel	to 240	Orinoco, Amazon basins (S America)	produces powerful electric shocks
electric ray (or torpedo ray)	to 180	tropical, temperate	produces powerful electric shocks
file fish	5–13	tropical, warm temperate	food fish
flounder	to 51	temperate (Europe)	flatfish; locally important food fish
flying fish	25–50	tropical, warm temperate	can jump and glide above water surface
goat fish ► red mullet			
goby	1–27	tropical, temperate	pelvic fins form single sucker-like fin
goldfish	to 30	temperate	popular ornamental fish
grenadier ► rat-tail			
grey mullet	to 75	tropical, temperate	food fish
grouper	5–370	tropical, warm temperate	prized sport and food fish
gurnard (or sea robin)	to 75	tropical, warm temperate	many produce audible sounds
hake	to 180	temperate	large head and jaws; food fish
halibut	to 250	temperate (Atlantic)	food fish
herring	to 40	temperate (N Atlantic, Arctic)	important food fish
lamprey	to 91	temperate (N Atlantic)	primitive jawless fish; food fish
lantern fish	2–15	tropical, temperate	body has numerous light organs
lemon sole	to 66	temperate	flatfish; feeds on polychaete worms; food fish
loach	to 15	temperate (Europe, Asia)	popular aquarium fish

Name	Size (cm)[1]	Range and habitat	Special features
mackerel	to 66	temperate (N Atlantic)	important food fish
manta ray (or devil ray)	120–900 (width)	tropical	fleshy 'horns' at side of head
minnow	to 12	temperate (N Europe, Asia)	locally abundant
monkfish	to 180	temperate (N Atlantic, Mediterranean)	cross between shark and ray in shape
moorish idol	to 22	tropical (Indo-Pacific)	bold black and white stripes with some yellow
moray eel	to 130	temperate, tropical	pointed snout; long sharp teeth
parrot fish	25–190	tropical	teeth fused to form parrot-like beak
perch	30–50	temperate	food fish; sport fish
pike	to 130	temperate	prized by anglers
pilchard (or sardine)	to 25	temperate (N Atlantic, Mediterranean)	important food fish, often canned
pipefish	15–160	tropical, warm temperate	males of some species carry eggs in brood pouch
plaice	50–90	temperate (Europe)	flatfish; important food fish
puffer	3–25	tropical, warm temperate	body often spiny; food delicacy in Japan
rat-tail (or grenadier)	40–110	temperate, tropical	large head, tapering body
ray	39–113	temperate	front flattened with large pectoral fins
red mullet (or goat fish)	to 40	tropical, temperate	food fish
remora	12–46	tropical, warm temperate	large sucking disc on head
roach	35–53	temperate (Europe, former USSR)	popular sport fish
sailfish	to 360	tropical, warm temperate	long tall dorsal fin; prized sport fish
salmon	to 150	temperate	prized sport and food fish
sand eel	to 20	temperate (N hemisphere)	very important food for seabirds
sardine ► pilchard			
scorpion-fish	to 50	tropical, temperate	distinctive fin and body spines
sea bass	60–100	tropical, temperate	food fish; sport fish
sea robin ► gurnard			
sea bream	35–51	tropical, temperate	food fish; sport fish
seahorse	to 15	tropical, warm temperate	horse-like head; swims upright
shark, basking	870–1350	tropical, temperate	second largest living fish
shark, great white	to 630	tropical	fierce; young born, not hatched

Name	Size (cm)[1]	Range and habitat	Special features
shark, hammer-head	360–600	tropical, warm temperate	head flattened into hammer shape
shark, tiger	360–600	tropical, warm temperate	vertical stripes on body; fierce
shark, whale	1 020–1 800	tropical	largest living fish; feeds on plankton
skate	200–285	temperate	food fish
smelt	20–30	temperate	related to salmon and trout
sole	30–60	tropical, temperate	flatfish; food fish
sprat	13–16	temperate	food fish; called whitebait when small
squirrel fish	12–30	tropical	brightly coloured; nocturnal
stickleback	5–10	temperate (N hemisphere)	male builds nest, guards eggs
sting ray	106–140	tropical, temperate	tail whip-like with poisonous spine(s)
sturgeon	100–500	temperate (N hemisphere)	eggs prized as caviar
sunfish	to 400	tropical, warm temperate	tail fin absent; body almost circular
surgeon fish (or tang)	20–45	tropical, subtropical	spine on tail can be erected for defence
swordfish	200–500	tropical, temperate	upper jaw forms flathead 'sword'
tang ▶ surgeon fish			
triggerfish	10–60	tropical	dorsal spine can be erected for defence
trout	23–140	temperate	prized food fish
tuna, skipjack	to 100	tropical, temperate	important food fish
tuna, yellow fin	to 200	tropical, warm temperate	elongated body; important food fish
turbot	50–100	temperate (N Atlantic)	flatfish; prized food fish
wrasse	7–210	tropical, warm temperate	brightly coloured

[1] To convert cm to inches, multiply by 0.3937.

Invertebrates

Invertebrates are animals with no backbone. Some have no skeleton at all, but many have external skeletons or shells that give them a rigid shape and provide anchorage for their muscles. There are about 30 major groups or phyla of invertebrates although the great majority of species belong to just two phyla — the Mollusca and the Arthropoda. The latter includes the insects, spiders, crustaceans and several other groups, all of which have segmented bodies and jointed legs. The majority of invertebrates are quite small, but examples of the largest — the giant squid — have been recorded as much as 15m/49ft long and may weigh well over a tonne.

For molluscs, lengths given are normally maximum shell lengths, but (b) indicates body length; for spiders, lengths are body lengths, although legs may be much longer; for insects, sizes given are normally body lengths, but (w) indicates wingspan.

Name	Size (cm)[1]	Range and habitat	Special features
MOLLUSCS: Phylum Mollusca			
❑ Slugs and snails/Gastropoda (c.50 000 species)			
abalone (several species)	<30	warm seas worldwide	collected for food and for the pearly shells
conch (several species)	<33	tropical seas	shells often used as trumpets
cone shell (c.600 species)	<23	warm seas worldwide	some species dangerous to humans; beautiful shells much sought after
cowrie (c.150 species in several genera)	<10	warm seas worldwide	shiny china-like shells were once used as money
limpet, common	<5.5	worldwide	conical shell pulled tightly down on rocks when tide is out
limpet, slipper	<6	originally N America, now common on coasts of Europe	serious pest in oyster and mussel farms, settling on the shells and cutting off their food supplies
periwinkle, common	<2.5	N Atlantic and adjacent seas; rocky shores	thick dull brown shell; the fishmonger's winkle
sea butterfly (c.100 species in several genera)	<5	oceans worldwide; most common in warm waters	swims by flapping wing-like extensions of the foot
slug, great grey	<20 (b)	Europe	common in gardens; mates in mid-air, hanging from a rope of slime
snail, giant African	<15	originally Africa, now tropical Asia and Pacific	agricultural pest; lays hard-shelled eggs as big as those of a thrush
snail, great ramshorn	<3	Europe; still and slow-moving freshwater	shell forms a flat spiral; body has bright red blood
snail, roman	<5	C and S Europe; lime soils	often a pest, but cultivated for food in some areas

Name	Size (cm)[1]	Range and habitat	Special features
whelk	< 12	N Atlantic and neighbouring seas	collected for human consumption

□ Bivalves/Lamellibranchia (c.8 000 species)

Name	Size (cm)[1]	Range and habitat	Special features
cockle, common	< 5	European coasts	important food for fish and wading birds
mussel, common	< 11	coasts of Europe and eastern N America	farmed on a large scale for human consumption
oyster	< 15	coasts of Europe and Africa	large numbers farmed for human consumption
piddock	< 12	coasts of Europe and eastern N America	uses rasp-like shell to bore into soft rocks and wood
razor-shell, pod	< 20	European coasts	long straight shell, shaped like a cut-throat razor
scallop, great	< 15	European coasts; usually below tide level	strongly ribbed, eared shells with one valve flatter than the other

□ Squids and octopuses/Cephalopoda (c.750 species)

Name	Size (cm)[1]	Range and habitat	Special features
cuttlefish, common	< 30	coastal waters of Atlantic and neighbouring seas	flat oval body can change colour
octopus, blue-ringed	10 (span)	Australian coasts	only octopus known to have killed humans
octopus, common	< 300 (span)	Atlantic and Mediterranean coastal waters	not dangerous to humans
squid, common	< 50	Atlantic and Mediterranean coastal waters	deep pink in life, fading to grey after death
squid, giant	< 1 500	oceans worldwide	main food of the sperm whale

CRUSTACEANS: Phylum Arthropoda

□ Crustacea (c.30 000 species)

Name	Size (cm)[1]	Range and habitat	Special features
barnacle, acorn	< 1.5 (diam.)	worldwide	cemented to intertidal rocks
crab, edible	< 20	eastern N Atlantic and neighbouring seas	widely caught for human consumption
crab, fiddler (many species)	< 3	tropical seashores and mangrove swamps	male has one big colourful claw
crab, hermit (several species and genera)	< 15	worldwide; mainly in coastal waters	soft-bodied crab that uses empty seashells as portable homes
crab, robber	< 45	islands and coasts of Indian and Pacific oceans	related to hermit crab
crayfish, noble	< 15	Europe	reared in large numbers for human consumption, especially in France

Name	Size (cm)[1]	Range and habitat	Special features
krill	<5	mainly the southern oceans	main food of the whalebone whales
lobster, common	<70	European coasts	now rare in many places through overfishing
lobster, Norway	<25	European seas	marketed as scampi
lobster, spiny	<45	Mediterranean and Atlantic; rocky coasts	popular food in S Europe; also known as crayfish
prawn, common	<10	European coasts; usually stony or rocky shores	scavenger; almost transparent in life
shrimp, common	<7	coasts of Europe and eastern N America	widely caught for human consumption
water flea (many species)	<0.5	worldwide; freshwater	major food of small fish
woodlouse (many genera and species)	<2.5	worldwide	only major group of terrestrial crustaceans; also called sow-bugs and slaters

SPIDERS: Phylum Arthropoda
❑ Arachnida (c.40 000 species)

bird-eating spider (c.800 species in several genera)	<10	warmer parts of the Americas and southern Africa	often in trees, where they sometimes capture nestling birds; venom not dangerous to humans
black widow	<1.6	most warm climates, including S Europe	has caused many human deaths, but bites are now cured with antivenin
bolas spider (several species and genera)	<1.5	N and S America, Africa and Australasia	catches moths by whirling a single thread of silk
crab spider (c.3 000 species in numerous genera)	<2	worldwide	mostly squat crab-like spiders that lie in wait for prey — often in flowers
funnel-web spider (3 species)	<5	Australia	among the deadliest spiders; inhabit tubular webs
garden spider	<1.2	N hemisphere	black to ginger, with a white cross on the back
gladiator spider (several species)	<2.5	warm regions and some cooler parts of N America and Australia	makes sticky webs which it throws at passing prey, usually at night
house spider (c.90 species)	<2	mostly N hemisphere	long-legged; fast-running; harmless
jumping spider (c.4 000 species in many genera)	<1.5	worldwide	large-eyed spiders that leap onto their prey; often brilliantly coloured

Name	Size (cm)[1]	Range and habitat	Special features
orb-web spider (c.2 500 species in many genera)	<3	worldwide	makers of the familiar wheel-shaped webs, up to a metre or more in diameter
raft spider (c.100 species)	<2.5	worldwide	hunting spiders that lurk at the edge of pools or on floating objects
spitting spider	<0.6	worldwide; normally only in buildings	catches prey by spitting strands of sticky, venom-coated gum at them
tarantula	<3	S Europe	wolf spider whose bite was believed to be curable only by performing a frantic dance — the tarantella; although painful, the bite is not really dangerous
trapdoor spider (c.700 species in several genera)	<3	most warm parts of the world, including S Europe	lives in burrows closed by hinged lids of silk and debris
water spider	<1.5	Eurasia; in ponds and slow-moving streams	world's only truly aquatic spider; lives in an air-filled, thimble-shaped web fixed to water plants
wolf spider (c.2 500 species in many genera)	<3	worldwide, but most common in cooler parts of N hemisphere	large-eyed hunting spiders; generally harmless but some of the larger species have dangerous bites
zebra spider	<0.6	N hemisphere; often in and around houses	black and white jumping spider, commonly hunts on rocks and walls

INSECTS: Phylum Arthropoda

□ Bristletails/Thysanura (c.600 species)

silverfish	1	worldwide	wingless scavenger of starchy foods in houses

□ Mayflies/Ephemeroptera (c.2 500 species)

mayfly	2	worldwide	flimsy insects with 2 or 3 long 'tails'; adults only live for a few hours

□ Dragonflies/Odonata (c.5 000 species)

dragonfly	<2–13	worldwide	long-bodied insects, with gauzy wings; most catch insects in mid-air

□ Crickets and grasshoppers/Orthoptera (c.17 000 species)

cricket, bush (thousands of species)	<15	worldwide, apart from coldest areas	like grasshoppers but with very long antennae; several N American species are called katydids

Name	Size (cm)[1]	Range and habitat	Special features
cricket, house	<2	worldwide	scavenger in houses and rubbish dumps
locust, desert	8.5	Africa and S Asia	swarms periodically destroy crops in Africa
locust, migratory	<5	Africa and S Europe	swarm in Africa, but solitary in Europe

❑ Stick insects and leaf insects/Phasmida (c.2 500 species, mostly tropical)

Name	Size (cm)[1]	Range and habitat	Special features
insect, leaf (c.50 species)	<9	SE Asia	very flat, leaf-like, green or brown bodies
insect, stick (over 2 400 species)	<35	warm areas, including S Europe	stick-like green or brown bodies with or without wings; often kept as pets

❑ Earwigs/Dermaptera (c.1 300 species)

Name	Size (cm)[1]	Range and habitat	Special features
earwig (many species)	<3	originally Africa, now worldwide	slender brownish insects with prominent pincers at the rear

❑ Cockroaches and mantids/Dictyoptera (c.5 500 species)

Name	Size (cm)[1]	Range and habitat	Special features
American cockroach	4	worldwide	scavenger, living outside (if warm) or in buildings; chestnut brown
praying mantis (c.2 000 species)	<15	all warm areas	catches other insects with spiky front legs

❑ Termites/Isoptera (over 2 000 species)

Name	Size (cm)[1]	Range and habitat	Special features
termites (many species)	<2.2	mostly tropical	colonies in mounds of earth, in dead wood or underground; many are timber pests

❑ Bugs/Hemiptera (c.70 000 species)

Name	Size (cm)[1]	Range and habitat	Special features
aphid (numerous species)	<0.5	worldwide	sap-sucking insects; many are serious pests
bedbug	0.5	worldwide	bloodsucking; feeds at night
cicada (numerous species)	<20 (w)	worldwide, mainly in warm climates	males make loud shrill sounds; young stages live underground
froghopper	0.6	N hemisphere	young stages live in froth, often called cuckoo-spit
pondskater	1	N hemisphere	skims across the surface of still water

❑ Thrips/Thysanoptera (over 3 000 species)

Name	Size (cm)[1]	Range and habitat	Special features
thrips (many species)	0.25	worldwide	cause much crop damage; fly in huge numbers in thundery weather

❑ Lacewings/Neuroptera (over 6 000 species)

Name	Size (cm)[1]	Range and habitat	Special features
antlion	9 (w)	Eurasia	larvae make small pits in sandy soil and feed on insects that fall into them

Name	Size (cm)[1]	Range and habitat	Special features
green lacewing (several genera and many species)	<5	worldwide	predators of aphids and other small insects

□ Scorpion flies/Mecoptera (c.400 species)

scorpion fly	2	worldwide	male abdomen is usually turned up like a scorpion's tail; harmless

□ Butterflies and moths/Lepidoptera (c.150 000 species)

Butterflies (c. 18 000 species)

birdwing butterfly (several genera and species)	<30 (w)	SE Asia and N Australia	include the world's largest butterflies; many are becoming rare through collecting and loss of habitat
cabbage white butterfly	<7 (w)	Eurasia and N Africa	caterpillar is a serious pest of cabbages and other brassicas
fritillary butterfly (many genera and species)	<8 (w)	mostly N hemisphere	mostly orange with black spots above and silvery spots below
monarch butterfly	<10 (w)	mostly Pacific area and N America	orange with black markings; it hibernates in huge swarms in Mexico and southern USA
skipper butterfly (many genera and species)	<8 (w)	worldwide	mostly small brown or orange grassland insects with darting flight
swallowtail butterfly (many genera and species)	<12 (w)	worldwide, but mostly tropical	prominent 'tails' on hindwings; many becoming rare through collecting and loss of habitat

Moths (c. 132 000 species)

burnet moth (many species)	<4 (w)	Eurasia and N Africa	protected by foul-tasting body fluids and gaudy black and red colours
clothes moth (several species)	<1.5 (w)	worldwide	caterpillars damage woollen fabrics
death's head hawkmoth	<13.5 (w)	Africa and Eurasia	skull-like pattern on its thorax
hummingbird hawkmoth	<6 (w)	Eurasia	produces a loud hum as it hovers
pine processionary moth	<4 (w)	S and C Europe	larvae feed in long processions at night; forest pest
silk moth	<6 (w)	native of China; now unknown in the wild	cream-coloured moth bred for the fine silk obtained from its cocoon; all cultured moths flightless

Name	Size (cm) [1]	Range and habitat	Special features
tiger moth (many genera and species)	< 10 (w)	worldwide	mostly brightly coloured and hairy, with evil-tasting body fluids

□ **True flies/Diptera** (c.90 000 species, a few without wings)

Name	Size (cm) [1]	Range and habitat	Special features
crane fly (or leather-jacket) (many genera and species)	< 6 (w)	worldwide	slender long-legged flies; larvae of many are leather-jackets that damage crop roots
house fly	0.7	worldwide	abundant on farms and rubbish dumps; becoming less common in houses; breeds in dung and other decaying matter and carries germs
hover fly (many genera and species)	< 4	worldwide	many have amazing hovering ability; adults feed on pollen and nectar; many are black and yellow mimics of bees and wasps
mosquito (many genera and species)	< 1.5	worldwide	females are bloodsuckers; spread malaria and other diseases
tsetse fly (c.20 species)	1	tropical Africa	bloodsuckers; spread human sleeping sickness and cattle diseases

□ **Fleas/Siphonaptera** (c.1 800 species)

Name	Size (cm) [1]	Range and habitat	Special features
European flea (many species)	0.3	worldwide	wingless, bloodsucking parasites; long hind legs enable them to jump many times their own lengths

□ **Bees, wasps and ants/Hymenoptera** (over 120 000 species)

Name	Size (cm) [1]	Range and habitat	Special features
ant, army (several genera and species)	< 4	tropics	live in mobile colonies, some of over a million ants
ant, honeypot (several genera and species)	2	deserts across the world	some workers gorge themselves with sugar-rich food and become living food for other ants
ant, weaver (several species)	1	Old World tropics	nest made from leaves, joined by sticky silk
bee, bumble (many species)	< 3.5	worldwide, except Australia	plump hairy bees living in annual colonies; only mated queen survives winter to start new colonies in spring
bee, honey	< 2	worldwide (probably native of SE Asia)	less hairy than bumble bee; lives in permanent colonies, mostly in artificial hives; stores honey for winter

Name	Size (cm)[1]	Range and habitat	Special features
hornet, European	<3.5	Eurasia and now N America	large brown and yellow wasp; nests in hollow trees
ichneumon (thousands of genera and species)	<5	worldwide	parasites; the young grow inside their hosts and gradually kill them
sawfly (numerous families)	<5	worldwide	saw-like ovipositor in most females, used to cut slits in plants before laying eggs

▫ Beetles/Coleoptera (over 350 000 species; front wings usually form casing over body)

Name	Size	Range	Special features
sexton beetle (several species)	<2.5	worldwide	often orange and black; beetles work in pairs to bury small dead animals, near which they then lay their eggs
click beetle (or wireworm) (many genera and species)	<4	worldwide	bullet-shaped; flick into the air to turn over, making a loud click; larvae damage crop roots
Colorado beetle	1	N America and now Europe	black and yellow adults and pink grubs both seriously damage potato crops
deathwatch beetle	0.7	N hemisphere	tunnelling larvae do immense damage to old building timbers; adults tap wood as mating call
devil's coach-horse	2.5	Eurasia	called cocktail because it raises its rear end
glow-worm	1.5	Europe	wingless female glows with greenish light to attract males
furniture beetle (or woodworm)	0.5	worldwide	causes much damage to furniture and building timbers
goliath beetle (several species)	<15	Africa	world's heaviest beetles
grain weevil	0.3	worldwide	destroys all kinds of stored grain
ladybird (c.3 500 species in many genera)	1	worldwide	aphid-eating habits make them friends of gardeners
scarab beetle (many species)	<3	most warm parts of the world	some form dung into balls and roll it around before burying it; introduced into Australia to deal with sheep and cattle dung
stag beetle	5	Eurasia	males have huge antler-like jaws, with which they wrestle rivals

woodworm ► furniture beetle

[1] To convert cm to inches, multiply by 0.3937.

HUMAN  LIFE

Main types of vitamin

Vitamin	Chemical name	Deficiency symptoms	Source
❑ Fat soluble vitamins			
A	retinol (carotene)	night blindness; rough skin; impaired bone growth	milk, butter, cheese, egg yolk, liver, fatty fish, dark green vegetables, yellow/red fruits and vegetables, especially carrots
D	cholecalciferol	rickets; osteomalacia	egg yolk, liver, fatty fish; made on skin in sunlight
E	tocopherols	multiple diseases produced in laboratory animals; in humans, multiple symptoms follow impaired fat absorption	vegetable oils
K	phytomenadione	haemorrhagic problems	green leafy vegetables, beef, liver
❑ Water soluble vitamins			
B_1	thiamin	beri-beri, Korsakov's syndrome	germ and bran of seeds, grains, yeast
B_2	riboflavin	skin disorders; failure to thrive	liver, milk, cheese, eggs, green leafy vegetables, pulses, yeast
B_6	pyridoxine	dermatitis; neurological disorders	liver, meats, fruits, cereals, leafy vegetables
	pantothenic acid	dermatitis; neurological disorders	widespread in plants and animals; destroyed in heavily-processed food
	biotin	dermatitis	liver, kidney, yeast extract; made by micro-organisms in large intestine
B_{12}	cyanocobalamin	anaemia; neurological disturbance	liver, kidney, milk; none found in plants
	folic acid	anaemia	liver, green leafy vegetables, peanuts; cooking and processing can cause serious losses in food
C	ascorbic acid	scurvy	blackcurrants, citrus fruits, other fruits, green leafy vegetables, potatoes; losses occur during storage and cooking

Main trace minerals

Mineral	Deficiency symptoms	Source
calcium	rickets in children; osteoporosis in adults	milk, butter, cheese, sardines, green leafy vegetables, citrus fruits
chromium	adult-onset diabetes	brewer's yeast, black pepper, liver, wholemeal bread, beer
copper	anaemia; Menkes' syndrome	green vegetables, fish, oysters, liver
fluorine	tooth decay; possibly osteoporosis	fluoridated drinking water, seafood, tea
iodine	goitre; cretinism in new-born children	seafood, saltwater fish, seaweed, iodized salt, table salt
iron	anaemia	liver, kidney, green leafy vegetables, egg yolk, dried fruit, potatoes, molasses
magnesium	irregular heart beat; muscular weakness; insomnia	green leafy vegetables (eaten raw), nuts, whole grains
manganese	not known in humans	legumes, cereal grains, green leafy vegetables, tea
molybdenum	not known in humans	legumes, cereal grains, liver, kidney, some dark green vegetables
phosphorus	muscular weakness; bone pain; loss of appetite	meat, poultry, fish, eggs, dried beans and peas, milk products
potassium	irregular heart beat; muscular weakness; fatigue; kidney and lung failure	fresh vegetables, meat, orange juice, bananas, bran
selenium	not known in humans	seafood, cereals, meat, egg yolk, garlic
sodium	impaired acid-base balance in body fluids (very rare)	table salt, other naturally occurring salts
zinc	impaired wound healing; loss of appetite; impaired sexual development	meat, whole grains, legumes, oysters, milk

Infectious diseases and infections

Name	Cause	Transmission	Incubation	Symptoms
AIDS (Acquired Immune Deficiency Syndrome)	human immunodeficiency virus (HIV)	sexual intercourse, sharing of syringes, blood transfusion	several years	fever, lethargy, weight loss, diarrhoea, lymph node enlargement, viral and fungal infections
amoebiasis	*Entamoeba histolytica*	organism in contaminated food	up to several years	fever, diarrhoea, exhaustion, rectal bleeding
anthrax	*Bacillus antracis* bacterium	animal hair	1–3 days	small red pimple on hand or face enlarges and discharges pus
appendicitis	usually *E. coli* organism	not transmitted	sudden onset	abdominal pain which moves from left to right after a few hours, nausea
bilharziasis (schistosomiasis)	*Schistosoma haematobium* (also called Bilharzia), *S. mansoni* or *S. japonicum*	certain snails living in calm water	varies with lifespan of parasite	fever, muscle aches, abdominal pain, headaches
bronchiolitis (babies only)	respiratory syncytical virus (RSV)	droplet infection	1–3 days	blocked or runny nose, irritability
brucellosis	*Brucella abortus* or *B. meliteusis* bacteria	cattle or goats	3–6 days	fever, drenching sweats, weight loss, muscle and joint pains, confusion and poor memory
bubonic plague	*Yersinia pestis* bacterium	fleas	3–6 days	fever, muscle aches, headaches, exhaustion, enlarged lymph glands ('buboes')
chicken pox (varicella)	varicella-zoster virus	droplet infection	14–21 days	blister-like eruptions, lethargy, headaches, sore throat
cholera	*Vibrio cholerae*	contaminated water	a few hours to 5 days	severe diarrhoea, vomiting

Name	Cause	Transmission	Incubation	Symptoms
common cold (coryza)	Rhinoviruses	droplet infection	1–3 days	blocked or runny nose, sneezing, sore throat, runny eyes
conjunctivitis	virus, bacterium or allergy	variable	variable	if viral, water discharge from eyes; if bacterial, sticky yellow discharge from eyes
dengue fever (break-bone fever)	B group of arboviruses	mosquito	5–6 days	fever, severe muscle cramps, enlarged lymph nodes
diphtheria	Corynebacterium diphtheriae	droplet infection	4–6 days	grey exudate across throat; swelling of throat tissues may lead to asphyxiation; toxin secreted by bacteria may seriously damage heart
dysentery	Shigella genus of bacteria	contaminated food or water	variable; can cause death within 48 hours	diarrhoea, with or without bleeding
gastro-enteritis	bacteria, viruses and food poisoning	droplet infection of food	variable	varies from nausea to severe fever, vomiting and diarrhoea
German measles (rubella)	togavirus	droplet infection	18 days	1–2 days catarrh and sore throat, then red rash, enlargement of lymph nodes
glandular fever (infectious mononucleosis)	Epstein-Barr virus	saliva of infected person	1–6 weeks	sore throat, fever, enlargement of tonsils and lymph nodes, lethargy, depression
gonorrhoea	Neisseria gonorrhoeae bacterium	usually sexually transmitted	2–10 days	in men, burning sensation on urination and discharge from urethra; in women (if any), vaginal discharge

Name	Cause	Transmission	Incubation	Symptoms
hepatitis	hepatitis A, B or C virus	contaminated food or water (type A); sexual relations, sharing syringes, transfusion (type B)	3–6 weeks (type A); up to a few weeks (type B)	often no symptoms, otherwise similar to 'flu; loss of appetite, tenderness below right ribs, jaundice
influenza ('flu)	influenza A, B or C virus	droplet infection	1–3 days	fever, sweating, muscle aches
kala-azar (leishmaniasis)	parasites, genus Leishmania	sandfly	usually 1–2 months; can be up to 10 years	lymph gland, spleen and liver enlargement
laryngitis	same viruses that cause colds and 'flu, ie adeno and rhinoviruses	droplet infection	1–3 days	sore throat, coughing, hoarseness
lassa fever	arenavirus	urine	3 weeks	fever, sore throat, muscle aches and pains, haemorrhage into the skin
Legionnaire's disease	Legionella pneumophila bacterium	water droplets in infected humidifiers, cooling towers; stagnant water in cisterns and shower heads	1–3 days	'flu and pneumonia-like symptoms, fever, diarrhoea, mental confusion
leprosy	Mycobacterium leprae bacterium	droplet infection; minimally contagious	variable	insensitive white patches on skin, nodules, thickening of and damage to nerves
malaria	Plasmodium falciparium, P. vivax, P. ovale, P. malariae	anopheles mosquito	several weeks for P. falciparium; up to several months for P. vivax	severe swinging fever, cold sweats, shivers
Marburg (or green monkey) disease	unclassified virus	monkeys, body fluids	5–9 days	fever, diarrhoea; affects brain, kidneys and lungs

Name	Cause	Transmission	Incubation	Symptoms
measles	paramyxovirus	droplet infection	14 days	fever, severe cold symptoms, bloody red rash
meningitis	various bacteria, viruses or fungi eg *Cryptococcus*	droplet infection	variable	severe headache, stiffness in neck muscles, dislike of the light, nausea, vomiting, confusion
mumps	paramyxovirus	droplet infection	18 days	lethargy, fever, pain at the angle of the jaw, swelling of parotid gland(s)
orchitis	bacterium or virus; if bacterial, urinary infection due to eg gonorrhoea; if viral, due to eg mumps	see cause	variable	painful red and swollen testes, fever, nausea
osteomyelitis	usually staphylococci organisms	infection spreads from eg boil or impetigo	1–10 days	abrupt onset of fever, and pain at site of infected bone (usually tibia or femur)
parotitis	bacterium or virus	common in mumps (viral), may follow severe febrile illness or abdominal operation	1–10 days	inflammation of one or both parotid glands
pericarditis	bacterium or virus eg *Coxsackie B*	infection follows a chest disease or heart attack	variable	inflamed pericardium (fibrous bag which encloses the heart); tight chest pain
peritonitis	usually *E. coli* organism; sometimes chemical irritation	usually appendicitis; perforation of the gut allows escape of barrel contents into peritoneal cavity	1–10 days	severe abdominal pain, vomiting, rigidity, shock
pharyngitis	bacteria or virus	droplet infection	3–5 days	sore throat, fever, pain on swallowing, enlarged neck glands

Name	Cause	Transmission	Incubation	Symptoms
pneumonia	*Streptococcus pneumoniae* bacterium, *Legionella pneumophila* etc	droplet infection	1–3 weeks	cough, fever, chest pain
poliomyelitis	three types of polio virus	droplet infection and hand to mouth infection from faeces	7–14 days	affects spinal cord and brain; headache, fever, neck and muscle stiffness; may result in meningitis or paralysis
proctitis	fungal infection possible	contact	variable	inflammation of the rectum and anus resulting from thrush, piles or fissures; pain on defecation
psittacosis	*Chlamydis psittaci* infection within uterine cavity or vagina	infected birds (eg parrots)	1–2 weeks	headache, chest pain, fever, nausea
puerperal fever		follows childbirth	1–10 days	fever; often fatal in past, now rare
pylitis	bacteria	kidney infection	1–10 days	fever, rigor, loin pain, burning on passing urine
rabies	virus	bite or lick by infected animal	2–6 weeks	headache, sickness, excitability, fear of drinking water, convulsions, coma and death
river blindness (or onchocerciasis)	*Onchocerca volvulus* worm	bites of infected flies of genus *Simulium*	worms mature in 2–4 months; may live 12 years	worms inhabit skin, causing nodules and sometimes blindness
salpingitis	infection of the Fallopian tubes	usually gonorrhoea	variable	abdominal pain,* fever, irregular periods, vaginal discharge
scarlet fever	haemolytic streptococcus	droplet infection or streptococci-infected milk or ice cream	2–4 days	sudden onset; headache, sore throat, fever, vomiting, red skin rash

Name	Cause	Transmission	Incubation	Symptoms
shingles	*Herpes zoster* virus (also causes chicken pox)	dormant virus in body becomes active following a minor infection	variable	pain, numbness, blisters
sinusitis	virus or bacteria	droplet infection; common with a cold	1–3 days	fever, sinus pain, nasal discharge
sleeping sickness (or African trypanosomiasis)	1. *Trypanosoma brucei gambieuse* or 2. *Tb. rhodesieuse*	bites by infected tsetse fly	1. weeks–months; 2. 7–14 days	fever, lymph node enlargement, headache, behavioural change, drowsiness, coma, sometimes death
smallpox	variole major or minor virus	now eradicated worldwide	12 days	fever, rash followed by pustules on face and extremities
syphilis	*Treponema pallidum*	sexually transmitted: organism enters bloodstream through a mucous membrane, usually genital skin	ulcer after 2–6 weeks, skin rash after weeks or months	late syphilis damages brain, heart and main blood vessels, and unborn babies
tetanus	*Clostridium tetani*	bacteria from soil infect wounds	2 days–4 weeks	muscular spasms cause lockjaw and affect breathing
thrush	*Candida albicans* yeast	the yeast is present on skin of most people and multiplies when resistance to infection is low; during pregnancy or when taking contraceptive pill	variable	white spots on tongue and cheeks; irritant vaginal discharge; rash in genital area or between folds of skin
tonsillitis	usually same viruses responsible for colds; sometimes bacterial (streptococci)	droplet infection	1–3 days	red inflamed tonsils, sore throat
trachoma	*Chlamydia trachomatis* organism	poor hygiene: organism infects eye	5 days	conjunctivitis, swelling and scarring in cornea, often leading to blindness

Name	Cause	Transmission	Incubation	Symptoms
tuberculosis	*Myobacterium tuberculosis* bacterium	inhalation of bacterium from person with active tuberculosis pneumonia or from infected milk	up to several years	cough with bloodstained sputum, weight loss, chest pain
typhoid	*Salmonella typhi* bacillus	contaminated water or food	10–14 days	slow onset of fever, abdominal discomfort, cough, rash, constipation then diarrhoea, delirium, coma
typhus	*Rickettsiae* parasites	bite by infected flea, tick, mite or louse	7–14 days	fever, rigor, headache, muscular pain, rash
urethritis	virus or bacteria	may occur with cystitis or venereal infection	variable	bloody stools, abdominal pain, burning on urination
whooping cough	*Bordetella pertussis*	droplet infection	7–14 days	severe coughing followed by 'whoop' of respiration
yellow fever	zoonosis virus	mosquitoes infected by monkeys	3–6 days	rigor, high fever, bone pain, headache, nausea, jaundice, kidney failure, coma

Immunization schedule for children up to age 18

Age	Vaccine	How given
2 months	Diphtheria, whooping cough (pertussis), tetanus	Combined DPT injection
	Polio	By mouth
4 months	Diphtheria, whooping cough (pertussis), tetanus	Combined DPT injection
	Polio	By mouth
6 months	Diphtheria, whooping cough (pertussis), tetanus	Combined DPT injection
	Polio	By mouth
1–2 years	Measles, mumps, rubella (German measles)	Combined MMR injection
4–5 years	Diphtheria and tetanus boosters	Combined injection
	Polio booster	By mouth
10–13 years	BCG (tuberculosis)	Injection
13–14 years	German measles (for girls who did not have the MMR injection at 12–24 months)	Injection
16–18 years	Tetanus booster	Injection
	Polio booster	By mouth

Immunization for foreign travel

Immunization is recommended for travellers of all ages who are visiting countries where there is a chance of contracting serious or potentially fatal diseases. Travellers should check which immunizations are required for their destinations, and whether they require immunization certificates.

Disease	Area where immunization needed	Effective for	Level of protection[1]
Cholera	Immunization no longer required by WHO but some countries still require evidence of vaccination. Check with embassy prior to travel.	6 months	M
Hepatitis A	Countries with poor hygiene and sanitation.	1 or 10 years	M
Meningococcal meningitis	For areas recommended by your doctor.	3–5 years	H
Polio	For all areas, if no recent booster received.	10 years	H
Rabies	Vaccine not recommended as routine.	1–3 years	H
Tetanus	For all areas, if no recent booster received.	10 years	H
Tuberculosis	For areas recommended by your doctor.	over 15 years	H
Typhoid fever	Countries with poor hygiene and sanitation.	10 years	M
Yellow fever	Some African and South American countries.	10 years	H

[1] M = provides moderate level of protection; H = provides high level of protection.

Energy expenditure

During exercise, the amount of energy consumed depends on the age, sex, size and fitness of the individual, and how vigorous the exercise is. This table shows the approximate energy used up by a person of average size and fitness carrying out certain activities over a one-hour period.

Activity	Energy used per hour kcals[1]	kJ[1]
Badminton	340	1 428
Climbing stairs	620	2 604
Cycling	660	2 772
Football	540	2 268
Gardening, heavy	420	1 764
Gardening, light	270	1 134
Golf	270	1 134
Gymnastics	420	1 764
Hockey	540	2 268
Housework	270	1 134
Jogging	630	2 646
Rugby	540	2 268
Squash	600	2 520
Standing	120	504
Staying in bed	60	252
Swimming	720	3 024
Tennis	480	2 016
Walking, brisk	300	1 260
Walking, easy	180	756

[1] kcals = kilocalories; kJ = kilojoules.

Average daily energy requirements

CHILDREN Age	Energy used per day kcals[1]	kJ[1]
0–3 months	550	2 300
3–6 months	760	3 200
6–9 months	905	3 800
9–12 months	1 000	4 200
8 years	2 095	8 800
15 years (female)	2 285	9 600
15 years (male)	3 000	12 600

| ADULT FEMALES | Energy used per day | |
Age	kcals[1]	kJ[1]
18–55 years		
Inactive	1 900	7 980
Active	2 150	9 030
Very active	2 500	10 500
Pregnant	2 380	10 000
Breastfeeding	2 690	11 300
Over 56 years		
Inactive	1 700	7 140
Active	2 000	8 400

| ADULT MALES | Energy used per day | |
Age	kcals[1]	kJ[1]
18–35 years		
Inactive	2 500	10 500
Active	3 000	12 600
Very active	3 500	14 700
36–55 years		
Inactive	2 400	10 080
Active	2 800	11 760
Very active	3 400	14 280
Over 56 years		
Inactive	2 200	9 240
Active	2 500	10 500

[1] kcals = kilocalories; kJ = kilojoules.

Measuring your Body Mass Index

Body Mass Index (BMI) gives an accurate measure of obesity. In order to determine your BMI, find out your height in metres and weight in kilograms. To convert height in inches to metres, multiply the number of inches by 0.0254; to convert weight in pounds to kilos, multiply the number of pounds by 0.4536.

$$BMI = \frac{weight\ (kg)}{height\ (m) \times height\ (m)}$$

BMI values:
Less than 18 – underweight   25 to 30 – overweight
18 to 25 – in the ideal weight range   Over 30 – obese; endangering health

Optimum weight according to height

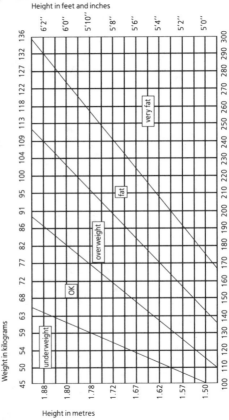

Height in feet and inches

| 6'2" | 6'0" | 5'10" | 5'8" | 5'6" | 5'4" | 5'2" | 5'0" |

Weight in kilograms

45 50 54 59 63 68 72 77 82 86 91 95 100 104 109 113 118 122 127 132 136

very fat

fat

overweight

OK

underweight

Weight in pounds

100 110 120 130 140 150 160 170 180 190 200 210 220 230 240 250 260 270 280 290 300

1.88 1.80 1.78 1.72 1.67 1.62 1.57 1.50

Height in metres

Dietary recommendations

❑ Dietary recommendations to protect the heart

Eat less fat, especially saturated fats.

Avoid sugary and processed foods.

Avoid obesity.

Eat plenty of fibre-rich foods.

Cut down on salt — too much salt can increase your blood pressure.

❑ Dietary recommendations to reduce cancer risks

Eat foods rich in fibre daily: these help to prevent bowel and colon cancers.

Eat fresh fruit and vegetables daily: these are rich in fibre and vitamins.

Eat less fat. There seems to be a close correlation between fat consumption and breast cancer.

Consume alcohol only in moderation. Excessive alcohol intake has been linked to cancers of the bowel, liver, mouth, oesophagus, stomach and throat, especially in smokers.

Eat fewer smoked and salted foods. High consumption of salt-cured meat and fish and nitrate-cured meat has been linked to throat and stomach cancers. There is also a link between eating pickled foods and stomach cancer.

Keep body weight at recommended level.

❑ Dietary recommendations to lose weight

To be healthy, a diet designed to reduce body weight needs to be in tune with the body's physiology. An effective diet should promote the loss of fatty, or adipose, tissue from the body so that its overall fat content is reduced. To do this successfully, the dieter should eat a well-balanced, high-carbohydrate, high-fibre, low-fat diet with an energy content of between 1 200 and 1 500 calories per day, combining this with regular exercise. Foods that can be consumed in this kind of low-calorie diet are shown (*overleaf*) as Type A and Type B foods; Type C foods should be avoided, and fat-containing Type B foods, such as meat, should be eaten in moderation.

❑ Dieting tips

Reduce alcohol intake to a minimum.

Avoid convenience foods because many contain 'hidden' fats and sugar.

Exercise at least three times a week.

Remove fat from meat, and fatty skin from poultry.

Avoid frying food — bake, grill, microwave or steam instead.

Avoid mayonnaise and rich sauces.

If you overeat, work out why you do it (eg through boredom or depression) and find other ways of relieving these feelings.

Plan meals for the next day the night before, or early in the morning, to avoid impulse eating of high-calorie foods.

Use a smaller plate to make smaller helpings look larger than they really are.

Eat regularly. Do not miss meals but try to eat 3–5 small meals each day.

Avoid second helpings.

Avoid between-meal snacks, except for raw fruit and vegetables if very hungry.

Eat at a table rather than eg in front of the television, which may encourage you to eat more and faster.

Take more time when eating — chew well.

Type A foods	Type B foods	Type C foods
Vegetarian foods	**Vegetarian foods**	**Meat, fish and dairy foods**
Cereals (unsweetened)	Dried fruit	Bacon
Fruits — all, except avocados	Margarine, polyunsaturated	Beef, fatty cuts
Vegetables — all, including potatoes	Nuts, except peanuts	Butter
Vegetable protein, eg tofu	Pasta, especially wholewheat	Cheeses, apart from low-fat
Wholemeal bread	Pulses, such as beans and lentils	Duck
Meat, fish and dairy foods	Rice, especially wholegrain	Fish, fried
Chicken and other poultry (not duck) with skin removed	Vegetable oils	Ice cream
Cod, haddock and other non-oily fish	**Meat, fish and dairy foods**	Lamb, fatty cuts
Mussels and other shellfish	Beef, lean cuts	Milk, full cream
Salmon (if tinned, in brine or water)	Eggs	Pâté
Tuna (if tinned, in brine or water)	Lamb, lean cuts	Pork, fatty cuts
Yoghurt (plain, low fat)	Oily fish such as herring or mackerel	Salami
	Pork, lean cuts	Sausages
	Sardines (if tinned, in brine)	**Convenience foods**
		Biscuits
		Burgers
		Cakes
		Chips
		Chocolate
		Crisps

HISTORY

Journeys of exploration

Date	Name	Exploration
490BC	Hanno	Makes voyage round part of the coast of Africa
325BC	Alexander the Great	Leads fleet along the N Indian coast and up the Persian Gulf
84AD	Agricola	Circumnavigates Britain
1003	Leif Ericsson	Voyages to N America and discovers 'Vinland' (possibly Nova Scotia)
1418	João Gonçalves Zarco	Discovers Madeira (dispatched by Henry the Navigator)
1434	Gil Eanes	Sails round Cape Bojador (dispatched by Henry the Navigator)
1446	Dinís Dias	Discovers Cape Verde and the Senegal River (dispatched by Henry the Navigator)
1488	Bartolomeu Dias	Sails round the Cape of Storms (Cape of Good Hope)
1492	Christopher Columbus	Discovers the New World
1493	Christopher Columbus	Discovers Puerto Rico, Antigua and Jamaica
1497	John Cabot	Explores the coast of Newfoundland
1497	Vasco da Gama	Voyages round the Cape of Good Hope
1498	Vasco da Gama	Explores coast of Mozambique and discovers sea route to India
1498	Christopher Columbus	Discovers Trinidad and Venezuela
1499	Amerigo Vespucci	Discovers mouth of the River Amazon
1500	Pedro Álvares Cabral	Discovers Brazil
1500	Diogo Dias	Discovers Madagascar
1500	Gaspar Corte Real	Explores east coast of Greenland and Labrador
1501	Amerigo Vespucci	Explores S American coast
1502	Christopher Columbus	Explores Honduras and Panama
1513	Vasco Núñez de Balboa	Crosses the Panama Isthmus to discover the Pacific Ocean
1520	Ferdinand Magellan	Discovers the Straits of Magellan
1521	Ferdinand Magellan	Discovers the Philippines
1524	Giovanni da Verrazano	Discovers New York Bay and the Hudson River
1526	Sebastian Cabot	Explores the Rio de la Plata
1534	Jacques Cartier	Explores the Gulf of St Lawrence
1535	Jacques Cartier	Navigates the St Lawrence River
1536	Pedro de Mendoza	Founds Buenos Aires and explores Parana and Paraguay rivers
1539	Hernando de Soto	Explores Florida
1540	García López de Cárdenas	Discovers the Grand Canyon
1580	Francis Drake	Completes circumnavigation of the globe

Date	Name	Exploration
1585	John Davis	Discovers Davis Strait on expedition to Greenland
1595	Walter Raleigh	Explores the Orinoco River
1610	Henry Hudson	Discovers Hudson's Bay
1616	William Baffin	Discovers Baffin Bay during search for the NW Passage
1617	Walter Raleigh	Begins expedition to Guiana
1642	Abel Janszoon Tasman	Discovers Tasmania and New Zealand
1678	Robert Cavelier de la Salle	Explores the Great Lakes of Canada
1692	Ijsbrand Iders	Explores the Gobi Desert
1736	Anders Celsius	Undertakes expedition to Lapland
1761	Carsten Niebuhr	Undertakes expedition to Arabia
1766	Louis de Bougainville	Voyage of discovery in Pacific; names Navigator Is
1769	James Cook	Names Society Is; charts coasts of New Zealand and E Australia
1770	James Cook	Lands at Botany Bay, Australia
1772	James Bruce	Explores Abyssinia and the confluence of the Blue Nile and White Nile
1774	James Cook	Discoveries and rediscoveries in the Pacific; discovers and names S Georgia and the S Sandwich Is
1778	James Cook	Discovers Hawaiian group; surveys coast of Bering Straits
1787	Horace Saussure	Makes first ascent of Mont Blanc
1790	George Vancouver	Explores the coast of NW America
1795	Mungo Park	Explores the course of the Niger
1818	John Ross	Attempts to discover NW Passage
1819	John Barrow	Enters Barrow Straits in the N Arctic
1823	Walter Oudney	Discovers Lake Chad in C Africa
1841	David Livingstone	Discovers Lake Ngami
1845	John Franklin	Attempts to discover NW Passage
1854	Richard Burton, John Speke	Explore interior of Somaliland
1855	David Livingstone	Discovers the Victoria Falls on the Zambesi River
1858	Richard Burton, John Speke	Discover Lake Tanganyika
1875	Henry Morton Stanley	Traces the Congo to the Atlantic
1888	Fridtjof Nansen	Crosses Greenland
1893	Fridtjof Nansen	Attempts to reach N Pole
1905	Roald Amundsen	Sails through NW Passage
1909	Robert Edwin Peary	Reaches N Pole
1911	Roald Amundsen	Reaches S Pole
1912	Robert Falcon Scott	Reaches S Pole
1914	Ernest Shackleton	Leads expedition to the Antarctic
1953	Edmund Hillary, Tenzing Norgay	Make first ascent of Mt Everest
1961	Yuri Gagarin	Becomes first man in space
1969	Neil Armstrong, Buzz Aldrin	Make first landing on the Moon

This table comprises mainly European explorers; 'discovers' is used to indicate the first recorded visit by a European.

Monarchs

Austria

Regnal dates	Name

Habsburg Dynasty

1440–93	Frederick III
1493–1519	Maximilian I
1519–58	Karl V
1558–64	Ferdinand I
1564–76	Maximilian II
1576–1612	Rudolf II
1612–19	Matthias
1619–37	Ferdinand II
1637–57	Ferdinand III
1658–1705	Leopold I
1705–11	Josef I
1711–40	Karl VI
1740–2	*Interregnum*
1742–5	Karl VII
1745–65	Franz I
1765–90	Josef II
1790–2	Leopold II
1792–1835	Franz II
1835–48	Ferdinand I
1848–1916	Franz Josef
1916–18	Karl I

Belgium

Belgium became an independent kingdom in 1831. A national congress elected Prince Leopold of Saxe-Coburg as king.

Regnal dates	Name
1831–65	Leopold I
1865–1909	Leopold II
1909–34	Albert I
1934–50	Leopold III
1950–93	Baudouin
1993–	Albert II

Denmark

Regnal dates	Name
1448–81	Kristian I
1481–1513	Johan
1513–23	Kristian II
1523–34	Frederik I
1534–59	Kristian III
1559–88	Frederik II
1588–1648	Kristian IV
1648–70	Frederik III
1670–99	Kristian V
1699–1730	Frederik IV
1730–46	Kristian VI
1746–66	Frederik V
1766–1808	Kristian VII
1808–39	Frederik VI
1839–48	Kristian VIII
1848–63	Frederik VII
1863–1906	Kristian IX
1906–12	Frederik VIII
1912–47	Kristian X
1947–72	Frederik IX
1972–	Margrethe II

England

Regnal dates	Name

West Saxon Kings

802–39	Egbert
839–58	Æthelwulf
858–60	Æthelbald
860–5	Æthelbert
866–71	Æthelred
871–99	Alfred
899–924	Edward (the Elder)
939–46	Edmund
946–55	Edred
955–9	Edwy
959–75	Edgar
975–8	Edward (the Martyr)
978–1016	Æthelred (the Unready)
1016	Edmund (Ironside)

Danish Kings

1016–35	Knut (Canute)
1035–7	Harold *Regent*
1037–40	Harold I (Harefoot)
1040–2	Hardaknut
1042–66	Edward (the Confessor)
1066	Harold II

House of Normandy

1066–87	William I (the Conqueror)
1087–1100	William II (Rufus)
1100–35	Henry I

House of Blois

1135–54	Stephen

House of Plantagenet

1154–89	Henry II
1189–99	Richard I (Cœur de Lion)
1199–1216	John
1216–72	Henry III
1272–1307	Edward I
1307–27	Edward II
1327–77	Edward III
1377–99	Richard II

House of Lancaster

1399–1413	Henry IV
1413–22	Henry V
1422–61	Henry VI

House of York

1461–70	Edward IV

House of Lancaster

1470–1	Henry VI

House of York

1471–83	Edward IV
1483	Edward V
1483–5	Richard III

House of Tudor

1485–1509	Henry VII
1509–47	Henry VIII
1547–53	Edward VI
1553–8	Mary I
1558–1603	Elizabeth I

Finland

Finland was under Swedish control from the 13th-c until it was ceded to Russia in 1809 by the Treaty of Friedrichsham. Russian rulers then assumed the title of Grand Duke of Finland. In 1917 it became an independent monarchy. However in November 1918, after initially accepting the throne the previous month, Landgrave Frederick Charles of Hesse, the brother-in-law of the German Emperor William II, withdrew his acceptance because of the Armistice and the ensuing abdication of William II. The previous regent remained in power until a Republic was declared in July 1919.

Regnal dates	Name
1918	Dr Pehr Evind Svinhufvud *Regent*
1918	Landgrave Frederick Charles of Hesse (withdrew acceptance)
1918–19	Dr Pehr Evind Svinhufvud

France

France became a republic in 1793, and an empire in 1804 under Napoleon Bonaparte. The monarchy was restored in 1814 and then once more dissolved in 1848.

Regnal dates	Name
987–996	Hugh Capet
996–1031	Robert II
1031–60	Henry I
1060–1108	Philip I
1108–37	Louis VI
1137–80	Louis VII
1180–1223	Philip II Augustus
1223–6	Louis VIII
1226–70	Louis IX
1270–85	Philip III
1285–1314	Philip IV
1314–16	Louis X
1316	John I
1316–22	Philip V

1322–8	Charles IV
1328–50	Philip VI
1350–64	John II
1364–80	Charles V
1380–1422	Charles VI
1422–61	Charles VII
1461–83	Louis XI
1483–98	Charles VIII
1498–1515	Louis XII
1515–47	Francis I
1547–59	Henry II
1559–60	Francis II
1560–74	Charles IX
1574–89	Henry III
1589–1610	Henry IV (of Navarre)
1610–43	Louis XIII
1643–1715	Louis XIV
1715–74	Louis XV
1774–92	Louis XVI
1814–24	Louis XVIII
1824–30	Charles X
1830–48	Louis-Philippe

Germany

Modern Germany was united under Prussia in 1871; it became a republic (1919) after World War I and the abdication of Wilhelm II in 1918.

Regnal dates	Name
1871–88	Wilhelm I
1888	Friedrich
1888–1918	Wilhelm II

Greece

In 1832 the Greek National Assembly elected Otto of Bavaria as King of modern Greece. In 1917 Constantine I abdicated the throne in favour of his son Alexander. In 1920 a plebiscite voted for his return. In 1922 he again abdicated. In 1923 the monarchy was deposed and a republic was proclaimed in 1924. In 1935 a plebiscite restored the monarchy until in 1967 a military junta staged a coup. The monarchy was formally abolished in 1973; Greece became a republic again in 1975.

Regnal dates	Name
1832–62	Otto of Bavaria
1863–1913	George I (of Denmark)
1913–17	Constantine I
1917–20	Alexander
1920–2	Constantine I
1922–3	George II
1935–47	George II
1947–64	Paul
1964–7	Constantine II

Italy

Modern Italy became a united kingdom in 1861; it voted by referendum to become a republic in 1946.

Regnal dates	Name
1861–78	Victor-Emanuel II
1878–1900	Umberto I
1900–46	Victor-Emanuel III
1946	Umberto II

Luxembourg

The Duchy of Luxembourg formally separated from the Netherlands in 1890.

Regnal dates	Name
1890–1905	Adolf of Nassau
1905–12	William
1912–19	Marie Adélaïde
1919–64	Charlotte
1964–2000	Jean
2000–	Henri

The Netherlands

Regnal dates	Name
1572–84	William the Silent
1584–1625	Maurice
1625–47	Frederick Henry
1647–50	William II
1672–1702	William III
1747–51	William IV
1751–95	William V
1806–10	Louis Bonaparte
1813–40	William I
1840–9	William II

1849–90	William III
1890–1948	Wilhelmina
1948–80	Juliana
1980–	Beatrix

Portugal

From 1383 to 1385 the Portuguese throne was the subject of a dispute between John of Castile and John of Aviz. In 1826 Peter IV (I of Brazil) renounced his right to the Portuguese throne in order to remain in Brazil. His abdication was contingent upon his successor and daughter, Maria II, marrying her uncle, Miguel. In 1828 Miguel usurped the throne on his own behalf. In 1834 Miguel was deposed and Maria II was restored to the throne. In 1910 Manuel II was deposed and Portugal became a republic.

Regnal dates	Name
1095–1112	Henry of Burgundy
1112–85	Alfonso I
1185–1211	Sancho I
1211–23	Alfonso II
1223–45	Sancho II
1245–79	Alfonso III
1279–1325	Diniz
1325–57	Alfonso IV
1357–67	Peter I
1367–83	Ferdinand
1385–1433	John I of Aviz
1433–8	Edward
1438–81	Alfonso V
1481–95	John II
1495–1521	Manuel I
1521–57	John III
1557–78	Sebastian
1578–80	Henry
1580–98	Philip I (II of Spain)
1598–1621	Philip II (III of Spain)
1621–40	Philip III (IV of Spain)
1640–56	John IV of Braganza
1656–83	Alfonso VI
1683–1706	Peter II
1706–50	John V
1750–77	Joseph

1777–1816	Maria I
1777–86	Peter III (King Consort)
1816–26	John VI
1826	Peter IV (I of Brazil)
1826–8	Maria II
1828–34	Miguel
1834–53	Maria II
1853–61	Peter V
1861–89	Luis
1889–1908	Charles
1908–10	Manuel II

Russia

In 1610 Vasili Shuisky was deposed as Tsar and the throne remained vacant until the election of Michael Romanov in 1613. In 1682 a condition of the succession was that the two step-brothers, Ivan V and Peter I (the Great) should jointly be proclaimed as Tsars. In 1917 the empire was overthrown and Tsar Nicholas II was forced to abdicate.

Regnal dates	Name
1283–1303	Daniel
1303–25	Yuri
1325–41	Ivan I
1341–53	Semeon
1353–9	Ivan II
1359–89	Dimitri Donskoy
1389–1425	Vasili I
1425–62	Vasili II
1462–1505	Ivan III (the Great)
1505–33	Vasili III
1533–84	Ivan IV (the Terrible)
1584–98	Feodor I
1598–1605	Boris Godunov
1605	Feodor II
1605–6	Dimitri II
1606–10	Vasili IV Shuisky
1613–45	Mikhail (Michael Romanov)
1645–76	Alexei
1676–82	Feodor III
1682–96	Ivan V
1682–1725	Peter I (the Great)
1725–7	Catherine I

1727–30	Peter II
1730–40	Anna
1740–1	Ivan VI
1741–62	Elizabeth
1762	Peter III
1762–96	Catherine II (the Great)
1796–1801	Paul
1801–25	Alexander I
1825–55	Nicholas I
1855–81	Alexander II
1881–94	Alexander III
1894–1917	Nicholas II

Scotland

Regnal dates	Name
1005–34	Malcolm II
1034–40	Duncan I
1040–57	Macbeth
1057–8	Lulach
1058–93	Malcolm III
1093–4	Donald Bane (Deposed 1094, Restored 1094–7)
1094	Duncan II
1097–1107	Edgar
1107–24	Alexander I
1124–53	David I
1153–65	Malcolm IV
1165–1214	William I
1214–49	Alexander II
1249–86	Alexander III
1286–90	Margaret
1290–2	Interregnum
1292–6	John Balliol
1296–1306	Interregnum
1306–29	Robert I (the Bruce)
1329–71	David II
1371–90	Robert II
1390–1406	Robert III
1406–37	James I
1437–60	James II
1460–88	James III
1488–1513	James IV
1513–42	James V
1542–67	Mary Queen of Scots
1567–1625	James VI [1]

[1] In 1603, James VI succeeded Elizabeth I to the English throne (Union of the Crowns) and united the thrones of Scotland and England.

Spain

Philip V abdicated in favour of Luis in 1724, but returned to the throne in the same year following Luis' death. After the French invasion of Spain in 1808, Napoleon set up Joseph Bonaparte as king. In 1814 Ferdinand was restored to the crown. In 1868 a revolution deposed Isabella II. In 1870 Amadeus of Savoy was elected as king. In 1873 he resigned the throne and a temporary republic was formed. In 1874 Alfonso XII restored the Bourbon dynasty to the throne. In 1931 Alfonso XIII was deposed and a republican constitution was proclaimed. From 1939 Franco ruled Spain under a dictatorship until his death in 1975 and the restoration of King Juan Carlos.

Regnal dates	Name
1516–56	Charles I (Emperor Charles V)
1556–98	Philip II
1598–1621	Philip III
1621–65	Philip IV
1665–1700	Charles II
1700–24	Philip V
1724	Luis
1724–46	Philip V
1746–59	Ferdinand VI
1759–88	Charles III
1788–1808	Charles IV
1808	Ferdinand VII
1808–14	Joseph Bonaparte
1814–33	Ferdinand VII
1833–68	Isabella II
1870–3	Amadeus of Savoy
1874–85	Alfonso XII
1886–1931	Alfonso XIII
1975–	Juan Carlos

Sweden

Regnal dates	Name
Vasa	
1523–60	Gustav I
1560–8	Erik XIV
1568–92	Johan III
1592–9	Sigismund
1599–1611	Karl IX
1611–32	Gustav II Adolf
1632–54	Kristina
Zweibrucken	
1654–60	Karl X Gustav
1660–97	Karl XI
1697–1718	Karl XII
1718–20	Ulrika Eleonora
Hesse	
1720–51	Fredrik
Oldenburg-Holstein-Gottorp	
1751–71	Adolf Fredrik
1771–92	Gustav III
1792–1809	Gustav IV Adolf
1809–18	Karl XIII
Bernadotte	
1818–44	Karl XIV Johan
1844–59	Oskar I
1859–72	Karl XV
1872–1907	Oskar II
1907–50	Gustav V
1950–73	Gustav VI Adolf
1973–	Karl XVI Gustav

United Kingdom

Regnal dates	Name
House of Stuart	
1603–25	James I (VI of Scotland)
1625–49	Charles I

Commonwealth and Protectorate

1649–53	Council of State
1653–8	Oliver Cromwell *Lord Protector*
1658–9	Richard Cromwell *Lord Protector*

House of Stuart (restored)

1660–85	Charles II
1685–8	James II
1689–94	William III (*jointly with* Mary II)
1694–1702	William III (*alone*)
1702–14	Anne

House of Hanover

1714–27	George I
1727–60	George II
1760–1820	George III
1820–30	George IV
1830–7	William IV
1837–1901	Victoria

House of Saxe-Coburg

1901–10	Edward VII

House of Windsor

1910–36	George V
1936	Edward VIII
1936–52	George VI
1952–	Elizabeth II

Roman kings

The founding of Rome by Romulus is a Roman literary tradition.

Regnal dates	Name
753–715BC	Romulus
715–673BC	Numa Pompilius
673–642BC	Tullus Hostilius
642–616BC	Ancus Marcius
616–578BC	Tarquinius Priscus
578–534BC	Servius Tullius
534–509BC	Tarquinius Superbus

Roman emperors

Dates overlap where there are periods of joint rule (eg Marcus Aurelius and Lucius Verus) and where the government of the empire divides between east and west.

Regnal dates	Name	Regnal dates	Name
27BC–14AD	Augustus (Caesar Augustus)	275–6	Tacitus
14–37	Tiberius	276	Florian
37–41	Caligula (Gaius Caesar)	276–82	Probus
41–54	Claudius	282–3	Carus
54–68	Nero	283–5	Carinus
68–9	Galba	283–4	Numerian
69	Otho	284–305	Diocletian – (East)
69	Vitellius	286–305	Maximian – (West)
69–79	Vespasian	305–11	Galerius – (East)
79–81	Titus	305–6	Constantius I
81–96	Domitian	306–7	Severus – (West)
96–8	Nerva	306–12	Maxentius – (West)
98–117	Trajan	306–37	Constantine I
117–38	Hadrian	308–24	Licinius – (East)
138–61	Antoninus Pius	337–40	Constantine II
161–80	Marcus Aurelius	337–50	Constans I
161–9	Lucius Verus	337–61	Constantius II
176–92	Commodus	350–1	Magnentius
193	Pertinax	360–3	Julian
193	Didius Julianus	364–75	Valentinian I – (West)
193–211	Septemius Severus	364–78	Valens – (East)
198–217	Caracalla	365–6	Procopius – (East)
209–12	Geta	375–83	Gratian – (West)
217–18	Macrinus	375–92	Valentinian II – (West)
218–22	Elagabalus	379–95	Theodosius I
222–35	Alexander Severus	395–408	Arcadius – (East)
235–8	Maximin	395–423	Honorius – (West)
238	Gordian I	408–50	Theodosius II – (East)
238	Gordian II	421–3	Constantius III – (West)
238	Maximus	423–55	Valentinian III – (West)
238	Balbinus	450–7	Marcian – (East)
238–44	Gordian III	455	Petronius Maximus – (West)
244–9	Philip	455–6	Avitus – (West)
249–51	Decius	457–74	Leo I – (East)
251	Hostilian	457–61	Majorian – (West)
251–3	Gallus	461–7	Libius Severus – (West)
253	Aemilian	467–72	Anthemius – (West)
253–60	Valerian	472–3	Olybrius – (West)
253–68	Gallienus	474–80	Julius Nepos – (West)
268–9	Claudius II (the Goth)	474	Leo II – (East)
269–70	Quintillus	474–91	Zeno – (East)
270–5	Aurelian	475–6	Romulus Augustus – (West)

Emperors of the Holy Roman Empire

Regnal dates	Name	Regnal dates	Name
800–14	Charlemagne (Charles I)	1247–56	William of Holland [2]
814–40	Louis I (the Pious)	1250–4	Conrad IV
840–3	*Civil War*	1254–73	*Great Interregnum*
843–55	Lothair	1257–72	Richard [2]
855–75	Louis II	1257–75	Alfonso (Alfonso X of
875–7	Charles II (the Bald)		Castile) [2]
877–81	*Interregnum*	1273–91	Rudolf I
881–7	Charles III (the Fat)	1292–8	Adolf
887–91	*Interregnum*	1298–1308	Albert I
891–4	Guido of Spoleto	1308–13	Henry VII
892–8	Lambert of Spoleto [1]	1314–26	Frederick (III) [3]
896–9	Arnulf [2]	1314–46	Louis IV
901–5	Louis III	1346–78	Charles IV
911–18	Conrad I [2]	1378–1400	Wenceslas
905–24	Berengar	1400–10	Rupert
919–36	Henry I	1410–37	Sigismund
936–73	Otto I (the Great)	1438–9	Albert II
973–83	Otto II	1440–93	Frederick III
983–1002	Otto III	1493–1519	Maximilian I
1002–24	Henry II (the Saint)	1519–56	Charles V
1024–39	Conrad II	1556–64	Ferdinand I
1039–56	Henry III (the Black)	1564–76	Maximilian II
1056–1106	Henry IV	1576–1612	Rudolf II
1077–80	Rudolf [2]	1612–19	Matthias
1081–93	Hermann [2]	1619–37	Ferdinand II
1093–1101	Conrad [2]	1637–57	Ferdinand III
1106–25	Henry V	1658–1705	Leopold I
1125–37	Lothair II	1705–11	Joseph I
1138–52	Conrad III	1711–40	Charles VI
1152–90	Frederick I (Barbarossa)	1740–2	*Interregnum*
1190–7	Henry VI	1742–5	Charles VII
1198–1208	Philip [2]	1745–65	Francis I
1198–1214	Otto IV	1765–90	Joseph II
1215–50	Frederick II	1790–2	Leopold II
1246–7	Henry Raspe [2]	1792–1806	Francis II

[1] Co-emperor.

[2] Rival.

[3] Co-regent.

Popes

Antipopes (who claimed to be pope in opposition to those canonically chosen) are given in square brackets.

until c.64	Peter
c.64–c.76	Linus
c.76–c.90	Anacletus
c.90–c.99	Clement I
c.99–c.105	Evaristus
c.105–c.117	Alexander I
c.117–c.127	Sixtus I
c.127–c.137	Telesphorus
c.137–c.140	Hyginus
c.140–c.154	Pius I
c.154–c.166	Anicetus
c.166–c.175	Soter
175–89	Eleutherius
189–98	Victor I
198–217	Zephyrinus
217–22	Callistus I
[217–c.235	Hippolytus]
222–30	Urban I
230–5	Pontian
235–6	Anterus
236–50	Fabian
251–3	Cornelius
[251–c.258	Novatian]
253–4	Lucius I
254–7	Stephen I
257–8	Sixtus II
259–68	Dionysius
269–74	Felix I
275–83	Eutychianus
283–96	Caius
296–304	Marcellinus
308–9	Marcellus I
310	Eusebius
311–14	Miltiades
314–35	Sylvester I
336	Mark
337–52	Julius I
352–66	Liberius
[355–65	Felix II]
366–84	Damasus I
[366–7	Ursinus]
384–99	Siricius
399–401	Anastasius I
402–17	Innocent I
417–18	Zosimus
418–22	Boniface I
[418–19	Eulalius]
422–32	Celestine I
432–40	Sixtus III
440–61	Leo I
461–8	Hilarus
468–83	Simplicius
483–92	Felix III (II)
492–6	Gelasius I
496–8	Anastasius II
498–514	Symmachus
[498, 501–5	Laurentius]
514–23	Hormisdas
523–6	John I
526–30	Felix IV (III)
530–2	Boniface II
[530	Dioscorus]
533–5	John II
535–6	Agapetus I
536–7	Silverius
537–55	Vigilius
556–61	Pelagius I
561–74	John III
575–9	Benedict I
579–90	Pelagius II
590–604	Gregory I
604–6	Sabinianus
607	Boniface III
608–15	Boniface IV
615–18	Deusdedit or Adeodatus I
619–25	Boniface V
625–38	Honorius I
640	Severinus
640–2	John IV
642–9	Theodore I
649–55	Martin I
654–7	Eugenius 1 [1]
657–72	Vitalian
672–6	Adeodatus II
676–8	Donus
678–81	Agatho

682–3	Leo II	903	Leo V
684–5	Benedict II	[903–4	Christopher]
685–6	John V	904–11	Sergius III
686–7	Cono	911–13	Anastasius III
[687	Theodore]	913–14	Lando
[687–92	Paschal]	914–28	John X
687–701	Sergius I	928	Leo VI
701–5	John VI	928–31	Stephen VII (VIII)
705–7	John VII	931–5	John XI
708	Sisinnius	936–9	Leo VII
708–15	Constantine	939–42	Stephen IX
715–31	Gregory II	942–6	Marinus II
731–41	Gregory III	946–55	Agapetus II
741–52	Zacharias	955–64	John XII
752	Stephen II (*not* *consecrated*)	[963–5	Leo VIII]
		964–6	Benedict V
752–7	Stephen II (III)	965–72	John XIII
757–67	Paul I	973–4	Benedict VI
[767–9	Constantine II]	[974, 984–5	Boniface VII]
[768	Philip]	974–83	Benedict VII
768–72	Stephen III (IV)	983–4	John XIV
772–95	Hadrian I	985–96	John XV
795–816	Leo III	996–9	Gregory V
816–17	Stephen IV (V)	[997–8	John XVI]
817–24	Paschal I	999–1003	Sylvester II
824–7	Eugenius II	1003	John XVII
827	Valentine	1004–9	John XVIII
827–44	Gregory IV	1009–12	Sergius IV
[844	John]	1012–24	Benedict VIII
844–7	Sergius II	[1012	Gregory]
847–55	Leo IV	1024–32	John XIX
855–8	Benedict III	1032–44	Benedict IX
[855	Anastasius Bibliothecarius]	1045	Sylvester III
		1045	Benedict IX (*second reign*)
858–67	Nicholas I		
867–72	Hadrian II	1045–6	Gregory VI
872–82	John VIII	1046–7	Clement II
882–4	Marinus I	1047–8	Benedict IX (*third reign*)
884–5	Hadrian III	1048	Damasus II
885–91	Stephen V (VI)	1048–54	Leo IX
891–6	Formosus	1055–7	Victor II
896	Boniface VI	1057–8	Stephen IX (X)
896–7	Stephen VI (VII)	[1058–9	Benedict X]
897	Romanus	1059–61	Nicholas II
897	Theodore II	1061–73	Alexander II
898–900	John IX	[1061–72	Honorius II]
900–3	Benedict IV	1073–85	Gregory VII

[1080, 1084–1100	
1086–7	Victor III
1088–99	Urban II
1099–1118	Paschal II
[1100–2	Theodoric]
[1102	Albert]
[1105–11	Sylvester IV]
1118–19	Gelasius II
[1118–21	Gregory VIII]
1119–24	Callistus II
1124–30	Honorius II
[1124	Celestine II]
1130–43	Innocent II
[1130–8	Anacletus II]
[1138	Victor IV][2]
1143–4	Celestine II
1144–5	Lucius II
1145–53	Eugenius III
1153–4	Anastasius IV
1154–9	Hadrian IV
1159–81	Alexander III
[1159–64	Victor IV][2]
[1164–8	Paschal III]
[1168–78	Callistus III]
[1179–80	Innocent III]
1181–5	Lucius III
1185–7	Urban III
1187	Gregory VIII
1187–91	Clement III
1191–8	Celestine III
1198–1216	Innocent III
1216–27	Honorius III
1227–41	Gregory IX
1241	Celestine IV
1243–54	Innocent IV
1254–61	Alexander IV
1261–4	Urban IV
1265–8	Clement IV
1271–6	Gregory X
1276	Innocent V
1276	Hadrian V
1276–7	John XXI [3]
1277–80	Nicholas III
1281–5	Martin IV
1285–7	Honorius IV
1288–92	Nicholas IV

1294	Celestine V
1294–1303	Boniface VIII
1303–4	Benedict XI
1305–14	Clement V
1316–34	John XXII
[1328–30	Nicholas V]
1334–42	Benedict XII
1342–52	Clement VI
1352–62	Innocent VI
1362–70	Urban V
1370–8	Gregory XI
1378–89	Urban VI
[1378–94	Clement VII]
1389–1404	Boniface IX
[1394–1423	Benedict XIII]
1404–6	Innocent VII
1406–15	Gregory XII
[1409–10	Alexander V]
[1410–15	John XXIII]
1417–31	Martin V
[1423–9	Clement VIII]
[1425–30	Benedict XIV]
1431–47	Eugenius IV
[1439–49	Felix V]
1447–55	Nicholas V
1455–8	Callistus III
1458–64	Pius II
1464–71	Paul II
1471–84	Sixtus IV
1484–92	Innocent VIII
1492–1503	Alexander VI
1503	Pius III
1503–13	Julius II
1513–21	Leo X
1522–3	Hadrian VI
1523–34	Clement VII
1534–49	Paul III
1550–5	Julius III
1555	Marcellus II
1555–9	Paul IV
1559–65	Pius IV
1566–72	Pius V
1572–85	Gregory XIII
1585–90	Sixtus V
1590	Urban VII
1590–1	Gregory XIV
1591	Innocent IX

1592–1605	Clement VIII	1758–69	Clement XIII
1605	Leo XI	1769–74	Clement XIV
1605–21	Paul V	1775–99	Pius VI
1621–3	Gregory XV	1800–23	Pius VII
1623–44	Urban VIII	1823–9	Leo XII
1644–55	Innocent X	1829–30	Pius VIII
1655–67	Alexander VII	1831–46	Gregory XVI
1667–9	Clement IX	1846–78	Pius IX
1670–6	Clement X	1878–1903	Leo XIII
1676–89	Innocent XI	1903–14	Pius X
1689–91	Alexander VIII	1914–22	Benedict XV
1691–1700	Innocent XII	1922–39	Pius XI
1700–21	Clement XI	1939–58	Pius XII
1721–4	Innocent XIII	1958–63	John XXIII
1724–30	Benedict XIII	1963–78	Paul VI
1730–40	Clement XII	1978	John Paul I
1740–58	Benedict XIV	1978–	John Paul II

[1] Elected during the banishment of Martin I.
[2] Different individuals.
[3] There was no John XX.

Japanese emperors

The first 14 emperors (to Chuai) are regarded as legendary, and the regnal dates for the 15th to the 28th emperor (Senka), taken from the early Japanese chronicle, 'Nihon Shoki', are not considered to be authentic.

660–585 BC	Jimmu	456–79	Yuryaku
581–549 BC	Suizei	480–4	Seinei
549–511 BC	Annei	485–7	Kenzo
510–477 BC	Itoku	488–98	Ninken
475–393 BC	Kosho	498–506	Buretsu
392–291 BC	Koan	507–31	Keitai
290–215 BC	Korei	531–5	Ankan
214–158 BC	Kogen	535–9	Senka
158–98 BC	Kaika	539–71	Kimmei
97–30 BC	Sujin	572–85	Bidatsu
29 BC–70 AD	Suinin	585–7	Yomei
71–130	Keiko	587–92	Sushun
131–90	Seimu	592–628	Suiko (Empress)
192–200	Chuai	629–41	Jomei
270–310	Ojin	642–5	Kogyoku (Empress)
313–99	Nintoku	645–54	Kotuko
400–5	Richu	655–61	Saimei (Empress)
406–10	Hanzei	662–71	Tenji
412–53	Ingyo	671–2	Kobun
453–6	Anko	673–86	Temmu

686–97	Jito (Empress)
697–707	Mommu
707–15	Gemmei (Empress)
715–24	Gensho (Empress)
724–49	Shomu
749–58	Koken (Empress)
758–64	Junnin
764–70	Shotoku (Empress)
770–81	Konin
781–806	Kammu
806–9	Heizei
809–23	Saga
823–33	Junna
833–50	Nimmyo
850–8	Montoku
858–76	Seiwa
876–84	Yozei
884–7	Koko
887–97	Uda
897–930	Daigo
930–46	Suzaku
946–67	Murakami
967–9	Reizei
969–84	En-yu
984–6	Kazan
986–1011	Ichijo
1011–16	Sanjo
1016–36	Go-Ichijo
1036–45	Go-Suzaku
1045–68	Go-Reizei
1068–72	Go-Sanjo
1072–86	Shirakawa
1086–1107	Horikawa
1107–23	Toba
1123–41	Sutoku
1141–55	Konoe
1155–8	Go-Shirakawa
1158–65	Nijo
1165–8	Rokujo
1168–80	Takakura
1180–3	Antoku
1183–98	Go-Toba
1198–1210	Tsuchimikado
1210–21	Juntoku
1221	Chukyo
1221–32	Go-Horikawa

1232–42	Shijo
1242–6	Go-Saga
1246–59	Go-Fukakusa
1259–74	Kameyama
1274–87	Go-Uda
1287–98	Fushimi
1298–1301	Go-Fushimi
1301–8	Go-Nijo
1308–18	Hanazono
1318–39	Go-Daigo
1339–68	Go-Murakami
1368–83	Chokei
1383–92	Go-Kameyama

Northern Court

1331–3	Kogon
1336–48	Komyo
1348–51	Suko
1352–71	Go-Kogon
1371–82	Go-Enyu
1382–1412	Go-Komatsu
1412–28	Shoko
1428–64	Go-Hanazono
1464–1500	Go-Tsuchimikado
1500–26	Go-Kashiwabara
1526–57	Go-Nara
1557–86	Ogimachi
1586–1611	Go-Yozei
1611–29	Go-Mizuno-o
1629–43	Meisho (Empress)
1643–54	Go-Komyo
1654–63	Go-Sai
1663–87	Reigen
1687–1709	Higashiyama
1709–35	Nakamikado
1735–47	Sakuramachi
1747–62	Momozono
1762–70	Go-Sakuramachi
1770–9	Go-Momozono
1779–1817	Kokaku
1817–46	Ninko
1846–66	Komei
1867–1912	Meiji
1912–26	Taisho
1926–89	Hirohito
1989–	Akihito

Ancient Egyptian dynasties

Date BC	Dynasty	Period
c.3100–2890	I	Early Dynastic Period
c.2890–2686	II	(First use of stone in building.)
c.2686–2613	III	Old Kingdom
c.2613–2494	IV	(The age of the great pyramid builders. Longest
c.2494–2345	V	reign in history: Pepi II, 90 years.)
c.2345–2181	VI	
c.2181–2173	VII	First Intermediate Period
c.2173–2160	VIII	(Social order upset; few monuments built.)
c.2160–2130	IX	
c.2130–2040	X	
c.2133–1991	XI	
1991–1786	XII	Middle Kingdom
1786–1633	XIII	(Golden age of art and craftsmanship.)
1786–c.1603	XIV	Second Intermediate Period
1674–1567	XV	(Country divided into principalities.)
c.1684–1567	XVI	
c.1660–1567	XVII	
1567–1320	XVIII	New Kingdom
1320–1200	XIX	(Began with colonial expansion, ended in divided
1200–1085	XX	rule.)
1085–945	XXI	Third Intermediate Period
945–745	XXII	(Revival of prosperity and restoration of cults.)
745–718	XXIII	
718–715	XXIV	
715–668	XXV	
664–525	XXVI	Late Period
525–404	XXVII	(Completion of Nile – Red Sea canal. Alexander the
404–399	XXVIII	Great reached Alexandria in 332BC.)
399–380	XXIX	
380–343	XXX	
343–332	XXXI	

Chinese dynasties

Regnal dates	Name	Regnal dates	Name
c.22nd – 18th-c BC	Hsia	317–420	Eastern Chin
c.18th – 12 th-c BC	Shang or Yin	420–589	Northern and
c.1111–256 BC	Chou		Southern
c.1111–770 BC	Western Chou		Dynasties
770–256 BC	Eastern Chou	581–618	Sui
770–476 BC	Ch'un Ch'iu Period	618–907	Tang
475–221 BC	Warring States	907–60	Five Dynasties and
	Period		Ten Kingdoms
221–206 BC	Ch'in		Period
206 BC –220 AD	Han	960–1279	Sung
206 BC –9 AD	Western Han	960–1127	Northern Sung
9–23	Hsin Interregnum	1127–1279	Southern Sung
25–220	Eastern Han	1115–1234	Chin (Jurchen
220–65	Three Kingdoms		Tartars)
	Period	1279–1368	Yuan (Mongol)
265–420	Chin	1368–1644	Ming
265–317	Western Chin	1644–1912	Ch'ing or Qing
			(Manchu)

Mughal emperors

The 2nd Mughal emperor, Humayun, lost his throne in 1540, became a fugitive, and did not regain his title until 1555.

Regnal dates	Name	Regnal dates	Name
1526–30	Babur	1719	Rafid-ud-Darajat
1530–56	Humayun	1719	Rafi-ud-Daulat
1556–1605	Akbar	1719	Nekusiyar
1605–27	Jahangir	1719	Ibrahim
1627–58	Shah Jahan	1719–48	Muhammad Shah
1658–1707	Aurangzeb (Alamgir)	1748–54	Ahmad Shah
1707–12	Bahadur Shah I (or Shah	1754–9	Alamgir II
	Alam I)	1759–1806	Shah Alam II
1712–13	Jahandar Shah	1806–37	Akbar II
1713–19	Farruksiyar	1837–57	Bahadur Shah II

Political leaders 1900–2000

Countries and organizations are listed alphabetically, with former or alternative names given in parentheses. Rulers are named chronologically since 1900 or (for new nations) since independence. For some major English-speaking nations, relevant details are also given of pre-20th-century rulers, along with a note of any political affiliation.

The list does not distinguish successive terms of office by a single ruler.

There is no universally agreed way of transliterating proper names in non-Roman alphabets; variations from the spellings given are therefore to be expected, especially in the case of Arabic rulers.

Minor variations in the titles adopted by Chiefs of State, or in the name of an administration, are not given; these occur most notably in countries under military rule.

Listings complete to May 2000.

Australia

Chief of State: British monarch, represented by Governor General

Prime Minister

1901–3	Edmund Barton *Prot*
1903–4	Alfred Deakin *Prot*
1904	John Christian Watson *Lab*
1904–5	George Houston Reid *Free*
1905–8	Alfred Deakin *Prot*
1908–9	Andrew Fisher *Lab*
1909–10	Alfred Deakin *Fusion*
1910–13	Andrew Fisher *Lab*
1913–14	Joseph Cook *Lib*
1914–15	Andrew Fisher *Lab*
1915–17	William Morris Hughes *Nat Lab*
1917–23	William Morris Hughes *Nat*
1923–9	Stanley Melbourne Bruce *Nat*
1929–32	James Henry Scullin *Lab*
1932–9	Joseph Aloysius Lyons *Un*
1939	Earle Christmas Page *Co*
1939–41	Robert Gordon Menzies *Un*
1941	Arthur William Fadden *Co*
1941–5	John Joseph Curtin *Lab*
1945	Francis Michael Forde *Lab*
1945–9	Joseph Benedict Chifley *Lab*
1949–66	Robert Gordon Menzies *Lib*
1966–7	Harold Edward Holt *Lib*
1967–8	John McEwen *Co*
1968–71	John Grey Gorton *Lib*
1971–2	William McMahon *Lib*
1972–5	Edward Gough Whitlam *Lab*
1975–83	John Malcolm Fraser *Lib*
1983–91	Robert James Lee Hawke *Lab*
1991–6	Paul Keating *Lab*
1996–	John Howard *Lib*

Co = Country
Free = Free Trade
Lab = Labor
Lib = Liberal
Nat = Nationalist
Nat Lab = National Labor
Prot = Protectionist
Un = United

Austria

President

1918–20	Karl Sätz
1920–8	Michael Hainisch
1928–38	Wilhelm Miklas
1938–45	*German rule*
1945–50	Karl Renner
1950–7	Theodor Körner
1957–65	Adolf Schärf
1965–74	Franz Jonas
1974–86	Rudolf Kirchsläger
1986–92	Kurt Waldheim
1992–	Thomas Klestil

Chancellor

1918–20	Karl Renner
1920–1	Michael Mayr
1921–2	Johann Schober
1922	Walter Breisky
1922	Johann Schober
1922–4	Ignaz Seipel
1924–6	Rudolph Ramek
1926–9	Ignaz Seipel
1929–30	Ernst Streeruwitz
1930	Johann Schober
1930	Carl Vaugoin
1930–1	Otto Ender
1931–2	Karl Buresch
1932–4	Engelbert Dollfuss
1934–8	Kurt von Schuschnigg
1938–45	*German rule*
1945	Karl Renner
1945–53	Leopold Figl
1953–61	Julius Raab
1961–4	Alfons Gorbach
1964–70	Josef Klaus
1970–83	Bruno Kreisky
1983–6	Fred Sinowatz
1986–97	Franz Vranitzky
1997–9	Viktor Klima
2000–	Wolfgang Schüssel

– Belgium –

Prime Minister

1899–1907	Paul de Smet de Nayer
1907–8	Jules de Trooz
1908–11	Frans Schollaert
1911–18	Charles de Broqueville
1918	Gerhard Cooreman
1918–20	Léon Delacroix
1920–1	Henri Carton de Wiart
1921–5	Georges Theunis
1925	Alois van de Vyvere
1925–6	Prosper Poullet
1926–31	Henri Jaspar
1931–2	Jules Renkin
1932–4	Charles de Broqueville
1934–5	Georges Theunis
1935–7	Paul van Zeeland

1937–8	Paul Émile Janson
1938–9	Paul Spaak
1939–45	Hubert Pierlot
1945–6	Achille van Acker
1946	Paul Spaak
1946	Achille van Acker
1946–7	Camille Huysmans
1947–9	Paul Spaak
1949–50	Gaston Eyskens
1950	Jean Pierre Duvieusart
1950–2	Joseph Pholien
1952–4	Jean van Houtte
1954–8	Achille van Acker
1958–61	Gaston Eyskens
1961–5	Théodore Lefèvre
1965–6	Pierre Harmel
1966–8	Paul Vanden Boeynants
1968–72	Gaston Eyskens
1973–4	Edmond Leburton
1974–8	Léo Tindemans
1978	Paul Vanden Boeynants
1979–81	Wilfried Martens
1981	Marc Eyskens
1981–91	Wilfried Martens
1992–9	Jean-Luc Dehaene
1999–	Guy Verhofstadt

– Canada –

Chief of State: British monarch, represented by Governor General

Prime Minister

1867–73	John A MacDonald *Con*
1873–8	Alexander Mackenzie *Lib*
1878–91	John A MacDonald *Con*
1891–2	John J C Abbot *Con*
1892–4	John S D Thompson *Con*
1894–6	Mackenzie Bowell *Con*
1896	Charles Tupper *Con*
1896–1911	Wilfrid Laurier *Lib*
1911–20	Robert Borden *Con*
1920–1	Arthur Meighen *Con*
1921–6	William Lyon Mackenzie King *Lib*
1926	Arthur Meighen *Con*
1926–30	William Lyon Mackenzie King *Lib*

1930–5	Richard Bedford Bennett Con	1931–2	Cheng Minxu (Ch'eng Ming-hsü) Acting President
1935–48	William Lyon Mackenzie King Lib	1932–43	Lin Sen (Lin Sen)
1948–57	Louis St Laurent Lib	1940–4	Wang Jingwei (Wang Ching-wei) In Japanese-occupied territory
1957–63	John George Diefenbaker Con		
1963–8	Lester Bowles Pearson Lib		
1968–79	Pierre Elliott Trudeau Lib	1943–9	Chiang K'ai-shek
1979–80	Joseph Clark Con	1945–9	Civil War
1980–4	Pierre Elliott Trudeau Lib	1949	Li Zongren (Li Tsung-jen)
1984	John Turner Lib		
1984–93	Brian Mulroney Con	*Premier*	
1993	Kim Campbell Con	1912	Tang Shaoyi (T'ang Shao-i)
1993–	Jean Chrétien Lib	1912–13	Zhao Bingjun (Chao Ping-chün)

Con = Conservative
Lib = Liberal

		1912–13	Xiong Xiling (Hsiung Hsi-ling)

— China ——————

		1914	Sun Baoyi (Sun Pao-chi)
❑ Qing (Ch'ing) dynasty		1915–16	no Premier
		1916–17	Duan Qirui (Tuan Ch'i-jui)
Emperor		1917–18	Wang Shizhen (Wang Shih-chen)
1875–1908	Guangxu (Kuang-hsü)		
1908–12	Xuantong (Hsüan-t'ung)	1918	Duan Qirui
		1918–19	Qian Nengxun (Ch'ien Neng-hsün)
Prime Minister			
1901–3	Ronglu (Jung-lu)	1919	Gong Xinzhan (Kung Hsin-chan)
1903–11	Prince Qing (Ch'ing)		
1912	Lu Zhengxiang (Lu Cheng-hsiang)	1919–20	Jin Yunpeng (Chin Yün-p'eng)
		1920	Sa Zhenbing (Sa Chen-ping)
1912	Yuan Shikai (Yüan Shih-k'ai)	1920–1	Jun Yunpeng
		1921–2	Liang Shiyi (Liang Shih-i)
❑ Republic of China		1922	Zhou Ziqi (Chow Tzu-ch'i) Acting Premier
President			
1912	Sun Yat-sen (Sun Yixian) Provisional	1922	Yan Huiqing (Yen Hui-ch'ing)
		1922	Wang Chonghui (Wang Ch'ung-hui)
1912–16	Yuan Shikai (Yüan Shih-k'ai)		
1916–17	Li Yuanhong (Li Yüan-hung)	1922–3	Wang Daxie (Wang Ta-hsieh)
1917–18	Feng Guozhang (Feng Kuo-chang)	1923	Zhang Shaozeng (Chang Shao-ts'eng)
		1923–4	Gao Lingwei (Kao Ling-wei)
1918–22	Xu Shichang (Hsü Shih-ch'ang)	1924	Sun Baoyi (Sun Pao-chi)
1921–5	Sun Yat-sen Canton Administration	1924	Gu Weijun (Ku Wei-chün) Acting Premier
1922–3	Li Yuanhong		
1923–4	Cao Kun (Ts'ao K'un)	1924	Yan Huiqing
1924–6	Duan Qirui (Tuan Ch'i-jui)	1924–5	Huang Fu (Huang Fu) Acting Premier
1926–7	Civil Disorder		
1927–8	Zhang Zuolin (Chang Tso-lin)	1925	Duan Qirui
1928–31	Chiang K'ai-shek (Jiang Jieshi)	1925–6	Xu Shiying (Hsü Shih-ying)
		1926	Jia Deyao (Chia Te-yao)

1926	Hu Weide (Hu Wei-te)
1926	Yan Huiqing
1926	Du Xigui (Tu Hsi-kuei)
1926–7	Gu Weijun
1927	*Civil Disorder*

President of the Executive Council

1928–30	Tan Yankai (T'an Yen-k'ai)
1930	T V Soong (Sung Tzu-wen) *Acting Premier*
1930	Wang Jingwei (Wang Ching-wei)
1930–1	Chiang K'ai-shek
1931–2	Sun Fo (Sun Fo)
1932–5	Wang Jingwei
1935–7	Chiang K'ai-shek
1937–8	Wang Chonghui (Wang Ch'ung-hui) *Acting Premier*
1938–9	Kong Xiangxi (K'ung Hsiang-hsi)
1939–44	Chiang K'ai-shek
1944–7	T V Soong
1945–9	*Civil War*
1948	Wang Wenhao (Wong Wen-hao)
1948–9	Sun Fo
1949	He Yingqin (Ho Ying-ch'in)
1949	Yan Xishan (Yen Hsi-shan)

◻ People's Republic of China

President

1949–59	Mao Zedong (Mao Tse-tung)
1959–68	Liu Shaoqi (Liu Shao-ch'i)
1968–75	Dong Biwu (Tung Pi-wu)
1975–6	Zhu De (Chu Te)
1976–8	Sung Qingling (Sung Ch'ing-ling)
1978–83	Ye Jianying (Yeh Chien-ying)
1983–8	Li Xiannian (Li Hsien-nien)
1988–93	Yang Shangkun (Yang Shang-k'un)
1993–	Jiang Zemin (Chiang Tse-min)

Prime Minister

1949–76	Zhou Enlai (Chou En-lai)
1976–80	Hua Guofeng (Huo Kuo-feng)
1980–7	Zhao Ziyang (Chao Tzu-yang)
1987–98	Li Peng (Li P'eng)
1998–	Zhu Rongji

Communist Party

Chairman

1935–76	Mao Zedong
1976–81	Hua Guofeng
1981–2	Hu Yaobang (Hu Yao-pang)

General Secretary

1982–7	Hu Yaobang
1987–9	Zhao Ziyang
1989–	Jiang Zemin

— Commonwealth —————

Secretary General

1965–75	Arnold Smith
1975–90	Shridath S Ramphal
1990–2000	Emeka Anyaoku
2000–	Donald C McKinnon

— Denmark —————

Prime Minister

1900–1	H Sehested
1901–5	J H Deuntzer
1905–8	J C Christensen
1908–9	N Neergaard
1909	L Holstein-Ledreborg
1909–10	C Th Zahle
1910–13	Klaus Berntsen
1913–20	C Th Zahle
1920	Otto Liebe
1920	M P Friis
1920–4	N Neergaard
1924–6	Thorvald Stauning
1926–9	Th Madsen-Mygdal
1929–42	Thorvald Stauning
1942	Wilhelm Buhl
1942–3	Erik Scavenius
1943–5	*No government*
1945	Wilhelm Buhl
1945–7	Knud Kristensen
1947–50	Hans Hedtoft
1950–3	Erik Eriksen
1953–5	Hans Hedtoft

1955–60	Hans Christian Hansen
1960–2	Viggo Kampmann
1962–8	Jens Otto Krag
1968–71	Hilmar Baunsgaard
1971–2	Jens Otto Krag
1972–3	Anker Jorgensen
1973–5	Poul Hartling
1975–82	Anker Jorgensen
1982–93	Poul Schlüter
1993–	Poul Nyrup Rasmussen

— European Commission —

President

1967–70	Jean Rey
1970–2	Franco M Malfatti
1972–3	Sicco L Mansholt
1973–7	Francois-Xavier Ortoli
1977–81	Roy Jenkins
1981–5	Gaston Thorn
1985–95	Jacques Delors
1995–9	Jacques Santer
1999–	Romano Prodi

— Finland —

President

1919–25	Kaarlo Juho Ståhlberg
1925–31	Lauri Kristian Relander
1931–7	Pehr Evind Svinhufvud
1937–40	Kyösti Kallio
1940–4	Risto Ryti
1944–6	Carl Gustaf Mannerheim
1946–56	Juho Kusti Paasikivi
1956–81	Urho Kekkonen
1982–94	Mauno Koivisto
1994–	Martti Ahtisaari

Prime Minister

1917–18	Pehr Evind Svinhufvud
1918	Juho Kusti Paasikivi
1918–19	Lauri Johannes Ingman
1919	Kaarlo Castrén
1919–20	Juho Vennola
1920–1	Rafael Erich
1921–2	Juho Vennola
1922	Aino Kaarlo Cajander
1922–4	Kyösti Kallio

1924	Aino Kaarlo Cajander
1924–5	Lauri Johannes Ingman
1925	Antti Agaton Tulenheimo
1925–6	Kyösti Kallio
1926–7	Väinö Tanner
1927–8	Juho Emil Sunila
1928–9	Oskari Mantere
1929–30	Kyösti Kallio
1930–1	Pehr Evind Svinhufvud
1931–2	Juhu Emil Sunila
1932–6	Toivo Kivimäki
1936–7	Kyösti Kallio
1937–9	Aino Kaarlo Cajander
1939–41	Risto Ryti
1941–3	Johann Rangell
1943–4	Edwin Linkomies
1944	Andreas Hackzell
1944	Urho Jonas Castrén
1944–5	Juho Kusti Paasikivi
1946–8	Mauno Pekkala
1948–50	Karl August Fagerholm
1950–3	Urho Kekkonen
1953–4	Sakari Tuomioja
1954	Ralf Törngren
1954–6	Urho Kekkonen
1956–7	Karl August Fagerholm
1957	Väinö Johannes Sukselainen
1957–8	Rainer von Fieandt
1958	Reino Lisakki Kuuskoski
1958–9	Karl August Fagerholm
1959–61	Väinö Johannes Sukselainen
1961–2	Martti Miettunen
1962–3	Ahti Karjalainen
1963–4	Reino Ragnar Lehto
1964–6	Johannes Virolainen
1966–8	Rafael Paasio
1968–70	Mauno Koivisto
1970	Teuvo Ensio Aura
1970–1	Ahti Karjalainen
1971–2	Teuvo Ensio Aura
1972	Rafael Paasio
1972–5	Kalevi Sorsa
1975	Keijo Antero Liinamaa
1975–7	Martti Miettunen
1977–9	Kalevi Sorsa
1979–82	Mauno Koivisto
1982–7	Kalevi Sorsa

1987–91	Harri Holkeri
1991–5	Esko Aho
1995–2000	Paavo Lipponen
2000–	Tarja Halonen

France

President

❏ Third Republic

1899–1906	Emile Loubet
1906–13	Armand Fallières
1913–20	Raymond Poincaré
1920	Paul Deschanel
1920–4	Alexandre Millerand
1924–31	Gaston Doumergue
1931–2	Paul Doumer
1932–40	Albert Lebrun

❏ Fourth Republic

1947–54	Vincent Auriol
1954–8	René Coty

❏ Fifth Republic

1958–69	Charles de Gaulle
1969–74	Georges Pompidou
1974–81	Valéry Giscard d'Estaing
1981–95	François Mitterrand
1995–	Jacques Chirac

Prime Minister

❏ Third Republic

1899–1902	Pierre Waldeck-Rousseau
1902–5	Emile Combes
1905–6	Maurice Rouvier
1906	Jean Sarrien
1906–9	Georges Clemenceau
1909–11	Aristide Briand
1911	Ernest Monis
1911–12	Joseph Caillaux
1912–13	Raymond Poincaré
1913	Aristide Briand
1913	Jean Louis Barthou
1913–14	Gaston Doumergue
1914	Alexandre Ribot
1914–15	René Viviani
1915–17	Aristide Briand
1917	Alexandre Ribot
1917	Paul Painlevé

1917–20	Georges Clemenceau
1920	Alexandre Millerand
1920–1	Georges Leygues
1921–2	Aristide Briand
1922–4	Raymond Poincaré
1924	Frédéric François-Marsal
1924–5	Édouard Herriot
1925	Paul Painlevé
1925–6	Aristide Briand
1926	Édouard Herriot
1926–9	Raymond Poincaré
1929	Aristide Briand
1929–30	André Tardieu
1930	Camille Chautemps
1930	André Tardieu
1930–1	Théodore Steeg
1931–2	Pierre Laval
1932	André Tardieu
1932	Édouard Herriot
1932–3	Joseph Paul-Boncour
1933	Édouard Daladier
1933	Albert Sarrault
1933–4	Camille Chautemps
1934	Édouard Daladier
1934	Gaston Doumergue
1934–5	Pierre-Étienne Flandin
1935	Fernand Bouisson
1935–6	Pierre Laval
1936	Albert Sarrault
1936–7	Léon Blum
1937–8	Camille Chautemps
1938	Léon Blum
1938–40	Édouard Daladier
1940	Paul Reynaud
1940	Philippe Pétain

❏ Vichy Government

1940–4	Philippe Pétain

❏ Provisional Government of the French Republic

1944–6	Charles de Gaulle
1946	Félix Gouin
1946	Georges Bidault

❏ Fourth Republic

1946–7	Léon Blum
1947	Paul Ramadier

1947–8	Robert Schuman
1948	André Marie
1948	Robert Schuman
1948–9	Henri Queuille
1949–50	Georges Bidault
1950	Henri Queuille
1950–1	René Pleven
1951	Henri Queuille
1951–2	René Pleven
1952	Edgar Faure
1952–3	Antoine Pinay
1953	René Mayer
1953–4	Joseph Laniel
1954–5	Pierre Mendès-France
1955–6	Edgar Faure
1956–7	Guy Mollet
1957	Maurice Bourgès-Maunoury
1957–8	Félix Gaillard
1958	Pierre Pflimlin
1958–9	Charles de Gaulle

❑ Fifth Republic

1959–62	Michel Debré
1962–8	Georges Pompidou
1968–9	Maurice Couve de Murville
1969–72	Jacques Chaban Delmas
1972–4	Pierre Mesmer
1974–6	Jacques Chirac
1976–81	Raymond Barre
1981–4	Pierre Mauroy
1984–6	Laurent Fabius
1986–8	Jacques Chirac
1988–91	Michel Rocard
1991–2	Édith Cresson
1992–3	Pierre Bérégovoy
1993–5	Édouard Balladur
1995–7	Alain Juppé
1997–	Lionel Jospin

—Germany——

❑ German Empire

Chancellor

1909–17	Theobald von Bethmann Hollweg
1917	Georg Michaelis
1917–18	Georg Graf von Hertling

1918	Prince Max von Baden
1918	Friedrich Ebert

❑ German Republic

President

1919–25	Friedrich Ebert
1925–34	Paul von Hindenburg

Reich Chancellor

1919	Philipp Scheidemann
1919–20	Gustav Bauer
1920	Hermann Müller
1920–1	Konstantin Fehrenbach
1921–2	Karl Joseph Wirth
1922–3	Wilhelm Cuno
1923	Gustav Stresemann
1923–4	Wilhelm Marx
1925–6	Hans Luther
1926–8	Wilhelm Marx
1928–30	Hermann Müller
1930–2	Heinrich Brüning
1932	Franz von Papen
1932–3	Kurt von Sleicher
1933	Adolf Hitler

Chancellor and Führer

1933–45	Adolf Hitler (*Führer from 1934*)
1945	Karl Dönitz

❑ German Democratic Republic (East Germany)

President

1949–60	Wilhelm Pieck

Chairman of the Council of State

1960–73	Walter Ernst Karl Ulbricht
1973–6	Willi Stoph
1976–89	Erich Honecker
1989	Egon Krenz
1989–90	Gregor Gysi *General Secretary as Chairman*

Premier

1949–64	Otto Grotewohl
1964–73	Willi Stoph
1973–6	Horst Sindermann

1976–89	Willi Stoph
1989–90	Hans Modrow
1990	Lothar de Maizière

❏ German Federal Republic (West Germany)

President

1949–59	Theodor Heuss
1959–69	Heinrich Lübke
1969–74	Gustav Heinemann
1974–9	Walter Scheel
1979–84	Karl Carstens
1984–90	Richard von Weizsäcker

Chancellor

1949–63	Konrad Adenauer
1963–6	Ludwig Erhard
1966–9	Kurt Georg Kiesinger
1969–74	Willy Brandt
1974–82	Helmut Schmidt
1982–90	Helmut Kohl

❏ Germany

President

1990–4	Richard von Weizsäcker
1994–9	Roman Herzog
1999–	Johannes Rau

Chancellor

1990–8	Helmut Kohl
1998–	Gerhard Schröder

──India──

President

1950–62	Rajendra Prasad
1962–7	Sarvepalli Radhakrishnan
1967–9	Zakir Husain
1969	Varahagiri Venkatagiri *Acting President*
1969	Mohammed Hidayatullah *Acting President*
1969–74	Varahagiri Venkatagiri
1974–7	Fakhruddin Ali Ahmed
1977	B D Jatti *Acting President*
1977–82	Neelam Sanjiva Reddy
1982–7	Giani Zail Singh

1987–92	Ramaswami Venkataraman
1992–7	Shankar Dayal Sharma
1997–	Kocheril Raman Narayanan

Prime Minister

1947–64	Jawaharlal Nehru
1964	Gulzari Lal Nanda *Acting Prime Minister*
1964–6	Lal Bahadur Shastri
1966	Gulzari Lal Nanda *Acting Prime Minister*
1966–77	Indira Gandhi
1977–9	Morarji Desai
1979–80	Charan Singh
1980–4	Indira Gandhi
1984–9	Rajiv Gandhi
1989–90	Vishwanath Pratap Singh
1990–1	Chandra Shekhar
1991–6	P V Narasimha Rao
1996	Atal Behari Vajpayee
1996–7	H D Deve Gowda
1997	Inder Kumar Gujral
1998–	Atal Behari Vajpayee

──Ireland──

Governor General

1922–7	Timothy Michael Healy
1927–32	James McNeill
1932–6	Donald Buckley

President

1938–45	Douglas Hyde
1945–59	Sean Thomas O'Kelly
1959–73	Éamon de Valera
1973–4	Erskine H Childers
1974–6	Carroll Daly
1976–90	Patrick J Hillery
1990–7	Mary Robinson
1997–	Mary McAleese

Prime Minister

1919–21	Éamon de Valera
1922	Arthur Griffiths
1922–32	William Cosgrave
1932–48	Éamon de Valera
1948–51	John Aloysius Costello
1951–4	Éamon de Valera

1954–7	John Aloysius Costello
1957–9	Éamon de Valera
1959–66	Sean Lemass
1966–73	John Lynch
1973–7	Liam Cosgrave
1977–9	John Lynch
1979–82	Charles Haughey
1982–7	Garrett Fitzgerald
1987–92	Charles Haughey
1992–4	Albert Reynolds
1994–7	John Bruton
1997–9	Bertie Ahern

— Italy —————————

❑ Italian Republic

President

1946–8	Enrico de Nicola
1948–55	Luigi Einaudi
1955–62	Giovanni Gronchi
1962–4	Antonio Segni
1964–71	Giuseppe Saragat
1971–8	Giovanni Leone
1978–85	Alessandro Pertini
1985–92	Francesco Cossiga
1992–9	Oscar Luigi Scalfaro
1999–2000	Carlo Azeglio Ciampi
2000	Massimo D'Alema
2000–	Giuliano Amato

❑ Kingdom of Italy

Prime Minister

1900–1	Giuseppe Saracco
1901–3	Giuseppe Zanardelli
1903–5	Giovanni Giolitti
1905–6	Alessandro Fortis
1906	Sydney Sonnino
1906–9	Giovanni Giolitti
1909–10	Sydney Sonnino
1910–11	Luigi Luzzatti
1911–14	Giovanni Giolitti
1914–16	Antonio Salandra
1916–17	Paolo Boselli
1917–19	Vittorio Emmanuele Orlando
1919–20	Francesco Saverio Nitti
1920–1	Giovanni Giolitti
1921–2	Ivanoe Bonomi

1922	Luigi Facta
1922–43	Benito Mussolini
1943–4	Pietro Badoglio
1944–5	Ivanoe Bonomi
1945	Ferrucio Parri
1945	Alcide de Gasperi

❑ Italian Republic

1946–53	Alcide de Gasperi
1953–4	Giuseppe Pella
1954	Amintore Fanfani
1954–5	Mario Scelba
1955–7	Antonio Segni
1957–8	Adone Zoli
1958–9	Amintore Fanfani
1959–60	Antonio Segni
1960	Fernando Tambroni
1960–3	Amintore Fanfani
1963	Giovanni Leone
1963–8	Aldo Moro
1968	Giovanni Leone
1968–70	Mariano Rumor
1970–2	Emilio Colombo
1972–4	Giulio Andreotti
1974–6	Aldo Moro
1976–9	Giulio Andreotti
1979–80	Francisco Cossiga
1980–1	Arnaldo Forlani
1981–2	Giovanni Spadolini
1982–3	Amintore Fanfani
1983–7	Bettino Craxi
1987	Amintore Fanfani
1987–8	Giovanni Goria
1988–9	Ciriaco de Mita
1989–92	Giulio Andreotti
1992–3	Giuliano Amato
1993–4	Carlo Azeglio Ciampi
1994	Silvio Berlusconi
1995–6	Lamberto Dini
1996–8	Romano Prodi
1998–	Massimo D'Alema

— Japan —————————

Chief of State (Emperor)

1867–1912	Mutsuhito (Meiji Era)
1912–26	Yoshihito (Taisho Era)
1926–89	Hirohito (Showa Era)

1989– Akihito (Heisei Era)

Prime Minister

1900–1	Hirobumi Ito
1901–6	Taro Katsura
1906–8	Kimmochi Saionji
1908–11	Taro Katsura
1911–12	Kimmochi Saionji
1912–13	Taro Katsura
1913–14	Gonnohyoe Yamamoto
1914–16	Shigenobu Okuma
1916–18	Masatake Terauchi
1918–21	Takashi Hara
1921–2	Korekiyo Takahashi
1922–3	Tomosaburo Kato
1923–4	Gonnohyoe Yamamoto
1924	Keigo Kiyoura
1924–6	Takaaki Kato
1926–7	Reijiro Wakatsuki
1927–9	Giichi Tanaka
1929–31	Osachi Hamaguchi
1931	Reijiro Wakatsuki
1931–2	Tsuyoshi Inukai
1932–4	Makoto Saito
1934–6	Keisuke Okada
1936–7	Koki Hirota
1937	Senjuro Hayashi
1937–9	Fumimaro Konoe
1939	Kiichiro Hiranuma
1939–40	Nobuyuki Abe
1940	Mitsumasa Yonai
1940–1	Fumimaro Konoe
1941–4	Hideki Tojo
1944–5	Kuniaki Koiso
1945	Kantaro Suzuki
1945	Naruhiko Higashikuni
1945–6	Kijuro Shidehara
1946–7	Shigeru Yoshida
1947–8	Tetsu Katayama
1948	Hitoshi Ashida
1948–54	Shigeru Yoshida
1954–6	Ichiro Hatoyama
1956–7	Tanzan Ishibashi
1957–60	Nobusuke Kishi
1960–4	Hayato Ikeda
1964–72	Eisaku Sato
1972–4	Kakuei Tanaka
1974–6	Takeo Miki
1976–8	Takeo Fukuda
1978–80	Masayoshi Ohira
1980–2	Zenko Suzuki
1982–7	Yasuhiro Nakasone
1987–9	Noburu Takeshita
1989	Sasuke Uno
1989–91	Toshiki Kaifu
1991–93	Kiichi Miyazawa
1993	Morihiro Hosokawa
1994	Tsutoma Hata
1994–6	Tomiichi Murayama
1996–8	Ryutaro Hashimoto
1998–2000	Keizo Obuchi
2000	Mikio Aoki *Interim Prime Minister*
2000–	Yoshiro Mori

—Liechtenstein —————

Prime Minister

1928–45	Franz Josef Hoop
1945–62	Alexander Friek
1962–70	Gérard Batliner
1970–4	Alfred J Hilbe
1974–8	Walter Kieber
1978–93	Hans Brunhart
1993	Markus Büchel
1994–	Mario Frick

—Luxembourg —————

Prime Minister

1889–1915	Paul Eyschen
1915	Mathias Mongenast
1915–16	Hubert Loutsch
1916–17	Victor Thorn
1917–18	Léon Kaufmann
1918–25	Emil Reuter
1925–6	Pierre Prum
1926–37	Joseph Bech
1937–53	Pierre Dupong (*in exile 1940–4*)
1953–8	Joseph Bech
1958	Pierre Frieden
1959–69	Pierre Werner
1969–79	Gaston Thorn

1979-84	Pierre Werner
1984-95	Jacques Santer
1995-	Jean-Claude Juncker

The Netherlands

Prime Minister

1897-1901	Nicholas G Pierson
1901-5	Abraham Kuyper
1905-8	Theodoor H de Meester
1908-13	Theodorus Heemskerk
1913-18	Pieter W A Cort van der Linden
1918-25	Charles J M Ruys de Beerenbrouck
1925-6	Hendrikus Colijn
1926	Dirk J de Geer
1926-33	Charles J M Ruys de Beerenbrouck
1933-9	Hendrikus Colijn
1939-40	Dirk J de Geer
1940-5	Pieter S Gerbrandy (*in exile*)
1945-6	Willem Schemerhorn / Willem Drees
1946-8	Louis J M Beel
1948-51	Willem Drees / Josephus R H van Schaik
1951-8	Willem Drees
1958-9	Louis J M Beel
1959-63	Jan E de Quay
1963-5	Victor G M Marijnen
1965-6	Joseph M L T Cals
1966-7	Jelle Zijlstra
1967-71	Petrus J S de Jong
1971-3	Barend W Biesheuvel
1973-7	Joop M Den Uyl
1977-82	Andreas A M van Agt
1982-94	Ruud F M Lubbers
1994-	Wim Kok

New Zealand

Chief of State: British monarch, represented by Governor General

Prime Minister

1893-1906	Richard John Seddon *Lib*
1906	William Hall-Jones *Lib*
1906-12	Joseph George Ward *Lib/Nat*
1912	Thomas Mackenzie *Nat*
1912-25	William Ferguson Massey *Ref*
1925	Francis Henry Dillon Bell *Ref*
1925-8	Joseph Gordon Coates *Ref*
1928-30	Joseph George Ward *Lib/Nat*
1930-5	George William Forbes *Un*
1935-40	Michael Joseph Savage *Lab*
1940-9	Peter Fraser *Lab*
1949-57	Sidney George Holland *Nat*
1957	Keith Jacka Holyoake *Nat*
1957-60	Walter Nash *Lab*
1960-72	Keith Jacka Holyoake *Nat*
1972	John Ross Marshall *Nat*
1972-4	Norman Eric Kirk *Lab*
1974-5	Wallace Edward Rowling *Lab*
1975-84	Robert David Muldoon *Nat*
1984-89	David Russell Lange *Lab*
1989-90	Geoffrey Palmer *Lab*
1990	Mike Moore *Lab*
1990-7	Jim Bolger *Nat*
1997-9	Jenny Shipley *Nat*
1999-	Helen Clark *Lab*

Lab = Labour
Lib = Liberal
Nat = National
Ref = Reform
Un = United

Norway

Prime Minister

1898-1902	Johannes Steen
1902-3	Otto Albert Blehr
1903-5	George Francis Hagerup
1905-7	Christian Michelsen
1907-8	Jørgen Løvland
1908-10	Gunnar Knudsen
1910-12	Wollert Konow

1912–13	Jens Bratlie
1913–20	Gunnar Knudsen
1920–1	Otto Bahr Halvorsen
1921–3	Otto Albert Blehr
1923	Otto Bahr Halvorsen
1923–4	Abraham Berge
1924–6	Johan Ludwig Mowinckel
1926–8	Ivar Lykke
1928	Christopher Hornsrud
1928–31	Johan Ludwig Mowinckel
1931–2	Peder L Kolstad
1932–3	Jens Hundseid
1933–5	Johan Ludwig Mowinckel
1935–45	Johan Nygaardsvold
1945–51	Einar Gerhardsen
1951–5	Oscar Torp
1955–63	Einar Gerhardsen
1963	John Lyng
1963–5	Einar Gerhardsen
1965–71	Per Borten
1971–2	Trygve Bratteli
1972–3	Lars Korvald
1973–6	Trygve Bratteli
1976–81	Odvar Nordli
1981	Gro Harlem Brundtland
1981–6	Kåre Willoch
1986–9	Gro Harlem Brundtland
1989–90	Jan P Syse
1990–6	Gro Harlem Brundtland
1996–7	Thorbjørn Jagland
1997–2000	Kjell Magne Bondevik
2000–	Jens Stoltenberg

Portugal

President

❑ First Republic

1910–11	Teófilo Braga
1911–15	Manuel José de Arriaga
1915	Teófilo Braga
1915–17	Bernardino Machado
1917–18	Sidónio Pais
1918–19	João do Canto e Castro
1919–23	António José de Almeida
1923–5	Manuel Teixeira Gomes
1925–6	Bernardino Machado

❑ New State

1926	*Military Junta* (José Mendes Cabeçadas)
1926	*Military Junta* (Manuel de Oliveira Gomes da Costa)
1926–51	António Oscar Fragoso Carmona
1951–8	Francisco Craveiro Lopes
1958–74	Américo de Deus Tomás

❑ Second Republic

1974	*Military Junta* (António Spínola)
1974–6	*Military Junta* (Francisco da Costa Gomes)

❑ Third Republic

1976–86	António dos Santos Ramalho Eanes
1986–96	Mario Soares
1996–	Jorge Sampaio

Prime Minister

1932–68	António de Oliveira Salazar
1968–74	Marcelo Caetano
1974	Adelino da Palma Carlos
1974–5	Vasco Gonçalves
1975–6	José Pinheiro de Azevedo
1976–8	Mário Soares
1978	Alfredo Nobre da Costa
1978–9	Carlos Alberto de Mota Pinto
1979	Maria de Lurdes Pintasilgo
1980–1	Francisco de Sá Carneiro
1981–3	Francisco Pinto Balsemão
1983–5	Mário Soares
1985–95	Aníbal Cavaço Silva
1995–	António Guterres

Russia

President

1991–9	Boris Yeltsin
2000–	Vladimir Putin

Prime Minister

1991–2	Boris Yeltsin
1992	Yegor Gaidar *Acting Prime Minister*

1992–8	Viktor Chernomyrdin
1998	Sergei Kiriyenko
1998	Viktor Chernomyrdin *Acting Prime Minister*
1998	Yevgeny Primakov
1999	Sergei Stephasin
1999–2000	Vladimir Putin
2000–	Mikhail Kasyanov

–Spain

□ Second Republic

President

| 1931–6 | Niceto Alcalá Zamora y Torres |
| 1936 | Diego Martínez Barrio *Acting President* |

Civil War

| 1936–9 | Manuel Azaña y Díez |
| 1936–9 | Miguel Cabanellas Ferrer |

□ Nationalist Government

Chief of State

| 1936–75 | Francisco Franco Bahamonde |

Monarch

| 1975– | Juan Carlos I |

Prime Minister

1900–1	Marcelo de Azcárraga y Palmero
1901–2	Práxedes Mateo Sagasta
1902–3	Francisco Silvela y Le-Vielleuze
1903	Raimundo Fernández Villaverde
1903–4	Antonio Maura y Montaner
1904–5	Marcelo de Azcárraga y Palmero
1905	Raimundo Fernández Villaverde
1905	Eugenio Montero Ríos
1905–6	Segismundo Moret y Prendergast
1906	José López Domínguez
1906	Segismundo Moret y Prendergast
1906–7	Antonio Aguilar y Correa
1907–9	Antonio Maura y Montaner

1909–10	Segismundo Moret y Prendergast
1910–12	José Canalejas y Méndez
1912	Álvaro Figueroa y Torres
1912–13	Manuel García Prieto
1913–15	Eduardo Dato y Iradier
1915–17	Álvaro Figueroa y Torres
1917	Manuel García Prieto
1917	Eduardo Dato y Iradier
1917–18	Manuel García Prieto
1918	Antonio Maura y Montaner
1918	Manuel García Prieto
1918–19	Álvaro Figueroa y Torres
1919	Antonio Maura y Montaner
1919	Joaquín Sánchez de Toca
1919–20	Manuel Allendesalazar
1920–1	Eduardo Dato y Iradier
1921	Gabino Bugallal Araujo *Acting Prime Minister*
1921	Manuel Allendesalazar
1921–2	Antonio Maura y Montaner
1922	José Sánchez Guerra y Martínez
1922–3	Manuel García Prieto
1923–30	Miguel Primo de Rivera y Oraneja
1930–1	Dámaso Berenguer y Fusté
1931	Juan Bautista Aznar-Cabañas
1931	Niceto Alcalá Zamora y Torres
1931–3	Manuel Azaña y Díez
1933	Alejandro Lerroux y García
1933	Diego Martínez Barrio
1933–4	Alejandro Lerroux y García
1934	Ricardo Samper Ibáñez
1934–5	Alejandro Lerroux y García
1935	Joaquín Chapaprieta y Terragosa
1935–6	Manuel Portela Valladares
1936	Manuel Azaña y Díez
1936	Santiago Casares Quiroga
1936	Diego Martínez Barrio
1936	José Giral y Pereyra
1936–7	Francisco Largo Caballero
1937–9	Juan Negrín

Chairman of the Council of Ministers

| 1939–73 | Francisco Franco Bahamonde |

Prime Minister

1973	Torcuato Fernández Miranda y Hevía *Acting Prime Minister*
1973–6	Carlos Arias Navarro
1976–81	Adolfo Suárez
1981–2	Calvo Sotelo
1982–96	Felipe González
1996–	José María Aznar

—Sweden—

Prime Minister

1900–2	Fredrik von Otter
1902–5	Erik Gustaf Boström
1905	Johan Ramstedt
1905	Christian Lundeberg
1905–6	Karl Staaf
1906–11	Arvid Lindman
1911–14	Karl Staaf
1914–17	Hjalmar Hammarskjöld
1917	Carl Swartz
1917–20	Nils Edén
1920	Hjalmar Branting
1920–1	Louis de Geer
1921	Oscar von Sydow
1921–3	Hjalmar Branting
1923–4	Ernst Trygger
1924–5	Hjalmar Branting
1925–6	Rickard Sandler
1926–8	Carl Gustaf Ekman
1928–30	Arvid Lindman
1930–2	Carl Gustaf Ekman
1932	Felix Hamrin
1932–6	Per Albin Hansson
1936	Axel Pehrsson-Branstorp
1936–46	Per Albin Hansson
1946–69	Tage Erlander
1969–76	Olof Palme
1976–8	Thorbjörn Fälldin
1978–9	Ola Ullsten
1979–82	Thorbjörn Fälldin
1982–6	Olof Palme
1986–91	Ingvar Carlsson
1991–4	Carl Bildt
1994–6	Ingvar Carlsson
1996–	Göran Persson

—Switzerland—

President

1900	Walter Hauser
1901	Ernst Brenner
1902	Joseph Zemp
1903	Adolf Deucher
1904	Robert Comtesse
1905	Marc-Emile Ruchet
1906	Ludwig Forrer
1907	Eduard Müller
1908	Ernst Brenner
1909	Adolf Deucher
1910	Robert Comtesse
1911	Marc-Emile Ruchet
1912	Ludwig Forrer
1913	Eduard Müller
1914	Arthur Hoffmann
1915	Giuseppe Motta
1916	Camille Decoppet
1917	Edmund Schulthess
1918	Felix Calonder
1919	Gustave Ador
1920	Giuseppe Motta
1921	Edmund Schulthess
1922	Robert Haab
1923	Karl Scheurer
1924	Ernest Chuard
1925	Jean-Marie Musy
1926	Heinrich Häberlin
1927	Giuseppe Motta
1928	Edmund Schulthess
1929	Robert Haab
1930	Jean-Marie Musy
1931	Heinrich Häberlin
1932	Giuseppe Motta
1933	Edmund Schulthess
1934	Marcel Pilet-Golaz
1935	Rudolf Minger
1936	Albert Meyer
1937	Giuseppe Motta
1938	Johannes Baumann
1939	Philipp Etter
1940	Marcel Pilet-Golaz
1941	Ernst Wetter
1942	Philipp Etter
1943	Enrico Celio

POLITICAL LEADERS 1900–2000

1944	Walter Stampfli
1945	Eduard von Steiger
1946	Karl Kobelt
1947	Philipp Etter
1948	Enrico Celio
1949	Ernst Nobs
1950	Max Petitpierre
1951	Eduard von Steiger
1952	Karl Kobelt
1953	Philipp Etter
1954	Rodolphe Rubattel
1955	Max Petitpierre
1956	Markus Feldmann
1957	Hans Streuli
1958	Thomas Holenstein
1959	Paul Chaudet
1960	Max Petitpierre
1961	Friedrich Wahlen
1962	Paul Chaudet
1963	Willy Spühler
1964	Ludwig von Moos
1965	Hans Peter Tschudi
1966	Hans Schaffner
1967	Roger Bonvin
1968	Willy Spühler
1969	Ludwig von Moos
1970	Hans Peter Tschudi
1971	Rudolf Gnägi
1972	Nello Celio
1973	Roger Bonvin
1974	Ernst Brugger
1975	Pierre Graber
1976	Rudolf Gnägi
1977	Kurt Furgler
1978	Willi Ritschard
1979	Hans Hürlimann
1980	Georges-André Chevallaz
1981	Kurt Furgler
1982	Fritz Honegger
1983	Pierre Aubert
1984	Leon Schlumpf
1985	Kurt Furgler
1986	Alphons Egli
1987	Pierre Aubert
1988	Otto Stich
1989	Jean-Pascal Delamuraz
1990	Arnold Koller

1991	Flavio Cotti
1992	René Felber
1993	Adolf Ogi
1994	Otto Stich
1995	Kaspar Villiger
1996	Jean-Pascal Delamuraz
1997	Arnold Koller
1998	Flavio Cotti
1999	Ruth Dreifuss
2000	Adolf Ogi

United Kingdom

Prime Minister

1721–42	Robert Walpole *Whig*
1742–3	Earl of Wilmington (Spencer Compton) *Whig*
1743–54	Henry Pelham *Whig*
1754–6	Duke of Newcastle (Thomas Pelham-Holles) *Whig*
1756–7	Duke of Devonshire (William Cavendish) *Whig*
1757–62	Duke of Newcastle *Whig*
1762–3	Earl of Bute (John Stuart) *Tory*
1763–5	George Grenville *Whig*
1765–6	Marquess of Rockingham (Charles Watson Wentworth) *Whig*
1766–70	Duke of Grafton (Augustus Henry Fitzroy) *Whig*
1770–82	Lord North (Frederick North) *Tory*
1782	Marquess of Rockingham *Whig*
1782–3	Earl of Shelburne (William Petty-Fitzmaurice) *Whig*
1783	Duke of Portland (William Henry Cavendish) *Coal*
1783–1801	William Pitt *Tory*
1801–4	Henry Addington *Tory*
1804–6	William Pitt *Tory*
1806–7	Lord Grenville (William Wyndham) *Whig*
1807–9	Duke of Portland *Tory*
1809–12	Spencer Perceval *Tory*
1812–27	Earl of Liverpool (Robert Banks Jenkinson) *Tory*

160

1827	George Canning *Tory*
1827–8	Viscount Goderich (Frederick John Robinson) *Tory*
1828–30	Duke of Wellington (Arthur Wellesley) *Tory*
1830–4	Earl Grey (Charles Grey) *Whig*
1834	Viscount Melbourne (William Lamb) *Whig*
1834–5	Robert Peel *Con*
1835–41	Viscount Melbourne *Whig*
1841–6	Robert Peel *Con*
1846–52	Lord John Russell *Lib*
1852	Earl of Derby (Edward George Stanley) *Con*
1852–5	Lord Aberdeen (George Hamilton-Gordon) *Peelite*
1855–8	Viscount Palmerston (Henry John Temple) *Lib*
1858–9	Earl of Derby *Con*
1859–65	Viscount Palmerston *Lib*
1865–6	Lord John Russell *Lib*
1866–8	Earl of Derby *Con*
1868	Benjamin Disraeli *Con*
1868–74	William Ewart Gladstone *Lib*
1874–80	Benjamin Disraeli *Con*
1880–5	William Ewart Gladstone *Lib*
1885–6	Marquess of Salisbury (Robert Gascoyne-Cecil) *Con*
1886	William Ewart Gladstone *Lib*
1886–92	Marquess of Salisbury *Con*
1892–4	William Ewart Gladstone *Lib*
1894–5	Earl of Rosebery (Archibald Philip Primrose) *Lib*
1895–1902	Marquess of Salisbury *Con*
1902–5	Arthur James Balfour *Con*
1905–8	Henry Campbell-Bannerman *Lib*
1908–15	Herbert Henry Asquith *Lib*
1915–16	Herbert Henry Asquith *Coal*
1916–22	David Lloyd George *Coal*
1922–3	Andrew Bonar Law *Con*
1923–4	Stanley Baldwin *Con*
1924	James Ramsay MacDonald *Lab*
1924–9	Stanley Baldwin *Con*
1929–31	James Ramsay MacDonald *Lab*
1931–5	James Ramsay MacDonald *Nat*
1935–7	Stanley Baldwin *Nat*
1937–40	Arthur Neville Chamberlain *Nat*
1940–5	Winston Churchill *Coal*
1945–51	Clement Attlee *Lab*
1951–5	Winston Churchill *Con*
1955–7	Anthony Eden *Con*
1957–63	Harold Macmillan *Con*
1963–4	Alec Douglas-Home *Con*
1964–70	Harold Wilson *Lab*
1970–4	Edward Heath *Con*
1974–6	Harold Wilson *Lab*
1976–9	James Callaghan *Lab*
1979–90	Margaret Thatcher *Con*
1990–7	John Major *Con*
1997–	Tony Blair *Lab*

Coal = Coalition
Con = Conservative
Lab = Labour
Lib = Liberal
Nat = Nationalist

—United Nations —————

Secretary General

1946–53	Trygve Lie *Norway*
1953–61	Dag Hammarskjöld *Sweden*
1962–71	U Thant *Burma*
1972–81	Kurt Waldheim *Austria*
1982–91	Javier Pérez de Cuéllar *Peru*
1992–6	Boutros Boutros-Ghali *Egypt*
1997–	Kofi Annan *Ghana*

—United States of America ———

President

Vice President in parentheses

1789–97	George Washington (1st) (John Adams)
1797–1801	John Adams (2nd) *Fed* (Thomas Jefferson)
1801–9	Thomas Jefferson (3rd) *Dem-Rep* (Aaron Burr, 1801–5) (George Clinton, 1805–9)

161

1809–17 James Madison (4th) *Dem-Rep* (George Clinton, 1809–12) *no Vice President 1812–13* (Elbridge Gerry, 1813–14) *no Vice President 1814–17*

1817–25 James Monroe (5th) *Dem-Rep* (Daniel D Tompkins)

1825–9 John Quincy Adams (6th) *Dem-Rep* (John C Calhoun)

1829–37 Andrew Jackson (7th) *Dem* (John C Calhoun, 1829–32) *no Vice President 1832–3* (Martin van Buren, 1833–7)

1837–41 Martin van Buren (8th) *Dem* (Richard M Johnson)

1841 William Henry Harrison (9th) *Whig* (John Tyler)

1841–5 John Tyler (10th) *Whig no Vice President*

1845–9 James Knox Polk (11th) *Dem* (George M Dallas)

1849–50 Zachary Taylor (12th) *Whig* (Millard Fillmore)

1850–3 Millard Fillmore (13th) *Whig no Vice President*

1853–7 Franklin Pierce (14th) *Dem* (William R King, 1853) *no Vice President 1853–7*

1857–61 James Buchanan (15th) *Dem* (John C Breckinridge)

1861–5 Abraham Lincoln (16th) *Rep* (Hannibal Hamlin, 1861–5) (Andrew Johnson, 1865)

1865–9 Andrew Johnson (17th) *Dem-Nat no Vice President*

1869–77 Ulysses Simpson Grant (18th) *Rep* (Schuyler Colfax, 1869–73) (Henry Wilson, 1873–5) *no Vice President 1875–7*

1877–81 Rutherford Birchard Hayes (19th) *Rep* (William A Wheeler)

1881 James Abram Garfield (20th) *Rep* (Chester A Arthur)

1881–5 Chester Alan Arthur (21st) *Rep no Vice President*

1885–9 Grover Cleveland (22nd) *Dem* (Thomas A Hendricks, 1885) *no Vice President 1885–9*

1889–93 Benjamin Harrison (23rd) *Rep* (Levi P Morton)

1893–7 Grover Cleveland (24th) *Dem* (Adlai E Stevenson)

1897–1901 William McKinley (25th) *Rep* (Garrat A Hobart, 1897–9) *no Vice President 1899–1901* (Theodore Roosevelt, 1901)

1901–9 Theodore Roosevelt (26th) *Rep no Vice President* 1901–5 (Charles W Fairbanks, 1905–9)

1909–13 William Howard Taft (27th) *Rep* (James S Sherman, 1909–12) *no Vice President 1912–13*

1913–21 Woodrow Wilson (28th) *Dem* (Thomas R Marshall)

1921–3 Warren Gamaliel Harding (29th) *Rep* (Calvin Coolidge)

1923–9 Calvin Coolidge (30th) *Rep no Vice President 1923–5* (Charles G Dawes, 1925–9)

1929–33 Herbert Clark Hoover (31st) *Rep* (Charles Curtis)

1933–45 Franklin Delano Roosevelt (32nd) *Dem* (John N Garner, 1933–41) (Henry A Wallace, 1941–5) (Harry S Truman, 1945)

1945–53 Harry S Truman (33rd) *Dem no Vice President 1945–9* (Alben W Barkley, 1949–53)

1953–61 Dwight David Eisenhower (34th) *Rep* (Richard M Nixon)

1961–3 John Fitzgerald Kennedy (35th) *Dem* (Lyndon B Johnson)

1963–9 Lyndon Baines Johnson (36th) *Dem no Vice President 1963–5* (Hubert H Humphrey, 1965–9)

1969–74	Richard Milhous Nixon (37th) Rep (Spiro T Agnew, 1969–73) no Vice President 1973, Oct–Dec (Gerald R Ford, 1973–4)
1974–7	Gerald Rudolph Ford (38th) Rep no Vice President 1974, Aug–Dec (Nelson A Rockefeller, 1974–7)
1977–81	Jimmy Carter (39th) Dem (Walter F Mondale)
1981–9	Ronald Wilson Reagan (40th) Rep (George H W Bush)
1989–93	George Herbert Walker Bush (41st) Rep (J Danforth Quayle)
1993–2001	William Jefferson Blythe IV Clinton (42nd) Dem (Albert Gore)

Dem = Democrat
Fed = Federalist
Nat = National Union
Rep = Republican

USSR (Union of Soviet Socialist Republics)

No longer in existence, but included for reference.

President

1917	Leo Borisovich Kamenev
1917–19	Yakov Mikhailovich Sverlov
1919–46	Mikhail Ivanovich Kalinin
1946–53	Nikolai Shvernik
1953–60	Klimentiy Voroshilov
1960–4	Leonid Brezhnev
1964–5	Anastas Mikoyan
1965–77	Nikolai Podgorny
1977–82	Leonid Brezhnev
1982–3	Vasily Kuznetsov Acting President
1983–4	Yuri Andropov
1984	Vasily Kuznetsov Acting

	President
1984–5	Konstantin Chernenko
1985	Vasily Kuznetsov Acting President
1985–8	Andrei Gromyko
1988–90	Mikhail Gorbachev

Executive President

1990–1	Mikhail Gorbachev
1991	Gennady Yanayev Acting President
1991	Mikhail Gorbachev

Chairman (Prime Minister)

Council of Ministers

| 1917 | Georgy Evgenyevich Lvov |
| 1917 | Aleksandr Fyodorovich Kerensky |

Council of People's Commissars

1917–24	Vladimir Ilyich Lenin
1924–30	Aleksei Ivanovich Rykov
1930–41	Vyacheslav Mikhailovich Molotov
1941–53	Josef Stalin

Council of Ministers

1953–5	Georgiy Malenkov
1955–8	Nikolai Bulganin
1958–64	Nikita Khrushchev
1964–80	Alexei Kosygin
1980–5	Nikolai Tikhonov
1985–90	Nikolai Ryzhkov
1990–1	Yuri Maslyukov Acting Chairman
1991	Valentin Pavlov

General Secretary

1922–53	Josef Stalin
1953	Georgiy Malenkov
1953–64	Nikita Khrushchev
1964–82	Leonid Brezhnev
1982–4	Yuri Andropov
1984–5	Konstantin Chernenko
1985–91	Mikhail Gorbachev

SOCIAL STRUCTURE

Nations of the world

Where more than one language is shown within a country, the status of the languages may not be equal. Some languages have a 'semi-official' status, or are used for a restricted set of purposes, such as trade or tourism.

Population census estimates are for 1996 or later.

English name	Capital	Official language(s)	Population
Afghanistan	Kabul	Dari, Pushtu	22 264 000
Albania	Tirana	Albanian	3 420 000
Algeria	Algiers	Arabic	28 566 000
Andorra	Andorra la Vella	Catalan, French, Spanish	64 311
Angola	Luanda	Portuguese	11 904 000
Antigua and Barbuda	St John's	English	64 400
Argentina	Buenos Aires	Spanish	34 995 000
Armenia	Yerevan	Armenian	3 754 000
Australia	Canberra	English	18 287 000
Austria	Vienna	German	8 102 000
Azerbaijan	Baku	Azeri	7 570 000
The Bahamas	Nassau	English	280 000
Bahrain	Manama	Arabic	598 000
Bangladesh	Dacca	Bengali	123 100 000
Barbados	Bridgetown	English	265 000
Belarus	Minsk	Belarusian, Russian	10 264 300
Belgium	Brussels	Flemish, French, German	10 140 000
Belize	Belmopan	English	219 000
Benin	Porto Novo	French	5 574 000
Bhutan	Thimphu	Dzongkha	1 622 000
Bolivia	La Paz	Spanish	7 593 000
Bosnia-Herzegovina	Sarajevo	Serbo-Croat	3 524 000
Botswana	Gaborone	English, Setswana	1 478 000
Brazil	Brasília	Portuguese	157 872 000
Brunei	Bandar Seri Begawan	Malay, English	290 000
Bulgaria	Sofia	Bulgarian	8 366 000
Burkina Faso	Ouagadougou	French	10 615 000
Burma ► Myanmar			
Burundi	Bujumbura	French, Kirundi	6 134 000
Cambodia	Phnom Penh	Khmer	10 081 000
Cameroon	Yaoundé	English, French	13 609 000
Canada	Ottawa	English, French	29 784 000
Cape Verde	Praia	Portuguese	403 000

English name	Capital	Official language(s)	Population
Central African Republic	Bangui	French, Sango	3 274 000
Chad	N'Djamena	French, Arabic	6 543 000
Chile	Santiago	Spanish	14 375 000
China	Beijing	Mandarin Chinese	1 218 709 000
Colombia	Bogotá	Spanish	35 652 000
Comoros	Moroni	French, Arabic	630 000
Congo	Brazzaville	French, Kongo	2 665 000
Congo, Democratic Republic of	Kinshasa	French, Lingala	45 259 000
Costa Rica	San José	Spanish	3 400 000
Côte d'Ivoire (Ivory Coast)	Yamoussoukro	French	14 733 000
Croatia	Zagreb	Serbo-Croat	4 775 000
Cuba	Havana	Spanish	11 117 000
Cyprus	Nicosia	Greek, Turkish	767 000
Czech Republic	Prague	Czech	10 316 000
Denmark	Copenhagen	Danish	5 244 000
Djibouti	Djibouti	Arabic, French	604 000
Dominica	Roseau	English, French Creole	73 800
Dominican Republic	Santo Domingo	Spanish	7 994 000
Ecuador	Quito	Spanish	11 698 000
Egypt	Cairo	Arabic	60 896 000
El Salvador	San Salvador	Spanish	5 897 000
Equatorial Guinea	Malabo	Spanish	406 000
Eritrea	Asmara	Arabic, Tigrinya	3 627 000
Estonia	Tallinn	Estonian	1 475 000
Ethiopia	Addis Ababa	Amharic	56 713 000
Federated States of Micronesia	Palikir, on Ponape	English	119 000
Fiji	Suva	English	802 000
Finland	Helsinki	Finnish, Swedish	5 132 000
France	Paris	French	58 392 000
Gabon	Libreville	French	1 173 000
The Gambia	Banjul	English	1 148 000
Georgia	Tbilisi	Georgian, Russian	5 361 000
Germany	Berlin	German	81 891 000
Ghana	Accra	English	16 904 000
Greece	Athens	Greek	10 493 000
Greenland	Nuuk	Danish, Greenlandic	56 000
Grenada	St George's	English	97 900
Guatemala	Guatemala City	Spanish	10 928 000
Guinea	Conakry	French	6 903 000
Guinea-Bissau	Bissau	Portuguese, Crioulo	1 096 000
Guyana	Georgetown	English	825 000
Haiti	Port-au-Prince	French, Creole	7 041 000

English name	Capital	Official language(s)	Population
Holland ► Netherlands, The			
Honduras	Tegucigalpa	Spanish	5 666 000
Hungary	Budapest	Hungarian	10 201 000
Iceland	Reykjavik	Icelandic	270 000
India	New Delhi	Hindi, English	952 969 000
Indonesia	Jakarta	Bahasa Indonesia	198 189 000
Iran	Tehran	Farsi	62 231 000
Iraq	Baghdad	Arabic	21 422 000
Ireland	Dublin	Irish, English	3 599 000
Israel	Tel Aviv-Jaffa	Hebrew, Arabic	5 481 000
Italy	Rome	Italian	57 500 000
Ivory Coast ► Côte d'Ivoire			
Jamaica	Kingston	English	2 505 000
Japan	Tokyo	Japanese	125 612 000
Jordan	Amman	Arabic	4 333 000
Jugoslavia ► Yugoslavia			
Kampuchea ► Cambodia			
Kazakhstan	Astana	Kazakh	17 155 000
Kenya	Nairobi	(Ki)Swahili	29 137 000
Kiribati	Bairiki, on Tarawa	English, Gilbertese	81 800
Korea, North	Pyongyang	Korean	23 904 000
Korea, South	Seoul	Korean	45 232 000
Kuwait	Kuwait City	Arabic	1 576 000
Kyrgyzstan	Bishkek	Kyrgyz, Russian	4 512 000
Laos	Vientiane	Lao	5 023 000
Latvia	Riga	Latvian	2 490 000
Lebanon	Beirut	Arabic	2 919 000
Lesotho	Maseru	English, Sesotho	2 017 000
Liberia	Monrovia	English	2 110 000
Libya	Tripoli	Arabic	5 445 000
Liechtenstein	Vaduz	German	31 400
Lithuania	Vilnius	Lithuanian	3 707 000
Luxembourg	Luxembourg	French, German, Letzebuergesch	415 000
Macedonia	Skopje	Macedonian	1 968 000
Madagascar	Antananarivo	Malagasy, French	13 671 000
Malawi	Lilongwe	Chichewa, English	9 453 000
Malaysia	Kuala Lumpur	Bahasa Malaysia	20 359 000
Maldives	Malé	Dhivehi	266 000
Mali	Bamako	French	10 400 000
Malta	Valletta	English, Maltese	373 000
Marshall Islands	Dalap-Uliga-Darrit, on Majuro	Marshallese	58 500
Mauritania	Nouakchott	French, Arabic	2 333 000
Mauritius	Port Louis	English	1 141 000
Mexico	Mexico City	Spanish	92 711 000

English name	Capital	Official language(s)	Population
Moldova	Kishinev	Moldovan	4 372 000
Monaco	Monaco	French	30 500
Mongolia	Ulan Bator	Khalkha	2 334 000
Morocco	Rabat	Arabic	26 736 000
Mozambique	Maputo	Portuguese	17 878 000
Myanmar (Burma)	Rangoon	Burmese	45 976 000
Namibia	Windhoek	English	1 709 000
Nauru	Yaren District	Nauruan, English	10 600
Nepal	Kathmandu	Nepali	20 892 000
The Netherlands	The Hague	Dutch	15 598 000
New Zealand	Wellington	English	3 619 000
Nicaragua	Managua	Spanish	4 272 000
Niger	Niamey	French	9 065 000
Nigeria	Abuja	English	103 912 000
Norway	Oslo	Norwegian	4 382 000
Oman	Muscat	Arabic	2 251 000
Pakistan	Islamabad	Urdu	133 500 000
Palau	Koror	Palauan, English	17 000
Panama	Panama City	Spanish	2 674 000
Papua New Guinea	Port Moresby	English, Tok Pïsin, Hiri Motu	4 400 000
Paraguay	Asunción	Spanish	4 964 000
Peru	Lima	Spanish, Quechua, Aymará	23 947 000
Philippines	Manila	Filipino, English	71 750 000
Poland	Warsaw	Polish	38 731 000
Portugal	Lisbon	Portuguese	9 927 000
Puerto Rico	San Juan	Spanish, English	3 766 000
Qatar	Doha	Arabic	590 000
Romania	Bucharest	Romanian	22 670 000
Russia	Moscow	Russian	148 070 000
Rwanda	Kigali	Kinyarwanda, French, English	8 430 000
St Kitts and Nevis	Basseterre	English	39 400
St Lucia	Castries	English	144 000
St Vincent and the Grenadines	Kingstown	English	113 000
Samoa	Apia	Samoan, English	214 000
San Marino	San Marino	Italian	25 300
São Tomé and Príncipe	São Tomé	Portuguese	134 000
Saudi Arabia	Riyadh	Arabic	18 426 000
Senegal	Dakar	French, Wolof	8 314 000
Seychelles	Victoria	Creole French, English, French	76 100
Sierra Leone	Freetown	English	4 617 000
Singapore	Singapore City	Mandarin Chinese, English, Malay, Tamil	3 045 000

English name	Capital	Official language(s)	Population
Slovakia	Bratislava	Slovak, Czech, Hungarian	5 372 000
Slovenia	Ljubljana	Slovene	1 959 000
Solomon Islands	Honiara	Afrikaans, English	396 000
Somalia	Mogadishu	Arabic, Somali	9 077 000
South Africa	Pretoria / Cape Town	Afrikaans, English, Ndebele, Pedi, Sotho, Swazi, Tsonga, Tswana, Venda, Xhosa, Zulu	41 734 000
Spain	Madrid	Spanish	39 270 000
Sri Lanka	Colombo	Sinhala, Tamil	18 318 000
The Sudan	Khartoum	Arabic	31 065 000
Suriname	Paramaribo	Dutch	436 000
Swaziland	Mbabane	Siswati, English	934 000
Sweden	Stockholm	Swedish	8 858 000
Switzerland	Berne	French, German, Italian, Romansch	7 087 000
Syria	Damascus	Arabic	14 798 000
Taiwan	Taipei	Mandarin Chinese	21 463 000
Tajikistan	Dushanbe	Tajik	5 945 000
Tanzania	Dodoma	(Ki)Swahili, English	29 165 000
Thailand	Bangkok	Thai	60 003 000
Togo	Lomé	French	4 269 000
Tonga	Nuku'alofa	English, Tongan	101 000
Trinidad and Tobago	Port of Spain	English	1 262 000
Tunisia	Tunis	Arabic	9 057 000
Turkey	Ankara	Turkish	62 650 000
Turkmenistan	Ashkhabad	Turkmenian	4 074 000
Tuvalu	Fongafale, on Funafuti	Tuvaluan, English	9 500
Uganda	Kampala	English, (Ki)Swahili	20 158 000
Ukraine	Kiev	Ukrainian, Russian	51 273 000
United Arab Emirates	Abu Dhabi	Arabic, English	2 500 000
United Kingdom	London	English	58 784 000
United States of America	Washington, DC	English	265 455 000
Uruguay	Montevideo	Spanish	3 140 000
Uzbekistan	Tashkent	Uzbek	23 206 000
Vanuatu	Port Vila	Bislama, English, French	172 000
Vatican City	Vatican City	Italian	1 000
Venezuela	Caracas	Spanish	22 311 000
Vietnam	Hanoi	Vietnamese	76 151 000
Western Samoa ► Samoa			
Yemen	San'a	Arabic	16 600 000
Yugoslavia	Belgrade	Serbo-Croat	10 473 000
Zaire ► Congo, Democratic Republic of			
Zambia	Lusaka	English	9 715 000
Zimbabwe	Harare	English	11 515 000

Counties of England

County[1]	Admin centre	Area sq km	Area sq mi	Population[2]
Avon[3]	Bristol	1 346	520	991 600
Bedfordshire[4]	Bedford	1 235	477	552 300
Berkshire	Reading	1 259	486	797 500
Buckinghamshire[4]	Aylesbury	1 883	727	677 500
Cambridgeshire	Cambridge	3 409	1 316	712 200
Cheshire	Chester	2 328	899	982 100
Cleveland[3]	Middlesbrough	583	225	555 800
Cornwall	Truro	3 564	1 376	487 600
Cumbria	Carlisle	6 810	2 629	492 100
Derbyshire[4]	Matlock	2 631	1 016	965 500
Devon	Exeter	6 711	2 591	1 063 900
Dorset[4]	Dorchester	2 654	1 025	687 500
Durham[4]	Durham	2 436	941	608 300
Essex	Chelmsford	3 672	1 418	1 595 300
Gloucestershire	Gloucester	2 643	1 020	559 300
Greater London	—	1 579	610	7 122 200
Greater Manchester	—	1 287	497	2 571 800
Hampshire[4]	Winchester	3 777	1 458	1 636 600
Hereford and Worcester	Worcester	3 926	1 516	701 700
Hertfordshire	Hertford	1 634	631	1 024 800
Humberside[3]	Hull	3 512	1 356	884 700
Isle of Wight	Newport	381	147	125 900
Kent	Maidstone	3 731	1 441	1 566 000
Lancashire	Preston	3 063	1 183	1 425 100
Leicestershire[4]	Leicester	2 553	986	929 000
Lincolnshire	Lincoln	5 915	2 284	619 400
Merseyside	Liverpool	652	252	1 413 400
Norfolk	Norwich	5 368	2 073	783 000
Northamptonshire	Northampton	2 367	914	610 300
Northumberland	Morpeth	5 032	1 943	308 800
Nottinghamshire	Nottingham	2 164	836	1 032 200
Oxfordshire	Oxford	2 608	1 007	610 800
Shropshire	Shrewsbury	3 490	1 347	424 600
Somerset	Taunton	3 451	1 332	486 700
Staffordshire[4]	Stafford	2 716	1 049	1 060 300
Suffolk	Ipswich	3 797	1 466	666 600
Surrey	Kingston upon Thames	1 679	648	1 057 100
Sussex, East[4]	Lewes	1 795	693	740 700
Sussex, West	Chichester	1 989	768	746 600
Tyne and Wear	Newcastle upon Tyne	540	208	1 121 400
Warwickshire	Warwick	1 981	765	503 600
West Midlands	Birmingham	899	347	2 630 600
Wiltshire[4]	Trowbridge	3 481	1 344	599 400

County[1]	Admin centre	Area sq km	sq mi	Population[2]
Yorkshire, North[3]	Northallerton	8 309	3 208	737 600
Yorkshire, South	Barnsley	1 560	602	1 304 500
Yorkshire, West	Wakefield	2 039	787	2 110 100

[1] Counties as at 31 March 1996.

[2] Mid-1997 estimated figures.

[3] The following counties were replaced by new unitary authorities (in parentheses) on 1 April 1996:
Avon (Bath and NE Somerset, City of Bristol, N Somerset, S Gloucestershire)
Cleveland (Hartlepool, Middlesbrough, Redcar and Cleveland, Stockton-on-Tees)
Humberside (East Riding of Yorkshire, Kingston Upon Hull, NE Lincolnshire, N Lincolnshire)
Yorkshire, North (York).

[4] The figures for the following counties include those for the new unitary authorities (in parentheses) created on 1 April 1997:
Bedfordshire (Luton)
Buckinghamshire (Milton Keynes)
Derbyshire (Derby)
Dorset (Bournemouth, Poole)
Durham (Darlington)
Hampshire (Portsmouth, Southampton)
Leicestershire (Leicester, Rutland)
Staffordshire (Stoke-on-Trent)
Sussex, East (Brighton and Hove)
Wiltshire (Swindon).

Population data source: ONS, © Crown Copyright 1998.

Council areas of Scotland

Unitary authority[1]	Admin centre	Area sq km	sq mi	Population[2]
Aberdeen City	Aberdeen	186	72	215 930
Aberdeenshire	Aberdeen	6 318	2 439	226 440
Angus	Forfar	2 181	842	110 230
Argyll and Bute	Lochgilphead	6 930	2 675	90 550
Clackmannanshire	Alloa	157	61	48 810
Dumfries and Galloway	Dumfries	6 439	2 485	147 300
Dundee City	Dundee	67	26	148 920
East Ayrshire	Kilmarnock	1 252	483	121 850
East Dunbartonshire	Kirkintilloch	172	66	110 870
East Lothian	Haddington	678	262	89 000
East Renfrewshire	Giffnock	173	67	88 600
Edinburgh, City of	Edinburgh	262	101	450 000
Eilean Siar[3]	Stornoway	3134	1210	28 240
Falkirk	Falkirk	299	115	143 210
Fife	Glenrothes	1 323	511	348 400
Glasgow City	Glasgow	175	68	611 680

Unitary authority [1]	Admin centre	Area sq km	sq mi	Population [2]
Highland	Inverness	25 784	9 953	208 600
Inverclyde	Greenock	182	70	86 500
Midlothian	Dalkeith	356	137	80 680
Moray	Elgin	2 238	864	86 030
North Ayrshire	Irvine	884	341	139 780
North Lanarkshire	Motherwell	474	183	326 520
Orkney Islands	Kirkwall	992	383	19 840
Perth and Kinross	Perth	5 311	2 050	133 250
Renfrewshire	Paisley	261	101	178 260
Scottish Borders	Newton St Boswells	4 734	1 827	106 200
Shetland Islands	Lerwick	1 438	555	23 020
South Ayrshire	Ayr	1 202	464	114 870
South Lanarkshire	Hamilton	1 771	684	307 350
Stirling	Stirling	2 196	848	83 580
West Dunbartonshire	Dumbarton	162	63	95 690
West Lothian	Livingston	425	164	152 320

[1] The counties of Scotland were replaced by 9 regional and 53 district councils in 1975; these in turn became 29 Unitary Authorities or Council Areas on 1 April 1996, the 3 island councils remaining as before.
[2] 30 June 1997 estimated figures.
[3] Formerly known as Western Isles.
Data obtained from the General Register Office for Scotland, © Crown Copyright 1998.

Council areas of Wales

Unitary authority	Admin centre	Area sq km	sq mi	Population [1]
Anglesey, Isle of	Llangefni	719	277	66 200
Blaenau Gwent	Ebbw Vale	109	42	72 800
Bridgend	Bridgend	246	95	130 600
Caerphilly	Hengoed	279	108	169 300
Cardiff	Cardiff	139	54	318 300
Carmarthenshire	Carmarthen	2 398	926	169 000
Ceredigion	Aberaeron	1 797	694	70 400
Conwy	Conwy	1 130	436	111 300
Denbighshire	Ruthin	844	326	90 300
Flintshire	Mold	437	169	145 400
Gwynedd	Caernarfon	2 548	984	117 800
Merthyr Tydfil	Merthyr Tydfil	111	43	57 300
Monmouthshire	Cwmbran	851	328	87 200
Neath Port Talbot	Port Talbot	442	171	139 100
Newport	Newport	191	74	137 300
Pembrokeshire	Haverfordwest	1 590	614	113 300
Powys	Llandrindod Wells	5 204	2 009	125 100

Unitary authority	Admin centre	Area sq km	sq mi	Population[1]
Rhondda, Cynon, Taff	Clydach Vale	424	164	241 300
Swansea	Swansea	378	146	230 100
Torfaen	Pontypool	126	49	90 400
Vale of Glamorgan	Barry	337	130	119 500
Wrexham	Wrexham	499	193	125 000

[1] Mid-1997 estimated figures.
Population data source: ONS, © Crown Copyright 1998.

UK islands

Name	Admin centre	Area sq km	sq mi	Population[1]
Isle of Man	Douglas	572	221	73 837
Jersey	St Helier	116	45	87 848
Guernsey	St Peter Port	63	24	58 681
Alderney (dependency of Guernsey)	St Anne	8	3	2 147
Sark (dependency of Guernsey)	—	4	2	550

[1] 1996 population estimates.

Districts of Northern Ireland

District	Admin centre	Area sq km	sq mi	Population[1]
Antrim	Antrim	563	217	50 800
Ards	Newtownards	369	142	67 800
Armagh	Armagh	672	259	53 400
Ballymena	Ballymena	638	246	58 500
Ballymoney	Ballymoney	419	162	24 900
Banbridge	Banbridge	444	171	37 700
Belfast	—	140	54	298 200
Carrickfergus	Carrickfergus	87	34	35 700
Castlereagh	Belfast	85	33	64 500
Coleraine	Coleraine	485	187	54 700
Cookstown	Cookstown	623	240	31 800
Craigavon	Craigavon	382	147	79 300
Derry	—	382	147	105 200
Down	Downpatrick	646	249	62 100
Dungannon	Dungannon	779	301	47 200
Fermanagh	Enniskillen	1 876	715	55 500
Larne	Larne	338	131	30 300

District	Admin centre	Area sq km	sq mi	Population[1]
Limavady	Limavady	587	227	31 000
Lisburn	Lisburn	444	171	109 800
Magherafelt	Magherafelt	573	221	37 900
Moyle	Ballycastle	495	191	15 000
Newry and Mourne	Newry	895	346	84 900
Newtownabbey	Newtownabbey	152	59	79 600
North Down	Bangor	73	28	74 100
Omagh	Omagh	1 129	436	48 100
Strabane	Strabane	870	336	36 800

[1] Mid-1997 estimated figures.
Population data source: Northern Ireland Statistics and Research Agency, ©1998.

Counties of Ireland

County	Admin centre	Area sq km	sq mi	Population[1]
Carlow	Carlow	896	346	41 616
Cavan	Cavan	1 891	730	52 944
Clare	Ennis	3 188	1 231	94 006
Cork	Cork	7 459	2 880	420 510
Donegal	Lifford	4 830	1 865	129 994
Dublin	Dublin	922	356	1 058 264
Galway	Galway	5 939	2 293	188 854
Kerry	Tralee	4 701	1 815	126 130
Kildare	Naas	1 694	654	134 992
Kilkenny	Kilkenny	2 062	796	75 336
Laoighis (Leix)	Portlaoise	1 720	664	52 945
Leitrim	Carrick	1 526	589	25 057
Limerick	Limerick	2 686	1 037	165 042
Longford	Longford	1 044	403	30 166
Louth	Dundalk	821	317	92 166
Mayo	Castlebar	5 398	2 084	111 524
Meath	Trim	2 339	903	109 732
Monaghan	Monaghan	1 290	498	51 313
Offaly	Tullamore	1 997	771	59 117
Roscommon	Roscommon	2 463	951	51 975
Sligo	Sligo	1 795	693	55 821
Tipperary	Clonmel	4 254	1 642	133 535
Waterford	Waterford	1 839	710	94 680
Westmeath	Mullingar	1 764	681	63 314
Wexford	Wexford	2 352	908	104 371
Wicklow	Wicklow	2 025	782	102 683

[1] 1996 population census figures.
Population data source: Central Statistics Office, Dublin, ©1997.

States of the USA

Population estimates for 1995.
Abbreviations are given after each state name: the first is the common abbreviation, the second the ZIP (postal) code.

Alabama (Ala; AL)
Entry to Union 1819 (22nd)
Pop 4 252 982
Nickname Camellia State, Heart of Dixie
Inhabitant Alabamian
Area 131 443 sq km / 50 750 sq mi
Capital Montgomery

Alaska (Alaska; AK)
Entry to Union 1959 (49th)
Pop 603 617
Nickname Mainland State, The Last Frontier
Inhabitant Alaskan
Area 1 477 268 sq km / 570 373 sq mi
Capital Juneau

Arizona (Ariz; AZ)
Entry to Union 1912 (48th)
Pop 4 217 940
Nickname Apache State, Grand Canyon State
Inhabitant Arizonan
Area 295 276 sq km / 114 006 sq mi
Capital Phoenix

Arkansas (Ark; AR)
Entry to Union 1836 (25th)
Pop 2 483 769
Nickname Bear State, Land of Opportunity
Inhabitant Arkansan
Area 137 754 sq km / 53 187 sq mi
Capital Little Rock

California (Calif; CA)
Entry to Union 1850 (31st)
Pop 31 589 153
Nickname Golden State
Inhabitant Californian
Area 403 971 sq km / 155 973 sq mi
Capital Sacramento

Colorado (Colo; CO)
Entry to Union 1876 (38th)
Pop 3 746 585
Nickname Centennial State
Inhabitant Coloradan
Area 268 658 sq km / 103 729 sq mi
Capital Denver

Connecticut (Conn; CT)
Entry to Union 1788 (5th)
Pop 3 274 662
Nickname Nutmeg State, Constitution State
Inhabitant Nutmegger
Area 12 547 sq km / 4 844 sq mi
Capital Hartford

Delaware (Del; DE)
Entry to Union 1787 (1st)
Pop 717 197
Nickname Diamond State, First State
Inhabitant Delawarean
Area 5 133 sq km / 1 982 sq mi
Capital Dover

District of Columbia (DC; DC)
Pop 554 256
Inhabitant Washingtonian
Area 159 sq km / 61 sq mi
Capital Washington

Florida (Fla; FL)
Entry to Union 1845 (27th)
Pop 14 165 570
Nickname Everglade State, Sunshine State
Inhabitant Floridian
Area 139 697 sq km / 53 937 sq mi
Capital Tallahassee

Georgia (Ga; GA)
Entry to Union 1788 (4th)
Pop 7 200 882
Nickname Empire State of the South, Peach State
Inhabitant Georgian
Area 152 571 sq km / 58 908 sq mi
Capital Atlanta

Hawaii (Hawaii; HI)
Entry to Union 1959 (50th)
Pop 1 186 815
Nickname Aloha State
Inhabitant Hawaiian
Area 16 636 sq km/6 423 sq mi
Capital Honolulu

Idaho (Idaho; ID)
Entry to Union 1890 (43rd)
Pop 1 163 261
Nickname Gem State
Inhabitant Idahoan
Area 214 325 sq km/82 751 sq mi
Capital Boise

Illinois (Ill; IL)
Entry to Union 1818 (21st)
Pop 11 829 940
Nickname Prairie State, Land of Lincoln
Inhabitant Illinoisan
Area 144 123 sq km/55 646 sq mi
Capital Springfield

Indiana (Ind; IN)
Entry to Union 1816 (19th)
Pop 5 803 471
Nickname Hoosier State
Inhabitant Hoosier
Area 92 903 sq km/35 870 sq mi
Capital Indianapolis

Iowa (Iowa; IA)
Entry to Union 1846 (29th)
Pop 2 841 764
Nickname Hawkeye State, Corn State
Inhabitant Iowan
Area 144 716 sq km/55 875 sq mi
Capital Des Moines

Kansas (Kans; KS)
Entry to Union 1861 (34th)
Pop 2 565 328
Nickname Sunflower State, Jayhawker State
Inhabitant Kansan
Area 211 922 sq km/81 823 sq mi
Capital Topeka

Kentucky (Ky; KY)
Entry to Union 1792 (15th)
Pop 3 860 219
Nickname Bluegrass State
Inhabitant Kentuckian
Area 102 907 sq km/39 732 sq mi
Capital Frankfort

Louisiana (La; LA)
Entry to Union 1812 (18th)
Pop 4 342 334
Nickname Pelican State, Sugar State, Creole State
Inhabitant Louisianian
Area 112 836 sq km/43 566 sq mi
Capital Baton Rouge

Maine (Maine; ME)
Entry to Union 1820 (23rd)
Pop 1 241 382
Nickname PineTree State
Inhabitant Downeaster
Area 79 931 sq km/30 861 sq mi
Capital Augusta

Maryland (Md; MD)
Entry to Union 1788 (7th)
Pop 5 042 438
Nickname Old Line State, Free State
Inhabitant Marylander
Area 25 316 sq km/9 775 sq mi
Capital Annapolis

Massachusetts (Mass; MA)
Entry to Union 1788 (6th)
Pop 6 073 550
Nickname Bay State, Old Colony
Inhabitant Bay Stater
Area 20 300 sq km/7 838 sq mi
Capital Boston

Michigan (Mich; MI)
Entry to Union 1837 (26th)
Pop 9 549 353
Nickname Wolverine State, Great Lake State
Inhabitant Michigander
Area 150 544 sq km/58 125 sq mi
Capital Lansing

Minnesota (Minn; MN)
Entry to Union 1858 (32nd)
Pop 4 609 548
Nickname Gopher State, North Star State
Inhabitant Minnesotan

Area 206 207 sq km/79 617 sq mi
Capital St Paul

Mississippi (Miss; MS)
Entry to Union 1817 (20th)
Pop 2 697 243
Nickname Magnolia State
Inhabitant Mississippian
Area 123 510 sq km/47 687 sq mi
Capital Jackson

Missouri (Mo; MO)
Entry to Union 1821 (24th)
Pop 5 323 523
Nickname Bullion State, Show Me State
Inhabitant Missourian
Area 178 446 sq km/68 898 sq mi
Capital Jefferson City

Montana (Mont; MT)
Entry to Union 1889 (41st)
Pop 870 281
Nickname Treasure State, Big Sky Country
Inhabitant Montanan
Area 376 991 sq km/145 556 sq mi
Capital Helena

Nebraska (Nebr; NE)
Entry to Union 1867 (37th)
Pop 1 637 112
Nickname Cornhusker State, Beef State
Inhabitant Nebraskan
Area 199 113 sq km/76 878 sq mi
Capital Lincoln

Nevada (Nev; NV)
Entry to Union 1864 (36th)
Pop 1 530 108
Nickname Silver State, Sagebrush State, Battle Born State
Inhabitant Nevadan
Area 273 349 sq km/105 540 sq mi
Capital Carson City

New Hampshire (NH; NH)
Entry to Union 1788 (9th)
Pop 1 148 253
Nickname Granite State
Inhabitant New Hampshirite
Area 23 292 sq km/8 993 sq mi
Capital Concord

New Jersey (NJ; NJ)
Entry to Union 1787 (3rd)
Pop 7 945 298
Nickname Garden State
Inhabitant New Jerseyite
Area 19 210 sq km/7 417 sq mi
Capital Trenton

New Mexico (N Mex; NM)
Entry to Union 1912 (47th)
Pop 1 685 401
Nickname Sunshine State, Land of Enchantment
Inhabitant New Mexican
Area 314 334 sq km/121 364 sq mi
Capital Santa Fe

New York (NY; NY)
Entry to Union 1788 (11th)
Pop 18 136 081
Nickname Empire State
Inhabitant New Yorker
Area 122 310 sq km/47 224 sq mi
Capital Albany

North Carolina (NC; NC)
Entry to Union 1789 (12th)
Pop 7 195 138
Nickname Old North State, Tar Heel State
Inhabitant North Carolinian
Area 126 180 sq km/48 718 sq mi
Capital Raleigh

North Dakota (N Dak; ND)
Entry to Union 1889 (39th)
Pop 641 367
Nickname Flickertail State, Sioux State, Peace Garden State
Inhabitant North Dakotan
Area 178 695 sq km/68 994 sq mi
Capital Bismarck

Ohio (Ohio; OH)
Entry to Union 1803 (17th)
Pop 11 150 506
Nickname Buckeye State
Inhabitant Ohioan
Area 106 067 sq km/40 952 sq mi
Capital Columbus

Oklahoma (Okla; OK)
Entry to Union 1907 (46th)

Pop 3 227 687
Nickname Sooner State
Inhabitant Oklahoman
Area 177 877 sq km / 68 678 sq mi
Capital Oklahoma City

Oregon (Oreg; OR)
Entry to Union 1859 (33rd)
Pop 3 140 585
Nickname Sunset State, Beaver State
Inhabitant Oregonian
Area 251 385 sq km / 97 060 sq mi
Capital Salem

Pennsylvania (Pa; PA)
Entry to Union 1787 (2nd)
Pop 12 071 842
Nickname Keystone State
Inhabitant Pennsylvanian
Area 116 083 sq km / 44 820 sq mi
Capital Harrisburg

Rhode Island (RI; RI)
Entry to Union 1790 (13th)
Pop 989 794
Nickname Little Rhody, Plantation State
Inhabitant Rhode Islander
Area 2 707 sq km / 1 045 sq mi
Capital Providence

South Carolina (SC; SC)
Entry to Union 1788 (8th)
Pop 3 673 287
Nickname Palmetto State
Inhabitant South Carolinian
Area 77 988 sq km / 30 111 sq mi
Capital Columbia

South Dakota (S Dak; SD)
Entry to Union 1889 (40th)
Pop 729 034
Nickname Sunshine State, Coyote State
Inhabitant South Dakotan
Area 196 576 sq km / 75 898 sq mi
Capital Pierre

Tennessee (Tenn; TN)
Entry to Union 1796 (16th)
Pop 5 256 051
Nickname Volunteer State
Inhabitant Tennessean
Area 106 759 sq km / 41 220 sq mi
Capital Nashville

Texas (Tex; TX)
Entry to Union 1845 (28th)
Pop 18 723 991
Nickname Lone Star State
Inhabitant Texan
Area 678 358 sq km / 261 914 sq mi
Capital Austin

Utah (Utah; UT)
Entry to Union 1896 (45th)
Pop 1 951 408
Nickname Mormon State, Beehive State
Inhabitant Utahn
Area 212 816 sq km / 82 168 sq mi
Capital Salt Lake City

Vermont (Vt; VT)
Entry to Union 1791 (14th)
Pop 584 771
Nickname Green Mountain State
Inhabitant Vermonter
Area 23 955 sq km / 9 249 sq mi
Capital Montpelier

Virginia (Va; VA)
Entry to Union 1788 (10th)
Pop 6 618 358
Nickname Old Dominion State, Mother of Presidents
Inhabitant Virginian
Area 102 558 sq km / 39 598 sq mi
Capital Richmond

Washington (Wash; WA)
Entry to Union 1889 (42nd)
Pop 5 430 940
Nickname Evergreen State, Chinook State
Inhabitant Washingtonian
Area 172 447 sq km / 66 582 sq mi
Capital Olympia

West Virginia (W Va; WV)
Entry to Union 1863 (35th)
Pop 1 828 140
Nickname Panhandle State, Mountain State
Inhabitant West Virginian
Area 62 758 sq km / 24 231 sq mi
Capital Charleston

Wisconsin (Wis; WI)
Entry to Union 1848 (30th)
Pop 5 122 871
Nickname Badger State, America's
Dairyland
Inhabitant Wisconsinite
Area 145 431 sq km / 56 151 sq mi
Capital Madison

Wyoming (Wyo; WY)
Entry to Union 1890 (44th)
Pop 480 184
Nickname Equality State
Inhabitant Wyomingite
Area 251 501 sq km / 97 105 sq mi
Capital Cheyenne

Australian states and territories

Name	Area sq km	sq mi	State Capital	Population (1996)
Australian Capital Territory	2 432	939	Canberra	308 500
New South Wales	801 263	309 431	Sydney	6 240 900
Northern Territory	1 346 200	519 768	Darwin	184 900
Queensland	1 732 700	668 995	Brisbane	3 374 300
South Australia	984 376	380 070	Adelaide	1 476 800
Tasmania	68 331	26 383	Hobart	474 200
Victoria	227 600	87 876	Melbourne	4 581 600
Western Australia	2 525 500	975 096	Perth	1 782 700

Canadian provinces

Name	Area sq km	sq mi	Provincial Capital	Population (1996)
Alberta	661 185	255 284	Edmonton	2 696 826
British Columbia	952 263	367 669	Victoria	3 724 500
Manitoba	649 947	250 945	Winnipeg	1 113 898
New Brunswick	73 439	28 355	Fredericton	738 133
Newfoundland and Labrador	405 720	156 648	St John's	551 792
Northwest Territories	1 224 920	472 819	Yellowknife	42 402
Nova Scotia	55 490	21 425	Halifax	909 282
Nunavut	2 201 400	849 740	Iqaluit	22 000 [1]
Ontario	1 068 472	412 537	Toronto	10 753 573
Prince Edward Island	5 660	2 185	Charlottetown	134 557
Quebec	1 540 667	594 852	Quebec City	7 138 795
Saskatchewan	652 324	251 862	Regina	990 237
Yukon Territory	483 450	186 660	Whitehorse	30 766

[1] Population (1999e)

United Nations membership

Grouped according to year of entry.

1945 Argentina, Australia, Belgium, Byelorussian SSR (Belarus, 1991), Bolivia, Brazil, Canada, Chile, China (Taiwan to 1971), Colombia, Costa Rica, Cuba, Czechoslavakia (to 1993), Denmark, Dominican Republic, Ecuador, Egypt, El Salvador, Ethiopia, France, Greece, Guatemala, Haiti, Honduras, India, Iran, Iraq, Lebanon, Liberia, Luxembourg, Mexico, Netherlands, New Zealand, Nicaragua, Norway, Panama, Paraguay, Peru, Philippines, Poland, Saudi Arabia, South Africa, Syria, Turkey, Ukrainian SSR (Ukraine, 1991), USSR (Russia, 1991), UK, USA, Uruguay, Venezuela, Yugoslavia (to 1992)

1946 Afghanistan, Iceland, Sweden, Thailand
1947 Pakistan, Yemen (N, to 1990)
1948 Burma (Myanmar, 1989)
1949 Israel
1950 Indonesia
1955 Albania, Austria, Bulgaria, Kampuchea (Cambodia, 1989), Ceylon (Sri Lanka, 1970), Finland, Hungary, Ireland, Italy, Jordan, Laos, Libya, Nepal, Portugal, Romania, Spain
1956 Japan, Morocco, The Sudan, Tunisia
1957 Ghana, Malaya (Malaysia, 1963)
1958 Guinea
1960 Cameroon, Central African Republic, Chad, Congo, Côte d'Ivoire (Ivory Coast), Cyprus, Dahomey (Benin, 1975), Gabon, Madagascar, Mali, Niger, Nigeria, Senegal, Somalia, Togo, Upper Volta (Burkina Faso, 1984), Zaïre (Democratic Republic of Congo, 1997)
1961 Mauritania, Mongolia, Sierra Leone, Tanganyika (within Tanzania, 1964)
1962 Algeria, Burundi, Jamaica, Rwanda, Trinidad and Tobago, Uganda
1963 Kenya, Kuwait, Zanzibar (within Tanzania, 1964)
1964 Malawi, Malta, Zambia, Tanzania
1965 The Gambia, Maldives, Singapore
1966 Barbados, Botswana, Guyana, Lesotho, Yemen (S, to 1990)
1968 Equatorial Guinea, Mauritius, Swaziland
1970 Fiji
1971 Bahrain, Bhutan, China (People's Republic), Oman, Qatar, United Arab Emirates
1973 The Bahamas, German Democratic Republic (within GFR, 1990), German Federal Republic
1974 Bangladesh, Grenada, Guinea-Bissau
1975 Cape Verde, Comoros, Mozambique, Papua New Guinea, São Tomé and Príncipe, Suriname
1976 Angola, Seychelles, Western Samoa (Samoa, 1997)
1977 Djibouti, Vietnam
1978 Dominica, Solomon Islands
1979 St Lucia
1980 St Vincent and the Grenadines, Zimbabwe
1981 Antigua and Barbuda, Belize, Vanuatu
1983 St Kitts and Nevis
1984 Brunei

1990 Liechtenstein, Namibia, Yemen (formerly N Yemen and S Yemen)
1991 Estonia, Federated States of Micronesia, Latvia, Lithuania, Marshall Islands, N Korea, S Korea
1992 Armenia, Azerbaijan, Bosnia-Herzegovina, Croatia, Georgia, Kazakhstan, Kyrgyzstan, Moldova, San Marino, Slovenia, Tajikistan, Turkmenistan, Uzbekistan
1993 Andorra, Czech Republic, Eritrea, Former Yugoslav Republic of Macedonia, Monaco, Slovakia
1994 Palau
1999 Kiribati, Nauru, Tonga

United Nations specialized agencies

Abbreviated form	Full title	Area of concern
ILO	International Labour Organization	Social justice
FAO	Food and Agriculture Organization	Improvement of the production and distribution of agricultural products
UNESCO	United Nations Educational, Scientific and Cultural Organization	Stimulation of popular education and the spread of culture
ICAO	International Civil Aviation Organization	Encouragement of safety measures in international flight
IBRD	International Bank for Reconstruction and Development	Aid of development through investment
IMF	International Monetary Fund	Promotion of international monetary co-operation
UPU	Universal Postal Union	Uniting members within a single postal territory
WHO	World Health Organization	Promotion of the highest standards of health for all people
ITU	International Telecommunication Union	Allocation of frequencies and regulation of procedures
WMO	World Meteorological Organization	Standardization and utilization of meteorological observations
IFC	International Finance Corporation	Promotion of the international flow of private capital
IMCO	Inter-governmental Maritime Consultative Organization	Co-ordination of safety at sea
IDA	International Development Association	Credit on special terms to provide assistance for less developed countries
WIPO	World Intellectual Property Organization	Protection of copyright, designs, inventions, etc
IFAD	International Fund for Agricultural Development	Increase of food production in developing countries by the generation of grants or loans

Commonwealth membership

The Commonwealth is an informal association of sovereign states.
Member countries are grouped by year of entry.

1931	Australia, Canada, New Zealand, United Kingdom, South Africa (left 1961, rejoined 1994)
1947	India, Pakistan (left 1972, rejoined 1989, suspended 1999)
1948	Sri Lanka
1957	Ghana, Malaysia
1960	Nigeria (suspended 1995, readmitted 1999)
1961	Cyprus, Sierra Leone, Tanzania
1962	Jamaica, Trinidad and Tobago, Uganda
1963	Kenya, Malawi
1964	Malawi, Malta, Zambia
1965	The Gambia, Singapore
1966	Barbados, Botswana, Guyana, Lesotho
1968	Mauritius, Nauru, Swaziland
1970	Tonga, Western Samoa, Fiji (left 1987, rejoined 1997, partially suspended 2000)
1972	Bangladesh
1973	The Bahamas
1974	Grenada
1975	Papua New Guinea
1976	Seychelles
1978	Dominica, Solomon Islands, Tuvalu
1979	Kiribati, St Lucia, St Vincent and the Grenadines
1980	Vanuatu, Zimbabwe
1981	Antigua and Barbuda, Belize
1982	Maldives
1983	St Kitts and Nevis
1984	Brunei
1990	Namibia
1995	Cameroon, Mozambique
1999	Nauru

The Republic of Ireland resigned from the Commonwealth in 1949.

European Union membership

Member countries are listed by year of entry.

1958	Belgium	1973	United Kingdom
1958	France	1981	Greece
1958	Germany	1986	Portugal
1958	Italy	1986	Spain
1958	Luxembourg	1995	Austria
1958	The Netherlands	1995	Finland
1973	Denmark	1995	Sweden
1973	Republic of Ireland		

Applications from Cyprus, Estonia, Hungary, Poland, Switzerland and the Czech Republic
are under consideration.

European Community organizations

Abbreviation	Full title	Area of concern
—	European Court of Justice	Adjudication of disputes arising from application of the Treaties
CAP	Common Agricultural Policy	Aiming to ensure reasonable standards of living for farmers; its policies have led to surpluses in the past
EMS	European Monetary System	Assistance of trading relations between member countries; all members of the community are in the EMS except Denmark, Greece, Sweden and the UK
EIB	European Investment Bank	Financing of capital investment projects to assist development of the Community
ECSC	European Coal and Steel Community	Regulation of prices and trade in these commodities
EURATOM	European Atomic Energy Community	Creation of technical and industrial conditions to produce nuclear energy on a large scale

COMMUNICATION

Language families

Estimates of the numbers of speakers in the main language families of the world in the early 1980s. The list includes Japanese and Korean, which are not clearly related to any other languages.

Main language families		Main language families	
Indo-European	2 000 000 000	Nilo-Saharan	30 000 000
Sino-Tibetan	1 040 000 000	Amerindian (North, Central, South America)	25 000 000
Niger-Congo	260 000 000	Uralic	23 000 000
Afro-Asiatic	230 000 000	Miao-Yao	7 000 000
Austronesian	200 000 000	Caucasian	6 000 000
Dravidian	140 000 000	Indo-Pacific	3 000 000
Japanese	120 000 000	Khoisan	50 000
Altaic	90 000 000	Australian aborigine	50 000
Austro-Asiatic	60 000 000	Palaeosiberian	25 000
Korean	60 000 000		
Tai	50 000 000		

Specific languages

The first column gives estimates (in millions) for mother-tongue speakers of the 20 most widely used languages. The second column gives estimates of the total population of all countries where the language has official or semi-official status; these totals are often over-estimates, as only a minority of people in countries where a second language is recognized may actually be fluent in it.

	Mother-tongue speakers			Official language populations	
1	Chinese	1 000	1	English	1 400
2	English	350	2	Chinese	1 000
3	Spanish	250	3	Hindi	700
4	Hindi	200	4	Spanish	280
5	Arabic	150	5	Russian	270
6	Bengali	150	6	French	220
7	Russian	150	7	Arabic	170
8	Portuguese	135	8	Portuguese	160
9	Japanese	120	9	Malay	160
10	German	100	10	Bengali	150
11	French	70	11	Japanese	120
12	Panjabi	70	12	German	100

Mother-tongue speakers			Official language populations		
13	Javanese	65	13	Urdu	85
14	Bihari	65	14	Italian	60
15	Italian	60	15	Korean	60
16	Korean	60	16	Vietnamese	60
17	Telugu	55	17	Persian	55
18	Tamil	55	18	Tagalog	50
19	Marathi	50	19	Thai	50
20	Vietnamese	50	20	Turkish	50

Speakers of English

The first column gives figures for countries where English is used as a mother-tongue or first language; for countries where no figure is given, English is not the first language of a significant number of people. (A question-mark indicates that no agreed estimates are available.) The second column gives total population figures (mainly 1996 estimates) for countries where English has official or semi-official status as a medium of communication. These totals are likely to bear little correlation with the real use of English in the area.

Country	First language speakers of English	Country population
Anguilla		1 650
Antigua and Barbuda	61 400	64 400
Australia	17 700 000	18 287 000
The Bahamas	230 000	280 000
Bangladesh	3 200 000	123 100 000
Barbados	265 000	265 000
Belize	111 000	219 000
Bermuda	61 000	61 400
Bhutan	?	1 622 000
Botswana	590 000	1 478 000
Brunei	10 000	290 000
Cameroon	2 720 000	13 609 000
Canada	18 112 000	29 784 000
Dominica	?	73 800
Fiji	160 000	802 000
Ghana	?	16 904 000
Gibraltar	24 000	27 100
Grenada	97 900	97 900
Guyana	700 000+	825 000
India	330 000	952 969 000
Ireland	3 599 000	3 599 000
Jamaica	2 505 000	2 505 000
Kenya		29 137 000
Kiribati		81 800
Lesotho		2 017 000
Liberia	570 000	2 110 000

Country	First language speakers of English	Country population
Malawi	540 000	9 453 000
Malaysia	100 000	20 359 000
Malta	8 000	373 000
Mauritius	2 000	1 141 000
Montserrat	12 000	12 000
Namibia	13 000	1 709 000
Nauru	800	10 600
Nepal	?	20 892 000
New Zealand	3 290 000	3 619 000
Nigeria	?	103 912 000
Pakistan	?	133 500 000
Papua New Guinea	70 000	4 400 000
Philippines		71 750 000
St Kitts and Nevis	39 400	39 400
St Lucia	29 000	144 000
St Vincent and the Grenadines	100 000+	113 000
Seychelles	2 000	76 100
Sierra Leone	700 000	4 617 000
Singapore	1 139 000	3 045 000
Solomon Islands		396 000
South Africa	3 800 000	41 734 000
Sri Lanka	10 000	18 318 000
Suriname		436 000
Swaziland		934 000
Tanzania	900 000	29 165 000
Tonga		101 000
Trinidad and Tobago	1 262 000	1 262 000
Tuvalu		9 500
Uganda	190 000	20 158 000
UK	57 190 000	58 784 000
USA	228 700 000	265 455 000
US territories in Pacific	?	196 300
Vanuatu	60 000	172 000
Samoa	1 000	214 000
Zambia	300 000	9 715 000
Zimbabwe	260 000	11 515 000
Other British territories	?	106 167
TOTALS	349 764 500	2 038 046 117

Foreign words and phrases

à bon marché (Fr) 'good market'; at a good bargain, cheap.

a cappella (Ital) 'in the style of the chapel'; sung without instrumental accompaniment.

achtung (Ger) 'Look out! Take care!'.

addendum *plural* addenda (Lat) 'that which is to be added'; supplementary material for a book.

à deux (Fr) 'for two'; often denotes a dinner or conversation of a romantic nature.

ad hoc (Lat) 'towards this'; for this special purpose.

ad hominem (Lat) 'to the man'; appealing not to logic or reason but to personal preferences or feelings.

ad infinitum (Lat) 'to infinity'; denotes endless repetition.

ad nauseam (Lat) 'to the point of sickness'; disgustingly endless or repetitive.

ad referendum (Lat) 'for reference'; to be further considered.

affaire (Fr) liaison, intrigue; an incident arousing speculation and scandal.

aficionado (Span) 'amateur'; an ardent follower; a 'fan'.

a fortiori (Lat) 'from the stronger' (argument); denotes the validity and stronger reason of a proposition.

agent provocateur (Fr) 'provocative agent'; someone who incites others, by pretended sympathy, to commit crimes.

aggiornamento (Ital) 'modernization'; reform (often political).

aide-de-camp (Fr) 'assistant on the field'; an officer who acts as a confidential personal assistant for an officer of higher rank.

aide-mémoire (Fr) 'help-memory'; a reminder; memorandum-book; a written summary of a diplomatic agreement.

à la carte (Fr) 'from the menu'; each dish individually priced.

à la mode (Fr) 'in fashion, fashionable'; also in cooking, of meat braised and stewed with vegetables; with ice-cream (American English).

al dente (Ital) 'to the tooth'; culinary term denoting (usually) pasta fully cooked but still firm.

al fresco (Ital) 'fresh'; painting on fresh or moist plaster; in the fresh, cool or open air.

alma mater (Lat) 'bountiful mother'; one's former school, college, or university; official college or university song (American English).

aloha (Hawaiian) 'love'; a salutation, 'hello' or 'goodbye'.

alumnus *plural* alumni (Lat) 'pupil' or 'foster son'; a former pupil or student.

ambiance (Fr) surroundings, atmosphere.

amende honorable (Fr) a public apology satisfying the honour of the injured party.

amour-propre (Fr) 'own love, self-love'; legitimate self-esteem, sometimes exaggerated; vanity, conceit.

ancien régime (Fr) 'old regime'; a superseded and outdated political system or ruling elite.

angst (Ger) 'anxiety'; an unsettling feeling produced by awareness of the uncertainties and paradoxes inherent in the state of being human.

anno Domini (Lat) 'in the year of the Lord'; used in giving dates of the Christian era, counting forward from the year of Christ's birth; abbreviated to AD.

annus mirabilis (Lat) 'year of wonders'; a remarkably successful or auspicious year.

anschluss (Ger) 'joining together'; union, especially the political union of Germany and Austria in 1938.

ante-bellum (Lat) 'before the war'; denotes a period before a specific war, especially the American Civil War.

ante meridiem (Lat) 'before midday'; between midnight and noon; abbreviated to am.

a posteriori (Lat) 'from the later'; applied to reasoning from experience, from effect to cause; inductive reasoning.

apparatchik (Russ) a Communist spy or agent; (humorous) any bureaucratic hack.

appellation contrôlée (Fr) 'certified name'; used in the labelling of French wines, a guarantee of specified conditions of origin, strength, etc.

après-ski (Fr) 'after-ski'; pertaining to the evening's amusements after skiing.

a priori (Lat) 'from the previous'; denotes argument from the cause to the effect; deductive reasoning.

atelier (Fr) a workshop; an artist's studio.

au contraire (Fr) 'on the contrary'.

au fait (Fr) 'to the point'; highly skilled; knowledgeable or familiar with something.

au fond (Fr) 'at the bottom'; fundamentally.

au naturel (Fr) 'in the natural state'; naked; also as a culinary term: cooked plainly, raw, or without dressing.

au pair (Fr) 'on an equal basis'; originally an arrangement of mutual service without payment; now used of a girl (usually foreign) who performs domestic duties for board, lodging and pocket money.

auto-da-fé (Port) 'act of the faith'; the public declaration or carrying out of a sentence imposed on heretics in Spain and Portugal by the Inquisition, eg burning at the stake.

avant-garde (Fr) 'front guard'; applied to those in the forefront of an artistic movement.

babushka (Russ) 'grandmother'; granny; a triangular headscarf worn under the chin.

bain-marie (Fr) 'bath of Mary'; a water-bath; a vessel of boiling water in which another is placed for slow and gentle cooking, or for keeping food warm.

banzai (Jap) a Japanese battle cry, salute to the emperor, or exclamation of joy.

barrio (Span) 'district, suburb'; a community (usually poor) of Spanish-speaking immigrants (esp American English).

batik (Javanese) 'painted'; method of producing patterns on fabric by drawing with wax before dyeing.

beau geste (Fr) 'beautiful gesture'; a magnanimous action.

belle époque (Fr) 'fine period'; the time of gracious living for the well-to-do immediately preceding World War I.

bête noire (Fr) 'black beast'; a bugbear; something one especially dislikes.

bildungsroman (Ger) 'educational novel'; a novel concerning its hero's early spiritual and emotional development and education.

blasé (Fr) 'cloyed'; dulled to enjoyment.

blitzkrieg (Ger) 'lightning war'; a sudden overwhelming attack by ground and air forces; a burst of intense activity.

bodega (Span) a wine shop that usually sells food as well; a building for wine storage.

bona fides (Lat) 'good faith'; genuineness.

bonsai (Jap) art of growing miniature trees in pots; a dwarf tree grown by this method.

bon vivant (Fr) 'good living (person)'; one who lives well, particularly enjoying good food and wine; a jovial companion.

bon voyage (Fr) have a safe and pleasant journey.

bourgeois (Fr) 'citizen'; a member of the middle class; a merchant; conventional, conservative.

camera obscura (Lat) 'dark room'; a light-free chamber in which an image of outside objects is thrown upon a screen.

canard (Fr) 'duck'; a false rumour; a second wing fitted as a horizontal stabilizer near the nose of an aircraft.

carpe diem (Lat) 'seize the day'; enjoy the pleasures of the present moment while they last.

carte blanche (Fr) 'blank sheet of paper'; freedom of action.

casus belli (Lat) 'occasion of war'; whatever sparks off or justifies a war or quarrel.

cause célèbre (Fr) a very notable or famous trial; a notorious controversy.

caveat emptor (Lat) 'let the buyer beware'; warns the buyer to examine carefully the article about to be purchased.

c'est la vie (Fr) 'that's life'; denotes fatalistic resignation.

chacun à son goût (Fr) 'each to his own taste'; implies surprise at another's choice.

chambré (Fr) 'put into a room'; (of red wine) at room temperature.

chargé-d'affaires (Fr) a diplomatic agent of lesser rank; an ambassador's deputy.

chef d'oeuvre (Fr) 'a masterpiece'; the best piece of work by a particular artist, writer, etc.

chicano (Span) *mejicano* 'Mexican'; or an American of Mexican descent.

chutzpah (Yiddish) 'effrontery'; nerve to do or say outrageous things.

cinéma vérité (Fr) 'cinema truth'; realism in films usually sought by photographic scenes of real life.

circa (Lat) 'surrounding'; of dates and numbers: approximately.

cliché (Fr) 'stereotype printing block'; the impression made by a die in any soft metal; a hackneyed phrase or concept.

coitus interruptus (Lat) 'interrupted intercourse'; coitus intentionally interrupted by withdrawal before semen is ejaculated; anticlimax when something ends prematurely.

comme il faut (Fr) 'as it is necessary'; correct; genteel.

compos mentis (Lat) 'having control of one's mind'; sane.

cordon bleu (Fr) 'blue ribbon'; denotes food cooked to a very high standard; a dish made with ham and cheese and a white sauce.

coup de foudre (Fr) 'flash of lightning'; a sudden and astonishing happening; ove at first sight.

coup de grâce (Fr) 'blow of mercy'; a finishing blow to end pain; a decisive action which ends a troubled enterprise.

coup d'état (Fr) 'blow of state'; a violent overthrow of a government or subversive stroke of state policy.

coupé (Fr) 'cut'; (usually) two-door motor-car with sloping roof.

crème de la crème (Fr) 'cream of the cream'; the very best.

cuisine minceur (Fr) 'slenderness cooking'; a style of cooking characterized by imaginative use of light, simple, low-fat ingredients.

cul-de-sac (Fr) 'bottom of the bag'; a road closed at one end.

curriculum vitae (Lat) 'course of life'; denotes a summary of someone's educational qualifications and work experience for presenting to a prospective employer.

décolleté (Fr) 'with bared neck and shoulders'; (of dress) low cut.

de facto (Lat) 'from the fact'; in fact; actually; irrespective of what is legally recognized.

de gustibus non est disputandum (Lat) (often in English shortened for convenience to *de gustibus*) 'there is no disputing about tastes'; there is no sense in challenging people's preferences.

déjà vu (Fr) 'already seen'; in any of the arts: original material; an illusion of having experienced something before; something seen so often it has become tedious.

de jure (Lat) 'according to law'; denotes the legal or theoretical position, which may not correspond with reality.

delirium tremens (Lat) 'trembling delirium'; psychotic condition caused by alcoholism, involving anxiety, shaking, hallucinations, etc.

deo volente (Lat) 'God willing'; a sort of good-luck talisman.

de rigueur (Fr) 'of strictness'; compulsory; required by strict etiquette.

derrière (Fr) 'behind'; the buttocks.

déshabillé (Fr) 'undressed'; state of being only partially dressed, or of being casually dressed.

de trop (Fr) 'of too much'; superfluous; in the way.

deus ex machina (Lat) 'a god from a machine'; a contrived solution to a difficulty in a plot.

distingué (Fr) 'distinguished'; having an aristocratic or refined demeanour; striking.

dolce far niente (Ital) 'sweet doing nothing'; denotes the pleasure of idleness.

doppelgänger (Ger) 'double goer'; a ghostly duplicate of a living person; a wraith; someone who looks exactly like someone else.

double entendre (Fr) 'double meaning'; ambiguity (normally with indecent connotations).

doyen (Fr) 'dean'; most distinguished member or representative by virtue of seniority, experience, and often also excellence.

droit du seigneur (Fr) 'the lord's right'; originally the alleged right of a feudal superior to take the virginity of a vassal's bride; any excessive claim imposed on a subordinate.

dummkopf (Ger) 'dumb-head'; blockhead; idiot.

élan (Fr) 'dash, rush, bound'; flair; flamboyance.

el dorado (Span) 'the gilded man'; the golden land (or city) imagined by the Spanish conquerors of America; any place which offers the opportunity of acquiring fabulous wealth.

embarras de richesse (Fr) 'embarrassment of wealth'; a perplexing amount of wealth or an abundance of any kind.

embonpoint (Fr) *en bon point* 'in fine form'; well-fed; stout; plump.

emeritus (Lat) 'having served one's time'; eg of a retired professor, honourably discharged from a public duty; holding a position on an honorary basis only.

éminence grise (Fr) 'grey eminence'; someone exerting power through their influence over a superior.

enfant terrible (Fr) 'terrible child'; a precocious child whose sayings embarrass its parents; a person whose behaviour is indiscreet, embarrassing to his associates.

ennui (Fr) 'boredom'; world-weary listlessness.

en passant (Fr) 'in passing'; by the way; incidentally; applied in chess to the taking of a pawn that has just moved two squares as if it had moved only one.

en route (Fr) 'on the way, on the road'; let us go.

entente (Fr) 'understanding'; a friendly agreement between nations.

erratum *plural*errata (Lat) an error in writing or printing.

ersatz (Ger) 'replacement, substitute'; connotes a second-rate substitute; a supplementary reserve from which waste can be made good.

et al (Lat) *et alii* 'and other things'; used to avoid giving a complete and possibly over-lengthy list of all items, eg of authors.

eureka (Gr) *heureka* 'I have found!'; cry of triumph at a discovery.

ex cathedra (Lat) 'from the seat'; from the chair of office; authoritatively; judicially.

ex gratia (Lat) 'from favour'; of a payment; one that is made as a favour, without any legal obligation and without admitting legal liability.

ex officio (Lat) 'from office, by virtue of office'; used as a reason for membership of a body.

ex parte (Lat) 'from (one) part, from (one) side'; on behalf of one side only in legal proceedings; partial; prejudiced.

fait accompli (Fr) 'accomplished fact'; already done or settled, and therefore irreversible.

fata Morgana (Ital) a striking kind of mirage, attributed to witchcraft.

fatwa (Arabic) 'the statement of a formal legal opinion'; a formal legal opinion delivered by an Islamic religious leader.

faute de mieux (Fr) 'for lack of anything better'.

faux pas (Fr) 'false step'; a social blunder.

femme fatale (Fr) 'fatal woman'; an irresistibly attractive woman who brings difficulties or disasters on men; a siren.

film noir (Fr) 'black film'; a bleak and pessimistic film.

fin de siècle (Fr) 'end of the century'; of the end of the 19th-c in Western culture or of an era; decadent.

floruit (Lat) 'he or she flourished'; denotes a period during which a person lived

force de frappe (Fr) 'strike force'; equivalent of the 'independent nuclear deterrent'.

force majeure (Fr) 'superior force'; an unforeseeable or uncontrollable course of events, excusing one from fulfilling a contract; a legal term.

führer (Ger) 'leader, guide'; an insulting term for anyone bossily asserting authority.

gastarbeiter (Ger) 'guest-worker'; an immigrant worker, especially one who does menial work.

gauleiter (Ger) 'district leader'; a chief official of a district under the Nazi régime; an overbearing wielder of petty authority.

gemütlich (Ger) amiable; comfortable; cosy.

gestalt (Ger) 'form, shape'; original whole or unit, more than the sum of its parts.

gesundheit (Ger) 'health', 'your health'; said to someone who has just sneezed.

glasnost (Russ) 'publicity'; the policy of openness and forthrightness followed by the Soviet government, initiated by Mikhail Gorbachev.

götterdämmerung (Ger) 'twilight of the gods'; the downfall of any once powerful system.

grand mal (Fr) 'large illness'; a violently convulsive form of epilepsy.

grand prix (Fr) 'great prize'; any of several international motor races; any competition of similar importance in other sports.

gran turismo (Ital) 'great touring, touring on a grand scale'; a motor car designed for high speed touring in luxury; abbreviated to GT.

gratis (Lat) *gratiis* 'kindness, favour'; free of charge.

gravitas (Lat) 'weight'; seriousness; weight of demeanour; avoidance of unseemly frivolity.

gringo (Mexican-Spanish) 'foreigner'.

guru (Hindi) a spiritual leader; a revered instructor or mentor.

habeas corpus (Lat) 'you should have the body'; a writ to a jailer to produce a prisoner in person, and to state the reasons for detention; maintains the right of the subject to protection from unlawful imprisonment.

hajj (Arabic) 'pilgrimage'; the Muslim pilgrimage to Mecca.

haka (Maori) a Maori ceremonial war dance; a similar dance performed by New Zealanders, eg before a rugby game.

halal (Arabic) 'lawful'; meat from an animal killed in strict accordance with Islamic law.

haute couture (Fr) 'higher tailoring'; fashionable, expensive dress designing and tailoring.

haut monde (Fr) 'high world'; high society; fashionable society; composed of the aristocracy and the wealthy.

hoi polloi (Gr) 'the many'; the rabble; the vulgar.

hombre (Span) 'man'.

hors concours (Fr) 'out of the competition'; not entered for a contest; unequalled.

ibidem (Lat) 'in the same place'; used in footnotes to indicate that the same book (or chapter) has been cited previously.

id (Lat) 'it'; the sum total of the primitive instinctive forces in an individual.

idée fixe (Fr) 'a fixed idea'; an obsession.

ikebana (Jap) 'living flowers'; the Japanese art of flower arrangement.

in absentia (Lat) 'in absence'; used for occasions, such as the receiving of a degree award, when the recipient would normally be present.

in camera (Lat) 'in the room'; in a private room; in secret.

incommunicado (Span) 'unable to communicate'; deprived of the right to communicate with others.

in extremis (Lat) 'in the last'; at the point of death; in desperate circumstances.

in flagrante delecto (Lat) 'with the crime blazing'; in the very act of committing the crime.

infra dig (Lat) 'below dignity'; below one's dignity.

in loco parentis (Lat) 'in place of a parent'.

in shallah (Arabic) 'if God wills'; ► deo volente

inter alia (Lat) 'among other things'; used to show that a few examples have been chosen from many possibilities.

in vitro (Lat) 'in glass'; in the test tube.

ipso facto (Lat) 'by the fact itself'; thereby.

je ne sais quoi (Fr) 'I do not know what'; an indefinable something.

jihad (Arabic) 'struggle'; a holy war undertaken by Muslims against unbelievers.

kamikaze (Jap) 'divine wind'; Japanese pilots making a suicide attack; any reckless, potentially self-destructive act.

karaoke (Jap) 'empty orchestra'; in bars, clubs, etc members of the public sing a solo to a recorded backing.

karma (Sanskrit) 'act'; the concept that the actions in a life determine the future condition of an individual.

kibbutz (Hebrew) a Jewish communal agricultural settlement in Israel.

kitsch (Ger) 'rubbish'; work in any of the arts that is pretentious and inferior or in bad taste.

la dolce vita (Ital) 'the sweet life'; the name of a film made by Federico Fellini in 1960 showing a life of wealth, pleasure and self-indulgence.

laissez-faire (Fr) 'let do'; a general principle of non-interference.

lebensraum (Ger) 'life space'; room to live; used by Hitler to justify his acquisition of land for Germany.

leitmotiv (Ger) 'leading motive'; a recurrent theme.

lèse-majesté (Fr) 'injured majesty'; offence against the sovereign power; treason.

lingua franca (Ital) 'Frankish language'; originally a mixed Italian trading language used in the Levant, subsequently any language chosen as a means of communication among speakers of different languages.

macho (Mexican-Spanish) 'male'; originally a positive term denoting masculinity or virility, it has come in English to describe an ostentatious virility.

magnum opus (Lat) 'great work'; a person's greatest achievement, especially a literary work.

maharishi (Sanskrit) a Hindu sage or spiritual leader; a guru.

mañana (Span) 'tomorrow'; an unspecified time in the future.

mea culpa (Lat) 'through my fault'; originally part of the Latin mass; an admission of fault and an expression of repentance.

ménage à trois (Fr) 'household of three'; a household comprising a husband and wife and the lover of one of them.

mens sana in corpore sano (Lat) 'a sound mind in a sound body' (Juvenal *Satires* X, 356); the guiding rule of the 19th-c English educational system.

mot juste (Fr) 'exact word'; the word which fits the context exactly.

mutatis mutandis (Lat) 'with the necessary changes made'.

négociant (Fr) 'merchant, trader'; often used for *négociant en vins* 'wine merchant'.

ne plus ultra (Lat) 'not more beyond'; extreme perfection.

netsuke (Jap) a small Japanese carved ornament used to fasten small objects, eg a purse, tobacco pouch, or medicine box, to the sash of a kimono. They are now collectors' pieces.

noblesse oblige (Fr) 'nobility obliges'; rank imposes obligations.

non sequitur (Lat) 'it does not follow'; a conclusion that does not follow logically from the premise; a remark that has no relation to what has gone before.

nostalgie de la boue (Fr) 'hankering for mud'; a craving for a debased physical life without civilized refinements.

nota bene (Lat) 'observe well, note well'; abbreviated to NB.

nouveau riche (Fr) 'new rich'; one who has only lately acquired wealth (without acquiring good taste).

nouvelle cuisine (Fr) 'new cooking'; a style of simple French cookery that aims to produce dishes that are light and healthy, utilizing fresh fruit and vegetables, and avoiding butter and cream.

nouvelle vague (Fr) 'new wave'; a movement in the French cinema aiming at imaginative quality films.

origami (Jap) 'paper-folding'; Japanese art of folding paper to make shapes suggesting birds, boats, etc.

outré (Fr) 'gone to excess'; beyond what is customary or proper; eccentric.

passim (Lat) 'everywhere, throughout'; dispersed through a book.

per capita (Lat) 'by heads'; per head of the population in statistical contexts.

perestroika (Russ) 'reconstruction'; restructuring of an organization.

pied à terre (Fr) 'foot to the ground'; a flat, small house etc kept for temporary or occasional accommodation.

plus ça change (Fr) abbreviated form of plus ça change, plus c'est la même chose'the more things change, the more they stay the same'; a comment on the unchanging nature of the world.

post meridiem (Lat) 'after midday, after noon'; abbreviated to pm.

post mortem (Lat) 'after death'; an examination of a body in order to determine the cause of death; an after-the-event discussion.

poule de luxe (Fr) 'luxurious hen'; a sexually attractive promiscuous young woman; a prostitute.

pour encourager les autres (Fr) 'to encourage the others' (Voltaire *Candide*, on the execution of Admiral Byng); exemplary punishment.

premier cru (Fr) 'first growth'; wine of the highest quality in a system of classification.

prêt-à-porter (Fr) 'ready to wear'; refers to 'designer' clothes that are made in standard sizes as opposed to made-to-measure clothes.

prima donna (Ital) 'first lady'; leading female singer in an opera; a person who is temperamental and hard to please.

prima facie (Lat) 'at first sight'; a legal term for evidence that is assumed to be true unless disproved by other evidence.

primus inter pares (Lat) 'first among equals'.

prix fixe (Fr) 'fixed price'; used of a meal in a restaurant offered at a set price for a restricted choice. Compare table d'hôte.

pro bono publico (Lat) 'for the public good'; something done for no fee.

quid pro quo (Lat) 'something for something'; something given or taken as equivalent to another, often as retaliation.

quod erat demonstrandum (Lat) 'which was to be shown'; often used in its abbreviated form qed.

raison d'être (Fr) 'reason for existence'.

realpolitik (Ger) 'politics of realism'; practical politics based on the realities and necessities of life, rather than moral or ethical ideas.

recherché (Fr) 'sought out'; carefully chosen; particularly choice; rare or exotic.

reductio ad absurdum (Lat) 'reduction to absurdity'; originally used in logic to mean the proof of a proposition by proving the falsity of its contradictory; the application of a principle so strictly that it is carried to absurd lengths.

répondez, s'il vous plaît (Fr) 'reply, please'; in English mainly in its abbreviated form, RSVP, on invitations.

revenons à nos moutons (Fr) 'let us return to our sheep'; let us get back to our subject.

rijsttafel (Dutch) 'rice table'; an Indonesian rice dish served with a variety of foods.

risqué (Fr) 'risky, hazardous'; audaciously bordering on the unseemly.

rus in urbe (Lat) 'the country in the town' (Martial *Epigrams* XII, 57); the idea of country charm in the centre of a city.

salus populi suprema est lex (Lat) 'let the welfare of the people be the chief law' (Cicero *De Legibus* III, 3).

samizdat (Russ) 'self-publisher'; the secret printing and distribution of banned literature in the former USSR and other Eastern European countries previously under Communist rule.

sang froid (Fr) 'cold blood'; self possession; coolness under stress.

savoir faire (Fr) 'knowing what to do'; knowing what to do and how to do it in any situation.

schadenfreude (Ger) 'hurt joy'; pleasure in others' misfortunes.

shlock (Yiddish) 'broken or damaged goods'; inferior; shoddy.

shmaltz (Yiddish) 'melted fat, grease'; showy sentimentality, particularly in writing, music, art, etc

shmuck (Yiddish) 'penis'; a (male) stupid person.

shogun (Jap) 'leader of the army'; ruler of feudal Japan.

sic (Lat) 'so, thus'; used in brackets within printed matter to show that the original is faithfully reproduced even if incorrect.

sine qua non (Lat) 'without which not'; an indispensable condition.

sotto voce (Ital) 'below the voice'; in an undertone; aside.

status quo (Lat) 'the state in which'; the existing condition.

sub judice (Lat) 'under a judge'; under consideration by a judge or a court of law.

subpoena (Lat) 'under penalty'; a writ commanding attendance in court.

sub rosa (Lat) 'under the rose'; in secret; privately.

succès de scandale (Fr) 'success of scandal'; the success of a book, film, etc due not to merit but to its connection with, or reference to, a scandal.

summa cum laude (Lat) 'with the highest praise'; with great distinction; the highest class of degree award that can be gained by a US college student.

summum bonum (Lat) 'the chief good'.

table d'hôte (Fr) 'host's table'; a set meal at a fixed price. Compare prix fixe

tabula rasa (Lat) 'scraped table'; a cleaned tablet; a mind not yet influenced by outside impressions and experience.

t'ai chi (Chin) 'great art of boxing'; a system of exercise and self-defence in which good use of balance and co-ordination allows effort to be minimized.

tempus fugit (Lat) 'time flies'; delay cannot be tolerated.

touché (Fr) 'touched'; claiming or acknowledging a hit made in fencing; claiming or acknowledging a point scored in an argument.

tour de force (Fr) 'turning movement'; feat of strength or skill.

trompe l'oeil (Fr) 'deceives the eye'; an appearance of reality achieved by the use of perspective and detail in painting, architecture, etc.

tsunami (Jap) 'wave in harbour'; a wave generated by movement of the earth's surface underwater; commonly (and erroneously) called a 'tidal wave'.

übermensch (Ger) 'over-person'; superman.

ultra vires (Lat) 'beyond strength, beyond powers'; beyond one's power or authority.

urbi et orbi (Lat) 'to the city and the world'; used of the Pope's pronouncements; to everyone.

vade-mecum (Lat) 'go with me'; a handbook; pocket companion.

vin du pays (Fr) 'wine of the country'; a locally produced wine for everyday consumption.

vis-à-vis (Fr) 'face to face'; one who faces or is opposite another; in relation to.

volte-face (Fr) 'turn-face'; a sudden and complete change in opinion or in views expressed.

vox populi (Lat); 'voice of the people'; public or popular opinion.

weltschmerz (Ger) 'world pain'; sympathy with universal misery; thoroughgoing pessimism.

wunderkind (Ger) 'wonder-child'; a 'child prodigy'; one who shows great talent and/or achieves great success at an early (or comparatively early) age.

zeitgeist (Ger) 'time-spirit'; the spirit of the age.

Symbols in general use

Symbol	Meaning
&	ampersand (*and*)
&c	et cetera
@	at; per (in costs)
×	by (measuring dimensions, eg 3 × 4)
£	pound
$	dollar (also peso, escudo, etc in certain countries)
¢	cent (also centavo, etc in certain countries)
©	copyright
®	registered
¶	new paragraph
§	new section
"	ditto
*	born (in genealogy)
†	died
*	hypothetical or unacceptable form (in linguistics)
☠	poison; danger
♂, □	male
♀, ○	female
✠	bishop's name follows
☎	telephone number follows

Symbol	Meaning
☞	this way
✂ ✂⋯	cut here

In astronomy

Symbol	Meaning
●	new moon
)	moon, first quarter
○	full moon
(	moon, last quarter

In meteorology

Symbol	Meaning
▲▲▲	cold front
●●●	warm front
▲●▲●	stationary front
▲▲▲	occluded front

In cards

Symbol	Meaning
♥	hearts
♦	diamonds
♠	spades
♣	clubs

Clothes care symbols

☒ Do not iron

☲ Can be ironed with *cool* iron (up to 110°C)

☲ Can be ironed with *warm* iron (up to 150°C)

☲ Can be ironed with *hot* iron (up to 200°C)

♨ Hand wash only

\60°/ Can be washed in a washing machine. The number shows the most effective washing temperature (in °C)

\60°/ Reduced (medium) washing conditions

\60°/ Much reduced (minimum) washing conditions (for wool products)

☒ Do not wash

◉ Can be tumble dried (one dot within the circle means a low temperature setting; two dots for higher temperatures)

☒ Do not tumble dry

☒ Do not dry clean

Ⓐ Dry cleanable (letter indicates which solvents can be used)

A: all solvents
Dry cleanable

Ⓕ F: white spirit and solvent 11 can be used
Dry cleanable

Ⓟ P: perchloroethylene (tetra-chloroethylene), white spirit, solvent 113 and solvent 11 can be used

Ⓟ Dry cleanable, if special care taken

△ Chlorine bleach may be used with care

☒ Do not use chlorine bleach

First name meanings in the UK and USA

The meanings of the most popular first names in the UK and USA are given below, along with a few other well-known names.

Name	Original meaning
Aaron	high mountain (*Hebrew*)
Adam	redness (*Hebrew*)
Alan	harmony (*Celtic*)
Albert	nobly bright (*Germanic*)
Alexander	defender of men (*Greek*)
Alexis	helper (*Greek*)
Alison	*French diminutive of* Alice; *of noble kind*
Amanda	fit to be loved (*Latin*)
Amy	loved (*French*)
Andrea	*female form of* Andrew
Andrew	manly (*Greek*)
Angela	messenger, angel (*Greek*)
Ann(e)	*English forms of* Hannah
Anthony	*Roman family name*
April	name of the month
Arthur	?bear, stone (*Celtic*)
Ashley	*Germanic place name;* ashwood
Austin	*English form of* Augustus; venerated
Barbara	strange, foreign (*Greek*)
Barry	spear, javelin (*Celtic*)
Beatrice	bringer of joy (*Latin*)
Benjamin	son of my right hand (*Hebrew*)
Bernard	bear + brave (*Germanic*)
Beth	*pet form of* Elizabeth
Betty	*pet form of* Elizabeth
Bill/Billy	*pet form of* William
Bob	*pet form of* Robert
Brandi	*variant of* Brandy, *from the common noun*
Brandon	*place name;* broom-covered hill (*Germanic*)
Brian	?hill (? *Celtic*)
Candice	meaning unknown
Carl	man, husbandman (*Germanic*)
Carol(e)	*forms of* Caroline, *Italian female form of* Charles
Catherine	pure (*Greek*)
Charles	man, husbandman (*Germanic*)

Name	Original meaning
Christine	*French form of* Christina, ultimately from Christian; anointed
Christopher	carrier of Christ (*Greek*)
Claire	bright, shining (*Latin*)
Colin	*form of* Nicholas
Craig	rock (*Celtic*)
Crystal	*female use of the common noun*
Daniel	God is my judge (*Hebrew*)
Danielle	*female form of* Daniel
Darren	*Irish surname*
Darryl	*surname; uncertain origin*
David	beloved, friend (*Hebrew*)
Dawn	*female use of the common noun*
Dean	*surname;* valley *or* leader
Deborah	bee (*Hebrew*)
Dennis	of Dionysus (*Greek*), the god of wine
Derek	*form of* Theodoric; ruler of the people (*Germanic*)
Diane	*French form of* Diana; divine (*Latin*)
Donald	world mighty (*Gaelic*)
Donna	lady (*Latin*)
Doreen	from Dora, a short form of Dorothy; gift of God
Doris	woman from Doris (*Greek*)
Dorothy	gift of God (*Greek*)
Ebony	*female use of the common noun*
Edward	property guardian (*Germanic*)
Eileen	*Irish form of* ?Helen
Elizabeth	oath/perfection of God (*Hebrew*)
Emily	*Roman family name*
Emma	all-embracing (*Germanic*)
Eric	ruler of all (*Norse*)
Erica	*female form of* Eric

Name	Original meaning	Name	Original meaning
Eugenie	*French form of* Eugene; *well-born* (*Greek*)	Joanne	*French form of* Johanna, *from* John
Frank	*pet form of* Francis; *Frenchman*	John	Jehovah has been gracious (*Hebrew*)
Frederick	*peaceful ruler* (*Germanic*)	Jonathan	*Jehovah's gift* (*Hebrew*)
Gail	*pet form of* Abigail; *father rejoices* (*Hebrew*)	Jordan	*flowing down* (*Hebrew*)
		Joseph	*Jehovah adds* (*Hebrew*)
Gareth	*gentle* (*Welsh*)	Joshua	*Jehovah is gracious* (*Hebrew*)
Gary	*US place name*	Joyce	*?joyful* (*?Latin*)
Gavin	*Scottish form of* Gawain; *hawk + white* (*Welsh*)	Julie	*French female form of Latin* Julius; *descended from Jove*
Gemma	*gem* (*Italian*)	Karen	*Danish form of* Katarina (*Catherine*)
Geoffrey	*?peace* (*Germanic*)		
George	*husbandman, farmer* (*Greek*)	Katherine	*US spelling of* Catherine
Graham	*Germanic place name*	Kathleen	*English form of Irish* Caitlin (*from* Catherine)
Hannah	*grace, favour* (*Hebrew*)		
Harold	*army power/ruler* (*Germanic*)	Kelly	*Irish surname; warlike one*
Harry	*pet form of* Henry; *home ruler* (*Germanic*)	Kenneth	*English form of Gaelic; fair one or fire-sprung*
		Kerry	*Irish place name*
Hayley	*English place name; hay-meadow*	Kevin	*handsome at birth* (*Irish*)
		Kimberly	*South African place name*
Heather	*plant name*	Lakisha	*La +?Aisha; woman* (*Arabic*)
Helen	*bright/shining one* (*Greek*)	Latoya	*La + form of* Tonya (*Antonia*)
Ian	*modern Scottish form of* John	Laura	*bay, laurel* (*Latin*)
Irene	*peace* (*Greek*)	Lauren	*diminutive of* Laura
Jacob	*he seized the heel* (*Hebrew*)	Lee	*Germanic place name; wood, clearing*
Jacqueline	*French female form of* Jacques (*James*)		
		Leslie	*Scottish place name*
James	*Latin form of* Jacob	Lilian	*lily* (*Italian*)
Jane	*from Latin* Johanna, *female form of* John	Linda	*serpent (symbol of wisdom)* (*Germanic*)
Janet	*diminutive form of* Jane	Lindsay	*Scottish place name*
Jasmine	*flower name* (*Persian*)	Lisa	*pet form of* Elizabeth
Jason	*form of* Joshua; *Jehovah is salvation* (*Hebrew*)	Margaret	*pearl* (*Greek*)
		Marjorie	*from* Marguerite, *French form of* Margaret
Jeffrey	*US spelling of* Geoffrey		
Jean	*French form of* Johanna, *from* John	Mark	*English form of* Marcus, *from* Mars, *god of war*
Jennifer	*fair/white + yielding/smooth* (*Celtic*)	Martin	*from* Mars, *god of war* (*Latin*)
		Mary	*Greek form of* Miriam (*Hebrew*); *unknown meaning*
Jeremy	*English form of* Jeremiah; *Jehova exalts* (*Hebrew*)		
Jessica	*he beholds* (*Hebrew*)	Matthew	*gift of the Lord* (*Hebrew*)
Joan	*contracted form of* Johanna, *from* John	Megan	*pet form of* Margaret
		Melissa	*bee* (*Greek*)
		Michael	*like the Lord* (*Hebrew*)

Name	Original meaning	Name	Original meaning
Michelle	English spelling of French Michèle, from Michael	Sarah	princess (Hebrew)
		Scott	surname; from Scotland
Morgan	?sea + ?circle (Welsh)	Sharon	the plain (Hebrew)
Nancy	pet form of Ann	Shaun	English spelling of Irish Sean, from John
Natalie	birthday of the Lord (Latin)		
Neil	champion (Irish)	Shirley	bright clearing (Germanic)
Nicholas	victory people (Greek)	Simon	form of Simeon; listening attentively (Hebrew)
Nicola	Italian female form of Nicholas		
Nicole	French female form of Nicholas	Stephanie	French female form of Stephen
Pamela	?all honey (Greek)		
Patricia	noble (Latin)	Stephen	crown (Greek)
Paul	small (Latin)	Stuart	steward (Germanic)
Pauline	French female form of Paul	Susan	short form of Susannah; lily (Hebrew)
Peter	stone, rock (Greek)		
Philip	fond of horses (Greek)	Teresa	woman of Theresia (Greek)
Rachel	ewe (Hebrew)	Thomas	twin (Hebrew)
Rebecca	?noose (Hebrew)	Tiffany	manifestation of God (Greek)
Richard	strong ruler (Germanic)	Timothy	honouring God (Greek)
Robert	fame bright (Germanic)	Trac(e)y	?pet form of Teresa
Ronald	counsel + power (Germanic)	Vera	faith (Slavic)
Ruth	?vision of beauty (Hebrew)	Victoria	victory (Latin)
Ryan	Irish surname	Vincent	conquer (Latin)
Sally	pet form of Sarah	Virginia	maiden (Latin)
Samantha	female form of Samuel; heard / name of God (Hebrew)	Walter	ruling people (Germanic)
		Wayne	surname; wagon-maker
		William	will + helmet (Germanic)
		Zachary	Jehovah has remembered (Hebrew)
Sandra	pet form of Alexandra	Zoë	life (Greek)

National newspapers (Europe)

Name	Location	Circulation[1]	Date founded
ABC	Madrid	350 000	1905
Algemeen Dagblad	Rotterdam	415 800	1946
Apogevmatini	Athens	67 300	1956
Avriani	Athens	115 000	1980
B T	Copenhagen	175 600	1916
Berliner Zeitung	Berlin	230 600	1877
Berlingske Tidende	Copenhagen	155 400	1749
Bild am Sonntag (s)	Hamburg	2 639 000	1956
Bild Zeitung	Hamburg	4 643 900	1952
Blick	Zürich	335 100	1959
Correio do Manha	Lisbon	90 000	1979
Corriere della Sera	Milan	720 200	1876

Name	Location	Circulation[1]	Date founded
Dagbladet	Oslo	228 000	1869
De Standaard/Het Nieuwsblad/De Gentenaar	Brussels	331 000	n/a
De Telegraaf	Amsterdam	743 000	1893
De Volkskrant	Amsterdam	361 200	1919
Diario de Noticias	Lisbon	41 900	1864
Diario Popular	Lisbon	29 200	1942
Die Welt	Bonn	214 700	1946
Die Zeit (weekly)	Hamburg	494 100	1946
Ekstra Bladet	Copenhagen	190 600	1904
El Pais	Madrid	412 300	1976
El Periodico	Barcelona	215 600	1978
Ethnos	Athens	58 800	1981
Evening Herald	Dublin	99 200	1891
Evening Press	Dublin	52 600	1954
Expressen	Stockholm	566 600	1944
France-Dimanche (s)	Paris	721 000	n/a
France-Soir	Paris	424 000	1944
Frankfurter Allgemeine Zeitung	Frankfurt	360 000	1949
Gazeta Wyborcza	Warsaw	500 000	n/a
Gazet Van Antwerpen	Antwerp	170 000	1891
Helsingin Sanomat	Helsinki	463 500	1889
Het Laatste Nieuws	Brussels	306 800	1888
Il Giornale	Milan	238 800	1974
Il Giorno	Milan	255 400	1965
Il Messaggero	Rome	426 100	1878
Il Sole 24 Ore	Milan	340 000	1865
International Herald Tribune	Paris	190 700	1887
Irish Independent	Dublin	147 100	1905
Irish Times	Dublin	95 300	1859
La Libre Belgique	Brussels	82 800	1884
La Dernière Heure	Brussels	93 400	1906
La Lanterne	Brussels	132 800	1944
La Repubblica	Rome	620 000	1976
La Stampa	Turin	420 600	1867
La Vanguardia	Barcelona	208 000	1881
La Voix du Nord	Lille	400 000	1944
Le Figaro	Paris	424 000	1828
Le Monde	Paris	379 100	1944
Le Parisien Libère	Paris	339 300	1944
Les Echos	Paris	121 000	1908
Le Soir	Brussels	148 900	1887
L'Humanité	Paris	117 000	1904
L'Humanité Dimanche (s)	Paris	360 000	1946
Libération	Paris	171 100	1973

NATIONAL NEWSPAPERS (UK)

Name	Location	Circulation[1]	Date founded
Luxemburger Wort / La Voix du Luxembourg	Luxembourg	82 800	1848
Népszabadság	Budapest	320 000	1942
Neue Kronenzeitung	Vienna	1 047 800	n/a
Ouest France	Rennes	790 000	1944
Politiken	Copenhagen	150 300	1884
Rude Pravo	Prague	400 000	1920
Süddeutsche Zeitung	Munich	405 400	1945
Sunday Independent (s)	Dublin	276 200	1905
Sunday Press (s)	Dublin	154 100	1949
Sunday World (s)	Dublin	232 100	1973
Täglich Alles	Vienna	542 000	1992
Ta Nea	Athens	135 000	1944
Vers L'Avenir	Namur	119 600	1918
Welt am Sonntag (s)	Hamburg	394 400	n/a
Ya	Madrid	380 000	1935

(s) published on Sundays only

[1] 1997 figures (rounded to nearest 100).

National newspapers (UK)

Name	Location	Circulation[1]	Date founded
Daily Mail	London	2 267 000	1896
Daily Record	Glasgow	674 000	1895
Daily Star	London	574 000	1978
Daily Telegraph	London	1 070 000	1855
The Express	London	1 142 000	1900
The Express on Sunday (s)	London	1 069 000	1918
Financial Times	London	358 000	1880
The Guardian	London	396 000	1821
The Independent	London	220 000	1986
Independent on Sunday (s)	London	255 000	1990
The Mail on Sunday (s)	London	2 191 000	1982
The Mirror	London	2 292 000	1903
News of the World (s)	London	4 206 000	1843
Observer (s)	London	402 000	1791
The People (s)	London	1 733 000	1881
Scotland on Sunday (s)	Edinburgh	123 000	1988
The Scotsman	Edinburgh	81 000	1817
The Sun	London	3 651 000	1964
Sunday Mirror (s)	London	2 033 000	1963
Sunday Post (s)	Dundee	764 000	1920
Sunday Sport (s)	Manchester	275 000	1986

Name	Location	Circulation [1]	Date founded
The SundayTelegraph (s)	London	826 000	1961
The SundayTimes (s)	London	1 340 000	1822
TheTimes	London	753 000	1785

(s) published on Sundays only

[1] 1998 figures (rounded to nearest 1 000).

Major newspapers (USA)

Includes national newspapers and local newspapers having an all-day, morning, or evening circulation of 250 000 or more.

Name	Location	Circulation [1]	Date founded
Arizona Republic	Phoenix, Ariz	342 300	1890
Atlanta Constitution	Atlanta, Ga	302 600	1868
Baltimore Sun	Baltimore, Md	406 000	1837
Boston Globe	Boston, Mass	507 600	1872
Boston Herald	Boston, Mass	364 000	1892
Buffalo News	Buffalo, NY	312 000	1880
Chicago Sun-Times	Chicago, Ill	535 800	1948
ChicagoTribune	Chicago, Ill	724 300	1847
Cleveland Plain Dealer	Cleveland, Ohio	432 400	1842
Columbus Dispatch	Columbus, Ohio	252 000	1871
Dallas Morning News	Dallas, Texas	520 400	1885
Denver Post	Denver, Colo	269 300	1892
Denver Rocky Mountain News	Denver, Colo	353 000	1859
Detroit Free Press	Detroit, Mich	638 000	1831
Detroit News	Detroit, Mich	526 000	1873
Forth Worth Star-Telegram	Fort Worth, Texas	254 000	1906
Houston Chronicle	Houston, Texas	439 600	1901
Houston Post	Houston, Texas	324 000	1885
Kansas City Star	Kansas City, Mo	287 100	1880
Los Angeles Times	Los Angeles, Cal	1 117 300	1881
Miami Herald	Miami, Fla	425 300	1910
Milwaukee Sentinel	Milwaukee, Wisc	276 000	1837
Minneapolis StarTribune	Minneapolis, Minn	408 000	1867
New OrleansTimes-Picayune	New Orleans, La	278 000	1837
NewYork Daily News	NewYork, NY	1 212 000	1919
NewYork Post	NewYork, NY	521 000	1801
NewYorkTimes [2]	NewYork, NY	1 209 200	1851
Newark Star-Ledger	Newark, NJ	483 400	1832
Newsday	Melville, NY	699 000	1940
Orange County Register	Santa Ana, Cal	353 800	1905

Name	Location	Circulation[1]	Date founded
Orlando Sentinel	Orlando, Fla	271 400	1876
Philadelphia Inquirer	Philadelphia, Pa	741 500	1829
Portland Oregonian	Portland, Ore	321 000	1850
Sacramento Bee	Sacramento, Cal	261 000	1857
San Diego Union	San Diego, Cal	270 000	1868
San Francisco Chronicle	San Francisco, Cal	693 800	1865
San Jose Mercury News	San Jose, Cal	270 200	1851
Seattle Times	Seattle, Wash	447 900	1886
St Louis Post-Dispatch	St Louis, Mo	380 000	1878
St Petersburg Times	St Petersburg, Fla	326 100	1884
Tampa Tribune	Tampa, Fla	275 600	1893
USA Today[2]	Arlington, Va	1 356 000	1982
Wall Street Journal[2]	New York, NY	1 847 000	1889
Washington Post	Washington, DC	930 800	1877

[1] 1997 figures (rounded to nearest 100).

[2] National newspapers.

Car index marks (International)

A	Austria	CZ	Czech Republic	GBZ	Gibraltar
ADN	Yemen	D	Germany	GCA	Guatemala
AFG	Afghanistan	DK	Denmark	GE	Georgia
AL	Albania	DOM	Dominican Republic	GH	Ghana
AND	Andorra	DY	Benin	GR	Greece
AUS	Australia*	DZ	Algeria	GUY	Guyana*
B	Belgium	E	Spain[1]	H	Hungary
BD	Bangladesh*	EAK	Kenya*	HK	Hong Kong*
BDS	Barbados*	EAT	Tanzania*	HKJ	Jordan
BG	Bulgaria	EAU	Uganda*	HR	Croatia
BH	Belize	EC	Ecuador	I	Italy
BIH	Bosnia-Herzegovina	ES	El Salvador	IL	Israel
BR	Brazil	EST	Estonia	IND	India*
BRN	Bahrain	ET	Egypt	IR	Iran
BRU	Brunei*	ETH	Ethiopia	IRL	Ireland*
BS	The Bahamas*	F	France[2]	IRQ	Iraq
BUR	Myanmar (Burma)	FIN	Finland	IS	Iceland
C	Cuba	FJI	Fiji*	J	Japan*
CDN	Canada	FL	Liechtenstein	JA	Jamaica*
CH	Switzerland	FO	Faroe Is	K	Cambodia
CI	Côte d'Ivoire	GB	UK*	KS	Kyrgyzstan
CL	Sri Lanka*	GBA	Alderney*	KWT	Kuwait
CO	Colombia	GBG	Guernsey*	KZ	Kazakhstan
CR	Costa Rica	GBJ	Jersey*	L	Luxembourg
CY	Cyprus*	GBM	Isle of Man*	LAO	Laos

203

LAR	Libya	RCA	Central African Republic	T	Thailand*
LB	Liberia			TG	Togo
LS	Lesotho*	RCB	Congo	TJ	Tajikistan
LT	Lithuania	RCH	Chile	TM	Turkmenistan
LV	Latvia	RH	Haiti	TN	Tunisia
M	Malta*	RI	Indonesia*	TR	Turkey
MA	Morocco	RIM	Mauritania	TT	Trinidad and Tobago*
MAL	Malaysia*	RL	Lebanon	UA	Ukraine
MC	Monaco	RM	Madagascar	USA	USA
MEX	Mexico	RMM	Mali	UZ	Uzbekistan
MGL	Mongolia	RN	Niger	V	Vatican City
MK	Macedonia	RO	Romania	VN	Vietnam
MS	Mauritius*	ROK	Korea, Republic of (South Korea)	WAG	The Gambia
MW	Malawi*			WAL	Sierra Leone
N	Norway	ROU	Uruguay	WAN	Nigeria
NA	Netherlands Antilles	RP	Philippines	WD	Dominica*
NAM	Namibia*	RSM	San Marino	WG	Grenada*
NIC	Nicaragua	RU	Burundi	WL	St Lucia*
NL	Netherlands	RUS	Russia	WS	Samoa
NZ	New Zealand*	RWA	Rwanda	WV	St Vincent and the Grenadines*
P	Portugal	S	Sweden		
PA	Panama	SD	Swaziland*	YU	Yugoslavia, Federal Republic of
PE	Peru	SGP	Singapore*		
PK	Pakistan*	SK	Slovakia	YV	Venezuela
PL	Poland	SLO	Slovenia	Z	Zambia*
PNG	Papua New Guinea*	SME	Suriname*	ZA	South Africa*
PY	Paraguay	SN	Senegal	ZRE	Congo, Democratic Republic of
RA	Argentina	SU	Belarus		
RB	Botswana*	SY	Seychelles*	ZW	Zimbabwe*
RC	China	SYR	Syria		

*In countries so marked, the rule of the road is to drive on the left; in other countries, vehicles drive on the right.

[1] Including Balearic Islands, Canary Islands and Spanish enclaves.

[2] Including French Overseas Possessions.

UK airports

Alderney	Channel Is	Leeds-Bradford	
Barra	Hebrides	Liverpool	
Belfast City		London City	
Belfast International		Luton	Bedfordshire
Bembridge	Isle of Wight	Lydd	Kent
Benbecula	Hebrides	Manchester	
Biggin Hill	Kent	Newcastle	
Birmingham International		North Bay	Barra, Hebrides
Blackpool	Lancashire	North Ronaldsay	Orkneys
Bournemouth	Dorset	Norwich	Norfolk
Bristol	Avon	Oronsay	Hebrides
Cambridge		Papa Stour	Orkneys
Campbeltown	Strathclyde	Papa Westray	Orkneys
Cardiff		Plymouth (Roborough)	Devon
Colonsay	Hebrides	Prestwick	Ayrshire
Coventry	West Midlands	Ronaldsway	Isle of Man
		St Mary's	Scilly Isles
Derry City		Sanday	Orkneys
Dundee		Sandown	Isle of Wight
Dyce	Aberdeen	Scatsa	Shetlands
East Midlands	Derbyshire	Sheffield	South Yorkshire
Eday	Orkneys	Shoreham	East Sussex
Exeter	Devon	Southampton	Hampshire
Fair Isle	Shetlands	Southend	Essex
Fetlar	Shetlands	Stansted	London
Foula	Shetlands	Stornoway	Hebrides
Gatwick	London	Stronsay	Orkneys
Glasgow		Sumburgh	Shetlands
Gloucester-Cheltenham		Swansea	
Guernsey	Channel Is	Teeside International	Cleveland
Heathrow	London	Tingwall	Lerwick, Shetlands
Hoy	Orkneys		
Humberside		Tiree	Hebrides
Inverness		Tresco	Scilly Isles
Ipswich	Suffolk	Turnhouse	Edinburgh
Islay	Hebrides	Unst	Shetlands
Jersey	Channel Is	West Midlands	Birmingham
Kent International	Manston	Westray	Orkneys
Kirkwall	Orkneys	Wick	Caithness
Land's End	Cornwall		

UK road distances

Road distances between British centres are given in statute miles, using routes recommended by the Automobile Association based on the quickest travelling time. To convert to kilometres, multiply number given by 1.6093.

	Aberdeen	Birmingham	Bristol	Cambridge	Cardiff	Dover	Edinburgh	Exeter	Glasgow	Holyhead	Hull	Leeds	Liverpool	Manchester	Newcastle	Norwich	Nottingham	Oxford	Penzance	Plymouth	Shrewsbury	Southampton	Stranraer	York
Birmingham	430																							
Bristol	511	85																						
Cambridge	468	101	156																					
Cardiff	532	119	45	198																				
Dover	591	203	202	121	234																			
Edinburgh	130	293	373	337	395	457																		
Exeter	584	157	81	233	119	248	457																	
Glasgow	149	291	372	349	393	488	45	465																
Holyhead	457	151	232	246	209	362	290	305	325															
Hull	361	136	227	157	246	278	229	297	325	305														
Leeds	336	115	216	143	236	265	205	288	305	222	59													
Liverpool	361	98	178	200	188	295	167	250	220	72	127	75												
Manchester	354	88	167	153	188	283	148	239	214	96	110	43	34											
Newcastle	239	198	291	224	311	348	105	361	150	218	120	95	167	141										
Norwich	501	161	217	62	252	167	341	281	379	260	153	173	232	183	258									
Nottingham	402	48	151	82	170	202	281	220	272	123	91	73	92	72	156	123								
Oxford	497	63	74	82	109	148	365	152	354	218	153	116	164	153	253	144	92							
Penzance	696	272	195	346	232	362	561	112	559	419	411	401	366	355	477	407	336	265						
Plymouth	624	199	125	275	164	290	488	45	486	347	341	328	294	281	410	336	265	193	78					
Shrewsbury	412	48	142	110	123	276	290	152	281	88	116	118	64	71	216	205	85	113	227	242				
Southampton	571	128	75	133	122	155	437	114	436	296	235	232	241	226	319	192	171	67	315	155	190			
Stranraer	241	221	307	386	361	503	130	457	88	332	253	259	234	226	164	393	295	371	572	502	287	447		
York	325	128	221	153	241	274	191	291	208	130	37	24	100	71	83	86	85	113	406	340	144	252	228	
London	543	118	119	60	155	77	405	170	402	263	215	196	210	199	280	115	128	56	283	215	162	76	419	209

SCIENCE, ENGINEERING AND MEASUREMENT

Electromagnetic spectrum

Radiation	Approximate wavelengths	Uses
Radio waves	> 10 cm	communications; radio and TV broadcasting
Microwaves	1 mm-10 cm	communications; radar; microwave ovens
Infrared	$10^{-3}-7.8 \times 10^{-7}$ m	night and smoke vision systems; intruder alarms; weather forecasting; missile guidance systems
Visible	$7.8 \times 10^{-7}-3 \times 10^{-7}$ m	human eyesight
Ultraviolet	$3 \times 10^{-7}-10^{-8}$ m	forensic science; medical treatment
X-rays	$10^{-8}-3 \times 10^{-11}$ m	medical X-ray photographs; material structure analysis
Gamma rays	$< 3 \times 10^{-11}$ m	medical diagnosis

Temperature conversion

To convert	To	Equation
°Fahrenheit	°Celsius	$-32, \times 5, \div 9$
°Fahrenheit	°Rankine	$+459.67$
°Fahrenheit	°Réaumur	$-32, \times 4, \div 9$
°Celsius	°Fahrenheit	$\times 9, \div 5, + 32$
°Celsius	Kelvin	$+273.15$
°Celsius	°Réaumur	$\times 4, \div 5$
Kelvin	°Celsius	-273.15
°Rankine	°Fahrenheit	-459.67
°Réaumur	°Fahrenheit	$\times 9, \div 4, + 32$
°Réaumur	°Celsius	$\times 5, \div 4$

Carry out operations in sequence.

Temperature conversion

Degrees Fahrenheit (F) converted to Degrees Celsius (Centigrade) (C)

°F → °C	°F → °C	°F → °C	°F → °C	°F → °C
1 -17.2	44 6.7	87 30.5	130 54.4	173 78.3
2 -16.7	45 7.2	88 31.1	131 55.0	174 78.9
3 -16.1	46 7.8	89 31.7	132 55.5	175 79.4
4 -15.5	47 8.3	90 32.2	133 56.1	176 80.0
5 -15.0	48 8.9	91 32.8	134 56.7	177 80.5
6 -14.4	49 9.4	92 33.3	135 57.2	178 81.1
7 -13.9	50 10.0	93 33.9	136 57.8	179 81.7
8 -13.3	51 10.5	94 34.4	137 58.3	180 82.2
9 -12.8	52 11.1	95 35.0	138 58.9	181 82.8
10 -12.2	53 11.7	96 35.5	139 59.4	182 83.3
11 -11.6	54 12.2	97 36.1	140 60.0	183 83.9
12 -11.1	55 12.8	98 36.7	141 60.5	184 84.4
13 -10.5	56 13.3	99 37.2	142 61.1	185 85.0
14 -10.0	57 13.9	100 37.8	143 61.7	186 85.5
15 -9.4	58 14.4	101 38.3	144 62.2	187 86.1
16 -8.9	59 15.0	102 38.9	145 62.8	188 86.7
17 -8.3	60 15.5	103 39.4	146 63.3	189 87.2
18 -7.8	61 16.1	104 40.0	147 63.9	190 87.8
19 -7.2	62 16.7	105 40.5	148 64.4	191 88.3
20 -6.7	63 17.2	106 41.1	149 65.0	192 88.8
21 -6.1	64 17.8	107 41.7	150 65.5	193 89.4
22 -5.5	65 18.3	108 42.2	151 66.1	194 90.0
23 -5.0	66 18.9	109 42.8	152 66.7	195 90.5
24 -4.4	67 19.4	110 43.3	153 67.2	196 91.1
25 -3.9	68 20.0	111 43.9	154 67.8	197 91.7
26 -3.3	69 20.5	112 44.4	155 68.3	198 92.2
27 -2.8	70 21.1	113 45.0	156 68.9	199 92.8
28 -2.2	71 21.7	114 45.5	157 69.4	200 93.3
29 -1.7	72 22.2	115 46.1	158 70.0	201 93.9
30 -1.1	73 22.8	116 46.7	159 70.5	202 94.4
31 -0.5	74 23.3	117 47.2	160 71.1	203 95.0
32 0.0	75 23.9	118 47.8	161 71.7	204 95.5
33 0.5	76 24.4	119 48.3	162 72.2	205 96.1
34 1.1	77 25.0	120 48.9	163 72.8	206 96.7
35 1.7	78 25.5	121 49.4	164 73.3	207 97.2
36 2.2	79 26.1	122 50.0	165 73.9	208 97.8
37 2.8	80 26.7	123 50.5	166 74.4	209 98.3
38 3.3	81 27.2	124 51.1	167 75.0	210 98.9
39 3.9	82 27.8	125 51.7	168 75.5	211 99.4
40 4.4	83 28.3	126 52.2	169 76.1	212 100.0
41 5.0	84 28.9	127 52.8	170 76.7	
42 5.5	85 29.4	128 53.3	171 77.2	
43 6.1	86 30.0	129 53.9	172 77.8	

Degrees Celsius (Centigrade) (C) converted to Degrees Fahrenheit (F)

°C → °F		°C → °F		°C → °F	
1	33.8	35	95.0	69	156.2
2	35.6	36	96.8	70	158.0
3	37.4	37	98.6	71	159.8
4	39.2	38	100.4	72	161.6
5	41.0	39	102.2	73	163.4
6	42.8	40	104.0	74	165.2
7	44.6	41	105.8	75	167.0
8	46.4	42	107.6	76	168.8
9	48.2	43	109.4	77	170.6
10	50.0	44	111.2	78	172.4
11	51.8	45	113.0	79	174.2
12	53.6	46	114.8	80	176.0
13	55.4	47	116.6	81	177.8
14	57.2	48	118.4	82	179.6
15	59.0	49	120.2	83	181.4
16	60.8	50	122.0	84	183.2
17	62.6	51	123.8	85	185.0
18	64.4	52	125.6	86	186.8
19	66.2	53	127.4	87	188.6
20	68.0	54	129.2	88	190.4
21	69.8	55	131.0	89	192.2
22	71.6	56	132.8	90	194.0
23	73.4	57	134.6	91	195.8
24	75.2	58	136.4	92	197.6
25	77.0	59	138.2	93	199.4
26	78.8	60	140.0	94	201.2
27	80.6	61	141.8	95	203.0
28	82.4	62	143.6	96	204.8
29	84.2	63	145.4	97	206.6
30	86.0	64	147.2	98	208.4
31	87.8	65	149.0	99	210.2
32	89.6	66	150.8	100	212.0
33	91.4	67	152.6		
34	93.2	68	154.4		

Periodic table

H 1 hydrogen								
Li 3 lithium	Be 4 beryllium							
Na 11 sodium	Mg 12 magnesium							
K 19 potassium	Ca 20 calcium	Sc 21 scandium	Ti 22 titanium	V 23 vanadium	Cr 24 chromium	Mn 25 manganese	Fe 26 iron	Co 27 cobalt
Rb 37 rubidium	Sr 38 strontium	Y 39 yttrium	Zr 40 zirconium	Nb 41 niobium	Mo 42 moly- bdenum	Tc 43 technetium	Ru 44 ruthenium	Rh 45 rhodium
Cs 55 caesium	Ba 56 barium	57–71 *	Hf 72 hafnium	Ta 73 tantalum	W 74 tungsten	Re 75 rhenium	Os 76 osmium	Ir 77 iridium
Fr 87 francium	Ra 88 radium	89–103 **	Rf 104 ruther- fordium	Db 105 dubnium	Sg 106 sea- borgium	Bh 107 bohrium	Hs 108 hassium	Mt 109 meitnerium

element symbol — atomic number
element name

*Lanthanide series	La 57 lanthanum	Ce 58 cerium	Pr 59 praseo- dymium	Nd 60 neo- dymium	Pm 61 pro- methium	Sm 62 samarium	Eu 63 europium
**Actinide series	Ac 89 actinium	Th 90 thorium	Pa 91 pro- tactinium	U 92 uranium	Np 93 neptunium	Pu 94 plutonium	Am 95 americium

He 2					
helium					

B 5	C 6	N 7	O 8	F 9	Ne 10
boron	carbon	nitrogen	oxygen	fluorine	neon
Al 13	Si 14	P 15	S 16	Cl 17	Ar 18
aluminium	silicon	phosphorus	sulphur	chlorine	argon

Ni 28	Cu 29	Zn 30	Ga 31	Ge 32	As 33	Se 34	Br 35	Kr 36
nickel	copper	zinc	gallium	germanium	arsenic	selenium	bromine	krypton
Pd 46	Ag 47	Cd 48	In 49	Sn 50	Sb 51	Te 52	I 53	Xe 54
palladium	silver	cadmium	indium	tin	antimony	tellurium	iodine	xenon
Pt 78	Au 79	Hg 80	Tl 81	Pb 82	Bi 83	Po 84	At 85	Rn 86
platinum	gold	mercury	thallium	lead	bismuth	polonium	astatine	radon
Uun 110	Uuu 111	Uub 112						
ununnilium	unununium	ununbium						

Gd 64	Tb 65	Dy 66	Ho 67	Er 68	Tm 69	Yb 70	Lu 71
gadolinium	terbium	dysprosium	holmium	erbium	thulium	ytterbium	lutetium
Cm 96	Bk 97	Cf 98	Es 99	Fm 100	Md 101	No 102	Lr 103
curium	berkelium	californium	einsteinium	fermium	mendelevium	nobelium	lawrencium

Numerical equivalents

Arabic	Roman	Greek	Binary numbers
1	I	α'	1
2	II	β'	10
3	III	γ'	11
4	IV	δ'	100
5	V	ε'	101
6	VI	ς'	110
7	VII	ζ'	111
8	VIII	η'	1000
9	IX	θ'	1001
10	X	ι'	1010
11	XI	$\iota\alpha'$	1011
12	XII	$\iota\beta'$	1100
13	XIII	$\iota\gamma'$	1101
14	XIV	$\iota\delta'$	1110
15	XV	$\iota\varepsilon'$	1111
16	XVI	$\iota\varsigma'$	10000
17	XVII	$\iota\zeta'$	10001
18	XVIII	$\iota\eta'$	10010
19	XIX	$\iota\theta'$	10011
20	XX	κ'	10100
30	XXX	λ'	11110
40	XL	μ'	101000
50	L	ν'	110010
60	LX	ξ'	111100
70	LXX	o'	1000110
80	LXXX	π'	1010000
90	XC	$.o'$	1011010
100	C	ρ'	1100100
200	CC	σ'	11001000
300	CCC	τ'	100101100
400	CD	υ'	110010000
500	D	ϕ'	111110100
1 000	M	$.\alpha$	1111101000
5 000	$\overline{V}$	$.\varepsilon$	1001110001000
10 000	$\overline{X}$	$.\iota$	10011100001000
100 000	$\overline{C}$	$.\rho$	11000011010100000

NUMERICAL EQUIVALENTS

%	D[1]	F[2]	%	D[1]	F[2]	%	D[1]	F[2]
1	0.01	$\frac{1}{100}$	20	0.20	$\frac{1}{5}$	41	0.41	$\frac{41}{100}$
2	0.02	$\frac{1}{50}$	21	0.21	$\frac{21}{100}$	42	0.42	$\frac{21}{50}$
3	0.03	$\frac{3}{100}$	22	0.22	$\frac{11}{50}$	43	0.43	$\frac{43}{100}$
4	0.04	$\frac{1}{25}$	23	0.23	$\frac{23}{100}$	44	0.44	$\frac{11}{25}$
5	0.05	$\frac{1}{20}$	24	0.24	$\frac{6}{25}$	45	0.45	$\frac{9}{20}$
6	0.06	$\frac{3}{50}$	25	0.25	$\frac{1}{4}$	46	0.46	$\frac{23}{50}$
7	0.07	$\frac{7}{100}$	26	0.26	$\frac{13}{50}$	47	0.47	$\frac{47}{100}$
8	0.08	$\frac{2}{25}$	27	0.27	$\frac{27}{100}$	48	0.48	$\frac{12}{25}$
$8\frac{1}{3}$	0.083	$\frac{1}{12}$	28	0.28	$\frac{7}{25}$	49	0.49	$\frac{49}{100}$
9	0.09	$\frac{9}{100}$	29	0.29	$\frac{29}{100}$	50	0.50	$\frac{1}{2}$
10	0.10	$\frac{1}{10}$	30	0.30	$\frac{3}{10}$	55	0.55	$\frac{11}{20}$
11	0.11	$\frac{11}{100}$	31	0.31	$\frac{31}{100}$	60	0.60	$\frac{3}{5}$
12	0.12	$\frac{3}{25}$	32	0.32	$\frac{8}{25}$	65	0.65	$\frac{13}{20}$
$12\frac{1}{2}$	0.125	$\frac{1}{8}$	33	0.33	$\frac{33}{100}$	70	0.70	$\frac{7}{10}$
13	0.13	$\frac{13}{100}$	$33\frac{1}{3}$	0.333	$\frac{1}{3}$	75	0.75	$\frac{3}{4}$
14	0.14	$\frac{7}{50}$	34	0.34	$\frac{17}{50}$	80	0.80	$\frac{4}{5}$
15	0.15	$\frac{3}{20}$	35	0.35	$\frac{7}{20}$	85	0.85	$\frac{17}{20}$
16	0.16	$\frac{4}{25}$	36	0.36	$\frac{9}{25}$	90	0.90	$\frac{9}{10}$
$16\frac{2}{3}$	0.167	$\frac{1}{6}$	37	0.37	$\frac{37}{100}$	95	0.95	$\frac{19}{20}$
17	0.17	$\frac{17}{100}$	38	0.38	$\frac{19}{50}$	100	1.00	1
18	0.18	$\frac{9}{50}$	39	0.39	$\frac{39}{100}$			
19	0.19	$\frac{19}{100}$	40	0.40	$\frac{2}{5}$			

[1] Decimal.

[2] Fraction.

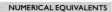

Fraction	Decimal	Fraction	Decimal	Fraction	Decimal
$\frac{1}{2}$	0.5000	$\frac{8}{9}$	0.8889	$\frac{15}{16}$	0.9375
$\frac{1}{3}$	0.3333	$\frac{1}{10}$	0.1000	$\frac{1}{20}$	0.0500
$\frac{2}{3}$	0.6667	$\frac{3}{10}$	0.3000	$\frac{3}{20}$	0.1500
$\frac{1}{4}$	0.2500	$\frac{7}{10}$	0.7000	$\frac{7}{20}$	0.3500
$\frac{3}{4}$	0.7500	$\frac{9}{10}$	0.9000	$\frac{9}{20}$	0.4500
$\frac{1}{5}$	0.2000	$\frac{1}{11}$	0.0909	$\frac{11}{20}$	0.5500
$\frac{2}{5}$	0.4000	$\frac{2}{11}$	0.1818	$\frac{13}{20}$	0.6500
$\frac{3}{5}$	0.6000	$\frac{3}{11}$	0.2727	$\frac{17}{20}$	0.8500
$\frac{4}{5}$	0.8000	$\frac{4}{11}$	0.3636	$\frac{19}{20}$	0.9500
$\frac{1}{6}$	0.1667	$\frac{5}{11}$	0.4545	$\frac{1}{32}$	0.0312
$\frac{5}{6}$	0.8333	$\frac{6}{11}$	0.5454	$\frac{3}{32}$	0.0937
$\frac{1}{7}$	0.1429	$\frac{7}{11}$	0.6363	$\frac{5}{32}$	0.1562
$\frac{2}{7}$	0.2857	$\frac{8}{11}$	0.7272	$\frac{7}{32}$	0.2187
$\frac{3}{7}$	0.4286	$\frac{9}{11}$	0.8181	$\frac{9}{32}$	0.2812
$\frac{4}{7}$	0.5714	$\frac{10}{11}$	0.9090	$\frac{11}{32}$	0.3437
$\frac{5}{7}$	0.7143	$\frac{1}{12}$	0.0833	$\frac{13}{32}$	0.4062
$\frac{6}{7}$	0.8571	$\frac{5}{12}$	0.4167	$\frac{15}{32}$	0.4687
$\frac{1}{8}$	0.1250	$\frac{7}{12}$	0.5833	$\frac{17}{32}$	0.5312
$\frac{3}{8}$	0.3750	$\frac{11}{12}$	0.9167	$\frac{19}{32}$	0.5937
$\frac{5}{8}$	0.6250	$\frac{1}{16}$	0.0625	$\frac{21}{32}$	0.6562
$\frac{7}{8}$	0.8750	$\frac{3}{16}$	0.1875	$\frac{23}{32}$	0.7187
$\frac{1}{9}$	0.1111	$\frac{5}{16}$	0.3125	$\frac{25}{32}$	0.7812
$\frac{2}{9}$	0.2222	$\frac{7}{16}$	0.4375	$\frac{27}{32}$	0.8437
$\frac{4}{9}$	0.4444	$\frac{9}{16}$	0.5625	$\frac{29}{32}$	0.9062
$\frac{5}{9}$	0.5556	$\frac{11}{16}$	0.6875	$\frac{31}{32}$	0.9687
$\frac{7}{9}$	0.7778	$\frac{13}{16}$	0.8125		

Multiplication table

×	2	3	4	5	6	7	8	9	10	11	12	13	14	15	16	17	18	19	20	21	22	23	24	25
2	4	6	8	10	12	14	16	18	20	22	24	26	28	30	32	34	36	38	40	42	44	46	48	50
3	6	9	12	15	18	21	24	27	30	33	36	39	42	45	48	51	54	57	60	63	66	69	72	75
4	8	12	16	20	24	28	32	36	40	44	48	52	56	60	64	68	72	76	80	84	88	92	96	100
5	10	15	20	25	30	35	40	45	50	55	60	65	70	75	80	85	90	95	100	105	110	115	120	125
6	12	18	24	30	36	42	48	54	60	66	72	78	84	90	96	102	108	114	120	126	132	138	144	150
7	14	21	28	35	42	49	56	63	70	77	84	91	98	105	112	119	126	133	140	147	154	161	168	175
8	16	24	32	40	48	56	64	72	80	88	96	104	112	120	128	136	144	152	160	168	176	184	192	200
9	18	27	36	45	54	63	72	81	90	99	108	117	126	135	144	153	162	171	180	189	198	207	216	225
10	20	30	40	50	60	70	80	90	100	110	120	130	140	150	160	170	180	190	200	210	220	230	240	250
11	22	33	44	55	66	77	88	99	110	121	132	143	154	165	176	187	198	209	220	231	242	253	264	275
12	24	36	48	60	72	84	96	108	120	132	144	156	168	180	192	204	216	228	240	252	264	276	288	300
13	26	39	52	65	78	91	104	117	130	143	156	169	182	195	208	221	234	247	260	273	286	299	312	325
14	28	42	56	70	84	98	112	126	140	154	168	182	196	210	224	238	252	266	280	294	308	322	336	350
15	30	45	60	75	90	105	120	135	150	165	180	195	210	225	240	255	270	285	300	315	330	345	360	375
16	32	48	64	80	96	112	128	144	160	176	192	208	224	240	256	272	288	304	320	336	352	368	384	400
17	34	51	68	85	102	119	136	153	170	187	204	221	238	255	272	289	306	323	340	357	374	391	408	425
18	36	54	72	90	108	126	144	162	180	198	216	234	252	270	288	306	324	342	360	378	396	414	432	450
19	38	57	76	95	114	133	152	171	190	209	228	247	266	285	304	323	342	361	380	399	418	437	456	475
20	40	60	80	100	120	140	160	180	200	220	240	260	280	300	320	340	360	380	400	420	440	460	480	500
21	42	63	84	105	126	147	168	189	210	231	252	273	294	315	336	357	378	399	420	441	462	483	504	525
22	44	66	88	110	132	154	176	198	220	242	264	286	308	330	352	374	396	418	440	462	484	506	528	550
23	46	69	92	115	138	161	184	207	230	253	276	299	322	345	368	391	414	437	460	483	506	529	552	575
24	48	72	96	120	144	168	192	216	240	264	288	312	336	360	384	408	432	456	480	504	528	552	576	600
25	50	75	100	125	150	175	200	225	250	275	300	325	350	375	400	425	450	475	500	525	550	575	600	625

Squares and roots

Number	Square	Cube	Square root	Cube root
1	1	1	1.000	1.000
2	4	8	1.414	1.260
3	9	27	1.732	1.442
4	16	64	2.000	1.587
5	25	125	2.236	1.710
6	36	216	2.449	1.817
7	49	343	2.646	1.913
8	64	512	2.828	2.000
9	81	729	3.000	2.080
10	100	1 000	3.162	2.154
11	121	1 331	3.317	2.224
12	144	1 728	3.464	2.289
13	169	2 197	3.606	2.351
14	196	2 744	3.742	2.410
15	225	3 375	3.873	2.466
16	256	4 096	4.000	2.520
17	289	4 913	4.123	2.571
18	324	5 832	4.243	2.621
19	361	6 859	4.359	2.668
20	400	8 000	4.472	2.714
25	625	15 625	5.000	2.924
30	900	27 000	5.477	3.107
40	1 600	64 000	6.325	3.420
50	2 500	125 000	7.071	3.684

Common measures

□ Metric units Length		Imperial equivalent
	1 millimetre	0.03937 in
10 mm	1 centimetre	0.39 in
10 cm	1 decimetre	3.94 in
100 cm	1 metre	39.37 in
1 000 m	1 kilometre	0.62 mile
Area		
	1 square millimetre	0.0016 sq in
	1 square centimetre	0.155 sq in
100 sq cm	1 square decimetre	15.5 sq in
10 000 sq cm	1 square metre	10.76 sq ft
10 000 sq m	1 hectare	2.47 acres

❏ Metric units Volume		Imperial equivalent
	1 cubic centimetre	0.016 cu in
1 000 cu cm	1 cubic decimetre	61.024 cu in
1 000 cu dm	1 cubic metre	35.31 cu ft
		1.308 cu yds
Liquid volume		
	1 litre	1.76 pints
100 litres	1 hectolitre	22 gallons
Weight		
	1 gram	0.035 oz
1 000 g	1 kilogram	2.2046 lb
1 000 kg	1 tonne	0.9842 ton

❏ Imperial units Length		Metric equivalent
	1 inch	2.54 cm
12 in	1 foot	30.48 cm
3 ft	1 yard	0.9144 m
1 760 yd	1 mile	1.6093 km
Area		
	1 square inch	6.45 cm^2
144 sq in	1 square foot	0.0929 m^2
9 sq ft	1 square yard	0.836 m^2
4 840 sq yd	1 acre	0.405 ha
640 acres	1 square mile	259 ha
Volume		
	1 cubic inch	16.3871 cm^3
1 728 cu in	1 cubic foot	0.028 m^3
27 cu ft	1 cubic yard	0.765 m^3
Liquid volume		
	1 pint	0.57 litre
2 pints	1 quart	1.14 litres
4 quarts	1 gallon	4.55 litres
Weight		
	1 ounce	28.3495 g
16 oz	1 pound	0.4536 kg
14 lb	1 stone	6.35 kg
8 stones	1 hundredweight	50.8 kg
20 cwt	1 ton	1.016 tonnes

Conversion factors

◻ Imperial to metric

Length			Multiply by
inches	→	millimetres	25.4
inches	→	centimetres	2.54
feet	→	metres	0.3048
yards	→	metres	0.9144
statute miles	→	kilometres	1.6093
nautical miles	→	kilometres	1.852

Area			
square inches	→	square centimetres	6.4516
square feet	→	square metres	0.0929
square yards	→	square metres	0.8361
acres	→	hectares	0.4047
square miles	→	square kilometres	2.5899

Volume			
cubic inches	→	cubic centimetres	16.3871
cubic feet	→	cubic metres	0.0283
cubic yards	→	cubic metres	0.7646

Capacity			
UK fluid ounces	→	litres	0.0284
US fluid ounces	→	litres	0.0296
UK pints	→	litres	0.5682
US pints	→	litres	0.4732
UK gallons	→	litres	4.546
US gallons	→	litres	3.7854

Weight			
ounces (avoirdupois)	→	grams	28.3495
ounces (troy)	→	grams	31.1035
pounds	→	kilograms	0.4536
tons (long)	→	tonnes	1.016

□ Metric to imperial

Length			Multiply by
millimetres	→	inches	0.0394
centimetres	→	inches	0.3937
metres	→	feet	3.2808
metres	→	yards	1.0936
kilometres	→	statute miles	0.6214
kilometres	→	nautical miles	0.54

Area			
square centimetres	→	square inches	0.155
square metres	→	square feet	10.764
square metres	→	square yards	1.196
hectares	→	acres	2.471
square kilometres	→	square miles	0.386

Volume			
cubic centimetres	→	cubic inches	0.061
cubic metres	→	cubic feet	35.315
cubic metres	→	cubic yards	1.308

Capacity			
litres	→	UK fluid ounces	35.1961
litres	→	US fluid ounces	33.8150
litres	→	UK pints	1.7598
litres	→	US pints	2.1134
litres	→	UK gallons	0.2199
litres	→	US gallons	0.2642

Weight			
grams	→	ounces (avoirdupois)	0.0353
grams	→	ounces (troy)	0.0322
kilograms	→	pounds	2.2046
tonnes	→	tons (long)	0.9842

Conversion tables: length

in	cm	cm	in	in	mm	mm	in
⅛	0.3	1	0.39	⅛	3.2	1	0.04
¼	0.6	2	0.79	¼	6.4	2	0.08
⅜	1.0	3	1.18	⅜	9.5	3	0.12
½	1.3	4	1.57	½	12.7	4	0.16
⅝	1.6	5	1.97	⅝	15.9	5	0.20
¾	1.9	6	2.36	¾	19.0	6	0.24
⅞	2.2	7	2.76	⅞	22.2	7	0.28
1	2.5	8	3.15	1	25.4	8	0.31
2	5.1	9	3.54	2	50.8	9	0.35
3	7.6	10	3.94	3	76.2	10	0.39
4	10.2	11	4.33	4	101.6	11	0.43
5	12.7	12	4.72	5	127.0	12	0.47
6	15.2	13	5.12	6	152.4	13	0.51
7	17.8	14	5.51	7	177.8	14	0.55
8	20.3	15	5.91	8	203.2	15	0.59
9	22.9	16	6.30	9	228.6	16	0.63
10	25.4	17	6.69	10	254.0	17	0.67
16	40.6	24	9.45				
17	43.2	25	9.84				
18	45.7	26	10.24				
19	48.3	27	10.63				
20	50.8	28	11.02				
21	53.3	29	11.42				
22	55.9	30	11.81				
23	58.4	31	12.20				
24	61.0	32	12.60				
25	63.5	33	12.99				
26	66.0	34	13.39				
27	68.6	35	13.78				
28	71.1	36	14.17				
29	73.7	37	14.57				
30	76.2	38	14.96				
40	101.6	39	15.35				
50	127.0	40	15.75				

Exact conversions

1 in = 2.54 cm
1 cm = 0.3937 in
1 in = 25.40 mm
1 mm = 0.0394 in

ft	m	m	ft	yd	m	m	yd
1	0.3	1	3.3	1	0.9	1	1.1
2	0.6	2	6.6	2	1.8	2	2.2
3	0.9	3	9.8	3	2.7	3	3.3
4	1.2	4	13.1	4	3.7	4	4.4
5	1.5	5	16.4	5	4.6	5	5.5
6	1.8	6	19.7	6	5.5	6	6.6
7	2.1	7	23.0	7	6.4	7	7.7
8	2.4	8	26.2	8	7.3	8	8.7
9	2.7	9	29.5	9	8.2	9	9.8
10	3.0	10	32.8	10	9.1	10	10.9
15	4.6	15	49.2	15	13.7	15	16.4
20	6.1	20	65.5	20	18.3	20	21.9
25	7.6	25	82.0	25	22.9	25	27.3
30	9.1	30	98.4	30	27.4	30	32.8
35	10.7	35	114.8	35	32.0	35	38.3
40	12.2	40	131.2	40	36.6	40	43.7
45	13.7	45	147.6	45	41.1	45	49.2
50	15.2	50	164.0	50	45.7	50	54.7
75	22.9	75	246.1	75	68.6	75	82.0
100	30.5	100	328.1	100	91.4	100	109.4
200	61.0	200	656.2	200	182.9	200	218.7
300	91.4	300	984.3	220	201.2	220	240.6
400	121.9	400	1 312.3	300	274.3	300	328.1
500	152.4	500	1 640.4	400	365.8	400	437.4
600	182.9	600	1 968.5	440	402.3	440	481.2
700	213.4	700	2 296.6	500	457.2	500	546.8
800	243.8	800	2 624.7	600	548.6	600	656.2
900	274.3	900	2 952.8	700	640.1	700	765.5
1 000	304.8	1 000	3 280.8	800	731.5	800	874.9
1 500	457.2	1 500	4 921.3	880	804.7	880	962.4
2 000	609.6	2 000	6 561.7	900	823.0	900	984.2
2 500	762.0	2 500	8 202.1	1 000	914.4	1 000	1 093.6
3 000	914.4	3 000	9 842.5	1 500	1 371.6	1 500	1 640.4
3 500	1 066.8	3 500	11 482.9	2 000	1 828.8	2 000	2 187.2
4 000	1 219.2	4 000	13 123.4	2 500	2 286.0	2 500	2 734.0
5 000	1 524.0	5 000	16 404.2	5 000	4 572.0	5 000	5 468.1

Exact conversions

1 ft = 0.3048 m   1 yd = 0.9144 m
1 m = 3.2808 ft   1 m = 1.0936 yd

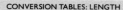
mi[1]	km		km	mi[1]
1	1.6		1	0.6
2	3.2		2	1.2
3	4.8		3	1.9
4	6.4		4	2.5
5	8.0		5	3.1
6	9.7		6	3.7
7	11.3		7	4.3
8	12.9		8	5.0
9	14.5		9	5.6
10	16.1		10	6.2
15	24.1		15	9.3
20	32.2		20	12.4
25	40.2		25	15.5
30	48.3		30	18.6
35	56.3		35	21.7
40	64.4		40	24.9
45	72.4		45	28.0
50	80.5		50	31.1
55	88.5		55	34.2
60	96.6		60	37.3
65	104.6		65	40.4
70	112.7		70	43.5
75	120.7		75	46.6
80	128.7		80	49.7
85	136.8		85	52.8
90	144.8		90	55.9
95	152.9		95	59.0
100	160.9		100	62.1
200	321.9		200	124.3
300	482.8		300	186.4
400	643.7		400	248.5
500	804.7		500	310.7
750	1 207.0		750	466.0
1 000	1 609.3		1 000	621.4
2 500	4 023.4		2 500	1 553.4
5 000	8 046.7		5 000	3 106.9

[1] Statute miles.

Exact conversions

1 mi = 1.6093 km
1 km = 0.6214 mi

Conversion tables: area

sq in	sq cm	sq cm	sq in	sq ft	sq m	sq m	sq ft
1	6.45	1	0.16	1	0.09	1	10.8
2	12.90	2	0.31	2	0.19	2	21.5
3	19.35	3	0.47	3	0.28	3	32.3
4	25.81	4	0.62	4	0.37	4	43.1
5	32.26	5	0.78	5	0.46	5	53.8
6	38.71	6	0.93	6	0.56	6	64.6
7	45.16	7	1.09	7	0.65	7	75.3
8	51.61	8	1.24	8	0.74	8	86.1
9	58.06	9	1.40	9	0.84	9	96.9
10	64.52	10	1.55	10	0.93	10	107.6
11	70.97	11	1.71	11	1.02	11	118.4
12	77.42	12	1.86	12	1.11	12	129.2
13	83.87	13	2.02	13	1.21	13	139.9
14	90.32	14	2.17	14	1.30	14	150.7
15	96.77	15	2.33	15	1.39	15	161.5
16	103.23	16	2.48	16	1.49	16	172.2
17	109.68	17	2.64	17	1.58	17	183.0
18	116.13	18	2.79	18	1.67	18	193.8
19	122.58	19	2.95	19	1.77	19	204.5
20	129.03	20	3.10	20	1.86	20	215.3
25	161.29	25	3.88	25	2.32	25	269.1
50	322.58	50	7.75	50	4.65	50	538.2
75	483.87	75	11.63	75	6.97	75	807.3
100	645.16	100	15.50	100	9.29	100	1 076.4
125	806.45	125	19.38	250	23.23	250	2 691.0
150	967.74	150	23.25	500	46.45	500	5 382.0
				750	69.68	750	8 072.9
				1 000	92.90	1 000	10 763.9

Exact conversions

$1 \text{ in}^2 = 6.4516 \text{ cm}^2$ $1 \text{ ft}^2 = 0.0929 \text{ m}^2$
$1 \text{ cm}^2 = 0.155 \text{ in}^2$ $1 \text{ m}^2 = 10.7639 \text{ ft}^2$

acres	hectares	hectares	acres	sq mi[1]	sq km	sq km	sq mi[1]
1	0.40	1	2.5	1	2.6	1	0.39
2	0.81	2	4.9	2	5.2	2	0.77
3	1.21	3	7.4	3	7.8	3	1.16
4	1.62	4	9.9	4	10.4	4	1.54
5	2.02	5	12.4	5	12.9	5	1.93
6	2.43	6	14.8	6	15.5	6	2.32
7	2.83	7	17.3	7	18.1	7	2.70
8	3.24	8	19.8	8	20.7	8	3.09
9	3.64	9	22.2	9	23.3	9	3.47
10	4.05	10	24.7	10	25.9	10	3.86
11	4.45	11	27.2	20	51.8	20	7.72
12	4.86	12	29.7	21	54.4	21	8.11
13	5.26	13	32.1	22	57.0	22	8.49
14	5.67	14	34.6	23	59.6	23	8.88
15	6.07	15	37.1	24	62.2	24	9.27
16	6.47	16	39.5	25	64.7	25	9.65
17	6.88	17	42.0	30	77.7	30	11.58
18	7.28	18	44.5	40	103.6	40	15.44
19	7.69	19	46.9	50	129.5	50	19.31
20	8.09	20	49.4	100	259.0	100	38.61
25	10.12	25	61.8	200	518.0	200	77.22
50	20.23	50	123.6	300	777.0	300	115.83
75	30.35	75	185.3	400	1 036.0	400	154.44
100	40.47	100	247.1	500	1 295.0	500	193.05
250	101.17	250	617.8	600	1 554.0	600	231.66
500	202.34	500	1 235.5	700	1 813.0	700	270.27
750	303.51	750	1 853.3	800	2 072.0	800	308.88
1 000	404.69	1 000	2 471.1	900	2 331.0	900	347.49
1 500	607.03	1 500	3 706.6	1 000	2 590.0	1 000	386.10
				1 500	3 885.0	1 500	579.15
				2 000	5 180.0	2 000	772.20

[1] Statute miles.

Exact conversions

1 acre = 0.4047 hectares   1 sq mi = 2.589999 sq km
1 hectare = 2.471 acres   1 sq km = 0.3861 sq mi

Conversion tables: volume

cu in	cu cm	cu cm	cu in	cu ft	cu m	cu m	cu ft
1	16.39	1	0.06	1	0.03	1	35.3
2	32.77	2	0.12	2	0.06	2	70.6
3	49.16	3	0.18	3	0.08	3	105.9
4	65.55	4	0.24	4	0.11	4	141.3
5	81.93	5	0.31	5	0.14	5	176.6
6	93.32	6	0.37	6	0.17	6	211.9
7	114.71	7	0.43	7	0.20	7	247.2
8	131.10	8	0.49	8	0.23	8	282.5
9	147.48	9	0.55	9	0.25	9	317.8
10	163.87	10	0.61	10	0.28	10	353.1
15	245.81	15	0.92	15	0.42	15	529.7
20	327.74	20	1.23	20	0.57	20	706.3
50	819.35	50	3.05	50	1.41	50	1 765.7
100	1 638.71	100	6.10	100	2.83	100	3 531.5

cu yd	cu m	cu m	cu yd
1	0.76	1	1.31
2	1.53	2	2.62
3	2.29	3	3.92
4	3.06	4	5.23
5	3.82	5	6.54
6	4.59	6	7.85
7	5.35	7	9.16
8	6.12	8	10.46
9	6.88	9	11.77
10	7.65	10	13.08
15	11.47	15	19.62
20	15.29	20	26.16
50	38.23	50	65.40
100	76.46	100	130.80

Exact conversions
$1 \text{ in}^3 = 16.3871 \text{ cm}^3$
$1 \text{ ft}^3 = 0.0283 \text{ m}^3$
$1 \text{ yd}^3 = 0.7646 \text{ m}^3$
$1 \text{ cm}^3 = 0.0610 \text{ in}^3$
$1 \text{ m}^3 = 35.3147 \text{ ft}^3$
$1 \text{ m}^3 = 1.3080 \text{ yd}^3$

Conversion tables: capacity

▫ Liquid measures

UK fluid ounces	litres	US fluid ounces	litres
1	0.0284	1	0.0296
2	0.0568	2	0.0592
3	0.0852	3	0.0888
4	0.114	4	0.118
5	0.142	5	0.148
6	0.170	6	0.178
7	0.199	7	0.207
8	0.227	8	0.237
9	0.256	9	0.266
10	0.284	10	0.296
11	0.312	11	0.326
12	0.341	12	0.355
13	0.369	13	0.385
14	0.397	14	0.414
15	0.426	15	0.444
20	0.568	20	0.592
50	1.42	50	1.48
100	2.84	100	2.96

litres	UK fluid ounces	US fluid ounces
1	35.2	33.8
2	70.4	67.6
3	105.6	101.4
4	140.8	135.3
5	176.0	169.1
6	211.2	202.9
7	246.4	236.7
8	281.6	270.5
9	316.8	304.3
10	352.0	338.1
11	387.2	372.0
12	422.4	405.8
13	457.5	439.6
14	492.7	473.4
15	527.9	507.2
20	703.9	676.3
50	1 759.8	1 690.7
100	3 519.6	3 381.5

Exact conversions

1 UK fl oz = 0.0284 l   1 US fl oz = 0.0296 l
1 l = 35.1961 UK fl oz   1 l = 33.8140 US fl oz

UK pints	litres		US pints	litres
1	0.57		1	0.47
2	1.14		2	0.95
3	1.70		3	1.42
4	2.27		4	1.89
5	2.84		5	2.37
6	3.41		6	2.84
7	3.98		7	3.31
8	4.55		8	3.78
9	5.11		9	4.26
10	5.68		10	4.73
11	6.25		11	5.20
12	6.82		12	5.68
13	7.38		13	6.15
14	7.95		14	6.62
15	8.52		15	7.10
20	11.36		20	9.46
50	28.41		50	23.66
100	56.82		100	47.32

litres	UK pints	US pints
1	1.76	2.11
2	3.52	4.23
3	5.28	6.34
4	7.04	8.45
5	8.80	10.57
6	10.56	12.68
7	12.32	14.79
8	14.08	16.91
9	15.84	19.02
10	17.60	21.13
11	19.36	23.25
12	21.12	25.36
13	22.88	27.47
14	24.64	29.59
15	26.40	31.70
20	35.20	105.67
50	87.99	211.34
100	175.98	422.68

Exact conversions

1 UK pt = 0.5682 l   1 UK pt = 1.20 US pt
1 US pt = 0.4732 l   1 US pt = 0.83 UK pt
1 l = 1.7598 UK pt, 2.1134 US pt   1 US cup = 8 fl oz

UK gallons	litres	US gallons	litres
1	4.55	1	3.78
2	9.09	2	7.57
3	13.64	3	11.36
4	18.18	4	15.14
5	22.73	5	18.93
6	27.28	6	22.71
7	31.82	7	26.50
8	36.37	8	30.28
9	40.91	9	34.07
10	45.46	10	37.85
11	50.01	11	41.64
12	54.55	12	45.42
13	59.10	13	49.21
14	63.64	14	52.99
15	68.19	15	56.78
20	90.92	20	75.71
25	113.65	25	94.63
50	227.30	50	189.27
75	340.96	75	283.90
100	454.61	100	378.54

litres	UK gallons	US gallons
1	0.22	0.26
2	0.44	0.53
3	0.66	0.79
4	0.88	1.06
5	1.10	1.32
6	1.32	1.58
7	1.54	1.85
8	1.76	2.11
9	1.98	2.38
10	2.20	2.64
11	2.42	2.91
12	2.64	3.17
13	2.86	3.43
14	3.08	3.70
15	3.30	3.96
20	4.40	5.28
25	5.50	6.60
50	11.00	13.20
75	16.50	19.81
100	22.00	26.42

Exact conversions

1 UK gal = 4.546 l   1 l = 0.220 UK gal, 0.2642 US gal
1 US gal = 3.7854 l

CONVERSION TABLES: CAPACITY

UK gallons	US gallons
1	1.2
2	2.4
3	3.6
4	4.8
5	6.0
6	7.2
7	8.4
8	9.6
9	10.8
10	12.0
11	13.2
12	14.4
13	15.6
14	16.8
15	18.0
20	24.0
25	30.0
50	60.0

US gallons	UK gallons
1	0.8
2	1.7
3	2.5
4	3.3
5	4.2
6	5.0
7	5.8
8	6.7
9	7.5
10	8.3
11	9.2
12	10.0
13	10.8
14	11.7
15	12.5
20	16.6
25	20.8
50	41.6

Exact conversions

1 UK gal = 1.200929 US gal

1 US gal = 0.832688 UK gal

□ Dry capacity measures

UK bushels	cu m	litres
1	0.037	36.4
2	0.074	72.7
3	0.111	109.1
4	0.148	145.5
5	0.184	181.8
10	0.369	363.7

US bushels	cu m	litres
1	0.035	35.2
2	0.071	70.5
3	0.106	105.7
4	0.141	140.9
5	0.175	176.2
10	0.353	352.4

Exact conversions

1 UK bushel = 0.0369 m^3
1 US bushel = 0.9353 m^3

1 UK bushel = 36.3677 l
1 US bushel = 35.2381 l

❏ Dry capacity measures

cu m	UK bushels	US bushels
1	27.5	28.4
2	55.0	56.7
3	82.5	85.1
4	110.0	113.0
5	137.0	142.0
10	275.0	284.0

litres	UK bushels	US bushels
1	0.027	0.028
2	0.055	0.057
3	0.082	0.085
4	0.110	0.114
5	0.137	0.142
10	0.275	0.284

Exact conversions

$1 \, m^3 = 27.4962$ UK bu
$1 \, l = 0.0275$ UK bu

$1 \, m^3 = 28.3776$ US bu
$1 \, l = 0.0284$ US bu

UK pecks	litres	US pecks	litres
1	9.1	1	8.8
2	18.2	2	17.6
3	27.3	3	26.4
4	36.4	4	35.2
5	45.5	5	44.0
10	90.9	10	88.1

litres	UK pecks	US pecks
1	0.110	0.113
2	0.220	0.226
3	0.330	0.339
4	0.440	0.454
5	0.550	0.567
10	1.100	1.135

Exact conversions

1 UK pk = $9.0919 \, l$
1 US pk = $8.8095 \, l$

$1 \, l = 0.1100$ UK pk, 0.1135 US pk

US quarts	cu m	litres
1	1 101	1.1
2	2 202	2.2
3	3 304	3.3
4	4 405	4.4
5	5 506	5.5
10	11 012	11.0

US pints	cu m	litres
1	551	0.55
2	1 101	1.10
3	1 652	1.65
4	2 202	2.20
5	2 753	2.75
10	5 506	5.51

Exact conversions

1 US qt = $1 \, 101.2209 \, cm^3$
1 US pt = $550.6105 \, cm^3$

1 US qt = $1.1012 \, l$
1 US pt = $0.5506 \, l$

Conversion tables: weight

ounces[1]	grams	grams	ounces[1]	pounds	kilograms	kilograms	pounds
1	28.3	1	0.04	1	0.45	1	2.2
2	56.7	2	0.07	2	0.91	2	4.4
3	85.0	3	0.11	3	1.36	3	6.6
4	113.4	4	0.14	4	1.81	4	8.8
5	141.7	5	0.18	5	2.27	5	11.0
6	170.1	6	0.21	6	2.72	6	13.2
7	198.4	7	0.25	7	3.18	7	15.4
8	226.8	8	0.28	8	3.63	8	17.6
9	255.1	9	0.32	9	4.08	9	19.8
10	283.5	10	0.35	10	4.54	10	22.0
11	311.7	20	0.71	11	4.99	11	24.3
12	340.2	30	1.06	12	5.44	12	26.5
13	368.5	40	1.41	13	5.90	13	28.7
14	396.9	50	1.76	14	6.35	14	30.9
15	425.2	60	2.12	15	6.80	15	33.1
16	453.6	70	2.47	16	7.26	16	35.3
		80	2.82	17	7.71	17	37.5
		90	3.18	18	8.16	18	39.7
		100	3.53	19	8.62	19	41.9
				20	9.07	20	44.1
				25	11.34	25	55.1
				30	13.61	30	66.1
				35	15.88	35	77.2
				40	18.14	40	88.2
				45	20.41	45	99.2
				50	22.68	50	110.2
				60	27.24	60	132.3
				70	31.78	70	154.4
				80	36.32	80	176.4
				90	40.86	90	198.5
				100	45.36	100	220.5
				200	90.72	200	440.9
				250	113.40	250	551.2
				500	226.80	500	1 102.3
				750	340.19	750	1 653.5
				1 000	453.59	1 000	2 204.6

[1] avoirdupois.

Exact conversions

1 oz (avdp) = 28.3495 g   1 lb = 0.454 kg
1 g = 0.0353 oz (avdp)   1 kg = 2.205 lb

Tons: long, UK 2 240 lb; short, US 2 000 lb

UK tons	tonnes	US tons	tonnes	UK tons	US tons	US tons	UK tons
1	1.02	1	0.91	1	1.12	1	0.89
2	2.03	2	1.81	2	2.24	2	1.79
3	3.05	3	2.72	3	3.36	3	2.68
4	4.06	4	3.63	4	4.48	4	3.57
5	5.08	5	4.54	5	5.6	5	4.46
10	10.16	10	9.07	10	11.2	10	8.93
15	15.24	15	13.61	15	16.8	15	13.39
20	20.32	20	18.14	20	22.4	20	17.86
50	50.80	50	45.36	50	56	50	44.64
75	76.20	75	68.04	75	84	75	66.96
100	101.60	100	90.72	100	102	100	89.29

	tonnes	UK tons	US tons
	1	0.98	1.10
	2	1.97	2.20
	3	2.95	3.30
	4	3.94	4.40
	5	4.92	5.50
	10	9.84	11.02
	15	14.76	16.53
	20	19.68	22.05
	50	49.21	55.11
	75	73.82	82.67
	100	98.42	110.23

Exact conversions

1 UK ton = 1.0160 tonnes   1 tonne = 0.9842 UK ton, 1.1023 US tons
1 US ton = 0.9072 tonne   1 US ton = 0.8929 UK ton
1 UK ton = 1.1199 US tons

Hundredweights: long, UK 112 lb; short, US 100 lb

UK cwt	kilograms	US cwt	kilograms	UK cwt	US cwt	US cwt	UK cwt
1	50.8	1	45.4	1	1.12	1	0.89
2	102	2	90.7	2	2.24	2	1.79
3	152	3	136	3	3.36	3	2.68
4	203	4	181	4	4.48	4	3.57
5	254	5	227	5	5.6	5	4.46
10	508	10	454	10	11.2	10	8.93
15	762	15	680	15	16.8	15	13.39
20	1 016	20	907	20	22.4	20	17.86
50	2 540	50	2 268	50	56	50	44.64
75	3 810	75	3 402	75	84	75	66.96
100	5 080	100	4 536	100	102	100	89.29

kilograms	UK cwt	US cwt
1	0.0197	0.022
2	0.039	0.044
3	0.059	0.066
4	0.079	0.088
5	0.098	0.11
10	0.197	0.22
15	0.295	0.33
20	0.394	0.44
50	0.985	1.10
75	1.477	1.65
100	1.970	2.20

Exact conversions

1 UK cwt = 50.8023 kg
1 US cwt = 45.3592 kg
1 UK cwt = 1.1199 US cwt

1 kg = 0.0197 UK cwt, 0.0220 US cwt
1 US cwt = 0.8929 UK cwt

stones	pounds	stones	kilograms
1	14	1	6.35
2	28	2	12.70
3	42	3	19.05
4	56	4	25.40
5	70	5	31.75
6	84	6	38.10
7	98	7	44.45
8	112	8	50.80
9	126	9	57.15
10	140	10	63.50
11	154		
12	168		
13	182		
14	196		
15	210		
16	224		
17	238		
18	252		
19	266		
20	280		

1 st = 14 lb
1 lb = 0.07 st

1 st = 6.350 kg
1 kg = 0.1575 st

Engineering: bridges

Name	Location	Length (m)[1]	Type
Akashi-Kaikyo	Honshu−Shikoku, Japan	1990	(longest) suspension
Alex Fraser (previously called Annacis)	Vancouver, Canada	465	cable-stayed
Ambassador	Detroit, Michigan, USA	564	suspension
Angostura	Cuidad Bolivar, Venezuela	712	suspension
Astoria	Astoria, Oregon, USA	376	truss
Bayonne (Kill van Kull)	New Jersey−Staten Island, USA	504	steel arch
Bendorf	Rhine River, Coblenz, Germany	1 030	cement girder
Benjamin Franklin	Philadelphia−Camden, USA	534	suspension
Bosporus I	Istanbul, Turkey	1 074	suspension
Bosporus II	Istanbul, Turkey	1 090	suspension
Bridge of Sighs	Doge's Palace−Pozzi Prison, Venice, Italy	c.5	enclosed arch
Britannia	Menai Strait, Wales	420	plate girder
Brooklyn	Brooklyn−Manhattan Island, New York City, USA	486	suspension
Chao Phraya	Bangkok, Thailand	450	(longest single-plane) cable-stayed
Commodore Barry	Chester, Pennsylvania, USA	501	cantilever
Cooper River	Charleston, S Carolina, USA	488	truss
Delaware River	Chester, Pennsylvania, USA	501	cantilever
Evergreen	Seattle, Washington, USA	2 293	floating pontoon
Forth (rail)	South Queensferry, Scotland	1 658 (spans 521)	cantilever
Forth (road)	South Queensferry, Scotland	1 006	suspension
George Washington	Hudson River, New York City, USA	1 067	suspension
Gladesville	Sydney, Australia	305	concrete arch
Golden Gate	San Francisco, California, USA	1 280	suspension
Grand Trunk	Niagara Falls, New York, USA (survived until 1897)	250	suspension
Great Belt (Storebælt) East	Halsskov−Kudshoved, Denmark	1 624	suspension
Greater New Orleans	Mississippi River, Louisiana, USA	480	cantilever
High Coast	Västernorrland, Sweden	1 210	suspension
Howrah	Hooghly River, Calcutta, India	457	cantilever
Humber Estuary	Hull−Grimsby, England	1 410	suspension
Humen	Humen, China	888	suspension
Jiangsu Yangtze	Jiangsu Province, China	1 385	suspension

Name	Location	Length (m) [1]	Type
Kap Shui Mun	Lantau Island – Ma Wan Island, Hong Kong	430	cable-stayed (double-deck road/rail)
Kincardine	Forth River, Scotland	822 (swing span 111)	movable
Lake Pontchartrain Causeway	Maudeville – Jefferson, Louisiana, USA	38km [2]	twin concrete trestle
Lion's Gate	Vancouver, Canada	473	suspension
London	Southwark – City of London	centre span 46	concrete arch
Mackinac	Michigan, USA	1 158	suspension
McCall's Ferry	Susquehanna River, Lancaster, Pennsylvania, USA	110	wooden covered
Meiko Chuo	Tokyo Bay, Japan	590	cable-stayed
Menai Strait	Menai Strait, N Wales	177	suspension
Minami Bisan-Seto	Honshu – Shikoku, Japan	1118	suspension
New River Gorge	Fayetteville, West Virginia	518	(longest) steel arch
Nord Sundet	Norway	223	lattice
Normandie	Le Havre, France	856	cable-stayed
Øresund	Flinterenden, Denmark – Malmö, Sweden	1 092 (main span 490)	cable-stayed
Plauen	Plauen, Germany	span 90	(longest) masonry arch
Pont d'Avignon	Rhône River, France	c.60	arch
Pontypridd	S Wales	43	single-span arch
Quebec	St Lawrence, Canada	549	(largest) cantilever
Rainbow	Canada – USA, Niagara Falls	300	steel arch
Ravenswood	West Virginia, USA	525	cantilever
Rialto	Grand Canal, Venice, Italy	25	single-span arch
Rio-Niteroi	Guanabara Bay, Brazil	centre span 300, length 14km [2]	box and plate girder
Salazar	Tagus River, Lisbon, Portugal	1 014	suspension
Severn	Ironbridge, Shropshire, England	31	(first) cast-iron arch
Severn	Beachley, England	988	suspension
Severn II	Severn Estuary, England	456	cable-stayed
Skarnsundet	Norway	530	cable-stayed
SkyTrain Bridge	Vancouver, Canada	340	cable-stayed
Sydney Harbour	Sydney, Australia	503	steel arch
Tacoma Narrows II	Puget Sound, Washington, USA	854	suspension
Tagus II	Lisbon, Portugal	420	cable-stayed
Tatara, Great	Japan	890	cable-stayed
Tay	Dundee, Scotland	2 246	box girder
Thatcher Ferry	Panama Canal, C America	344	arch

Name	Location	Length (m)[1]	Type
Tower	Thames River, London	76	movable
Transbay	San Francisco, California, USA	705	suspension
Trans-Tokyo Bay Highway	Kawasaki–Kisarazu, Japan	590	box girder
Trois-Rivières	St Lawrence River, Quebec, Canada	336	steel arch
Tsing Ma	Tsing Yi Island – Ma Wan Island, Hong Kong	1 377	suspension (double deck)
Verrazano Narrows	Brooklyn – Staten Island, New York Harbour, USA	1 298	suspension
Victoria Jubilee	St Lawrence River, Montreal, Canada	2 742	open steel
Wheeling	Wheeling, Virginia, USA	308	suspension
Xiling Yangtze	Three Gorges Dam, China	900	suspension
Yokohama Bay	Japan	855	suspension
Zoo	Cologne, Germany	259	steel box girder

[1] To convert m to ft, multiply by 3.2808.

[2] To convert km to mi, multiply by 0.6214.

Engineering: tunnels

Name	Use	Location	Length (km)[1]
Aki	rail	Japan	13
Box	rail	Wiltshire, England	3
Cascade	rail	Washington, USA	13
Channel	rail	Cheriton, England – Sargette, France	50
Chesapeake Bay Bridge-Tunnel	road	USA	28
Chesbrough	water supply	Chicago, USA	3
Cumberland Mountain	underground parking	Cumberland Gap, USA	1.40
Dai-shimizu	rail	Honshu, Japan	22
Delaware Aqueduct	water supply	Catskill Mountains, New York, USA	169
Detroit River	rail	Detroit, Michigan, USA – Windsor, Ontario, Canada	2
Eupalinus	water supply	Samos, Greece	1.04
FATIMA (Magerøy)	road	Norway	6.82 (longest undersea road)
Flathead	rail	Washington, USA	13
Fréjus	rail	Modane, France – Bardonecchia, Italy	13
Fucino	drainage	Lake Fucino, Italy	6

[1]

Name	Use	Location	Length (km) [1]
Great Apennine	rail	Vernio, Italy	19
Hokuriku	rail	Japan	15
Holland	road	Hudson River, New York City—Jersey City, New Jersey, USA	3
Hoosac	rail	Massachusetts	8
Hyperion	sewer	Los Angeles, California, USA	8
Kanmon	rail	Kanmon Strait, Japan	19
Keijo	rail	Japan	11
Kilsby Ridge	rail	London—Birmingham line, England	2
Languedoc (Canal du Midi)	canal	Malpas, France	0.157
Lierasen	rail	Norway	11
London and Southwark Subway	rail	London, England	11
Lötschberg	rail	Switzerland	15
Mersey	road	Mersey River, Birkenhead—Liverpool, England	4
Moffat	rail	Colorado, USA	10
Mont Blanc	road	France—Italy	12
Mt MacDonald	rail	Canada	15
NEAT (St Gotthard)	rail	Switzerland	57
NEAT (Bern—Lötschberg—Simplon)	rail	Switzerland	38
Orange-Fish River	irrigation	South Africa	82 (longest irrigation tunnel)
Øresund	road—rail	Copenhagen, Denmark—Malmö, Sweden	3.75 (longest immersed tube)
Owingsburg Landing	canal	Pennsylvania, USA	0.137
Posilipo	road	Naples—Pozzuoli, Italy	6
Rogers Pass	rail	Calgary—Vancouver, Canada	15
Rogers Pass	road	British Columbia, Canada	35
Rokko	rail	Osaka—Kobe, Japan	16
Seikan	rail	Tsugaru Strait, Honshu—Hokkaido, Japan	54 (longest undersea rail)
Severn	rail	Bristol—Newport, England	4.5
Shin-shimizu	rail	Japan	13
Simplon I and II	rail	Brigue, Switzerland—Iselle, Italy	20
St Gotthard	rail	Switzerland	15
St Gotthard	road	Göschenen, Switzerland—Airolo, Italy	16

Name	Use	Location	Length (km)[1]
(First) Thames	pedestrian, rail after 1865	Wapping – Rotherhithe, London, England	0.366
Tower Subway	rail	London, England	0.411
Tronquoy	canal	France	1.1

[1]To convert km to mi, multiply by 0.6214.

Engineering: dams

Name	River, country	Height (m)[1]
Afsluitdijk Sea	Zuider Zee, Netherlands	20 (largest sea dam, length 31km)
Aguamilpa	Santiago, Mexico	187
Aswan High	Nile, Egypt	111
Atatürk	Euphrates, Turkey	184
Bakun	Rajang, Malaysia	204
Chapetón	Paraná, Argentina	296
Chicoasén	Grijalva, Mexico	263
Chivor	Cundinamarca, Colombia	237
Cipasang	Cimanuk, Indonesia	200
Daniel Johnson	Manicouagan, Canada	214
Ertan	Yalong, China	240
Grand Coulee	Columbia (Franklin D Roosevelt Lake), USA	168
Grand Dixence	Dixence, Switzerland	285
Guavio	Guaviare, Colombia	245
Hoover	Colorado (Lake Mead), USA	221
Inguri	Inguri, Georgia	272
Itaipú	Paraná, Paraguay/Brazil border	189
Kambarantinsk	Naryn, Kyrgyzstan	255
Katse	Malibamatso, Lesotho	182
Kiev	Dneiper, Ukraine	256
Kishau	Tons, India	253
La Grande 2A	La Grande, Canada	168
Lhakwar	Yamuna, India	204
Longtan	Hongshui, China	285
Mauvoisin	Drance de Bagnes, Switzerland	237
Mica	Columbia, Canada	244
New China (Three Gorges)	Chang Jiang (Yangzte), China	175
Nurek	Vakhsh, Tajikistan	310
Oroville	Feather, California, USA	235
Pati	Paraná, Argentina	109
Piedra del Aguila	Limay, Argentina	163
Rogun	Vakhsh, Tajikistan	335 (tallest)

238

Name	River, country	Height (m) [1]
San Roque	Agno, Philippines	210
Sardar Sarovar	Narmada, India	163
Sayansk	Yenisey, Russia	236
Tehri	Bhagirathi, India	261
Thames Barrier	Thames, England	spans 520 (largest tidal barrier)
Vaiont	Vaiont, Italy	265
Xiaolangdi	Huang He, China	154
Yacyretá-Apipe	Paraná, Paraguay-Argentina	43 (longest, length 70km)

[1] To convert m to ft, multiply by 3.2808.

Engineering: tallest buildings

Name	Location	Height (m) [1]	Date
Taipei Financial Center	Taipei, Japan	508	2003
Petronas I and II	Kuala Lumpur, Malaysia	452	1996
Sears Tower	Chicago, USA	443	1973–4
Jin Mao	Shanghai, China	420	1998
International Finance Center	Hong Kong	420	2003
World Trade Centre	New York City, USA	417	1972
Fairwell International Centre	Xiamen, China	397	2002
Empire State Building	New York City, USA	381	1931
Central Plaza	Hong Kong	374	1992
Bank of China	Hong Kong	368	1988–9
Emirates Tower I	Dubai, United Arab Emirates	350	1999
The Centre	Hong Kong	350	1998
T&C Tower	Kaohsiung, Taiwan	347	1997
Amoco Building	Chicago, USA	346	1973
John Hancock Center	Chicago, USA	344	1967
Shun Hing Square	Shenzen, China	325	1996

[1] To convert m to ft, multiply by 3.2808.

Inventions

Name	Date	Inventor (nationality)*
adding machine	1642	Blaise Pascal (Fr)
adhesive (rubber-based glue)	1850	anon
adhesive (epoxy resin)	1958	Certas Co
aeroplane (steam powered)	1886	Clement Ader (Fr)
aeroplane	1903	Orville and Wilbur Wright (US)
aeroplane (swing-wing)	1954	Grumman Co (US)
aerosol	1926	Erik Rotheim (Nor)
airship (non-rigid)	1851	Henri Giffard (Fr)
airship (rigid)	1900	Graf Ferdinand von Zeppelin (Ger)

Name	Date	Inventor (nationality)*
ambulance	1792	Jean Dominique Larrey (Fr)
aspirin (synthesization)	1859	Heinrich Kolbe (Ger)
aspirin (introduction into medicine)	1899	Felix Hoffmann (Ger)
atomic bomb	1939–45	Otto Frisch (Aus), Niels Bohr (D) and Rudolf Peierls (Ger)
balloon	1783	Jacques and Joseph Montgolfier (Fr)
barbed wire (first patent)	1867	Lucien B Smith (US)
barbed wire (manufacture)	1874	Joseph Glidden (US)
barbiturates (preparation of barbituric acid)	1863	Adolf von Baeyer (Ger)
barometer	1643	Evangelista Torricelli (Ital)
battery (electric)	1800	Alessandro Volta (Ital)
bicycle	1839–40	Kirkpatrick MacMillan (UK)
bifocal lens	1780	Benjamin Franklin (US)
blood (artificial)	1966	Clark and Gollan (US)
bronze (copper with tin)	c.3700BC	Pre-dynastic Egypt
bunsen burner	1855	Robert Wilhelm Bunsen (Pruss)
burglar alarm	1858	Edwin T Holmes (US)
cable-car	1866	W Ritter (Ger) or anon (US)
calendar (modern)	525	Dionysius Exiguus (Scythian)
camera (polaroid)	1947	Edwin Land (US)
canning	1810	Nicolas Appert (Fr)
cannon	2nd-c BC	Archimedes (Gr)
car (three-wheeled steam tractor)	1769	Nicolas Cugnot (Fr)
car (internal combustion)	1884	Gottlieb Daimler (Ger)
car (petrol)	1886	Karl Benz (Ger)
car (air-conditioning)	1902	J Wilkinson (US)
car (disc brakes)	1902	Frederick W Lanchester (UK)
car (speedometer)	1902	Thorpe and Salter (UK)
carbon fibres	1964	Courtaulds Ltd (UK)
carburettor	1876	Gottlieb Daimler (Ger)
carpet sweeper	1876	Melville Bissell (US)
cash register	1892	William Burroughs (US)
celluloid	1870	John W Hyatt (US)
cement (Portland)	1824	Joseph Aspdin (UK)
chocolate (solid)	1819	François-Louis Cailler (Swiss)
chocolate (solid, milk)	1875	Daniel Peter (Swiss)
chronometer	1735	John Harrison (UK)
cinema	1895	Auguste and Louis Lumière (Fr)
cinema (wide screen)	1900	Raoul Grimoin-Sanson (Fr)
clock (mechanical)	725	I-Hsing (Chinese)
clock (pendulum)	1657	Christiaan Huygens (NL)
clock (quartz)	1929	Warren Alvin Marrison (US)
coffee (instant)	1937	Nestlé (Swiss)
compact disc	1979	Philips (NL) and Sony (Japanese)
compass (discovery of magnetite)	1st-c	China

Name	Date	Inventor (nationality)*
compass (first record of mariner's compass)	1187	Alexander Neckam (UK)
computer	1835	Charles Babbage (UK)
computer (electronic, digital)	1946	J Presper Eckert and John W Mauchly (US)
concrete	1st-c	Rome
concrete (reinforced)	1892	François Hennebique (Fr)
contact lenses	1887	Adolph E Fick (Ger)
contraceptive pill	1950	Gregor Pincus (US)
corrugated iron	1853	Pierre Carpentier (Fr)
credit card	1950	Ralph Scheider (US)
crossword	1913	Arthur Wynne (US) in *New York World*
crystal	c.1450	anon, Venice
decompression chamber	1929	Robert H Davis (UK)
dental plate	1817	Anthony A Plantson (US)
dental plate (rubber)	1854	Charles Goodyear (US)
detergents	1916	anon, Germany
diesel engine	1892	Rudolf Diesel (Ger)
dishwasher (automatic)	1889	Mrs W A Cockran (US)
drill (pneumatic)	1861	Germain Sommelier (Fr)
drill (electric, hand)	1895	Wilhelm Fein (Ger)
electric chair	1888	Harold P Brown and E A Kenneally (US)
electric flat iron	1882	Henry W Seeley (US)
electric generator	1831	Michael Faraday (UK)
electric guitar	1931	Adolph Rickenbacker, Barth and Beauchamp (US)
electric heater	1887	W Leigh Burton (US)
electric light bulb	1879	Thomas Alva Edison (US)
electric motor (AC)	1888	Nikola Tesla (US)
electric motor (DC)	1870	Zenobe Gramme (Belg)
electric oven	1889	Bernina Hotel, Switzerland
electrocardiography	1903	Willem Einthoven (NL)
electromagnet	1824	William Sturgeon (UK)
encyclopedia	c.47BC	Marcus Terentius Varro (Roman)
endoscope	1827	Pierre Segalas (Fr)
escalator	1892	Jesse W Reno (US)
explosives (nitroglycerine)	1847	Ascanio Sobrero (Ital)
explosives (dynamite)	1866	Alfred Nobel (Swed)
extinguisher	1866	François Carlier (Fr)
facsimile machine (fax)	1907	Arthur Korn (Ger)
ferrofluids	1968	Ronald Rosensweig (US)
film (moving outlines)	1874	Jules Janssen (Fr)
	1888	Louis Le Prince (Fr)
	1891	Thomas Alva Edison (US)
film (with soundtrack)	1896	Lee De Forest (US)
forceps (obstetric)	c.1630	Peter Chamberlen (UK)
freeze-drying	1906	Arsene D'Arsonval and Georges Bordas (Fr)

Name	Date	Inventor (nationality)*
galvanometer	1834	André Marie Ampère (Fr)
gas lighting	1792	William Murdock (UK)
gearbox (automatic)	1910	Hermann Fottinger (Ger)
glass (heat-resistant)	1884	Carl Zeiss (Ger)
glass (stained)	pre-850	Europe
glass (toughened)	1893	Leon Appert (Fr)
glass fibre	1713	René de Réaumur (Fr)
glass fibre (industrial)	1931	Owens Illinois Glass Co (US)
glassware	c.2600BC	Egypt
glider	1853	George Cayley (UK)
gramophone	1877	Thomas Alva Edison (US)
gun	245BC	Ctesibius (Gr)
gyro-compass	1911	Elmer A Sperry (US)
heart (artificial)	1937	Vladimir P Demikhov (USSR)
	1982	Robert Jarvik (US)
heat pump	1851	William Thompson, Lord Kelvin (UK)
helicopter	1907	Louis and Jacques Breguet (Fr)
holography	1948	Denis Gabor (Hung/UK)
hovercraft	1955	Christopher Cockerell (UK)
integrated circuit (concept)	1952	Geoffrey Dummer (UK)
interferometry	1802	Thomas Young (UK)
interferometer	1856	J-C Jamin (Fr)
iron (working of)	c.1323BC	Hittites, Anatolia
jeans	1872	Levi-Strauss (US)
kidney (artificial)	1945	Willem Kolff (NL)
laser	1960	Theodore Maiman (US)
launderette	1934	J F Cantrell (US)
lawnmower	1902	James Edward Ransome (UK)
lift (mechanical)	1851	Elisha G Otis (US)
lightning conductor	1752	Benjamin Franklin (US)
linoleum	1860	Frederick Walton (UK)
lithography	1796	Aloys Senefelder (Bav)
locomotive (railed)	1804	Richard Trevithick (UK)
lock	c.4000BC	Mesopotamia
loom (power)	1785	Edmund Cartwright (UK)
loudspeaker	1900	Horace Short (UK)
machine gun	1718	James Puckle (UK)
maps	c.2250BC	Mesopotamia
margarine	1868	Hippolyte Mergé-Mouriès (Fr)
match	1680	Robert Boyle (UK)
match (safety)	1845	Anton von Schrotter (Ger)
microchip	1958	Jack Saint Clair Kilby (US)
microphone	1876	Alexander Graham Bell and Thomas Alva Edison (US)
microprocessor	1971	Marcian E Hoff (US)
microscope	1590	Zacharias Janssen (NL)

Name	Date	Inventor (nationality)*
microscope (electron)	1933	Max Knoll and Ernst Ruska (Ger)
microscope (scanning tunnelling)	1982	Gerd Binnig and Heinrich Rohrer (Swiss)
microscope (atomic force)	1985	Gerd Binnig and Heinrich Rohrer (Swiss)
microwave oven	1945	Percy Le Baron Spencer (US)
missile (air-to-air)	1943	Herbert Wagner (Ger)
motorcycle	1885	Gottlieb Daimler (Ger)
neon lamp	1910	Georges Claude (Fr)
newspaper	59BC	Julius Caesar (Roman)
non-stick pan	1954	Marc Grégoir (Fr)
novel (serialized)	1836	Charles Dickens, Chapman and Hall Publishers (UK)
nylon	1938	Wallace H Carothers (US)
optical fibres	c.1955	Navinder S Kapany (Ind)
optical sound recording	1920	Lee De Forest (US)
pacemaker (implantable)	1956	Wilson Greatbach (US)
paint (fluorescent)	1933	Joe and Bob Switzer (US)
paint (acrylic)	1964	Reeves Ltd (UK)
paper	AD105	Ts'ai Lun (Chinese)
paper clip	1900	Johann Vaaler (Nor)
parachute	c.2nd-c BC	China
parachute (jump)	1797	André-Jacques Garnerin (Fr)
parachute (patent)	1802	André-Jacques Garnerin (Fr)
parchment	2nd-c BC	Eumenes II of Pergamum (reigned 197–159BC)
parking meter	1932	Carlton C Magee (US)
pasteurization	1863	Louis Pasteur (Fr)
pen (fountain)	1884	Lewis Waterman (US)
pen (ball-point)	1938	Laszlo Biro (Hung)
pencil	1795	Nicholas Jacques Conté (Fr)
pentium processor	1995	Intel (US)
phonograph	1877	Thomas Alva Edison (US)
photoelectric cell	1896	Julius Elster and Hans F Geitel (Ger)
phototypesetting	1894	Eugene Porzott (Hung)
photographic lens (for camera obscura)	1812	William H Wollaston UK)
photographic film	1889	George Eastman (US)
photography (on metal)	1816	Joseph Nicéphore Niepce (Fr)
photography (on paper)	1838	William Henry Fox Talbot (UK)
photography (colour)	1861	James Clerk Maxwell (UK)
pianoforte	1720	Bartolomeo Cristofori (Ital)
plastics	1868	John W Hyatt (US)
pocket calculator	1972	Jack Saint Clair Kilby, James Van Tassell and Jerry D Merryman (US)
porcelain	c.960	China
pressure cooker	1679	Denis Papin (Fr)
printing press (wooden)	c.1450	Johannes Gutenberg (Ger)
printing press (rotary)	1845	Richard Hoe (US)
propeller (boat, hand-operated)	1775	David Bushnell (US)

Name	Date	Inventor (nationality)*
propeller (ship)	1844	Isambard Kingdom Brunel (UK)
radar (theory)	1900	Nikola Tesla (Croat)
radar (theory)	1922	Guglielmo Marconi (Ital)
radar (application)	c.1930	A Hoyt Taylor and Leo C Young (US)
radio telegraphy (discovery and production of sound waves)	1888	Heinrich Hertz (Ger)
radio (transatlantic)	1901	Guglielmo Marconi (Ital)
rails (iron)	1738	Abraham Barby (UK)
railway (underground)	1843	Charles Pearson (UK)
railway (electric)	1878	Ernst Werner von Siemens (Ger)
rayon	1883	Joseph Swan (UK)
razor (safety)	1895	King Camp Gillette (US)
razor (electric)	1928	Jacob Schick (US)
record (flat disc)	1888	Emil Berliner (Ger)
record (long-playing microgroove)	1948	Peter Goldmark (US)
refrigerator (compressed ether)	1855	James Harrison (UK)
refrigerator (absorption)	1857	Ferdinand Carré (Fr)
revolver	1835	Samuel Colt (US)
Richter seismographic scale	1935	Charles Francis Richter (US)
rocket (missile)	1232	Mongols, China
rubber (latex foam)	1929	E A Murphy, W H Chapman and John Dunlop (US)
rubber (butyl)	1937	Robert Thomas and William Sparks, Exxon (US)
rubber (vulcanized)	1939	Charles Goodyear (US)
Rubik cube	1975	Erno Rubik (Hung)
safety-pin	1849	Walter Hunt (US)
satellite (artificial)	1957	USSR
saw	c.4000 BC	Egypt
scanner	1973	Godfrey N Hounsfield (UK)
scotch tape	1930	Richard Drew (US)
screw	3rd-c BC	Archimedes (Gr)
serotherapy	1890	Emil von Behring (Ger)
sewing machine	1830	Barthelemy Thimonnier (Fr)
ship (steam)	1775	Jacques C Perier (Fr)
ship (turbine)	1894	Charles Parsons (UK)
ship (metal hull and propeller)	1844	Isambard Kingdom Brunel (UK)
silicon chip	1961	Texas Instruments (US)
silk (reeling)	c.2640 BC	Hsi Ling Shi (Chinese)
skin (artificial)	c.1980	John Tanner (US), Bell (US), Neveu (Fr), Ioannis Yannas (Gr), Howard Green (US) and Jacques Thivolet (Fr)
skyscraper	1882	William Le Baron Jenney (US)
slide rule	1621	William Oughtred (UK)
soap	c.2500 BC	Sumer, Babylonia
soda (extraction of)	c.16th-c BC	Egypt

Name	Date	Inventor (nationality)*
space shuttle	1981	NASA (US)
spectacles	c.1280	Alessandro della Spina and Salvino degli Armati (Ital)
spinning frame	1768	Richard Arkwright (UK)
spinning jenny	c.1764	James Hargreaves (UK)
spinning-mule	1779	Samuel Crompton (UK)
stapler	1868	Charles Henry Gould (UK)*
starter motor	1912	Charles F Kettering (US)
steam engine	1698	Thomas Savery (UK)
steam engine (condenser)	1769	James Watt (UK)
steam engine (piston)	1705	Thomas Newcomen (UK)
steel (production)	1854	Henry Bessemer (UK) and William Kelly (US)
steel (stainless)	1913	Henry Brearley (UK)
stethoscope	1816	René Théophile Hyacinthe Laënnec (Fr)
stereotype	1725	William Ged (UK)
submarine	c.1620	Cornelis Brebbel or Van Drebbel (NL)
sun-tan cream	1936	Eugène Schueller (Fr)
suspension bridge	25BC	China
syringe (scientific)	1646	Blaise Pascal (Fr)
syringe (hypodermic)	c.1835	Charles Gabriel Pravaz (Fr)
table tennis	1890	James Gibb (UK)
tampon	1930	Earl Hass (US)
tank	1916	Ernest Swinton (UK)
telegraph (electric)	1774	Georges Louis Lesage (Swiss)
telegraph (transatlantic cable)	1866	William Thompson, Lord Kelvin (UK)
telegraph code	1837	Samuel F B Morse (US)
telephone (first practical)	1876	Alexander Graham Bell (US)
telephone (automatic exchange)	1889	Alman B Strowger (US)
telescope (refractor)	1608	Hans Lippershey (NL)
telescope (space)	1990	Edwin Hubble (US)
television (mechanical)	1926	John Logie Baird (UK)
television (colour)	1940	Peter Goldmark (US)
tennis	1873	Walter G Wingfield (UK)
thermometer	3rd-cBC	Ctesibius (Gr)
thermometer (mercury)	1714	Gabriel Fahrenheit (Ger)
timeclock	1894	Daniel M Cooper (US)
toaster	1927	Charles Strite (US)
traffic lights	1868	J P Knight (UK)
traffic lights (automatic)	1914	Alfred Benesch (US)
transformer	1831	Michael Faraday (UK)
tranquillizers	1952	Henri Laborit (Fr)
transistor	1948	John Bardeen, Walter Brattain and William Shockley (US)
travel agency	1841	Thomas Cook (UK)
traveller's cheques	1891	American Express Travel Agency (US)
turbojet	1928	Frank Whittle (UK)

Name	Date	Inventor (nationality)*
typewriter	1829	William Burt (US)
typewriter (electric)	1872	Thomas Alva Edison (US)
tyre (pneumatic, coach)	1845	Robert William Thomson (UK)
tyre (pneumatic, bicycle)	1888	John Boyd Dunlop (UK)
ultrasonography (obstetric)	1958	Ian Donald (UK)
universal joint	c.140BC	Fang Feng (Chinese)
vacuum cleaner (steam powered)	1871	Ives W McGaffrey (US)
vacuum cleaner (electric)	1901	Hubert Cecil Booth (UK)
vending machine	1883	Percival Everitt (UK)
ventilator	1858	Théophile Guibal (Fr)
videophone	1927	American Telegraph and Telephone Co
video recorder	1956	Ampex Co (US)
washing machine (electric)	1907	Hurley Machine Co (US)
watch	1462	Bartholomew Manfredi (Ital)
watch (waterproof)	1927	Rolex (Swiss)
wheel	c.3500BC	Mesopotamia
windmill	c.600	Syria
word processor	1965	IBM (US)
writing (pictography)	c.3000BC	Egypt
xerography	1938	Chester Carbon (US)
zip-fastener	1893	Whitcomb L Judson (US)

*Aus: Austrian	Bav: Bavarian	Belg: Belgian
Croat: Croatian	D: Danish	Fr: French
Ger: German	Gr: Greek	Hung: Hungarian
Ind: Indian	Ital: Italian	NL: Dutch
Nor: Norwegian	Pruss: Prussian	Swed: Swedish

Scientists

Airy, Sir George Biddell (1802–92) English astronomer and geophysicist, born Alnwick. Astronomer Royal (1835–81) who reorganized the Greenwich Observatory. Initiated measurement of Greenwich Mean Time, determined the mass of the Earth from gravity experiments in mines and carried out extensive work in optics.

Alzheimer, Alois (1864–1915) German psychiatrist and neuropathologist, born Markbreit. Gave full clinical and pathological description of pre-senile dementia (Alzheimer's disease) (1907).

Ampère, André Marie (1775–1836) French mathematician and physicist, born Lyons. Laid the foundations of the science of electrodynamics. His name is given to the basic SI unit of electric current (ampere, amp).

Archimedes (c.287–212BC) Greek mathematician, born Syracuse. Discovered formulae for the areas and volumes of plane and solid geometrical figures using methods which anticipated theories of integration to be developed 1 800 years later. Also founded the science of hydrostatics; in popular tradition remembered for the cry of 'Eureka' when he discovered the principle of upthrust on a floating body.

Aristotle (384–322 BC) Greek philosopher and scientist, born Stagira. One of the most influential figures in the history of Western thought and scientific tradition. Wrote enormous amounts on biology, zoology, physics and psychology.

Avogadro, Amedeo (1776–1856) Italian physicist, born Turin. Formulated the hypothesis (Avogadro's law) that equal volumes of gas contain equal numbers of molecules when at the same temperature and pressure.

Babbage, Charles (1791–1871) English mathematician, born Teignmouth. Attempted to build two calculating machines — the 'difference engine', to calculate logarithms and similar functions by repeated addition performed by trains of gear wheels, and the 'analytical engine', to perform much more varied calculations. Babbage is regarded as the pioneer of modern computers.

Bacon, Francis, Baron Verulam of Verulam, Viscount St Albans (1561–1626) English statesman and natural philosopher, born London. Creator of scientific induction; stressed the importance of experiment in interpreting nature, giving significant impetus to future scientific investigation.

Baird, John Logie (1888–1946) Scottish engineer, born Helensburgh. Gave first demonstration of a television image in 1926. Also researched radar and infrared television, and succeeded in producing 3-D and colour images (1944), as well as projection onto a screen and stereophonic sound.

Barnard, Christiaan Neethling (1922–) South African surgeon, born Beaufort West. Performed first successful heart transplant in December 1967 at Groote Schuur Hospital. Although the recipient died 18 days later from pneumonia, a second patient operated on in January 1968 survived for 594 days.

Becquerel, Antoine Henri (1852–1908) French physicist, born Paris. While researching fluorescence (the ability of substances to give off visible light), discovered radioactivity in the form of rays emitted by uranium salts, leading to the beginnings of modern nuclear physics. For this he shared the 1903 Nobel Prize for physics with Marie and Pierre Curie.

Bell, Alexander Graham (1847–1922) Scottish–American inventor, born Edinburgh. After researching and teaching methods in speech therapy and experimenting with various acoustical devices, produced the first intelligible telephonic transmission on 5 June 1875, and patented the telephone in 1876. Founded the Bell Telephone Company in 1877.

Bohr, Niels Henrik David (1885–1962) Danish physicist, born Copenhagen. Greatly extended the theory of atomic structure by explaining the spectrum of hydrogen by means of an atomic model and quantum theory (1913). Awarded the Nobel Prize for physics in 1922. Assisted in atom bomb research in America during World War II.

Boyle, The Hon Robert (1627–91) Irish physicist and chemist, born Munster. One of the first members of the Royal Society. Carried out experiments on air, vacuum, combustion and respiration, and in 1662 arrived at Boyle's law, which states that the pressure and volume of a gas are inversely proportional at constant temperature.

Brahe, Tycho or **Tyge** (1546–1601) Danish astronomer, born Knudstrup, Sweden (then under Danish crown). After seeing the partial solar eclipse of 1569, became obsessed with astronomy. Accurately measured and compiled catalogues of the positions of stars, providing vital information for later astronomers, and recorded unique observations of a new star in Cassiopeia in 1572 (a nova now known as Tycho's star).

Brunel, Isambard Kingdom (1806–59) English engineer and inventor, born Portsmouth. Helped to plan the Thames Tunnel and later planned the Clifton Suspension Bridge. Designed the first steamship to cross the Atlantic, the first ocean screw-steamer. In 1833 appointed engineer to the Great Western Railway and constructed all tunnels, bridges and viaducts on that line; also constructed and improved many docks.

Celsius, Anders (1701–44) Swedish astronomer, born Uppsala. Devised the centigrade, or 'Celsius', scale of temperature. Also advocated the introduction of the Gregorian calendar, and made observations of the aurora borealis, or northern lights.

Copernicus, Nicolaus (1473–1543) Polish astronomer, born Torún. Studied mathematics, optics, perspective and canon law before a varied career involving law, medicine and astronomy. Published theory in 1543 that the Sun is at the centre of the Universe; this was not initially accepted due to opposition from the Church which held that the Universe was Earth-centred.

Crick, Francis Harry Compton (1916–   ) English biologist, born Northampton. Constructed a molecular model of the complex genetic material deoxyribonucleic acid (DNA). Later research on nucleic acids led to far-reaching discoveries concerning the genetic code. Joint winner of the Nobel Prize for physiology or medicine in 1962 with James Watson (1928–   ).

Curie, Marie (originally Manya, née Sklodowska) (1867–1934) Polish–French physicist, born Warsaw. After graduating from the Sorbonne, worked on magnetism and radioactivity, isolating radium and polonium. Shared the Nobel Prize for physics in 1903 with her husband, Pierre Curie, and Antoine Henri Becquerel. Became professor of physics at the Sorbonne in 1906; awarded the Nobel Prize for chemistry in 1911. Element 96 is named curium after the Curies.

Curie, Pierre (1859–1906) French chemist and physicist, born Paris. Carried out research on magnetism and radioactivity with his wife, Marie Curie, for which they were jointly awarded the Nobel Prize for physics in 1903, with Antoine Henri Becquerel.

Cuvier, Georges (Léopold Chrétien Frédéric Dagobert) (1769–1832) French anatomist, born Montbéliard. Known as the father of comparative anatomy and palaeontology. Opponent of the theory of descent, he originated the natural system of animal classification. Linked comparative anatomy and palaeontology through studies of animal and fish fossils.

Dalton, John (1766–1844) English chemist, born Eaglesfield, near Cockermouth. Researched mixed gases, the force of steam and the elasticity of vapours, and deduced the law of partial pressures, or Dalton's law. Also made important contributions to atomic theory.

Darwin, Charles Robert (1809–82) English naturalist, born Shrewsbury. Recommended as naturalist for a scientific survey of South American waters (1831–6) on HMS *Beagle*, during which he made many geological and zoological discoveries which led him to speculate on the origin of species. In 1859 published theory of evolution in *The Origin of Species by Means of Natural Selection.*

Davy, Sir Humphry (1778–1829) English chemist, born Penzance. Experimented with newly discovered gases and discovered the anaesthetic effect of laughing gas. Discovered the new metals potassium, sodium, barium, strontium and magnesium, and the metallic element calcium. Also investigated volcanic action, devised safety lamps for use in mining and was important in promoting science within industry.

Descartes, René (1596–1650) French philosopher and mathematician, born near Tours. Creator of analytical or co-ordinate geometry, also named after him as Cartesian geometry. Also theorized extensively in physics and physiology, and is regarded as the father of modern philosophy.

Doppler, Christian Johann (1803–53) Austrian physicist, born Salzburg. The Doppler effect, described in a paper in 1842, explains the increase and decrease of wave frequency observed when a wave source and the observer respectively approach or recede from one another.

Edison, Thomas Alva (1847–1931) American inventor and physicist, born Milan, Ohio. Took out more than 1 000 patents, including the gramophone (1877), the incandescent light bulb (1879) and an improved microphone for Bell's telephone. Also discovered thermionic emission, formerly called the Edison effect.

Ehrlich, Paul (1854–1915) German bacteriologist, born Strehlen (now Strzelin), Silesia. Pioneer in haematology and chemotherapy, he synthesized salvarsan as a treatment for syphilis and propounded the side-chain theory in immunology. Joint winner of the 1908 Nobel Prize for physiology or medicine.

Einstein, Albert (1879–1955) German–Swiss–American mathematical physicist, born Ulm, Bavaria. Achieved world fame through his special and general theories of relativity; also studied gases and discovered the photoelectric effect, for which he was awarded the Nobel Prize for physics in 1921. Element 99 was named einsteinium after him.

Euler, Leonhard (1707–83) Swiss mathematician, born Basel. Published over 800 different books and papers on mathematics, physics and astronomy, introducing many new functions and carrying out important work in calculus. Introduced the notations e and gp, still used today. Also studied motion and celestial mechanics.

Fahrenheit, Gabriel Daniel (1686–1736) German physicist, born Danzig. Devised the alcohol thermometer (1709) and later invented the mercury thermometer (1714). Also devised the temperature scale named after him, and was the first to show that the boiling point of liquids varies at different atmospheric pressures.

Faraday, Michael (1791–1867) English chemist and physicist, born Grenoble. Discovered electromagnetic induction (1831), the laws of electrolysis (1833) and the rotation of polarized light by magnetism (1845). First to isolate benzene and to synthesize chlorocarbons.

Fermi, Enrico (1901–54) Italian–American nuclear physicist, born Rome. Published method of calculating atomic particles, and in 1943 succeeded in splitting the nuclei of uranium atoms, producing artificial radioactive substances. Awarded the 1938 Nobel Prize for physics, and constructed the first American nuclear reactor at Chicago (1942). Element 100 was named fermium after him.

Feynman, Richard Phillips (1918–88) American physicist, born New York City. Made considerable theoretical advances in quantum electrodynamics, for which he was joint winner of the Nobel Prize for physics in 1965. Involved in building the first atomic bomb during World War II.

Fleming, Sir Alexander (1881–1955) Scottish bacteriologist, born Loudoun, Ayrshire. First to use anti-typhoid vaccines on humans and pioneered the use of salvarsan to treat syphilis. In 1928 discovered penicillin by chance, for which he was joint winner of the 1945 Nobel Prize for physiology or medicine.

Galilei, Galileo, known as **Galileo** (1564–1642) Italian astronomer, mathematician and natural philosopher, born Pisa. Inferred the value of a pendulum for exact measurement of time and proved that all falling bodies, great or small, descend due to gravity at the same rate. Also perfected the refracting telescope and pursued astronomical observations which revealed mountains and valleys on the Moon, four satellites of Jupiter, and sunspots, convincing him of the correctness of the Copernican theory. His advocacy of the Copernican theory led to his imprisonment by the Inquisition; he remained under house arrest until his death.

Geiger, Hans Wilhelm (1882–1945) German physicist, born Neustadt-an-der-Haart. Investigated beta-ray radioactivity and, with Walther Müller, devised a counter to measure it.

Halley, Edmond (1656–1742) English astronomer and mathematician, born London. Studied the Solar System and correctly predicted the return (in 1758, 1835 and 1910) of a comet that had been observed in 1583, and is now named after him.

Harvey, William (1578–1657) English physician, born Folkestone. Discovered the circulation of the blood.

Hawking, Stephen William (1942–) English theoretical physicist, born Oxford. Research on relativity led him to study gravitational singularities such as the 'big bang', out of which the Universe originated, and 'black holes', which result from the death of stars. His book *A Brief History of Time* is a popular account of modern cosmology. Since the 1960s he has suffered from a highly disabling progressive neuromotor disease.

Heisenberg, Werner Karl (1901–76) German theoretical physicist, born Würzburg. Developed quantum mechanics and formulated the principle of indeterminacy (uncertainty principle). Awarded the 1932 Nobel Prize for physics. In 1958, with Wolfgang Pauli, announced the formulation of a unified field theory.

Henle, Friedrich Gustav Jakob (1809–85) German anatomist, born Fürth. Discovered the tubules in the kidney, which are now named after him, and wrote treatises on systematic anatomy.

Herschel, Sir John Frederick William (1792–1871) English astronomer, born Slough. Son of Sir William Herschel; continued his father's research and discovered 525 nebulae and clusters. Pioneered celestial photography and researched photoactive chemicals and the wave theory of light.

Herschel, Sir (Frederick) William (1738–1822) German–British astronomer, born Hanover. Made a reflecting telescope (1773–4) with which he discovered the planet Uranus in 1781. Also discovered satellites of Uranus and Saturn, the rotation of Saturn's rings and Saturn's rotation period. Researched binary stars, nebulae and the Milky Way.

Hertz, Heinrich Rudolph (1857–94) German physicist, born Hamburg. Confirmed James Clerk Maxwell's predictions in 1887 with his discovery of invisible electromagnetic waves of the same fundamental form as light waves.

Hooke, Robert (1635–1703) English chemist, physicist and architect, born Freshwater, Isle of Wight. Anticipated the invention of the steam engine, formulated Hooke's law of the extension and compression of elastic bodies, and anticipated Isaac Newton's inverse square law of gravitation. Constructed first Gregorian telescope and inferred rotation of Jupiter. Materially invented the microscope, the quadrant and a marine barometer.

Hubble, Edwin Powell (1889–1953) American astronomer, born Marshfield, Missouri. Demonstrated that some nebulae are independent galaxies, and in 1929 discovered galaxy 'redshift': distant galaxies are receding from us and the apparent speed of recession of a galaxy is proportional to its distance from us.

Hutton, James (1726–97) Scottish geologist, born Edinburgh. Formed the basis of modern geology with the Huttonian theory, emphasizing the igneous origin of many rocks and deprecating the assumption of causes other than those still seen at work.

Huxley, Thomas Henry (1825–95) English biologist, born Ealing. Assistant surgeon on surveying expedition to the South Seas (1846–50), during which he collected marine animal specimens; became foremost scientific supporter of Charles Darwin's theory of evolution. Also studied fossils and later turned to philosophy.

Huygens, Christiaan (1629–93) Dutch physicist, born The Hague. Made pendulum clock (1657) and developed the doctrine of accelerated motion under gravity. Discovered the rings and fourth satellite of Saturn, and the laws of collision of elastic bodies.

Jansky, Karl Guthe (1905–50) American radio engineer, born Norman, Oklahoma. Discovered astronomical radio sources by chance while investigating interference on short-wave radio telephone transmissions, initiating the science of radio astronomy. The SI unit of radio emission strength, the jansky, is named after him.

Jeans, Sir James Hopwood (1877–1946) English physicist and astronomer, born Ormskirk, near Southport. Made important contributions to the dynamical theory of gases, radiation, quantum theory and stellar evolution; best known for his role in popularizing physics and astronomy.

Joule, James Prescott (1818–89) English physicist, born Salford. Showed experimentally that heat is a form of energy and established the mechanical equivalent of heat; this became the basis for the theory of conservation of energy. With Lord Kelvin, he studied temperatures of gases and formulated the absolute scale of temperature. The joule, a unit of work or energy, is named after him.

Kant, Immanuel (1724–1804) German philosopher, born Königsberg, Prussia (now Kaliningrad, Russia). Researched astronomy and geophysics, and predicted the existence of the planet Uranus before its discovery. His philosophical works had enormous influence.

Kelvin, William Thomson, 1st Baron (1824–1907) Irish–Scottish physicist and mathematician, born Belfast. Solved important problems in electrostatics, proposed the absolute, or Kelvin, temperature scale, and established the second law of thermodynamics simultaneously with Rudolf Clausius. Also investigated geomagnetism and hydrodynamics, and invented innumerable instruments.

Kepler, Johannes (1571–1630) German astronomer, born Weil der Stadt, Württemberg. Formulated laws of planetary motion describing elliptical orbits and forming the starting point of modern astronomy. Also made discoveries in optics, general physics and geometry.

Kirchhoff, Gustav Robert (1824–87) German physicist, born Königsberg. Carried out important research in electricity, heat, optics and spectrum analysis, his work leading to the discovery of caesium and rubidium (1859).

Lamarck, Jean (Baptiste Pierre Antoine de Monet) Chevalier de (1744–1829) French naturalist, born Bazentin. Made the basic distinction between vertebrates and invertebrates. On evolution he postulated that acquired characteristics can be inherited by later generations, preparing the way for the Darwinian theory of evolution.

Langmuir, Irving (1881–1959) American physical chemist, born New York City. He worked at the General Electric Company for 41 years, and his many inventions include the gas-filled tungsten lamp and an improved vacuum pump. He was awarded the 1932 Nobel Prize for chemistry for his work on solid and liquid surfaces.

Leibniz, Gottfried Wilhelm (1646–1716) German mathematician and philosopher, born Leipzig. Discovered calculus around the same time as Isaac Newton; also made original contributions in the fields of optics, mechanics, statistics, logic and probability, and laid the foundations of 18th-century philosophy.

Leishman, Sir William Boog (1865–1926) Scottish bacteriologist, born Glasgow. Discovered an effective vaccine for inoculation against typhoid and was first to discover the parasite of the disease kala-azar.

Linnaeus, Carolus (Carl von Linné) (1707–78) Swedish naturalist and physician, born Raceshult. Founder of modern scientific nomenclature for plants and animals.

Lorentz, Hendrik Antoon (1853–1928) Dutch physicist, born Arnhem. Carried out important work in electromagnetism; joint winner of the Nobel Prize for physics in 1902 for explaining the effect whereby atomic spectral lines are split in the presence of magnetic fields.

Lorenz, Konrad Zacharias (1903–89) Austrian zoologist and ethologist, born Vienna. Regarded as the father of ethology, favouring the study of the instinctive behaviour of animals in the wild. In 1935 published observations on imprinting in young birds by which hatchlings 'learn' to recognize substitute parents, and argued that while aggressive behaviour in humans is inborn, it may be channelled into other forms of activity, whereas in other animals it is purely survival-motivated.

Lyell, Sir Charles (1797–1875) Scottish geologist, born Kinnordy, Fife. Established the principle of uniformitarianism in geology: geological changes have been gradual, produced by forces still at work and not by catastrophic changes. His work significantly influenced Charles Darwin, although Lyell never accepted the theory of evolution by natural selection.

Mach, Ernst (1838–1916) Austrian physicist and philosopher, born Turas, Moravia. Carried out experimental work on projectiles and the flow of gases. His name has been given to the ratio of the speed of flow of a gas to the speed of sound (Mach number) and to the angle of a shock wave to the direction of motion (Mach angle).

Marconi, (Marquis) Guglielmo (1874–1937) Italian physicist and inventor, born Bologna. Experimented with converting electromagnetic waves into electricity and achieved wireless telegraphy in 1895. In 1898 transmitted signals across the English Channel and in 1901 succeeded in sending Morse code signals across the Atlantic. Joint winner of the 1909 Nobel Prize for physics. Later developed short-wave radio equipment and established a worldwide radio telegraph network for the British government.

Maxwell, James Clerk (1831–79) Scottish physicist, born Edinburgh. Produced mathematical theory of electromagnetism and identified light as electromagnetic radiation. Also suggested that invisible electromagnetic waves could be generated in a laboratory, as later carried out by Hertz. Other research included the kinetic theory of gases, the nature of Saturn's rings, colour perception and colour photography.

Medawar, Sir Peter Brian (1915–87) British zoologist and immunologist, born Rio de Janeiro. Pioneered experiments in skin grafting and the prevention of rejection in transplant operations. Joint winner of the Nobel Prize for physiology or medicine in 1960.

Mendel, Gregor Johann (1822–84) Austrian biologist and botanist, born near Udrau, Silesia. Became abbot in 1868. Researched inheritance characteristics in plants leading to the formulation of Mendel's law of segregation and the law of independent assortment; his principles became the basis of modern genetics.

Mendeleyev, Dmitri Ivanovich (1834–1907) Russian chemist, born Tobolsk. Formulated the periodic law from which he predicted the existence of several elements which were subsequently discovered. Element 101 was named mendelevium after him.

Michelson, Albert Abraham (1852–1931) German–American physicist, born Strelno (now Strzelno, Poland). Carried out famous Michelson–Morley experiment which confirmed the non-existence of 'ether', a result which set Einstein on the road to the theory of relativity. First American scientist to win a Nobel Prize (physics) in 1907.

Napier, John (1550–1619) Scottish mathematician, born Edinburgh. He is famous for the invention of logarithms to simplify computation and for devising a calculating machine using a set of rods, known as 'Napier's Bones'.

Newton, Sir Isaac (1642–1727) English scientist and mathematician, born Woolsthorpe, Lincolnshire. Formulated complete theory of gravitation by 1684; also carried out important work in optics, concluding that the different colours of light making up white light have different refrangibility, developed the reflecting telescope, and invented calculus around the same time as Leibniz.

Pascal, Blaise (1623–62) French mathematician and physicist, born Clermont-Ferrand. Carried out important work in geometry, invented a calculating machine, demonstrated that air pressure decreases with altitude as previously predicted, and developed probability theory. The SI unit of pressure (pascal) and the modern computer programming language, Pascal, are named after him.

Pasteur, Louis (1822–95) French chemist, born Dôle. Father of modern bacteriology. Discovered possibility of attenuating the virulence of injurious micro-organisms by exposure to air, by variety of culture, or by transmission through various animals, and demonstrated that the attenuated organisms could be used for immunization. From this he developed vaccinations against anthrax and rabies. Also introduced pasteurization (moderate heating) to kill disease-producing organisms in wine, milk and other foods, and disymmetry in molecules.

Pauli, Wolfgang (1900–58) Austrian–American theoretical physicist, born Vienna. Formulated the exclusion principle (1924), that no two electrons can be in the same energy state, producing important advances in the application of quantum theory to the periodic table of elements; for this he was awarded the Nobel Prize for physics in 1945.

Pauling, Linus (1901–94) American chemist, born Portland, Oregon. He made important discoveries concerning chemical bonding and complex molecular structures; this led him into work on the chemistry of biological molecules and the chemical basis of hereditary disease. He was awarded the 1954 Nobel Prize for chemistry and the 1962 Nobel Peace Prize.

Pavlov, Ivan Petrovich (1849–1936) Russian physiologist, born near Ryazan. Studied physiology of circulation, digestion and 'conditioned' or acquired reflexes, believing the brain's only function to be to couple neurons to produce reflexes. Awarded the Nobel Prize for physiology or medicine in 1904.

Planck, Max Karl Ernst (1858–1947) German theoretical physicist, born Kiel. Researched thermodynamics and black-body radiation, leading him to formulate quantum theory (1900), which assumes energy changes take place in abrupt instalments or quanta. Awarded the Nobel Prize for physics in 1918.

Ptolemy or Claudius Ptolemaeus (c.90–168) Egyptian astronomer and geographer, believed born Ptolemaeus Hermion. Corrected and improved the astronomical work of his predecessors to form the Ptolemaic system, described by Plato and Aristotle, with the Earth at the centre of the Universe and heavenly bodies revolving round it; beyond this lay the sphere of the fixed stars. Also compiled geographical catalogues and maps.

Pythagoras (6th century BC) Greek mathematician and philosopher, born Samos. Associated with mathematical discoveries involving the chief musical intervals, the relations of numbers and the relations between the lengths of sides of right-angled triangles (Pythagoras's theorem). Profoundly influenced Plato and later astronomers and mathematicians.

Ramón y Cajal, Santiago (1852–1934) Spanish physician and histologist, born Petilla de Aragon. Carried out important work on the brain and nerves, isolated the neuron and discovered how nerve impulses are transmitted to brain cells. Joint winner of the 1906 Nobel Prize for physiology or medicine.

Rayleigh, John William Strutt, 3rd Baron (1842–1919) English physicist, born near Maldon, Essex. Carried out valuable research on vibratory motion, the theory of sound and the wave theory of light. With Sir William Ramsay (1852–1916) discovered argon (1894). Awarded the Nobel Prize for physics in 1904.

Richter, Charles Francis (1900–85) American seismologist, born near Hamilton, Ohio. Devised the scale of earthquake strength which bears his name (1927–35).

Röntgen, Wilhelm Konrad von (1845–1923) German physicist, born Lennep, Prussia. Discovered the electromagnetic rays which he called X-rays (also known as Röntgen rays) in 1895. For his work on X-rays he was joint winner of the Rumford Medal in 1896 and winner of the 1901 Nobel Prize for physics. Also carried out important work on the heat conductivity of crystals, the specific heat of gases, and the electromagnetic rotation of polarized light.

Rutherford, Ernest Rutherford, 1st Baron Rutherford of Nelson (1871–1937) New Zealand–British physicist, born Spring Grove, near Nelson. Made first successful wireless transmissions over two miles, discovered the three types of uranium radiations, formulated a theory of atomic disintegration and determined the nature of alpha particles; this led to a new atomic model in which the mass is concentrated in the nucleus. Also discovered that alpha-ray bombardment could produce atomic transformation and predicted the existence of the neutron. Awarded the Nobel Prize for chemistry in 1908.

Schrödinger, Erwin (1887–1961) Austrian physicist, born Vienna. Originated the study of wave mechanics as part of the quantum theory with the celebrated Schrödinger wave equation, for which he was joint winner of the 1933 Nobel Prize for physics. Also made contributions to field theory.

Szent-Györgyi, Albert von Nagyrapolt (1893–1986) Hungarian–American biochemist, born Budapest. Discovered actin, isolated vitamin C, and was awarded the Nobel Prize for physiology or medicine in 1937. Also made important studies of biological combustion, muscular contraction and cellular oxidation.

Thomson, Sir Joseph John (1856–1940) English physicist, born Cheetham Hill, near Manchester. Studied gaseous conductors of electricity and the nature of cathode rays; this led to his discovery of the electron. Also pioneered mass spectrometry and discovered the existence of isotopes of elements. Awarded the Nobel Prize for physics in 1906.

Thomson, Sir William   Kelvin, 1st Baron

Tinbergen, Nikolaas (1907–88) Dutch ethologist, born The Hague. Co-founder with Konrad Lorenz of the science of ethology (study of animal behaviour in natural surroundings). Analysed social behaviour of certain animals and insects as an evolutionary process with considerable relevance to human behaviour, especially courtship and aggression. Joint winner of the 1973 Nobel Prize for physiology or medicine.

Van de Graaff, Robert Jemison (1901–67) American physicist, born Tuscaloosa, Alabama. Conceived of an improved type of electrostatic generator, in which electric charge could be built up on a hollow metal sphere; constructed first model, later to be known as the Van de Graaff generator, giving possibility of generating potentials of over a million volts. Developed the generator for use as a particle accelerator for atomic and nuclear physicists. Generator was also adapted to produce high-energy X-rays for cancer treatment and examination of the interior structure of heavy ordnance.

Volta, Alessandro Giuseppe Anastasio, Count (1745–1827) Italian physicist, born Como. Developed the theory of current electricity, discovered the electric composition of water, invented an electric battery, the electrophorus, an electroscope, and made investigations into heat and gases. His name is given to the SI unit of electric potential difference, the volt.

Watt, James (1736–1819) Scottish engineer and inventor, born Greenock. Developed and improved early models of the steam engine, and manufactured it from 1774. The watt, a unit of power, is named after him, and the term horsepower was first used by him.

Young, Thomas (1773–1829) English physicist and physician, born Milverton, Somerset. Expounded the phenomenon of interference, which established the undulatory theory of light. Also made valuable contributions in insurance, haemodynamics and deciphering the inscriptions on the Rosetta Stone.

Nobel Prizes 1980–2000

Year	Chemistry	Physics	Physiology/Medicine
1980	Paul Berg Walter Gilbert Frederick Sanger	James W Cronin Val L Fitch	Baruj Benacerraf Jean Dausset George D Snell
1981	Kenichi Fukui Roald Hoffmann	Nicolaas Bloembergen Arthur L Schawlow Kai M Siegbahn	Roger W Sperry David H Hubel Torsten Wiesel
1982	Aaron Klug	Kenneth G Wilson	Sune K Bergström Bengt I Samuelsson John R Vane
1983	Henry Taube	Subrahmanyan Chandrasekhar William A Fowler	Barbara McClintock
1984	Robert B Merrifield	Carlo Rubbia Simon van der Meer	Niels K Jerne Georges J F Köhler César Milstein
1985	Herbert Hauptman Jerome Karle	Klaus von Klitzing	Michael S Brown Joseph L Goldstein
1986	Dudley R Herschbach Yuan Tseh Lee John C Polanyi	Gerd Binnig Heinrich Rohrer Ernst Ruska	Stanley Cohen Rita Lévi-Montalcini
1987	Donald J Cram Jean-Marie Lehn Charles Pedersen	Georg Bednorz Alex Müller	Susumu Tonegawa
1988	Johann Deisenhofer Robert Huber Hartmut Michel	Leon Lederman Melvin Schwartz Jack Steinberger	James Black Gertrude Elion George Hitchings
1989	Sydney Altman Thomas R Cech	Hans Dehmelt Wolfgang Paul Norman Ramsey	J Michael Bishop Harold E Varmus
1990	Elias James Corey	Jerome Friedman Henry Kendall Richard Taylor	Joseph E Murray E Donnall Thomas
1991	Richard R Ernst	Pierre-Gilles de Gennes	Erwin Neher Bert Sakmann
1992	Rudolph A Marcus	Georges Charpak	Edmond H Fischer Edwin G Krebs
1993	Kary Banks Mullis Michael Smith	Russell Hulse Joseph Hooton Taylor Jr	Richard Roberts Phillip Allen Sharp
1994	George Olah	Clifford Shull Bertram Brockhouse	Alfred G Gilman Martin Rodbell
1995	Paul Crutzen Mario Molina F Sherwood Rowland	Martin L Perl Frederick Reines	Edward B Lewis Eric F Wieschaus Christiane Nüsslein- Volhard

Year	Chemistry	Physics	Physiology/Medicine
1996	Robert Curl Jr	David Lee	Peter Doherty
	Harold Kroto	Douglas Osheroff	Rolf M Zinkernagel
	Richard Smalley	Robert Richardson	
1997	Paul Boyer	Steven Chu	Stanley Prusiner
	Jens Skou	William D Phillips	
	John E Walker	Claude Cohen-Tannoudji	
1998	Walter Kohn	Robert B Laughlin	Robert F Furchgott
	John A Pople	Horst L Störmer	Louis J Ignarro
		Daniel C Tsui	Ferid Murad
1999	Ahmed Zewail	Gerardus 't Hooft	Günter Blobel
		Martinus J G Veltman	
2000	Alan J Heeger	Zhores I Alferov	Arvid Carlsson
	Alan G MacDiarmid	Herbert Kroemer	Paul Greengard
	Hideki Shirakawa	Jack S Kilby	Eric Kandel

ARTS AND CULTURE

Novelists

Selected works are listed.

Achebe, Chinua (originally Albert Chinualumogu) (1930–) Nigerian novelist, born Ogidi; *Things Fall Apart* (1959), *Anthills of the Savannah* (1987), *Deadly Voyage* (1996).

Adams, Douglas (Noël) (1952–) English novelist, short-story writer, born Cambridge; *The Hitch Hiker's Guide to the Galaxy* (1979), *Dirk Gently's Holistic Detective Agency* (1987), *Mostly Harmless* (1992).

Adams, Richard (George) (1920–) English novelist, short-story writer, born Newbury, Berkshire; *Watership Down* (1972), *Shardik* (1974), *The Girl in a Swing* (1980), *The Day Gone By* (autobiography) (1990).

Aldiss, Brian (Wilson) (1925–) English novelist, poet, short-story writer, playwright, critic, born East Dereham, Norfolk; *The Helliconia Trilogy* (1985), *Forgotten Life* (1988), *Dracula Unbound* (1991), *Remembrance Day* (1993), *The Detached Retina* (1995).

Ambler, Eric (1909–98) English novelist, playwright, screenwriter, born London; *The Mask of Dimitrios* (1939), *The Intercom Conspiracy* (1970), *The Care of Time* (1981), *The Story So Far* (1993).

Amis, Kingsley (William) (1922–95) English novelist, poet, born London; *Lucky Jim* (1954), *That Uncertain Feeling* (1955), *Jake's Thing* (1978), *The Old Devils* (1986, Booker Prize).

Amis, Martin (Louis) (1949–) English novelist, short-story writer, born Oxford; *The Rachel Papers* (1973), *Money* (1984), *London Fields* (1990), *Time's Arrow* (1991), *The Information* (1995).

Angelou, Maya (pseudonym of Marguerite Annie Johnson) (1928–) American novelist, poet, playwright, born St Louis, Missouri; *I Know Why the Caged Bird Sings* (1969), *All God's Children Need Travelling Shoes* (1986), *Wouldn't Take Nothing for My Journey Now* (1993).

Archer, Jeffrey (Howard Archer, Baron) (1940–) English novelist, short-story writer, born Somerset; *Not a Penny More, Not a Penny Less* (1975), *Kane and Abel* (1979), *First Among Equals* (1984), *A Twist in the Tale* (short stories) (1989), *Honour Among Thieves* (1993), *The Fourth Estate* (1996).

Asimov, Isaac (1920–92) American novelist, short-story writer, born Petrovichi, Russia; *I Robot* (1950), *Foundation* (1951), *The Disappearing Man and Other Stories* (1985), *Nightfall* (1990).

Atwood, Margaret (Eleanor) (1939–) Canadian novelist, poet, short-story writer, born Ottowa; *Bluebeard's Egg* (1983), *The Handmaid's Tale* (1986), *Cat's Eye* (1989), *The Robber Bride* (1993), *Alias Grace* (1996).

Austen, Jane (1775–1817) English novelist, born Steventon, Hampshire; *Sense and Sensibility* (1811), *Pride and Prejudice* (1813), *Mansfield Park* (1814), *Emma* (1816), *Persuasion* (1818).

Bainbridge, Dame Beryl (Margaret) (1934–) English novelist, born Liverpool; *The Dressmaker* (1973), *The Bottle Factory Outing* (1974), *Injury Time* (1977), *An Awfully Big Adventure* (1989), *Every Man for Himself* (1996).

Ballantyne, R(obert) M(ichael) (1825–94) Scottish novelist, born Edinburgh; *The Coral Island* (1857), *The Gorilla Hunters* (1862).

Ballard, J(ames) G(raham) (1930–) English novelist, born Shanghai, China; *The Drowned World* (1962), *The Terminal Beach* (1964), *Empire of the Sun* (1984), *The Kindness of Women* (1991), *A User's Guide to the Millennium* (1996).

Balzac, Honoré de (1799–1850) French novelist, born Tours; *Comédie humaine* (1827–47), *Illusions perdues* (1837–43).

Banks, Iain M (1954–) Scottish novelist, born Dunfermline; *The Wasp Factory* (1984), *The Bridge* (1986), *The Crow Road* (1992), *Whit* (1995), *Excession* (1996), *Barbaric Castle: a Song of Stone* (1997).

Barker, Pat (Patricia Margaret) (1943–) English novelist, short-story writer, born Thornaby-on-Tees; *Union Street* (1982), *Blow Your House Down* (1984), *The Century's Daughter* (1986), *The Man Who Wasn't There* (1989), *Regeneration* (1991), *The Eye in the Door* (1993), *The Ghost Road* (1995, Booker Prize).

Bates, H(erbert) E(rnest) (1905–74) English novelist, short-story writer, born Rushden, Northamptonshire; *Fair Stood the Wind for France* (1944), *The Jacaranda Tree* (1949), *Love for Lydia* (1952), *The Darling Buds of May* (1958).

Bellow, Saul (1915–) Canadian novelist, born Lachine, Quebec; *Henderson the Rain King* (1959), *Herzog* (1964), *Humboldt's Gift* (1975, Pulitzer Prize 1976) *The Dean's December* (1982), *The Actual* (1997); Nobel Prize for literature 1976.

Berger, John (Peter) (1926–) English novelist, playwright, born Stoke Newington, London; *A Painter of Our Time* (1958), *A Fortunate Man* (non-fiction) (1967), *G* (1972, Booker Prize), *To The Wedding* (1995), *Photocopies* (1996).

Berger, Thomas (Louis) (1924–) American novelist, born Cincinnati, Ohio; *Reinhart in Love* (1962), *Arthur Rex* (1978), *The Houseguest* (1988), *Suspects* (1996).

Binchy, Maeve (1940–) Irish novelist, short-story writer, born Dublin; *Light a Penny Candle* (1982), *Echoes* (1985), *Firefly Summer* (1987), *Circle of Friends* (1990), *Copper Beech* (1992), *The Glass Lake* (1994), *Evening Class* (1996).

Blackmore, R(ichard) D(odderidge) (1825–1900) English novelist, born Longworth, Berkshire; *Lorna Doone* (1869).

Bleasdale, Alan (1946–) English novelist, playwright, born Liverpool; *Scully* (1975), *The Boys from the Blackstuff* (TV series) (1982), *Are You Lonesome Tonight?* (musical) (1985), *GBH* (TV series) (1991), *Jake's Progress* (TV series) (1995).

Böll, Heinrich (1917–85) German novelist, born Cologne; *And Never Said a Solitary Word* (1953), *The Unguarded House* (1954), *The Bread of Our Early Years* (1955); Nobel Prize for literature 1972.

Borges, Jorge Luis (1899–1986) Argentinian poet, short-story writer, born Buenos Aires; *Ficciones* (1944), *El Aleph* (1949), *Labyrinths* (1962).

Boyd, William (Andrew Murray) (1952–) Scottish novelist, short-story writer, born Accra, Ghana; *A Good Man in Africa* (1982), *An Ice-Cream War* (1983), *Brazzaville Beach* (1990), *The Blue Afternoon* (1993), *The Destiny of Nathalie X* (stories) (1995).

Bradbury, Malcolm (Stanley) (1932–) English novelist, born Sheffield; *Eating People is Wrong* (1959), *The History Man* (1975).

Bradbury, Ray(mond) (Douglas) (1920–) American novelist, short-story writer, born Waukegan, Illinois; *The Martian Chronicles* (short stories) (1950), *Fahrenheit 451* (1954), *Something Wicked This Way Comes* (1962), *A Graveyard for Lunatics* (1990).

Bradford, Barbara Taylor (1933–) English novelist, born Leeds; *A Woman of Substance* (1979), *Hold the Dream* (1985), *Love in Another Town* (1995).

Brink, André (Philippus) (1935–) South African novelist, short-story writer, playwright, born Vrede, Orange Free State; *Looking on Darkness* (1974), *Rumours of Rain* (1978), *A Dry White Season* (1979), *States of Emergency* (1988), *On the Contrary* (1993), *Imaginings of Sand* (1996).

Brontë, Anne (1820–49) English novelist, poet, born Thornton, Yorkshire; *Agnes Grey* (1847), *The Tenant of Wildfell Hall* (1848).

Brontë, Charlotte (1816–55) English novelist, poet, born Thornton, Yorkshire; *Jane Eyre* (1847), *Shirley* (1849), *Villette* (1853).

Brontë, Emily (1818–48) English novelist, poet, born Thornton, Yorkshire; *Wuthering Heights* (1847).

Brooke-Rose, Christine (1926–) English novelist, born Geneva, Switzerland; *The Languages of Love* (1957), *Thru* (1975), *Amalgamemnon* (1984), *Textermination* (1991), *Remake* (1996).

Brookner, Anita (1928–) English novelist, born London; *Hotel du Lac* (1984, Booker Prize), *Family and Friends* (1985), *Brief Lives* (1991), *Altered States* (1996), *Visitors* (1997).

Buchan, John (1875–1940) Scottish novelist, poet, born Perth; *The Thirty-Nine Steps* (1915), *Greenmantle* (1916), *Sir Walter Scott* (biography) (1932).

Buck, Pearl (née Sydenstricker) (1892–1973) American novelist, born Hillsboro, West Virginia; *The Good Earth* (1913), *Pavilion of Women* (1946); Nobel Prize for literature 1938.

Bunyan, John (1628–88) English novelist, born Elstow, near Bedford; *Pilgrim's Progress* (1678).

Burgess, Anthony (pseudonym of John Anthony Burgess Wilson) (1917–93) English novelist, born Manchester; *A Clockwork Orange* (1962), *The Malayan Trilogy* (1972), *Earthly Powers* (1980), *Kingdom of the Wicked* (1985), *Any Old Iron* (1989).

Burney, Fanny (Frances, later Mme d'Arblay) (1752–1840) English novelist, born King's Lynn; *Evelina* (1778), *Cecilia* (1782).

Burroughs, Edgar Rice (1875–1950) American novelist, born Chicago; *Tarzan of the Apes* (1914), *The Land That Time Forgot* (1924).

Burroughs, William S(eward) (1914–97) American novelist, born St Louis, Missouri; *The Naked Lunch* (1959), *The Soft Machine* (1961), *The Wild Boys* (1971), *Exterminator!* (1974), *My Education: a Book of Dreams* (1995).

Byatt, Dame A(ntonia) S(usan) (1936–) English novelist, born Sheffield; *The Shadow of a Sun* (1964), *The Virgin in the Garden* (1978), *Possession* (1989, Booker Prize 1990), *Babel Tower* (1996).

Camus, Albert (1913–60) French novelist, playwright, born Mondovi, Algeria; *The Outsider* (1942), *The Plague* (1948), *The Fall* (1957); Nobel Prize for literature 1957.

Canetti, Elias (1905–94) Bulgarian novelist, born Russe, Bulgaria; *Auto da Fé* (1935, trans 1946), *Crowds and Power* (1960, trans 1962); Nobel Prize for literature 1981.

Capote, Truman (1924–84) American playwright, novelist, short-story writer, born New Orleans; *Other Voices, Other Rooms* (1948), *Breakfast at Tiffany's* (1958).

Carey, Peter (Philip) (1943–) Australian novelist, short-story writer, born Bacchus Marsh, Victoria; *Bliss* (1981), *Illywhacker* (1985), *Oscar and Lucinda* (1989, Booker Prize), *The Tax Inspector* (1991), *The Big Bazoohley* (1995).

Carr, Philippa ► Holt, Victoria

Cartland, (Mary) Barbara (Hamilton) (1901–2000) English novelist, born Birmingham; *The Husband Hunters* (1976), *Wings on My Heart* (1954), *The Castle Made for Love* (1985), *Love Solves the Problem* (1995).

Cather, Willa (Silbert) (1876–1947) American novelist, poet, born near Winchester, Virginia; *O Pioneers!* (1913), *My Antonia* (1918), *One of Ours* (1922), *The Professor's House* (1925), *My Mortal Enemy* (1926), *Death Comes for the Archbishop* (1927), *Sapphira and the Slave Girl* (1940).

Cela, Camilo José (1916–) Spanish novelist, born Iria Flavia; *La Familia de Pascual Duarte* (1942), *Mazurca para dos muertos* (1984, trans *Mazurka for Two Dead People*); Nobel Prize for literature 1989.

Cervantes (Saavedra), Miguel de (1547–1616) Spanish novelist and poet, born Alcala de Henares; *La Galatea* (1585), *Don Quixote* (1605–15).

Chandler, Raymond (1888–1959) American novelist, born Chicago; *The Big Sleep* (1939), *Farewell, My Lovely* (1940), *The High Window* (1942), *The Lady in the Lake* (1943), *The Long Goodbye* (1953).

Chesterton, G(ilbert) K(eith) (1874–1936) English novelist, poet, born London; *The Napoleon of Notting Hill* (1904), *The Innocence of Father Brown* (1911).

Christie, Dame Agatha (Mary Clarissa) (née Miller) (1890–1976) English novelist, born Torquay, Devon; *Murder on the Orient Express* (1934), *Death on the Nile* (1937), *Ten Little Niggers* (1939), *Curtain* (1975).

Clarke, Sir Arthur C(harles) (1917–) English novelist, short-story writer, born Minehead, Somerset; *Childhood's End* (1953), *The Fountains of Paradise* (1979), *The Garden of Rama* (1991), *The Hammer of God* (1993).

Clavell, James (du Maresq) (1922–94) American novelist, playwright, born England; *King Rat* (1962), *Tai-Pan* (1966), *Shogun* (1975).

Coetzee, J(ohn) M(ichael) (1940–) South African novelist, born Cape Town; *Life and Times of Michael K* (1983, Booker Prize), *Foe* (1986), *The Master of Petersburg* (1994).

Collins, (William) Wilkie (1824–89) English novelist, born London; *The Woman in White* (1860), *No Name* (1862), *Armadale* (1866), *The Moonstone* (1868).

Condon, Richard (Thomas) (1915–96) American novelist, born New York City; *The Manchurian Candidate* (1959), *Winter Kills* (1974), *Prizzi's Honor* (1982).

Conrad, Joseph (originally Jozef Teodor Konrad Nalecz Korzeniowski) (1857–1924) Anglo-Polish novelist, short-story writer, born Berdichev, Poland, (now Ukraine); *Lord Jim* (1900), *Heart of Darkness* (1902), *Nostromo* (1904), *The Secret Agent* (1907), *Chance* (1914).

Cookson, Dame Catherine (Ann) (1906–98) English novelist, born Tyne Dock, County Durham; *Tilly Trotter* (1956), *The Glass Virgin* (1969), *The Black Candle* (1989).

Davies, (William) Robertson (1913–95) Canadian novelist, short-story writer, playwright, born Thamesville, Ontario; *The Rebel Angels* (1981), 'The Deptford Trilogy' (1970–5), *What's Bred in the Bone* (1985).

de Beauvoir, Simone (1908–86) French novelist, born Paris; *The Second Sex* (1949, trans 1953), *Les Mandarins* (1954), *Memoirs of a Dutiful Daughter* (1959).

Defoe, Daniel (1660–1731) English novelist, born Stoke Newington, London; *Robinson Crusoe* (1719), *Moll Flanders* (1722), *A Journal of the Plague Year* (1722).

Deighton, Len (Leonard Cyril) (1929–) English novelist, born London; *The Ipcress File* (1962), *Spy Hook* (1988), *Spy Line* (1989), *Spy Sinker* (1990), *Faith* (1994), *Hope* (1995), *Charity* (1996).

de Quincey, Thomas (1785–1859) English novelist, born Manchester; *Confessions of an English Opium Eater* (1822).

Desai, Anita (née Mazumbar) (1937–) Indian novelist, short-story writer, born Mussoorie; *Cry, The Peacock* (1963), *Fire on the Mountain* (1977), *In Custody* (1984), *Baumgartner's Bombay* (1988), *Journey to Ithaca* (1995).

Dickens, Charles (1812–70) English novelist, born Landport, Portsmouth; *Oliver Twist* (1837–9), *David Copperfield* (1849–50), *Bleak House* (1852–3), *Great Expectations* (1860–1).

Disraeli, Benjamin (1804–81) English novelist, born London; *Coningsby* (1844), *Sybil* (1846), *Tancred* (1847).

Donleavy, J(ames) P(atrick) (1926–) Irish–American novelist, playwright, born Brooklyn, New York City; *The Ginger Man* (1955), *Shultz* (1980), *Are You Listening, Rabbi Low?* (1987), *The Lady Who Liked Clean Rest Rooms* (1995).

Dos Passos, John Roderigo (1896–1970) American novelist, born Chicago; *Manhattan Transfer* (1925), *USA* (1930–6).

Dostoyevsky, Fyodor Mikhailovich (1821–81) Russian novelist, born Moscow; *Notes from the Underground* (1864), *Crime and Punishment* (1866), *The Brothers Karamazov* (1880).

Doyle, Sir Arthur Conan (1859–1930) Scottish novelist, short-story writer, born Edinburgh; *The Memoirs of Sherlock Holmes* (1894), *The Hound of the Baskervilles* (1902), *The Lost World* (1912).

Doyle, Roddy (1958–) Irish novelist, born Dublin; *The Commitments* (1987), *Paddy Clarke Ha Ha Ha* (1993, Booker Prize), *The Woman Who Walked into Doors* (1996).

Drabble, Margaret (1939–) English novelist, short-story writer, born Sheffield; *The Millstone* (1965), *Jerusalem the Golden* (1967), *The Ice Age* (1977), *The Gates of Ivory* (1991).

Duffy, Maureen (Patricia) (1933–) English novelist, playwright, born Worthing, Sussex; *That's How It Was* (1962), *The Microcosm* (1966), *The Paradox Players* (1967), *Occam's Razor* (1993).

Dumas, Alexandre (in full Alexandre Dumas Davy de la Pailleterie), known as Dumas père (1802–70) French novelist and playwright, born Villers-Cotterêts, Aisne; *The Three Musketeers* (1844–5).

Dumas, Alexandre, known as Dumas fils (1824–95) French novelist, playwright, born Paris; *La Dame aux camélias* (1848).

du Maurier, Dame Daphne (1907–89) English novelist, born London; *Rebecca* (1938), *My Cousin Rachel* (1951).

Durrell, Gerald Malcolm (1925–95) English writer, born Jamshedpur, India; *The Overloaded Ark* (1953), *My Family and Other Animals* (1956).

Durrell, Lawrence George (1912–90) English novelist, poet, born Julundur, India; *'Alexandria Quartet'* (1957–60).

Eco, Umberto (1932–) Italian novelist, born Alessandria, Piedmont; *The Name of the Rose* (1980), *Foucault's Pendulum* (1989), *The Island of the Day Before* (1995).

Eliot, George (originally Mary Ann, later Marian Evans) (1819–80) English novelist, born Arbury, Warwickshire; *Adam Bede* (1858), *The Mill on the Floss* (1860), *Middlemarch* (1871–2), *Daniel Deronda* (1874–6).

Elton, Ben (Benjamin Charles) (1959–) English novelist, born Catford, South London; *Stark* (1989), *Gridlock* (1991), *Popcorn* (1996).

Farmer, Philip José (1918–) American novelist, short-story writer, born Indiana; *To Your Scattered Bodies Go* (1977), *The Magic Labyrinth* (1980), *Nothing Burns in Hell* (1998).

Faulkner, William Harrison (1897–1962) American novelist, born near Oxford, Mississippi; *Sartoris* (1929), *The Sound and the Fury* (1929), *Absalom, Absalom!* (1936); Nobel Prize for literature 1949.

Fielding, Henry (1707–54) English novelist, born Sharpham Park, near Glastonbury, Somerset; *Joseph Andrews* (1742), *Tom Jones* (1749).

Fitzgerald, F(rancis) Scott (Key) (1896–1940) American novelist, short-story writer, born St Paul, Minnesota; *The Great Gatsby* (1925), *Tender is the Night* (1934).

Fitzgerald, Penelope (Mary) (née Knox) (1916–2000) English novelist, born Lincoln; *The Bookshop* (1978), *Offshore* (1979, Booker Prize), *The Gate of Angels* (1990), *The Blue Flower* (1995).

Flaubert, Gustave (1821–80) French novelist, born Rouen; *Madame Bovary* (1857), *Salammbô* (1862).

Fleming, Ian (Lancaster) (1908–64) English novelist, born London; author of the 'James Bond' novels, eg *Casino Royale* (1953), *From Russia with Love* (1957), *Dr No* (1958), *Goldfinger* (1959), *The Man with the Golden Gun* (1965).

Ford, Richard (1944–) American novelist, born Jackson, Mississippi; *A Piece of My Heart* (1976), *The Sportswriter* (1986), *Independence Day* (1995, Pulitzer Prize 1996).

Forester, C(ecil) S(cott) (1899–1966) British novelist, born Cairo, Egypt; *Payment Deferred* (1926), *The African Queen* (1935), *The Happy Return* (1937).

Forster, E(dward) M(organ) (1879–1970) English novelist, short-story writer, born London; *A Room with a View* (1908), *Howards End* (1910), *A Passage to India* (1922–4).

Forsyth, Frederick (1938–) English novelist, short-story writer, born Ashford, Kent; *The Day of the Jackal* (1971), *The Odessa File* (1972), *The Fourth Protocol* (1984), *The Fist of God* (1993), *Icon* (1996).

Fowles, John (Robert) (1926–) English novelist, born Leigh-on-Sea, Essex; *The Magus* (1965, revised 1977), *The French Lieutenant's Woman* (1969), *The Ebony Tower* (1974), *The Tree* (1991).

Frame, Janet Paterson (1924–) New Zealand novelist, short-story writer, born Dunedin; *The Lagoon: Stories* (1952), *Scented Gardens for the Blind* (1963), *Living in the Maniototo* (1979), *The Carpathians* (1988); autobiography: *To the Island* (1982), *An Angel at My Table* (1984), *The Envoy from Mirror City* (1985).

Francis, Dick (Richard Stanley) (1920–) English novelist, born Tenby, Pembrokeshire; *Dead Cert* (1962), *Slay-Ride* (1973), *The Edge* (1988), *Comeback* (1991), *To The Hilt* (1996), *10 lb Penalty* (1997).

Fraser, Lady Antonia (née Pakenham) (1932–) English novelist, born London; *Mary, Queen of Scots* (1969), *Quiet as a Nun* (1977), *A Splash of Red* (1981), *Have a Nice Death* (1983), *Political Death* (1994).

French, Marilyn (1929–) American novelist, born New York City; *The Women's Room* (1977), *The Bleeding Heart* (1980), *Her Mother's Daughter* (1987), *The War Against Women* (1992).

Fuller, Roy (Broadbent) (1912–91) English novelist, poet, born Failsworth, Lancashire; *The Second Curtain* (1953), *The Ruined Boys* (1959), *My Child, My Sister* (1965).

Galsworthy, John (1867–1933) English novelist, playwright, born Coombe, Surrey; *The Man of Property* (1906), *The Forsyte Saga* (1906–31); Nobel Prize for literature 1932.

García Márquez, Gabriel (1928–) Colombian novelist, born Aracataca; *One Hundred Years of Solitude* (1970), *Chronicle of a Death Foretold* (1982), *The General in His Labyrinth* (1991), *Of Love and Other Demons* (1995), *News of a Kidnapping* (non-fiction, 1997); Nobel Prize for literature 1982.

Gaskell, Mrs Elizabeth (Cleghorn) (née Stevenson) (1810–65) English novelist, born Cheyne Row, Chelsea, London; *Mary Barton* (1848), *Cranford* (1853), *North and South* (1855), *Sylvia's Lovers* (1863).

Gibbon, Lewis Grassic (pseudonym of James Leslie Mitchell) (1901–35) Scottish novelist, born near Auchterless, Aberdeenshire; *Sunset Song* (1932), *Cloud Howe* (1933), *Grey Granite* (1934).

Gibbons, Stella (Dorothea) (1902–89) English novelist, born London; *Cold Comfort Farm* (1933).

Gide, André (Paul Guillaume) (1860–1951) French novelist, born Paris; *The Immoralist* (1902), *The Vatican Cellars* (1914).

Godden, (Margaret) Rumer (1907–98) English novelist, poet, children's author, born Eastbourne, Sussex; *Black Narcissus* (1939), *Breakfast with the Nikolides* (1942), *The Greengage Summer* (1958), *Coromandel Sea Change* (1991), *Pippa Passes* (1994).

Godwin, William (1756–1836) English novelist, born Wisbech, Cambridgeshire; *Caleb Williams* (1794), *Mandeville* (1817).

Goethe, Johann Wolfgang von (1749–1832) German novelist, poet, born Frankfurt am Main; *The Sorrows of Young Werther* (1774).

Gogol, Nikolai Vasilievich (1809–52) Russian novelist, short-story writer, playwright, born Sorochinstsi, Poltava; *The Overcoat* (1835), *Diary of a Madman* (1835), *Dead Souls* (1842), *The Odd Women* (1893).

Golding, (Sir) William (Gerald) (1911–93) English novelist, born St Columb Minor, Cornwall; *The Lord of the Flies* (1954), *The Inheritors* (1955), *Pincher Martin* (1956), *The Spire* (1964), *Darkness Visible* (1979), *Rites of Passage* (1980, Booker Prize), *The Paper Men* (1984), *Close Quarter* (1987), *Fire Down Below* (1989); Nobel Prize for literature 1983.

Goldsmith, Oliver (1728–74) Anglo-Irish playwright, novelist, poet, born Pallasmore, County Longford; *The Vicar of Wakefield* (1766).

Gordimer, Nadine (1923–) South African novelist, short-story writer, born Springs, Transvaal; *Occasion for Loving* (1963), *A Guest of Honour* (1970), *The Conservationist* (1974, Booker Prize), *A Sport of Nature* (1987), *None to Accompany Me* (1994); Nobel Prize for literature 1991.

Gorky, Maxim (pseudonym of Aleksei Maksimovich Peshkov) (1868–1936) Russian novelist, short-story writer, born Nizhni Novgorod (New Gorky); *The Mother* (1906–7), *Childhood* (1913), *The Life of Klim Samgin* (1925–36).

Grass, Günter (Wilhelm) (1927–) German novelist, born Danzig; *The Tin Drum* (1959), *The Meeting at Telgte* (1979), *A Wide Field* (1995).

Graves, Robert (Ranke) (1895–1985) English novelist, poet, born London; *I Claudius* (1934), *Claudius the God* (1934).

Gray, Alasdair (James) (1934–) Scottish novelist, short-story writer, poet, born Glasgow; *Lanark* (1981), *Unlikely Stories, Mostly* (stories) (1983), *Janine* (1984), *Poor Things* (1992), *A History Maker* (1994).

Greene, (Henry) Graham (1904–91) English novelist, playwright, born Berkhamstead, Hertfordshire; *Brighton Rock* (1938), *The Power and the Glory* (1940), *The Third Man* (1950), *The Honorary Consul* (1973).

Haggard, Sir (Henry) Rider (1856–1925) English novelist, born Bradenham Hall, Norfolk; *King Solomon's Mines* (1885), *She* (1887), *Allan Quatermain* (1887).

Hailey, Arthur (1920–) Anglo-Canadian novelist, playwright, born Luton, Bedfordshire; *Flight into Danger* (1958), *Airport* (1968), *The Evening News* (1990), *Detective* (1997).

Hammond Innes, Ralph (1913–98) English novelist, playwright, born Horsham, Sussex; *The Trojan Horse* (1940), *Atlantic Fury* (1962), *Isvik* (1991), *Delta Connection* (1996).

Hardy, Thomas (1840–1928) English novelist, poet, born Higher Bockhampton, Dorset; *Far from the Madding Crowd* (1874), *The Mayor of Casterbridge* (1886), *Tess of the D'Urbervilles* (1891), *Jude the Obscure* (1895).

Hartley, L(eslie) P(oles) (1895–1972) English novelist, short-story writer, born near Peterborough; *The Shrimp and the Anemone* (1944), *The Go-Between* (1953), *The Hireling* (1957).

Hawthorne, Nathaniel (1804–64) American novelist, short-story writer, born Salem, Massachusetts; *The Scarlet Letter* (1850), *The House of the Seven Gables* (1851).

Heller, Joseph (1923–99) American novelist, born Brooklyn, New York City; *Catch-22* (1961), *Something Happened* (1974), *Picture This* (1988), *Closing Time* (1994).

Hemingway, Ernest (Millar) (1899–1961) American novelist, short-story writer, born Oak Park (Chicago), Illinois; *A Farewell to Arms* (1929), *For Whom the Bell Tolls* (1940), *The Old Man and the Sea* (1952); Nobel Prize for literature 1954.

Hesse, Hermann (1877–1962) German novelist, born Calw, Württemberg; *Rosshalde* (1914), *Steppenwolf* (1927), *The Glass Bead Game* (1943); Nobel Prize for literature 1946.

Heyer, Georgette (1902–74) English novelist, born London; *The Black Moth* (1929), *Footsteps in the Dark* (1932), *Regency Buck* (1935), *The Corinthian* (1940), *Friday's Child* (1944), *The Grand Sophy* (1950), *Bath Tangle* (1955), *Venetia* (1958), *The Nonesuch* (1962), *Frederica* (1965).

Highsmith, (Mary) Patricia (née Plangman) (1921–95) American novelist, short-story writer, born Fort Worth, Texas; *This Sweet Sickness* (1960), *The Cry of the Owl* (1962), *The Boy Who Followed Ripley* (1980).

Hilton, James (1900–54) English novelist, born Leigh, Lancashire; *Lost Horizon* (1933), *Goodbye Mr Chips* (1934).

Hines, (Melvin) Barry (1939–) English novelist, playwright, born Barnsley, S Yorkshire; *A Kestrel for a Knave* (1968), *The Gamekeeper* (1975), *The Heart of It* (1994).

Hoban, Russell (Conwell) (1925–) American novelist, playwright, children's writer, born Lansdale, Pennsylvania; *Turtle Diary* (1975), *Riddley Walker* (1980), *Pilgermann* (1983), *The Trokeville Way* (1996).

Hogg, James ('the Ettrick Shepherd') (1770–1835) Scottish novelist, poet, born Ettrick, Selkirkshire; *Confessions of a Justified Sinner* (1824).

Holt, Victoria (pseudonym of Eleanor Alice Burford Hibbert) (1906–93) English novelist, born London, also writes as Philippa Carr, Jean Plaidy; *Catherine de' Medici* (1969, as JP), *Will You Love Me in September* (1981, as PC), *The Captive* (1989, as VH).

Hughes, Thomas (1822–96) English novelist, born Uffington, Berkshire; *Tom Brown's Schooldays* (1857).

Hugo, Victor (Marie) (1802–85) French novelist, dramatist, poet, born Besançon; *Notre Dame de Paris* (1831), *Les Misérables* (1862).

Hulme, Keri (1947–) New Zealand novelist, born Christchurch; *The Bone People* (1983, Booker Prize 1985), *Lost Possessions* (1985).

Hunter, Evan (originally Salvatore A Lambino) (1926–) American novelist, playwright, short-story writer, born New York City; *The Blackboard Jungle* (1954), *Strangers When We Meet* (1958), *The Paper Dragon* (1966), *Last Summer* (1968), *Privileged Conversation* (1996); also writes as Ed McBain.

Hurston, Zora Neale (1903–60) American novelist, born Eatonville, Florida; *Their Eyes Were Watching God* (1937), *Moses, Man of the Mountain* (1939).

Huxley, Aldous (Leonard) (1894–1963) English novelist, born Godalming, Surrey; *Brave New World* (1932), *Eyeless in Gaza* (1936), *Island* (1962).

Irving, John (Winslow) (1942–) American novelist, short-story writer, born Exeter, New Hampshire; *The World According to Garp* (1978), *The Hotel New Hampshire* (1981), *A Prayer for Owen Meany* (1989), *A Son of the Circus* (1994).

Isherwood, Christopher (William Bradshaw) (1904–86) Anglo-American novelist, born Disley, Cheshire; *Mr Norris Changes Trains* (1935), *Goodbye to Berlin* (1939), *Down There on a Visit* (1962).

Ishiguro, Kazuo (1954–) British novelist, short-story writer, born Japan; *The Remains of the Day* (1989, Booker Prize), *The Unconsoled* (1995).

James, Henry (1843–1916) American novelist, born New York City; *Portrait of a Lady* (1881), *The Bostonians* (1886), *The Turn of the Screw* (1889), *The Awkward Age* (1899), *The Ambassadors* (1903), *The Golden Bowl* (1904).

James, P(hyliss) D(orothy) (1920–) English novelist, born Oxford; *Cover Her Face* (1966), *Taste for Death* (1986), *Devices and Desires* (1989), *Original Sin* (1994).

Jhabvala, Ruth Prawer (1927–) Anglo-Polish novelist, born Cologne, Germany; *Heat and Dust* (1975, Booker Prize), *In Search of Love and Beauty* (1983), *Poet and Dancer* (1993).

Jong, Erica (née Mann) (1942–) American novelist, poet, born New York City; *Fear of Flying* (1973), *Fanny* (1980), *Serenissima* (1987).

Joyce, James (Augustine Aloysius) (1882–1941) Irish novelist, poet, born Dublin; *Dubliners* (1914), *A Portrait of the Artist as a Young Man* (1914–15), *Ulysses* (1922), *Finnegan's Wake* (1939).

Kafka, Franz (1883–1924) Austrian novelist, short-story writer, born Prague (now in Czech Republic); *Metamorphosis* (1916), *The Trial* (1925), *The Castle* (1926), *America* (1927).

Kazantazakis, Nikos (1883–1957) Greek novelist, poet, playwright, born Heraklion, Crete; *Zorba the Greek* (1946).

Kelman, James (Alexander) (1946–) Scottish novelist, short-story writer, playwright, born Glasgow; *The Busconductor Hines* (1984), *A Chancer* (1985), *Greyhound for Breakfast* (1987), *A Disaffection* (1989), *How late it was, how late* (1994, Booker Prize).

Keneally, Thomas (Michael) (1935–) Australian novelist, short-story writer, playwright, born Sydney; *Bring Larks and Heroes* (1967), *Three Cheers for a Paraclete* (1968), *The Survivor* (1969), *Schindler's Ark* (1982, Booker Prize), *Woman of the Inner Sea* (1992), *A River Town* (1995).

Kerouac, Jack (Jean-Louis) (1922–69) American novelist, born Lowell, Massachusetts; *On the Road* (1957), *The Dharma Bums* (1958).

Kesey, Ken (Elton) (1935–) American novelist, short-story writer, born La Junta, Colorado; *One Flew Over the Cuckoo's Nest* (1962), *Demon Box* (stories) (1987), *Sailor Song* (1990).

King, Stephen (Edwin) (1947–) American novelist, short-story writer, born Portland, Maine; *Carrie* (1974), *The Shining* (1977), *Christine* (1983), *Pet Sematary* (1983), *Four Past Midnight* (1990).

Kingsley, Charles (1819–75) English novelist, born Holne vicarage, Dartmoor; *Westward Ho!* (1855), *The Water-Babies* (1863), *Hereward the Wake* (1866).

Kipling, Rudyard (1865–1936) English novelist, poet, short-story writer, born Bombay, India; *Barrack-room Ballads* (1892), *The Jungle Book* (1894), *Kim* (1901), *Just So Stories* (1902); Nobel Prize for literature 1907.

Kundera, Milan (1929–) French–Czech novelist, born Brno; *Life is Elsewhere* (1973), *The Farewell Party* (1976), *The Unbearable Lightness of Being* (1984), *Immortality* (1991), *Testaments Betrayed* (1995), *Slowness* (1996).

Laclos, Pierre (Ambroise François) Choderlos de (1741–1803) French novelist, born Amiens; *Les Liaisons Dangereuses* (1782, trans Dangerous Liaisons 1784).

La Fayette, Marie Madeleine Pioche de Lavergne, Comtesse de (1634–93) French novelist, born Paris; *Zaïde* (1670), *La Princesse de Clèves* (1678).

Lampedusa, Giuseppe Tomasi di (1896–1957) Italian novelist, born Palermo, Sicily; *Il Gattopardo* (1958, transThe Leopard 1960).

Lawrence, D(avid) H(erbert) (1885–1930) English novelist, poet, short-story writer, born Eastwood, Nottinghamshire; *Sons and Lovers* (1913), *The Rainbow* (1915), *Women in Love* (1920), *Lady Chatterley's Lover* (1928).

Le Carré, John (pseudonym of David John Moore Cornwell) (1931–) English novelist, born Poole, Dorset; *Tinker, Tailor, Soldier, Spy* (1974), *Smiley's People* (1980), *The Little Drummer Girl* (1983), *A Perfect Spy* (1986), *The Russia House* (1989), *The Secret Pilgrim* (1991), *The Night Manager* (1993), *Our Game* (1995), *The Tailor of Panama* (1996).

Lee, (Nelle) Harper (1926–) American novelist, born Monroeville, Alabama; *To Kill a Mockingbird* (1960, Pulitzer Prize 1961).

Lee, Laurie (1914–97) English novelist, poet, born Slad, Gloucestershire; *Cider with Rosie* (1959), *As I Walked Out One Midsummer Morning* (1969).

Le Fanu, (Joseph) Sheridan (1814–73) Irish novelist, short-story writer, born Dublin; *Uncle Silas* (1864), *In a Glass Darkly* (1872).

Le Guin, Ursula K(roeber) (1929–) American novelist, poet, short-story writer, born Berkeley, California; *Rocannon's World* (1966), *The Left Hand of Darkness* (1969), *Searoad* (1991), *Fish Soup* (1992).

Lessing, Doris May (néeTayler) (1919–) Rhodesian novelist, short-story writer, born Kermanshah, Iran; *The Grass is Singing* (1950), *The Golden Notebook* (1962), *Canopus in Argus Archives* (1979–83), *The Good Terrorist* (1985), *Playing the Game* (1996).

Levi, Primo (1919–87) Italian novelist, born Turin; *If this is a Man* (1947), *The Periodic Table* (1984).

Lewis, C(live) S(taples) (1898–1963) English novelist, religious writer, born Belfast; *Out of the Silent Planet* (1938), *Perelandra* (1939), *That Hideous Strength* (1945), *The Chronicles of Narnia* —a series of seven books beginning with *The Lion, The Witch and The Wardrobe* (1950) and ending with *The Last Battle* (1956).

Lewis, (Harry) Sinclair (1885–1951) American novelist, born Sauk Center, Minnesota; *Main Street* (1920), *Babbitt* (1922), *Martin Arrowsmith* (1925), *Elmer Gantry* (1927); Nobel Prize for literature 1930.

Lively, Penelope (Margaret) (née Low) (1933–) English, born Cairo, Egypt; *The Road to Lichfield* (1977), *Moon Tiger* (1987, Booker Prize), *City of the Mind* (1991), *Heat Wave* (1996).

Lodge, David (John) (1935–) English novelist, born London; *The British Museum is Falling Down* (1965), *Changing Places* (1975), *Small World* (1984), *Nice Work* (1988), *Paradise News* (1991), *Therapy* (1995).

London, Jack (John) Griffith (1876–1916) American novelist, born San Francisco; *Call of the Wild* (1903), *White Fang* (1907), *Martin Eden* (1909).

Lowry, (Clarence) Malcolm (1909–57) English novelist, born New Brighton, Merseyside; *Under The Volcano* (1947).

Lurie, Alison (1926–) American novelist, born Chicago; *Love and Friendship* (1962), *The War Between the Tates* (1974), *Foreign Affairs* (1984, Pulitzer Prize 1985), *The Truth about Lorin Jones* (1988), *Women and Ghosts* (short stories) (1994).

Macaulay, Dame (Emilie) Rose (1881–1958) English novelist, born Rugby, Warwickshire; *Dangerous Ages* (1921), *The World, My Wilderness* (1950), *The Towers of Trebizond* (1956).

McEwan, Ian (Russell) (1948–) English novelist, short-story writer, playwright, born Aldershot, Hampshire; *First Love, Last Rites* (1975), *The Cement Garden* (1978), *The Child in Time* (1987), *The Innocent* (1990), *Enduring Love* (1997).

MacKenzie, Sir (Edward Montague) Compton (1883–1972) English novelist, born West Hartlepool, Cleveland; *Whisky Galore* (1942).

MacLean, Alistair (1922–87) Scottish novelist, born Glasgow; *The Guns of Navarone* (1957), *Ice Station Zebra* (1963), *Where Eagles Dare* (1967), *Force Ten from Navarone* (1968).

Mahfouz, Naguib (1911–) Egyptian novelist, born Cairo; *The Thief and the Dogs* (1961), *Adrift on the Nile* (1966), *God's World* (1973), *The Cairo Trilogy* (1956–7); Nobel Prize for literature 1988.

Mailer, Norman (Kingsley) (1923–) American novelist, born Long Beach, New Jersey; *The Naked and the Dead* (1949), *Barbary Shore* (1951), *An American Dream* (1965), *The Executioner's Song* (1979, Pulitzer Prize 1980), *Harlot's Ghost* (1991), *Portrait of Picasso as a Young Man* (1995), *Oswald's Tale* (1995).

Mann, Thomas (1875–1955) German novelist, born Lübeck; *Death in Venice* (1912), *The Magic Mountain* (1924).

Mansfield, Katherine (pseudonym of Katherine Mansfield Beauchamp) (1888–1923) New Zealand short-story writer, born Wellington; *Prelude* (1918), *Bliss, and Other Stories* (1920), *The Garden Party, and Other Stories* (1922).

Marsh, Ngaio (1899–1982) New Zealand novelist, born Christchurch; *Death in a White Tie* (1958), *A Grave Mistake* (1978).

Maugham, (William) Somerset (1874–1965) English novelist, born Paris; *Of Human Bondage* (1915), *The Moon and Sixpence* (1919), *The Razor's Edge* (1945).

Maupassant, Guy de (1850–93) French short-story writer, novelist, born Miromesnil; *Claire de Lune* (1884), *Bel Ami* (1885).

Mauriac, François (1885–1970) French novelist, born Bordeaux; *Le Baiser au lépreux* (1922, trans The Kiss to the Leper 1923); Nobel Prize for literature 1952.

Melville, Herman (1819–1909) American novelist, poet, born New York City; *Moby Dick* (1851).

Meredith, George (1828–1909) English novelist, poet, born Portsmouth; *The Egoist* (1879), *Diana of the Crossways* (1885).

Michener, James A(lbert) (1907–97) American novelist, short-story writer, born New York City; *Tales of the South Pacific* (1947, Pulitzer Prize 1948), *Hawaii* (1959), *Chesapeake* (1978), *Miracle in Seville* (1995).

Miller, Henry Valentine (1891–1980) American novelist, born New York City; *Tropic of Cancer* (1934), *Tropic of Capricorn* (1938), *The Rosy Crucifixion Trilogy* (1949–60).

Mishima, Yukio (pseudonym of Hiraoka Kimitake) (1925–70) Japanese novelist, born Tokyo; *Confessions of a Mask* (1960), *The Temple of the Golden Pavilion* (1959), *The Sea of Fertility* (1969–71).

Mitchell, Margaret (1900–49) American novelist, born Atlanta, Georgia; *Gone with the Wind* (1936).

Mitford, Nancy (1904–73) English novelist, born London; *Love in a Cold Climate* (1949), *Don't Tell Alfred* (1960).

Mo, Timothy (Peter) (1950–) British novelist, born Hong Kong; *The Monkey King* (1978), *Sour Sweet* (1982), *An Insular Possession* (1986), *The Redundancy of Courage* (1991), *Brownout on Breadfruit Boulevard* (1995).

Monsarrat, Nicholas (John Turney) (1910–79) English novelist, born Liverpool; *The Cruel Sea* (1951), *The Story of Esther Costello* (1953).

Morrison, Toni (Chloe Anthony) (née Wofford) (1931–) American novelist, born Lorain, Ohio; *The Bluest Eye* (1970), *Song of Solomon* (1977), *Tar Baby* (1981), *Beloved* (1987, Pulitzer Prize 1988).

Mortimer, Sir John (Clifford) (1923–) English novelist, short-story writer, playwright, born London; *A Cat Among the Pigeons* (1964), *Rumpole of the Bailey* (1978), *Paradise Postponed* (1985), *Under the Hammer* (1994).

Murdoch, Dame (Jean) Iris (1919–99) Irish novelist, philosopher, born Dublin; *The Bell* (1958), *The Sea, The Sea* (1978, Booker Prize), *The Philosopher's Pupil* (1983), *The Green Knight* (1993).

Nabokov, Vladimir Vladimirovich (1899–1977) Russian–American novelist, poet, born St Petersburg; *Lolita* (1955), *Look at the Harlequins!* (1974).

Naipaul, Sir V(idiadhar) S(urajprasad) (1932–) Trinidadian novelist, born Chaguanas; *A House for Mr Biswas* (1961), *In a Free State* (1971, Booker Prize), *A Bend in the River* (1979), *A Way in the World* (1994).

O'Brien, Edna (1932–) Irish novelist, short-story writer, born Tuamgraney, County Clare; *The Country Girls* (1960), *August is a Wicked Month* (1964), *A Pagan Place* (1971), *Lantern Slides* (stories) (1990), *Time and Tide* (1992).

Oë, Kenzaburo (1935–) Japanese novelist, born Shikoku; *Hiroshima Notes* (1981), *A Personal Matter* (1968), *The Silent Cry* (1974); Nobel Prize for literature 1994.

Okri, Ben (1959–) Nigerian novelist, born Minna; *The Famished Road* (1991, Booker Prize), *Dangerous Love* (1996).

Ondaatje, (Philip) Michael (1943–) Canadian novelist, poet, born Ceylon (now Sri Lanka); *Coming Through Slaughter* (1976), *In the Skin of a Lion* (1987), *The English Patient* (1991, Booker Prize 1992).

Orwell, George (pseudonym of Eric Arthur Blair) (1903–50) English novelist, born Bengal, India; *Down and Out in Paris and London* (1933), *The Road to Wigan Pier* (1937), *Animal Farm* (1945), *Nineteen Eighty-Four* (1949).

Pasternak, Boris (Leonidovich) (1890–1960) Russian novelist, born Moscow; *Doctor Zhivago* (1957); Nobel Prize for literature 1958.

Paton, Allan (Stewart) (1903–88) South African novelist, short-story writer, born Pietermaritzburg, Natal; *Cry, the Beloved Country* (1948).

Peake, Mervyn (Laurence) (1911–68) English novelist, poet, born Kuling, China; *Titus Groan* (1946), *Gormenghast* (1950), *Titus Alone* (1959).

Plaidy, Jean ▶ Holt, Victoria

Poe, Edgar Allan (1809–49) American short-story writer, poet, born Boston, Massachusetts; *Tales of the Grotesque and Arabesque* (eg 'The Fall of the House of Usher') (1840), *The Pit and the Pendulum* (1843).

Porter, Katherine Anne (Maria Veronica Callista Russell) (1890–1980) American novelist, short-story writer, born Indian Creek, Texas; *Pale Horse, Pale Rider* (1939), *Ship of Fools* (1962).

Powell, Anthony (Dymoke) (1905–2000) English novelist, born London; *A Dance to the Music of Time* (1951–75), *The Fisher King* (1986).

Powys, John Cowper (1872–1963) English novelist, born Shirley, Derbyshire; *Wolf Solent* (1929), *Owen Glendower* (1940).

Priestley, J(ohn) B(oynton) (1894–1984) English novelist, playwright, born Bradford, Yorkshire; *The Good Companions* (1929), *Angel Pavement* (1930).

Pritchett, Sir V(ictor) S(awdon) (1900–97) English novelist, short-story writer, playwright, born Ipswich, Suffolk; *Nothing like Leather* (1935), *Dead Man Leading* (1937), *Mr Beluncle* (1951), *The Key to My Heart* (1963), *Man of Letters* (essays) (1985).

Proulx, E Annie (1935–) American novelist, short-story writer, born Connecticut; *Postcards* (1993), *The Shipping News* (1993, Pulitzer Prize 1994), *Heart Songs* (1996), *Accordion Crimes* (1996).

Proust, Marcel (1871–1922) French novelist, born Paris; *Remembrance of Things Past* (1913–27).

Puzo, Mario (1920–99) American novelist, born New York City; *The Godfather* (1969), *The Last Don* (1996).

Pynchon, Thomas (1937–) American novelist, born Long Island, New York; *V* (1963), *Gravity's Rainbow* (1973), *Vineland* (1989), *Mason & Dixon* (1996).

Queen, Ellery (pseudonym of Patrick Dannay (1905–82) and his cousin Manfred B Lee (1905–71)) American novelists and short-story writers, both born Brooklyn, New York City; *The French Powder Mystery* (1930), *The Tragedy of X* (1940), *The Glass Village* (1954).

Remarque, Erich Maria (1898–1970) German novelist, born Osnabrück; *All Quiet on the Western Front* (1929), *The Road Back* (1931), *The Black Obelisk* (1957).

Rendell, Ruth (Barbara) Rendell, Baroness (1930–) English novelist, born London; *A Judgement in Stone* (1977), *The Killing Doll* (1980), *Heartstones*, (1987), *Blood Linen* (short stories) (1995); as Barbara Vine: *The House of Stairs* (1989).

Richardson, Samuel (1689–1761) English novelist, born near Derby; *Pamela* (1740), *Clarissa* (1747–8), *Sir Charles Grandison* (1753–4).

Robbins, Harold (pseudonym of Francis Kane) (1916–97) American novelist, born Hell's Kitchen, New York City; *Never Love a Stranger* (1948), *A Stone for Danny Fisher* (1951), *The Carpetbaggers* (1961), *The Betsy* (1971), *Tycoon* (1996).

Roth, Philip Milton (1933–) American novelist, short-story writer, born Newark, New Jersey; *Goodbye Columbus* (1959), *Portnoy's Complaint* (1969), *The Great American Novel* (1973), *My Life as a Man* (1974), *Patrimony* (1991), *Sabbath's Theater* (1995), *American Pastoral* (1997, Pulitzer Prize 1998).

Rushdie, (Ahmed) Salman (1947–) British novelist, short-story writer, born Bombay, India; *Midnight's Children* (1981, Booker Prize), *Shame* (1983), *The Satanic Verses* (1988), *Haroun and the Sea of Stories* (1990), *The Moor's Last Sigh* (1995).

Sackville-West, Vita (Victoria May) (1892–1962) English poet, novelist, short-story writer, born Knole, Kent; *The Edwardians* (1930), *All Passion Spent* (1931).

Sade, Donatien Alphonse François, Comte de, known as **Marquis** (1740–1814) French novelist, born Paris; *Les 120 Journées de Sodome* (1784), *Justine* (1791), *La Philosophie dans le boudoir* (1793), *Juliette* (1798), *Les Crimes de l'amour* (1800).

Saki (pseudonym of Hector Hugh Munro) (1870–1916) British novelist, short-story writer, born Akyab, Burma; *The Chronicles of Clovis* (1912), *The Unbearable Bassington* (1912).

Salinger, J(erome) D(avid) (1919–) American novelist, born New York; *The Catcher in the Rye* (1951), *Franny and Zooey* (1961), *Hapworth 16, 1924* (1997).

Sartre, Jean-Paul (1905–80) French novelist, playwright, born Paris; *Nausea* (1949), *The Roads to Freedom* (1945–7); Nobel Prize for literature 1964.

Sayers, Dorothy Leigh (1893–1957) English novelist, short-story writer, born Oxford; *Lord Peter Views the Body* (1928), *Gaudy Night* (1935).

Scott, Sir Walter (1771–1832) Scottish novelist, poet, born Edinburgh; *Waverley* (1814), *Rob Roy* (1817), *The Heart of Midlothian* (1818), *The Bride of Lammermoor* (1819), *Ivanhoe* (1820).

Sharpe, Tom (Thomas Ridley) (1928–) English novelist, born London; *Riotous Assembly* (1971), *Porterhouse Blue* (1974), *Blott on the Landscape* (1975), *Wilt* (1976), *Grantchester Grind* (1995), *The Midden* (1996).

Shelley, Mary (Wollstonecraft) (née Godwin) (1797–1851) English novelist, born London; *Frankenstein* (1818), *The Last Man* (1826), *Perkin Warbeck* (1830).

Shields, Carol (née Warner) (1935–) Canadian–American novelist, born Oak Park, Illinois; *Small Ceremonies* (1976), *Happenstance* (1980), *Swann: A Mystery* (1987), *The Republic of Love* (1992), *The Stone Diaries* (1993, Pulitzer Prize 1995), *Larry's Party* (1997, Orange Prize 1998).

Sholokhov, Mikhail Alexandrovich (1905–84) Russian novelist, born near Veshenskayal; *And Quiet Flows the Don* (1928–40), *The Upturned Soil* (1940); Nobel Prize for literature 1965.

Shute, Nevil (pseudonym of Nevil Shute Norway) (1899–1960) Anglo-Australian novelist, born Ealing, London; *The Pied Piper* (1942), *A Town Like Alice* (1950), *On the Beach* (1957).

Sillitoe, Alan (1928–) English novelist, poet, short-story writer, born Nottingham; *Saturday Night and Sunday Morning* (1958), *The Loneliness of the Long Distance Runner* (1959), *Alligator Playground* (1997).

Simenon, Georges (1903–89) French writer, born Liège, Belgium; almost 100 novels featuring Jules Maigret, and 400 other novels: *The Death of Monsieur Gallet* (1932), *The Crime of Inspector Maigret* (1933).

Simon, Claude (Henri Eugène) (1913–) French novelist, born Tananarive, Madagascar; *The Wind* (1959), *The Flanders Road* (1962), *Triptych* (1977); Nobel Prize for literature 1985.

Smollett, Tobias George (1721–71) Scottish novelist, born Dalquharn, Dunbartonshire; *Roderick Random* (1748), *The Adventures of Peregrine Pickle* (1751), *The Expedition of Humphry Clinker* (1771).

Snow, C(harles) **P**(ercy) (1905–80) English novelist, born Leicester; *Strangers and Brothers* (1940–70).

Solzhenitsyn, Aleksandr Isayevich (1918–) Russian novelist, born Kislovodsk, Caucasus; *One Day in the Life of Ivan Denisovich* (1962), *Cancer Ward* (1968), *The First Circle* (1969), *The Gulag Archipelago 1918–56* (3 vols 1973–6); Nobel Prize for literature 1970.

Spark, Dame Muriel (Sarah) (née Camberg) (1918–) Scottish novelist, short-story writer, poet, born Edinburgh; *The Ballad of Peckham Rye* (1960), *The Prime of Miss Jean Brodie* (1962), *The Girls of Slender Means* (1963), *The Mandelbaum Gate* (1965), *A Far Cry from Kensington* (1988).

Stein, Gertrude (1874–1946) American novelist, short-story writer, born Allegheny, Pennsylvania; *Three Lives* (1909), *Tender Buttons* (1914).

Steinbeck, John Ernest (1902–68) American novelist, born Salinas, California; *Of Mice and Men* (1937), *The Grapes of Wrath* (1939), *Cannery Row* (1945), *East of Eden* (1952); Nobel Prize for literature 1962.

Stendhal (pseudonym of Henri Marie Beyle) (1788–1842) French novelist, born Grenoble; *Le Rouge et le noir* (1830), *La Chartreuse de Parme* (1839).

Sterne, Lawrence (1713–68) Irish novelist, born Clonmel, Tipperary; *Tristram Shandy* (1759–67), *A Sentimental Journey* (1768).

Stevenson, Robert Louis (Balfour) (1850–94) Scottish novelist, short-story writer, poet, born Edinburgh; *Travels with a Donkey* (1879), *Treasure Island* (1883), *Kidnapped* (1886), *The Strange Case of Dr Jekyll and Mr Hyde* (1886), *Weir of Hermiston* (1896).

Stewart, Mary (Florence Elinor) (1916–) English novelist born Sunderland; *This Rough Magic* (1964), *The Last Enchantment* (1979), *The Prince and the Pilgrim* (1995).

Stoker, Bram (Abraham) (1847–1912) Irish novelist, short-story writer, born Dublin; *Dracula* (1897).

Storey, David (Malcolm) (1933–) English novelist, playwright, born Wakefield, Yorkshire; *This Sporting Life* (1960), *Radcliffe* (1963), *Saville* (1976, Booker Prize), *A Prodigal Child* (1982).

Stowe, Harriet (Elizabeth) **Beecher** (1811–96) American novelist, born Litchfield, Connecticut; *Uncle Tom's Cabin* (1852).

Styron, William (Clark) (1925–) American novelist, born Newport News, Virginia; *Lie Down in Darkness* (1951), *The Confessions of Nat Turner* (1967), *Sophie's Choice* (1979), *A Tidewater Morning* (1993).

Swift, Graham (Colin) (1949–   ) English novelist, born London; *The Sweet Shop Owner* (1980), *Waterland* (1983), *Out of This World* (1988), *Ever After* (1992), *Last Orders* (1996, Booker Prize).

Swift, Jonathan (1667–1754) Irish novelist, poet, born Dublin; *A Tale of a Tub* (1704), *Gulliver's Travels* (1726).

Tennant, Emma (Christina) (1937–   ) English novelist, born London; *Hotel de Dream* (1978), *Alice Fell* (1980), *Pemberley* (1993), *Elinor and Marianne* (1996).

Thackeray, William Makepeace (1811–63) English novelist, born Calcutta, India; *Vanity Fair* (1847–8), *Pendennis* (1848–50).

Theroux, Paul (Edward) (1941–   ) American novelist, short-story writer, travel writer, born Medford, Massachusetts; *The Mosquito Coast* (1981), *The Kingdom by the Sea* (travel) (1983), *Doctor Slaughter* (1984), *Riding the Iron Rooster* (travel) (1988), *My Secret History* (1989), *My Other Life* (1996).

Thomas, D(onald) M(ichael) (1935–   ) English novelist, poet, born Redruth, Cornwall; *The White Hotel* (1981); Russian Nights (quintet): *Ararat* (1983), *Swallow* (1984), *Sphinx* (1986), *Summit* (1987), *Lying Together* (1990); *Eating Pavlova* (1994).

Tolkien, J(ohn) R(onald) R(euel) (1892–1973) English novelist, born Bloemfontein, South Africa; *The Hobbit* (1937), *The Lord of the Rings* (1954–5).

Tolstoy, Count Leo Nikolayevich (1828–1910) Russian novelist, born Yasnaya Polyana, Central Russia; *War and Peace* (1863–9), *Anna Karenina* (1873–7), *Resurrection* (1899).

Tranter, Nigel Godwin (1909–99) Scottish novelist, born Glasgow; over 100 novels including *The Steps to the Empty Throne* (1969), *The Path of the Hero King* (1970), *The Price of the King's Peace* (1971), *Honours Even* (1995).

Trollope, Anthony (1815–82) English novelist, born London; *Barchester Towers* (1857), *Can You Forgive Her?* (1864), *The Way We Live Now* (1875).

Trollope, Joanna (1943–   ) English novelist; *Eliza Stanhope* (1978), *The Choir* (1988), *A Village Affair* (1989), *The Rector's Wife* (1991), *Next of Kin* (1996).

Turgenev, Ivan Sergeevich (1818–83) Russian novelist, born province of Oryel; *Sportsman's Sketches* (1952), *Fathers and Children* (1862).

Twain, Mark (pseudonym of Samuel Langhorne Clemens) (1835–1910) American novelist, born Florida, Missouri; *The Celebrated Jumping Frog of Calaveras County* (1865), *The Adventures of Tom Sawyer* (1876), *The Prince and the Pauper* (1882), *The Adventures of Huckleberry Finn* (1884), *A Connecticut Yankee in King Arthur's Court* (1889).

Updike, John (Hoyer) (1932–   ) American novelist, short-story writer, born Shillington, Pennsylvania; *Rabbit, Run* (1960), *Pigeon Feathers and Other Stories* (1962), *Rabbit is Rich* (1982, Pulitzer Prize), *The Witches of Eastwick* (1984), *Rabbit at Rest* (1990, Pulitzer Prize 1991), *In the Beauty of the Lilies* (1996).

Uris, Leon (Marcus) (1924–   ) American novelist, born Baltimore, Maryland; *Battle Cry* (1953), *Exodus* (1958), *The Haj* (1984), *Redemption* (1995).

Van der Post, Sir Laurens (Jan) (1906–96) South African novelist, playwright, born Philippolis; *Flamingo Feather* (1955), *Journey into Russia* (1964), *A Far-Off Place* (1974).

Vargas Llosa, Mario (1936–) Peruvian novelist, born Arequipa; *The Time of the Hero* (1963), *Aunt Julia and the Scriptwriter* (1977), *The War at the End of the World* (1982), *The Green House* (1986).

Verne, Jules (1828–1905) French novelist, born Nantes; *Voyage to the Centre of the Earth* (1864), *Twenty Thousand Leagues under the Sea* (1870).

Vidal, Gore (Eugene Luther, Jr) (1925–) American novelist, short-story writer, playwright, born West Point, New York; *Williwaw* (1946), *The City and the Pillar* (1948), *The Judgement of Paris* (1952), *Myra Breckenridge* (1968), *Kalki* (1978), *Empire* (1987), *Hollywood* (1989), *The Season of Conflict* (1996).

Vine, Barbara ► Rendell, Ruth

Voltaire, François-Marie Arouet de (1694–1778) French novelist, poet, born Paris; *Zadig* (1747), *Candide* (1759).

Vonnegut, Kurt, Jr (1922–) American novelist, short-story writer, born Indianapolis, Indiana; *Cat's Cradle* (1963), *Slaughterhouse-Five* (1969), *Hocus Pocus* (1990).

Wain, John (Barrington) (1925–94) English novelist, poet, short-story writer, playwright, born Stoke-on-Trent, Staffordshire; *Hurry on Down* (1953), *The Young Visitors* (1965), *Where the Rivers Meet* (1988).

Walker, Alice (Malsenior) (1944–) American novelist, short-story writer, born Eatonville, Georgia; *The Third Life of Grange Copeland* (1970), *In Love and Trouble* (1973), *The Color Purple* (1983, Pulitzer Prize), *Everyday Use* (1994).

Walpole, Horace (1717–97) English novelist, poet, born London; *Letter from Xotto to His Friend Lien Chi at Pekin* (1757), *Anecdotes of Painting in England* (1761–71), *The Castle of Otranto* (1764), *The Mysterious Mother* (1768), *Historic Doubts on the Life and Reign of King Richard the Third* (1768).

Waterhouse, Keith (Spencer) (1929–) English novelist, playwright, born Leeds, Yorkshire; *Billy Liar* (1959), *Office Life* (1978), *Bimbo* (1990), *Unsweet Charity* (1992).

Waugh, Evelyn (Arthur St John) (1903–66) English novelist, born Hampstead, London; *Decline and Fall* (1928), *A Handful of Dust* (1934), *Brideshead Revisited* (1945).

Weldon, Fay (originally Franklin Birkinshaw) (1933–) English novelist, born Alvechurch, Worcestershire; *Down Among the Women* (1971), *Female Friends* (1975), *Life and Loves of a She-Devil* (1983), *Worst Fears* (1996).

Wells, H(erbert) G(eorge) (1866–1946) English novelist, born Bromley, Kent; *The Time Machine* (1895), *The War of the Worlds* (1898), *The History of Mr Polly* (1910).

Welty, Eudora (1909–) American novelist, short-story writer, born Jackson, Mississippi; *A Curtain of Green* (1941), *The Robber Bridegroom* (1944), *The Golden Apples* (1949), *The Ponder Heart* (1954), *The Optimist's Daughter* (1972, Pulitzer Prize 1973), *A Writer's Eye: Collected Book Reviews* (1994).

Wesley, Mary (pseudonym of Mary Aline Siepmann) (née Farmar) (1912–) English novelist, born Englefield Green, Berkshire; *The Camomile Lawn* (1984), *A Sensible Life* (1990), *Part of the Furniture* (1997).

Wharton, Edith (Newbold) (1862–1937) American novelist, short-story writer, born New York; *The House of Mirth* (1905), *Ethan Frome* (1911), *The Age of Innocence* (1920).

White, Patrick Victor Martindale (1912–90) Australian novelist, playwright, short-story writer, born London; *Voss* (1957), *The Vivisector* (1970), *A Fringe of Leaves* (1976); Nobel Prize for literature 1973.

Wilde, Oscar (Fingal O'Flahertie Wills) (1854–1900) Irish novelist, short-story writer, playwright, poet, born Dublin; *The Happy Prince and Other Tales* (1888), *The Picture of Dorian Gray* (1890).

Wilder, Thornton Niven (1897–1976) American novelist, playwright, born Madison, Wisconsin; *The Bridge of San Luis Rey* (1927), *The Woman of Andros* (1930), *Heaven's My Destination* (1935).

Winterson, Jeanette (1959–) English novelist, born Manchester; *Oranges Are Not the Only Fruit* (1987), *The Passion* (1987), *Sexing the Cherry* (1989), *Gut Symmetries* (1997).

Wodehouse, Sir P(elham) G(renville) (1881–1975) English novelist, short-story writer, born Guildford, Surrey; *The Inimitable Jeeves* (1923), *Carry on, Jeeves* (1925).

Wolfe, Thomas Clayton (1900–38) American novelist, born Asheville, North Carolina; *Look Homeward, Angel* (1929), *Of Time and the River* (1935), *From Death to Morning* (1935).

Wolfe, Tom (Thomas Kennerly) (1931–) American novelist, journalist, born Richmond, Virginia; *The Kandy-Kolored Tangerine-Flake Streamline Baby* (1965), *The Electric Kool-Aid Acid Test* (1968), *The Right Stuff* (1979), *The Bonfire of the Vanities* (1988).

Woolf, (Adeline) Virginia (1882–1941) English novelist, born London; *Mrs Dalloway* (1925), *To The Lighthouse* (1927), *Orlando* (1928), *A Room of One's Own* (1929), *The Waves* (1931).

Wouk, Herman (1915–) American novelist, playwright, born New York City; *The Caine Mutiny* (1951), *The Winds of War* (1971), *War and Remembrance* (1978), *Inside, Outside* (1985), *The Hope* (1993), *The Glory* (1994).

Yerby, Frank (Garvin) (1916–91) American novelist, born Augusta, Georgia; *The Golden Hawk* (1948), *The Dahomean* (1971), *A Darkness at Ingraham's Crest* (1979).

Yourcenar, Marguerite (pseudonym of Marguerite de Crayencour) (1903–87) French novelist, poet, born Brussels; *Memoirs of Hadrian* (1941).

Zola, Émile (1840–1902) French novelist, born Paris; *Thérèse Raquin* (1867), *Les Rougon-Macquart* (1871–93), *Germinal* (1885).

Poets

Selected volumes of poetry are listed.

Abse, Dannie (Daniel) (1923–) Welsh, born Cardiff; *After Every Green Thing* (1948), *Tenants of the House* (1957), *There Was a Young Man from Cardiff* (1991), *The Man Behind the Smile* (1996).

Adcock, (Karen) Fleur (1934–) New Zealander, born Papakura; *The Eye of the Hurricane* (1964), *In Focus* (1977), *The Incident Book* (1986).

Aiken, Conrad (Potter) (1889–1973) American, born Georgia; *Earth Triumphant* (1914), *Preludes for Memnon* (1931).

Akhamatova, Anna (pseudonym of Anna Andreevna Gorenko) (1889–1966) Russian, born Odessa; *Evening* (1912), *Poem without a Hero* (1940–62), *Requiem* (1963).

Angelou, Maya (pseudonym of Marguerite Annie Johnson) (1928–) American, born St Louis, Missouri; *And Still I Rise* (1978), *I Shall Not Be Moved* (1990), *Complete Collected Poems of Maya Angelou* (1995).

Apollinaire, Guillaume (1880–1918) French, born Rome; *Alcools* (1913), *Calligrammes* (1918).

Ariosto, Ludovico (1474–1535) Italian, born Reggio; *Furioso* (1532).

Auden, W(ystan) H(ugh) (1907–73) British, naturalized American citizen, born York; *Another Time* (1940), *The Sea and the Mirror* (1944), *The Age of Anxiety* (1947).

Baudelaire, Charles (Pierre) (1821–67) French, born Paris; *Les Fleurs du mal* (1857).

Beer, Patricia (1919–99) English, born Exmouth, Devon; *The Loss of the Magyar* (1959), *The Lie of the Land* (1983), *Friend of Heraclitus* (1993).

Belloc, (Joseph) Hillaire (Pierre) (1870–1953) British, born St Cloud, France; *Cautionary Tales* (1907), *Sonnets and Verse* (1923).

Berryman, John (1914–72) American, born McAlester, Oklahoma; *Homage to Mistress Bradsheet* (1966), *Dream Songs* (1969).

Betjeman, Sir John (1906–84) English, born Highgate, London; *Mount Zion* (1931), *New Bats in Old Belfries* (1945), *A Nip in the Air* (1972).

Bishop, Elizabeth (1911–79) American, born Worcester, Massachusetts; *North and South* (1946), *Geography III* (1978).

Blake, William (1757–1827) English, born London; *The Marriage of Heaven and Hell* (1793), *The Vision of the Daughter of Albion* (1793), *Songs of Innocence and Experience* (1794), *Vala, or The Four Zoas* (1800), *Milton* (1810).

Blunden, Edmund (Charles) (1896–1974) English, born Yalding, Kent; *The Waggoner and Other Poems* (1920), *Undertones of War* (1928).

Brodsky, Joseph (originally Iosif Aleksandrovich Brodsky) (1940–96) Russian–American, born Leningrad (now St Petersburg); *Longer and Shorter Poems* (1965), *To Urania: Selected Poems 1965–1985* (1988); Nobel Prize for literature 1987.

Brooke, Rupert (Chawner) (1887–1915) English, born Rugby; *Poems* (1911); *1914 and Other Poems* (1915), *New Numbers* (1915).

Brooks, Gwendolyn (Elizabeth) (1917–) American, born Topeka, Kansas; *A Street in Bronzeville* (1945), *Annie Allen* (1949, Pulitzer Prize 1950), *In The Mecca* (1968), *Blacks* (1987).

Browning, Elizabeth Barrett (née Barrett) (1806–61) English, born Coxhoe Hall, near Durham; *Sonnets from the Portuguese* (1850), *Aurora Leigh* (1855).

Browning, Robert (1812–89) English, born Camberwell, London; *Bells and Pomegranates* (1841–6), *Men and Women* (1855), *The Ring and the Book* (1868–9).

Burns, Robert (1759–96) Scottish, born Alloway, Ayr; *Poems, Chiefly in the Scottish Dialect* (1786), *Tam o'Shanter* (1790).

Byron (of Rochdale), George Gordon, 6th Baron (1788–1824) English, born London; *Hours of Idleness* (1807), *Childe Harolde* (1817), *Don Juan* (1819–24).

Carver, Raymond (1939–88) American, born Clatskanie, Oregon; *Where Water Comes Together with Other Water* (1985), *Ultramarine* (1985).

Catullus, Gaius Valerius (c.84–c.54BC) Roman, born Verona; lyric poet, over 100 poems survive.

Causley, Charles (1917–) English, born Lanceton, Cornwall; *Union St* (1957), *Johnny Alleluia* (1961), *Underneath the Water* (1968), *All Day Saturday* (1994).

Chaucer, Geoffrey (c.1343–1400) English, born London; *Book of the Duchess* (1370), *Troilus and Cressida* (c.1385), *The Canterbury Tales* (1387–1400).

Clampitt, Amy (1920–94) American, born Iowa; *The Kingfisher* (1983), *Archaic Figure* (1987), *Westward* (1990).

Clare, John (1793–1864) English, born Helpstone, Northamptonshire; *Poems Descriptive of Rural Life* (1820), *The Shepherd's Calendar* (1827).

Coleridge, Samuel Taylor (1772–1834) English, born Otterly St Mary, Devon; *Poems on Various Subjects* (1796), 'Kubla Khan' (1797), 'The Rime of the Ancient Mariner' (1798), *Christabel and Other Poems* (1816), *Sybylline Leaves* (1817).

Cowper, William (1731–1800) English, born Great Berkhampstead, Hertfordshire; *The Task* (1785).

Crabbe, George (1754–1823) English, born Aldeburgh, Suffolk; *The Village* (1783).

cummings, e(dward) e(stlin) (1894–1962) American, born Cambridge, Massachusetts; *Tulips and Chimneys* (1923), *XLI Poems* (1925), *is 5* (1926).

Dante, Alighieri (1265–1321) Italian, born Florence; *Vita nuova* (1294), *Divine Comedy* (1321).

Day Lewis, Cecil (1904–72) Irish, born Ballintogher, Sligo; *Overtures to Death* (1938), *The Aeneid of Virgil* (1952).

de la Mare, Walter (1873–1956) English, born Charleston, Kent; *The Listeners* (1912), *The Burning Glass and Other Poems* (1945).

Dickinson, Emily (Elizabeth) (1830–86) American, born Amherst, Massachusetts; only 7 poems published in her lifetime; posthumous publications, eg *Poems* (1890).

Donne, John (c.1572–1631) English, born London; *Satires & Elegies* (1590s), *Holy Sonnets* (1610–11), *Songs and Sonnets*; most verse published posthumously.

Doolittle, Hilda (known as H D) (1886–1961) American, born Bethlehem, Pennsylvania; *Sea Garden* (1916), *The Walls Do Not Fall* (1944), *Helen in Egypt* (1961).

Dryden, John (1631–1700) English, born Adwinckle All Saints, Northamptonshire; 'Astrea Redux' (1660), 'Absalom and Achitophel' (1681), 'MacFlecknoe' (1684).

Duffy, Carol Ann (1955–) Scottish, born Glasgow; *Standing Female Nude* (1985), *Mean Time* (1993).

Dunbar, William (c.1460–c.1520) Scottish, birthplace probably E Lothian; 'The Thrissill and the Rois' (1503), 'Lament for the Makaris' (c.1507).

Dunn, Douglas (Eaglesham) (1942–) Scottish, born Inchinnan, Strathclyde; *Love or Nothing* (1974), *Elegies* (1985), *Dante's Drum-kit* (1993).

Dutton, Geoffrey (Piers Henry) (1922–) Australian, born Kapunda; *Antipodes in Shoes* (1955), *Poems, Soft and Loud* (1968), *A Body of Words* (1977).

Eliot, T(homas) S(tearns) (1888–1965) American (British citizen 1927), born St Louis, Missouri; *Prufrock and Other Observations* (1917), *The Waste Land* (1922), *Ash Wednesday* (1930), *Four Quartets* (1944).

Éluard, Paul (pseudonym of Eugène Grindal) (1895–1952) French, born Saint-Denis; *La Vie immédiate* (1934), *Poésie et vérité* (1942).

Emerson, Ralph Waldo (1803–84) American, born Boston, Massachusetts; poems published posthumously in *Complete Works* (1903–4).

Empson, Sir William (1906–84) English, born Yokefleet, E Yorkshire; *Poems* (1935), *The Gathering Storm* (1940).

Fitzgerald, Edward (1809–83) English, born near Woodbridge, Suffolk; translator of *The Rubaiyat of Omar Khayyam* (1859).

Fitzgerald, Robert (David) (1902–87) Australian, born Hunters Hill, New South Wales; *To Meet the Sun* (1929), *The Wind at Your Door* (1959), *Product* (1974).

Frost, Robert (Lee) (1874–1963) American, born San Francisco; *North of Boston* (1914), *Mountain Interval* (1916), *New Hampshire* (1923), *In the Clearing* (1962).

Ginsberg, Allen (1926–97) American, born Newark, New Jersey; *Howl and Other Poems* (1956), *Empty Mirror* (1961), *The Fall of America* (1973).

Graves, Robert (Ranke) (1895–1985) English, born London; *Fairies and Fusiliers* (1917).

Gunn, Thom(son William) (1929–) English, born Gravesend, Kent; *The Sense of Movement* (1957), *Touch* (1967), *Jack Straw's Castle* (1976), *The Passages of Joy* (1982), *The Man with Night Sweats* (1992).

Heaney, Seamus (Justin) (1939–) Irish, born Castledawson, County Derry; *Death of a Naturalist* (1966), *Door into the Dark* (1969), *Field Work* (1979), *Seeing Things* (1991), *The Spirit Level* (1996); Nobel Prize for literature 1995.

Henri, Adrian (Maurice) (1932–) English, born Birkenhead; *Tonight at Noon* (1968), *City* (1969), *From the Loveless Motel* (1980), *Wish You Were Here* (1990), *Not Fade Away* (1994).

Henryson, Robert (c.1430–1506) Scottish, birthplace unknown; *Testament of Cresseid, Morall Fables of Esope the Phrygian*.

Herbert, George (1593–1633) English, born Montgomery, Wales; *The Temple* (1633).

Herrick, Robert (1591–1674) English, born London; *Hesperides* (1648).

Hill, Geoffrey (William) (1932–) English, born Bromsgrove, Worcestershire; *King Log* (1968), *Mercian Hymns* (1971), *Tenebrae* (1978).

Hodgson, Ralph (Edwin) (1871–1962) English, born Yorkshire; *Poems* (1917), *The Skylark and Other Poems* (1958).

Homer (10th–8th-cBC) Greek, birthplace and existence disputed; he is credited with the writing or writing down of *The Iliad* and *The Odyssey*.

Hopkins, Gerard Manley (1844–89) English, born Stratford, London; 'The Wreck of the Deutschland' (1876), posthumously published *Poems* (1918).

Horace, Quintus Horatius Flaccus (65–8BC) Roman, born Venusia, Apulia; *Epodes* (30BC), *Odes* (23–13BC).

Housman, A(lfred) E(dward) (1859–1936) English, born Flockbury, Worcestershire; *A Shropshire Lad* (1896), *Last Poems* (1922).

Hughes, Ted (1930–98) English, born Mytholmroyd, Yorkshire; *The Hawk in the Rain* (1957), *Lupereal* (1960), *Wodwo* (1967), *Crow* (1970), *Care Birds* (1975), *Season Songs* (1976), *Gaudete* (1977), *Moortown* (1979), *Wolfwatching* (1989), *Birthday Letters* (1998).

Jennings, Elizabeth (Joan) (1926–) English, born Boston, Lincolnshire; *Poems* (1953), *The Mind Has Mountains* (1966), *The Animals' Arrival* (1969), *Relationships* (1972).

Johnson, Samuel (1709–84) English, born Lichfield, Staffordshire; *The Vanity of Human Wishes* (1749).

Kavanagh, Patrick (1905–67) Irish, born Inniskeen; *Ploughman and Other Poems* (1936), *The Great Hunger* (1942).

Keats, John (1795–1821) English, born London; *Endymion* (1818), *Lamia and Other Poems* (1820).

Keyes, Sidney (Arthur Kilworth) (1922–43) English, born Dartford, Kent; *The Iron Laurel* (1942), *The Cruel Solstice* (1943).

La Fontaine, Jean de (1621–95) French, born Château-Thierry, Champagne; *Contes et nouvelles en vers* (1665), *Fables choisies mises en vers* (1668).

Langland or Langley, William (c.1332–c.1400) English, birthplace uncertain, possibly Ledbury, Herefordshire; *Vision of William Concerning Piers the Plowman* (1362–99).

Larkin, Philip (Arthur) (1922–85) English, born Coventry; *The North Ship* (1945), *The Whitsun Weddings* (1964), *High Windows* (1974).

Longfellow, Henry (Wadsworth) (1807–82) American, born Portland, Maine; *Voices of the Night* (1839), *Ballads and Other Poems* (1842), *Hiawatha* (1855), 'Divina Comedia' (1872).

Lowell, Amy (Laurence) (1874–1925) American, born Brookline, Massachusetts; *A Dome of Many-Colored Glass* (1912), *Legends* (1921).

Lowell, Robert (Traill Spence, Jr) (1917–77) American, born Boston, Massachusetts; *Lord Weary's Castle* (1946), *Life Studies* (1959), *Prometheus Bound* (1967).

Macaulay, Thomas (Babington) (1800–59) English, born Rothey Temple, Leicestershire; *The Lays of Ancient Rome* (1842).

MacCaig, Norman (Alexander) (1910–96) Scottish, born Edinburgh; *Far Cry* (1943), *Riding Lights* (1955), *A Round of Applause* (1962), *A Man in My Position* (1969), *Voice-Over* (1988).

MacDiarmid, Hugh (pseudonym of Christopher Murray Grieve) (1892–1978) Scottish, born Langholm, Dumfriesshire; *A Drunk Man Looks at the Thistle* (1926).

McGough, Roger (1937–) English, educated Liverpool; *The Mersey Sound: Penguin Modern Poets 10* (with Adrian Henri and Brian Patten) (1967), *Gig* (1973), *Waving at Trains* (1982), *An Imaginary Menagerie* (1988).

MacLean, Sorley (Gaelic Somhairle MacGill-Eain) (1911–96) Scottish, born Isle of Raasay, off Skye; *Reothairt is Contraigh* (Spring Tide and Neap Tide) (1977).

MacNeice, (Frederick) Louis (1907–63) Irish, born Belfast; *Blind Fireworks* (1929), *Solstices* (1961).

Mallarmé, Stéphane (1842–98) French, born Paris; *L'Après-midi d'un faune* (1876), *Poésies* (1899).

Marvell, Andrew (1621–78) English, born Winestead, near Hull; *Miscellaneous Poems by Andrew Marvell, Esq* (1681).

Masefield, John (Edward) (1878–1967) English, born Ledbury, Herefordshire; *Salt-Water Ballads* (1902).

Millay, Edna St Vincent (1892–1950) American, born Rockland, Maine; *A Few Figs from Thistles* (1920), *The Ballad of Harp-Weaver* (1922).

Milton, John (1608–74) English, born London; *Lycidas* (1637), *Paradise Lost* (1667), *Samson Agonistes* (1671).

Moore, Marianne (Craig) (1887–1972) American, born Kirkwood, Missouri; *The Pangolin and Other Verse* (1936).

Muir, Edwin (1887–1959) Scottish, born Deerness, Orkney; *First Poems* (1925), *Chorus of the Newly Dead* (1926), *Variations on a Time Theme* (1934), *The Labyrinth* (1949), *New Poems* (1949–51).

Nash, (Frederick) Ogden (1902–71) American, born Rye, New York; *Free Wheeling* (1931).

O'Hara, Frank (Francis Russell) (1926–66) American, born Baltimore, Maryland; *A City Winter and Other Poems* (1952), *Lunch Poems* (1964).

Ovid (in full Publius Ovidius Naso) (43BC–c.17AD) Roman, born Sulmo; *Amores* (c.16BC), *Metamorphoses*, *Ars Amatoria*.

Owen, Wilfred (Edward Salter) (1893–1918) English, born Oswestry, Shropshire; most poems published posthumously, 1920, by Siegfried Sassoon; 'Dulce et decorum est'.

Patten, Brian (1946–) English, born Liverpool; *The Mersey Sound: Penguin Modern Poets 10* (with Adrian Henri and Roger McGough) (1967), *Notes to the Hurrying Man* (1969), *Grinning Jack* (1990), *Armada* (1996).

Paz, Octavio (1914–98) Mexican, born Mexico City; *Sun Stone* (1963), *The Bow and the Lyre* (1973), *Collected Poems 1957–87* (1987), *Glimpses of India* (1995); Nobel Prize for literature 1990.

Petrarch, Francesco Petrarca (1304–74) Italian, born Arezzo; *Canzoniere*.

Plath, Sylvia (1932–63) American, born Boston, Massachusetts; *The Colossus and Other Poems* (1960), *Ariel* (1965), *Crossing the Water* (1971), *Winter Trees* (1972).

Porter, Peter (Neville Frederick) (1929–) Australian, born Brisbane; *Poems, Ancient and Modern* (1964), *English Subtitles* (1981), *The Automatic Oracle* (1987).

Pound, Ezra (Weston Loomis) (1885–1972) American, born Haile, Idaho; *The Cantos* (1917, 1948, 1959).

Pushkin, Aleksandr (Sergeyevich) (1799–1837) Russian, born Moscow; *Eugene Onegin* (1828), *Ruslam and Lyudmilla* (1820).

Raine, Kathleen (Jessie) (1908–) English, born London; *Stone and Flower* (1943), *The Hollow Hill* (1965), *Living with Mystery* (1992).

Rich, Adrienne (Cecile) (1929–) American, born Baltimore, Maryland; *The Diamond Cutters and Other Poems* (1955), *Snapshots of a Daughter-in-Law* (1963), *The Will to Change* (1971), *Dark Fields of the Republic* (1995).

Riding, Laura (née Reichenfeld) (1901–91) American, born New York; *The Close Chaplet* (1926).

Rilke, Rainer Maria (1875–1926) Austrian, born Prague; *Die Sonnettean Orpheus* (1923).

Rimbaud, (Jean Nicholas) Arthur (1854–91) French, born Charleville, Ardennes; *Les Illuminations* (1886).

Rochester, John Wilmot, Earl of (1647–80) English, born Ditchley, Oxfordshire; *A Satyre Against Mankind* (1675).

Roethke, Theodore Huebner (1908–63) American, born Saginaw, Michigan; *Open House* (1941), *The Lost Son and Other Poems* (1948).

Rosenberg, Isaac (1890–1918) English, born Bristol; *Night and Day* (1912), *Youth* (1915), *Poems* (1922).

Saint-John Perse (pseudonym of Marie René Auguste Alexis Saint-Léger Léger) (1887–1975) French, born St Léger des Feuilles; *Anabase* (1924), *Exil* (1942), *Chroniques* (1960); Nobel Prize for literature 1960.

Sassoon, Siegfried (Lorraine) (1886–1967) English, born Brenchley, Kent; *Counter-Attack and Other Poems* (1917), *The Road to Ruin* (1933).

Schwarz, Delmore (1913–66) American, born New York City; *In Dreams Begin Responsibilities* (1938), *Vaudeville for a Princess and Other Poems* (1950).

Seifert, Jaroslav (1901–86) Czech, born Prague; *City of Tears* (1921), *All Love* (1923), *A Helmet of Earth* (1945); Nobel Prize for literature 1984.

Shelley, Percy Bysshe (1792–1822) English, born Field Place, Horsham, Sussex; *Alastor* (1816), *The Revolt of Islam* (1818), *Julian and Maddalo* (1818), *The Triumph of Life* (1822).

Sidney, Sir Philip (1554–86) English, born Penshurst, Kent; *Arcadia* (1580), *Astrophel and Stella* (1591).

Sitwell, Dame Edith (Louisa) (1887–1964) English, born Scarborough; *Façade* (1922), *Colonel Fantock* (1926).

Smart, Christopher (1722–71) English, born Shipbourne, Kent; *Jubilate Agno* (first published 1939).

Smith, Stevie (pseudonym of Florence Margaret Smith) (1902–71) English, born Hull; *Not Waving but Drowning: Poems* (1957).

Spender, Sir Stephen (Harold) (1909–95) English, born London; *Poems* (1933).

Spenser, Edmund (1552–99) English, born London; *The Shepheardes Calender* (1579), *The Faerie Queene* (1590, 1596).

Stevens, Wallace (1879–1955) American, born Reading, Pennsylvania; *Harmonium* (1923), *Transport to Summer* (1947).

Szymborska, Wislawa (1923–) Polish, born Bnin; *A Great Number* (1976), *People on a Bridge* (1986), *View with a Grain of Sand* (1995); Nobel Prize for literature 1996.

Tennyson, Alfred, Lord (1809–92) English, born Somersby Rectory, Lincolnshire; *Poems* (1832) (eg 'The Lotus-Eaters' and 'The Lady of Shalott'), *The Princess* (1847), *In Memoriam* (1850), *Idylls of the King* (1859), *Maud* (1885).

Thomas, Dylan (Marlais) (1914–53) Welsh, born Swansea; *Twenty-five Poems* (1936), *Deaths and Entrances* (1946), *In Country Sleep and Other Poems* (1952).

Thomas, (Philip) Edward (1878–1917) English, born London; *Six Poems* (1916), *Last Poems* (1918).

Thomas, R(onald) S(tuart) (1913–2000) Welsh, born Cardiff; *Stones of the Field* (1947), *Song at the Year's Turning* (1955), *The Bread of Truth* (1963), *Between Here and Now* (1981), *Counterpoint* (1990), *No Truce with The Furies* (1995).

Thomson, James (1700–48) Scottish, born Ednam, Roxburghshire; *The Seasons* (1730), *The Castle of Indolence* (1748).

Verlaine, Paul (1844–96) French, born Metz; *Fêtes galantes* (1869), *Sagesse* (1881).

Virgil, Publius Vergilius Maro (70–19BC) Roman, born near Mantua; *Eclogues* (37BC), *Georgics* (29BC), *The Aeneid* (19BC).

Walcott, Derek Alton (1930–) West Indian, born St Lucia; *Castaway* (1965), *Fortunate Traveller* (1981), *Selected Poetry* (1993); Nobel Prize for literature (1992).

Webb, Francis Charles (1925–73) Australian, born Adelaide; *A Drum for Ben Boyd* (1948), *The Ghost of the Cock* (1964).

Whitman, Walt (1819–92) American, born West Hills, Long Island, New York; *Leaves of Grass* (1855–89).

Wordsworth, William (1770–1850) English, born Cockermouth; *Lyrical Ballads* (with S T Coleridge, 1798), *The Prelude* (1799, 1805, 1850), *The Excursion* (1814).

Wright, Judith (Arundell) (1915–2000) Australian, born Armidale, New South Wales; *The Moving Image* (1946), *The Two Fires* (1955), *Birds* (1962), *Alive* (1973), *The Cry for the Dead* (1981).

Wyatt, Sir Thomas (1503–42) English, born Allington Castle, Kent; poems first published in *Tottel's Miscellany* (1557).

Yeats, W(illiam) B(utler) (1865–1939) Irish, born Sandymount, County Dublin; *The Wanderings of Oisin and Other Poems* (1889), *The Wind Among the Reeds* (1894), *The Wild Swans at Coole* (1917), *Michael Robartes and the Dancer* (1921), *The Winding Stair and Other Poems* (1933); Nobel Prize for literature 1923.

Playwrights

Selected plays are listed.

Aeschylus (c.525–c.456BC) Athenian; *The Oresteia Trilogy (Agamemnon, Choephoroe, Eumenides)* (458BC), *Prometheus Bound, Seven Against Thebes*.

Albee, Edward Franklin, III (1928–) American, born Washington DC; *The American Dream* (1961), *Who's Afraid of Virginia Woolf?* (1962), *A Delicate Balance* (1966, Pulitzer Prize), *Seascape* (1974), *Three Tall Women* (1991, Pulitzer Prize 1994), *Fragments* (1993).

Amos, Robert (1920–) Australian, born Austria; *When the Gravediggers Come* (1961).

Anouilh, Jean (1910–87) French, born Bordeaux; *Antigone* (1944), *Médée* (1946), *L'Alouette* (1953), *Beckett; or, the Honour of God* (1960).

Aristophanes (c.448–c.385BC) Athenian; *The Acharnians* (425BC), *The Knights* (424BC), *The Clouds* (423BC), *The Wasps* (422BC), *The Birds* (414BC), *Lysistrata* (411BC), *The Frogs* (405BC).

Ayckbourn, Sir Alan (1939–) English, born London; *Absurd Person Singular* (1973), *Absent Friends* (1975), *Joking Apart* (1979), *Way Upstream* (1982), *Woman in Mind* (1985), *Henceforward* (1987), *Man of the Moment* (1988), *Wildest Dreams* (1991), *Communicating Doors* (1994), *The Champion of Paribanou* (1996).

Beaumont, Sir Francis (1584–1616) English, born Grace-Dieu, Leicestershire, and John Fletcher; *Philaster* (1609), *The Maid's Tragedy* (1610).

Beckett, Samuel (Barclay) (1906–89) Irish, born Foxrock, near Dublin; *Waiting for Godot* (1955), *Endgame* (1958), *Krapp's Last Tape* (1958), *Happy Days* (1961), *Not I* (1973); Nobel Prize for literature 1969.

Beynon, Richard (1925–) Australian, born Carlton, Melbourne; *The Shifting Heart* (1956), *Time and Mr Strachan* (1958).

Bond, (Thomas) Edward (1934–) English, born North London; *Early Morning* (1969), *Lear* (1971), *Summer* (1982), *The War Plays* (1985), *Olly's Prison* (1992), *Coffee: a tragedy* (1995).

Brecht, (Eugen) Bertolt (Friedrich) (1898–1956) German, born Augsburg; *Galileo* (1938–9), *Mutter Courage and ihre Kinder* (1941, trans Mother Courage and Her Children 1961), *Der gute Mensch von Setzuan* (1943, trans The Good Woman of Setzuan 1948), *Der kaukasische Kreidekreis* (1947, trans The Caucasian Chalk Circle 1948).

Brieux, Eugène (1858–1932) French, born Paris; *Les Trois Filles de M Dupont* (1897), *The Red Robe* (1900).

Chapman, George (c.1559–1634) English, born near Hitchin, Hertfordshire; *Bussy D'Ambois* (1607).

Chekhov, Anton Pavlovich (1860–1904) Russian, born Taganrog; *The Seagull* (1895), *Uncle Vanya* (1900), *Three Sisters* (1901), *The Cherry Orchard* (1904).

Congreve, William (1670–1729) English, born Bardsey, near Leeds; *Love for Love* (1695), *The Way of the World* (1700).

Corneille, Pierre (1606–84) French, born Rouen; *Le Cid* (1636), *Horace* (1639), *Polyeucte* (1640).

Coward, Sir Noël Peirce (1899–1973) English, born Teddington, Middlesex; *Hay Fever* (1925), *Private Lives* (1933), *Blithe Spirit* (1941).

Dekker, Thomas (c.1570–1632) English, born London; *The Whore of Babylon* (1606).

Dryden, John (1631–1700) English, born Aldwinkle; *The Indian Queen* (1664), *Marriage à la Mode* (1672), *All for Love* (1678), *Amphitryon* (1690).

Eliot, T(homas) S(tearns) (1888–1965) American naturalized British, born St Louis, Missouri; *Murder in the Cathedral* (1935), *The Family Reunion* (1939), *The Cocktail Party* (1950).

Esson, (Thomas) Louis (Buvelot) (1879–1943) Australian, born Edinburgh; *The Drovers* (1920), *Andeganora* (1937).

Euripides (c.480–406BC) Athenian; *Medea* (431BC), *Electra* (413BC), *The Bacchae* (407BC).

Fletcher, John (1579–1625) English, born Rye, Sussex, *The Faithful Shepherdess* (1610), *A Wife for a Month* (1624).

Fo, Dario (1926–) Italian, born Lombardy; *Accidental Death of an Anarchist* (1970), *Can't Pay! Won't Pay!* (1974), *The Pope and the Witch* (1989), *The Tricks of the Trade* (1991).

Ford, John (1586–c.1640) English, born Devon; *'Tis Pity She's a Whore* (1633), *Perkin Warbeck* (1634).

Galsworthy, John (1867–1933) English, born Coombe, Surrey; *Strife* (1909), *Justice* (1910); Nobel Prize for literature 1932.

Genet, Jean (1910–86) French, born Paris; *The Maids* (1948), *The Balcony* (1956).

Giraudoux, (Hippolyte) Jean (1882–1944) French, born Bellac; *Judith* (1931), *Ondine* (1939).

Goethe, Johann Wolfgang von (1749–1832) German, born Frankfurt am Main; *Faust* (1808, 1832).

Gogol, Nikolai (Vasilievich) (1809–52) Russian, born Ukraine; *The Inspector General* (1836).

Goldsmith, Oliver (1728–74) Irish, born Pallas, County Longford; *She Stoops to Conquer* (1773).

Gray, Oriel (1921–) Australian, born Sydney; *The Torrents* (1955), *Burst of Summer* (1960).

Greene, Robert (1558–92) English, born Norwich; *Orlando Furioso* (1594), *James the Fourth* (1598).

Hauptmann, Gerhart Johann Robert (1862–1946) German, born Obersalzbrunn, Silesia; *Before Sunrise* (1889), *The Weavers* (1892); Nobel Prize for literature 1912.

Hayes, Alfred (1911–85) American, born England; *The Girl on the Via Flaminia* (1954).

Hebbel, (Christian) Friedrich (1813–63) German, born Wesselburen, Dithmarschen; *Judith* (1841), *Maria Magdalena* (1844).

Hewett, Dorothy (Coade) (1923–) Australian, born Wickepin, West Australia; *The Chapel Perilous* (1972), *This Old Man Comes Rolling Home* (1976), *Golden Valley* (1984).

Heywood, Thomas (c.1574–1641) English, born Lincolnshire; *A Woman Killed with Kindness* (1603), *The Fair Maid of the West* (1631), *The English Traveller* (1633).

Hibberd, Jack (1940–) Australian, born Warracknabeal, Victoria; *Dimboola* (1969), *White with Wire Wheels* (1970), *A Stretch of the Imagination* (1973), *Squibs* (1984).

Howard, Sidney (Coe) (1891–1939) American, born Oakland, California; *They Knew What They Wanted* (1924), *The Silver Cord* (1926).

Ibsen, Henrik (1828–1906) Norwegian, born Skien; *Peer Gynt* (1867), *A Doll's House* (1879), *The Pillars of Society* (1880), *The Wild Duck* (1884), *Hedda Gabler* (1890), *The Master Builder* (1892).

Inge, William Motter (1913–73) American, born Kansas; *Picnic* (1953), *Where's Daddy?* (1966).

Ionesco, Eugène (1912–94) French, born Romania; *The Bald Prima Donna* (1948), *The Picture* (1958), *Le Rhinocéros* (1960).

Jonson, Ben(jamin) (c.1572–1637) English, born Westminster, London; *Every Man in His Humour* (1598), *Sejanus* (1603), *Volpone* (1606), *The Alchemist* (1610), *Bartholomew Fair* (1614).

Kaiser, Georg (1878–1945) German, born Magdeburg; *The Burghers of Calais* (1914), *Gas* (1920).

Kushner, Tony (1956–) American, born New York City; *Yes, Yes, No, No* (1985), *Angels in America* (1992, Pulitzer Prize 1993), *Slavs!* (1995), *Henry Box Brown* (1997).

Kyd, Thomas (1558–94) English, born London; *The Spanish Tragedy* (1587).

Lawler, Ray(mond Evenor) (1922–) Australian, born Melbourne; *The Summer of the Seventeenth Doll* (1955), *The Man Who Shot the Albatross* (1970), *Kid Stakes* (1975), *Other Times* (1976), *Godsend* (1982).

Lorca, Federico García (1899–1936) Spanish, born Fuente Vaqueros; *Blood Wedding* (1933), *The House of Bernarda Alba* (1945).

Maeterlinck, Maurice, Count (1862–1949) Belgian, born Ghent; *La Princesse Maleine* (1889), *Pélleas et Mélisande* (1892), *The Blue Bird* (1909); Nobel Prize for literature 1911.

Mamet, David Alan (1947–) American, born Chicago; *Sexual Perversity in Chicago* (1974), *Duck Variations* (1974), *American Buffalo* (1975), *Edmond* (1982), *Glengarry Glen Ross* (1983, Pulitzer Prize), *Oleanna* (1992), *Death Defying Acts* (1996).

Marlowe, Christopher (1564–93) English, born Canterbury; *Tamburlaine the Great* (in two parts, 1587), *Dr Faustus* (1588), *The Jew of Malta* (c.1589), *Edward II* (1592).

Marston, John (1576–1634) English, born Wardington, Oxfordshire; *Antonio's Revenge* (1602), *The Malcontent* (1604).

Miller, Arthur (1915–) American, born New York City; *All My Sons* (1947), *Death of a Salesman* (1949), *The Crucible* (1952), *A View from the Bridge* (1955), *The Misfits* (1961), *After the Fall* (1964), *The Creation of the World and Other Business* (1972), *Playing for Time* (1981), *Danger: Memory!* (1987), *The Ride Down Mount Morgan* (1991), *The Last Yankee* (1992), *Broken Glass* (1994).

Molière (pseudonym of Jean-Baptiste Poquelin) (1622–73) French, born Paris; *Le Bourgeois Gentilhomme* (1660, trans The Bourgeois Gentleman), *Tartuffe* (1664), *Le Misanthrope* (1666, trans The Misanthropist), *Le Malade Imaginaire* (1673, trans The Hypochondriac).

Oakley, Barry (1931–) Australian, born Melbourne; *The Feet of Daniel Mannix* (1975), *Bedfellows* (1975).

O'Casey, Sean (originally John Casey) (1880–1964) Irish, born Dublin; *Juno and the Paycock* (1924), *The Plough and the Stars* (1926).

O'Neill, Eugene Gladstone (1888–1953) American, born New York City; *Beyond the Horizon* (1920), *Desire under the Elms* (1924), *Mourning Becomes Electra* (1931), *Long Day's Journey into Night* (1941), *The Iceman Cometh* (1946); Nobel Prize for literature 1936.

Orton, Joe (John Kingsley) (1933–67) English, born Leicester; *Entertaining Mr Sloane* (1964), *Loot* (1965), *What the Butler Saw* (1969).

Osborne, John (James) (1929–94) Welsh, born Fulham, London; *Look Back in Anger* (1956), *The Entertainer* (1957), *Inadmissible Evidence* (1965), *The Hotel in Amsterdam* (1968), *West of Suez* (1971), *Almost a Vision* (1976), *Déjà Vu* (1989).

Otway, Thomas (1652–85) English, born Milland, Sussex; *Don Carlos* (1676), *The Orphan* (1680), *Venice Preserv'd* (1682).

Patrick, John (1905–95) American, born Louisville, Kentucky; *The Teahouse of the August Moon* (1953).

Pinter, Harold (1930–) English, born East London; *The Birthday Party* (1958), *The Caretaker* (1960), *The Homecoming* (1965), *Landscape* (1967), *Old Times* (1970), *No Man's Land* (1974), *Betrayal* (1978), *A Kind of Alaska* (1982), *One for the Road* (1984), *Party Time* (1991), *Ashes to Ashes* (1996).

Pirandello, Luigi (1867–1936) Italian, born near Agrigento, Sicily; *Six Characters in Search of an Author* (1921), *Henry IV* (1922); Nobel Prize for literature 1934.

Plautus, Titus Maccius (c.250–184BC) Roman; *Menachmi, Miles Gloriosus.*

Porter, Hal (1911–84) Australian, born Melbourne; *The Tower* (1963), *The Professor* (1966), *Eden House* (1969).

Potter, Dennis (Christopher George) (1935–94) English, born Forest of Dean; *Vote, Vote, Vote for Nigel Barton* (1965), *Brimstone and Treacle* (1978), *Pennies from Heaven* (1978), *The Singing Detective* (1986), *Lipstick on Your Collar* (1993), *Karaoke* (1994).

Racine, Jean (1639–99) French, born near Soissons; *Andromaque* (1667), *Phèdre* (1677), *Bajazet* (1672), *Esther* (1689).

Romeril, John (1945–) Australian, born Melbourne; *Chicago, Chicago* (1970), *I Don't Know Who to Feel Sorry For* (1973), *The Kelly Dance* (1986).

Russell, Willy (William) (1947–) English, born Whiston, Merseyside; *Educating Rita* (1979), *Blood Brothers* (1983), *Shirley Valentine* (1986).

Sackville, Thomas (1553–1608) English, born Buckhurst, Sussex; *Gorboduc* (1592).

Sartre, Jean-Paul (1905–80) French, born Paris; *The Flies* (1943), *Huis Clos* (1945), *The Condemned of Altona* (1961).

Schiller, Johann Christoph Friedrich von (1759–1805) German, born Marbach; *The Robbers* (1781), *Wallenstein* (1799), *Maria Stuart* (1800).

Seneca, Lucius Annaeus (c.4BC–AD65) Roman, born Corduba; *Hercules, Medea, Thyestes.*

Seymour, Alan (1927–) Australian, born Perth; *The One Day of the Year* (1962), *Swamp Creatures* (1958), *Danny Johnson* (1960).

Shaffer, Peter (Levin) (1926–) English, born Liverpool; *The Royal Hunt of the Sun* (1964), *Equus* (1973), *Amadeus* (1979), *Yonadab* (1985), *The Gift of the Gorgon* (1992).

Shakespeare, William ► Plays of Shakespeare p289

Shaw, George Bernard (1856–1950) Irish, born Dublin; *Arms and the Man* (1894), *Man and Superman* (1903), *Pygmalion* (1913), *Saint Joan* (1924); Nobel prize for literature 1925.

Shepard, Sam (originally Samuel Shepard Rogers) (1943–) American, born Fort Sheridan, Illinois; *La Turista* (1967), *Forensic and the Navigators* (1968), *The Tooth of Crime* (1972), *Buried Child* (1978), *The Curse of the Starving Class* (1976), *True West* (1979), *Fool for Love* (1983).

Sheridan, Richard Brinsley (1751–1816) Irish, born Dublin; *The Rivals* (1775), *The School for Scandal* (1777), *The Critic* (1779).

Sherwood, Robert (Emmet) (1896–1955) American, born New Rochelle, New York; *Idiot's Delight* (1936), *Abe Lincoln in Illinois* (1938), *There Shall Be No Night* (1940).

Sophocles (496–406BC) Athenian, born Colonus; *Antigone, Oedipus Rex, Oedipus at Colonus.*

Soyinka, Wole (in full Akinwande Oluwole Soyinka) (1934–) Nigerian, born Abeokata, West Nigeria; *The Swamp Dwellers* (1958), *The Strong Breed* (1962), *The Road* (1964), *The Bacchae of Euripides* (1973), *Opera Wonyosi* (1978), *From Zia, with Love* (1991); Nobel prize for literature 1986.

Stoppard, Sir Tom (Thomas Straussler) (1937–) English, born Czechoslovakia; *Rosencrantz and Guildenstern are Dead* (1966), *The Real Inspector Hound* (1968), *Travesties* (1974), *New-Found-Land* (1976), *Undiscovered Country* (1980), *Rough Crossing* (1984), *Arcadia* (1993), *Indian Ink* (1995).

Strindberg, (Johan) August (1849–1912) Swedish, born Stockholm; *Master Olof* (1877), *Miss Julie* (1888), *The Dance of Death* (1901).

Synge, (Edmund) J(ohn) M(illington) (1871–1909) Irish, born near Dublin; *The Well of Saints* (1905), *The Playboy of the Western World* (1907).

Webster, John (c.1578–c.1632) English, born London; *The White Devil* (1612), *The Duchess of Malfi* (1614).

Wilde, Oscar (Fingal O'Flahertie Wills) (1854–1906) Irish, born Dublin; *Lady Windermere's Fan* (1892), *The Importance of Being Earnest* (1895), *Salomé* (1896).

Wilder, Thornton (Niven) (1897–1975) American, born Wisconsin; *Our Town* (1938), *The Merchant of Yonkers* (1938), *The Skin of Our Teeth* (1942), *The Matchmaker* (1954, later a musical *Hello, Dolly!* 1964).

Williams, Tennessee (originally Thomas Lanier Williams) (1911–83) American, born Mississippi; *The Glass Menagerie* (1944), *A Streetcar Named Desire* (1947), *Cat on a Hot Tin Roof* (1955), *Sweet Bird of Youth* (1959).

Williamson, David Keith (1942–) Australian, born Melbourne; *The Removalists* (1971), *Don's Party* (1971), *The Club* (1977), *The Perfectionist* (1981), *Sons of Cain* (1985).

Plays of Shakespeare

William Shakespeare (1564–1616), English playwright and poet, born Stratford-upon-Avon.

Title	Date	Category
The Two Gentlemen of Verona	1590–1	comedy
Henry VI Part One	1592	history
Henry VI Part Two	1592	history
Henry VI Part Three	1592	history
Titus Andronicus	1592	tragedy
Richard III	1592–3	history
The Taming of the Shrew	1593	comedy
The Comedy of Errors	1594	comedy
Love's Labours Lost	1594–5	comedy
Richard II	1595	history
Romeo and Juliet	1595	tragedy
A Midsummer Night's Dream	1595	comedy
King John	1596	history
The Merchant of Venice	1596–7	comedy
Henry IV Part One	1596–7	history
The Merry Wives of Windsor	1597–8	comedy
Henry IV Part Two	1597–8	history
Much Ado About Nothing	1598	dark comedy
Henry V	1598–9	history
Julius Caesar	1599	tragedy
As You Like It	1599–1600	comedy
Hamlet, Prince of Denmark	1600–1	tragedy
Twelfth Night, or What You Will	1601	comedy
Troilus and Cressida	1602	tragedy
Measure for Measure	1603	dark comedy
Othello	1603–4	tragedy
All's Well That Ends Well	1604–5	dark comedy
Timon of Athens	1605	romance
The Tragedy of King Lear	1605–6	tragedy
Macbeth	1606	tragedy
Antony and Cleopatra	1606	tragedy
Pericles	1607	romance
Coriolanus	1608	tragedy
The Winter's Tale	1609	romance
Cymbeline	1610	comedy
The Tempest	1611	comedy
Henry VIII	1613	history

Poets laureate

1617	Ben Jonson*
1638	Sir William Davenant*
1668	John Dryden
1689	Thomas Shadwell
1692	Nahum Tate
1715	Nicholas Rowe
1718	Laurence Eusden
1730	Colley Cibber
1757	William Whitehead
1785	Thomas Warton
1790	Henry Pye
1813	Robert Southey
1843	William Wordsworth
1850	Alfred, Lord Tennyson
1896	Alfred Austin
1913	Robert Bridges
1930	John Masefield
1968	Cecil Day Lewis
1972	Sir John Betjeman
1984	Ted Hughes
1999	Andrew Motion

*The post was not officially established until 1668.

Literary prizes

Booker Prize (UK)

1980 William Golding, *Rites of Passage*
1981 Salman Rushdie, *Midnight's Children*
1982 Thomas Keneally, *Schindler's Ark*
1983 J M Coetzee, *Life and Times of Michael K*
1984 Anita Brookner, *Hotel du Lac*
1985 Keri Hulme, *The Bone People*
1986 Kingsley Amis, *The Old Devils*
1987 Penelope Lively, *Moon Tiger*
1988 Peter Carey, *Oscar and Lucinda*
1989 Kazuo Ishiguro, *The Remains of the Day*
1990 A S Byatt, *Possession*
1991 Ben Okri, *The Famished Road*
1992 Michael Ondaatje, *The English Patient;*
Barry Unsworth, *Sacred Hunger*
1993 Roddy Doyle, *Paddy Clarke Ha Ha Ha*
1994 James Kelman, *How late it was, how late*

1995 Pat Barker, *The Ghost Road*
1996 Graham Swift, *Last Orders*
1997 Arundhati Roy, *The God of Small Things*
1998 Ian McEwan, *Amsterdam*
1999 J M Coetzee, *Disgrace*

Orange Prize for Fiction (women writers)
1996 Helen Dunmore, *A Spell of Winter*
1997 Anne Michaels, *Fugitive Pieces*
1998 Carol Shields, *Larry's Party*
1999 Suzanne Berne, *A Crime in the Neighborhood*
2000 Linda Grant, *When I Lived in Modern Times*

Prix Goncourt (France)
1980 Yves Navarre, *Le Jardin d'acclimatation*
1981 Lucien Bodard, *Anne Marie*
1982 Dominique Fernandez, *Dans la Main de l'ange*
1983 Frédérick Tristan, *Les Égarés*
1984 Marguerite Duras, *L'Amant*
1985 Yann Queffelec, *Les Noces barbares*
1986 Michel Host, *Valet de Nuit*
1987 Tahar ben Jalloun, *La Nuit sacrée*
1988 Erik Orsenna, *L'Exposition coloniale*
1989 Jean Vautrin, *Un Grand Pas vers le Bon Dieu*
1990 Jean Rouaud, *Les Champs d'Honneur*
1991 Pierre Combescot, *Les Filles du Calvaire*
1992 Patrick Chamoiseau, *Texaco*
1993 Amin Maalouf, *Le Rocher de Tanios*
1994 Didier van Cauwelaert, *Un Aller simple*
1995 Andréï Makine, *Le Testament français*
1996 Pascale Roze, *Le Chasseur Zéro*
1997 Patrick Rambaud, *La Bataille*
1998 Paule Constant, *Confidence pour confidence*
1999 Jean Echenoz, *Je m'en vais*

Pulitzer Prize in Letters: Fiction (USA)
1980 Norman Mailer, *The Executioner's Song*
1981 John Kennedy Toole, *A Confederacy of Dunces*
1982 John Updike, *Rabbit is Rich*
1983 Alice Walker, *The Color Purple*
1984 William Kennedy, *Ironweed*
1985 Alison Lurie, *Foreign Affairs*
1986 Larry McMurtry, *Lonesome Dove*

1987 Peter Taylor, *A Summons to Memphis*

1988 Toni Morrison, *Beloved*

1989 Anne Tyler, *Breathing Lessons*

1990 Oscar Hijuelos, *The Mambo Kings Play Songs of Love*

1991 John Updike, *Rabbit at Rest*

1992 Jane Smiley, *A Thousand Acres*

1993 Robert Olen Butler, *A Good Scent from a Strange Mountain*

1994 E Annie Proulx, *The Shipping News*

1995 Carol Shields, *The Stone Diaries*

1996 Richard Ford, *Independence Day*

1997 Steven Millhauser, *Martin Dressler: The Tale of an American Dreamer*

1998 Philip Roth, *American Pastoral*

1999 Michael Cunningham, *The Hours*

2000 Jhumpa Lahiri, *Interpreter of Maladies*

Film and TV actors

Selected films and television productions are listed. Original and full names of actors are given in parentheses.

Allen, Woody (Allen Stewart Konigsberg) (1935–   ) American, born Brooklyn, New York City; *What's New, Pussycat?* (1965), *Casino Royale* (1967), *Bananas* (1971), *Play it Again Sam* (1972), *Sleeper* (1973), *Annie Hall* (1977), *Manhattan* (1979), *Stardust Memories* (1980), *Hannah and Her Sisters* (1986), *New York Stories* (1989), *Crimes and Misdemeanors* (1989), *Scenes from a Mall* (1991), *Shadows and Fog* (1992), *Husbands and Wives* (1992), *Manhattan Murder Mystery* (1993), *Mighty Aphrodite* (1995), *Anna Oz* (1996), *Deconstructing Harry* (1997).

Andrews, Dame Julie (Julia Elizabeth Wells) (1935–   ) British, born Walton-on-Thames, Surrey; *Mary Poppins* (1964), *The Americanization of Emily* (1964), *The Sound of Music* (1965), *Torn Curtain* (1966), *Thoroughly Modern Millie* (1967), *Star!* (1968), *SOB* (1981), *Victor/Victoria* (1982), *The Man Who Loved Women* (1983), *Tchin Tchin* (1990).

Astaire, Fred (Frederick Austerlitz) (1899–1987) American, born Omaha, Nebraska; *Flying Down to Rio* (1933), *The Gay Divorcee* (1934), *Top Hat* (1935), *Funny Face* (1957), *It Takes a Thief* (TV 1965–9), *Finian's Rainbow* (1968).

Attenborough, Richard Samuel Attenborough, Baron (1923–   ) British, born Cambridge; *In Which We Serve* (1942), *The Man Within* (1942), *Brighton Rock* (1947), *The Guinea Pig* (1949), *The Great Escape* (1963), *Brannigan* (1975), *Jurassic Park* (1993), *Miracle on 34th Street* (1994), *E=MC^2* (1995).

Bacall, Lauren (Betty Joan Perske) (1924–   ) American, born New York City; *To Have and Have Not* (1944), *The Big Sleep* (1946), *How to Marry a Millionaire* (1953), *The Fan* (1981), *Mr North* (1988), *Misery* (1990), *Prêt-À-Porter* (1994), *The Mirror Has Two Faces* (1996).

Bardot, Brigitte (Camille Javal) (1934–   ) French, born Paris; *And God Created Woman* (1956), *En Cas de Malheur* (1958), *Viva Maria!* (1965).

Basinger, Kim (1953–) American, born Athens, Georgia; *From Here to Eternity* (TV 1980), *Hard Country* (1981), *Never Say Never Again* (1983), *The Natural* (1984), *9½ Weeks* (1985), *No Mercy* (1986), *Blind Date* (1987), *Nadine* (1987), *Batman* (1989), *My Stepmother is an Alien* (1989), *The Marrying Man* (1990), *Wayne's World 2* (1993), *Prêt-À-Porter* (1994), *Kansas City* (1996), *LA Confidential* (1997).

Beatty, Warren (Henry Warren Beaty) (1937–) American, born Richmond, Virginia; *Splendor in the Grass* (1961), *The Roman Spring of Mrs Stone* (1961), *All Fall Down* (1962), *Bonnie and Clyde* (1967), *The Parallax View* (1974), *Shampoo* (1975), *Heaven Can Wait* (1978), *Reds* (1981), *Ishtar* (1987), *Dick Tracy* (1990), *Bugsy* (1991), *Love Affair* (1994).

Bergman, Ingrid (1915–82) Swedish, born Stockholm; *Intermezzo* (1939), *Dr Jekyll and Mr Hyde* (1941), *Casablanca* (1943), *For Whom the Bell Tolls* (1943), *Gaslight* (1943), *Spellbound* (1945), *Anastasia* (1946), *Notorious* (1946), *Stromboli* (1950), *Indiscreet* (1958), *Cactus Flower* (1969), *Murder on the Orient Express* (1974), *Autumn Sonata* (1978).

Bogarde, Dirk (Derek Niven van den Bogaerde) (1921–99) Anglo-Dutch, born Hampstead, London; *A Tale of Two Cities* (1958), *Victim* (1961), *The Servant* (1963), *Darling* (1965), *Death in Venice* (1973), *Providence* (1977), *These Foolish Things* (1990).

Bogart, Humphrey (De Forest) (1899–1957) American, born New York City; *Broadway's Like That* (1930), *The Petrified Forest* (1936), *High Sierra* (1941), *The Maltese Falcon* (1941), *Casablanca* (1942), *To Have and Have Not* (1944), *The Big Sleep* (1946), *The Treasure of the Sierra Madre* (1947), *The African Queen* (1952), *The Barefoot Contessa* (1954), *The Caine Mutiny* (1954).

Branagh, Kenneth (1960–) British, born Belfast; *High Season* (1987), *A Month in the Country* (1988), *Henry V* (1989), *Dead Again* (1991), *Peter's Friends* (1992), *Much Ado About Nothing* (1993), *Frankenstein* (1994), *In the Bleak Mid Winter* (1995), *Othello* (1995), *Hamlet* (1996).

Brando, Marlon (1924–) American, born Omaha, Nebraska; *A Streetcar Named Desire* (1951), *Viva Zapata* (1952), *Julius Caesar* (1953), *The Wild One* (1953), *On the Waterfront* (1954), *Guys and Dolls* (1955), *The Teahouse of the August Moon* (1956), *The Young Lions* (1958), *One-Eyed Jacks* (1961), *Mutiny on the Bounty* (1962), *The Chase* (1966), *The Godfather* (1972), *Last Tango in Paris* (1972), *Superman* (1978), *Apocalypse Now* (1979), *A Dry White Season* (1988), *The Freshman* (1990), *Hearts of Darkness* (doc) (1991), *Christopher Columbus: The Discovery* (1992), *Don Juan de Marco and the Centerfold* (1995).

Bronson, Charles (Charles Buchinski) (1920–) American, born Ehrenfield, Pennsylvania; *Drumbeat* (1954), *Vera Cruz* (1954), *The Magnificent Seven* (1960), *This Property is Condemned* (1966), *The Dirty Dozen* (1967), *Chato's Land* (1972), *The Mechanic* (1972), *The Valachi Papers* (1972), *Death Wish* (1974), *Hard Times* (1975), *Telefon* (1977), *Death Wish II* (1982), *Death Wish III* (1985), *Death Wish IV* (1987), *Murphy's Law* (1987), *Messenger of Death* (1988), *Kinjite: Forbidden Subjects* (1989), *The Indian Runner* (1991), *Death Wish V* (1993).

Brynner, Yul (1915–85) Swiss-Russian, naturalized American, born Sakhalin, Siberia; *The King and I* (1956), *The Brothers Karamazov* (1958), *The Magnificent Seven* (1960), *Return of the Seven* (1966).

Burton, Richard (Richard Walter Jenkins) (1925–84) British, born Pontrhydfen, S Wales: *My Cousin Rachel* (1952), *Alexander the Great* (1956), *Look Back in Anger* (1959), *Cleopatra* (1962), *The Night of the Iguana* (1964), *The Spy Who Came in from the Cold* (1965), *Who's Afraid of Virginia Woolf?* (1966), *The Taming of the Shrew* (1967), *Where Eagles Dare* (1969), *Equus* (1977), *Exorcist II: The Heretic* (1977), *Absolution* (1979), *1984* (1984).

Cagney, James (Francis Jr) (1899–1986) American, born New York City; *Public Enemy* (1931), *Lady Killer* (1933), *A Midsummer Night's Dream* (1935), *The Roaring Twenties* (1939), *Yankee Doodle Dandy* (1942), *White Heat* (1949), *Love Me or Leave Me* (1955), *Mister Roberts* (1955), *One, Two, or Three* (1961), *Ragtime* (1981).

Caine, Sir Michael (Maurice Micklewhite) (1933–) British, born London; *Zulu* (1963), *The Ipcress File* (1965), *Alfie* (1966), *The Italian Job* (1969), *Sleuth* (1972), *The Man Who Would Be King* (1975), *The Eagle Has Landed* (1976), *California Suite* (1978), *Beyond the Poseidon Adventure* (1979), *Dressed to Kill* (1980), *Death Trap* (1983), *Educating Rita* (1983), *Hannah and Her Sisters* (1986), *The Whistle Blower* (1987), *Without a Clue* (1988), *Bullseye* (1990), *Shock to the System* (1990), *Mr Destiny* (1990), *Noises Off* (1992), *Blue Ice* (1992), *Blood and Wine* (1996).

Chaplin, Charlie (Sir Charles Spencer) (1889–1977) British, born London; *The Champion* (1915), *The Tramp* (1915), *Easy Street* (1917), *A Dog's Life* (1918), *Shoulder Arms* (1918), *The Kid* (1920), *The Idle Class* (1921), *The Gold Rush* (1924), *City Lights* (1931), *Modern Times* (1936), *The Great Dictator* (1940), *Limelight* (1952), *A King in New York* (1957).

Christie, Julie (1941–) British, born Chukua, Assam, India; *The Fast Lady* (1963), *Billy Liar* (1963), *Doctor Zhivago* (1965), *Darling* (1965), *Farenheit 451* (1966), *Far from the Madding Crowd* (1967), *The Go-Between* (1971), *Don't Look Now* (1974), *Shampoo* (1975), *Heaven Can Wait* (1978), *Heat and Dust* (1982), *Power* (1985), *The Gold Diggers* (1988), *Dragon Heart* (1996), *Hamlet* (1996).

Clift, (Edward) Montgomery (1920–66) American, born Omaha, Nebraska; *Red River* (1946), *The Search* (1948), *A Place in the Sun* (1951), *From Here to Eternity* (1953), *Freud* (1962).

Close, Glenn (1947–) American, born Greenwich, Connecticut; *The World According to Garp* (1982), *The Big Chill* (1983), *The Natural* (1984), *Something About Amelia* (TV 1984), *Jagged Edge* (1985), *Maxie* (1985), *Fatal Attraction* (1987), *Dangerous Liaisons* (1988), *Immediate Family* (1989), *Reversal of Fortune* (1990), *Hamlet* (1990), *Meeting Venus* (1991), *Hook* (1991), *The Paper* (1994), *Mary Reilly* (1996), *101 Dalmatians* (1996), *Mars Attacks!* (1996).

Cobb, Lee J (Lee Jacoby) (1911–76) American, born New York City; *Golden Boy* (1939), *The Moon is Down* (1943), *Anna and the King of Siam* (1946), *The Dark Past* (1948), *On the Waterfront* (1954), *The Man in the Grey Flannel Suit* (1956), *Twelve Angry Men* (1957), *The Brothers Karamazov* (1958), *The Virginian* (TV 1962–6), *Come Blow Your Horn* (1963), *Death of a Salesman* (TV 1966), *Coogan's Bluff* (1968), *They Came to Rob Las Vegas* (1968), *The Young Lawyers* (TV 1970–1), *The Exorcist* (1973).

Connery, Sir Sean (Thomas Connery) (1930–) British, born Edinburgh; *Dr No* (1963), *Marnie* (1964), *From Russia With Love* (1964), *Goldfinger* (1965), *The Hill* (1965), *Thunderball* (1965), *A Fine Madness* (1966), *You Only Live Twice* (1967), *The Molly Maguires* (1969), *The Anderson Tapes* (1970), *Diamonds are Forever* (1971), *The*

Offence (1972), *Zardoz* (1973), *Murder on the Orient Express* (1974), *The Man Who Would Be King* (1975), *Robin and Marian* (1976), *Meteor* (1979), *Outland* (1981), *Time Bandits* (1981), *Never Say Never Again* (1983), *Highlander* (1985), *The Name of the Rose* (1986), *The Untouchables* (1987), *The Presidio* (1988), *Indiana Jones and the Last Crusade* (1989), *Family Business* (1989), *The Hunt for Red October* (1990), *The Russia House* (1990), *Highlander II: The Quickening* (1991), *Robin Hood: Prince of Thieves* (1991), *Medicine Man* (1991), *The Rising Sun* (1992), *Dreadnought* (1992), *Broken Dreams* (1992), *First Knight* (1995), *Dragon Heart* (1996), *The Avengers* (1998).

Cooper, Gary (Frank J Cooper) (1901–61) American, born Helena, Montana; *The Winning of Barbara Worth* (1926), *Lilac Time* (1928), *The Virginian* (1929), *A Farewell to Arms* (1932), *City Streets* (1932), *The Lives of a Bengal Lancer* (1935), *Sergeant York* (1941), *For Whom the Bell Tolls* (1943), *The Fountainhead* (1949), *High Noon* (1952), *Friendly Persuasion* (1956).

Costner, Kevin (1955–) American, born Los Angeles; *Night Shift* (1982), *American Flyers* (1984), *Silverado* (1985), *The Untouchables* (1987), *No Way Out* (1987), *Bull Durham* (1988), *Field of Dreams* (1989), *Revenge* (1990), *Dances with Wolves* (1990), *Robin Hood: Prince of Thieves* (1991), *JFK* (1991), *The Bodyguard* (1992), *A Perfect World* (1993), *The War* (1994), *Waterworld* (1995), *Tin Cup* (1996).

Crawford, Joan (Lucille Le Sueur) (1906–77) American, born San Antonio, Texas; *Our Dancing Daughters* (1928), *Our Blushing Brides* (1933), *Dancing Lady* (1933), *The Women* (1939), *Mildred Pierce* (1945), *Possessed* (1947), *What Ever Happened to Baby Jane?* (1962), *Trog* (1970).

Crosby, Bing (Harry Lillis Crosby) (1904–77) American, born Tacoma, Washington; *King of Jazz* (1930), *Mississippi* (1935), *Anything Goes* (1936), *Road to Singapore* (1940), *Road to Zanzibar* (1941), *Holiday Inn* (1942), *Road to Morrocco* (1942), *Going My Way* (1944), *The Bells of St Mary's* (1945), *Blue Skies* (1946), *A Connecticut Yankee in King Arthur's Court* (1949), *White Christmas* (1954), *The Country Girl* (1954), *High Society* (1956), *Road to Hong Kong* (1962).

Cruise, Tom (Tom Cruise Mapother IV) (1962–) American, born Syracuse, New York; *Taps* (1981), *Endless Love* (1981), *The Outsiders* (1983), *Legend* (1984), *Risky Business* (1984), *Top Gun* (1985), *The Color of Money* (1986), *Cocktail* (1988), *Rain Man* (1988), *Born on the Fourth of July* (1989), *Days of Thunder* (1990), *Far and Away* (1992), *A Few Good Men* (1992), *The Firm* (1993), *Interview with the Vampire* (1994), *Mission: Impossible* (1996), *Jerry Maguire* (1996), *Eyes Wide Shut* (1997).

Curtis, Tony (Bernard Schwarz) (1925–) American, born New York City; *Houdini* (1953), *Trapeze* (1956), *The Vikings* (1958), *Some Like It Hot* (1959), *Spartacus* (1960), *The Boston Strangler* (1968), The Persuaders (TV 1971–2).

Cushing, Peter (1913–94) British, born Kenley, Surrey; *The Man in the Iron Mask* (1939), *Hamlet* (1947), *1984* (TV 1955), *The Curse of Frankenstein* (1957), *Dracula* (1958), *The Mummy* (1959), *The Hound of the Baskervilles* (1959), *Cash on Demand* (1963), *Dr Who and the Daleks* (1965), Sherlock Holmes (TV 1968), *Tales from the Crypt* (1972), *Horror Express* (1972), *Star Wars* (1977), *Biggles* (1988).

Dafoe, Willem (1955–) American, born Appleton, Wisconsin; *Heaven's Gate* (1980), *Platoon* (1986), *The Last Temptation of Christ* (1988), *Mississippi Burning* (1988), *Triumph of the Spirit* (1989), *Born on the Fourth of July* (1989), *Wild At Heart* (1990), *Cry*

Baby (1990), *Flight of the Intruder* (1990), *Light Sleeper* (1992), *Body of Evidence* (1992), *Tom and Viv* (1994), *Clear and Present Danger* (1994), *The English Patient* (1996).

Davis, Bette (Ruth Elizabeth Davis) (1908–89) American, born Lowell, Massachusetts; *Bad Sister* (1931), *Dangerous* (1935), *Jezebel* (1938), *The Great Lie* (1941), *All About Eve* (1950), *What Ever Happened to Baby Jane?* (1962), *Strangers* (TV 1979), *The Whales of August* (1987).

Day, Doris (Doris von Kappelhoff) (1924–) American, born Cincinnati, Ohio; *Romance on the High Seas* (1948), *Storm Warning* (1950), *Calamity Jane* (1953), *Young at Heart* (1954), *Love Me or Leave Me* (1955), *The Pajama Game* (1957), *Pillow Talk* (1959), *That Touch of Mink* (1962), *With Six You Get Egg Roll* (1968), *The Doris Day Show* (TV 1968–73).

Day-Lewis, Daniel (1958–) Irish, born London; *Gandhi* (1983), *My Beautiful Laundrette* (1985), *Room with a View* (1985), *The Unbearable Lightness of Being* (1988), *Stars and Bars* (1988), *Nanou* (1988), *My Left Foot* (1989), *The Last of the Mohicans* (1992), *Age of Innocence* (1993), *In the Name of the Father* (1993), *The Crucible* (1996), *The Boxer* (1998).

Dean, James (Byron) (1931–55) American, born Fairmount, Indiana; *East of Eden* (1955), *Rebel without a Cause* (1955), *Giant* (1956).

De Havilland, Olivia (1916–) British, born Tokyo, Japan; *Midsummer Night's Dream* (1935), *The Adventures of Robin Hood* (1938), *Gone with the Wind* (1939), *The Dark Mirror* (1946), *To Each His Own* (1946), *The Heiress* (1949).

Dench, Dame Judi (Judith Olivia Dench) (1934–) British, born York; *The Third Secret* (1964), *Four in the Morning* (1966), *A Fine Romance* (TV 1981–4), *A Room With a View* (1985), *84 Charing Cross Road* (1987), *A Handful of Dust* (1988), *Henry V* (1989), *Behaving Badly* (TV 1989), *Jack and Sarah* (1995), *Hamlet* (1996), *Mrs Brown* (1997).

Deneuve, Catherine (Catherine Dorleac) (1943–) French, born Paris; *Les Parapluies de Cherbourg* (1964), *Repulsion* (1965), *Belle de Jour* (1967), *Tristana* (1970), *The Hunger* (1983), *Indochine* (1991), *Les Voleurs* (1996).

De Niro, Robert (1943–) American, born New York City; *Bang the Drum Slowly* (1973), *Mean Streets* (1973), *The Godfather, Part II* (1974), *1900* (1976), *Taxi Driver* (1976), *The Deer Hunter* (1978), *Raging Bull* (1980), *King of Comedy* (1982), *Brazil* (1985), *Angel Heart* (1987), *The Untouchables* (1987), *Midnight Run* (1988), *Jacknife* (1989), *Stanley & Iris* (1989), *We're No Angels* (1990), *Goodfellas* (1990), *Awakenings* (1990), *Backdraft* (1991), *Cape Fear* (1991), *The Mistress* (1992), *Mad Dog and Glory* (1992), *Night and The City* (1992), *This Boy's Life* (1992), *Frankenstein* (1994), *Casino* (1995), *Heat* (1995), *Sleepers* (1996), *Jackie Brown* (1998).

Depardieu, Gérard (1948–) French, born Châteauroux; *1900* (1976), *Get Out Your Handkerchiefs* (1977), *Loulou* (1980), *The Last Metro* (1980), *The Return of Martin Guerre* (1981), *Danton* (1982), *The Moon in the Gutter* (1983), *Police* (1985), *Jean de Florette* (1986), *Streets of Departure* (1986), *Under the Sun of Satan* (1987), *The Woman Next Door* (1987), *Cyrano de Bergerac* (1990), *Green Card* (1990), *Uranus* (1991), *Merci la Vie* (1991), *Mon Père, Ce Héros* (1991), *Tous les Matins du Monde* (1991), *Christopher Columbus* (1992), *Germinal* (1992), *Le Colonel Chabert* (1994), *Les Anges Gardiens* (1995), *Unhook The Stars* (1996), *Hamlet* (1996), *Le Gaulois* (1997).

De Vito, Danny (1944–   ) American, born Neptune, New Jersey; *One Flew Over the Cuckoo's Nest* (1975), *Taxi* (TV 1978–82), *Romancing the Stone* (1983), *Terms of Endearment* (1984), *The Jewel of the Nile* (1985), *Ruthless People* (1986), *Tin Men* (1987), *Throw Momma from the Train* (1987), *Twins* (1988), *War of the Roses* (1989), *Batman Returns* (1992), *Renaissance Man* (1994), *Junior* (1994), *Get Shorty* (1995), *Matilda* (1996), *LA Confidential* (1997).

Douglas, Kirk (Issur Danielovitch Demsky) (1916–   ) American, born Amsterdam, New York; *The Strange Love of Martha Ivers* (1946), *Lust for Life* (1956), *Gunfight at the OK Corral* (1957), *Paths of Glory* (1957), *The Vikings* (1958), *Spartacus* (1960), *The Man from Snowy River* (1982), *Oscar* (1991), *Greedy* (1994).

Douglas, Michael (1944–   ) American, born New Brunswick, New Jersey; *The Streets of San Francisco* (TV 1972–5), *Coma* (1978), *The China Syndrome* (1980), *The Star Chamber* (1983), *Romancing the Stone* (1984), *The Jewel of the Nile* (1985), *Fatal Attraction* (1987), *Wall Street* (1987), *Black Rain* (1989), *War of the Roses* (1989), *Shining Through* (1991), *Basic Instinct* (1992), *Falling Down* (1993), *Disclosure* (1994), *The American President* (1995), *The Ghost in the Darkness* (1996), *The Game* (1997).

Dreyfuss, Richard (1947–   ) American, born Brooklyn, New York City; *American Graffiti* (1973), *The Apprenticeship of Duddy Kravitz* (1974), *Jaws* (1975), *Close Encounters of the Third Kind* (1977), *The Goodbye Girl* (1977), *Whose Life is it Anyway?* (1981), *Down and Out in Beverly Hills* (1986), *Stakeout* (1987), *Tin Men* (1987), *Moon over Parador* (1988), *Always* (1989), *The Proud and the Free* (1991), *What About Bob?* (1991), *Prisoners of Honor* (1991), *Rosencrantz and Guilderstern are Dead* (1991), *Lost in Yonkers* (1993), *Another Stakeout* (1993), *The American President* (1995), *Trigger Happy* (1996).

Dunaway, (Dorothy) Faye (1941–   ) American, born Bascom, Florida; *Bonnie and Clyde* (1967), *Little Big Man* (1970), *The Getaway* (1972), *Chinatown* (1974), *The Towering Inferno* (1974), *Network* (1976), *The Eyes of Laura Mars* (1978), *The Champ* (1979), *Mommie Dearest* (1981), *Barfly* (1987), *Midnight Crossing* (1988), *Burning Secret* (1988), *The Handmaid's Tale* (1990), *Scorchers* (1991), *Silhouette* (TV 1991), *Three Weeks in Jerusalem* (1991), *American Dreamers* (1992), *Don Juan de Marco and the Centerfold* (1995), *Albino Alligator* (1996).

Eastwood, Clint (1930–   ) American, born San Francisco, California; *Rawhide* (TV 1958–65), *A Fistful of Dollars* (1964), *For a Few Dollars More* (1965), *The Good, The Bad, and the Ugly* (1966), *Paint Your Wagon* (1969), *Coogan's Bluff* (1968), *Where Eagles Dare* (1969), *Play Misty for Me* (1971), *Dirty Harry* (1972), *High Plains Drifter* (1973), *Magnum Force* (1973), *The Enforcer* (1976), *The Outlaw Josey Wales* (1976), *Every Which Way But Loose* (1978), *Escape from Alcatraz* (1979), *Any Which Way You Can* (1980), *Firefox* (1982), *Honky Tonk Man* (1982), *Sudden Impact* (1983), *Tightrope* (1984), *Heartbreak Ridge* (1986), *Pink Cadillac* (1989), *The Dead Pool* (1989), *White Hunter Black Heart* (1990), *The Rookie* (1990), *Unforgiven* (1992), *In the Line of Fire* (1993), *A Perfect World* (1993), *The Bridges of Madison County* (1995), *Absolute Power* (1997).

Fairbanks, Douglas, Jr (1909–2000) American, born New York City; *Catherine the Great* (1934), *The Prisoner of Zenda* (1937), *Sinbad the Sailor* (1947).

Fairbanks, Douglas, Sr (Douglas Elton Ullman) (1883–1939) American, born Denver, Colorado; *The Mark of Zorro* (1920), *The Three Musketeers* (1921), *Robin Hood* (1922), *The Thief of Baghdad* (1924), *The Black Pirate* (1926).

Fields, W C (William Claude Dunkenfield) (1879–1946) American, born Philadelphia, Pennsylvania; *Pool Sharks* (1915), *International House* (1933), *It's a Gift* (1934), *The Old Fashioned Way* (1934), *David Copperfield* (1935), *My Little Chickadee* (1940), *The Bank Dick* (1940), *Never Give a Sucker an Even Break* (1941).

Fiennes, Ralph (Ralph Nathanial Fiennes) (1962–) British; *Wuthering Heights* (1992), *Schindler's List* (1994), *Quiz Show* (1994), *The English Patient* (1996), *Oscar and Lucinda* (1998), *The Avengers* (1998).

Finch, Peter (Frederick George Peter Ingle Finch) (1916–77) British, born London; *The Shiralee* (1957), *The Nun's Story* (1959), *No Love for Johnnie* (1961), *Far from the Madding Crowd* (1967), *Sunday Bloody Sunday* (1971), *Network* (1976).

Finney, Albert (1936–) British, born Salford, Lancashire; *The Entertainer* (1960), *Saturday Night and Sunday Morning* (1960), *Tom Jones* (1963), *Charlie Bubbles* (1968), *Murder on the Orient Express* (1974), *Shoot the Moon* (1981), *Annie* (1982), *The Dresser* (1983), *Under the Volcano* (1984), *The Green Man* (TV 1990), *Miller's Crossing* (1990), *The Playboys* (1992), *Karaoke* (TV 1996), *Cold Lazarus* (TV1996).

Flynn, Errol (1909–59) Australian–American, born Hobart, Tasmania; *In the Wake of the Bounty* (1933), *Captain Blood* (1935), *The Charge of the Light Brigade* (1936), *The Adventures of Robin Hood* (1938), *The Sea Hawk* (1940), *The Sun Also Rises* (1957).

Fonda, Henry (James) (1905–82) American, born Grand Island, Nebraska; *The Moon's Our Home* (1936), *A Farmer Takes A Wife* (1938), *Young Mr Lincoln* (1939), *The Grapes of Wrath* (1940), *The Lady Eve* (1941), *The Oxbow Incident* (1943), *My Darling Clementine* (1946), *Twelve Angry Men* (1957), *Stage Struck* (1957), *Fail Safe* (1964), *The Boston Strangler* (1968), *On Golden Pond* (1981).

Fonda, Jane (Seymour) (1937–) American, born New York City; *Walk on the Wild Side* (1961), *Barbarella* (1968), *They Shoot Horses Don't They?* (1969), *Klute* (1971), *Julia* (1977), *Coming Home* (1978), *The Electric Horseman* (1979), *The China Syndrome* (1980), *Nine to Five* (1981), *On Golden Pond* (1981), *The Dollmaker* (TV 1983), *The Morning After* (1986), *Old Gringo* (1989), *Stanley and Iris* (1989).

Ford, Harrison (1942–) American, born Chicago; *Dead Heat on a Merry-Go-Round* (1966), *American Graffiti* (1974), *Star Wars* (1977), *Heroes* (1977), *Force 10 from Navarone* (1978), *The Frisco Kid* (1979), *Hanover Street* (1979), *Apocalypse Now* (1979), *The Empire Strikes Back* (1980), *Raiders of the Lost Ark* (1981), *Blade Runner* (1982), *Return of the Jedi* (1983), *Indiana Jones and the Temple of Doom* (1984), *Witness* (1985), *Mosquito Coast* (1986), *Frantic* (1988), *Working Girl* (1988), *Indiana Jones and the Last Crusade* (1989), *Presumed Innocent* (1990), *Regarding Henry* (1991), *Patriot Games* (1992), *The Fugitive* (1993), *Clear and Present Danger* (1994), *The Devil's Own* (1996).

Foster, Jodie (Ariane Munker) (1962–) American, born The Bronx, New York City; *Bob and Carol and Ted and Alice* (TV 1973), *Paper Moon* (TV 1974), *Alice Doesn't Live Here Anymore* (1974), *Bugsy Malone* (1976), *Taxi Driver* (1976), *The Little Girl Who Lives Down the Lane* (1976), *Candleshoe* (1977), *Freaky Friday* (1977), *Siesta* (1987), *The Accused* (1988), *5 Corners* (1988), *Stealing Home* (1988), *Catchfire* (1990), *Silence of the Lambs*

(1991), *Little Man Tate* (1991), *Shadows and Fog* (1992), *Sommersby* (1993), *Maverick* (1994), *Nell* (1994), *Contact* (1997).

Fox, Michael J (1961–) Canadian, born Edmonton, Alberta; *Letters from Frank* (TV 1979), *Family Ties* (TV 1982–9), *Poison Ivy* (TV 1985), *Back to the Future* (1985), *Teenwolf* (1985), *The Secret of My Success* (1987), *Bright Lights Big City* (1988), *Casualties of War* (1989), *Back to the Future Ii* (1989), *Back to the Future III* (1990), *The Hard Way* (1991), *'Doc' Hollywood* (1991), *For Love or Money* (1993), *Life with Mikey* (1993), *Don't Drink the Water* (TV 1994), *The American President* (1995), *Blue in the Face* (1995).

Gable, (William) Clark (1901–60) American, born Cadiz, Ohio; *Red Dust* (1932), *It Happened One Night* (1934), *Mutiny on the Bounty* (1935), *San Francisco* (1936), *Gone with the Wind* (1939), *The Hucksters* (1947), *Mogambo* (1953), *Never Let Me Go* (1953), *Teacher's Pet* (1958), *The Misfits* (1961).

Garbo, Greta (Greta Lovisa Gustafsson) (1905–90) Swedish–American, born Stockholm; *Flesh and the Devil* (1927), *Anna Christie* (1930), *Grand Hotel* (1932), *Queen Christina* (1933), *Anna Karenina* (1935), *Camille* (1936), *Ninotchka* (1939).

Gardner, Ava (Lucy Johnson) (1922–90) American, born Smithfield, North Carolina; *The Killers* (1946), *The Hucksters* (1947), *Show Boat* (1951), *Pandora and the Flying Dutchman* (1951), *The Snows of Kilimanjaro* (1952), *Mogambo* (1953), *The Barefoot Contessa* (1954), *The Sun Also Rises* (1957), *The Night of the Iguana* (1964).

Garland, Judy (Frances Gumm) (1922–69) American, born Grand Rapids, Minnesota; *The Wizard of Oz* (1939), *Babes in Arms* (1939), *For Me and My Gal* (1942), *Meet Me in St Louis* (1944), *Ziegfeld Follies* (1945), *The Clock* (1945), *Easter Parade* (1948), *Summer Stock* (1950), *A Star is Born* (1954).

Gere, Richard (1949–) American, born Philadelphia, Pennsylvania; *Yanks* (1979), *American Gigolo* (1980), *An Officer and a Gentleman* (1982), *Breathless* (1983), *The Cotton Club* (1984), *No Mercy* (1986), *Miles from Home* (1988), *Internal Affairs* (1990), *Pretty Woman* (1990), *Rhapsody in August* (1991), *Final Analysis* (1992), *Mr North* (1992), *Sommersby* (1993), *First Knight* (1995), *Primal Fear* (1996), *The Jackal* (1997).

Gibson, Mel (1956–) American–Australian, born Peekshill, NewYork; *Tim* (1979), *Mad Max* (1979), *Gallipoli* (1981), *Mad Max 2: The Road Warrior* (1982), *The Year of Living Dangerously* (1982), *Mad Max Beyond Thunderdome* (1985), *Lethal Weapon* (1987), *Tequila Sunrise* (1988), *Lethal Weapon 2* (1989), *Bird on a Wire* (1990), *Air America* (1990), *Hamlet* (1990), *Lethal Weapon 3* (1992), *The Rest of Daniel* (1992), *Forever Young* (1992), *The Man Without a Face* (1993), *Maverick* (1994), *Braveheart* (1995), *Ransom* (1996), *Conspiracy Theory* (1997).

Gielgud, Sir John (Arthur) (1904–2000) British, born London; also stage; *Julius Caesar* (1953), *The Charge of the Light Brigade* (1968), *Oh What a Lovely War* (1969), *Murder on the Orient Express* (1974), *Providence* (1977), *Brideshead Revisited* (TV 1981), *Arthur* (1981), *Gandhi* (1982), *The Whistle Blower* (1987), *Arthur 2: On the Rocks* (1988), *Loser Takes All* (1989), *Prospero's Books* (1991), *First Knight* (1995), *Haunted* (1995), *Hamlet* (1996).

Gish, Lillian (Diana) (Lillian de Guiche) (1896–1993) American, born Springfield, Ohio; *An Unseen Enemy* (1912), *Birth of a Nation* (1914), *Intolerance* (1916), *Broken Blossoms*

(1919), *Way Down East* (1920), *Duel in the Sun* (1946), *Night of the Hunter* (1955), *The Whales of August* (1987).

Glover, Danny (1947–) American, born San Francisco, California; *Silverado* (1985), *Witness* (1985), *Lethal Weapon* (1987), *Bat 21* (1988), *Lethal Weapon 2* (1989), *Predator 2* (1990), *Lethal Weapon 3* (1992), *The Saint of Fort Washington* (1993), *Bopha!* (1993).

Goldberg, Whoopi (Caryn Johnson) (1949–) American, born Manhattan, New York City; *The Color Purple* (1985), *Burglar* (1985), *Jumping Jack Flash* (1986), *Clara's Heart* (1988), *The Telephone* (1988), *Ghost* (1990), *Soapdish* (1991), *Sister Act* (1992), *Change of Heart* (1992), *The Player* (1992), *Made in America* (1993), *Sister Act 2: Back in the Habit* (1993), *Corrina Corrina* (1994).

Goldblum, Jeff (1952–) American, born Pittsburgh, Pennsylvania; *California Split* (1974), *Death Wish* (1974), *Nashville* (1975), *Invasion of the Body Snatchers* (1978), *Escape from Athena* (1979), *The Right Stuff* (1983), *The Big Chill* (1983), *Into the Night* (1985), *Silverado* (1985), *The Fly* (1985), *Life Story* (TV 1987), *Vibes* (1988), *The Tall Guy* (1989), *Earth Girls Are Easy* (1989), *Mister Frost* (1990), *The Player* (1992), *Fathers and Sons* (1992), *Jurassic Park* (1993), *Nine Months* (1995), *Independence Day* (1996).

Granger, Stewart (James Lablanche Stewart) (1913–93) British, born London; *The Man in Grey* (1943), *Waterloo Road* (1944), *Love Story* (1944), *Caesar and Cleopatra* (1945), *Captain Boycott* (1947), *King Solomon's Mines* (1950), *Scaramouch* (1952), *The Prisoner of Zenda* (1952), *Beau Brummell* (1954), *The Wild Geese* (1977).

Grant, Cary (Archibald Alexander Leach) (1904–86) Anglo-American, born Bristol, England; *This is the Night* (1932), *She Done Him Wrong* (1933), *The Awful Truth* (1937), *Bringing Up Baby* (1938), *His Girl Friday* (1940), *Arsenic and Old Lace* (1944), *Notorious* (1946), *To Catch a Thief* (1953), *North by Northwest* (1959).

Guinness, Sir Alec (1914–2000) British, born London; *Oliver Twist* (1948), *Kind Hearts and Coronets* (1949), *The Mudlark* (1950), *The Lavender Hill Mob* (1951), *The Man in the White Suit* (1951), *The Card* (1952), *Father Brown* (1954), *The Ladykillers* (1955), *The Bridge on the River Kwai* (1957), *The Horse's Mouth* (1958), *Our Man in Havana* (1960), *Tunes of Glory* (1962), *Lawrence of Arabia* (1962), *Doctor Zhivago* (1966), *Star Wars* (1977), *Tinker, Tailor, Soldier, Spy* (TV 1979), *Smiley's People* (TV 1981), *Return of the Jedi* (1983), *A Passage to India* (1984), *Little Dorrit* (1987), *A Handful of Dust* (1988), *Kafka* (1991), *Foreign Field* (TV 1993).

Hackman, Gene (1931–) American, born San Bernardino, California; *Bonnie and Clyde* (1967), *I Never Sang for My Father* (1969), *French Connection* (1971), *The Poseidon Adventure* (1972), *Young Frankenstein* (1974), *French Connection II* (1975), *A Bridge Too Far* (1977), *Superman* (1978), *Superman II* (1981), *Target* (1985), *Superman IV* (1987), *Another Woman* (1988), *Bat 21* (1988), *Full Moon in Blue Water* (1988), *Split Decisions* (1988), *Mississippi Burning* (1989), *The Package* (1989), *Loose Cannons* (1990), *Postcards from the Edge* (1990), *Narrow Margin* (1990), *Class Action* (1990), *Company Business* (1991), *Unforgiven* (1992), *The Firm* (1993), *Geronimo: An American Legend* (1993), *Get Shorty* (1995), *The Birdcage* (1996), *The Chamber* (1996), *Extreme Measures* (1996), *Absolute Power* (1997).

Hanks, Tom (1957–) American, born Oakland, California; *Bachelor Party* (1983), *Splash!* (1984), *The Man With One Red Shoe* (1985), *Dragnet* (1987), *Big* (1988),

Punchline (1988), *The 'Burbs* (1989), *Turner and Hooch* (1990), *Joe Versus the Volcano* (1990), *Bonfire of the Vanities* (1991), *A League of Their Own* (1992), *Benny and Joon* (1992), *Sleepless in Seattle* (1993), *Philadelphia* (1993), *Forrest Gump* (1994), *Apollo 13* (1995), *That Thing You Do* (1996), *Saving Private Ryan* (1998).

Hardy, Oliver (Norvell Hardy Junior) (1892–1957) American, born near Atlanta, Georgia; many Laurel and Hardy films including *Putting Pants on Philip* (1927), *The Battle of the Century* (1927), *Two Tars* (1928), *The Perfect Day* (1929), *Laughing Gravy* (1931), *The Music Box* (1932), *Babes in Toyland* (1934), *Bonnie Scotland* (1935), *Way Out West* (1937), *The Flying Deuces* (1939), *Atoll K* (1950).

Harlow, Jean (Harlean Carpentier) (1911–37) American, born Kansas City, Missouri; *Red Dust* (1932), *Hell's Angels* (1930), *Platinum Blonde* (1931), *Red-Headed Woman* (1932), *Bombshell* (1933), *Dinner at 8* (1933), *Libelled Lady* (1936).

Harris, Richard (1930–) Irish, born County Limerick; *The Guns of Navarone* (1961), *Mutiny on the Bounty* (1962), *This Sporting Life* (1963), *Camelot* (1967), *A Man Called Horse* (1969), *Cromwell* (1970), *The Cassandra Crossing* (1977), *Orca — Killer Whale* (1977), *The Wild Geese* (1978), *Tarzan the Ape Man* (1981), *The Field* (1990).

Hayworth, Rita (Margarita Carmen Cansino) (1918–87) American, born New York City; *Only Angels Have Wings* (1939), *The Lady in Question* (1940), *The Strawberry Blonde* (1940), *Blood and Sand* (1941), *You'll Never Get Rich* (1941), *Cover Girl* (1944), *Gilda* (1946), *The Lady from Shanghai* (1948), *Separate Tables* (1958).

Hepburn, Audrey (Audrey Hepburn-Ruston) (1929–93) Anglo-Dutch, born Brussels, Belgium; *Roman Holiday* (1953), *War and Peace* (1956), *Funny Face* (1957), *The Nun's Story* (1959), *Breakfast at Tiffany's* (1961), *My Fair Lady* (1964), *How to Steal a Million* (1966), *Wait Until Dark* (1967), *Robin and Marian* (1976), *Always* (1989).

Hepburn, Katharine (1907–) American, born Hartford, Connecticut; *A Bill of Divorcement* (1932), *Morning Glory* (1933), *Stage Door* (1937), *Bringing Up Baby* (1938), *Holiday* (1938), *The Philadelphia Story* (1940), *Woman of the Year* (1942), *Adam's Rib* (1949), *The African Queen* (1951), *Long Day's Journey into Night* (1962), *Guess Who's Coming to Dinner?* (1967), *Suddenly Last Summer* (1968), *The Lion in Winter* (1968), *The Glass Menagerie* (TV 1973), *Rooster Cogburn* (1975), *On Golden Pond* (1981), *Love Affair* (1994).

Heston, Charlton (John Charlton Carter) (1922–) American, born Evanston, Illinois; *Arrowhead* (1953), *The Ten Commandments* (1956), *Touch of Evil* (1958), *Ben Hur* (1959), *El Cid* (1961), *The Greatest Story Ever Told* (1965), *The War Lord* (1965), *Khartoum* (1966), *Planet of the Apes* (1968), *Will Penny* (1968), *Earthquake* (1973), *Airport* (1975), *The Four Musketeers* (1975), *Almost an Angel* (1990), *Wayne's World 2* (1993), *Tombstone* (1993), *Hamlet* (1996).

Hoffman, Dustin (1937–) American, born Los Angeles; *The Graduate* (1967), *Midnight Cowboy* (1969), *Little Big Man* (1970), *Papillon* (1973), *Lenny* (1974), *All the President's Men* (1976), *Kramer vs Kramer* (1979), *Tootsie* (1982), *Death of a Salesman* (TV 1984), *Rain Man* (1988), *Dick Tracy* (1990), *Billy Bathgate* (1991), *Hook* (1991), *Hero* (1992), *Outbreak* (1995), *Sleepers* (1996).

Holden, William (William Franklin Beedle Jr) (1918–82) American, born O'Fallon, Illinois; *Golden Boy* (1939), *Rachel and the Stranger* (1948), *Sunset Boulevard* (1950), *Born Yesterday* (1950), *Stalag 17* (1953), *Love is a Many-Splendored Thing* (1955), *Picnic*

(1955), *The Bridge on the River Kwai* (1957), *Casino Royale* (1967), *The Wild Bunch* (1969), *The Towering Inferno* (1974), *Network* (1976), *Damien: Omen II* (1978), *Escape to Athena* (1979), *The Earthling* (1980), *SOB* (1981), *When Time Ran Out* (1981).

Hope, Bob (Leslie Townes Hope) (1903–) Anglo-American, born Eltham, London; *Thanks for the Memory* (1938), *The Cat and the Canary* (1939), *Road to Singapore* (1940), *The Ghost Breakers* (1940), *Road to Zanzibar* (1941), *My Favorite Blonde* (1942), *Road to Morocco* (1942), *The Paleface* (1948), *Fancy Pants* (1950), *The Facts of Life* (1960), *Road to Hong Kong* (1961), *How to Commit Marriage* (1969).

Hopkins, Anthony (1941–) Welsh–American, born Port Talbot, Wales; *The Lion in Winter* (1968), *When Eight Bells Toll* (1971), *War and Peace* (TV 1972), *The Lindbergh Kidnapping Case* (TV 1976), *Magic* (1978), *The Elephant Man* (1980), *The Bunker* (TV 1981), *The Bounty* (1983), *84 Charing Cross Road* (1986), *Desperate Hours* (1991), *Silence of the Lambs* (1991), *Spotswood* (1991), *Freejack* (1992), *Howards End* (1992), *Charlie* (1992), *The Innocent* (1992), *Dracula* (1992), *The Remains of the Day* (1993), *Shadowlands* (1993), *The Road to Wellville* (1994), *Legends of the Fall* (1994), *Nixon* (1995), *Surviving Picasso* (1996), *Bookworm* (1997).

Hopper, Dennis (1936–) American, born Dodge City, Kansas; *Rebel Without a Cause* (1955), *Giant* (1956), *Cool Hand Luke* (1967), *Easy Rider* (1969), *Apocalypse Now* (1979), *Blue Velvet* (1986), *River's Edge* (1986), *Blood Red* (1990), *Catchfire* (1990), *Paris Trout* (1991), *The Indian Runner* (1991), *Money Men* (1992), *True Romance* (1993), *Speed* (1994), *Waterworld* (1995).

Hoskins, Bob (Robert William) (1942–) British, born Bury St Edmunds, Suffolk; *Pennies from Heaven* (TV 1978), *The Long Good Friday* (1980), *Pink Floyd: The Wall* (1982), *The Honorary Consul* (1983), *The Cotton Club* (1984), *Brazil* (1985), *Sweet Liberty* (1985), *Mona Lisa* (1986), *A Prayer for the Dying* (1987), *Who Framed Roger Rabbit?* (1988), *Heart Condition* (1990), *Mermaids* (1990), *Shattered* (1991), *Hook* (1991), *The Favour, the Watch and the Very Big Fish* (1991), *The Inner Circle* (1992), *Rainbow* (1995), *Nixon* (1995), *The Secret Agent* (1996).

Howard, Trevor (Wallace) (1916–88) British, born Cliftonville, Kent; *The Way Ahead* (1944), *Brief Encounter* (1946), *Green for Danger* (1946), *The Third Man* (1949), *The Heart of the Matter* (1953), *The Key* (1958), *Sons and Lovers* (1960), *Mutiny on the Bounty* (1962), *The Charge of the Light Brigade* (1968), *Ryan's Daughter* (1970), *The Night Visitor* (1971), *Catholics* (TV 1973), *Conduct Unbecoming* (1975), *Meteor* (1979), *Staying On* (TV 1980), *Gandhi* (1982), *White Mischief* (1987), *The Unholy* (1988).

Hudson, Rock (Roy Scherer Jr) (1925–85) American, born Winnetka, Illinois; *Magnificent Obsession* (1954), *Giant* (1956), *Written on the Wind* (1956), *The Tarnished Angel* (1957), *Pillow Talk* (1959), *Send Me No Flowers* (1964), *Seconds* (1966), *Darling Lili* (1969), *McMillan and Wife* (TV 1971–5), *McMillan* (TV 1976), *Embryo* (1976), *The Martian Chronicles* (TV 1980), *Dynasty* (TV 1985).

Hurt, John (1940–) British, born Chesterfield, Derbyshire; *A Man for All Seasons* (1966), *10 Rillington Place* (1971), *The Naked Civil Servant* (TV 1975), *Midnight Express* (1978), *Alien* (1979), *The Elephant Man* (1980), *History of the World Part One* (1981), *Champions* (1983), *1984* (1984), *Spaceballs* (1987), *Aria* (1987), *White Mischief* (1987), *Scandal* (1989), *Frankenstein Unbound* (1990), *King Ralph* (1991), *Resident Alien* (1991), *Dark at Noon* (1992), *Rob Roy* (1995), *Darkening* (1996).

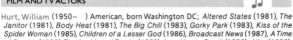

Hurt, William (1950–) American, born Washington DC; *Altered States* (1981), *The Janitor* (1981), *Body Heat* (1981), *The Big Chill* (1983), *Gorky Park* (1983), *Kiss of the Spider Woman* (1985), *Children of a Lesser God* (1986), *Broadcast News* (1987), *A Time of Destiny* (1988), *The Accidental Tourist* (1989), *Love You to Death* (1990), *Alice* (1990), *Until the End of the World* (1991), *The Doctor* (1991), *The Plague* (1992), *Second Best* (1994), *Smoke* (1995), *Jane Eyre* (1995).

Huston, Angelica (1952–) Irish–American, born Ireland; *The Last Tycoon* (1976), *Frances* (1982), *This is Spinal Tap* (1984), *Prizzi's Honor* (1985), *The Dead* (1987), *Gardens of Stone* (1987), *A Handful of Dust* (1988), *Mr North* (1988), *The Witches* (1990), *The Grifters* (1990), *The Addams Family* (1991), *Bitter Moon* (1992), *Addams Family Values* (1993), *Manhattan Murder Mystery* (1994), *The Crossing Guard* (1995).

Irons, Jeremy (1948–) British, born Cowes; *The French Lieutenant's Woman* (1981), *Brideshead Revisited* (TV 1981), *Swann in Love* (1984), *The Mission* (1985), *Dead Ringers* (1988), *Reversal of Fortune* (1990), *Kafka* (1991), *Waterland* (1992), *Damage* (1992), *M Butterfly* (1992), *Die Hard with a Vengeance* (1995), *Stealing Beauty* (1995), *Lolita* (1996).

Jackson, Glenda (1936–) British, born Liverpool; *Women in Love* (1969), *Sunday Bloody Sunday* (1971), *Mary Queen of Scots* (1971), *Elizabeth R* (TV 1971), *A Touch of Class* (1972), *Hedda* (1975), *Stevie* (1978), *The Patricia Neal Story* (TV 1981), *Turtle Diary* (1985), *Business as Usual* (1987), *Salome's Last Dance* (1988), *The Rainbow* (1989), *Doombeach* (1990), *A Murder of Quality* (TV 1991).

Karloff, Boris (William Henry Pratt) (1887–1969) Anglo-American, born London; *Frankenstein* (1931), *The Mask of Fu Manchu* (1931), *The Lost Patrol* (1934), *The Raven* (1935), *The Bride of Frankenstein* (1935), *The Body Snatcher* (1945).

Keaton, Buster (Joseph Francis Keaton) (1895–1966) American, born Piqua, Kansas; *Our Hospitality* (1923), *The Navigator* (1924), *The General* (1927), *San Diego I Love You* (1944), *Sunset Boulevard* (1950), *Limelight* (1952), *It's a Mad, Mad, Mad, Mad World* (1963).

Keaton, Diane (Diane Hall) (1946–) American, born Los Angeles, California; *The Godfather* (1972), *The Godfather, Part II* (1974), *Sleeper* (1973), *Annie Hall* (1977), *Manhattan* (1979), *Reds* (1981), *Shoot the Moon* (1982), *Mrs Soffel* (1984), *Baby Boom* (1987), *The Good Mother* (1988), *The Godfather, Part III* (1990), *Success* (1991), *Father of the Bride* (1991), *Manhattan Murder Mystery* (1993), *Father of the Bride II* (1995), *The First Wives Club* (1996).

Keitel, Harvey (1947–) American, born Brooklyn, New York City; *Mean Streets* (1973), *Taxi Driver* (1976), *Bad Timing* (1980), *The Men's Club* (1986), *The Last Temptation of Christ* (1988), *The January Man* (1989), *Bugsy* (1991), *Thelma and Louise* (1991), *Reservoir Dogs* (1992), *The Bad Lieutenant* (1992), *Sister Act* (1992), *The Piano* (1993), *Pulp Fiction* (1994), *Smoke* (1995), *Clockers* (1995), *Ulysses' Gaze* (1995), *Get Shorty* (1995), *Head Above Water* (1996), *Copland* (1997).

Kelly, Gene (Eugene Curran Kelly) (1912–96) American, born Pittsburgh, Pennsylvania; *For Me and My Girl* (1942), *Cover Girl* (1944), *Anchors Aweigh* (1945), *Ziegfeld Follies* (1946), *The Pirate* (1948), *The Three Musketeers* (1948), *Take Me Out to the Ball Game* (1949), *On the Town* (1949), *Summer Stock* (1950), *An American in Paris* (1951), *Singin' in the Rain* (1952), *Brigadoon* (1954), *Invitation to Dance* (1956), *Les Girls* (1957), *Marjorie Morningstar* (1958), *Inherit the Word* (1960), *Sins* (TV 1987).

Kelly, Grace (Patricia) (1928–82) American, born Philadelphia, Pennsylvania; *High Noon* (1952), *Mogambo* (1953), *Dial M for Murder* (1954), *Rear Window* (1954), *The Country Girl* (1954), *To Catch a Thief* (1955), *High Society* (1956).

Kennedy, George (1925–   ) American, born New York City; *Charade* (1963), *The Flight of the Phoenix* (1967), *The Dirty Dozen* (1967), *Cool Hand Luke* (1967), *Sarge* (TV 1971), *Thunderbolt and Lightfoot* (1974), *Earthquake* (1974), *The Blue Knight* (TV 1975–6), *The Eiger Sanction* (1977), *Death on the Nile* (1979), *Bolero* (1984), *Delta Force* (1985), *Creepshow 2* (1987), *Dallas* (TV 1988–91), *Naked Gun* (1989), *Naked Gun 2½: The Smell of Fear* (1991), *Naked Gun 33⅓: The Final Insult* (1994).

Kerr, Deborah (Deborah Jane Kerr-Trimmer) (1921–   ) British, born Helensburgh, Scotland; *Major Barbara* (1940), *Love on the Dole* (1941), *The Life and Death of Colonel Blimp* (1943), *Perfect Strangers* (1945), *I See a Dark Stranger* (1945), *Black Narcissus* (1947), *From Here to Eternity* (1953), *The King and I* (1956), *Tea and Sympathy* (1956), *An Affair to Remember* (1957), *Separate Tables* (1958), *The Sundowners* (1960), *The Innocents* (1961), *The Night of the Iguana* (1964), *Casino Royale* (1967), *Prudence and the Pill* (1968), *The Assam Garden* (1985).

Lancaster, Burt (Stephen Burton) (1913–94) American, born New York City; *The Killers* (1946), *Brute Force* (1947), *The Flame and the Arrow* (1950), *Come Back Little Sheba* (1953), *From Here to Eternity* (1953), *Vera Cruz* (1954), *Gunfight at the OK Corral* (1957), *Elmer Gantry* (1960), *Birdman of Alcatraz* (1962), *The Professionals* (1966), *The Swimmer* (1967), *1900* (1976), *Atlantic City* (1980), *Local Hero* (1983), *Rocket Gibraltar* (1988), *Field of Dreams* (1988).

Lansbury, Angela (Brigid) (1925–   ) American, born London; *National Velvet* (1944), *Gaslight* (1944), *The Picture of Dorian Gray* (1945), *The Private Affairs of Bel Ami* (1947), *The Three Musketeers* (1948), *The Reluctant Debutante* (1958), *The Long Hot Summer* (1958), *The Dark at the Top of the Stairs* (1960), *The Manchurian Candidate* (1962), *The Greatest Story Ever Told* (1965), *Bedknobs and Broomsticks* (1971), *Death on the Nile* (1978), *The Lady Vanishes* (1979), *Lace* (TV 1984), *Company of Wolves* (1984), *Murder She Wrote* (TV 1984–96).

Laughton, Charles (1899–1962) British, born Scarborough; *The Sign of the Cross* (1932), *The Private Life of Henry VIII* (1932), *The Barretts of Wimpole Street* (1934), *Ruggles of Red Gap* (1935), *Mutiny on the Bounty* (1935), *Les Misérables* (1935), *Rembrandt* (1936), *The Hunchback of Notre Dame* (1939), *Hobson's Choice* (1954), *Witness for the Prosecution* (1957), *Advise and Consent* (1962).

Laurel, Stan (Arthur Stanley Jefferson) (1890–1965) Anglo-American, born Ulverston, Lancashire; *Nuts in May* (1917), *Monsieur Don't Care* (1925); for films with Hardy ► Hardy, Oliver

Lee, Christopher (1922–   ) British, born London; *The Curse of Frankenstein* (1956), *Dracula* (1958), *The Man Who Could Cheat Death* (1959), *The Mummy* (1959), *The Face of Fu Manchu* (1965), *Rasputin the Mad Monk* (1965), *Horror Express* (1972), *The Three Musketeers* (1973), *The Man With the Golden Gun* (1974), *Return from Witch Mountain* (1976), *Howling II* (1985), *The Land of Faraway* (1988), *Gremlins 2: The New Batch* (1990), *Police Academy 7: Mission to Moscow* (1994), *The Knot* (1996), *Ivanhoe* (TV 1997).

Leigh, Vivien (Vivien Hartley) (1913–67) British, born Darjeeling, India; *Dark Journey* (1937), *A Yank at Oxford* (1938), *Gone with the Wind* (1939), *Lady Hamilton* (1941), *Caesar and Cleopatra* (1945), *Anna Karenina* (1948), *A Streetcar Named Desire* (1951), *The Roman Spring of Mrs Stone* (1961), *Ship of Fools* (1965).

Lemmon, Jack (John Uhler Lemmon III) (1925–   ) American, born Boston, Massachusetts; *It Should Happen to You* (1953), *Mister Roberts* (1955), *Some Like It Hot* (1959), *The Apartment* (1960), *Irma La Douce* (1963), *The Great Race* (1965), *The Odd Couple* (1968), *The Prisoner of Second Avenue* (1975), *The China Syndrome* (1979), *Missing* (1982), *Dad* (1990), *JFK* (1991), *The Player* (1992), *Glengarry Glen Ross* (1992), *Short Cuts* (1993), *The Grass Harp* (1995), *Hamlet* (1996).

Lewis, Jerry (Joseph Levitch) (1926–   ) American, born Newark, New Jersey; *My Friend Irma* (1949), *The Bellboy* (1960), *Cinderfella* (1960), *The Nutty Professor* (1963), *It's a Mad, Mad, Mad, Mad World* (1963), *The Family Jewels* (1965), *King of Comedy* (1983), *Smorgasbord* (1983), *Cookie* (1988), *Funny Bones* (1995).

Lloyd, Harold (Clayton) (1893–1971) American, born Burchard, Nebraska; *High and Dizzy* (1920), *Grandma's Boy* (1922), *Safety Last* (1923), *Why Worry?* (1923), *The Freshman* (1925), *The Kid Brother* (1927), *Feet First* (1930), *Movie Crazy* (1932).

Lom, Herbert (Herbert Charles Angelo Kuchacevich ze Schluderpacheru) (1917–   ) Czech, born Prague; *The Seventh Veil* (1946), *Duel Alibi* (1947), *State Secret* (1950), *The Ladykillers* (1950), *El Cid* (1961), *Phantom of the Opera* (1962), *A Shot in the Dark* (1964), *Murders in the Rue Morgue* (1972), *The Return of the Pink Panther* (1974), *The Pink Panther Strikes Again* (1977), *Revenge of the Pink Panther* (1978), *The Lady Vanishes* (1979), *Hopscotch* (1980), *The Dead Zone* (1983), *Whoops Apocalypse* (1986), *Going Bananas* (1988), *Ten Little Indians* (1989), *The Pope Must Die* (1991), *Son of the Pink Panther* (1993).

Loren, Sophia (Sofia Scicolone) (1934–   ) Italian, born Rome; *Woman of the River* (1955), *Boy on a Dolphin* (1957), *The Key* (1958), *El Cid* (1961), *Two Women* (1961), *The Millionairess* (1961), *Marriage Italian Style* (1964), *Cinderella Italian Style* (1967), *A Special Day* (1977), *Prêt-À-Porter* (1994), *Grumpier Old Men* (1995).

Lorre, Peter (Laszlo Lowenstein) (1904–64) Hungarian, born Rosenberg; *M* (1931), *Mad Love* (1935), *Crime and Punishment* (1935), *The Maltese Falcon* (1941), *Casablanca* (1942), *The Mask of Dimitrios* (1944), *Arsenic and Old Lace* (1944), *The Beast With Five Fingers* (1946), *My Favourite Brunette* (1947), *20 000 Leagues Under the Sea* (1954), *The Raven* (1963).

Lugosi, Bela (Bela Ferenc Denzso Blasko) (1882–1956) Hungarian–American, born Lugos (now Romania); *Dracula* (1930), *The Murders in the Rue Morgue* (1931), *White Zombie* (1932), *International House* (1933), *The Black Cat* (1934), *Son of Frankenstein* (1939), *Abbott and Costello Meet Frankenstein* (1948), *Plan 9 from Outer Space* (1956).

McGregor, Ewan (1971–   ) British, born Creiff; *Lipstick on Your Collar* (TV1993), *Scarlet and Black* (TV1993), *Shallow Grave* (1994), *Blue Juice* (1995), *The Pillow Book* (1995), *Emma* (1995), *Trainspotting* (1996), *Brassed Off* (1996), *The Serpent's Kiss* (1997), *A Life Less Ordinary* (1997).

MacLaine, Shirley (Shirley Beaty) (1934–   ) American, born Richmond, Virginia; *The Trouble with Harry* (1955), *Ask any Girl* (1959), *The Apartment* (1959), *Irma La Douce* (1963), *Sweet Charity* (1968), *Terms of Endearment* (1983), *Madame Sousatzka* (1988),

Postcards from the Edge (1990), *Defending Your Life* (1991), *Used People* (1992), *Guarding Tess* (1994), *The Evening Star* (1996).

McQueen, Steve (Terence Steven McQueen) (1930–80) American, born Slater, Missouri; *Wanted Dead or Alive* (TV 1958), *The Blob* (1958), *The Magnificent Seven* (1960), *The Great Escape* (1962), *Love with the Proper Stranger* (1963), *The Cincinnatti Kid* (1965), *Bullitt* (1968), *Le Mans* (1971), *Getaway* (1972), *Papillon* (1973), *The Towering Inferno* (1974), *An Enemy of the People* (1977).

Martin, Steve (1945–) American, born Waco, Texas; *Sgt Pepper's Lonely Hearts Club Band* (1978), *The Jerk* (1978), *Muppet Movie* (1979), *Pennies from Heaven* (1981), *Dead Men Don't Wear Plaid* (1982), *The Man With Two Brains* (1983), *The Lonely Guy* (1984), *All of Me* (1984), *The Three Amigos* (1986), *The Little Shop of Horrors* (1986), *Planes, Trains and Automobiles* (1987), *Roxanne* (1987), *Dirty, Rotten Scoundrels* (1989), *Parenthood* (1989), *My Blue Heaven* (1990), *LA Story* (1991), *Father of the Bride* (1991), *Grand Canyon* (1991), *Housesitter* (1992), *A Simple Twist of Faith* (1994), *Sgt Bilko* (1995).

Marvin, Lee (1924–87) American, born New York City; *The Wild One* (1954), *Attack* (1957), *The Killers* (1964), *Cat Ballou* (1965), *The Dirty Dozen* (1967), *Paint Your Wagon* (1969), *Gorky Park* (1983), *Dirty Dozen 2: The Next Mission* (TV 1985).

Marx Brothers, The: Chico (Leonard Marx) (1886–1961); Harpo (Adolph Marx) (1888–1964); Groucho (Julius Henry Marx) (1890–1977); Zeppo (Herbert Marx) (1901–79) all American, born New York City; (joint) *The Cocoanuts* (1929), *Monkey Business* (1931), *Horse Feathers* (1932), *Duck Soup* (1933), *A Night at the Opera* (1935), *A Day at the Races* (1937), *A Night in Casablanca* (1946).

Mason, James (1909–84) British, born Huddersfield; *I Met a Murderer* (1939), *The Night Has Eyes* (1942), *The Man in Grey* (1943), *Fanny by Gaslight* (1944), *The Seventh Veil* (1945), *The Wicked Lady* (1946), *Odd Man Out* (1946), *Pandora and the Flying Dutchman* (1951), *The Desert Fox* (1951), *Five Fingers* (1952), *The Prisoner of Zenda* (1952), *Julius Caesar* (1953), *20 000 Leagues Under the Sea* (1954), *A Star is Born* (1954), *Journey to the Center of the Earth* (1959), *Lolita* (1962), *The Pumpkin Eater* (1964), *Georgy Girl* (1966), *The Blue Max* (1966), *The Deadly Affair* (1967), *Voyage of the Damned* (1976), *Heaven Can Wait* (1978), *The Boys from Brazil* (1978), *Murder by Decree* (1979), *Evil Under the Sun* (1982), *The Verdict* (1982), *Yellowbeard* (1983), *The Shooting Party* (1984).

Mastroianni, Marcello (1924–96) Italian, born Fontana Liri, near Frosinone; *I Miserabili* (1947), *White Nights* (1957), *La Dolce Vita* (1959), *Divorce Italian Style* (1962), *Yesterday, Today and Tomorrow* (1963), $8\frac{1}{2}$ (1963), *Casanova* (1970), *Diamonds for Breakfast* (1968), *Ginger and Fred* (1985), *Black Eyes* (1987), *The Two Lives of Mattia Pascal* (1988), *Traffic Jam* (1988), *Used People* (1992), *Prêt-À-Porter* (1994), *Beyond the Clouds* (1996).

Matthau, Walter (Matuschanskavasky) (1920–2000) American, born New York City; *A Face in the Crowd* (1957), *King Creole* (1958), *Charade* (1963), *Mirage* (1965), *The Fortune Cookie* (1966), *A Guide to the Married Man* (1967), *The Odd Couple* (1968), *Hello Dolly* (1969), *Cactus Flower* (1969), *Kotch* (1971), *Earthquake* (1974), *The Taking of Pelham One Two Three* (1974), *Hopscotch* (1980), *Pirates* (1986), *The Couch Trip* (1988), *JFK* (1991), *Grumpy Old Men* (1993), *Grumpier Old Men* (1995), *Out to Sea* (1997).

Mature, Victor (1913–99) American, born Louisville, Kentucky; *One Million BC* (1940), *My Darling Clementine* (1946), *Kiss of Death* (1947), *Samson and Delilah* (1949), *The Robe* (1953), *The Egyptian* (1954), *Safari* (1956), *The Long Haul* (1957), *After the Fox* (1966).

Midler, Bette (1945–) American, born Honolulu, Hawaii; *The Rose* (1979), *Down and Out in Beverly Hills* (1986), *Ruthless People* (1986), *Outrageous Fortune* (1987), *Beaches* (1988), *Big Business* (1988), *Stella* (1989), *Scenes from a Mall* (1991), *For the Boys* (1991), *Hocus Pocus* (1993), *Gypsy* (1993), *Get Shorty* (1995), *The First Wives Club* (1996).

Mills, Hayley (1946–) British, born London; *Tiger Bay* (1959), *Pollyanna* (1960), *The Parent Trip* (1961), *Whistle Down the Wind* (1961), *The Moonspinners* (1965), *Forbush and the Penguins* (1971), *Deadly Strangers* (1974), *After Midnight* (1989).

Mills, Sir John (Lewis Ernest Watts) (1908–) British, born Felixstowe, Suffolk; *Those Were the Days* (1934), *Cottage to Let* (1941), *In Which We Serve* (1942), *Waterloo Road* (1944), *The Way to the Stars* (1945), *Great Expectations* (1946), *The October Man* (1947), *Scott of the Antarctic* (1948), *The History of Mr Polly* (1949), *The Rocking Horse Winner* (1950), *The Colditz Story* (1954), *Hobson's Choice* (1954), *Town on Trial* (1957), *Tiger Bay* (1959), *Swiss Family Robinson* (1959), *Tunes of Glory* (1960), *Ryan's Daughter* (1970), *Lady Caroline Lamb* (1972), *The Big Sleep* (1978), *The 39 Steps* (1978), *Quatermass* (TV 1979), *Young at Heart* (TV 1980–1), *Gandhi* (1982), *Sahara* (1983), *Who's That Girl?* (1987), *Hamlet* (1996).

Minnelli, Liza (1946–) American, born Los Angeles; *Cabaret* (1972), *New York New York* (1977), *Arthur* (1981), *Arthur 2: On the Rocks* (1988), *Rent-a-Cop* (1988), *Stepping Out* (1991).

Mitchum, Robert (1917–97) American, born Bridgeport, Connecticut; *The Story of G I Joe* (1945), *Pursued* (1947), *Crossfire* (1947), *Out of the Past* (1947), *The Big Steal* (1949), *Night of the Hunter* (1955), *Home from the Hill* (1960), *The Sundowners* (1960), *Cape Fear* (1962), *The List of Adrian Messenger* (1963), *Ryan's Daughter* (1970), *Farewell My Lovely* (1975), *The Big Sleep* (1978), *The Winds of War* (TV 1983), *War and Remembrance* (TV 1987), *Mr North* (1988), *Scrooged* (1988), *Cape Fear* (1991), *Tombstone* (1993), *Backfire* (1994).

Monroe, Marilyn (Norma Jean Mortenson or Baker) (1926–62) American, born Los Angeles; *How to Marry a Millionaire* (1953), *Gentlemen Prefer Blondes* (1953), *The Seven Year Itch* (1955), *Bus Stop* (1956), *Some Like It Hot* (1959), *The Misfits* (1960).

Montand, Yves (Ivo Levi) (1921–91) French, born Monsumagno, Italy; *The Wages of Fear* (1953), *Let's Make Love* (1962), *Jean de Florette* (1986), *Manon des Sources* (1986).

Moore, Demi (Demi Guines) (1962–) American, born Roswell, New Mexico; *St Elmo's Fire* (1986), *About Last Night* (1987), *The Seventh Sign* (1988), *We're No Angels* (1990), *Ghost* (1990), *The Butcher's Wife* (1991), *A Few Good Men* (1992), *Indecent Proposal* (1993), *Disclosure* (1994), *The Scarlet Letter* (1995), *Striptease* (1996), *G I Jane* (1997).

Moore, Roger (George) (1927–) British, born London; *Ivanhoe* (TV 1957), *The Saint* (TV 1963–8), *The Persuaders* (TV 1971–2), *Live and Let Die* (1973), *The Man with the Golden Gun* (1974), *Shout at the Devil* (1976), *The Spy Who Loved Me* (1977), *The Wild Geese* (1978), *Escape to Athena* (1979), *Moonraker* (1979), *For Your Eyes Only* (1981), *The Cannonball Run* (1981), *Octopussy* (1983), *A View to a Kill* (1985), *The Quest* (1996).

FILM AND TV ACTORS

Moreau, Jeanne (1928–) French, born Paris; *Les Amants* (1958), *Ascenseur Pour L'Échafaud* (1957), *Jules et Jim* (1961), *Eva* (1962), *The Trial* (1963), *Journal D'une Femme de Chambre* (1964), *Viva Maria* (1965), *Nikita* (1990), *La Vieille Qui Marchait Dans La Mer* (1991).

Murphy, Eddie (1961–) American, born Brooklyn, New York City; *48 Hours* (1982), *Trading Places* (1983), *Beverly Hills Cop* (1985), *The Golden Child* (1986), *Beverly Hills Cop II* (1987), *Coming to America* (1988), *Harlem Nights* (1989), *Another 48 Hours* (1990), *Boomerang* (1992), *Distinguished Gentleman* (1992), *Beverly Hills Cop III* (1994), *The Nutty Professor* (1995), *The Metro* (1997).

Neeson, Liam (1952–) British, born Ballymena, Northern Ireland; *Excalibur* (1981), *Suspect* (1987), *Satisfaction* (1988), *High Spirits* (1988), *The Good Mother* (1988), *The Dead Pool* (1988), *The Big Man* (1990), *Dark Man* (1990), *Husbands and Wives* (1992), *Schindler's List* (1994), *Nell* (1994), *Rob Roy* (1995), *Michael Collins* (1996).

Newman, Paul (1925–) American, born Cleveland, Ohio; *Somebody Up There Likes Me* (1956), *The Long Hot Summer* (1958), *The Hustler* (1961), *Hud* (1963), *The Prize* (1963), *Torn Curtain* (1966), *Cool Hand Luke* (1967), *Butch Cassidy and the Sundance Kid* (1969), *Judge Roy Bean* (1972), *The Sting* (1973), *Absence of Malice* (1981), *The Verdict* (1982), *The Color of Money* (1986), *Blaze* (1990), *Mr and Mrs Bridge* (1990), *The Hudsucker Proxy* (1994), *Nobody's Fool* (1994), *Magic Hour* (1997).

Nicholson, Jack (1937–) American, born Neptune, New Jersey; *The Little Shop of Horrors* (1960), *Easy Rider* (1969), *Five Easy Pieces* (1970), *Carnal Knowledge* (1971), *The Last Detail* (1974), *Chinatown* (1974), *One Flew Over the Cuckoo's Nest* (1975), *Tommy* (1975), *The Shining* (1980), *The Postman Always Rings Twice* (1981), *Reds* (1981), *Terms of Endearment* (1983), *Prizzi's Honor* (1985), *Broadcast News* (1987), *Ironweed* (1987), *The Witches of Eastwick* (1987), *Batman* (1989), *Two Jakes* (1990), *The Death of Napoleon* (1991), *Man Trouble* (1992), *A Few Good Men* (1992), *Hoffa* (1992), *Wolf* (1994), *The Crossing Guard* (1995), *Blood and Wine* (1996), *Mars Attacks!* (1996), *As Good as It Gets* (1997).

Niven, David (James David Graham Niven) (1910–83) British, born London; *Thank You Jeeves* (1936), *The Prisoner of Zenda* (1937), *Wuthering Heights* (1939), *Bachelor Mother* (1939), *Raffles* (1940), *The Way Ahead* (1944), *A Matter of Life and Death* (1946), *Carrington VC* (1955), *Around the World in Eighty Days* (1956), *Separate Tables* (1958), *The Guns of Navarone* (1961), *The Pink Panther* (1964), *Casino Royale* (1967), *Candleshoe* (1977), *Death on the Nile* (1978), *Escape to Athena* (1979), *Trail of the Pink Panther* (1982), *Curse of the Pink Panther* (1983).

Nolte, Nick (1940–) American, born Omaha, Nebraska; *Rich Man Poor Man* (TV 1976), *Cannery Row* (1982), *48 Hours* (1982), *Down and Out in Beverly Hills* (1986), *Weeds* (1987), *New York Stories* (1989), *Three Fugitives* (1989), *Another 48 Hours* (1990), *Cape Fear* (1991), *Prince of Tides* (1991), *The Player* (1992), *Lorenzo's Oil* (1992), *Blue Chips* (1993), *I'll Do Anything* (1994), *I Love Trouble* (1994), *Jefferson in Paris* (1995), *Nightwatch* (1996).

Oldman, Gary (1959–) British, born New Cross, South London; *Sid and Nancy* (1986), *Prick Up Your Ears* (1987), *We Think the World of You* (1988), *Track 29* (1988), *Rosencrantz and Guilderstern are Dead* (1990), *JFK* (1991), *Bram Stoker's Dracula* (1992), *True Romance* (1993), *Leon* (1994), *The Scarlet Letter* (1995), *The Fifth Element* (1996).

Olivier, Sir Laurence (Kerr) (1907–89) British, born Dorking; *The Divorce of Lady X* (1938), *Wuthering Heights* (1939), *Rebecca* (1940), *Pride and Prejudice* (1940), *Henry V* (1944), *Hamlet* (1948), *Richard III* (1956), *The Prince and the Showgirl* (1958), *The Devil's Disciple* (1959), *The Entertainer* (1960), *Sleuth* (1972), *Marathon Man* (1976), *A Bridge Too Far* (1977), *Brideshead Revisited* (TV 1981), *A Voyage Round My Father* (TV 1982), *The Last Days of Pompeii* (1984), *The Jigsaw Man* (1984), *The Bounty* (1984), *A Talent for Murder* (TV 1986), *War Requiem* (1988).

O'Toole, Peter (Seamus) (1932–) Irish, born Kerry, Connemara; *Lawrence of Arabia* (1962), *How to Steal a Million* (1966), *The Lion in Winter* (1968), *Goodbye Mr Chips* (1969), *The Ruling Class* (1972), *The Stunt Man* (1980), *My Favourite Year* (1982), *The Last Emperor* (1987), *High Spirits* (1988), *Wings of Fame* (1989), *Isabelle Eberhardt* (1990), *King Ralph* (1991), *World's Apart* (1992).

Pacino, Al (Alfredo Pacino) (1940–) American, born New York City; *The Godfather* (1972), *The Godfather, Part II* (1974), *Dog Day Afternoon* (1975), *Scarface* (1983), *Revolution* (1984), *Sea of Love* (1990), *Dick Tracy* (1990), *The Godfather, Part III* (1990), *Frankie and Johnny* (1991), *Glengarry Glen Ross* (1992), *Scent of a Woman* (1992), *Damon* (1992), *Carlito's Way* (1993), *Heat* (1995), *Donnie Brasco* (1997).

Peck, Gregory (Eldred) (1916–) American, born La Jolla, California; *The Keys to the Kingdom* (1944), *Spellbound* (1945), *Duel in the Sun* (1946), *Gentleman's Agreement* (1947), *The Macomber Affair* (1947), *The Paradine Case* (1947), *Twelve O'Clock High* (1949), *The Gunfighter* (1950), *Captain Horatio Hornblower* (1951), *The Million Pound Note* (1954), *The Purple Plain* (1955), *The Man in the Grey Flannel Suit* (1956), *The Big Country* (1958), *The Guns of Navarone* (1961), *Cape Fear* (1962), *To Kill a Mockingbird* (1963), *The Omen* (1976), *Old Gringo* (1989), *Other People's Money* (1991), *Cape Fear* (1991).

Penn, Sean (1960–) American, born Burbank, California; *Taps* (1981), *Fast Times at Ridgemont High* (1982), *Racing with the Moon* (1984), *The Falcon and the Snowman* (1985), *At Close Range* (1986), *Shanghai Surprise* (1986), *Colors* (1988), *Judgement in Berlin* (1988), *Casualties of War* (1989), *We're No Angels* (1989), *State of Grace* (1990), *Carlito's Way* (1993), *Dead Man Walking* (1995).

Pfeiffer, Michelle (1957–) American, born Santa Ana, California; *Grease 2* (1982), *Scarface* (1983), *Sweet Liberty* (1982), *Into the Night* (1985), *The Witches of Eastwick* (1987), *Dangerous Liaisons* (1988), *Tequila Sunrise* (1988), *Married to the Mob* (1989), *The Fabulous Baker Boys* (1989), *The Russia House* (1990), *Frankie and Johnny* (1991), *Batman Returns* (1992), *Age of Innocence* (1993), *My Posse Don't Do Homework* (1994), *Wolf* (1994), *Up Close and Personal* (1995).

Phoenix, River (1970–93) American, born Madras, Oregon; *Explorers* (1985), *Mosquito Coast* (1986), *Running on Empty* (1988), *Jimmy Reardon* (1988), *Little Nikita* (1988), *Indiana Jones and the Last Crusade* (1989), *I Love You to Death* (1990), *Dogfight* (1991), *My Own Private Idaho* (1991), *Sneakers* (1992), *The Thing Called Love* (1993).

Pickup, Ronald (Alfred) (1940–) British, born Chester; *Day of the Jackal* (1973), *The 39 Steps* (1978), *Nijinski* (1980), *Never Say Never Again* (1983), *Fortunes of War* (TV 1987), *Testimony* (1987).

Pitt, Brad (William Bradley Pitt) (1963–) American, born Shawnee, Oklahoma; *Thelma and Louise* (1991), *A River Runs Through It* (1992), *Kalifornia* (1993), *True Romance*

(1993), *Interview with the Vampire* (1994), *Legends of the Fall* (1994), *Seven* (1995), *Twelve Monkeys* (1995), *Sleepers* (1996), *Seven Years in Tibet* (1997).

Pleasence, Donald (1919–95) British, born Worksop; *Robin Hood* (TV 1955–7), *Battle of the Sexes* (1959), *Dr Crippen* (1962), *The Great Escape* (1963), *The Caretaker* (1964), *Cul-de-Sac* (1966), *Fantastic Voyage* (1966), *You Only Live Twice* (1967), *Escape to Witch Mountain* (1975), *The Eagle Has Landed* (1977), *Oh God* (1977), *Telefon* (1977), *Halloween* (1978), *Sgt Pepper's Lonely Hearts Club Band* (1978), *Escape from New York* (1981), *Halloween 4* (1988), *Hanna's War* (1988), *Ground Zero* (1988), *Halloween 5* (1989), *Ten Little Indians* (1989), *Shadows and Fog* (1992), *Halloween 6* (1995).

Price, Vincent (1911–93) American, born St Louis, Missouri; *Tower of London* (1940), *Dragonwyck* (1946), *His Kind of Woman* (1941), *House of Wax* (1953), *The Story of Mankind* (1957), *The Fly* (1958), *The Fall of the House of Usher* (1961), *The Raven* (1963), *The Tomb of Ligeia* (1964), *City Under the Sea* (1965), *House of a Thousand Dolls* (1967), *The House of Long Shadows* (1983), *The Whales of August* (1987), *Dead Heat* (1988), *Edward Scissorhands* (1991).

Quinn, Anthony (Rudolph Oaxaca) (1915–) Irish–American, born Chihuahua, Mexico; *Viva Zapata* (1952), *La Strada* (1954), *Lust for Life* (1956), *The Guns of Navarone* (1961), *Zorba the Greek* (1964), *The Shoes of the Fisherman* (1968), *Revenge* (1989), *Ghosts Can't Do It* (1990), *Jungle Fever* (1991), *Mobsters* (1991), *Last Action Hero* (1993), *A Walk in the Clouds* (1995).

Rathbone, Basil (Philip St John) (1892–1967) British, born Johannesburg, South Africa; *David Copperfield* (1935), *Anna Karenina* (1935), *Captain Blood* (1935), *Romeo and Juliet* (1936), *The Adventures of Robin Hood* (1938), *The Hound of the Baskervilles* (1939), *The Adventures of Sherlock Holmes* (1939), *Spider Woman* (1944), *Heartbeat* (1946), *The Court Jester* (1956).

Redford, (Charles) Robert (1937–) American, born Santa Monica, California; *Barefoot in the Park* (1967), *Butch Cassidy and the Sundance Kid* (1969), *The Candidate* (1972), *The Great Gatsby* (1973), *The Sting* (1973), *The Way We Were* (1973), *All the President's Men* (1976), *The Electric Horseman* (1979), *The Natural* (1984), *Out of Africa* (1985), *Legal Eagles* (1986), *Havana* (1990), *Sneakers* (1992), *Indecent Proposal* (1993), *Up Close and Personal* (1995), *The Horse Whisperer* (1998).

Redgrave, Sir Michael (Scudamore) (1908–85) British, born Bristol; *The Lady Vanishes* (1938), *The Way to the Stars* (1945), *The Browning Version* (1951), *The Importance of Being Earnest* (1952), *The Dam Busters* (1955), *The Quiet American* (1958), *The Innocents* (1961), *Nicholas and Alexandra* (1971).

Redgrave, Vanessa (1937–) British, born London; also stage; *Morgan!* (1965), *Blow-Up* (1966), *Camelot* (1967), *Mary, Queen of Scots* (1971), *Julia* (1977), *Playing for Time* (TV 1980), *The Bostonians* (1984), *Wetherby* (1985), *Three Sovereigns for Sarah* (TV 1985), *Prick Up Your Ears* (1987), *Consuming Passions* (1988), *The Ballad of The Sad Café* (1991), *What Ever Happened to Baby Jane?* (1991), *Howards End* (1992), *Little Odessa* (1994), *Mission: Impossible* (1996).

Reeve, Christopher (1952–) American, born New York City; *Superman* (1978), *Superman II* (1980), *Somewhere in Time* (1980), *Monsignor* (1982), *Death Trap* (1982), *Superman III* (1983), *The Bostonians* (1984), *Superman IV* (1987), *Switching Channels*

(1988), *Noises Off* (1992), *The Remains of the Day* (1993), *The Sea Wolf* (TV 1993), *Morning Glory* (1993), *Speechless* (1994), *Village of the Damned* (1995).

Reeves, Keanu (1964–   ) American, born Beirut, Lebanon; *River's Edge* (1986), *Prince of Pennsylvania* (1988), *The Night Before* (1988), *Dangerous Liaisons* (1988), *Permanent Record* (1988), *Bill and Ted's Excellent Adventure* (1989), *Parenthood* (1989), *Love You to Death* (1990), *Bill and Ted's Bogus Journey* (1991), *My Own Private Idaho* (1991), *Dracula* (1992), *Much Ado About Nothing* (1993), *Little Buddha* (1993), *Speed* (1994), *Even Cowgirls Get the Blues* (1994), *A Walk in the Clouds* (1995), *Feeling Minnesota* (1995), *Johnny Mnemonic* (1995).

Reynolds, Burt (1935–   ) American, born Waycross, Georgia; *Gunsmoke* (TV 1965–7), *Hunters are for Killing* (TV 1970), *Deliverance* (1972), *Nickelodeon* (1976), *Smokey and the Bandit* (1977), *Hooper* (1978), *Starting Over* (1979), *Smokey and the Bandit II* (1980), *The Cannonball Run* (1981), *Sharkey's Machine* (1981), *The Best Little Whorehouse in Texas* (1982), *Stroker Ace* (1983), *The Man Who Loved Women* (1983), *City Heat* (1984), *Rent-a-Cop* (1988), *Switching Channels* (1988), *Breaking In* (1989), *Evening Shade* (TV 1990–4), *Modern Love* (1990), *Cop-and-a-Half* (1992), *The Player* (1992), *The Maddening* (1995), *Striptease* (1996), *Trigger Happy* (1996).

Richardson, Sir Ralph (1902–83) British, born Cheltenham; *Bulldog Jack* (1935), *Q Planes* (1939), *The Four Feathers* (1939), *Anna Karenina* (1948), *The Fallen Idol* (1948), *The Heiress* (1949), *Richard III* (1956), *Oscar Wilde* (1960), *Long Day's Journey into Night* (1962), *Dr Zhivago* (1966), *The Wrong Box* (1967), *A Doll's House* (1973), *The Man in the Iron Mask* (1977), *Time Bandits* (1980), *Dragonslayer* (1981), *Greystoke* (1984).

Robbins, Tim (Timothy Francis) (1958–   ) American, born New York City; *Bull Durham* (1988), *Cadillac Man* (1990), *Jacob's Ladder* (1990), *The Player* (1992), *Bob Roberts* (1992), *Short Cuts* (1993), *The Hudsucker Proxy* (1994), *The Shawshank Redemption* (1994), *Nothing to Lose* (1996).

Roberts, Julia (1967–   ) American, born Smyrna, Georgia; *Mystic Pizza* (1988), *Steel Magnolias* (1989), *Flatliners* (1990), *Pretty Woman* (1990), *Sleeping with the Enemy* (1991), *Dying Young* (1991), *Hook* (1991), *The Player* (1992), *The Pelican Brief* (1993), *I Love Trouble* (1994), *Prêt-À-Porter* (1994), *Mary Reilly* (1995), *Michael Collins* (1996), *My Best Friend's Wedding* (1997).

Robinson, Edward G (Emanuel Goldenberg) (1893–1973) American, born Bucharest, Romania; *Little Caesar* (1930), *Five Star Final* (1931), *The Whole Town's Talking* (1935), *The Last Gangster* (1937), *A Slight Case of Murder* (1938), *The Amazing Dr Clitterhouse* (1938), *Dr Ehrlich's Magic Bullet* (1940), *Brother Orchid* (1940), *The Sea Wolf* (1941), *Double Indemnity* (1944), *The Woman in the Window* (1944), *Scarlet Street* (1945), *All My Sons* (1948), *Key Largo* (1948), *House of Strangers* (1949), *Two Weeks in Another Town* (1962), *The Cincinnati Kid* (1965), *Soylent Green* (1973).

Rogers, Ginger (Virginia Katherine McMath) (1911–95) American, born Independence, Missouri; *Young Man of Manhattan* (1930), *42nd Street* (1933), *Flying Down to Rio* (1933), *The Gay Divorcee* (1934), *Top Hat* (1935), *Follow the Fleet* (1936), *Stage Door* (1937), *Bachelor Mother* (1939), *Kitty Foyle* (1940), *Roxie Hart* (1942), *Lady in the Dark* (1944).

Rooney, Mickey (Joe Yule Jr) (1920–   ) American, born Brooklyn, New York City; *A Midsummer Night's Dream* (1935), *Ah Wilderness* (1935), *A Family Affair* (1937), *Judge*

Hardy's Children (1938), *Boys Town* (1938), *Babes in Arms* (1939), *The Human Comedy* (1943), *National Velvet* (1944), *Summer Holiday* (1948), *The Bold and the Brave* (1956), *Breakfast at Tiffany's* (1961), *It's a Mad, Mad, Mad, Mad World* (1963), *Leave 'Em Laughing* (TV 1980), *Bill* (TV 1981), *Erik the Viking* (1989), *Home for Christmas* (TV 1990), *The Toy Maker* (1991), *The Legend of Wolf Mountain* (1992), *That's Entertainment! III* (1994), *Heidi* (1996).

Rutherford, Dame Margaret (1892–1972) British, born London; *Blithe Spirit* (1945), *The Happiest Days of Your Life* (1950), *The Importance of Being Earnest* (1952), *The Smallest Show on Earth* (1957), *Murder She Said* (1961), *The VIPs* (1963), *Murder Most Foul* (1964), *Murder Ahoy* (1964).

Ryder, Winona (1971–) American, born Winona, Michigan; *Beetlejuice* (1988), *1969* (1988), *Heathers* (1989), *Great Balls of Fire* (1989), *Mermaids* (1990), *Night on Earth* (1992), *Dracula* (1992), *Age of Innocence* (1993), *Reality Bites* (1994), *Little Women* (1994), *How to Make an American Quilt* (1995), *The Crucible* (1996), *Alien: Resurrection* (1997).

Sarandon, Susan (Susan Abigail Tomalin) (1946–) American, born New York City; *The Front Page* (1974), *Dragonfly* (1977), *Atlantic City* (1981), *Tempest* (1982), *The Hunger* (1983), *The Witches of Eastwick* (1987), *Bull Durham* (1988), *A Dry White Season* (1989), *White Palace* (1991), *Thelma and Louise* (1991), *Light Sleeper* (1991), *Lorenzo's Oil* (1992), *The Client* (1994), *Little Women* (1995), *Dead Man Walking* (1995).

Schwarzenegger, Arnold (1947–) American, born Thal, near Graz, Austria; *Stay Hungry* (1976), *Pumping Iron* (1977), *Conan the Barbarian* (1982), *Conan the Destroyer* (1984), *The Terminator* (1984), *Red Sonja* (1985), *Commando* (1985), *Raw Deal* (1986), *Predator* (1987), *The Running Man* (1987), *Twins* (1988), *Red Heat* (1989), *Total Recall* (1990), *Kindergarten Cop* (1990), *Terminator 2: Judgement Day* (1991), *The Last Action Hero* (1993), *True Lies* (1994), *Junior* (1994), *Jingle All the Way* (1996), *Eraser* (1996), *Batman and Robin* (1997).

Scott, George C (1927–99) American, born Wise, Virginia; *Anatomy of a Murder* (1959), *The Hustler* (1962), *The List of Adrian Messenger* (1963), *Dr Strangelove* (1963), *Patton* (1970), *The Hospital* (1972), *Fear on Trial* (TV 1976), *The Changeling* (1980), *Taps* (1981), *Oliver Twist* (1982), *Firestarter* (1984), *A Christmas Carol* (TV 1984), *The Last Days of Patton* (TV 1986), *The Exorcist III* (1990), *Malice* (1993), *Family Rescue* (TV 1996).

Selleck, Tom (1945–) American, born Detroit, Michigan; *Coma* (1977), *Magnum* (TV 1981–9), *High Road to China* (1983), *Lassiter* (1984), *Runaway* (1984), *Three Men and a Baby* (1988), *Three Men and a Little Lady* (1990), *Tokyo Diamond* (1991), *Christopher Columbus: The Discovery* (1992), *Mr Baseball* (1992), *Open Season* (1994).

Sellers, Peter (1925–80) British, born Southsea; *The Smallest Show on Earth* (1957), *The Ladykillers* (1959), *I'm Alright Jack* (1959), *Only Two Can Play* (1962), *Lolita* (1962), *Dr Strangelove* (1963), *The Pink Panther* (1963), *A Shot in the Dark* (1964), *Return of the Pink Panther* (1975), *The Pink Panther Strikes Again* (1976), *Revenge of the Pink Panther* (1978), *Being There* (1979).

Shatner, William (1931–) Canadian, born Montreal, Quebec; *Star Trek* (TV 1966–8), *Horror at 37 000 Feet* (TV 1974), *Big Bad Mama* (1974), *Star Trek: The Motion Picture* (1979), *The Kidnapping of the President* (1980), *Star Trek II: The Wrath of Khan* (1982), *T J Hooker* (TV 1982–6), *Star Trek III: The Search for Spock* (1984), *Star Trek IV: The Voyage*

Home (1987), *Star Trek V: The Final Frontier* (1989), *Star Trek VI: The Undiscovered Country* (1991), *Star Trek Generations* (1994).

Sheen, Martin (Ramon Estevez) (1940–   ) American, born Dayton, Ohio; *Catch 22* (1970), *Badlands* (1973), *The Execution of Private Slovik* (TV 1974), *The Little Girl Who Lives Down the Lane* (1976), *Apocalypse Now* (1979), *Gandhi* (1982), *That Championship Season* (1982), *The Dead Zone* (1983), *Firestarter* (1984), *Wall Street* (1987), *Siesta* (1987), *Da* (1988), *Judgement in Berlin* (1988), *Stockade* (1990), *JFK* (1991), *Gettysburg* (1993), *Finnegan's Wake* (1993), *A Hundred and One Nights* (1994), *The American President* (1995).

Signoret, Simone (Simon-Henriette Charlotte Kaminker) (1921–85) French, born Wiesbaden, Germany; *La Ronde* (1950), *Casque d'Or* (1952), *Les Diaboliques* (1952), *Room at the Top* (1959), *Ship of Fools* (1965), *Le Chat* (1971), *Madame Rosa* (1973).

Sim, Alastair (1900–76) British, born Edinburgh; *Inspector Hornleigh* (1939), *Green for Danger* (1946), *The Happiest Days of Your Life* (1950), *Scrooge* (1951), *Laughter in Paradise* (1951), *The Bells of St Trinians* (1954).

Sinatra, Frank (Francis Albert Sinatra) (1915–98) American, born Hoboken, New Jersey; *Anchors Aweigh* (1945), *On the Town* (1949), *From Here to Eternity* (1953), *The Man With the Golden Gun* (1955), *Pal Joey* (1957), *The Manchurian Candidate* (1962), *The Detective* (1963).

Smith, Maggie (1934–   ) British, born Ilford, Essex; *The VIPs* (1963), *The Pumpkin Eater* (1964), *The Prime of Miss Jean Brodie* (1969), *Travels with My Aunt* (1972), *California Suite* (1978), *A Private Function* (1984), *A Room with a View* (1985), *The Lonely Passion of Judith Hearne* (1987), *Hook* (1991), *Sister Act* (1992), *The Secret Garden* (1993), *Sister Act 2: Back in the Habit* (1993), *Richard III* (1995), *The First Wives Club* (1996), *Washington Square* (1997).

Stallone, Sylvester (1946–   ) American, born New York City; *The Lords of Flatbush* (1973), *Rocky* (1976), *Paradise Alley* (1978), *Rocky II* (1979), *Victory* (1981), *Nighthawks* (1981), *First Blood* (1981), *Rocky III* (1981), *Rambo* (1985), *Rocky IV* (1985), *Rambo II* (1986), *Over the Top* (1987), *Rambo III* (1988), *Lock Up* (1989), *Tango and Cash* (1990), *Rocky V* (1990), *Oscar* (1991), *Stop, Or My Mom Will Shoot* (1992), *Bartholomew vs Neff* (1992), *Cliffhanger* (1992), *Demolition Man* (1993), *The Specialist* (1994), *Judge Dredd* (1995), *Daylight* (1996), *Copland* (1997).

Stanwyck, Barbara (Ruby Shaw) (1907–90) American, born Brooklyn, New York City; *Broadway Nights* (1927), *Miracle Woman* (1931), *Night Nurse* (1931), *The Bitter Tea of General Yen* (1933), *Baby Face* (1933), *Annie Oakley* (1935), *Stella Dallas* (1937), *Union Pacific* (1939), *The Lady Eve* (1941), *Meet John Doe* (1941), *Ball of Fire* (1941), *Double Indemnity* (1944), *The Strange Love of Martha Ivers* (1946), *Sorry Wrong Number* (1948), *The Furies* (1950), *Executive Suite* (1954), *Walk on the Wild Side* (1962), *The Big Valley* (TV 1965–9), *The Thorn Birds* (TV 1983).

Stewart, James (Maitland) (1908–97) American, born Indiana, Pennsylvania; *Seventh Heaven* (1937), *You Can't Take It With You* (1938), *Mr Smith Goes to Washington* (1939), *Destry Rides Again* (1939), *The Shop around the Corner* (1940), *The Philadelphia Story* (1940), *It's a Wonderful Life* (1946), *Harvey* (1950), *Broken Arrow* (1950), *The Glen Miller Story* (1953), *Rear Window* (1954), *The Man from Laramie* (1955), *Vertigo* (1958),

Anatomy of a Murder (1959), *Mr Hobbs Takes a Vacation* (1962), *Shenandoah* (1965), *The Big Sleep* (1978), *North and South II* (TV 1986).

Stone, Sharon (1964–) American, born Meadsville, Pennsylvania; *Deadly Blessing* (1981), *Action Jaction* (1987), *Total Recall* (1990), *He Said She Said* (1991), *Basic Instinct* (1992), *Diary of a Hitman* (1992), *Sliver* (1993), *Last Action Hero* (1993), *Intersection* (1994), *Casino* (1995), *Diabolique* (1996).

Streep, Meryl (Mary Louise Streep) (1949–) American, born Summit, New Jersey; *Julia* (1977), *The Deer Hunter* (1978), *Kramer vs Kramer* (1979), *Manhattan* (1979), *The French Lieutenant's Woman* (1981), *Sophie's Choice* (1982), *Still of the Night* (1982), *Silkwood* (1983), *Plenty* (1985), *Out of Africa* (1986), *Ironweed* (1987), *A Cry in the Dark* (1988), *Evil Angels* (1988), *She-Devil* (1989), *Postcards from the Edge* (1990), *Defending Your Life* (1991), *Death Becomes Her* (1992), *The River Wild* (1994), *The Bridges of Madison County* (1995).

Streisand, Barbra (Joan) (1942–) American, born Brooklyn, New York City; *Funny Girl* (1968), *Hello Dolly* (1969), *On a Clear Day You Can See Forever* (1970), *What's Up, Doc?* (1972), *The Way We Were* (1973), *A Star is Born* (1976), *Yentl* (1983), *Nuts* (1987), *Prince of Tides* (1991), *The Mirror Has Two Faces* (1996).

Sutherland, Donald (1934–) Canadian, born St John, New Brunswick; *The Dirty Dozen* (1967), *M*A*S*H* (1970), *Klute* (1971), *Casanova* (1976), *1900* (1976), *The Eagle Has Landed* (1977), *Animal House* (1978), *Invasion of the Body Snatchers* (1978), *Ordinary People* (1980), *Apprentice to Murder* (1988), *Lock Up* (1989), *A Dry White Season* (1989), *Backdraft* (1991), *Buffy the Vampire Slayer* (1992), *Benefit of the Doubt* (1993), *The Shadow Conspiracy* (1995), *The Poet* (1996).

Taylor, Dame Elizabeth (Rosemond) (1932–) British, born London; *National Velvet* (1944), *Little Women* (1949), *The Father of the Bride* (1950), *A Place in the Sun* (1951), *Giant* (1956), *Raintree Country* (1957), *Cat on a Hot Tin Roof* (1958), *Butterfield 8* (1960), *Cleopatra* (1962), *Who's Afraid of Virginia Woolf?* (1966), *Reflections in a Golden Eye* (1967), *The Taming of the Shrew* (1967), *Suddenly Last Summer* (1968), *A Little Night Music* (1977), *The Mirror Crack'd* (1981), *Malice in Wonderland* (TV 1985), *Poker Alice* (TV 1986), *Young Toscanini* (1988), *Sweet Bird of Youth* (TV 1989), *Faithful* (1992), *The Flintstones* (1994).

Temple, Shirley (1928–) American, born Santa Monica, California; *Little Miss Marker* (1934), *Curly Top* (1935), *Dimples* (1936), *Heidi* (1937), *The Little Princess* (1939).

Thompson, Emma (1959–) British, born Cambridge; *The Tall Guy* (1989), *Henry V* (1989), *Dead Again* (1989), *Impromptu* (1991), *Howards End* (1992), *Peter's Friends* (1992), *Much Ado About Nothing* (1993), *The Remains of the Day* (1993), *In the Name of the Father* (1993), *Junior* (1994), *My Father the Hero* (1994), *Carrington* (1995), *Sense and Sensibility* (1995), *The Well of Loneliness* (1997).

Tracy, Spencer (1900–67) American, born Milwaukee, Wisconsin; *Twenty Thousand Years in Sing Sing* (1932), *The Power and the Glory* (1933), *A Man's Castle* (1933), *Fury* (1936), *San Francisco* (1936), *Libeled Lady* (1936), *Captains Courageous* (1937), *Boys Town* (1938), *Stanley and Livingstone* (1939), *Northwest Passage* (1939), *Edison the Man* (1940), *Dr Jekyll and Mr Hyde* (1941), *Woman of the Year* (1942), *The Seventh Cross* (1944), *State of the Union* (1948), *Adam's Rib* (1949), *Father of the Bride* (1950), *Bad Day at Black Rock* (1955), *The Last Hurrah* (1958), *Inherit the Wind* (1960), *Judgement* at Nuremberg (1961), It's a Mad, Mad, Mad, Mad World (1963), Guess Who's Coming to Dinner? (1967).

Travolta, John (1954–) American, born Englewood, New Jersey; Welcome Back Kotter (TV 1975–8), Carrie (1976), Saturday Night Fever (1977), Grease (1978), Blow Out (1981), Staying Alive (1983), Two of a Kind (1984), Perfect (1985), Look Who's Talking (1989), Look Who's Talking Too (1991), Chains of Gold (1991), Pulp Fiction (1994), White Man's Burden (1995), Get Shorty (1995), Broken Arrow (1996), Phenomenon (1996), Michael (1996).

Turner, Kathleen (1954–) American, born Springfield, Missouri; The Doctors (TV 1977–8), Body Heat (1981), The Man With Two Brains (1983), Romancing the Stone (1984), Crimes of Passion (1984), The Jewel of the Nile (1985), Prizzi's Honor (1985), Peggy Sue Got Married (1986), Switching Channels (1988), Julia and Julia (1988), The Accidental Tourist (1989), War of the Roses (1989), V I Warshawski (1991), House of Cards (1992), Serial Mom (1994), Moonlight and Valentino (1995).

Ullmann, Liv (1939–) Norwegian, born Tokyo, Japan; Persona (1966), The Emigrants (1972), Face to Face (1975), Autumn Sonata (1978), Dangerous Moves (1983), Gaby — The True Story (1987), La Amiga (1988), The Rose Garden (1989), Mindwalk (1990), The Ox (1991), The Long Shadow (1992), Private Confessions (1996).

Ustinov, Peter (Alexander) (1921–) British, born London; Private Angelo (1949), Hotel Sahara (1951), Quo Vadis (1951), Beau Brummell (1954), The Sundowners (1960), Spartacus (1960), Romanoff and Juliet (1961), Topkapi (1964), Logan's Run (1976), Death on the Nile (1978), Evil Under the Sun (1982), Appointment with Death (1988), Lorenzo's Oil (1992), Stiff Upper Lips (1997).

Valentino, Rudolph (Rodolpho Alphonso Guglielmi di Valentina d'Antonguolla) (1895–1926) Italian–American, born Castellaneta, Italy; The Four Horsemen of the Apocalypse (1921), The Sheikh (1921), Blood and Sand (1922), The Young Rajah (1922), Monsieur Beaucaire (1924), The Eagle (1925), The Son of the Sheikh (1926).

Van Damme, Jean-Claude (1961–) Belgian, born Brussels; No Retreat No Surrender (1985), Kickboxer (1989), Universal Soldier (1992), Nowhere to Run (1993), Last Action Hero (1993), Timecop (1993), Streetfighter (1994), The Quest (1996).

von Sydow, Max (Carl Adolf) (1929–) Swedish, born Lund; The Seventh Seal (1956), The Face (1959), The Greatest Story Ever Told (1965), Hawaii (1966), Through a Glass Darkly (1966), Hour of the Wolf (1967), The Shame (1968), The Emigrants (1972), The Exorcist (1973), Exorcist II: The Heretic (1977), Flash Gordon (1980), Never Say Never Again (1983), Hannah and Her Sisters (1986), Pelle, the Conquerer (1988), Awakenings (1990), Dr Grassler (1990), The Father (1990), The Ox (1991), The Touch (1991), Needful Things (1993), Judge Dredd (1995).

Walken, Christopher (1943–) American, born Astoria, New York; The Anderson Tapes (1970), Annie Hall (1977), The Deer Hunter (1978), The Dogs of War (1981), Pennies from Heaven (1981), The Dead Zone (1983), Brainstorm (1983), A View to a Kill (1984), At Close Range (1986), The Milagro Beanfield War (1987), Biloxi Blues (1988), Puss in Boots (1988), The Comfort of Strangers (1990), Batman Returns (1992), True Romance (1993), Wayne's World 2 (1993), Pulp Fiction (1994), Things to Do in Denver When You're Dead (1995), Darkening (1996).

Washington, Denzel (1954–) American, born Mt Vernon, New York; *St Elsewhere* (TV 1982–9), *Cry Freedom* (1987), *Queen and Country* (1988), *Glory* (1989), *Mo' Better Blues* (1990), *Mississippi Masala* (1991), *Ricochet* (1991), *Malcolm X* (1992), *Philadelphia* (1993), *The Pelican Brief* (1993), *Much Ado About Nothing* (1993), *Devil in a Blue Dress* (1995), *Crimson Tide* (1995), *Courage Under Fire* (1996), *The Preacher's Wife* (1996), *He Got Game* (1998).

Wayne, John (Marion Michael Morrison) (1907–79) American, born Winterset, Iowa; *The Big Trail* (1930), *Stagecoach* (1939), *The Long Voyage Home* (1940), *Red River* (1948), *She Wore a Yellow Ribbon* (1949), *Sands of Iwo Jima* (1949), *The Quiet Man* (1952), *The High and the Mighty* (1954), *The Searchers* (1956), *Rio Bravo* (1959), *The Alamo* (1960), *True Grit* (1969), *The Shootist* (1976).

Welles, Orson (1915–85) American, born Kenosha, Wisconsin; *Citizen Kane* (1941), *Journey into Fear* (1942), *The Stranger* (1945), *The Lady from Shanghai* (1947), *The Third Man* (1949), *The Trial* (1962), *Touch of Evil* (1965), *A Man For All Seasons* (1966), *Casino Royale* (1967), *Voyage of the Damned* (1976), *History of the World Part One* (1981).

West, Mae (1892–1980) American, born Brooklyn, New York City; *She Done Him Wrong* (1933), *I'm No Angel* (1933), *My Little Chickadee* (1939), *Myra Breckenridge* (1970).

Williams, Robin (1952–) American, born Chicago; *Mork and Mindy* (TV 1978–82), *Popeye* (1980), *The World According to Garp* (1982), *Good Morning Vietnam* (1987), *Dead Poets Society* (1989), *Cadillac Man* (1990), *Awakenings* (1990), *Dead Again* (1991), *The Fisher King* (1991), *Hook* (1991), *Toys* (1992), *Ferngully* (1992), *Being Human* (1992), *Mrs Doubtfire* (1993), *Jumanji* (1995), *Hamlet* (1996), *Father's Day* (1997), *Good Will Hunting* (1997).

Willis, Bruce (1955–) American, born Penns Grove, New Jersey; *Moonlighting* (TV 1985–9), *Blind Date* (1987), *Die Hard* (1988), *Sunset* (1988), *In Country* (1989), *Die Hard 2: Die Harder* (1990), *Bonfire of the Vanities* (1990), *Hudson Hawk* (1991), *Billy Bathgate* (1991), *The Last Boy Scout* (1991), *Death Becomes Her* (1992), *Striking Distance* (1993), *Pulp Fiction* (1994), *Nobody's Fool* (1994), *Die Hard with a Vengeance* (1995), *Twelve Monkeys* (1995), *The Fifth Element* (1996), *The Jackal* (1997).

Wood, Natalie (Natasha Gurdin) (1938–81) American, born San Francisco, California; *Miracle on 34th Street* (1947), *The Ghost and Mrs Muir* (1947), *Rebel Without a Cause* (1955), *The Searchers* (1956), *Marjorie Morningstar* (1958), *All The Fine Young Cannibals* (1959), *Splendor in the Grass* (1961), *West Side Story* (1961), *Love with the Proper Stranger* (1964), *The Great Race* (1965), *This Property is Condemned* (1966), *Bob and Carol and Ted and Alice* (1969), *From Here to Eternity* (TV 1979), *Meteor* (1979), *Brainstorm* (1983).

Woodward, Joanne (1930–) American, born Thomasville, Georgia; *Three Faces of Eve* (1957), *No Down Payment* (1957), *The Long Hot Summer* (1958), *The Stripper* (1963), *A Big Hand for the Little Lady* (1966), *Rachel, Rachel* (1968), *Summer Wishes, Winter Dreams* (1973), *The Glass Menagerie* (1987), *Mr and Mrs Bridge* (1990), *Philadelphia* (1993), *Breathing Lessons* (TV 1994).

Film directors

Selected films are listed.

Aldrich, Robert (1918–83) American, born Cranston, Rhode Island; *Apache* (1954), *Vera Cruz* (1954), *Kiss Me Deadly* (1955), *Attack!* (1957), *What Ever Happened to Baby Jane?* (1962), *The Dirty Dozen* (1967).

Allen, Woody (Allen Stewart Konigsberg) (1935–) American, born Brooklyn, New York City; *What's Up Tiger Lily?* (1966), *Bananas* (1971), *Everything You Wanted to Know About Sex, But Were Afraid to Ask* (1972), *Play it Again, Sam* (1972), *Sleeper* (1973), *Love and Death* (1975), *Annie Hall* (1977), *Interiors* (1978), *Manhattan* (1979), *Stardust Memories* (1980), *A Midsummer Night's Sex Comedy* (1982), *Broadway Danny Rose* (1984), *The Purple Rose of Cairo* (1985), *Hannah and Her Sisters* (1986), *Radio Days* (1987), *Crimes and Misdemeanors* (1990), *Alice* (1991), *Shadows and Fog* (1992), *Husbands and Wives* (1992), *Manhattan Murder Mystery* (1993), *Bullets Over Broadway* (1994), *Mighty Aphrodite* (1996), *Anna Oz* (1996), *Deconstructing Harry* (1997).

Almodóvar, Pedro (1951–) Spanish, born Calzada de Calatrava; *Dark Habits* (1983), *Law of Desire* (1987), *Women on the Verge of a Nervous Breakdown* (1988), *Tie Me Up! Tie Me Down!* (1990), *High Heels* (1991), *Kika* (1993), *Live Flesh* (1998).

Altman, Robert (1925–) American, born Kansas City, Missouri; *The James Dean Story* (1957), *M*A*S*H* (1970), *McCabe and Mrs Miller* (1971), *The Long Goodbye* (1973), *Nashville* (1975), *A Wedding* (1978), *Popeye* (1980), *Come Back to the 5 & Dime Jimmy Dean Jimmy Dean* (1982), *Streamers* (1983), *Fool for Love* (1985), *Aria* (1987), *Vincent and Theo* (1990), *The Player* (1992), *Short Cuts* (1993), *Prêt-À-Porter* (1994), *Kansas City* (1996).

Antonioni, Michelangelo (1912–) Italian, born Ferrara; *L'Avventura* (1959), *La Notte* (1960), *L'Eclisse* (1962), *Blow-Up* (1966), *The Passenger* (1975).

Attenborough, Richard Samuel Attenborough, Baron (1923–) British, born Cambridge; *Oh! What a Lovely War* (1968), *A Bridge Too Far* (1977), *Gandhi* (1982), *A Chorus Line* (1985), *Cry Freedom* (1987), *Chaplin* (1992), *Shadowlands* (1993), *In Love and War* (1996).

Bergman, (Ernst) Ingmar (1918–) Swedish, born Uppsala; *Crisis* (1945), *Prison* (1948), *Sawdust and Tinsel* (1953), *The Face* (1955), *Smiles of a Summer Night* (1955), *The Seventh Seal* (1957), *Wild Strawberries* (1957), *The Virgin Spring* (1959), *Through a Glass Darkly* (1961), *The Silence* (1963), *Shame* (1968), *Cries and Whispers* (1972), *The Magic Flute* (1974), *Autumn Sonata* (1978), *Fanny and Alexander* (1983).

Bertolucci, Bernardo (1940–) Italian, born Parma; *Love and Anger* (1969), *The Conformist* (1970), *Last Tango in Paris* (1972), *1900* (1976), *The Last Emperor* (1987), *The Sheltering Sky* (1990), *Little Buddha* (1993).

Besson, Luc (1959–) French, born Paris; *The Last Battle* (1983), *Subway* (1985), *The Big Blue* (1988), *Nikita* (1990), *Leon* (1994), *The Fifth Element* (1997).

Bogdanovich, Peter (1939–) American, born Kingston, New York; *Targets* (1967), *The Last Picture Show* (1971), *Paper Moon* (1973), *What's Up, Doc?* (1972), *Nickelodeon* (1976), *Mask* (1985), *Illegally Yours* (1987), *Texasville* (1990), *Noises Off* (1992), *The Thing Called Love* (1993).

Boorman, John (1933–) English, born Epsom, Surrey; *Point Blank* (1967), *Hell in the Pacific* (1969), *Deliverance* (1972), *Zardoz* (1974), *Exorcist II: The Heretic* (1977), *Excalibur* (1981), *The Emerald Forest* (1984), *Hope and Glory* (1987), *Where the Heart Is* (1990), *Beyond Rangoon* (1995).

Bresson, Robert (1901–99) French, born Bromon-Lamothe; *Les Dames du Bois de Boulogne* (1946), *Journal du Cure de Campagne* (1950), *Pickpocket* (1959), *Au hasard Balthazar* (1966), *Une Femme douce* (1969), *L'Argent* (1983).

Brooks, Mel (Melvin Kaminski) (1926–) American, born Brooklyn, New York City; *The Producers* (1966), *Blazing Saddles* (1974), *Young Frankenstein* (1974), *High Anxiety* (1978), *History of the World Part One* (1981), *Spaceballs* (1987), *Life Stinks* (1991), *Robin Hood: Men in Tights* (1993), *Dracula: Dead and Loving It* (1995).

Buñuel, Luis (1900–83) Spanish, born Calanda; *Un Chien Andalou* (with Salvador Dali) (1928), *L'Âge d'Or* (1930), *Los Olvidados* (1950), *Robinson Crusoe* (1952), *El* (1953), *Nazarin* (1958), *Viridiana* (1961), *The Exterminating Angel* (1962), *Belle de Jour* (1967), *The Discreet Charm of the Bourgeoisie* (1972), *The Phantom of the Liberty* (1974), *That Obscure Object of Desire* (1977).

Burton, Tim (1958–) American, born Burbank, California; *Peewee's Big Adventure* (1985), *Beetlejuice* (1988), *Batman* (1989), *Edward Scissorhands* (1990), *Batman Returns* (1992), *Ed Wood* (1994), *Mars Attacks!* (1996).

Capra, Frank (1897–1991) Italian–American, born Bisacquino, Sicily; *Platinum Blonde* (1932), *American Madness* (1932), *Lady for a Day* (1933), *It Happened One Night* (1934), *Mr Deeds Goes to Town* (1936), *Lost Horizon* (1937), *You Can't Take It with You* (1938), *Mr Smith Goes to Washington* (1939), *Meet John Doe* (1941), *Arsenic and Old Lace* (1944), *It's a Wonderful Life* (1946).

Carpenter, John (1948–) American, born Carthage, New York; *Dark Star* (1974), *Assault on Precinct 13* (1976), *Halloween* (1978), *Elvis — the Movie* (TV 1979), *The Fog* (1979), *Escape from New York* (1981), *The Thing* (1982), *Christine* (1983), *Starman* (1984), *Big Trouble in Little China* (1986), *Prince of Darkness* (1987), *Memoirs of an Invisible Man* (1992), *Escape From LA* (1996).

Carné, Marcel (1909–96) French, born Batignolles, Paris; *Quai des Brumes* (1938), *Le Jour se lève* (1939), *Les Enfants du Paradis* (1944).

Clair, René (René Lucien Chomette) (1891–1981) French, born Paris; *An Italian Straw Hat* (1927), *Sous Les Toits de Paris* (1929), *Le Million* (1931), *À Nous la liberté* (1931), *I Married a Witch* (1942), *It Happened Tomorrow* (1944), *And Then There Were None* (1945), *Les Belles de Nuit* (1952), *Porte des Lila* (1956), *Tout l'or du Monde* (1961).

Cocteau, Jean (1889–1963) French, born Maisons-Lafitte; *Le Sang d'un poète* (1930), *La Belle et La Bête* (1946), *Orphée* (1950), *Le Testament d'Orphée* (1959).

Cohen, Ethan (1958–) and **Joel** (1955–) American, both born St Louis Park, Minnesota; *Blood Simple* (1984), *Raising Arizona* (1987), *Miller's Crossing* (1990), *Barton Fink* (1991), *The Hudsucker Proxy* (1994), *Fargo* (1995).

Coppola, Francis Ford (1939–) American, born Detroit, Michigan; *The Godfather* (1972), *The Godfather, Part II* (1974), *Apocalypse Now* (1979), *One from the Heart* (1982), *The Outsiders* (1983), *Rumble Fish* (1983), *The Cotton Club* (1984), *Peggy Sue Got Married* (1987), *Gardens of Stone* (1987), *Tucker: The Man and His Dream* (1988), *The Godfather, Part III* (1991), *Dracula* (1992).

Corman, Roger (1926–) American, born Detroit, Michigan; *Not of This Earth* (1957), *Bucket of Blood* (1960), *Fall of the House of Usher* (1960), *The Little Shop of Horrors* (1960), *The Intruder* (1961), *The Raven* (1963), *The Man with the X-ray Eyes* (1963), *The Masque of the Red Death* (1964), *The Tomb of Ligeia* (1965), *Frankenstein Unbound* (1990), *The Pit and the Pendulum* (1990).

Cronenberg, David (1943–) Canadian, born Toronto, Ontario; *Shivers* (1976), *Rabid* (1977), *The Brood* (1978), *Scanners* (1980), *Videodrome* (1983), *The Dead Zone* (1983), *The Fly* (1985), *Dead Ringers* (1988), *Naked Lunch* (1991), *M Butterfly* (1992), *Crash* (1996).

Curtiz, Michael (Mihály Kertész) (1888–1962) American–Hungarian, born Budapest, Hungary; *Noah's Ark* (1929), *Mammy* (1930), *Doctor X* (1932), *The Mystery of the Wax Museum* (1933), *British Agent* (1934), *Black Fury* (1935), *Captain Blood* (1935), *Charge of the Light Brigade* (1936), *The Adventures of Robin Hood* (1938), *Angels with Dirty Faces* (1938), *The Sea Hawk* (1940), *The Sea Wolf* (1941), *Yankee Doodle Dandy* (1942), *Casablanca* (1943), *Mildred Pierce* (1945), *White Christmas* (1954), *We're No Angels* (1955), *King Creole* (1958).

de Mille, Cecil B(lount) (1881–1959) American, born Ashfield, Massachusetts; *Male and Female* (1919), *King of Kings* (1927), *The Ten Commandments* (1923 & 1956), *The Greatest Show on Earth* (1952).

Demme, Jonathan (1944–) American, born Long Island, New York; *Citizen Band* (1977), *Swing Shift* (1984), *Something Wild* (1987), *Swimming to Cambodia* (1987), *Married to the Mob* (1988), *The Silence of the Lambs* (1991), *Philadelphia* (1993).

de Palma, Brian (1940–) American, born Newark, New Jersey; *Greetings* (1968), *Carrie* (1976), *The Fury* (1978), *Dressed to Kill* (1980), *Blow Out* (1981), *Scarface* (1983), *Body Double* (1984), *The Untouchables* (1987), *Casualties of War* (1989), *Bonfire of the Vanities* (1990), *Carlito's Way* (1993), *Mission: Impossible* (1996).

Donner, Richard (1930–) American; *The Omen* (1976), *Superman* (1978), *Inside Moves* (1980), *The Final Conflict* (1981), *The Toy* (1982), *Ladyhawke* (1984), *The Goonies* (1985), *Lethal Weapon* (1987), *Scrooged* (1988), *Lethal Weapon 2* (1989), *Lethal Weapon 3* (1992), *Maverick* (1994).

Eastwood, Clint (1930–) American, born San Francisco, California; *Play Misty for Me* (1971), *The Outlaw Josey Wales* (1976), *Pale Rider* (1985), *Birdy* (1988), *Unforgiven* (1992), *The Bridges of Madison County* (1995).

Edwards, Blake (William Blake McEdwards) (1922–) American, born Tulsa, Oklahoma; *Operation Petticoat* (1959), *Breakfast at Tiffany's* (1961), *Days of Wine and Roses* (1962), *The Pink Panther* (1964), *The Great Race* (1965), '*10*' (1979), *Victor/Victoria* (1982).

Eisenstein, Sergei Mikhailovich (1898–1948) Russian, born Riga; *Stride* (1924), *Battleship Potemkin* (1925), *Alexander Nevsky* (1938), *Ten Days that Shook the World* (1928), *The Magic Seed* (1941), *Ivan the Terrible* (1942–6).

Fassbinder, Rainer Werner (1946–82) German, born Bad Wörishofen; *Warnung von einer heiligen Nutte* (1971), *Satan's Brew* (1976).

Fellini, Federico (1920–93) Italian, born Rimini; *I Vitelloni* (1953), *La Strada* (1954), *La Dolce Vita* (1960), *8½* (1963), *Satyricon* (1969), *Fellini's Rome* (1972), *Casanova* (1976),

Orchestra Rehearsal (1979), *City of Women* (1981), *The Ship Sails On* (1983), *Ginger and Fred* (1986).

Fleming, Victor (1883–1949) American, born Pasadena, California; *Mantrap* (1926), *The Virginian* (1929), *The Wet Parade* (1932), *Red Dust* (1932), *Treasure Island* (1934), *Test Pilot* (1938), *Gone with the Wind* (1939), *The Wizard of Oz* (1939), *Dr Jekyll and Mr Hyde* (1941), *A Guy Named Joe* (1943).

Ford, John (1895–73) American, born Cape Elizabeth, Maine; *The Tornado* (1917), *The Iron Horse* (1924), *Arrowsmith* (1931), *The Informer* (1935), *Stagecoach* (1939), *Young Mr Lincoln* (1939), *The Grapes of Wrath* (1940), *My Darling Clementine* (1946), *The Quiet Man* (1952), *The Searchers* (1956), *The Man Who Shot Liberty Valance* (1962).

Forman, Miloš (1932–) Czech, born Kaslov; *The Fireman's Ball* (1967), *Taking Off* (1971), *One Flew Over the Cuckoo's Nest* (1975), *Amadeus* (1984), *The People vs Larry Flynt* (1996).

Forsyth, Bill (William David) (1946–) British, born Whiteinch, Glasgow; *That Sinking Feeling* (1979), *Gregory's Girl* (1980), *Local Hero* (1983), *Housekeeping* (1987), *Being Human* (1994).

Frears, Stephen (1941–) British, born Leicester; *Gumshoe* (1971), *The Hit* (1984), *My Beautiful Laundrette* (1985), *Prick Up Your Ears* (1987), *Sammy and Rosie Get Laid* (1987), *Dangerous Liaisons* (1988), *The Grifters* (1990), *The Snapper* (1993), *Mary Reilly* (1995).

Friedkin, William (1939–) American, born Chicago; *The French Connection* (1971), *The Exorcist* (1973), *The Guardian* (1990).

Gilliam, Terry (1940–) American, born Minneapolis, Minnesota; *Jabberwocky* (1977), *Time Bandits* (1980), *Brazil* (1985), *The Adventures of Baron Munchausen* (1988), *The Fisher King* (1991), *Twelve Monkeys* (1995).

Godard, Jean-Luc (1930–) French, born Paris; *À Bout de Souffle* (1960), *Alphaville* (1965), *Le Plus Vieux Métier du Monde* (1967), *Sauve Qui Peut La Vie* (1980), *Hail Mary* (1985), *Nouvelle Vague* (1990).

Greenaway, Peter (1942–) British, born London; *The Draughtman's Contract* (1982), *The Belly of an Architect* (1987), *Drowning by Numbers* (1988), *The Cook, The Thief, His Wife and Her Lover* (1989), *Prospero's Books* (1991), *The Baby of Macon* (1993), *The Pillow Book* (1995).

Griffith, D(avid) W(ark) (1875–1948) American, born La Grange, Kentucky; *Judith of Bethulia* (1913), *The Birth of a Nation* (1915), *Intolerance* (1916), *Hearts of the World* (1918), *Broken Blossoms* (1919), *Orphans of the Storm* (1922).

Hawks, Howard Winchester (1896–1977) American, born Goshen, Indiana; *The Dawn Patrol* (1930), *Scarface* (1932), *Twentieth Century* (1934), *Barbary Coast* (1935), *Bringing Up Baby* (1938), *His Girl Friday* (1940), *To Have and Have Not* (1944), *The Big Sleep* (1946), *Red River* (1948), *Gentlemen Prefer Blondes* (1953), *Rio Bravo* (1959).

Hill, George Roy (1921–) American, born Minneapolis, Minnesota; *The World of Henry Orient* (1964), *Thoroughly Modern Millie* (1967), *Butch Cassidy and the Sundance Kid* (1969), *Slaughterhouse 5* (1972), *The Sting* (1973), *The World According to Garp* (1982).

Hitchcock, Sir Alfred Joseph (1899–1980) British, born Leytonstone, London; *The Lodger* (1926), *Blackmail* (1929), *Murder* (1930), *The Thirty-Nine Steps* (1935), *The Lady Vanishes* (1938), *Rebecca* (1940), *Lifeboat* (1944), *Spellbound* (1945), *Notorious* (1946), *The Paradine Case* (1947), *Strangers on a Train* (1951), *Dial M for Murder* (1955), *Vertigo* (1958), *North by Northwest* (1959), *Psycho* (1960), *The Birds* (1963), *Marnie* (1964), *Frenzy* (1972), *Alfred Hitchcock Presents* (TV 1955–61).

Huston, John Marcellus (1906–87) Irish–American, born Nevada, Missouri; *Murders in the Rue Morgue* (1932), *Juarez* (1939), *High Sierra* (1941), *The Maltese Falcon* (1941), *Key Largo* (1948), *The Treasure of the Sierra Madre* (1948), *The Asphalt Jungle* (1950), *The African Queen* (1951), *Moulin Rouge* (1952), *The Misfits* (1960), *Freud* (1962), *Night of the Iguana* (1964), *Casino Royale* (1967), *Fat City* (1972), *The Man Who Would Be King* (1975), *Annie* (1982), *Prizzi's Honor* (1985), *The Dead* (1987).

Ivory, James Francis (1928–) American, born Berkeley, California; *Shakespeare Wallah* (1965), *Heat and Dust* (1982), *The Bostonians* (1984), *A Room with a View* (1985), *Maurice* (1987), *Mr and Mrs Bridge* (1990), *Howards End* (1992), *The Remains of the Day* (1993), *Jefferson in Paris* (1995), *Surviving Picasso* (1996).

Jarman, (Michael) Derek (1942–94) British, born Northwood, Middlesex; *Sebastiane* (1976), *Jubilee* (1977), *The Tempest* (1979), *Caravaggio* (1985), *The Last of England* (1987), *The Garden* (1990), *Edward II* (1991), *Wittgenstein* (1993).

Jarmusch, Jim (1953–) American, born Akron, Ohio; *Stranger than Paradise* (1984), *Down by Law* (1986), *Mystery Train* (1989), *Night on Earth* (1992).

Jordan, Neil (1950–) Irish, born Sligo; *Angel* (1982), *The Company of Wolves* (1984), *Mona Lisa* (1986), *High Spirits* (1988), *The Crying Game* (1992), *Interview with the Vampire* (1994), *Michael Collins* (1996), *The Butcher Boy* (1997).

Kasdan, Lawrence (1949–) American, born Miami Beach, Florida; *Body Heat* (1981), *The Big Chill* (1983), *Silverado* (1985), *The Accidental Tourist* (1989), *Love You to Death* (1990), *Grand Canyon* (1991), *Wyatt Earp* (1994), *French Kiss* (1995).

Kaufman, Philip (1936–) American, born Chicago; *Invasion of the Body Snatchers* (1978), *The Wanderers* (1979), *The Right Stuff* (1983), *The Unbearable Lightness of Being* (1988), *Henry and June* (1990).

Kazan, Elia (Elia Kazanjoglou) (1909–) American, born Istanbul, Turkey; *Boomerang* (1947), *Gentleman's Agreement* (1947), *Pink* (1949), *A Streetcar Named Desire* (1951), *Viva Zapata* (1952), *On the Waterfront* (1954), *East of Eden* (1955), *Baby Doll* (1956), *A Face in the Crowd* (1957), *Splendor in the Grass* (1962), *America, America* (1963), *The Arrangement* (1969), *The Visitors* (1972), *The Last Tycoon* (1976).

Kieslowski, Krzystof (1941–96) Polish, born Warsaw; *The Scar* (1976), *Camera Buff* (1979), *No End* (1984), *A Short Film About Killing* (1988), *The Double Life of Veronique* (1991), *Three Colours: Blue* (1993), *White* (1993), *Red* (1994).

Kubrick, Stanley (1928–99) American, born The Bronx, New York City; *The Killing* (1956), *Paths of Glory* (1958), *Spartacus* (1960), *Lolita* (1962), *Dr Strangelove* (1964), *2001: A Space Odyssey* (1968), *A Clockwork Orange* (1971), *Barry Lyndon* (1975), *The Shining* (1980), *Full Metal Jacket* (1987).

Kurosawa, Akira (1910–98) Japanese, born Tokyo; *Rashomon* (1950), *The Idiot* (1951), *Living* (1952), *Seven Samurai* (1954), *Throne of Blood* (1957), *The Lower Depths*

(1957), *The Hidden Fortress* (1958), *Dersu Uzala* (1975), *The Shadow Warrior* (1981), *Ran* (1985), *Dreams* (1990), *Rhapsody in August* (1991).

Landis, John (1950–) American, born Chicago; *Schlock* (1971), *Kentucky Fried Movie* (1977), *Animal House* (1978), *The Blues Brothers* (1980), *An American Werewolf in London* (1981), *Twilight Zone* (1983), *Trading Places* (1983), *Into the Night* (1985), *Spies Like Us* (1985), *The Three Amigos* (1986), *Coming to America* (1988), *Oscar* (1991), *Innocent Blood* (1992), *Beverly Hills Cop III* (1994).

Lang, Fritz (1890–1976) German, born Vienna, Austria; *Destiny* (1921), *Dr Mabuse the Gambler* (1922), *Siegfried* (1923), *Metropolis* (1926), *Spies* (1927), *M* (1931), *The Testament of Dr Mabuse* (1932), *You Only Live Once* (1937), *The Return of Frank James* (1940), *The Woman in the Window* (1944), *The Big Heat* (1953), *Beyond a Reasonable Doubt* (1956), *While the City Sleeps* (1955).

Lean, Sir David (1908–91) English, born Croydon; *Pygmalion* (1938), *In Which We Serve* (1942), *Blithe Spirit* (1945), *Brief Encounter* (1946), *Great Expectations* (1946), *The Sound Barrier* (1952), *Hobson's Choice* (1954), *Summer Madness* (1955), *Bridge on the River Kwai* (1957), *Lawrence of Arabia* (1962), *Doctor Zhivago* (1965), *Ryan's Daughter* (1970), *A Passage to India* (1984).

Lee, Spike (Shelton Jackson Lee) (1957–) American, born Atlanta, Georgia; *She's Gotta Have It* (1986), *School Daze* (1988), *Do the Right Thing* (1989), *Mo' Better Blues* (1990), *Jungle Fever* (1991), *Malcolm X* (1992), *Crooklyn* (1994), *Clockers* (1995), *Girl 6* (1996), *He Got Game* (1998).

Leigh, Mike (1943–) British, born Salford; *Bleak Moments* (1971), *Nuts in May* (1976), *Abigail's Party* (1977), *High Hopes* (1988), *Life is Sweet* (1990), *Naked* (1993), *Secrets and Lies* (1996), *Career Girls* (1997).

Leone, Sergio (1929–89) Italian, born Rome; *A Fistful of Dollars* (1964), *Once Upon a Time in the West* (1968), *Once Upon a Time in America* (1983).

Levinson, Barry (1942–) American, born Baltimore, Maryland; *Diner* (1982), *The Natural* (1984), *The Young Sherlock Holmes* (1985), *Tin Men* (1987), *Good Morning Vietnam* (1987), *Rain Man* (1988), *Avalon* (1990), *Bugsy* (1991), *Toys* (1992), *Disclosure* (1994), *Sleepers* (1996).

Lucas, George (1944–) American, born Modesto, California; *THX–1138:4EB/ Electronic Labyrinth* (1965), *American Graffiti* (1973), *Star Wars* (1977).

Lumet, Sidney (1924–) American, born Philadelphia; *Twelve Angry Men* (1957), *The Pawnbroker* (1965), *The Hill* (1965), *Murder on the Orient Express* (1974), *Dog Day Afternoon* (1975), *Network* (1976), *The Verdict* (1982), *Q & A* (1990), *Night Falls on Manhattan* (1996).

Lynch, David K (1946–) American, born Missoula, Montana; *Eraserhead* (1976), *The Elephant Man* (1980), *Dune* (1984), *Blue Velvet* (1986), *Wild at Heart* (1990), *Twin Peaks* (TV 1990–1), *Twin Peaks: Fire Walk With Me* (1992).

McBride, Jim (1941–) American, born New York City; *Breathless* (1983), *The Big Easy* (1986), *Great Balls of Fire* (1989), *The Wrong Man* (1992).

Mankiewicz, Joseph Leo (1909–93) American, born Wilkes-Barre, Pennsylvania; *All About Eve* (1950), *The Barefoot Contessa* (1954), *Guys and Dolls* (1954), *Suddenly Last Summer* (1959), *Sleuth* (1972).

Miller, George (1945–) Australian, born Brisbane; *Mad Max* (1979), *Mad Max 2: The Road Warrior* (1982), *Mad Max Beyond Thunderdome* (1985), *The Witches of Eastwick* (1987).

Miller, Jonathan Wolfe (1934–) British, born London; *The Magic Flute* (1986), *The Tempest* (1988), *Lorenzo's Oil* (1992).

Minnelli, Vincente (1913–86) American, born Chicago; *Ziegfeld Follies* (1946), *An American in Paris* (1951), *Lust for Life* (1956), *Gigi* (1958).

Nichols, Mike (Michael Igor Peschkowsky) (1931–) American–German, born Berlin, Germany; *Who's Afraid of Virginia Woolf?* (1966), *The Graduate* (1967), *Catch 22* (1970), *Working Girl* (1988), *Postcards from the Edge* (1990), *Wolf* (1994), *The Birdcage* (1996).

Olivier, Laurence Kerr Olivier, Baron (1907–89) British, born Dorking, Surrey; *Henry V* (1944), *Hamlet* (1948), *Richard III* (1956), *The Prince and the Showgirl* (1958), *The Entertainer* (1960).

Parker, Alan (1944–) British, born London; *Bugsy Malone* (1976), *Midnight Express* (1978), *Fame* (1980), *Shoot the Moon* (1981), *Pink Floyd: The Wall* (1982), *Birdy* (1985), *Angel Heart* (1987), *Mississippi Burning* (1988), *Come See the Paradise* (1990), *The Commitments* (1991), *Evita* (1996).

Pasolini, Pier Paolo (1922–75) Italian, born Bologna; *Accatone!* (1961), *The Gospel According to St Matthew* (1964), *Oedipus Rex* (1967), *Medea* (1970).

Peckinpah, (David) Sam(uel) (1925–84) American, born Fresno, California; *Ride the High Country* (1962), *The Wild Bunch* (1969), *Straw Dogs* (1971).

Polanski, Roman (1933–) Polish, born Paris; *Knife in the Water* (1962), *Repulsion* (1965), *Cul-de-Sac* (1966), *Rosemary's Baby* (1968), *Macbeth* (1971), *Chinatown* (1974), *Tess* (1979), *Pirates* (1985), *Frantic* (1988), *Bitter Moon* (1992), *Death and the Maiden* (1994).

Pollack, Sydney (1934–) American, born South Bend, Indiana; *They Shoot Horses Don't They?* (1969), *The Electric Horseman* (1979), *Absence of Malice* (1981), *Tootsie* (1982), *Out of Africa* (1985), *Havana* (1990), *The Firm* (1993).

Powell, Michael Latham (1905–90) British, born Bekesbourne, near Canterbury; with Emeric Pressburger (1902–88) Hungarian–British, born Miskolc, Hungary; *The Spy in Black* (1939), *The Thief of Baghdad* (1940), *The Life and Death of Colonel Blimp* (1943), *Black Narcissus* (1946), *The Red Shoes* (1948), *A Matter of Life and Death* (1946), *Peeping Tom* (1959).

Redford, (Charles) Robert (1937–) American, born Santa Monica, California; *Ordinary People* (1980), *The Milagro Beanfield War* (1987), *A River Runs Through It* (1992), *Quiz Show* (1994), *The Horse Whisperer* (1998).

Reed, Sir Carol (1906–76) British, born London; *The Young Mr Pitt* (1942), *The Way Ahead* (1944), *The Fallen Idol* (1948), *The Third Man* (1949), *An Outcast of the Islands* (1952), *The Man Between* (1953), *Our Man in Havana* (1959), *Oliver!* (1968).

Reiner, Carl (1922–) American, born The Bronx, New York City; *Oh God* (1977), *The Jerk* (1979), *Dead Men Don't Wear Plaid* (1982), *The Man with Two Brains* (1983), *Summer School* (1987).

Reiner, Rob (1945–) American, born The Bronx, New York City; *This is Spinal Tap* (1984), *Stand by Me* (1987), *The Princess Bride* (1988), *When Harry Met Sally ...* (1989), *Misery* (1990), *A Few Good Men* (1992), *The American President* (1995), *North* (1994).

Renoir, Jean (1894–1979) French, born Paris; *Une Partie de Campagne* (1936), *La Règle du Jeu* (1939), *The Southerner* (1945).

Robbins, Tim (Timothy Francis) (1958–) American, born West Covina, California; *No Small Affair* (1984), *Bob Roberts* (1992), *Dead Man Walking* (1995).

Roeg, Nicolas Jack (1928–) British, born London; *Performance* (1970), *Walkabout* (1971), *Don't Look Now* (1973), *The Man Who Fell to Earth* (1976), *Bad Timing* (1979), *Eureka* (1983), *Insignificance* (1985), *Castaway* (1986), *Black Widow* (1988), *Track 29* (1988), *The Witches* (1990), *Heart of Darkness* (1994).

Rossellini, Roberto (1906–77) Italian, born Rome; *The White Ship* (1940), *Rome, Open City* (1945), *Paisan* (1946), *Germany, Year Zero* (1947), *Stromboli* (1950), *Voyage to Italy* (1953), *General Della Rovera* (1959).

Russell, Ken (Henry Kenneth Alfred Russell) (1927–) British, born Southampton; *Women in Love* (1969), *The Music Lovers* (1970), *The Devils* (1971), *Crimes of Passion* (1984), *Gothic* (1987), *Lair of the White Worm* (1989), *The Rainbow* (1990), *Whore* (1991).

Schlesinger, John Richard (1926–) British, born London; *A Kind of Loving* (1962), *Billy Liar!* (1963), *Midnight Cowboy* (1969), *Sunday Bloody Sunday* (1971), *Marathon Man* (1976), *Honky Tonk Freeway* (1981), *An Englishman Abroad* (TV 1982), *Madame Sousatzka* (1988), *Pacific Heights* (1990), *The Innocent* (1993).

Scorsese, Martin (1942–) American, born Queens, New York; *Boxcar Bertha* (1972), *Mean Streets* (1973), *Alice Doesn't Live Here Any More* (1974), *Taxi Driver* (1976), *Raging Bull* (1980), *King of Comedy* (1982), *After Hours* (1985), *The Mission* (1986), *The Color of Money* (1986), *The Last Temptation of Christ* (1988), *Goodfellas* (1990), *Cape Fear* (1991), *Age of Innocence* (1992), *Casino* (1995), *Kundun* (1997).

Scott, Ridley (1937–) British, born South Shields; *Alien* (1979), *Blade Runner* (1982), *No Way Out* (1989), *Thelma and Louise* (1991), *1492* (1992).

Siegel, Don (1912–91) American, born Chicago; *Riot in Cell Block 11* (1954), *Invasion of the Body Snatchers* (1956), *Baby Face Nelson* (1957), *Coogan's Bluff* (1968), *Two Mules for Sister Sara* (1969), *Dirty Harry* (1971), *Charley Varrick* (1973), *The Shootist* (1976), *Telefon* (1977), *Escape from Alcatraz* (1979).

Spielberg, Steven (1946–) American, born Cincinnati, Ohio; *Duel* (TV 1972), *Sugarland Express* (1973), *Jaws* (1975), *1941* (1979), *Close Encounters of the Third Kind* (1977), *Raiders of the Lost Ark* (1981), *ET* (1982), *Twilight Zone* (1983), *The Color Purple* (1985), *Indiana Jones and the Temple of Doom* (1984), *Empire of the Sun* (1987), *Indiana Jones and the Last Crusade* (1989), *Hook* (1992), *Jurassic Park* (1993), *Schindler's List* (1993), *The Lost World: Jurassic Park* (1997), *Saving Private Ryan* (1998).

Stevenson, Robert (1905–86) British, born Buxton, Derbyshire; *King Solomon's Mines* (1937), *Mary Poppins* (1964), *The Love Bug* (1968), *Bedknobs and Broomsticks* (1971).

Stone, Oliver (1946–) American, born New York City; *Platoon* (1987), *Wall Street* (1987), *Born on the Fourth of July* (1989), *The Doors* (1991), *JFK* (1991), *Heaven and Earth* (1993), *Natural Born Killers* (1994), *Nixon* (1995).

Tarantino, Quentin (1963–) American, born Knoxville, Tennessee; *Reservoir Dogs* (1993), *Pulp Fiction* (1994), *Four Rooms* (co-director, 1995), *Jackie Brown* (1998).

Tati, Jacques (Jacques Tatischeff) (1908–82) French, born Le Pecq; *Jour de fête* (1947), *Monsieur Hulot's Holiday* (1952), *Mon Oncle* (1958), *Playtime* (1968), *Traffic* (1981).

Tavernier, Bertrand (1941–) French, born Lyons; *L'Horloger de Saint-Paul* (1973), *Dimanche à la Campagne* (1984), *La Mort en direct* (1979), *La Vie et rien d'autre* (1989), *Daddy Nostalgie* (1990), *L 627* (1992), *Capitaine Conan* (1996).

Truffaut, François (1932–84) French, born Paris; *Jules et Jim* (1961), *The Bride Wore Black* (1967), *Baisers volés* (1968), *L'Enfant Sauvage* (1969), *Day for Night* (1973), *The Last Metro* (1980).

Visconti, Luchino (Count Don Luchino Visconti Di Morone) (1906–76) Italian, born Milan; *The Leopard* (1963), *Ossessione* (1942), *The Damned* (1969), *Death in Venice* (1971).

Weir, Peter (1944–) Australian, born Sydney; *The Cars That Ate Paris* (1974), *Picnic at Hanging Rock* (1975), *The Last Wave* (1977), *Gallipoli* (1981), *The Year of Living Dangerously* (1982), *Witness* (1985), *Mosquito Coast* (1986), *Dead Poets Society* (1989), *Green Card* (1990), *Fearless* (1993).

Welles, (George) Orson (1915–85) American, born Kenosha, Wisconsin; *Citizen Kane* (1941), *The Magnificent Ambersons* (1942), *Jane Eyre* (1943), *Macbeth* (1948), *Othello* (1951), *Touch of Evil* (1958), *The Trial* (1962), *Chimes at Midnight* (1966).

Wenders, Wim (Wilhelm) (1945–) German, born Düsseldorf; *Summer in the City* (1970), *Alice in the Cities* (1974), *Kings of the Road* (1976), *Paris, Texas* (1984), *Wings of Desire* (1987), *Until the End of the World* (1991), *Faraway, So Close* (1993), *Beyond the Clouds* (co-director 1995), *The End of Violence* (1997).

Wilder, Billy (Samuel) (1906–) Austrian–American, born Sucha, Austria; *Double Indemnity* (1944), *The Lost Weekend* (1945), *Sunset Boulevard* (1950), *The Seven Year Itch* (1955), *Some Like It Hot* (1959), *The Apartment* (1960), *Avanti!* (1972), *Buddy Buddy* (1981).

Wise, Robert (1914–) American, born Winchester, Indiana; *The Body Snatcher* (1945), *The Day the Earth Stood Still* (1951), *West Side Story* (1961), *The Sound of Music* (1965), *Star Trek: The Motion Picture* (1979).

Wyler, William (1902–81) American, born Mülhausen, Alsace-Lorraine; *Mrs Miniver* (1932), *The Best Years of Our Lives* (1946), *Ben Hur* (1959), *Funny Girl* (1968).

Zeffirelli, Franco (Gianfranco Corsi) (1923–) Italian, born Florence; *The Taming of the Shrew* (1966), *Romeo and Juliet* (1968), *Brother Sun, Sister Moon* (1973), *Jesus of Nazareth* (TV 1977), *The Champ* (1979), *Endless Love* (1981), *La Traviata* (1982), *Otello* (1986), *Hamlet* (1990), *Jane Eyre* (TV 1995).

Zemeckis, Robert (1951–) American, born Chicago; *I Wanna Hold Your Hand* (1978), *Romancing The Stone* (1984), *Back to the Future* (1985), *Who Framed Roger Rabbit?* (1988), *Back to the Future II* (1989), *Back to the Future III* (1990), *Death Becomes Her* (1992), *Forrest Gump* (1994).

Zinnemann, Fred (1907–97) Austrian–American, born Vienna, Austria; *High Noon* (1952), *From Here to Eternity* (1953), *A Man for All Seasons* (1966), *Five Days One Summer* (1982).

Motion picture Academy Awards

Best film	Best actor	Best actress
1972 *The Godfather* (Francis Ford Coppola)	Marlon Brando *The Godfather*	Liza Minnelli *Cabaret*
1973 *The Sting* (George Roy Hill)	Jack Lemmon *Save the Tiger*	Glenda Jackson *A Touch of Class*
1974 *The Godfather, Part II* (Francis Ford Coppola)	Art Carney *Harry and Tonto*	Ellen Burstyn *Alice Doesn't Live Here Anymore*
1975 *One Flew Over the Cuckoo's Nest* (Miloš Forman)	Jack Nicholson *One Flew Over the Cuckoo's Nest*	Louise Fletcher *One Flew Over the Cuckoo's Nest*
1976 *Rocky* (John G Avildsen)	Peter Finch *Network*	Faye Dunaway *Network*
1977 *Annie Hall* (Woody Allen)	Richard Dreyfuss *The Goodbye Girl*	Diane Keaton *Annie Hall*
1978 *The Deer Hunter* (Michael Cimino)	Jon Voight *Coming Home*	Jane Fonda *Coming Home*
1979 *Kramer vs Kramer* (Robert Beaton)	Dustin Hoffman *Kramer vs Kramer*	Sally Field *Norma Rae*
1980 *Ordinary People* (Robert Redford)	Robert de Niro *Raging Bull*	Sissy Spacek *Coal Miner's Daughter*
1981 *Chariots of Fire* (Hugh Hudson)	Henry Fonda *On Golden Pond*	Katharine Hepburn *On Golden Pond*
1982 *Gandhi* (Richard Attenborough)	Ben Kingsley *Gandhi*	Meryl Streep *Sophie's Choice*
1983 *Terms of Endearment* (James L Brooks)	Robert Duval *Tender Mercies*	Shirley MacLaine *Terms of Endearment*
1984 *Amadeus* (Miloš Forman)	F Murray Abraham *Amadeus*	Sally Field *Places in the Heart*
1985 *Out of Africa* (Sydney Pollack)	William Hurt *Kiss of the Spider Woman*	Geraldine Page *The Trip to Bountiful*
1986 *Platoon* (Oliver Stone)	Paul Newman *The Color of Money*	Marlee Matlin *Children of a Lesser God*
1987 *The Last Emperor* (Bernardo Bertolucci)	Michael Douglas *Wall Street*	Cher *Moonstruck*
1988 *Rain Man* (Barry Levinson)	Dustin Hoffman *Rain Man*	Jodie Foster *The Accused*
1989 *Driving Miss Daisy* (Bruce Beresford)	Daniel Day-Lewis *My Left Foot*	Jessica Tandy *Driving Miss Daisy*
1990 *Dances with Wolves* (Kevin Costner)	Jeremy Irons *Reversal of Fortune*	Kathy Bates *Misery*
1991 *The Silence of the Lambs* (Jonathan Demme)	Anthony Hopkins *The Silence of the Lambs*	Jodie Foster *The Silence of the Lambs*
1992 *Unforgiven* (Clint Eastwood)	Al Pacino *Scent of a Woman*	Emma Thompson *Howards End*

	Best film	Best actor	Best actress
1993	*Schindler's List* (Steven Spielberg)	Tom Hanks *Philadelphia*	Holly Hunter *The Piano*
1994	*Forrest Gump* (Robert Zemeckis)	Tom Hanks *Forrest Gump*	Jessica Lange *Blue Sky*
1995	*Braveheart* (Mel Gibson)	Nicolas Cage *Leaving Las Vegas*	Susan Sarandon *Dead Man Walking*
1996	*The English Patient* (Anthony Minghella)	Geoffrey Rush *Shine*	Frances McDormand *Fargo*
1997	*Titanic* (James Cameron)	Jack Nicholson *As Good as It Gets*	Helen Hunt *As Good as It Gets*
1998	*Shakespeare in Love* (Guy Madden)	Roberto Benigni *Life is Beautiful*	Gwyneth Paltrow *Shakespeare in Love*
1999	*American Beauty* (Sam Mendes)	Kevin Spacey *American Beauty*	Hilary Swank *Boys Don't Cry*

Composers

Selected works are listed.

Adams, John Coolidge (1947–) American, born Worcester, Massachusetts; works include opera (eg *Nixon in China*) and compositions for chorus and orchestra (eg *Harmonium*).

Albéniz, Isaac (1860–1909) Spanish, born Camprodón, Catalonia; works include operas and works for piano based on Spanish folk music (eg *Iberia*).

Arnold, Sir Malcolm Henry (1921–) English, born Northampton; works include concertos, ballets, operas, vocal, choral, chamber and orchestral music (eg *Tam O'Shanter*) and film scores (eg *Bridge over the River Kwai*).

Bach, Johann Sebastian (1685–1750) German, born Eisenach; prolific composer, works include over 190 cantatas and oratorios, concertos, chamber music, keyboard music, and orchestral works (eg *Toccata and Fugue in D minor*, *The Well-tempered Clavier*, *Six Brandenburg Concertos*, *St Matthew Passion*, *Mass in B minor*, *Goldberg Variations*, *The Musical Offering*, *The Art of Fugue*).

Bartók, Béla (1881–1945) Hungarian, born Nagyszentmiklós; works include six string quartets, *Sonata for 2 pianos and percussion*, concertos (for piano, violin, viola and notably the *Concerto for Orchestra*), opera (*Duke Bluebeard's Castle*), two ballets (*The Wooden Prince*, *The Miraculous Mandarin*), songs, choruses, folksong arrangements.

Beethoven, Ludwig van (1770–1827) German, born Bonn; works include 33 piano sonatas (eg the 'Pathétique', 'Moonlight', *Waldstein*, *Appassionata*), nine symphonies (eg *Eroica*, 'Pastoral', *Choral Symphony No.9*), string quartets, concertos, *Lebewohl* and the opera *Fidelio*.

Berg, Alban (1885–1935) Austrian, born Vienna; works include songs (*Four Songs*), operas (*Wozzeck*, *Lulu*, unfinished), a violin concerto and a string quartet (*Lyric Suite*).

Berio, Luciano (1925–) Italian, born Oneglia; works include compositions using tapes and electronic music (eg *Mutazioni*, *Omaggio a James Joyce*), works for solo instruments (*Sequenzas*), stage works (eg *Laborintus II*, *Opera*) and symphonies (*Synfonia*).

Berlioz, (Louis) Hector (1803–69) French, born Côte St André, near Grenoble; works include the overture *Le carnival romain*, the cantata (*La Damnation de Faust*), symphonies (eg *Symphonie Fantastique, Romeo et Juliette*) and operas (eg *Béatrice et Bénédict, Les Toyens*).

Bernstein, Leonard (1918–90) American, born Laurence, Massachusetts; works include ballets (*Jeremiah, The Age of Anxiety, Kaddish*), symphonies (eg *Fancy Free, The Dybbuk*), and musicals, (eg *Candide, West Side Story, On The Town, Songfest, Halil*).

Birtwistle, Sir Harrison (1934–   ) English, born Accrington, Lancashire; works include operas (eg *The Mask of Orpheus*), 'dramatic pastorals' (eg *Down by the Greenwood Side*) and orchestral pieces (eg *The Triumph of Time*).

Bizet, Georges (1838–75) French, born Paris; works include opera (eg *Carmen, Les Pêcheurs de Perles, La Jolie Fille de Perth*), incidental music to Daudet's play *L'Arlésienne* and a symphony.

Boulez, Pierre (1925–   ) French, born Montbrison; works include three piano sonatas, and works for piano and flute (eg *Sonatine*).

Brahms, Johannes (1833–97) German, born Hamburg; works include songs, four symphonies, two piano concertos, choral work (eg *German Requiem*), orchestral work (eg *Variations on a Theme of Haydn*), programme work (eg *Tragic Overture*), also the *Academic Festival Overture* and *Hungarian Dances*.

Bruckner, Anton (1824–96) Austrian, born Ansfelden; works include nine symphonies, a string quartet, choral-orchestral Masses and other church music (eg *Te Deum*).

Cage, John (1912–92) American, born Los Angeles; works include unorthodox modern compositions, eg *Sonatas and Interludes for the Prepared Piano*.

Carter, Elliott Cook, Jr (1908–   ) American, born New York City; works include quartets, symphonies, concertos, songs and chamber music.

Chabrier, Emmanuel (1841–94) French, born Ambert; works include operas (*Gwendoline, Le Roi malgré lui, Briséis*) and an orchestral rhapsody (*España*).

Chausson, Ernest (1855–99) French, born Paris; works include songs and orchestral works (eg *Poème*).

Chopin, Frédéric François (1810–49) Polish, born Zelazowa Wola, near Warsaw; wrote almost exclusively for piano — nocturnes, polonaises, mazurkas, preludes, concertos and a funeral march.

Copland, Aaron (1900–90) American, born Brooklyn, New York City; ballets (eg *Billy The Kid, Appalachian Spring*), film scores (eg *Our Town, The Hucis*), symphonies (eg *Symphonie Ode, Connotations, Clarinet Concerto*).

Corelli, Arcangelo (1653–1713) Italian, born Fusignano, near Bologna; works include 12 concertos (eg *Concerto for Christmas Night*), and solo and trio sonatas for violin.

Couperin, François (1668–1733) French, born Paris; works include chamber music, four books containing 240 harpsichord pieces, motets and other church music.

Debussy, Claude Achille (1862–1918) French, born St Germaine-en-Laye, near Paris; songs (eg the cantata *L'Enfant prodigue*), opera (*Pelléas et Mélisande*), orchestral works (eg *Prélude à l'après-midi d'un faune, La Mer*), chamber and piano music (eg *Feux d'artifice, La Cathédrale engloutie*).

Delius, Frederick (1862–1934) English (of German Scandinavian descent), born Bradford; works include songs (eg *A Song of Summer, Idyll, Songs of Farewell*), concertos, operas (eg *Koanga, A Village Romeo and Juliette*), chamber music and orchestral variations (eg *Appalachia, Sea Drift, A Mass of Life*).

Dukas, Paul (1865–1935) French, born Paris; works include a symphonic poem (*L'Apprenti sorcier*) and opera (*Ariane et Barbe-Bleue*).

Dutilleux, Henri (1916–) French, born Angers; works include a piano sonata, two symphonies, a violin concerto, a string quartet (*Ainsi la nuit*), compositions for two pianos and other orchestral works.

Dvořák, Antonin Leopold (1841–1904) Czech, born near Prague; works include songs, concertos, choral (eg *Hymnus*) and chamber music, symphonies (notably 'From the New World'), operas (eg *Rusalka, Armida, Slavonic Dances*).

Elgar, Sir Edward (William) (1857–1934) English, born Broadheath, near Worcester; works include chamber music, two symphonies, oratorios (eg *The Dream of Gerontius, The Apostles, The Kingdom*), and the orchestral work *Enigma Variations*.

Falla, Manuel de (1876–1946) Spanish, born Cádiz; works include opera (eg *La Vida Breve, Master Peter's Puppet Show*), ballet (eg *The Three-Cornered Hat, Love the Magician*) and orchestral suites (eg *Nights in the Gardens of Spain*).

Fauré, Gabriel Urbain (1845–1924) French, born Pamiers; works include songs (eg *Après un rêve*), chamber music, choral music (eg the *Requiem*), operas and orchestral music (eg *Masques et bergamasques*).

Franck, César Auguste (1822–90) naturalized French, born Liège, Belgium; works include tone-poems, (eg *Les Béatitudes*), sonatas for violin and piano, *Symphony in D minor* and *Variations symphoniques* for piano and orchestra.

Gershwin, George (1898–1937) American, born Brooklyn, New York City; Broadway musicals (eg *Lady Be Good, Of Thee I Sing*), symphonies, songs (notably 'I Got Rhythm', 'The Man I Love'), operas (eg *Porgy and Bess*), and concert works (eg *Rhapsody in Blue, Concerto in F, An American in Paris*).

Glass, Philip (1937–) American, born Baltimore, Maryland; works include stage pieces (eg *Einstein on the Beach*), film scores (eg *Hamburger Hill*) and the opera *Orphee*.

Grainger, Percy Aldridge (1882–1961) Australian, born Melbourne; works include songs, piano and chamber music (eg *Molly on the Shore, Mock Morris, Shepherd's Hey*).

Grieg, Edvard Hagerup (1843–1907) Norwegian, born Bergen; works include songs, a piano concerto, orchestral suites, violin sonatas, choral music, and incidental music for *Peer Gynt* and *Sigurd Jorsalfar*.

Handel, George Friederic (1685–1759) naturalized English, born Halle, Saxony; prolific output including over 27 operas (eg *Almira, Rinaldo*), 20 oratorios (eg *The Messiah, Saul, Israel in Egypt, Samson, Jephthah*), orchestral suites (eg the *Water Music* and *Music for the Royal Fireworks*), organ concertos and chamber music.

Haydn, (Franz) Joseph (1732–1809) Austrian, born Rohrau, Lower Austria; prolific output including 104 symphonies (eg the 'Salomon' or 'London' Symphonies), string quartets and oratorios (notably *The Creation, The Seasons*).

Holst, Gustav Theodore (originally von Holst) (1874–1934) English of Swedish origin, born Cheltenham; works include choral and ballet music, operas (eg *The Perfect Fool, At the Boar's Head*), orchestral suites (eg *The Planets, St Paul's Suite for Strings*), choral music (eg *The Hymn of Jesus, Ode to Death*), and *Concerto for Two Violins*.

Honegger, Arthur (1892–1955) French, born Le Havre; works include five symphonies and dramatic oratorios (*King David, Joan of Arc at the Stake*).

Ireland, John Nicholson (1879–1962) English, born Bowden, Cheshire; works include sonatas (eg Violin Sonata in A), piano music, songs (eg 'Sea Fever'), the rhapsody *Mai-dun* and orchestral works (eg *The Forgotten Rite, These Things Shall Be*).

Ives, Charles (1874–1954) American, born Danbury, Connecticut; works include five symphonies, chamber music (eg *Concord Sonata*) and many songs.

Janáček, Leoš (1854–1928) Czech, born Hukvaldy, Moravia; works include chamber, orchestral and choral music (eg the song cycle *The Diary of One Who Has Vanished*), operas (eg *Janufa, The Cunning Little Vixen, The Excursions of Mr Brouček, From the House of the Dead*), two string quartets and a mass.

Lalo, (Victor Antoine) Édouard (1823–92) French, born Lille. Works include compositions for violin (eg *Symphonie espagnole*), opera (eg *Le Roi d'Ys*) and ballet (*Namouna*).

Ligeti, Györgi Sándor (1923–) Hungarian, born Dicsöszentmárton; works include orchestral compositions (eg *Apparitions, Lontano, Double Concerto*), choral works (eg *Requiem*) and music for harpsichord, organ and wind and string ensembles.

Liszt, Franz (1811–86) Hungarian, born Raiding; 400 original compositions including symphonic poems, piano music and masses (eg *The Legend of St Elizabeth, Christus*).

Lloyd-Webber, Andrew Lloyd Webber, Baron (1948–) English, born London; works include the 'rock opera' *Jesus Christ Superstar* and the musicals *Cats, Evita* and *Aspects of Love*.

Mahler, Gustav (1860–1911) Austrian, born Kalist, Bohemia; works include 10 symphonies, songs, the cantata *Das klagende Lied* and the song-symphony *Das Lied von der Erde* (The Song of the Earth).

Mendelssohn, (Jacob Ludwig) Felix (1809–47) German, born Hamburg; prolific output, including concerto overtures (eg *Fingal's Cave, A Midsummer Night's Dream, Hebrides*), symphonies (*Symphony in C minor, Scottish, Italian*), quartets (B minor Quartet), operas (eg *Camacho's Wedding*) and oratorios (eg *Elijah*).

Messiaen, Olivier Eugène Prosper Charles (1908–92) French, born Avignon; works include compositions for piano (*Vingt regards sur l'enfant Jésus, Catalogue d'oiseaux*), the symphony *Turangalila*, an oratorio (*La Transfiguration de Notre Seigneur Jésus-Christ*) and an opera (*St François d'Assisi*).

Milhaud, Darius (1892–1974) French, born Aix-en-Provence; works include several operas, incidental music for plays, ballets (eg the jazz ballet *La Création du monde*), symphonies and orchestral, choral and chamber works.

Monteverdi, Claudio (Giovanni Antonio) (1567–1643) Italian, born Cremona; works include masses (eg *Mass* and *Vespers* of the Virgin), cantatas and operas (eg *Orfeo, Il Ritorno d'Ulisse, L'Incoronazione di Poppea*).

Mozart, (Johann Chrysostom) Wolfgang Amadeus (1756–91) Austrian, born Salzburg; 600 compositions including symphonies (eg 'Jupiter', *Linz, Prague*), concertos, string quartets, sonatas, operas (eg *Marriage of Figaro, Don Giovanni, Così fan tutte*) and the Singspiels *The Abductions from the Seraglio, Die Zauberflöte*.

Mussorgsky, Modeste (1839–81) Russian, born Karevo; works include operas (eg *Boris Godunov*), song cycles and instrumental works (eg *Pictures from an Exhibition, Night on the Bare Mountain*).

Nielsen, Carl August (1865–1931) Danish, born Furen; works include operas (eg *Saul and David, Masquerade*), symphonies (eg 'The Four Temperaments'), string quartets, choral and piano music.

Palestrina, Giovanni Pierluigi da (c.1525–1594) Italian, born Palestrina, near Rome; works include chamber music and the organ work *Commotion*, masses, choral music (eg *Song of Songs*), madrigals.

Pendericki, Krzysztof (1933–   ) Polish, born Debica; works include compositions for strings (eg *Trenofiarom Hiroszimy*), operas (eg *Die schwarze Maske*) and concertos (eg *Flute Concerto*).

Prokofiev, Sergei (1891–1953) Russian, born Sontsovka, Ukraine; works include 11 operas (eg *The Gambler, The Love for Three Oranges, The Fiery Angels, Semyon Kotko, Betrothal in a Monastery, War and Peace, The Story of a Real Man*), ballets (eg *Romeo and Juliet, Cinderella*), concertos, sonatas, cantatas (eg *We are Seven, Hail to Stalin*), film scores (eg *Alexander Nevsky*), and the 'children's piece' *Peter and the Wolf*.

Puccini, Giacomo (Antonio Domenico Michele Secondo Maria) (1858–1924) Italian, born Lucca; 12 operas (eg *Manon Lescaut, La Bohème, Tosca, Madama Butterfly, Turandot*).

Purcell, Henry (1659–95) English, born London; works include songs (eg 'Nymphs and Shepherds', 'Arise, ye Subterranean Winds'), sonatas, string fantasies, church music and opera (eg *Dido and Aeneas*).

Rachmaninov, Sergei Vasilyevich (1873–1943) Russian, born Nizhny Novgorod; works include operas, three symphonies, four piano concertos (eg *Prelude in C Sharp Minor*), the tone-poem *The Isle of the Dead* and *Rhapsody on a Theme of Paganini* for piano and orchestra.

Rameau, Jean Philippe (1683–1764) French, born Dijon; works include over 30 ballets and operas (eg *Hippolyte et Aricie, Castor et Pollux*) and harpsichord pieces.

Ravel, Maurice (1875–1937) French, born Ciboure; works include piano compositions (eg *Sonatina, Miroirs, Ma Mère L'Oye, Gaspard de la nuit*), string quartets, operas (eg *L'Heure espagnol, L'Enfant et les sortilèges*), ballets (eg *Daphnis and Chloé*), the 'choreographic poem' *La Valse* and the miniature ballet *Boléro*.

Rimsky-Korsakov, Nikolai Andreyevich (1844–1908) Russian, born Tikhvin, Novgorod; works include orchestral music (eg the symphonic suite *Sheherazade, Capriccio Espagnol, Easter Festival*) and 15 operas (eg *Sadko, The Snow Maiden, The Tsar Sultan, The Invisible City of Kitesh, The Golden Cockerel*).

Rossini, Gioacchino Antonio (1792–1868) Italian, born Pesaro; works include many operas (eg *Il Barbiere de Seviglia, Otella, Guillaume Tell*) and a number of vocal and piano pieces.

Roussel, Albert (1869–1937) French, born Tourcoing; works include four symphonies, numerous choral works (eg *Évocations*), ballets (eg *Bacchus and Ariane, Le Festin de l'araignée*) and an opera (*Padmâvati*).

Saint-Saëns, (Charles) Camille (1835–1921) French, born Paris; works include four symphonic poems (eg *Danse macabre*), piano (*Le Rouet d'Omphale, Phaëton, La Jeunesse d'Hercule*), violin and cello concertos, symphonies, the opera *Samson et Dalila*, church music (eg *Messe solennelle*) and *Carnival des animaux* for two pianos and orchestra.

Satie, Erik Alfred Leslie (1866–1925) French, born Hornfleur; works include ballets (eg *Parade*), lyric dramas and whimsical pieces.

Scarlatti, (Guiseppe) Domenico (1685–1757) Italian, born Naples; works include over 600 harpsichord sonatas.

Schönberg, Arnold (1874–1951) naturalized American, born Vienna, Austria; works include chamber music (eg *Chamber Symphony*), concertos (eg *Piano Concerto*), symphonic poems (eg *Pelleas and Melisande*), the choral-orchestral *Gurrelieder*, string quartets, the oratorio *Die Jacobsiter* and opera (*Von Heute auf Morgen, Moses und Aaron*).

Schubert, Franz Peter (1797–1828) Austrian, born Vienna; prolific output, works include symphonies, piano sonatas, string quartets and songs (eg *Gretchen am Spinnrade, Erlkönig, Die schöne Müllerin, Winterreise, Who is Sylvia?, Hark, Hark the Lark, Schwanengesang*).

Schumann, Robert Alexander (1810–56) German, born Zwickau, Saxony; works include piano music (eg *Fantasiestücke*), songs (eg The Fool's Song in *Twelfth Night*, the Chamisso songs *Frauenliebe und Leben* or 'Woman's Love and Life'), chamber music and four symphonies (eg the *Rhenish*).

Scriabin, Alexander (1872–1915) Russian, born Moscow; works include a piano concerto, three symphonies, two tone-poems (eg *Poem of Ecstasy*), 10 sonatas, studies and preludes.

Shostakovich, Dmitri (1906–75) Russian, born St Petersburg; works include 15 symphonies, operas (eg *The Nose, A Lady Macbeth of Mtensk*), concertos, string quartets and film music.

Sibelius, Jean (1865–1957) Finnish, born Tavastehus; works include symphonic poems (eg *Swan of Tuonela, En Saga*), songs, a violin concerto and seven symphonies.

Simpson, Robert Wilfred Levick (1921–97) English, born Leamington Spa, Warwickshire; works include 11 symphonies, concertos for violin, piano, flute and cello, 15 string quartets, other chamber pieces, brass band music and two choral compositions; also wrote on music, eg *The Essence of Bruckner* (1966).

Stockhausen, Karlheinz (1928–   ) German, born Mödrath, near Cologne; works include orchestral music (eg *Gruppen*), choral and instrumental compositions.

Strauss, Johann, (the Younger) (1825–99) Austrian, born Vienna; works include over 400 waltzes (eg *The Blue Danube, Wine, Women, and Song, Perpetuum Mobile, Artist's Life, Tales from the Vienna Woods, Voices from Spring, The Emperor*), and operettas (eg *Die Fledermaus, A Night in Venice*).

Strauss, Richard (1864–1949) German, born Munich; works include symphonic poems (eg *Don Juan, Till Eulenspiegels lustige Streiche, Also Sprach Zarathustra, Tod und Verklärung* ('Death and Transfiguration'), *Don Quixote, Ein Heldenleben*) and operas (eg *Der Rosenkavalier, Ariadne auf Naxos, Capriccio*).

Stravinsky, Igor (1882–1971) Russian, born Oranienbaum, near St Petersburg (naturalized French, then American); works include operas (eg *The Rake's Progress*), oratorios (eg *Oedipus Rex, Symphony of Psalms*), concertos, ballets (eg *The Firebird, The Rite of*

Spring, Petrushka, Pulcinella, Apollo Musogetes, The Card Game, Orpheus, Agon) and a musical play *Elegy for JFK* for voice and clarinets.

Tchaikovsky, Piotr Ilyich (1840–93) Russian, born Kamsko-Votkinsk; works include 10 operas (eg *Eugene Onegin, The Queen of Spades*), a violin concerto, six symphonies, two piano concertos, three ballets (*The Nutcracker, Swan Lake, The Sleeping Beauty*) and tone-poems (eg *Romeo and Juliet, Italian Capriccio*).

Telemann, George Philipp (1681–1767) German, born Magdeburg; prolific composer, works include 600 overtures, 40 operas, 200 concertos, sonatas, suites and overtures (eg *Der Tag des Gerichts, Die Tageszeiten*).

Tippett, Sir Michael Kemp (1905–98) English, born London; works include operas (eg *The Midsummer Marriage, King Priam, The Knot Garden, The Ice Break*), concertos, symphonies, cantatas and oratorios (eg *A Child of Our Time, The Vision of St Augustine*).

Varèse, Edgar (1883–1965) American, born Paris; works are almost entirely orchestral (eg *Metal, Ionization, Hyperprism*).

Vaughan Williams, Ralph (1872–1958) English, born Down Ampney, Gloucestershire; works include songs, symphonies (eg *London Symphony, Pastoral Symphony*), choral-orchestral works (eg *Sea Symphony, Magnificat*), operas (eg *Hugh the Drover, The Pilgrim's Progress*), a ballet (*Job*) and film music (eg *Scott of the Antarctic*).

Verdi, Giuseppe (1813–1901) Italian, born le Roncole, near Busseto; works include church music (eg *Requiem*) and operas (eg *Oberto, Nabucco, Rigoletto, Il Trovatore, La Traviata, Un Ballo in Maschera, La Forza del Destino, Aïda, Otello, Falstaff*).

Vivaldi, Antonio (1678–1741) Italian, born Venice; prolific output, works include over 400 concertos (eg *L'Estro Armonico, The Four Seasons*), 40 operas and an oratorio *Juditha triumphans*.

Wagner, (Wilhelm) Richard (1813–83) German, born Leipzig; operas include *Lohengrin, Rienzi*, the *Ring* cycle (*Das Rheingold, Die Walküre, Siegfried, Götterdämmerung*), *Die Meistersinger, Tristan und Isolde, Parsifal*.

Walton, Sir William Turner (1902–83) English, born Oldham; works include concertos, operas (*Troilus and Cressida, The Bear*), a cantata (*Belshazzar's Feast*), ballet music for *The Wise Virgins*, a song-cycle (*Anon in Love*) and film music.

Weber, Carl Maria Friedrich von (1786–1826) German, born Eutin, near Lübeck; works include operas (eg *Oberon, Euryanthe, Silvana*), concertos, symphonies, sonatas, scenas, cantatas (eg *Kampf und Sieg*) and songs.

Webern, Anton Friedrich Wilhelm von (1883–1945) Austrian, born Vienna; works include a symphony, three cantatas, *Four Pieces for Violin and Pianoforte, Five Pieces for Orchestra* and a concerto for nine instruments and songs.

Whitehead, Gillian (1941–) New Zealand, born Whangarei; works include compositions for choir and chamber orchestra (eg *Inner Harbour*), for soprano and instrumental ensemble (eg *Hotspur*) for opera (eg *Eleanor of Aquitaine*) and for strings (eg *Pakuru*).

Xenakis, Iannis (1922–) Greek, born Romania; works include compositions for piano and orchestra (eg *Erikhthon*), *Shaar* for strings, *Tetras* for string quartet and solo pieces (eg *Nomos Alpha* for cello, *Herma* for piano), and *Pithoprakta* for 50 instruments.

Layout of an orchestra

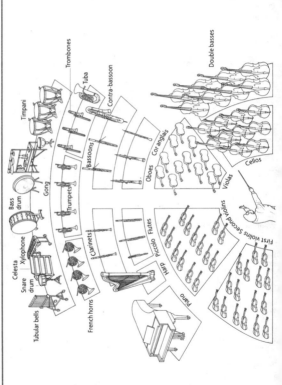

Artists

Selected paintings are listed.

Altdorfer, Albrecht (c.1480–1538) German, born Regensburg; *Danube Landscape* (1520), *Alexander's Victory* (1529).

Andrea del Sarto (properly Andrea d'Agnolo di Francesco) (1486–1530) Italian, born Florence; *Miracles of S Filippo Benizzi* (1509–10), *Madonna del Saeco* (1525).

Angelico, Fra (real name Guido di Pietro) (c.1400–55) Italian, born Vicchio, Tuscany; *Coronation of the Virgin* (1430–5), *San Marco altarpiece* (c.1440).

Auerbach, Frank (1931–) Anglo-German, born Berlin; *Mornington Crescent* (1967).

Bacon, Francis (1909–92) British, born Dublin; *Three Figures at the Base of a Crucifixion* (1945), *Two Figures with a Monkey* (1973), *Triptych Inspired by the Oresteia of Aeschylus* (1981).

Beardsley, Aubrey (Vincent) (1872–98) British, born Brighton; illustrations to Malory's *Morte d'Arthur* (1893), Wilde's *Salome* (1894).

Bell, Vanessa (1879–1961) British, born Kensington, London; *Still Life on Corner of a Mantlepiece* (1914).

Bellini, Gentile (c.1429–1507) Italian, born Venice; *Procession of the Relic of the True Cross* (1496), *Miracle at Ponte di Lorenzo* (1500).

Blackadder, Elizabeth (1931–) British, born Falkirk; *Interior with Self-Portrait* (1972), *White Anemones* (1983), *Texas Flame* (1986).

Blake, Peter (1932–) British, born Dartford, Kent; *On the Balcony* (1955–7), design for the Beatles' album *Sergeant Pepper's Lonely Hearts Club Band* (1967).

Blake, William (1757–1827) British, born London; illustrations for his own *Songs of Innocence and Experience* (1794), *Newton* (1795), illustrations for the *Book of Job* (1826).

Böcklin, Arnold (1827–1901) Swiss, born Basel; *Pan in the Reeds* (1857), *The Island of the Dead* (1880).

Bomberg, David (1890–1957) British, born Birmingham; *In the Hold* (1913–14), *The Mud Bath* (1913–14).

Bonnard, Pierre (1867–1947) French, born Paris; *Young Woman in Lamplight* (1900), *Dining Room in the Country* (1913), *Seascape of the Mediterranean* (1941).

Bosch, Hieronymus (real name Jerome van Aken) (c.1460–1516) Dutch, born 's-Hertogenbosch, Brabant; *The Temptation of St Anthony*, *The Garden of Earthly Delights* (work undated).

Botticelli, Sandro (originally Alessandro di Mariano Filipepi) (1444–1510) Italian, born Florence; *Primavera* (c.1478), *The Birth of Venus* (c.1485), *Mystic Nativity* (1500).

Boucher, François (1703–70) French, born Paris; *Reclining Girl* (1751), *The Rising* and *The Setting of the Sun* (1753).

Braque, Georges (1882–1963) French, born Argenteuil-sur-Seine; *Still Life with Violin* (1910), *The Portuguese* (1911), *Blue Wash-Basin* (1942).

Brueghel, Pieter, (the Elder), (c.1525–69) Dutch, born Bruegel, near Breda; *Road to Calvary* (1564), *Massacre of the Innocents* (c.1566), *The Blind Leading the Blind* (1568), *The Peasant Wedding* (1568), *The Peasant Dance* (1568).

Burne-Jones, Sir Edward (Coley) (1833–98) British, born Birmingham; *The Beguiling of Merlin* (1874), *The Arming of Perseus* (1877), *King Cophetea and the Beggar Maid* (1880–4).

Burra, Edward (1905–76) British, born London; *Dancing Skeletons* (1934), *Soldiers* (1942), *Scene in Harlem (Simply Heavenly)* (1952).

Canaletto (properly Giovanni Antonio Canal) (1697–1768) Italian, born Venice; *Stone Mason's Yard* (c.1730).

Caravaggio (properly Michelangelo Merisi da Caravaggio) (1573–1610) Italian, born Caravaggio, near Burgamo; *The Supper at Emmaus* (c.1598–1600), *Martyrdom of St Matthew* (1599–1600), *The Death of the Virgin* (1605–6).

Cassatt, Mary (1844–1926) American, born Pittsburgh, Pennsylvania; *The Blue Room* (1878), *Lady at the Tea Table* (1885), *Morning Toilette* (1886), *The Tramway* (1891), *The Bath* (1892).

Cézanne, Paul (1839–1906) French, born Aix-en-Provence; *The Black Marble Clock* (c.1869–70), *Maison du Pendu* (c.1873), *Bathing Women* (1900–5), *Le Jardinier* (1906).

Chagall, Marc (1887–1985) Russian–French, born Vitebsk; *The Musician* (1912–13), *Bouquet of Flying Lovers* (1947).

Chicago, Judy (originally Judy Gerowitz) (1939–) American, born Chicago; *The Dinner Party* (1974–9).

Chirico, Giorgio de (1888–1978) Italian, born Volos, Greece; *Portrait of Guillaume Apollinaire* (1914), *The Jewish Angel* (1916), *The Return of Ulysses* (1968).

Christo (originally Christo Javachef) (1935–) American, born Gabovra, Bulgaria; *Surrounded Islands* (1980–3), *Wrapped Reichstag* (1995).

Cimabue (originally Bencivieni di Pepo) (c.1240–c.1302) Italian, born Florence; *Crucifix* (date unknown), *St John the Evangelist* (1302).

Claude Lorrain(e) (in full Claude le Lorrain) (real name Claude Gêllée) (1600–82) French, born near Nancy; *The Mill* (1631), *The Embarkation of St Ursula* (1641), *Ascanius Shooting the Stag of Silvia* (1682).

Constable, John (1776–1837) British, born East Bergholt, Suffolk; *A Country Lane* (c.1810), *The White Horse* (1819), *The Hay Wain* (1821), *Stonehenge* (1835).

Corot, Jean Baptiste Camille (1796–1875) French, born Paris; *Bridge at Narni* (1827), *Souvenir de Marcoussis* (1869), *Woman Reading in a Landscape* (1869).

Correggio (Antonio Allegri da) (c.1494–1534) Italian, born Correggio; *The Agony in the Garden* (c.1528).

Courbet, (Jean Désiré) Gustave (1819–77) French, born Ornans; *The After-Dinner at Ornans* (1848–9), *The Bathers* (1853), *The Painter's Studio* (1855), *The Stormy Sea* (1869).

Cranach, Lucas, (the Elder) (1472–1553) German, born Kronach, near Bamberg; *The Crucifixion* (1503), *The Fountain of Youth* (1550).

Dalí, Salvador (Felipe Jacinto) (1904–89) Spanish, born Figueras, Gerona; *The Persistence of Memory* (1931), *The Transformation of Narcissus* (1934), *Christ of St John of the Cross* (1951).

Daumier, Honoré (1808–78) French, born Marseilles; many caricatures and lithographs; *The Legislative Paunch* (1834), *The Third Class Carriage* (1840s), paintings on the theme of *Don Quixote*.

David, Jacques Louis (1748–1825) French, born Paris; *Death of Socrates* (1788), *The Death of Marat* (1793), *The Rape of the Sabines* (1799), *Madame Récamier* (1800).

Davis, Stuart (1894–1964) American, born Philadelphia; *The President* (1917), *House and Street* (1931), *Visa* (1951), *Premiere* (1957).

Degas, (Hilaire Germain) Edgar (1834–1917) French, born Paris; *Cotton-brokers Office* (1873), *L'Absinthe* (1875–6), *Little Fourteen-year-old Dancer* (sculpture) (1881), *Dancer at the Bar* (c.1900).

de Kooning, Willem (1904–97) American, born Rotterdam, the Netherlands; *Woman I–V* (1952–3), *Montauk Highway* (1958), *Pastorale* (1963).

Delacroix, (Ferdinand Victor) Eugène (1798–1863) French, born St-Maurice-Charenton; *Dante and Virgil in Hell* (1822), *Liberty Guiding the People* (1831), *Jacob and the Angel* (1853–61).

Delvaux, Paul (1897–1994) Belgian, born Antheit, near Huys; *Vénus endormie* (1932), *Phases of the Moon* (1939), *In Praise of Melancholy* (1951).

Derain, André Louis (1880–1954) French, born Chatou; *Mountains at Collioure* (1905), *Westminster Bridge* (1907), *The Bagpiper* (1910–11).

Doré, (Louis Auguste) Gustave (1832–83) French, born Strasbourg; Illustrations to Dante's *Inferno* (1861), Milton's *Paradise Lost* (1866).

Duccio di Buoninsegna (c.1260–c.1320) Italian; *Maestà* (Siena Cathedral alterpiece) (1308–11).

Duchamp, (Henri Robert) Marcel (1887–1968) French–American, born Blainville, Normandy; *Nude Descending a Staircase* (1912), *The Bride Stripped Bare by Her Bachelors Even* (1915–23).

Dufy, Raoul (1877–1953) French, born Le Havre; *Posters at Trouville* (1906), illustrations to Guillaume Apollinaire's *Bestiary* (1911), *Riders in the Wood* (1931).

Dürer, Albrecht (1471–1528) German, born Nuremberg; *Adam and Eve* (1507), *Adoration of the Magi* (1504), *Adoration of the Trinity* (1511).

Eardley, Joan (1921–63) British, born Warnham, Sussex; *Winter Sea IV* (1958), *Two Children* (1962).

Ernst, Max(imillian) (1891–1976) German–American–French, born Brühl, near Cologne, Germany; *Europe After the Rain* (1940–2), *The Elephant Célébes* (1921), *Moonmad* (1944) (sculpture), *The King Playing with the Queen* (1959) (sculpture).

Eyck, Jan van (c.1389–1441) Dutch, born Maaseyck, near Maastricht; *The Adoration of the Holy Lamb* (Ghent altarpiece) (1432), *Man in a Red Turban* (1433), *Arnolfni Marriage Portrait* (1434), *Madonna by the Fountain* (1439).

Fini, Léonor (1908–96) Italian–Argentinian, born Buenos Aires; *The End of the World* (1944).

Fragonard, Jean Honoré (1732–1806) French, born Grasse; *Coroesus Sacrificing Himself to Save Callirhoe* (1765), *The Swing* (c.1766), four canvases for Mme du Barry entitled *The Progress of Love* (1771–3).

Freud, Lucian (1922–) German–British, born Berlin; *Woman with a Daffodil* (1945), *Interior in Paddington* (1951), *Hotel Room* (1953–4).

Friedrich, Caspar David (1774–1840) German, born Pomerania; *The Cross in the Mountains* (1807–8).

Fuseli, Henri (originally Johann Heinrich Füssli) (1741–1825) Anglo-Swiss, born Zurich; *The Nightmare* (1781), *Appearance of the Ghost* (1796).

Gainsborough, Thomas (1727–88) British, born Sudbury, Suffolk; *Peasant Girl Gathering Sticks* (1782), *The Watering Place* (1777).

Gauguin, (Eugène Henri) Paul (1848–1903) French, born Paris; *The Vision After the Sermon* (1888), *Still Life with Three Puppies* (1888), *The White Horse* (1898), *Women of Tahiti* (1891), *Tahitian Landscape* (1891), *Where Do We Come From? What Are We? Where Are We Going?* (1897–8), *Golden Bodies* (1901).

Géricault, Théodore (1791–1824) French, born Rouen; *Officer of Light Horse* (c.1812), *Raft of the Medusa* (1819).

Ghirlandaio, Domenico (properly Domenico di Tommaso Bigordi) (1449–94) Italian, born Florence; *Virgin of Mercy* (1472), *St Jerome* (1480), *Nativity* (1485).

Giorgione (de Castelfranco) or Giorgio Barbarelli (c.1478–1511) Italian, born Castelfranco; *The Tempest* (c.1508), *Three Philosophers* (c.1508), *Portrait of a Man* (1510).

Giotto (di Bondone) (c.1266–1337) Italian, born near Florence; frescoes in *Arena Chapel*, Padua (1304–12), *Ognissanti Madonna* (1311–12).

Goes, Hugo van der (c.1440–82) Dutch, born probably Ghent; *Portinari Alterpiece* (1475).

Gorky, Arshile (originally Vosdanig Manoog Adoian) (1905–48) American, born Khorkom Vari, Turkish Armenia; *The Artist and His Mother* (c.1926–36), series *Image in Xhorkam* (from 1936), *The Liver is the Cock's Comb* (1944), *The Betrothal II* (1947).

Goya (y Lucientes), Francisco (José) de (1746–1828) Spanish, born Fuendetotos; *Family of Charles IV* (1799), *Los Desastres de la Guerra* (1810–14), *Black Paintings* (1820s).

Greco, El (originally Domenico Theotocopoulos) (1541–1614) Greek, born Candia, Crete; *Lady in Fur Wrap* (c.1577–8), *El Espolio* ('The Disrobing of Christ') (1577–9), *The Saviour of the World* (1600), *Portrait of Brother Hortensio Felix Paravicino* (1609), *Toledo Landscape* (c.1610).

Gris, Juan, (pseudonym of José Victoriano González) (1887–1927) Spanish, born Madrid; *Sunblind* (1914), *Still Life with Dice* (1922), *Violin and Fruit Dish* (1924).

Grünewald, Matthias (originally perhaps Mathis Nithardt or Gothardt) (c.1480–1528) German, born probably Würzburg; *Isenheim Altarpiece* (1515).

Hals, Frans (c.1580–1666) Dutch, born Antwerp; *The Laughing Cavalier* (1624), *Banquet of the Company of St Adrian* (1627), *Gypsy Girl* (c.1628–30), *Man in a Slouch Hat* (c.1660–6).

Hamilton, Richard (1922–) British, born London; *Hommage à Chrysler Corp* (1952), *Just What is it That Makes Today's Homes so Different, so Appealing?* (1956), *Study of Hugh Gaitskell as a Famous Monster of Film Land* (1964).

Hilliard, Nicholas (c.1547–1619) British, born Exeter; miniature of *Queen Elizabeth I* (1572), *Henry Wriothesley* (1594).

Hirst, Damien (1965–) British, born Bristol; *The Physical Impossibilty of Death in the Mind of Someone Living* (1991), *The Asthmatic Escaped* (1991), *Mother and Child, Divided* (1993).

Hockney, David (1937–) British, born Bradford, Yorkshire; *We Two Boys Together Clinging* (1961), *The Rake's Progress* (1963), *A Bigger Splash* (1967), *Invented Man Revealing a Still Life* (1975), *Dancer* (1980).

Hogarth, William (1697–1764) British, born Smithfield, London; *Before and After* (1731), *A Rake's Progress* (1733–5).

Hokusai, Katsushika (1760–1849) Japanese, born Tokyo; *Tametomo and the Demon* (1811), *Mangwa* (1814–19), *Hundred Views of Mount Fuji* (1835).

Holbein, Hans, (the Younger) (1497–1543) German, born Augsburg; *Bonifacius Amerbach* (1519), *Solothurn Madonna* (1522), *Anne of Cleves* (1539).

Hundertwasser, Friedensreich (Friedrich Stowasser) (1928–2000) Austrian, born Vienna; *Many Transparent Heads* (1949–50), *The End of Greece* (1963), *The Court of Sulaiman* (1967).

Hunt, (William) Holman (1827–1910) British, born London; *Our English Coasts* (1852), *Claudio and Isabella* (1853), *The Light of the World* (1854), *Isabella and the Pot of Basil* (1867).

Ingres, Jean August Dominique (1780–1867) French, born Montauban; *Gilbert* (1805), *La Source* (1807–59), *Bather* (1808), *Turkish Bath* (1863).

John, Augustus (Edwin) (1878–1961) British, born Tenby; *The Smiling Woman* (1908), *Portrait of a Lady in Black* (1917).

John, Gwen (1876–1939) British, born Haverfordwest, Pembrokeshire; *Girl with Bare Shoulders* (1909–10).

Johns, Jasper (1930–) American, born Allendale, South Carolina; *Target with Four Faces* (1955), *Beer Cans* (1961) (sculpture).

Kandinsky, Wassily (1866–1944) Russian–French, born Moscow; *Kossacks* (1910–11), *Swinging* (1925), *Two Green Points* (1935), *Sky Blue* (1940).

Kiefer, Anselm (1945–) German, born Donaueschingen, Baden; *Parsifal III* (1973), *Innenraum* (1982), *Lilith* (1989).

Kirchner, Ernst Ludwig (1880–1938) German, born Aschaffenburg; *Recumbent Blue Nude with Straw Hat* (1908–9), *The Drinker* (1915), *Die Amselfluh* (1923).

Kitaj, R(onald) B(rooks) (1932–) American, born Cleveland, Ohio; *The Ohio Gang* (1964), *If Not, Not* (1975–6).

Klee, Paul (1879–1940) Swiss, born Münchenbuchsee, near Berne; *Der Vollmond* (1919), *Rosegarden* (1920), *Twittering Machine* (1922), *A Tiny Tale of a Tiny Dwarf* (1925), *Fire in the Evening* (1929).

Klimt, Gustav (1862–1918) Austrian, born Baumgarten, near Vienna; *Music* (1895), *The Kiss* (1907–8), *Judith II (Salome)* (1909).

Kline, Franz Joseph (1910–62) American, born Wilkes-Barre, Pennsylvania; *Orange and Black Wall* (1939), *Chief* (1950), *Mahoning* (1956).

Kokoschka, Oskar (1886–1980) Anglo-Austrian, born Pöchlarn; *The Dreaming Boys* (1908).

Kupka, Frantisek (1871–1957) Czech, born in Opocno, East Bohemia; *Girl with a Ball* (1908), *Amorpha: Fugue in Two Colours* (1912), *Working Steel* (1921–9).

Landseer, Sir Edwin (Henry) (1803–73) British, born London; *The Old Shepherd's Chief Mourner* (1837), *The Monarch of the Glen* (1850).

La Tour, Georges (Dumesnil) de (1593–1652) French, born Vic-sur-Seille, Lorraine; *St Jerome Reading* (1620s), *The Denial of St Peter* (1650).

Léger, Fernand (1881–1955) French, born Argentan; *Contrast of Forms* (1913), *Black Profile* (1928), *The Great Parade* (1954).

Lely, Sir Peter (originally Pietar van der Faes) (1618–80) Anglo-Dutch, born Soest, Westphalia; *The Windsor Beauties* (1668), *Admirals* series (1666–7).

Leonardo da Vinci (1452–1519) Italian, born Vinci; *The Last Supper* (1495–7), *Madonna and Child with St Anne* (begun 1503), *Mona Lisa* (1500–6), *The Virgin of the Rocks* (c.1508).

Lichtenstein, Roy (1923–97) American, born New York City; *Whaam!* (1963), *As I Opened Fire* (1964).

Lippi, Fra Filippo, called Lippo (c.1406–69) Italian, born Florence; *Tarquinia Madonna* (1437), *Barbadori Altarpiece* (begun 1437).

Lochner, Stefan (c.1400–51) German, born Meersburg am Bodensee; *The Adoration of the Magi* (c.1448), triptych in Cologne Cathedral.

Macke, August (1887–1914) German, born Meschede; *Greeting* (1912), *The Zoo* (1912), *Girls Under Trees* (1914).

Magritte, René (François Ghislain) (1898–1967) Belgian, born Lessines, Hainault; *The Menaced Assassin* (1926), *Loving Perspective* (1935), *Presence of Mind* (1960).

Manet, Édouard (1932–83) French, born Paris; *Le Déjeuner sur l'herbe* (1863), *La Brioche* (1870), *A Bar at the Folies-Bergères* (1882).

Mantegna, Andrea (1431–1506) Italian, born Vicenza; *Madonna of Victory* (altarpiece), *San Zeno Altarpiece* (1457–9), *Triumphs of Caesar* (c.1486–94).

Martin, John (1789–1854) British, born Haydon Bridge; *Joshua Commanding the Sun to Stand Still* (1816), *The Last Judgement* (1851–4).

Martini or Memmi, Simone (c.1284–1344) Italian, born Siena; *S Caterina Polyptych* (1319), *Annunciation* (1333).

Masaccio (real name Tamasso de Giovanni di Simone Guidi) (1401–28) Italian, born Castel San Giovanni di Val d'Arno; polyptych for the *Carmelite Church* in Pisa (1426), frescoes in *Sta Maria del Carmine*, Florence (1424–7).

Masson, André (Aimé René) (1896–1987) French, born Balgny, Oise; *Massacres* (1933), *The Labyrinth* (1939).

Matisse, Henri (Emile Benoît) (1869–1954) French, born Le Cateau-Cambrésis; *La Desserte* (1908), *Notre Dame* (1914), *The Large Red Studio* (1948), *L'Escargot* (1953).

Michelangelo (in full Michelangelo di Lodovico Buonarroti) (1475–1564) Italian, born Caprese, Tuscany; *The Pietà* (1497) (sculpture), *David* (1501–4) (sculpture), *Madonna* (c.1502), ceiling of the *Sistine Chapel*, Rome (1508–12), *The Last Judgement* (begun 1537).

Millais, Sir John Everett (1829–96) British, born Southampton; *Ophelia* (1851–2), *The Bridesmaid* (1851), *Tennyson* (1881), *Bubbles* (1886).

Millet, Jean-François (1814–75) French, born Grouchy; *Sower* (1850), *The Gleaners* (1857).

Miró, Joán (1893–1983) Spanish, born Montroig; *Catalan Landscape* (1923–4), *Maternity* (1924).

Modigliani, Amedeo (1884–1920) Italian, born Leghorn (Livorno),Tuscany; *The Jewess* (1908), *Moise Kisling* (1915), *Reclining Nude* (c.1919), *Jeanne Hébuterne* (1919).

Mondrian, Piet (properly Pieter Cornelis Mondriaan) (1872–1944) Dutch, born Amersfoot; *Still Life with Gingerpot II* (1911), *Composition with Red, Black, Blue,Yellow, and Grey* (1920), *Broadway Boogie-Woogie* (1942–3).

Monet, Claude (1840–1926) French, born Paris; *Impression: Sunrise* (1872), *Haystacks* (1890–1), *Rouen Cathedral* (1892–5), *Waterlilies* (1899 onwards).

Moreau, Gustave (1826–98) French, born Paris; *Oedipus and the Sphinx* (1864), *Apparition* (1876), *Jupiter and Semele* (1889–95).

Morisot, Berthe (Marie Pauline) (1841–95) French, born Bourges; *The Harbour at Cherbourg* (1874), *In the Dining Room* (1886).

Morris,William (1834–96) British, bornWalthamstow, London; *Queen Guinevere* (1858).

Motherwell, Robert (Burns) (1915–91) American, born Aberdeen, Washington; *Gauloises* (1967), *Opens* (1968–72).

Munch, Edvard (1863–1944) Norwegian, born Löten; *The Scream* (1893), *Mother and Daughter* (c.1897), *Self-Portrait between the Clock and the Bed* (1940–2).

Nash, Paul (1899–1946) British, born London; *We Are Making a New World* (1918), *Menin Road* (1919).

Newman, Barnett (1905–70) American, born NewYork; *The Moment* (1946), *Onement I* (1948), *Vir Heroicus Sublimis* (1950–1).

Nicholson, Ben (1894–1982) British, born Denham, London; *White Relief* (1935), *November 11, 1947* (1947).

Nicholson, Winifred (1893–1981) British, born Oxford; *Honeysuckle and Sweet Peas* (1950), *The Copper and Capari* (1967), *The Gate to the Isles* (1980).

Nolde, Emil (pseudonym of Emil Hansen) (1867–1956) German, born Nolde; *The Missionary* (1912), *Candle Dancers* (1912).

Oliver, Isaac (c.1560–1617) Anglo-French, born Rouen; *Self-Portrait* (c.1590), *Henry, Prince of Wales* (c.1612).

Palmer, Samuel (1805–81) British, born London; *Repose of the Holy Family* (1824), *The Magic Apple Tree* (1830), *Opening the Fold* (1880).

Parmigiano or Pamigianino (properly Girolamo Francesco Maria Mazzola) (1503–40) Italian, born Parma; frescoes in *S Giovanni Evangelista*, Parma (c.1522), *Self-Portrait in a Convex Mirror* (1524), *Vision of St Jerome* (1526–7), *Madonna Altarpiece*, Bologna (c.1528–30), *The Madonna of the Long Neck* (c.1535).

Pasmore, (Edwin John) Victor (1908–98) British, born Chelsham, Surrey; *The Evening Star* (1945–7), *Black Symphony — the Pistol Shot* (1977).

Peploe, S(amuel) J(ohn) (1871–1935) British, born Edinburgh; one of the 'Scottish colourists'; *Boats of Royan* (1910).

Perugino (properly Pietro di Cristoforo Vannucci) (c.1450–1523) Italian, born Città della Pieve, Umbria; *Christ Giving the Keys to Peter* (fresco in the Sistine Chapel) (c.1483).

Pevsner, Antoine (1886–1962) French, born Orël, Russia; *Torso* (1924–6), *Development Column* (1942).

Picabia, Francis (Marie) (1879–1953) French, born Paris; *I See Again in Memory My Dear Undine* (1913), *The Kiss* (1924).

Picasso, Pablo (Ruiz) (1881–1973) Spanish, born Malaga; *Mother and Child* (1921), *Three Dances* (1925), *Guernica* (1937), *The Charnel House* (1945), *The Artist and His Model* (1968).

Piero della Francesca (c.1420–92) Italian, born Borgo san Sepolcro; *Madonna of the Misericordia* (1445–8), *Resurrection* (c.1450).

Piper, John (1903–92) British, born Epsom; *Windsor Castle* watercolours (1941–2), *Council Chamber, House of Commons* (1941); also stage designs and illustrated publications.

Pissarro, Camille (Jacob) (1830–1903) French, born St Thomas, West Indies; *Landscape at Chaponval* (1880), *The Boieldieu Bridge at Rouen* (1896), *Boulevard Montmartre* (1897).

Pollock, (Paul) Jackson (1912–56) American, born Cody, Wyoming; *No 14* (1948), *Guardians of the Secret* (1943).

Pontormo, Jacopo da (1494–1552) Italian; frescoes eg of the *Passion* (1522–5), *Deposition* (c.1525).

Poussin, Nicolas (1594–1665) French, born Les Andelys, Normandy; *The Adoration of the Golden Calf* (1624), *Inspiration of the Poet* (c.1628), *Seven Sacraments* (1644–8), *Self-Portrait* (1650).

Raeburn, Sir Henry (1756–1823) British, born Edinburgh; *Rev Robert Walker Skating* (1784), *Isabella McLeod, Mrs James Gregory* (c.1798).

Ramsay, Allan (1713–84) British, born Edinburgh; *The Artist's Wife* (1754–5).

Raphael (properly Raffaello Santi or Sanzio) (1483–1520) Italian, born Urbino; *Assumption of the Virgin* (1504), *Madonna of the Meadow* (1505–6), *Transfiguration* (1518–20).

Redon, Odilon (1840–1916) French, born Bordeaux; *Woman with Outstretched Arms* (c.1910–14).

Redpath, Anne (1895–1965) British, born Galashiels; *Pinks* (1947).

Rembrandt (properly Rembrandt Harmensz van Rijn) (1606–69) Dutch, born Leiden; *Anatomy Lesson of Dr Tulp* (1632), *Blinding of Samson* (1636), *The Night Watch* (1642), *The Conspiracy of Claudius* (1661–2).

Renoir, (Jean Pierre) Auguste (1841–1919) French, born Limoges; *Woman in Blue* (1874), *Woman Reading* (1876), *The Bathers* (1887).

Reynolds, Sir Joshua (1723–92) British, born Plympton Earls, near Plymouth; *Portrait of Miss Bowles with Her Dog* (1775), *Master Henry Hoare* (1788).

Riley, Bridget (Louise) (1931–) British, born London; *Pink Landscapes* (1959–60), *Zig-Zag* (1961), *Fall* (1963), *Apprehend* (1970).

Rosa, Salvator (1615–73) Italian, born Arenella, near Naples; *Self-Portrait with a Skull* (1656), *Humana Fragilitas* (c.1657).

Rossetti, Dante Gabriel (1828–82) British, born London; *Beat Beatrix* (1849–50), *Ecce Ancilla Domini!* (1850), *Astarte Syriaca* (1877).

Rothko, Mark (Marcus Rothkovitch) (1903–70) Latvian–American, born Dvinsk; *The Omen of the Eagle* (1942), *Red on Maroon* (1959).

Rousseau, Henri (Julien Félix), known as Le Douanier (1844–1910) French, born Laval; *Monsieur et Madame Stevene* (1884), *Sleeping Gipsy* (1897), *Portrait of Joseph Brunner* (1909).

Rubens, Sir Peter Paul (1577–1640) Flemish, born Siegen, Westphalia; *Marchesa Brigida Spinola-Doria* (1606), *Hélène Fourment with Two of Her Children* (c.1637).

Sargent, John Singer (1856–1925) American, born Florence; *Madame X* (1884), *Lady Agnew* (1893), *Gassel* (1918).

Schiele, Egon (1890–1918) Austrian, born Tulln; *Autumn Tree* (1909), *Pregnant Woman and Death* (1911), *Edith Seated* (1917–18).

Schnabel, Julian (1951–) American, born New York City; *The Unexpected Death of Blinky Palermo in the Tropics* (1981), *Humanity Asleep* (1982).

Seurat, Georges (Pierre) (1859–91) French, born Paris; *Bathers at Asnières* (1884), *Sunday on the Island of La Grande Jatte* (1885–6), *Le Cirque* (1891).

Sickert, Walter (Richard) (1860–1942) British, born Munich; *La Hollandaise* (1905–6), *Ennui* (c.1914).

Sisley, Alfred (1839–99) French, born Paris; *Avenue of Chestnut Trees near La Celle Saint-Cloud* (1868), *Mosley Weir, Hampton Court* (1874).

Spencer, Sir Stanley (1891–1959) British, born Cookham-on-Thames, Berkshire; *The Resurrection* (1927), *The Leg of Mutton Nude* (1937).

Steen, Jan (Havicksz) (1627–79) Dutch, born Leiden; *A Woman at Her Toilet* (1663), *The World Upside Down* (1663).

Stubbs, George (1724–1806) British, born Liverpool; *James Stanley* (1755), *Anatomy of the Horse* (1766), *Hambletonian, Rubbing Town* (1799).

Sutherland, Graham (Vivian) (1903–80) British, born London; *Entrance to a Lane* (1939), *Crucifixion* (1946), *A Bestiary and Some Correspondences* (1968).

Tanguy, Yves (1900–55) French–American, born Paris; *He Did What He Wanted* (1927), *The Invisibles* (1951).

Tatlin, Vladimir Yevgrafovich (1885–1953) Russian, born Moscow; painted reliefs, relief constructions, corner reliefs (all 1914 onwards); design for *Monument to the Third International* (1920).

Tintoretto (properly Jacopo Robusti) (1518–94) Italian, born probably Venice; *The Miracle of the Slave* (1548), *St George and the Dragon* (c.1558), *The Golden Calf* (c.1560).

Titian (properly Tiziano Veccellio) (c.1488–1576) Italian, born Pieve di Cadore; *The Assumption of the Virgin* (1516–18), *Bacchus and Ariadne* (1522–3), *Pesaro Madonna* (1519–26), *Crowning with Thorns* (c.1570).

Toulouse-Lautrec, Henri (Marie Raymond de) (1864–1901) French, born Albi; *The Jockey* (1899), *At the Moulin Rouge* (1895), *The Modiste* (1900).

Turner, Joseph Mallord William (1775–1851) British, born London; *Frosty Morning* (1813), *The Shipwreck* (1805), *Crossing the Brook* (1815), *The Fighting Téméraire* (1839), *Rain, Steam and Speed* (1844).

Uccelo, Paolo (originally Paolo di Dono) (c.1396–1475) Italian, born Pratovecchio; *The Flood* (c.1445), *The Rout of San Romano* (1454–7).

Utamaro, Kitagawa (1753–1806) Japanese, born Edo (modern Tokyo); *Ohisa* (c.1788), *The Twelve Hours of the Green Houses* (c.1795).

Van Dyck, Sir Anthony (1599–1641) Flemish, born Antwerp; *Marchesa Elena Grimaldi* (c.1625), *The Deposition* (1634–5), *Le Roi à la chasse* (c.1638).

Van Gogh, Vincent (Willem) (1853–90) Dutch, born Groot-Zundert, near Breda; *The Potato Eaters* (1885), *Self-Portrait with Bandaged Ear* (1888), *The Harvest* (1888), *The Sunflowers* (1888), *Starry Night* (1889), *Cornfields with Flight of Birds* (1890).

Velázquez, Diego (Rodríguez de Silva y) (1599–1660) Spanish, born Seville; *The Immaculate Conception* (c.1618), *The Waterseller of Seville* (c.1620), *The Surrender of Breda* (1634–5), *Pope Innocent X* (1650), *Las Meninas* (c.1656).

Vermeer, Jan (Johannes) (1632–75) Dutch, born Delft; *The Astronomer* (1668), *Christ in the House of Mary and Martha* (date unknown), *A Lady with a Gentleman at the Virginals* (c.1665), *The Lacemaker* (date unknown).

Veronese (pseudonym of Paolo Caliari) (1528–88) Italian, born Verona; *The Feast in the House of Levi* (1573), *Marriage at Cana* (1573), *Triumph of Venice* (c.1585).

Verrocchio, Andrea del (properly Andrea del Cionie) (c.1435–c.1488) Italian, born Florence; *Baptism of Christ* (c.1470), *David* (c.1475) (sculpture).

Vlaminck, Maurice de (1876–1958) French, born Paris; *The Red Trees* (1906), *Tugboat at Chatou* (1906).

Warhol, Andy (originally Andrew Warhola) (1928–87) American, born McKeesport, Pennsylvania; *Marilyn* (1962), *Electric Chair* (1963).

Watteau, (Jean) Antoine (1684–1721) French, born Valenciennes; *The Pilgrimage to the Island of Cythera* (1717), *L'Enseigne de Gersaint* (1721).

Whistler, James (Abbott) McNeill (1834–1903) American, born Lowell, Massachusetts; *The Artist's Mother* (1871), *Nocturne in Blue and Silver: Old Battersea Bridge* (1872–5), *Falling Rocket* (1875).

Wilkie, Sir David (1785–1841) British, born Cults, Fife; *The Village Politicians* (1806), *Chelsea Pensioners Reading the Waterloo Despatch* (1822).

Wood, Grant (1891–1942) American, born Iowa; *American Gothic* (1930), *Spring Turning* (1936).

Wright, Joseph, ('of Derby') (1734–97) British, born Derby; *Experiment with an Air Pump* (1766), *The Alchemist in Search of the Philosopher's Stone Discovers Phosphorous* (1795).

Wyeth, Andrew (Newell) (1917–) American, born Chadds Ford, Pennsylvania; *Christina's World* (1948).

Architects

Selected works are listed.

Aalto, (Hugo) Alvar (Henrik) (1898–1976) Finnish, born Kuortane; *Convalescent Home*, Paimio, near Turku (1929–30), *Town Hall*, Saynatsab (1950–2), *Finlandia Concert Hall*, Helsinki (1971).

Adam, Robert (1728–92) Scottish, born Kirkcaldy; *Adelphi*, London (1769–71, demolished 1936), *General Register House* (begun 1774), *Charlotte Square* (1791), *University of Edinburgh, Old College* (1789–94), all Edinburgh; *Culzean Castle*, Ayrshire (1772–92).

Adam, William (1689–1748) Scottish, born Maryburgh; *Hopetoun House*, near Edinburgh (1721).

Alberti, Leone Battista (1404–72) Italian, born Genoa; façade of the *Palazzo Recellai*, Florence (1460), *San Andrea*, Mantua (1470).

Anthemias of Tralles (dates unknown) Greek, born Tralles, Lydia; *Hagia Sophia*, Constantinople (now Istanbul) (532–7).

Apollodorus of Damascus (dates unknown) Greek, born Syria; *Trajan's Forum*, Rome, *The Baths of Trajan*, Rome.

Arnolfo di Cambio (1232–1302) Italian, born Colle di Val d'Elsa, Tuscany; *Florence Cathedral* (1299–1310).

Asplund, Erik Gunnar (1885–1940) Swedish, born Stockholm; *Stockholm City Library* (1924–7), *Law Courts*, Gothenburg (1934–7).

Baker, Sir Herbert (1862–1946) English, born Kent; *Groote Schuur*, near Cape Town (1892–1902), *Union Government Buildings*, Pretoria (1907).

Barry, Sir Charles (1795–1860) English, born London; *Royal Institution of the Arts*, Manchester (1824), *Houses of Parliament*, London (opened 1852).

Behrens, Peter (1868–1940) German, born Hamburg; *Turbine Assembly Works*, Berlin (1909), *German Embassy*, St Petersburg (1912).

Berlage, Hendrick Petrus (1856–1934) Dutch, born Amsterdam; *Amsterdam Bourse* (1903), *Holland House*, London (1914), *Gemeente Museum*, The Hague (1934).

Bernini, Gian Lorenzo (1598–1680) Italian, born Naples; *St Peter's Baldacchino* (1625), *Cornaro Chapel* in the Church of Santa Maria della Vittoria (1645–52), both Rome.

Borromini, Francesco (1599–1667) Italian, born Bissone, on Lake Lugano; *S Carlo alle Quattro Fontane* (1637–41), *S Ivo della Sapienza* (1642–61), both Rome.

Boullée, Étienne-Louis (1728–99) French, born Paris; *Hôtel de Brunoy*, Paris (1772), *Monument to Isaac Newton* (never built) (1794).

Bramante, Donato (originally Donato di Pascuccio d'Antonio) (1444–1514) Italian, born near Urbino; *San Maria presso S Satiro*, Milan (begun 1482), *Tempietto of S Pietro*, Rome (1502).

Breuer, Marcel Lajos (1902–81) Hungarian–American, born Pécs, Hungary; *UNESCO Building*, Paris (1953–8).

Brosse, Salomon de (1565–1626) French, born Verneuil-sur-Oise; *Luxembourg Palace*, Paris (1615–20), *Louis XIII's Hunting Lodge*, Versailles (1624–6).

Brunelleschi, Filippo (1377–1446) Italian, born Florence; *San Lorenzo*, Florence (begun 1418), Dome of *Florence Cathedral* (begun 1420), *Ospedale degli Innocenti*, Florence (1419).

Bryce, David (1803–76) Scottish, born Edinburgh; *Fettes College* (1863–9), *Royal Infirmary* (begun 1870), both Edinburgh.

Burnham, David Hudson (1846–1912) American, born Henderson, New York; *Reliance Building*, Chicago (1890–5), *Monadnock Building*, Chicago (1890–1), *Selfridge Building*, London (1908).

Burton, Decimus (1800–81) English, born London; *Regent's Park Colosseum* (1823), *Arch at Hyde Park Corner* (1825), both London.

Butterfield, William (1814–1900) English, born London; *Keble College*, Oxford (1866–86), *St Augustine's College*, Canterbury (1844–73), *All Saints*, Margaret Street, London (1849–59).

Campen, Jacob van (1595–1657) Dutch, born Haarlem; *Maurithuis*, The Hague (1633), *Amsterdam Theatre* (1637), *Amsterdam Town Hall* (1647–55).

Candela, Felix (1910–97) Spanish–Mexican, born Madrid; *Sports Palace* for Olympic Games, Mexico City (1968).

Chambers, Sir William (1726–96) Scottish, born Stockholm; *Somerset House* (1776), pagoda in *Kew Gardens* (1757), both London.

Chermayeff, Serge (1900–96) American, born the Caucasus Mountains, Russia; *De La Warr Pavilion*, Bexhill (1933–5).

Churriguera, Don José (1650–1725) Spanish, born Salamanca; *Salamanca Cathedral* (1692–4).

Coates, Wells Wintemute (1895–1958) English, born Tokyo; *BBC Studios* (1932), *EKCO Laboratories* (1936), *Cinema*, Festival of Great Britain Exhibition (1951).

Cockerell, Charles Robert (1788–1863) English, born London; *Taylorian Institute*, Oxford (1841–5), *Fitzwilliam Museum*, Cambridge (1837–40).

Cortona, Pietro Berrettini da (1596–1669) Italian, born Cortona; *Villa Sacchetti*, Castel Fusano (1626–7), *San Firenze*, Florence (1645).

Cuvilliés, François de (1695–1768) Bavarian, born Belgium; *Amelienburg Pavilion* at Schloss Nymphenburg, near Munich (1734–9), *Residenztheater*, Munich (1750–3).

Dance, George, (the Elder) (1700–68) English, born London; *Mansion House*, London (1739).

Dance, George, (the Younger) (1741–1825) English, born London; rebuilt *Newgate Prison* (1770–83).

Delorme, Philibert (c.1510–70) French, born Lyons; *Tuileries* (1565–70), *Châteaux of Anet, Meudon, Saint Germain-en-Laye* (1547–55).

Doesburg, Theo van (originally Christian Emil Marie Kupper) (1883–1931) Dutch, born Utrecht; *L'Art Nouveau Shop*, Paris (1896), *Keller und Reiner Art Gallery*, Berlin (1898).

Doshi, Balkrishna Vithaldas (1927–) Indian, born Poona; *City Hall*, Toronto (1958), *Indian Institute of Management*, Ahmedabad (1951–7).

Dudok, Willem Marinus (1884–1974) Dutch, born Amsterdam; *Hilversum Town Hall* (1928–30), *Bijenkorf Department Store*, Rotterdam (1929).

Engel, Johann Carl Ludwig (1778–1840) Finnish, born Berlin; layout of *Helsinki* (1818–26).

Erickson, Arthur Charles (1924–) Canadian, born Vancouver; *Simon Fraser University Buildings*, British Columbia (1963), *Lethbridge University*, Alberta (1971).

Fischer von Erlach, Johann Bernard (1656–1723) Austrian, born Graz; *Karlskirche*, Vienna (1716), *Hofbibliotek*, Vienna (1723), *Kollegienkirche*, Salzburg (1707).

Foster, Sir Norman (1935–) English, born Manchester; *Willis Faber Dumas Building*, Ipswich (1975), *Sainsbury Centre*, University of East Anglia (1978), *Hong Kong and Shanghai Bank*, Hong Kong (1979–85).

Francesco di Giorgio (1439–1501/2) Italian, born Siena; *Church of San Bernardino all'Osservanza*, Siena (1474–84), *Palazzo Ducale*, Gubbio (1476–82).

Gabriel, Ange-Jacques (1698–1782) French, born Paris; *Pavillon de Pompadour*, Fontainebleau (begun 1749), Paris; layout of *Place de la Concorde*, Paris (1753), *Petit Trianon*, Versailles (1761–8).

Garnier, Tony (Antoine) (1869–1948) French, born Lyons; *Grange Blanche Hospital*, Lyons (1911–27), *Stadium*, Lyons (1913–18), *Hôtel de Ville*, Boulogne-Bilancourt (1931–3).

Gaudí (i Cornet), Antoni (1852–1926) Spanish, born Reus, Tarragona; *Casa Vicens* (1878–80), *Sagrada Familia* (1884 onwards), *Casa Batlló* (1904–17), *Casa Milá* (1905–9), all Barcelona.

Geddes, Sir Patrick (1854–1932) Scottish, born Perth; *Ramsay Garden, Edinburgh* (1892), *Edinburgh Zoo* (1913), *Scots College*, Montpelier, France (1924).

Gibbs, James (1682–1754) Scottish, born Aberdeen; *St-Martin-in-the-Fields*, London (1722–6), *King's College Fellows' Building*, Cambridge (1724–49).

Gilbert, Cass (1859–1934) American, born Zanesville, Ohio; *Woolworth Building*, New York City (1913).

Gilly, Friedrich (1772–1800) German, born Berlin; *Funerary Precinct and Temple* to Frederick II, the Great of Prussia (1796), *Prussian National Theatre*, Berlin (1798).

Giotto (di Bondone) (c.1266–1337) Italian, born Vespignano, near Florence; *Campanile*, Florence Cathedral (from 1334).

Giulio Romano (properly Giulio Pippi de' Giannuzzi) (c.1492–1546) Italian, born Rome; *Palazzo del Tè*, Mantua (1526), *Church of S Petronio* façade, Bologna (1546).

Greenway, Francis Howard (1777–1837) Anglo-Australian, born Bristol; *Macquarie Lighthouse*, Sydney Harbour (1818), *St James' Church*, Sydney (1824).

Gropius, Walter (1883–1969) German–American, born Berlin; *Fagus Shoe Factory*, Alfeld (1911), *The Bauhaus*, Dessau (1925), both Germany; *Harvard University Graduate Centre* (1950), Massachusetts.

Guarini, Guarino (originally Camillo) (1624–83) Italian, born Modena; *San Lorenzo* church, Turin (1668–80), *Capella della SS Sindone* church, Turin (1668), *Palazzo Carignano*, Racconigi (1679).

Hamilton, Thomas (1784–1858) Scottish, born Glasgow; *Royal High School* (1825–9), *Royal College of Physicians Hall* (1844–5), *George IV Bridge* (1827–34), all Edinburgh.

Haussmann, Georges Eugène (1809–91) French, born Paris; layout of *Bois de Boulogne*, *Bois de Vincennes*, Paris (1853–70).

Hawksmoor, Nicholas (1661–1736) English, born Nottinghamshire; *St Mary Woolnoth Church* (1716–24), *St George's*, Bloomsbury (1716–30), both London.

Hildebrandt, Johann Lukas von (1668–1745) Austrian, born Genoa; *Lower and Upper Belvedere*, Vienna, (1714–15, 1720–3).

Hoffmann, Josef (1870–1956) Austrian, born Pirnitz; *Purkersdorf Sanatorium* (1903–5), *Stociet House*, Brussels (1905–11).

Holland, Henry (1746–1806) English, born London; *Carlton House*, London (1783–96), *Brighton Pavilion* (1787).

Howard, Sir Ebenezer (1850–1928) English, born London; *Letchworth Garden City* (1903).

Itkinos and Callicrates (dates and place of birth unknown) Greek; *The Parthenon*, Athens (447/6–438BC).

Jacobsen, Arne (1902–71) Danish, born Copenhagen; *Town Hall of Aarhus* (with Erik Moller, 1938–42), *Town Hall of Rodovre* (1955–6), *SAS Tower*, Copenhagen (1960), all Denmark; new *St Catherine's College*, Oxford (1959).

Jefferson, Thomas (1743–1826) American, born Shadwell, Virginia; *Monticello*, Albemarle County (1769), *Virginia State Capitol* (1796).

Johnson, Philip Cortelyou (1906–) American, born Cleveland, Ohio; *Glass House*, New Canaan, Connecticut (1949–50), *Seagram Building*, New York City (1945), *Amon Carter Museum of Western Art*, Texas (1961), *New York State Theater*, Lincoln Center (1964).

Jones, Inigo (1573–1652) English, born London; *The Queen's House*, Greenwich (1616–18, 1629–35), *Banqueting House*, Whitehall, London (1619–22).

Kahn, Louis Isadore (1901–74) American architect, born Osel (now Saaremaa), Estonia; *Richards Medical Research Building*, Pennsylvania (1957–61), *City Tower Municipal Building*, Philadelphia (1952–7).

Kent, William (1685–1748) English, born Bridlington, *Holkham Hall* (begun 1734).

Labrouste, (Pierre François) Henri (1801–75) French, born Paris; *Bibliothèque Sainte Geneviève* (1838–50), *Bibliothèque Nationale* reading room (1860–7), both Paris.

Lasdun, Sir Denys Louis (1914–) English, born London; *Royal College of Musicians* (1958–64), *National Theatre* (1965–76), both London.

Le Corbusier (pseudonym of Charles Édouard Jeanneret) (1887–1965) French, born La Chaux-de-Fonds, Switzerland; *Salvation Army Hostel*, Paris (begun 1929), *Chapel of Ronchamp*, near Belfort (1950–4), *Chandigarh*, Punjab (1951–6), *Museum of Modern Art*, Tokyo (1957).

Ledoux, Claude Nicolas (1736–1806) French, born Dormans, Champagne; *Château*, Louveciennes (1771–3), *Theatre*, Besançon (1771–3).

Leonardo da Vinci (1452–1519) Italian, born Vinci; *Mariolo de Guiscardi House*, Milan (1497), *La Veruca Fortress*, near Pisa (1504), *Villa Melzi*, Vaprio, Milan (1513).

Lescot, Pierre (c.1510–78) French, born Paris; rebuilt one wing of the *Louvre*, Paris (1546), screen of *St Germain l'Auxerrois* (1541–4).

Lethaby, William Richard (1857–1931) English, born Barnstaple; *Avon Tyrell*, Christchurch, Hampshire (1891–2), *Eagle Insurance Buildings*, Birmingham (1899–1900).

Le Vau or Levau, Louis (1612–70) French, born Paris; *Hôtel Lambert*, Paris (1640–4), part of *Palace of Versailles* (from 1661), *Collège des Quatre Nations*, Paris (1661).

Loos, Adolf (1870–1933) Austrian, born Bruno, Moravia; *Steiner House*, Vienna (1910).

Lorimer, Sir Robert Stodart (1864–1929) Scottish, born Edinburgh; *Thistle Chapel, St Giles*, Edinburgh (1909–11), *Scottish National War Memorial*, Edinburgh Castle (1923–8).

Lutyens, Sir Edwin Landseer (1869–1944) English, born London; *Cenotaph*, Whitehall, London (1919–20), *Liverpool Roman Catholic Cathedral* (1929–c.1941), *Viceroy's House*, New Delhi (1921–5).

Mackintosh, Charles Rennie (1868–1928) Scottish, born Glasgow; *Glasgow School of Art* (1897–9), *Hill House*, Helensburgh (1902–3).

Mackmurdo, Arthur Heygate (1851–1942) English, born London; *Gordon Institute for Boys*, St Helens (1890).

Maderna or Maderno, Carlo (1556–1629) Italian, born Capalago; façade of *St Peter's* (1606–12), *S Susanna* (1597–1603), *Palazzo Barberini* (1628–38), all Rome.

Mansard or Mansart, François (1598–1666) French, born Paris; north wing of *Château de Blois* (1635), *Sainte-Marie de la Visitation*, Paris (1632).

Mansard or Mansart, Jules Hardouin (1645–1708) French, born Paris; *Grand Trianon*, *Palace of Versailles* (1678–89).

Mendelsohn, Eric (1887–1953) German, born Allenstein; *De La Warr Pavilion*, Bexhill (1933–5), *Anglo-Palestine Bank*, Jerusalem (1938).

Michelozzo di Bartolommeo (1396–1472) Italian, born Florence; *Villa Medici*, Fiesole (1458–61), *San Marco*, Florence (begun 1437).

Mies van der Rohe, Ludwig (1886–1969) German–American, born Aachen; *Seagram Building*, New York City (1956–8), *Public Library*, Washington (1967).

Moore, Charles Willard (1925–) American, born Benton Harbor, Michigan; *Sea Ranch Condominium Estate*, Glendale, California (1965), *Kresge College*, Santa Cruz, California (1974), *Piazza d'Italia*, New Orleans (1975–8), *Civic Center*, Beverly Hills, California (1990).

Nash, John (1752–1835) English, born London; layout of *Regent's Park* and *Regent Street*, London (1811 onwards), *Brighton Pavilion* (1815).

Nervi, Pier Luigi (1891–1979) Italian, born Sondrio; *Berta Stadium*, Florence (1930–2), *Olympic Stadia*, Rome (1960), *San Francisco Cathedral* (1970).

Neumann, (Johann) Balthasar (1687–1753) German, born Eger; *Würzburg Palace* (1730–43), *Schloss Bruchsal* (1738–53).

Niemeyer, Oscar (1907–) Brazilian, born Rio de Janeiro; *Church of St Francis of Assisi*, Pampúlha, Belo Horizonte (1942–4), *Niemeyer House*, Rio de Janeiro (1953).

Oud, Jacobus Johann Pieter (1890–1963) Dutch, born Purmerend; *Alida Hartog-Ond House*, Purmerend (1906), *Café de Unie*, Rotterdam (1924), *Convention Centre*, The Hague (1957–63).

Palladio, Andrea (1508–80) Italian, born Padua; *Godi-Porto* (villa at Lonedo) (1540), *La Malcontenta* (villa near Padua) (1560), *San Giorgio Maggiore*, Venice (begun 1566).

Paxton, Sir Joseph (1801–65) English, born Milton-Bryant, near Woburn; building for *Great Exhibition* of 1851, later re-erected as the *Crystal Palace*, Sydenham (1852–4).

Pei, Ieoh Meng (1917–) Chinese–American, born Canton; *Mile High Center*, Denver (1954–9), *John Hancock Tower*, Boston (1973), *Glass Pyramids*, the Louvre, Paris (1983–9).

Perret, Auguste (1874–1954) French, born Brussels; *Théâtre des Champs Élysées*, Paris (1911–13), *Musée des travaux publics*, Paris (1936).

Piranesi, Giambattista (1720–78) Italian, born Venice; *Santa Maria Arentina*, Rome (1764–6).

Pisano, Nicola (c.1225–c.1284) Italian, born Tuscany; *Pisa Baptistry* (1260), façade renovation of *Pisa Cathedral* (1260–70).

Playfair, William Henry (1789–1857) Scottish, born London; *National Gallery of Scotland* (1850–7), *Royal Scottish Academy* (1832–5), *Surgeon's Hall* (1829–32), all Edinburgh.

Poelzig, Hans (1869–1936) German, born Berlin; *Exhibition Hall*, Posen (1910–11), *Salzburg Festival Theatre* (1920–2).

Pugin, August Welby Northmore (1812–52) English, born London; drawings, decorations and sculpture for the *Houses of Parliament*, London (1836–7), *Birmingham Cathedral* (1839–41).

Renwick, James (1818–95) American, born New York; *Smithsonian Institution*, Washington (1844–55), *Grace Church*, New York (1846), *St Patrick's Cathedral*, New York (1858–79).

Rietveld, Gerrit Thomas (1888–1964) Dutch, born Utrecht; *Schröder House*, Utrecht (1924), *Van Gogh Museum*, Amsterdam (1963–4).

Rogers, Richard George Rogers, Baron (1933–) English, born Florence; *Pompidou Centre*, Paris (1971–9), *Lloyds*, London (1979–85).

Saarinen, (Gottlieb) Eliel (1873–1950) Finnish–American, born Rantasalmi; *Cranbrook Academy of Art*, Michigan (1934–40).

Saarinen, Eero (1910–61) Finnish–American, born Kirkkonummi; *Jefferson Memorial Arch*, St Louis (1948–64), *American Embassy*, London (1955–60).

Sanmichele, Michele (c.1484–1559) Italian, born Verona; *Capella Pelegrini*, Verona (1527–57), *Palazzo Grimani*, Venice (1551–9).

Sansovino, Jacopo (1486–1570) Italian, born Florence; *Library* and *Mint*, Venice.

Schinkel, Karl Friederich (1781–1841) German, born Neurippen, Brandenburg; *Old Museum*, Berlin (1823–30), *War Memorial on the Kreuzberg* (1818).

Scott, Sir George Gilbert (1811–78) English, born Gawcott, Buckinghamshire; *Albert Memorial*, London (1862–3), *St Pancras station and hotel*, London (1865), *Glasgow University* (1865).

Serlio, Sebastiano (1475–1554) Italian, born Bologna; *Grand Ferrare*, Fontainebleau (1541–8), *Château*, Ancy-le-Franc, Tonnerre (from 1546).

Shaw, (Richard) Norman (1831–1912) English, born Edinburgh; *Old Swan House*, Chelsea (1876), *New Scotland Yard*, London (1888).

Smirke, Sir Robert (1781–1867) English, born London; *Covent Garden Theatre*, London (1809), *British Museum*, London (1823–47).

Smythson, Robert (c.1535–1614) English, place of birth unknown; *Wollaton Hall*, Nottingham (1580–8), *Hardwick Hall*, Derbyshire (1591–7).

Soane, Sir John (1753–1837) English, born near Reading; altered interior of *Bank of England* (1788–1833), *Dulwich College Art Gallery* (1811–14).

Sottsass, Ettore, Jr (1917–) Italian, born Innsbruck; *Apartment Building*, Turin (1934), *Galleria del Cavallino*, Venice (1956).

Soufflot, Jacques Germain (1713–80) French, born Irancy; *Hôtel Dieu*, Lyons (1741), *St Geneviève* (Panthéon), Paris (begun 1757).

Spence, Sir Basil Urwin (1907–76) Scottish, born India; pavilions for *Festival of Britain*, London (1951), new *Coventry Cathedral* (1951).

Stirling, Sir James (1926–92) Scottish, born Glasgow; *Department of Engineering*, Leicester University (1959–63) (with James Gowan), *History Faculty*, Cambridge (1965–8), *Florey Building*, Queen's College, Oxford (1966), *Neue Staatsgalerie*, Stuttgart (1980–4).

Street, George Edmund (1824–81) English, born Woodford, Essex; *London Law Courts* (1870–81).

Stuart, James (1713–88) English, born London; rebuilt interior of *Chapel of Greenwich Hospital* (1779).

Sullivan, Louis Henry (1856–1924) American, born Boston, Massachusetts; *Wainwright Building*, St Louis (1890), *Carson, Pirie and Scott Store*, Chicago (1899–1904).

Tange, Kenzo (1913–) Japanese, born Tokyo; *Hiroshima Peace Centre* (1949–55), *Shizoka Press and Broadcasting Centre*, Tokyo (1966–7).

Utzon, Jørn (1918–) Danish, born Copenhagen; *Sydney Opera House* (1956–68), *Kuwait House of Parliament* (begun 1972).

Vanbrugh, Sir John (1664–1726) English, born London; *Castle Howard* (1699–1726), *Blenheim Palace* (1705–20).

Velde, Henri Clemens van de (1863–1957) Belgian, born Antwerp; *Werkbund Theatre*, Cologne (1914), *Museum Kröller-Muller*, Otterloo (1937–54).

Venturi, Robert Charles (1925–) American, born Philadelphia, Pennsylvania; *Brant-Johnson House*, Vail, Colorado (1976), *Sainsbury Wing*, National Gallery, London (1986–91).

Vignola, Giacomo Barozzi da (1507–73) Italian, born Vignola; *Villa di Papa Giulio* (1550–5), church of the *Il Gesu*, Rome (1586–73).

Viollet-le-Duc, Eugène Emmanuel (1814–79) French, born Paris; restored cathedral of *Notre Dame*, Paris (1845–64), *Château de Pierrefonds* (1858–70).

Voysey, Charles Francis Annesley (1857–1941) English, born London; *Grove Town Houses*, Kensington (1891–2), *Sanderson's Wallpaper Factory*, Chiswick (1902).

Wagner, Otto (1841–1918) Austrian, born Penzing, near Vienna; stations for *Vienna Stadtbahn* (1894–7), *Post Office Savings Bank*, Vienna (1904–6).

Waterhouse, Alfred (1830–1905) English, born Liverpool; *Manchester Town Hall* (1867–77), *Natural History Museum*, South Kensington, London (1873–81).

Webb, Sir Aston (1849–1930) English, born London; eastern façade of *Buckingham Palace* (1912), *Admiralty Arch* (1903–10), *Imperial College of Science* (1906), all London.

Webb, Philip (1831–1915) English, born Oxford; *Red House*, Bexley (1859), *Clouds*, Wiltshire (1881–6), *Standen*, East Grinstead (1891).

Wood, John, (the Elder) (1704–54) English. *Queen Square*, Bath (1729–36).

Wood, John, (the Younger) (1728–82) English. *Royal Crescent*, Bath (1767–75), *Assembly Rooms*, Bath (1769–71).

Wren, Sir Christopher (1632–1723) English, born East Knoyle, Wiltshire; *Pembroke College Chapel*, Cambridge (1663–5), *The Sheldonian Theatre*, Oxford (1664), *Royal Greenwich Observatory* (1675–6), *St Paul's*, London (1675–1710), *Greenwich Hospital* (1696).

Wright, Frank Lloyd (1869–1959) American, born Richland Center, Wisconsin; *Larkin Building*, Buffalo (1904), *Robie House*, Chicago (1908), *Johnson Wax Factory*, Racine, Wisconsin (1936–9), *Falling Water*, Mill Run, Pennsylvania (1936), *Guggenheim Museum*, New York (begun 1942).

Wyatt, James (1746–1813) English, born Staffordshire; *London Pantheon* (1772), *Gothic Revival Country House*, Fonthill Abbey, Wiltshire (1796–1813).

Sculptors

Selected works are listed.

Andre, Carl (1935–) American, born Quincy, Massachusetts; *144 Magnesium Square* (1969), *Twelfth Copper Corner* (1975), *Bloody Angle* (1985).

Armitage, Kenneth (1916–) British, born Leeds; *People in a Wind* (1951), *Sprawling Woman* (1958), *Figure and Clouds* (1972).

Arp, Hans (Jean) (1887–1966) French, born Strasbourg; *Eggboard* (1922), *Kore* (1958).

Barlach, Ernst (1870–1938) German, born Wedel; *Moeller-Jarke Tomb* (1901), *Have Pity!* (1919).

Bernini, Gianlorenzo (1598–1680) Italian, born Naples; *Neptune and Triton* (1620), *David* (1623), *Ecstasy of St Theresa* (1640s), *Fountain of the Four Rivers* (1648–51).

Bologna, Giovanni da (also called Giambologna) (1529–1608) French, born Douai; *Mercury* (1564–5), *Rape of the Sabines* (1579–83).

Brancusi, Constantin (1876–1957) Romanian–French, born Hobitza, Gorj; *The Kiss* (1909), *Torso of a Young Man* (1922).

Bourgeois, Louise (1911–) American, born Paris; *Labyrinthine Tower* (1963), *Destruction of the Father* (1974), *Spiders* (1995).

Calder, Alexander (1898–1976) American, born Philadelphia, Pennsylvania; *Stabiles and Mobiles* (1932), *A Universe* (1934).

Caro, Sir Anthony (1924–) British, born London; *Sailing Tonight* (1971–4), *Veduggio Sound* (1973), *Ledge Piece* (1978).

Cellini, Benvenuto (1500–71) Italian, born Florence; salt cellar of *Neptune and Ceres* (1543), *Cosimo de' Medici* (1545–7), *Perseus with the Head of Medusa* (1564).

Deacon, Richard (1949–) British, born Bangor, Wales; *Double Talk* (1987), *Kiss and Tell* (1989), *Never Mind* (1993).

Donatello (originally Donato di Betti Bardi) (c.1386–1466) Italian, born Florence; *St Mark* (1411–12), *St George Killing the Dragon* (c.1417), *Feast of Herod* (1423–37), *David, Judith and Holofernes*, Piazza della Signoria, Florence.

Epstein, Sir Jacob (1880–1959) Anglo-American, born New York City; *Rima* (1925), *Genesis* (1930), *Ecce Homo* (1934–5), *Adam* (1939), *Christ in Majesty* (Llandaff Cathedral), *St Michael and the Devil* (on the façade of Coventry Cathedral) (1958–9).

Frink, Dame Elizabeth (1930–93) British, born Thurlow, Suffolk; *Horse Lying Down* (1975), *Running Man* (1985), *Seated Man* (1986).

Gabo, Naum (originally Naum Neemia Pevsner) (1890–1977) American, born Bryansk, Russia; *Kinetic Construction* (1920), *No 1* (1943).

Gaudier-Brzeska, Henri (1891–1915) French, born St Jean de Braye, near Orléans; *Red Stone Dancer* (1913).

Ghiberti, Lorenzo (c.1378–1455) Italian, born in or near Florence; *St John the Baptist* (1412–15), *St Matthew* (1419–22), *The Gates of Paradise* (1425–52).

Giacometti, Alberto (1901–66) Swiss, born Bogonova, near Stampa; *Head* (c.1928),

Woman with Her Throat Cut (1932).

Goldsworthy, Andy (1956–) British, born Cheshire; *Hazel Stick Throws* (1980), *Slate Cone* (1988), *The Wall* (1988–9).

González, Julio (1876–1942) Spanish, born Barcelona; *Angel* (1933), *Woman Combing Her Hair* (1936), *Cactus People* (1930–40).

Hepworth, Dame (Jocelyn) Barbara (1903–75) British, born Wakefield, Yorkshire; *Figure of a Woman* (1929–30), *Large and Small Forms* (1945), *Single Form* (1963).

Leonardo da Vinci (1452–1519) Italian, born Vinci, between Pisa and Florence; *St John the Baptist*.

Michelangelo (in full Michelangelo di Lodovico Buonarotti) (1475–1564) Italian, born Caprese, Tuscany; *Cupid* (1495), *Bacchus* (1496), *Pieta* (1497), *David* (c.1500).

Moore, Henry (Spencer) (1898–1986) British, born Castleford, Yorkshire; *Recumbent Figure* (1938), *Fallen Warrior* (1956–7).

Oldenburg, Claes Thure (1929–) American, born Stockholm, Sweden; *Giant Clothespin* (1975), *The Course of the Knife* (1985), *Match Cover* (1992).

Paolozzi, Sir Eduardo Luigi (1924–) British, born Leith, Edinburgh; *Krokodeel* (c.1956–7), *Japanese War God* (1958), *Medea* (1964), *Piscator* (1981), *Manuscript of Monte Cassino*, Edinburgh (1991).

Pheidias (c.490–c.417BC) Greek, born Athens; *Athena Promachos* (460–450BC), marble sculptures of the *Parthenon* (447–432BC).

Pisano, Andrea (c.1270–1349) Italian, born Pontedera; bronze doors of the *Baptistry* of Florence (1330–6).

Pisano, Giovanni (c.1248–c.1320) Italian, born Pisa; *Fontana Magiore*, Perugia (1278), *Duomo Pulpit*, Pisa (1302–10).

Pisano, Nicola (c.1225–c.1284) Italian, birthplace unknown; *Baptistry* at Pisa (1260).

Praxiteles (5th-c BC) Greek, born probably Athens; *Hermes Carrying the Boy Dionysus* (date unknown).

Robbia, Luca della (c.1400–1482) Italian, born Florence; *Cantoria* (1432–7).

Rodin, (François) Auguste (René) (1840–1917) French, born Paris; *The Age of Bronze* (1875–6), *The Gates of Hell* (1880–1917), *The Burghers of Calais* (1884), *The Thinker* (1904).

Schwitters, Kurt (1887–1948) German, born Hannover; *Merzbau* (1920–43).

Tinguely, Jean (1925–91) Swiss, born Fribourg; *Baluba No 3* (1959), *Métamécanique No 9* (1959), *Homage to New York* (1960), *EOSX* (1967).

Whiteread, Rachel (1963–) British, born London; *Torso* (1991), *House* (1993), *Orange Bath* (1996).

Nobel Prizes 1980–2000

Year	Peace	Literature	Economic Science
1980	Adolfo Pérez Esquivel	Czeslaw Milosz	Lawrence R Klein
1981	Office of the UN High Commissioner for Refugees	Elias Canetti	James Tobin
1982	Alfonso García Robles Alva Myrdal	Gabriel García Márquez	George J Stigler
1983	Lech Walesa	William Golding	Gerald Debreu
1984	Desmond Tutu	Jaroslav Seifert	Richard Stone
1985	International Physicians for the Prevention of Nuclear War	Claude Simon	Franco Modigliani
1986	Elie Wiesel	Wole Soyinka	James M Buchanan
1987	Oscar Arias Sánchez	Joseph Brodsky	Robert M Solow
1988	UN Peacekeeping Forces	Naguib Mahfouz	Maurice Allais
1989	Tenzin Giyatso (Dalai Lama)	Camilo José Cela	Trygve Haavelmo
1990	Mikhail Gorbachev	Octavio Paz	Harry M Markovitz Merton Miller William Sharpe
1991	Aung San Suu Kyi	Nadine Gordimer	Ronald Coase
1992	Rigoberta Menchú	Derek Walcott	Gary S Becker
1993	Nelson Mandela F W de Klerk	Toni Morrison	Robert Fugel Douglas North
1994	Yasser Arafat Shimon Peres Yitzhak Rabin	Kenzaburo Oë	John Nash John Harsanyi Reinhard Selten
1995	Joseph Rotblat Pugwash Conferences on Science and World Affairs	Seamus Heaney	Robert E Lucas
1996	Carlos Filipe Ximenes Belo José Ramos-Horta	Wislawa Szymborska	James Mirrlees William Vickrey
1997	Jody Williams and the International Campaign to Ban Landmines	Dario Fo	Robert Merton Myron Scholes
1998	John Hume David Trimble	José Saramago	Amartya Sen
1999	Médecins Sans Frontières	Günter Grass	Robert A Mundell
2000	Kim Dae-jung	Gao Xingjian	James J Heckman Daniel L McFadden

SPORT AND GAMES

Olympic Games

First Modern Olympic Games took place in 1896, founded by Frenchman Baron de Coubertin (1863–1937); held every four years; women first competed in 1900; first separate Winter Games celebrations in 1924.

— Venues —

Summer Games

1896	Athens, Greece	1960	Rome, Italy
1900	Paris, France	1964	Tokyo, Japan
1904	St Louis, USA	1968	Mexico City, Mexico
1908	London, UK	1972	Munich, W Germany
1912	Stockholm, Sweden	1976	Montreal, Canada
1920	Antwerp, Belgium	1980	Moscow, USSR
1924	Paris, France	1984	Los Angeles, USA
1928	Amsterdam, Netherlands	1988	Seoul, South Korea
1932	Los Angeles, USA	1992	Barcelona, Spain
1936	Berlin, Germany	1996	Atlanta, USA
1948	London, UK	2000	Sydney, Australia
1952	Helsinki, Finland	2004	Athens, Greece
1956	Melbourne, Australia		

Winter Games

1924	Chamonix, France	1968	Grenoble, France
1928	St Moritz, Switzerland	1972	Sapporo, Japan
1932	Lake Placid, New York, USA	1976	Innsbruck, Austria
1936	Garmisch-Partenkirchen, Germany	1980	Lake Placid, New York, USA
		1984	Sarajevo, Yugoslavia
1948	St Moritz, Switzerland	1988	Calgary, Canada
1952	Oslo, Norway	1992	Albertville, France
1956	Cortina, Italy	1994	Lillehammer, Norway
1960	Squaw Valley, California, USA	1998	Nagano, Japan
		2002	Salt Lake City, USA
1964	Innsbruck, Austria	2006	Turin, Italy

The 1956 equestrian events were held at Stockholm, Sweden, due to quarantine laws in Australia.

Olympic Games were also held in 1906 in Athens, Greece, to commemorate the tenth anniversary of the birth of the modern Games.

In 1994, the Winter Games celebrations were re-adjusted to take place at the mid-point between the Summer Games years.

Leading Medal Winners

Figures for the Summer Games include medals won in 2000, and for the Winter Games medals won in 1998.

		Summer Games					Winter Games			
	Nation	Gold	Silver	Bronze	Total	Nation	Gold	Silver	Bronze	Total
1	USA	872	659	657	2 188	1 Russia[1]	108	77	74	259
2	Russia[1]	517	423	382	1 322	2 Norway	83	87	69	239
3	Germany[2]	221	262	290	773	3 Germany[2]	62	53	45	160
4	Great Britain	188	243	232	663	4 USA	59	59	41	159
5	France	189	195	216	600	5 Austria	39	53	53	145
6	Italy	179	144	155	478	6 Finland	38	49	48	135
7	Sweden	138	157	176	471	7 East Germany	39	36	35	110
8	Hungary	150	134	158	442	8 Sweden	39	28	35	102
9	East Germany	153	130	127	410	9 Switzerland	29	31	32	92
10	Australia	103	110	139	352	10 Canada	25	25	29	79

[1] Includes medals won by the former USSR team, and by the Unified Team (Armenia, Azerbaijan, Belarus, Georgia, Kazakhstan, Kyrgyzstan, Moldova, Russia, Tajikistan, Turkmenistan, Ukraine and Uzbekistan) in 1992.

[2] Includes medals won as West Germany 1968–88.

Commonwealth Games

First held as the British Empire Games in 1930; take place every four years and between Olympic celebrations; became the British Empire and Commonwealth Games in 1954; current title adopted in 1970. Figures for the Leading Medal Winners table include medals won in 1998.

Venues

1930	Hamilton, Canada
1934	London, England
1938	Sydney, Australia
1950	Auckland, New Zealand
1954	Vancouver, Canada
1958	Cardiff, Wales
1962	Perth, Australia
1966	Kingston, Jamaica
1970	Edinburgh, Scotland
1974	Christchurch, New Zealand
1978	Edmonton, Canada
1982	Brisbane, Australia
1986	Edinburgh, Scotland
1990	Auckland, New Zealand
1994	Victoria, Canada
1998	Kuala Lumpur, Malaysia
2002	Manchester, England
2006	Melbourne, Australia

Leading Medal Winners

	Nation	Gold	Silver	Bronze	Total
1	Australia	564	489	424	1 477
2	England	488	461	469	1 418
3	Canada	366	383	361	1 110
4	New Zealand	107	142	203	452
5	Scotland	65	78	126	269
6	South Africa	71	60	64	195
7	Wales	40	51	74	165
8	India	50	57	46	153
9	Kenya	50	34	43	127
10	Nigeria	30	38	39	107

Recent champions

For 1992 Summer Olympic events the designation (UT) is given for members of the Unified Team (Armenia, Azerbaijan, Belarus, Georgia, Kazakhstan, Kyrgyzstan, Moldova, Russia, Tajikistan, Turkmenistan, Ukraine and Uzbekistan).

— American football —

□ Super Bowl

First held in 1967; takes place each January; an end-of-season meeting between the champions of the two major US leagues, the National Football Conference (NFC) and the American Football Conference (AFC).

1988	Washington Redskins (NFC)
1989	San Francisco 49ers (NFC)
1990	San Francisco 49ers (NFC)
1991	New York Giants (NFC)
1992	Washington Redskins (NFC)
1993	Dallas Cowboys (NFC)
1994	Dallas Cowboys (NFC)
1995	San Francisco 49ers (NFC)
1996	Dallas Cowboys (NFC)
1997	Green Bay Packers (NFC)
1998	Denver Broncos (AFC)
1999	Denver Broncos (AFC)
2000	St Louis Rams (NFC)

— Association football —

□ FIFA World Cup

Association Football's premier event; first contested for the Jules Rimet Trophy in 1930; Brazil won it outright after winning for the third time in 1970; since then teams have competed for the FIFA (*Féderation Internationale de Football Association*) World Cup; held every four years.

Post-war winners

1950	Uruguay
1954	West Germany
1958	Brazil
1962	Brazil
1966	England
1970	Brazil
1974	West Germany
1978	Argentina
1982	Italy
1986	Argentina
1990	West Germany
1994	Brazil
1998	France

□ European Championship

Held every four years since 1960; qualifying group matches held over the two years preceding the final.

All winners

1960	USSR
1964	Spain
1968	Italy
1972	West Germany
1976	Czechoslovakia
1980	West Germany
1984	France
1988	Netherlands
1992	Denmark
1996	Germany
2000	France

□ South American Championship

Known as Copa de América; first held in 1916, for South American national sides; there were two tournaments in 1959, won by Argentina and Uruguay; discontinued in 1967, but revived eight years later; now played every two years.

1989	Brazil
1991	Argentina
1993	Argentina
1995	Uruguay
1997	Brazil
1999	Brazil

□ European Champions Cup

The leading club competition in Europe; open to the League champions of countries affiliated to UEFA (Union of European Football Associations); commonly known as the 'European Cup'; inaugurated in the 1955–6 season; played annually.

1988	PSV Eindhoven (Netherlands)
1989	AC Milan (Italy)
1990	AC Milan (Italy)
1991	Red Star Belgrade (Yugoslavia)
1992	Barcelona (Spain)
1993	Olympique Marseille (France)
1994	AC Milan (Italy)
1995	Ajax Amsterdam (Netherlands)
1996	Juventus (Italy)
1997	Borussia Dortmund (Germany)
1998	Real Madrid (Spain)
1999	Manchester United (England)
2000	Real Madrid (Spain)

□ Football Association Challenge Cup (FA Cup)

The world's oldest club knockout competition; held annually; first contested in the 1871–2 season; first final at the Kennington Oval on 16 March 1872; first winners were The Wanderers.

1988	Wimbledon
1989	Liverpool
1990	Manchester United
1991	Tottenham Hotspur
1992	Liverpool
1993	Arsenal
1994	Manchester United
1995	Everton
1996	Manchester United
1997	Chelsea
1998	Arsenal
1999	Manchester United
2000	Chelsea

□ Football League (Premier League)

The oldest league in the world, founded in 1888; consists of four divisions; the current complement of 92 teams achieved in 1950.

1987–8	Liverpool
1988–9	Arsenal
1989–90	Liverpool
1990–1	Arsenal
1991–2	Leeds United
1992–3	Manchester United
1993–4	Manchester United
1994–5	Blackburn Rovers
1995–6	Manchester United
1996–7	Manchester United
1997–8	Arsenal
1998–9	Manchester United
1999–2000	Manchester United

– Athletics

□ World Championships

First held in Helsinki, Finland in 1983, then in Rome, Italy in 1987; since 1993 every two years.

Event	Winners (Men)
1995	
100 m	Donovan Bailey (Canada)
200 m	Michael Johnson (USA)
400 m	Michael Johnson (USA)
800 m	Wilson Kipketer (Denmark)
1 500 m	Noureddine Morceli (Algeria)
5 000 m	Ismael Kirui (Kenya)
10 000 m	Haile Gebreselassie (Ethiopia)
Marathon	Martin Fiz (Spain)
3 000 m steeple-chase	Moses Kiptanui (Kenya)
110 m hurdles	Allen Johnson (USA)
400 m hurdles	Derrick Adkins (USA)
20 km walk	Michele Didoni (Italy)
50 km walk	Valentin Kononen (Finland)
4 × 100 m relay	Canada
4 × 400 m relay	USA
High jump	Troy Kemp (Bahamas)

Long jump	Ivan Pedroso (Cuba)
Triple jump	Jonathan Edwards (Great Britain)
Pole vault	Sergei Bubka (Ukraine)
Shot	John Godina (USA)
Discus	Lars Riedel (Germany)
Hammer	Andrei Abduvaliyev (Tajikistan)
Javelin	Jan Zelezny (Czech Republic)
Decathlon	Dan O'Brien (USA)

1997

100 m	Maurice Greene (USA)
200 m	Ato Boldon (Trinidad)
400 m	Michael Johnson (USA)
800 m	Wilson Kipketer (Denmark)
1 500 m	Hicham El Guerrouj (Morocco)
5 000 m	Daniel Komen (Kenya)
10 000 m	Haile Gebreselassie (Ethiopia)
Marathon	Abel Anton (Spain)
3 000 m steeple-chase	Wilson Boit Kipketer (Kenya)
110 m hurdles	Allen Johnson (USA)
400 m hurdles	Stephane Diagana (France)
20 km walk	Daniel Garcia (Mexico)
50 km walk	Robert Korzeniowski (Poland)
4 × 100 m relay	Canada
4 × 400 m relay	USA
High jump	Javier Sotomayor (Cuba)
Long jump	Ivan Pedroso (Cuba)
Triple jump	Yoelvis Quesada (Cuba)
Pole vault	Sergei Bubka (Ukraine)
Shot	Aleksandr Bagach[1] (Ukraine)
Discus	Lars Riedel (Germany)
Hammer	Heinz Weis (Germany)
Javelin	Marius Corbett (South Africa)
Decathlon	Tomás Dvorák (Czech Republic)

1999

100 m	Maurice Greene (USA)
200 m	Maurice Greene (USA)
400 m	Michael Johnson (USA)
800 m	Wilson Kipketer (Denmark)
1 500 m	Hicham El Guerrouj (Morocco)
5 000 m	Salah Hissou (Morocco)
10 000 m	Haile Gebreselassie (Ethiopia)
Marathon	Abel Antón (Spain)
3 000 m steeple-chase	Christopher Koskei (Kenya)
110 m hurdles	Colin Jackson (Great Britain)
400 m hurdles	Fabrizio Mori (Italy)
20 km walk	Ilya Markov (Russia)
50 km walk	German Skurygin (Russia)
4 × 100 m relay	USA
4 × 400 m relay	USA
High jump	Vyacheslav Voronin (Russia)
Long jump	Ivan Pedroso (Cuba)
Triple jump	Charles Michael Friedek (Germany)
Pole vault	Maksim Tarasov (Russia)
Shot	C J Hunter (USA)
Discus	Anthony Washington (USA)
Hammer	Karsten Kobs (Germany)
Javelin	Aki Parviainen (Finland)
Decathlon	Tomás Dvorák (Czech Republic)

[1] Stripped of gold medal following positive drugs test; medal awarded to John Godina (USA).

Event	*Winners (Women)*

1995

100 m	Gwen Torrence (USA)
200 m	Merlene Ottey (Jamaica)
400 m	Marie-José Pérec (France)
800 m	Ana Fidelia Quirot (Cuba)
1 500 m	Hassiba Boulmerka (Algeria)
5 000 m	Sonia O'Sullivan (Ireland)
10 000 m	Fernanda Ribeiro (Portugal)
Marathon	Manuela Machado (Portugal)
100 m hurdles	Gail Devers (USA)

400 m hurdles	Kim Batten (USA)
10 km walk	Irina Stankina (Russia)
4 × 100 m relay	USA
4 × 400 m relay	USA
High jump	Stefka Kostadinova (Bulgaria)
Long jump	Fiona May (Italy)
Triple jump	Inessa Kravets (Ukraine)
Shot	Astrid Kumbernuss (Germany)
Discus	Ellina Zvereva (Belarus)
Javelin	Natalya Shikolenko (Belarus)
Heptathlon	Ghada Shouaa (Syria)
1997	
100 m	Marion Jones (USA)
200 m	Zhanna Pintussevich (Ukraine)
400 m	Cathy Freeman (Australia)
800 m	Ana Fidelia Quirot (Cuba)
1 500 m	Carla Sacramento (Portugal)
5 000 m	Gabriela Szabo (Romania)
10 000 m	Sally Barsosio (Kenya)
Marathon	Hiromi Suzuki (Japan)
100 m hurdles	Ludmila Engquist (Sweden)
400 m hurdles	Nezha Bidouane (Morocco)
10 km walk	Annarita Sidoti (Italy)
4 × 100 m relay	USA
4 × 400 m relay	Germany
High jump	Hanne Haugland (Norway)
Long jump	Lyudmila Galkina (Russia)
Triple jump	Sarka Kasparkova (Czech Republic)
Shot	Astrid Kumbernuss (Germany)
Discus	Beatrice Faumuina (New Zealand)
Javelin	Trine Hattestad (Norway)
Heptathlon	Sabine Braun (Germany)
1999	
100 m	Marion Jones (USA)
200 m	Inger Miller (USA)
400 m	Cathy Freeman (Australia)
800 m	Ludmilla Formanova (Czech Republic)

1 500 m	Svetlana Masterkova (Russia)
5 000 m	Gabriela Szabo (Romania)
10 000 m	Gete Wami (Ethiopia)
Marathon	Jong Song-Ok (North Korea)
100 m hurdles	Gail Devers (USA)
400 m hurdles	Daimi Pernia (Cuba)
20 km walk	Liu Hongyu (China)
4 × 100 m relay	Bahamas
4 × 100 m relay	Russia
High jump	Inga Babakova (Ukraine)
Long jump	Niurka Montalvo (Spain)
Triple jump	Paraskevi Tsiamita (Greece)
Pole vault	Stacy Draglia (USA)
Shot	Astrid Kumbernuss (Germany)
Discus	Franka Dietzsch (Germany)
Hammer	Michaela Melinte (Romania)
Javelin	Mirela Manjani-Tzelili (Greece)
Heptathlon	Eunice Barber (France)

[1] Stripped of gold medal following positive drugs test; medal awarded to John Godina (USA).

—Australian rules football—

▫ Australian Football League Trophy

The top prize is the Australian Football League Trophy (Victoria Football League 1897–1989); inaugural winners in 1897 were Essendon.

1988	Hawthorn
1989	Hawthorn
1990	Collingwood
1991	Hawthorn
1992	West Coast
1993	Essendon
1994	West Coast
1995	Carlton
1996	North Melbourne
1997	Adelaide
1998	Adelaide
1999	North Melbourne
2000	Essendon

— Baseball ————————

□ World Series

First held in 1903; takes place each October, the best of seven matches; professional baseball's leading event, the end-of-season meeting between the winners of the two major baseball leagues in the USA, the National League (NL) and the American League (AL).

1988	Los Angeles Dodgers (NL)
1989	Oakland Athletics (AL)
1990	Cincinatti Reds (NL)
1991	MinnesotaTwins (AL)
1992	Toronto BlueJays (AL)
1993	Toronto BlueJays (AL)
1994	not held
1995	Atlanta Braves (NL)
1996	NewYorkYankees (AL)
1997	Florida Marlins (NL)
1998	NewYorkYankees (AL)
1999	NewYorkYankees (NL)

□ World Amateur Championship

Instituted in 1938; since 1990 held every four years.

1978	Cuba
1980	Cuba
1982	South Korea
1984	Cuba
1986	Cuba
1988	Cuba
1990	Cuba
1994	Cuba
1998	Cuba

— Basketball ————————

□ World Championship

First held 1950 for men, 1953 for women; takes place approximately every four years.

Men

1974	USSR
1978	Yugoslavia
1982	USSR
1986	USA
1990	Yugoslavia
1994	USA
1998	Yugoslavia

Women

1975	USSR
1979	USA
1983	USSR
1987	USA
1991	USA
1994	Brazil
1998	USA

□ National Basketball Association Championship

First held in 1947; the major competition in professional basketball in the USA, end-of-season NBA Play-off involving the champion teams from the Eastern Conference (EC) and Western Conference (WC).

1988	Los Angeles Lakers (WC)
1989	Detroit Pistons (EC)
1990	Detroit Pistons (EC)
1991	Chicago Bulls (EC)
1992	Chicago Bulls (EC)
1993	Chicago Bulls (EC)
1994	Houston Rockets (WC)
1995	Houston Rockets (WC)
1996	Chicago Bulls (EC)
1997	Chicago Bulls (EC)
1998	Chicago Bulls (EC)
1999	San Antonio Spurs (WC)
2000	Los Angeles Lakers (WC)

— Boxing ————————

□ World Heavyweight Champions

The first world heavyweight champion under Queensbury Rules with gloves was James J Corbett in 1892.

		Recognizing Body
1989	Francesco Damiani (Italy)	WBO
1990	James (Buster) Douglas (USA)	WBA/WBC/IBF
1990	Evander Holyfield (USA)	WBA/WBC/IBF

1991	Ray Mercer (USA)	WBO
1992	Riddick Bowe (USA) [1]	WBA/WBC/IBF
1992	Michael Moorer (USA)	WBO
1993	Evander Holyfield (USA)	WBA/IBF
1993	Lennox Lewis (UK)	WBC
1993	Tommy Morrison (USA)	WBO
1993	Michael Bentt (USA)	WBO
1994	Herbie Hide (UK)	WBO
1994	Michael Moorer (USA)	WBA/IBF
1994	Oliver McCall (USA)	WBC
1994	George Foreman (USA) [2,3]	WBA/IBF
1995	Riddick Bowe (USA)	WBO
1995	Bruce Seldon (USA)	WBA
1995	Frank Bruno (UK)	WBC
1995	Frans Botha (South Africa) [4]	IBF
1996	Mike Tyson (USA) [5]	WBA/WBC
1996	Henry Akinwande (UK)	WBO
1996	Michael Moorer (USA)	IBF
1996	Evander Holyfield (USA)	WBA
1997	Evander Holyfield (USA)	WBA/IBF
1997	Lennox Lewis (UK)	WBC
1997	Herbie Hide (UK)	WBO
1999	Vitali Klitschko (Ukraine)	WBO
1999	Lennox Lewis (UK)	WBA/WBC/IBF [6]
2000	Chris Byrd (USA)	WBO
2000	Evander Holyfield (USA)	WBA

[1] stripped of WBC title in 1992.

[2] gave up IBF title in 1995.

[3] stripped of WBA title in 1995.

[4] stripped of IBF title in 1996.

[5] gave up WBC title in 1996.

[6] stripped of WBA title in 2000.

UND = Undisputed Champion
WBC = World Boxing Council
WBA = World Boxing Association
IBF = International Boxing Federation
WBO = World Boxing Organization

Chess

□ World Champions

World Champions have been recognized since 1886. The first international tournament was held in London in 1851,

and won by Adolf Anderssen (Germany); first women's champion recognized in 1927.

Men

1985–93	Gary Kasparov (USSR)
1993–8	Anatoliy Karpov (Russia)
1999–	Alexander Khalifman (Russia)

Women

1978–91	Maya Chiburdanidze (USSR)
1991–6	Xie Jun (China)
1996–8	Zsuzsa Polgar (Hungary)
1999–	Xye Jun (China)

Cricket

□ World Cup

First played in England in 1975; usually held every four years; the 1987 competition, held in India and Pakistan, was the first to be played outside England.

1983	India
1987	Australia
1992	Pakistan
1996	Sri Lanka
1999	Australia

□ County Championship

The oldest cricket competition in the world; first won by Sussex in 1827; not officially recognized until 1890, when a proper points system was introduced.

1988	Worcestershire
1989	Worcestershire
1990	Middlesex
1991	Essex
1992	Essex
1993	Middlesex
1994	Warwickshire
1995	Warwickshire
1996	Leicestershire
1997	Glamorgan
1998	Leicestershire
1999	Surrey
2000	Surrey

❑ Norwich Union National Cricket League

First held in 1969; known as the John Player League until 1987, the Refuge Assurance League until 1991, the Axa Equity and Law League until 1999 and the CGU League until 2000.

1988	Worcestershire
1989	Lancashire
1990	Derbyshire
1991	Nottinghamshire
1992	Middlesex
1993	Glamorgan
1994	Warwickshire
1995	Kent
1996	Surrey
1997	Warwickshire
1999	Lancashire
2000	Gloucestershire

❑ NatWest Bank Trophy

First held in 1963; known as the Gillette Cup until 1981.

1988	Middlesex
1989	Warwickshire
1990	Lancashire
1991	Hampshire
1992	Northamptonshire
1993	Warwickshire
1994	Worcestershire
1995	Warwickshire
1996	Lancashire
1997	Essex
1998	Lancashire
1999	Gloucestershire
2000	Gloucestershire

❑ Benson and Hedges Cup

First held in 1972.

1988	Hampshire
1989	Nottinghamshire
1990	Lancashire
1991	Worcestershire
1992	Hampshire
1993	Derbyshire
1994	Warwickshire

1995	Lancashire
1996	Lancashire
1997	Surrey
1998	Essex
1999	Gloucestershire
2000	Gloucestershire

❑ Pura Milk Cup

Australia's leading domestic competition; contested inter-state since 1891–2, known as the Sheffield Shield until 1999.

1988	Western Australia
1989	Western Australia
1990	New South Wales
1991	Victoria
1992	Western Australia
1993	New South Wales
1994	New South Wales
1995	Queensland
1996	South Australia
1997	Queensland
1998	Western Australia
1999	Queensland

─ Cycling ─────────────

❑ Tour de France

World's premier cycling event; first held in 1903.

1988	Pedro Delgado (Spain)
1989	Greg LeMond (USA)
1990	Greg LeMond (USA)
1991	Miguel Indurain (Spain)
1992	Miguel Indurain (Spain)
1993	Miguel Indurain (Spain)
1994	Miguel Indurain (Spain)
1995	Miguel Indurain (Spain)
1996	Bjarne Riis (Denmark)
1997	Jan Ullrich (Germany)
1998	Marco Pantani (Italy)
1999	Lance Armstrong (USA)
2000	Lance Armstrong (USA)

❏ World Road Race Championships

Men's race first held in 1927; first women's race in 1958; takes place annually.

Professional Men

1988	Maurizio Fondriest (Italy)
1989	Greg LeMond (USA)
1990	Rudy Dhaenens (Belgium)
1991	Gianni Bugno (Italy)
1992	Gianni Bugno (Italy)
1993	Lance Armstrong (USA)
1994	Luc Leblanc (France)
1995	Abraham Olano (Spain)
1996	Johan Museeuw (Belgium)
1997	Laurent Brochard (France)
1998	Oskar Camenzind (Switzerland)
1999	Oscar Freire Gomez (Spain)

Women

1988	Jeannie Longo (France)
1989	Jeannie Longo (France)
1990	Catherine Marsal (France)
1991	Leontien van Moorsel (Netherlands)
1992	Kathryn Watt (Australia)
1993	Leontien van Moorsel (Netherlands)
1994	Monica Valvik (Norway)
1995	Jeannie Longo (France)
1996	Barbara Heeb (Switzerland)
1997	Alessandra Cappellotto (Italy)
1998	Diana Ziliute (Lithuania)
1999	Edita Pucinskaite (Lithuania)

Golf

❏ British Open

First held at Prestwick in 1860, and won by Willie Park; takes place annually; regarded as the world's leading golf tournament.

1988	Severiano Ballesteros (Spain)
1989	Mark Calcavecchia (USA)
1990	Nick Faldo (Great Britain)
1991	Ian Baker-Finch (Australia)
1992	Nick Faldo (Great Britain)
1993	Greg Norman (Australia)
1994	Nick Price (Zimbabwe)
1995	John Daly (USA)
1996	Tom Lehman (USA)
1997	Justin Leonard (USA)
1998	Mark O'Meara (USA)
1999	Paul Lawrie (Great Britain)
2000	Tiger Woods (USA)

❏ United States Open

First Held at Newport, Rhode Island, in 1895, and won by Horace Rawlins; takes place annually.

1988	Curtis Strange (USA)
1989	Curtis Strange (USA)
1990	Hale Irwin (USA)
1991	Payne Stewart (USA)
1992	Tom Kite (USA)
1993	Lee Janzen (USA)
1994	Ernie Els (South Africa)
1995	Corey Pavin (USA)
1996	Steve Jones (USA)
1997	Ernie Els (South Africa)
1998	Lee Janzen (USA)
1999	Payne Stewart (USA)
2000	Tiger Woods (USA)

❏ US Masters

First held in 1934; takes place at the Augusta National course in Georgia every April.

1988	Sandy Lyle (Great Britain)
1989	Nick Faldo (Great Britain)
1990	Nick Faldo (Great Britain)
1991	Ian Woosnam (Great Britain)
1992	Fred Couples (USA)
1993	Bernhard Langer (Germany)
1994	José-María Olazábal (Spain)
1995	Ben Crenshaw (USA)
1996	Nick Faldo (Great Britain)
1997	Tiger Woods (USA)
1998	Mark O'Meara (USA)
1999	José-María Olazábal (Spain)
2000	Vijay Singh (Fiji)

□ United States PGA Championship

The last of the season's four 'Majors'; first held in 1916, and a match-play event until 1958; takes place annually.

1988	Jeff Sluman (USA)
1989	Payne Stewart (USA)
1990	Wayne Grady (Australia)
1991	John Daly (USA)
1992	Nick Price (Zimbabwe)
1993	Paul Azinger (USA)
1994	Nick Price (Zimbabwe)
1995	Steve Elkington (Australia)
1996	Mark Brooks (USA)
1997	Davis Love III (USA)
1998	Vijay Singh (Fiji)
1999	Tiger Woods (USA)
2000	Tiger Woods (USA)

□ Ryder Cup

The leading international team tournament; first held at Worcester, Massachusetts in 1927; takes place every two years between teams from the USA and Europe (Great Britain 1927–71; Great Britain and Ireland 1973–7).

1989	Drawn	14–14
1991	USA	$14\frac{1}{2}$–$13\frac{1}{2}$
1993	USA	15–13
1995	Europe	$14\frac{1}{2}$–$13\frac{1}{2}$
1997	Europe	$14\frac{1}{2}$–$13\frac{1}{2}$
1999	USA	$14\frac{1}{2}$–$13\frac{1}{2}$

— Gymnastics ————————

□ World Championships

First held in 1903; took place every four years, 1922–78; since 1979, usually every two years.

Individual (Men)

1989	Igor Korobichensky (USSR)
1991	Vitaly Scherbo (USSR)
1993	Vitaly Scherbo (Belarus)
1994	Ivan Ivankov (Belarus)
1995	Li Xianoshuang (China)
1997	Ivan Ivankov (Belarus)
1999	Nikolay Krukov (Russia)

Team (Men)

1989	USSR
1991	USSR
1993	*no team prize*
1994	China
1995	China
1997	China
1999	China

Individual (Women)

1989	Svetlana Boginskaya (USSR)
1991	Kim Zmeskal (USA)
1993	Shannon Miller (USA)
1994	Shannon Miller (USA)
1995	Lilia Podkopayeva (Ukraine)
1997	Svetlana Khorkina (Russia)
1999	Maria Olaru (Romania)

Team (Women)

1989	USSR
1991	USSR
1993	*no team prize*
1994	Romania
1995	Romania
1997	Romania
1999	Romania

— Horse racing ————————

□ The Derby

The 'Blue Riband' of the Turf; run at Epsom over $1\frac{1}{2}$ miles; first run in 1780.

Horse (Jockey)

1988	Kahyasi (Ray Cochrane)
1989	Nashwan (Willie Carson)
1990	Quest For Fame (Pat Eddery)
1991	Generous (Alan Munro)
1992	Dr Devious (John Reid)
1993	Commander in Chief (Michael Kinane)
1994	Erhaab (Willie Carson)
1995	Lammtarra (Walter Swinburn)
1996	Shaamit (Michael Hills)
1997	Benny the Dip (Willie Ryan)
1998	High Rise (Olivier Peslier)
1999	Oath (Kieren Fallon)
2000	Sinndar (John Murtagh)

◻ The Oaks

Raced at Epsom over 1½ miles; for fillies only; first run in 1779.

	Horse (Jockey)
1988	Diminuendo (Steve Cauthen)
1989	Aliysa (Walter Swinburn)
1990	Salsabil (Willie Carson)
1991	Jet Ski Lady (Christy Roche)
1992	User Friendly (George Duffield)
1993	Intrepidity (Michael Roberts)
1994	Balanchine (Frankie Dettori)
1995	Moonshell (Frankie Dettori)
1996	Lady Carla (Pat Eddery)
1997	Reams of Verse (Kieren Fallon)
1998	Shahtoush (Michael Kinane)
1999	Ramruma (Kieren Fallon)
2000	Love Divine (Richard Quinn)

◻ One Thousand Guineas

Run over 1 mile at Newmarket; for fillies only; first run in 1814.

	Horse (Jockey)
1988	Ravinella (Gary Moore)
1989	Musical Bliss (Walter Swinburn)
1990	Salsabil (Willie Carson)
1991	Shadayid (Willie Carson)
1992	Hatoof (Walter Swinburn)
1993	Sayyedati (Walter Swinburn)
1994	Las Meninas (John Reid)
1995	Harayir (Richard Hills)
1996	Bosra Sham (Pat Eddery)
1997	Sleepytime (Kieren Fallon)
1998	Cape Verdi (Frankie Dettori)
1999	Wince (Kieren Fallon)
2000	Lahan (Richard Hills)

◻ Two Thousand Guineas

Run at Newmarket over 1 mile; first run in 1809.

	Horse (Jockey)
1988	Doyoun (Walter Swinburn)
1989	Nashwan (Willie Carson)
1990	Tirol (Michael Kinane)
1991	Mystiko (Michael Roberts)
1992	Rodrigo de Traiano (Lester Piggott)
1993	Zafonic (Pat Eddery)
1994	Mister Baileys (Jason Weaver)
1995	Pennekamp (Thierry Jarnet)
1996	Mark of Esteem (Frankie Dettori)
1997	Entrepreneur (Michael Kinane)
1998	King of Kings (Michael Kinane)
1999	Island Sands (Frankie Dettori)
2000	King's Best (Kieren Fallon)

◻ St Leger

The oldest of the five English classics; first run in 1776; raced at Doncaster annually over 1 mile 6 furlongs 127 yards.

	Horse (Jockey)
1988	Minster Son (Willie Carson)
1989	Michelozzo (Steve Cauthen)
1990	Snurge (Richard Quinn)
1991	Toulon (Pat Eddery)
1992	User Friendly (George Duffield)
1993	Bob's Return (Philip Robinson)
1994	Moonax (Pat Eddery)
1995	Classic Cliche (Frankie Dettori)
1996	Shantou (Frankie Dettori)
1997	Silver Patriarch (Pat Eddery)
1998	Nedawi (John Reid)
1999	Mutafaweq (Richard Hills)
2000	Millenary (Richard Quinn)

Grand National

Steeplechasing's most famous race; first run at Maghull in 1836; at Aintree since 1839; war-time races at Gatwick 1916–18.

Horse (Jockey)

1988	Rhyme 'N' Reason (Brendan Powell)
1989	Little Polveir (Jimmy Frost)
1990	Mr Frisk (Marcus Armytage)
1991	Seagram (Nigel Hawke)
1992	Party Politics (Carl Llewellyn)
1993	*race declared void* Esha Ness (John White) first past the post
1994	Minnehoma (Richard Dunwoody)
1995	Royal Athlete (Jason Titley)
1996	Rough Quest (Mick Fitzgerald)
1997	Lord Gyllene (Tony Dobbin)
1998	Earth Summit (Carl Llewellyn)
1999	Bobbyjo (Paul Carberry)
2000	Papillon (Ruby Walsh)

Prix de l'Arc de Triomphe

The leading end of season race in Europe; raced over 2400 metres at Longchamp; first run in 1920.

Horse (Jockey)

1988	Tony Bin (John Reid)
1989	Caroll House (Michael Kinane)
1990	Suamarez (Gerard Mosse)
1991	Suave Dancer (Cash Asmussen)
1992	Subotica (Thierry Jarnet)
1993	Urban Sea (Eric Saint-Martin)
1994	Carnegie (Thierry Jarnet)
1995	Lammtarra (Frankie Dettori)
1996	Helissio (Olivier Peslier)
1997	Peintre Celebre (Olivier Peslier)
1998	Sagamix (Olivier Peslier)
1999	Montieu (Michael Kinane)
2000	Sinndar (John Murtagh)

Ice hockey

World Championship

First held in 1930; takes place annually (except 1980); up to 1968 Olympic champions also regarded as world champions.

1988	USSR
1989	USSR
1990	USSR
1991	Sweden
1992	Sweden
1993	Russia
1994	Canada
1995	Finland
1996	Czech Republic
1997	Sweden
1998	Sweden
1999	Czech Republic
2000	Czech Republic

Stanley Cup

The most sought-after trophy at club level; the end-of-season meeting between the winners of the two conferences in the National Hockey League in the USA and Canada.

1988	Edmonton Oilers
1989	Calgary Flames
1990	Edmonton Oilers
1991	Pittsburgh Penguins
1992	Pittsburgh Penguins
1993	Montreal Canadiens
1994	New York Rangers
1995	New Jersey Devils
1996	Colorado Avalanche
1997	Detroit Red Wings
1998	Detroit Red Wings
1999	Dallas Stars
2000	New Jersey Devils

— Ice skating —

□ World Championships

First men's championships in 1896; first women's event in 1906; pairs first contested in 1908; Ice dance officially recognized in 1952.

Men

1988	Brian Boitano (USA)
1989	Kurt Browning (Canada)
1990	Kurt Browning (Canada)
1991	Kurt Browning (Canada)
1992	Viktor Petrenko (CIS)
1993	Kurt Browning (Canada)
1994	Elvis Stojko (Canada)
1995	Elvis Stojko (Canada)
1996	Todd Eldredge (USA)
1997	Elvis Stojko (Canada)
1998	Alexei Yagudin (Russia)
1999	Alexei Yagudin (Russia)
2000	Alexei Yagudin (Russia)

Women

1988	Katarina Witt (East Germany)
1989	Midori Ito (Japan)
1990	Jill Trenary (USA)
1991	Kristi Yamaguchi (USA)
1992	Kristi Yamaguchi (USA)
1993	Oksana Baiul (Ukraine)
1994	Yuka Sato (Japan)
1995	Lu Chen (China)
1996	Michelle Kwan (USA)
1997	Tara Lipinski (USA)
1998	Michelle Kwan (USA)
1999	Maria Butyrskaya (Russia)
2000	Michelle Kwan (USA)

Pairs

1988	Oleg Vasiliev/Yelena Valova (USSR)
1989	Sergei Grinkov/Yekaterina Gordeeva (USSR)
1990	Sergei Grinkov/Yekaterina Gordeeva (USSR)
1991	Artur Dmtriev/Natalya Mishkutienok (USSR)
1992	Artur Dmtriev/Natalya Mishkutienok (USSR)
1993	Lloyd Eisler/Isabelle Brasseur (Canada)
1994	Vadim Naumov/Evgenia Shiskova (Russia)
1995	Rene Novotny/Radka Kovarikova (Czech Republic)
1996	Andrei Bushkov/Marina Eltsova (Russia)
1997	Ingo Steuer/Mandy Woetzel (Germany)
1998	Anton Sikharulidze/Elena Berezhnaya (Russia)
1999	Anton Sikharulidze/Elena Berezhnaya (Russia)
2000	Alexei Tikhonov/Maria Petrova (Russia)

Ice Dance

1988	Andrei Bukin/Natalya Bestemianova (USSR)
1989	Sergei Ponomarenko/Marina Klimova (USSR)
1990	Sergei Ponomarenko/Marina Klimova (USSR)
1991	Isabelle and Paul Duchesnay (France)
1992	Sergei Ponomarenko/Marina Klimova (CIS)
1993	Alesandr Zhulin/Maia Usova (Russia)
1994	Yevgeni Platov/Oksana Gritschuk (Russia)
1995	Yevgeni Platov/Oksana Gritschuk (Russia)
1996	Yevgeni Platov/Oksana Gritschuk (Russia)
1997	Yevgeni Platov/Oksana Gritschuk (Russia)
1998	Angelika Krylova/Oleg Ovsyannikov (Russia)
1999	Angelika Krylova/Oleg Ovsyannikov (Russia)
2000	Marina Anissina/Gwendal Peizerat (France)

Motor racing

❑ World Championship

A Formula One drivers' world championship instituted in 1950; constructor's championship instituted in 1958.

1988	Ayrton Senna (Brazil)	*McLaren*
1989	Alain Prost (France)	*McLaren*
1990	Ayrton Senna (Brazil)	*McLaren*
1991	Ayrton Senna (Brazil)	*McLaren*
1992	Nigel Mansell (Great Britain)	*Williams*
1993	Alain Prost (France)	*Williams*
1994	Michael Schumacher (Germany)	*Benetton*
1995	Michael Schumacher (Germany)	*Benetton*
1996	Damon Hill (Great Britain)	*Williams*
1997	Jacques Villeneuve (Canada)	*Williams*
1998	Mika Hakkinen (Finland)	*McLaren*
1999	Mika Hakkinen (Finland)	*McLaren*

❑ Le Mans 24-Hour Race

The greatest of all endurance races; first held in 1923.

1988 Jan Lammers (Netherlands)
Johnny Dumfries (Great Britain)
Andy Wallace (Great Britain)
1989 Jochen Mass (West Germany)
Manuel Reuter (West Germany)
Stanley Dickens (Sweden)
1990 John Nielsen (Denmark)
Price Cobb (USA)
Martin Brundle (Great Britain)
1991 Volker Weidler (Germany)
Johnny Herbert (Great Britain)
Bertrand Gachot (Belgium)
1992 Derek Warwick (Great Britain)
Mark Blundell (Great Britain)
Yannick Dalmas (France)
1993 Geoff Brabham (Australia)
Christophe Bouchut (France)
Eric Helary (France)
1994 Yannick Dalmas (France)
Hurley Haywood (USA)
Mauro Baldi (Italy)

1995 Yannick Dalmas (France)
J J Lehto (Finland)
Masanori Sekiya (Japan)
1996 Manuel Reuter (Germany)
Davy Jones (USA)
Alexander Würz (Austria)
1997 Michele Alboreto (Italy)
Stefan Johansson (Sweden)
Tom Kristensen (Denmark)
1998 Allan McNish (Great Britain)
Laurent Aiello (France)
Stephane Ortelli (France)
1999 Pierluigi Martini (Italy)
Joachim Winkelhock (Germany)
Yannick Dalmas (France)
2000 Frank Biela (Germany)
Tom Kristensen (Denmark)
Emmanuele Pirro (Italy)

❑ Indianapolis 500

First held in 1911; raced over the Indianapolis Raceway as part of the Memorial Day celebrations at the end of May each year.

1988 Rick Mears (USA)
1989 Emerson Fittipaldi (Brazil)
1990 Arie Luyendyk (Netherlands)
1991 Rick Mears (USA)
1992 Al Unser (USA)
1993 Emerson Fittipaldi (Brazil)
1994 Al Unser (USA)
1995 Jacques Villeneuve (Canada)
1996 Buddy Lazier (USA)
1997 Arie Luyendyk (Netherlands)
1998 Eddie Cheever (USA)
1999 Kenny Brack (USA)
2000 Juan Montoya (Colombia)

❑ Monte Carlo Rally

The world's leading rally; first held in 1911.
1988 Bruno Saby (France)
Jean-François Fauchille (France)
1989 Miki Biasion (Italy)
Tiziano Siviero (Italy)
1990 Didier Auriol (France)
Bernard Occelli (France)

1991	Carlos Sainz (Spain)
	Luis Moya (Spain)
1992	Didier Auriol (France)
	Bernard Occelli (France)
1993	Didier Auriol (France)
	Bernard Occelli (France)
1994	François Delecour (France)
	Daniel Grataloup (France)
1995	Carlos Sainz (Spain)
	Luis Moya (Spain)
1996	Patrick Bernardini (France)
	Bernard Occelli (France)
1997	Piero Liatti (Italy)
	Fabrizia Pons (Italy)
1998	Carlos Sainz (Spain)
	Luis Moya (Spain)
1999	Tommi Mäkinen (Finland)
	Risto Mannisemäki (Finland)
2000	Tommi Mäkinen (Finland)
	Risto Mannisemäki (Finland)

Rowing

❏ World Championships

First held for men in 1962 and for women in 1974; Olympic champions assume the role of world champion in Olympic years; principal event is the single sculls.

Single Sculls (Men)

1988	Thomas Lange (East Germany)
1989	Thomas Lange (East Germany)
1990	Yuri Janson (USSR)
1991	Thomas Lange (Germany)
1992	Thomas Lange (Germany)
1993	Derek Porter (Canada)
1994	Andre Wilms (Germany)
1995	Iztok Cop (Slovenia)
1996	Xeno Müller (Switzerland)
1997	Jamie Koven (USA)
1998	Rob Waddell (New Zealand)
1999	Rob Waddell (New Zealand)
2000	Rob Waddell (New Zealand)

Single Sculls (Women)

1988	Jutta Behrendt (East Germany)
1989	Elisabeta Lipa (Romania)
1990	Brigit Peter (East Germany)

1991	Silke Laumann (Canada)
1992	Elisabeta Lipa (Romania)
1993	Jana Phieme (Germany)
1994	Trine Hansen (Denmark)
1995	Maria Brandin (Sweden)
1996	Yekatarina Khodotovich (Belarus)
1997	Yekatarina Khodotovich (Belarus)
1998	Irina Fedotova (Russia)
1999	Ekaterina Karsten (Belarus)
2000	Ekaterina Karsten (Belarus)

❏ The Boat Race

An annual contest between the crews from the Oxford and Cambridge University rowing clubs; first contested in 1829; the current course is from Putney to Mortlake.

1988	Oxford
1989	Oxford
1990	Oxford
1991	Oxford
1992	Oxford
1993	Cambridge
1994	Cambridge
1995	Cambridge
1996	Cambridge
1997	Cambridge
1998	Cambridge
1999	Cambridge
2000	Oxford

❏ Diamond Sculls

Highlight of Henley Royal Regatta held every July; first contested in 1884.

1988	Hamish McGlashan (Australia)
1989	Vaclav Chlupa (Czechoslovakia)
1990	Erik Verdonk (New Zealand)
1991	Wim van Belleghem (Belgium)
1992	Rorie Henderson (Great Britain)
1993	Thomas Lange (Germany)
1994	Xeno Müller (Switzerland)
1995	Juri Jaanson (Estonia)
1996	Merlin Vervoorn (Netherlands)
1997	Greg Searle (Great Britain)
1998	Jamie Koven (USA)
1999	Marcel Hacker (Germany)
2000	Aquil Abdullah (USA)

—Rugby league———————

□ Challenge Cup Final

First contested in 1897 and won by Batley;
first final at Wembley Stadium in 1929.

1988	Wigan
1989	Wigan
1990	Wigan
1991	Wigan
1992	Wigan
1993	Wigan
1994	Wigan
1995	Wigan
1996	St Helens
1997	St Helens
1998	Sheffield
1999	Leeds
2000	Bradford

□ Premiership Trophy

End-of-season knockout competition
involving the top eight teams in the first
division; first contested at the end of the
1974–5 season; discontinued in 1997.

1988	Widnes
1989	Widnes
1990	Widnes
1991	Hull
1992	Wigan
1993	St Helens
1994	Wigan
1995	Wigan
1996	Wigan
1997	Wigan

□ Regal Trophy

A knockout competition, first held in 1971–
2. Known as the John Player Special Trophy
until 1989–90; discontinued in 1996.

1988	St Helens
1989	Wigan
1990	Wigan
1991	Warrington
1992	Widnes
1993	Wigan
1994	Castleford

| 1995 | Wigan |
| 1996 | Wigan |

—Rugby union———————

□ World Cup

The first Rugby Union World Cup was staged
in 1987.

1987	New Zealand
1991	Australia
1995	South Africa
1999	Australia

□ Five Nations' Championship

A round robin competition involving
England, Ireland, Scotland, Wales and France
and from 2000, Italy; first contested in
1884.

1988	France and Wales
1989	France
1990	Scotland
1991	England
1992	England
1993	France
1994	Wales
1995	England
1996	England
1997	France
1998	France
1999	Scotland
2000	England

□ County Championship

First held in 1889.

1988	Lancashire
1989	Durham
1990	Lancashire
1991	Cornwall
1992	Lancashire
1993	Lancashire
1994	Yorkshire
1995	Warwickshire
1996	Gloucestershire
1997	Cumbria
1998	Cheshire
1999	Cornwall
2000	Yorkshire

❑ Tetley's Bitter Cup

An annual knockout competition for English Club sides; first held in the 1971–2 season; known as the John Player Special Cup until 1988, and the Pilkington Cup until 1997.

1988	Harlequins
1989	Bath
1990	Bath
1991	Harlequins
1992	Bath
1993	Leicester
1994	Bath
1995	Bath
1996	Bath
1997	Leicester
1998	Saracens
1999	Wasps
2000	Wasps

❑ Principality Cup

The knockout tournament for Welsh clubs; first held in 1971–2; formerly known as the Schweppes Welsh Cup and the Swalec Cup.

1988	Llanelli
1989	Neath
1990	Neath
1991	Llanelli
1992	Llanelli
1993	Llanelli
1994	Cardiff
1995	Swansea
1996	Pontypridd
1997	Cardiff
1998	Llanelli
1999	Swansea
2000	Llanelli

— Skiing —

❑ World Cup

A season-long competition first organized in 1967; champions are declared in downhill, slalom, giant slalom and super-giant slalom, as well as the overall champion; points are obtained for performances in each category.

Overall winners

Men

1988	Pirmin Zurbriggen (Switzerland)
1989	Marc Girardelli (Luxembourg)
1990	Pirmin Zurbriggen (Switzerland)
1991	Marc Girardelli (Luxembourg)
1992	Paul Accola (Switzerland)
1993	Marc Girardelli (Luxembourg)
1994	Kjetil-Andre Aamodt (Norway)
1995	Alberto Tomba (Italy)
1996	Lasse Kjus (Norway)
1997	Luc Alphand (France)
1998	Hermann Maier (Austria)
1999	Lasse Kjus (Norway)
2000	Hermann Maier (Austria)

Women

1988	Michela Figini (Switzerland)
1989	Vreni Schneider (Switzerland)
1990	Petra Kronberger (Austria)
1991	Petra Kronberger (Austria)
1992	Petra Kronberger (Austria)
1993	Anita Wachter (Austria)
1994	Vreni Schneider (Switzerland)
1995	Vreni Schneider (Switzerland)
1996	Katja Seizinger (Germany)
1997	Pernilla Wiberg (Sweden)
1998	Katja Seizinger (Germany)
1999	Alexandra Meissnitzer (Austria)
2000	Michaela Dorfmeister (Austria)

— Snooker —

❑ World Professional Championship

Instituted in the 1926–7 season; a knockout competition open to professional players who are members of the World Professional Billiards and Snooker Association; played at the Crucible Theatre, Sheffield.

1988	Steve Davis (England)
1989	Steve Davis (England)
1990	Stephen Hendry (Scotland)
1991	John Parrott (England)
1992	Stephen Hendry (Scotland)
1993	Stephen Hendry (Scotland)
1994	Stephen Hendry (Scotland)
1995	Stephen Hendry (Scotland)

1996	Stephen Hendry (Scotland)
1997	Ken Doherty (Ireland)
1998	John Higgins (Scotland)
1999	Stephen Hendry (Scotland)
2000	Mark Williams (Wales)

□ World Amateur Championship

First held in 1963; originally took place every two years, but annual since 1984.

1988	James Wattana (Thailand)
1989	Ken Doherty (Ireland)
1990	Stephen O'Connor (Ireland)
1991	Noppodol Noppajorn (Thailand)
1992	Neil Mosley (England)
1993	Chuchat Triratanapradit (Thailand)
1994	Mohamed Yusuf (Pakistan)
1995	Sakchai Sim-Nhan (Thailand)
1996	Stuart Bingham (England)
1997	Marco Fu (China/Hong Kong)
1998	Luke Simmonds (England)
1999	Ian Preece (Wales)

—Softball

□ World Championships

First held for women in 1965 and for men the following year; usually held every four years.

Men

1980	USA
1984	New Zealand
1988	USA
1992	Canada
1996	New Zealand
2000	New Zealand

Women

1978	USA
1982	New Zealand
1986	USA
1990	USA
1995	USA
1998	USA

—Squash

□ World Open Championship

First held in 1976; takes place annually for men and women; every two years for women 1976–89.

Men

1988	Jahangir Khan (Pakistan)
1989	Jansher Khan (Pakistan)
1990	Jansher Khan (Pakistan)
1991	Rodney Martin (Australia)
1992	Jansher Khan (Pakistan)
1993	Jansher Khan (Pakistan)
1994	Jansher Khan (Pakistan)
1995	Jansher Khan (Pakistan)
1996	Jansher Khan (Pakistan)
1997	Rodney Eyles (Australia)
1998	Jonathon Power (Canada)
1999	Peter Nicol (Great Britain)

Women

1989	Martine Le Moignan (Great Britain)
1990	Sue Devoy (New Zealand)
1991	*not held*
1992	Sue Devoy (New Zealand)
1993	Michelle Martin (Australia)
1994	Michelle Martin (Australia)
1995	Michelle Martin (Australia)
1996	Sarah FitzGerald (Australia)
1997	Sarah FitzGerald (Australia)
1998	Sarah FitzGerald (Australia)
1998	Jonathon Power (Canada)
1999	Cassie Campion (Great Britain)

—Surfing

□ World Professional Championship

A season-long series of Grand Prix events; first held in 1970.

Men

1988	Barton Lynch (Australia)
1989	Martin Potter (Great Britain)
1990	Tommy Curren (USA)
1991	Damien Hardman (Australia)
1992	Kelly Slater (USA)
1993	Derek Ho (Hawaii)

1994	Kelly Slater (USA)
1995	Kelly Slater (USA)
1996	Kelly Slater (USA)
1997	Kelly Slater (USA)
1998	Kelly Slater (USA)
1999	Mark Occhilupo (Australia)

Women

1988	Frieda Zamba (USA)
1989	Wendy Botha (South Africa)
1990	Pam Burridge (Australia)
1991	Wendy Botha (Australia)
1992	Wendy Botha (Australia)
1993	Pauline Menczer (Australia)
1994	Lisa Andersen (USA)
1995	Lisa Andersen (USA)
1996	Lisa Andersen (USA)
1997	Lisa Andersen (USA)
1998	Layne Beachley (Australia)
1999	Layne Beachley (Australia)

—Swimming and diving—————

□ World Championships

First held in 1973 and again in 1975; since 1978 take place approximately every four years; the complete list of 1998 world champions is given below.

Men

50 metres freestyle	Bill Pilczuk (USA)
100 metres freestyle	Alexander Popov (Russia)
200 metres freestyle	Michael Klim (Australia)
400 metres freestyle	Ian Thorpe (Australia)
1 500 metres freestyle	Grant Hackett (Australia)
100 metres backstroke	Lenny Krayzelburg (USA)
200 metres backstroke	Lenny Krayzelburg (USA)
100 metres breaststroke	Frederick Deburghgraeve (Belgium)
200 metres breaststroke	Kurt Grote (USA)

100 metres butterfly	Michael Klim (Australia)
200 metres butterfly	Denys Sylantyev (Ukraine)
200 metres individual medley	Marcel Wouda (Netherlands)
400 metres individual medley	Tom Dolan (USA)
4 × 100 metres freestyle relay	USA
4 × 200 metres freestyle relay	Australia
4 × 100 metres medley relay	Australia
Springboard diving	Zhuocheng Yu (China)
Highboard diving	Dmitri Sautin (Russia)

Women

50 metres freestyle	Amy Van Dyken (USA)
100 metres freestyle	Jenny Thompson (USA)
200 metres freestyle	Claudia Poll (Costa Rica)
400 metres freestyle	Chen Yan (China)
800 metres freestyle	Brooke Bennett (USA)
100 metres backstroke	Lea Maurer (USA)
200 metres backstroke	Roxanna Maracineanu (France)
100 metres breaststroke	Kristy Kowal (USA)
200 metres breaststroke	Agnes Kovacs (Hungary)
100 metres butterfly	Jenny Thompson (USA)
200 metres butterfly	Susie O'Neill (Australia)
200 metres individual medley	Wu Yanyan (China)
400 metres individual medley	Chen Yan (China)
4 × 100 metres freestyle relay	USA

4 × 200 metres
freestyle relay   Germany
4 × 100 metres
medley relay   USA
Springboard diving   Irina Lashko (Russia)
Highboard diving Oleana Zhupyna (Ukraine)

Synchronized swimming

Solo	Olga Sedakova (Russia)
Duet	Russia
Team	Russia

—Table tennis—

❑ World Championships

First held in 1926 and every two years since 1957.

Swaythling Cup (Men's Team)
1989	Sweden
1991	Sweden
1993	Sweden
1995	China
1997	China
1999	not held

Corbillon Cup (Women's Team)
1989	China
1991	Unified Korea
1993	China
1995	China
1997	China
1999	not held

Men's Singles
1989	Jan-Ove Waldner (Sweden)
1991	Jorgen Persson (Sweden)
1993	Jean-Philippe Gatien (France)
1995	Kong Linghui (China)
1997	Jan-Ove Waldner (Sweden)
1999	Liu Guoliang (China)

Women's Singles
1989	Qiao Hong (China)
1991	Deng Yaping (China)
1993	Hyun Jung-Hwa (South Korea)
1995	Deng Yaping (China)
1997	Deng Yaping (China)
1999	Wang Nan (China)

Men's Doubles
1989	Jaerg Rosskopf/Stefen Fetzner (West Germany)
1991	Peter Karlsson/Tomas von Scheele (Sweden)
1993	Wang Tao/Lu Lin (China)
1995	Wang Tao/Lu Lin (China)
1997	Jan-Ove Waldner/Jorgen Persson (Sweden)
1999	Liu Guoliang/Kong Linghui (China)

Women's Doubles
1989	Qiao Hong/Deng Yaping (China)
1991	Chen Zhie/Gao Jun (China)
1993	Liu Wei/Qiao Yunping (China)
1995	Qiao Hong/Deng Yaping (China)
1997	Li Ju/Wang Nan (China)
1999	Li Ju/Wang Nan (China)

Mixed Doubles
1989	Yoo Nam-Kyu/Hyun Jung-Hwa (South Korea)
1991	Wang Tao/Liu Wei (China)
1993	Wang Tao/Liu Wei (China)
1995	Wang Tao/Liu Wei (China)
1997	Kong Linghui/Deng Yaping (China)
1999	Zhang Yingying/Ma Lin (China)

—Tennis (Lawn)—

❑ All-England Championships at Wimbledon

The All-England Championships at Wimbledon are Lawn Tennis's most prestigious championships; first held in 1877.

Men's Singles
1988	Stefan Edberg (Sweden)
1989	Boris Becker (West Germany)
1990	Stefan Edberg (Sweden)
1991	Michael Stich (Germany)
1992	Andre Agassi (USA)
1993	Pete Sampras (USA)
1994	Pete Sampras (USA)
1995	Pete Sampras (USA)
1996	Richard Krajicek (Netherlands)
1997	Pete Sampras (USA)

1998 Pete Sampras (USA)
1999 Pete Sampras (USA)
2000 Pete Sampras (USA)

Women's Singles
1988 Steffi Graf (West Germany)
1989 Steffi Graf (West Germany)
1990 Martina Navratilova (USA)
1991 Steffi Graf (Germany)
1992 Steffi Graf (Germany)
1993 Steffi Graf (Germany)
1994 Conchita Martinez (Spain)
1995 Steffi Graf (Germany)
1996 Steffi Graf (Germany)
1997 Martina Hingis (Switzerland)
1998 Jana Novotna (Czech Republic)
1999 Lindsay Davenport (USA)
2000 Venus Williams (USA)

Men's Doubles
1988 Ken Flach / Robert Seguso (USA)
1989 John Fitzgerald (Australia) /
     Anders Jarryd (Sweden)
1990 Rick Leach / Jim Pugh (USA)
1991 John Fitzgerald (Australia) /
     Anders Jarryd (Sweden)
1992 John McEnroe (USA) /
     Michael Stich (Germany)
1993 Todd Woodbridge / Mark Woodforde
     (Australia)
1994 Todd Woodbridge / Mark Woodforde
     (Australia)
1995 Todd Woodbridge / Mark Woodforde
     (Australia)
1996 Todd Woodbridge / Mark Woodforde
     (Australia)
1997 Todd Woodbridge / Mark Woodforde
     (Australia)
1998 Jacco Eltingh / Paul Haarhuis
     (Netherlands)
1999 Mahesh Bhupathi / Leander Paes
     (India)
2000 Todd Woodbridge / Mark Woodforde
     (Australia)

Women's Doubles
1988 Steffi Graf (West Germany) /
     Gabriela Sabatini (Argentina)

1989 Jana Novotna / Helena Sukova
     (Czechoslovakia)
1990 Jana Novotna / Helena Sukova
     (Czechoslovakia)
1991 Natalya Zvereva / Larissa Savchenko
     (USSR)
1992 Gigi Fernandez (USA) / Natalya
     Zvereva (CIS)
1993 Gigi Fernandez (USA) / Natalya
     Zvereva (CIS)
1994 Gigi Fernandez (USA) / Natalya
     Zvereva (CIS)
1995 Arantxa Sanchez Vicario (Spain) /
     Jana Novotna (Czech Republic)
1996 Helena Sukova (Czech Republic) /
     Martina Hingis (Switzerland)
1997 Gigi Fernandez (USA) / Natalya
     Zvereva (Belarus)
1998 Jana Novotna (Czech Republic) /
     Martina Hingis (Switzerland)
1999 Lindsay Davenport / Corina Morariu
     (USA)
2000 Serena Williams / Venus Williams
     (USA)

Mixed Doubles
1988 Zina Garrison / Sherwood Stewart
     (USA)
1989 Jana Novotna (Czechoslovakia) /
     Jim Pugh (USA)
1990 Zina Garrison / Rick Leach (USA)
1991 Elizabeth Smylie / John Fitzgerald
     (Australia)
1992 Larissa Savchenko-Neiland (Latvia) /
     Cyril Suk (Czechoslovakia)
1993 Martina Navratilova (USA) /
     Mark Woodforde (Australia)
1994 Helena Sukova (Czech Republic) /
     Todd Woodbridge (Australia)
1995 Martina Navratilova / Jonathan Stark
     (USA)
1996 Helena Sukova / Cyril Suk (Czech
     Republic)
1997 Helena Sukova / Cyril Suk (Czech
     Republic)
1998 Serena Williams (USA) / Max Mirnyi
     (Belarus)

1999   Lisa Raymond (USA)/Leander Paes (India)

2000   Kimberly Po/Donald Johnson (USA)

❑ United States Open

First held in 1891 as the United States Championship; became the United States Open in 1968.

Men's Singles
1988   Mats Wilander (Sweden)
1989   Boris Becker (West Germany)
1990   Pete Sampras (USA)
1991   Stefan Edberg (Sweden)
1992   Stefan Edberg (Sweden)
1993   Pete Sampras (USA)
1994   Andre Agassi (USA)
1995   Pete Sampras (USA)
1996   Pete Sampras (USA)
1997   Pat Rafter (Australia)
1998   Pat Rafter (Australia)
1999   Andre Agassi (USA)
2000   Marat Safin (Russia)

Women's Singles
1988   Steffi Graf (West Germany)
1989   Steffi Graf (West Germany)
1990   Gabriela Sabatini (Argentina)
1991   Monica Seles (Yugoslavia)
1992   Monica Seles (Yugoslavia)
1993   Steffi Graf (Germany)
1994   Arantxa Sanchez Vicario (Spain)
1995   Steffi Graf (Germany)
1996   Steffi Graf (Germany)
1997   Martina Hingis (Switzerland)
1998   Lindsay Davenport (USA)
1999   Serena Williams (USA)
2000   Venus Williams (USA)

❑ Davis Cup

International team competition organized on a knockout basis; first held in 1900; contested on a challenge basis until 1972.

1988   West Germany
1989   West Germany
1990   USA
1991   France
1992   USA
1993   Germany
1994   Sweden
1995   USA
1996   France
1997   Sweden
1998   Sweden
1999   Australia

─ **Weightlifting** ──────────

❑ World Championships

First held in 1898; 11 weight divisions; the most prestigious is the 110kg-plus category (formerly known as Super Heavyweight); in 1993 the weight for this category was changed to 108kg-plus, and in 1998 it was reduced to 105kg-plus; Olympic champions are automatically world champions in Olympic years.

110kg-plus
1988   Aleksandr Kurlovich (USSR)
1989   Stefan Botev (Bulgaria)
1990   Stefan Botev (Bulgaria)
1991   Aleksandr Kurlovich (USSR)
1992   Aleksandr Kurlovich (UT)
1993   Ronnie Weller (Germany)
1994   Aleksandr Kurlovich (Belarus)
1995   Andrey Chemerkin (Russia)
1996   Andrey Chemerkin (Russia)
1997   Andrey Chemerkin (Russia)
1998   Andrey Chemerkin (Russia)
1999   Andrey Chemerkin (Russia)
2000   Hossein Rezazadeh (Iran)

Wrestling

□ World Championships

Graeco-Roman world championships first held in 1921; first freestyle championships in 1951; each style contests 10 weight divisions, the heaviest being the 130kg (formerly over 100kg) category; Olympic champions become world champions in Olympic years.

Super-heavyweight/130kg

Freestyle

1988	David Gobedzhishvilli (USSR)
1989	Ali Reiza Soleimani (Iran)
1990	David Gobedzhishvilli (USSR)
1991	Andreas Schroder (Germany)
1992	Bruce Baumgartner (USA)
1993	Bruce Baumgartner (USA)
1994	Mahmut Demir (Turkey)
1995	Bruce Baumgartner (USA)
1996	Mahmut Demir (Turkey)
1997	Zekeriya Güglü (Turkey)
1998	Alexis Rodriguez (Cuba)
1999	Stephen Neal (USA)
2000	David Moussoulbes (Russia)

Graeco-Roman

1988	Aleksandr Karelin (USSR)
1989	Aleksandr Karelin (USSR)
1990	Aleksandr Karelin (USSR)
1991	Aleksandr Karelin (USSR)
1992	Aleksandr Karelin (UT)
1993	Aleksandr Karelin (Russia)
1994	Aleksandr Karelin (Russia)
1995	Aleksandr Karelin (Russia)
1996	Aleksandr Karelin (Russia)
1997	Aleksandr Karelin (Russia)
1998	Aleksandr Karelin (Russia)
1999	Aleksandr Karelin (Russia)
2000	Rulon Gardener (USA)

Yachting

□ America's Cup

One of sport's famous trophies; first won by the schooner Magic in 1870; now held approximately every four years, when challengers compete in a series of races to find which of them races against the holder; all 25 winners up to 1983 were from the USA.

	Winning Yacht (Skipper)
1983	Australia II (Australia) (John Bertrand)
1987	Stars & Stripes (USA) (Dennis Conner)
1988	Stars & Stripes (USA) (Dennis Conner) [1]
1992	America (USA) (Bill Koch)
1995	Black Magic (New Zealand) (Russell Coutts)
2000	Black Magic (New Zealand) (Russell Coutts)

[1] Stars and Stripes (USA) skippered by Dennis Conner won a special challenge match but on appeal the race was awarded to the New Zealand boat. However the decision was reversed by the New York Appeals court in 1989.

□ Admiral's Cup

A two-yearly series of races in the English Channel, around Fastnet rock and at Cowes; four national teams of three boats per team; first held in 1957.

1989	Great Britain
1991	France
1993	Germany
1995	Italy
1997	USA
1999	Netherlands

THOUGHT AND BELIEF

Greek gods of mythology

Adonis	God of vegetation and rebirth	Hebe	Goddess of youth
Aeolus	God of the winds	Hecate	Goddess of the moon
Alphito	Barley goddess of Argos	Helios	God of the sun
Aphrodite	Goddess of love and beauty	Hephaestus	God of fire
Apollo	God of prophecy, music, youth, archery and healing	Hera	Goddess of marriage and childbirth; queen of heaven
Ares	God of war	Hermes	Messenger of the gods
Arethusa	Goddess of springs and fountains	Hestia	Goddess of the hearth
		Hypnos	God of sleep
Artemis	Goddess of fertility, chastity and hunting	Iris	Goddess of the rainbow
		Morpheus	God of dreams
Asclepius	God of healing	Nemesis	God of destiny
Athene	Goddess of prudence and wise council; protectress of Athens	Nereus	God of the sea
		Nike	Goddess of victory
Atlas	A Titan who bears up the earth	Oceanus	God of the river Oceanus
Attis	God of vegetation	Pan	God of male sexuality and of herds
Boreas	God of the north wind		
Cronus	Father of Zeus	Persephone	Goddess of the underworld and of corn
Cybele	Goddess of the earth		
Demeter	Goddess of the harvest	Poseidon	God of the sea
Dionysus	God of wine, vegetation and ecstasy	Rhea	The original mother goddess; wife of Cronus
Eos	Goddess of the dawn	Selene	Goddess of the moon
Eros	God of love	Thanatos	God of death
Gaia	Goddess of the earth	Zeus	Overlord of the Olympian gods and goddesses; god of the sky and all its properties
Ganymede	God of rain		
Hades	God of the underworld		

Roman gods of mythology

Apollo	God of the sun	Egreria	Goddess of fountains and childbirth
Bacchus	God of wine and ecstasy		
Bellona	Goddess of war	Epona	Goddess of horses
Ceres	Goddess of corn	Fauna	Goddess of fertility
Consus	God of seed sowing	Faunus	God of crops and herbs
Cupid	God of love	Feronia	Goddess of spring flowers
Diana	Goddess of fertility and hunting	Fides	God of honesty
		Flora	Goddess of fruitfulness and flowers

380

Fortuna	Goddess of chance and fate	Mithras	The sun god; god of regeneration
Genius	Protective god of individuals, groups and the state	Neptune	God of the sea
Janus	God of entrances, travel, the dawn	Ops	Goddess of the harvest
		Orcus	God of death
Juno	Goddess of marriage, child-birth, light	Pales	Goddess of flocks
Jupiter	God of the sky and its attributes (sun, moon, thunder, rain, etc)	Penates	Gods of food and drink
		Picus	God of woods
		Pluto	God of the underworld
Lares	Gods of the house	Pomona	Goddess of fruit trees
Liber Pater	God of agricultural and human fertility	Portunus	God of husbands
		Proserpina	Goddess of the underworld
Libitina	Goddess of funeral rites	Rumina	Goddess of nursing mothers
Luna	Goddess of the moon	Saturn	God of fertility and agriculture
Maia	Goddess of fertility	Silvanus	God of trees and forests
Mars	God of war	Venus	Goddess of spring, gardens and love
Mercury	Messenger of the gods; also god of merchants	Vertumnus	God of fertility
		Vesta	Goddess of the hearth
Minerva	Goddess of war, craftsmen, education and the arts	Victoria	Goddess of victory
		Vulcan	God of fire

Norse gods of mythology

Aegir	God of the sea	Idunn	Guardian goddess of the golden apples of youth; wife of Bragi
Aesir	Race of warlike gods, including Odin, Thor, Tyr		
Alcis	Twin gods of the sky	Kvasir	God of wise utterances
Balder	Son of Odin and favourite of the gods	Logi	Fire god
		Loki	God of mischief
Bor	Father of Odin	Mimir	God of wisdom
Bragi	God of poetry	Nanna	Goddess wife of Balder
Fafnir	Dragon god	Nehallenia	Goddess of plenty
Fjorgynn	Mother of Thor	Nerthus	Goddess of earth
Frey	God of fertility	Njord	God of ships and the sea
Freyja	Goddess of libido	Norns	Goddesses of destiny
Frigg	Goddess of fertility; wife of Odin	Odin (Woden, Wotan)	Chief of the Aesir family of gods, the 'father' god; the god of battle, death, inspiration
Gefion	Goddess who received virgins after death		
		Otr	Otter god
Heimdall	Guardian of the bridge Bifrost	Ran	Goddess of the sea
Hel	Goddess of death; Queen of Niflheim, the land of mists	Sif	Goddess wife of Thor
		Sigyn	Goddess wife of Loki
Hermod	Son of Odin	Thor (Donar)	God of thunder and sky; good crops
Hoder	Blind god who killed Balder		
Hoenir	Companion to Odin and Loki	Tyr	God of battle
		Ull	Stepson of Thor, an enchanter

Valkyries	Female helpers of the gods of war	Vidar	Slayer of the wolf, Fenrir
Vanir	Race of benevolent gods, including Njord, Frey, Freyja	Weland (Volundr, Wayland, Weiland)	Craftsman god

Egyptian gods of mythology

Amun-Re	Universal god	Khonsou	Son of Amun-Re
Anubis	God of funerals	Maat	Goddess of order
Apis	God of fertility	Nephthys	Goddess of funerals
Aten	Unique god	Nut	God of the sky
Geb	God of the earth	Osiris	God of vegetation
Hathor	Goddess of love	Ptah	God of creation
Horus	God of light	Sekhmet	Goddess of might
Isis	Goddess of magic	Seth	God of evil
Khnum	Goddess of creation	Thoth	Supreme scribe

Baha'i

Founded 1863 in Persia.

Founder Mirza Husayn Ali (1817–92), known as Baha Ullah (Glory of God). He declared himself the prophet foretold by Mirza ali Mohammed (1819–50), a direct descendant of Mohammed, who proclaimed himself to be the bab ('gate' or 'door').

Sacred texts Most Holy Book, The Seven Valleys, The Hidden Words and The Bayan.

Beliefs Baha'i teaches the oneness of God, the unity of all faiths, the inevitable unification of humankind, the harmony of all people, universal education and obedience to government. It does not predict an end to this world or any intervention by God but believes there will be a change within man and society.

Organization There is virtually no organization and Baha'i has no clergy or sacraments. Although there is little formal ritual (most assemblies are simply gatherings of the faithful), there are ceremonies for marriage, funerals and naming babies and there are shrines and temples.

Buddhism

Founded c.500BC in India.

Founder Prince Siddhartha Gautama (c.560–c.480BC) who became Buddha ('the enlightened') through meditation.

Sacred texts The Pali Canon or Tripitaka made up of the Vinaya Pitaka (monastic discipline), Sutta Pitaka (discourses of the Buddha) and the Abhidhamma Pitaka (analysis of doctrines). Other texts: the Mahayana Sutras, the Milindapanha (Questions of Milinda) and the Bardo Thodol (Tibetan Book of the Dead).

Beliefs Buddha's teaching is summarized in the Four Noble Truths; suffering is always present in life; desire is the cause of suffering; freedom from life can be achieved by

Nirvana (perfect peace and bliss); the Eightfold Path leads to Nirvana. Karma, by which good and evil deeds result in appropriate reward or punishment, and the cycle of rebirth can be broken by taking the Eightfold Path. All Buddhas are revered but particularly Gautama.

Organization There is a monastic system which aims to create favourable conditions for spiritual development. This involves meditation, personal discipline and spiritual exercises in the hope of liberation from self. Buddhism has proved very flexible in adapting its organization, ceremony and pattern of belief to different cultural and social conditions. There are numerous festivals and ceremonies, and pilgrimage is of great spiritual value.

Divisions There are two main traditions in Buddhism. Theravada Buddhism adheres to the teachings of the earliest Buddhist writings; salvation can be attained only by the few who accept the severe discipline and effort necessary to achieve it. Mahayana Buddhism developed later and is more flexible and creative, embracing popular piety. It teaches that salvation is possible for everyone and introduced the doctrine of the bodhisattva (one who attains enlightenment but out of compassion forestalls passing into Nirvana to help others achieve enlightenment). As Buddhism spread, other schools sprang up including Zen, Lamaism, Tendai, Nichiren and Soka Gakkai.

Major Buddhist festivals

Weekly Uposatha Days, Buddha's Birth, Enlightenment, First Sermon and Death are observed in the different countries where Buddhism is practised but often on different dates. In some of these countries there are additional festivals in honour of Buddha.

Christianity

Founded 1st-c AD.

Founder Jesus Christ 'the Son of God' (c.4BC–c.30AD).

Sacred texts The Bible consisting of the Old and New Testaments. The New Testament written between AD30 and 150 consists of the Gospels, the Acts of the Apostles, the Epistles and the Apocalypse.

Beliefs A monotheistic world religion, centred on the life and works of Jesus of Nazareth in Judaea, who proclaimed the most important rules of life to be love of God, followed by love of one's neighbour. Christians believe that Jesus was the Son of God who was put to death by crucifixion as a sacrifice in order to save humanity from the consequences of sin and death, and was raised from the dead; he makes forgiveness and reconciliation with God possible, and ensures eternal life for the repentant believer. The earliest followers of Jesus were Jews who believed him to be the Messiah or 'Saviour' promised by the prophets in the Old Testament. Christians believe he will come again to inaugurate the 'Kingdom of God'.

Organization Jesus Christ appointed 12 men to be his disciples:

1 Peter (brother of Andrew)

2 Andrew (brother of Peter)

3 James, son of Zebedee (brother of John)

4 John (brother of James)

5 Philip

6 Bartholomew

7 Thomas

8 Matthew

9 James of Alphaeus

10 Simon the Canaanite (in Matthew and Mark) or Simon 'the Zealot' (in Luke and the Acts)

11 Judas Iscariot

(Thaddeus in the book of Matthew and Mark is the twelfth disciple, while in Luke and the Acts the twelfth is Judas or James. Matthias succeeded to Judas's place.) Soon after the resurrection the disciples gathered for the festival of Pentecost and received special signs of the power of God, the Holy Spirit. The disciples became a defined new body, the Church. Through the witness of the Apostles and their successors, the Christian faith quickly spread and in AD315 became the official religion of the Roman Empire. It survived the 'Dark Ages' to become the basis of civilization in the Middle Ages in Europe.

Divisions Major divisions, separated as a result of differences of doctrine and practice, are the Orthodox or Eastern Church, the Roman Catholic Church, acknowledging the Bishop of Rome as head, and the Protestant Churches stemming from the split with the Roman Church in the 16th-c. All Christians recognize the authority of the Bible, read at public worship, which takes place at least every Sunday, to celebrate the resurrection of Jesus Christ. Most Churches recognize at least two sacraments (Baptism and the Eucharist, Mass, or Lord's Supper) as essential.

Major immovable Christian feasts

For Saints' days ► pp385–9

1 Jan	Solemnity of Mary, Mother of God	15 Aug	Assumption of the Virgin Mary
6 Jan	Epiphany	22 Aug	Queenship of Mary
7 Jan	Christmas Day (*Eastern Orthodox*)[1]	8 Sep	Birthday of the Virgin Mary
		14 Sep	Exaltation of the Holy Cross
11 Jan	Baptism of Jesus	2 Oct	Guardian Angels
25 Jan	Conversion of Apostle Paul	1 Nov	All Saints
2 Feb	Presentation of Jesus (*Candelmas Day*)	2 Nov	All Souls
		9 Nov	Dedication of the Lateran Basilica
22 Feb	The Chair of Peter, Apostle	21 Nov	Presentation of the Virgin Mary
25 Mar	Annunciation of the Virgin Mary	8 Dec	Immaculate Conception
24 Jun	Birth of John the Baptist	25 Dec	Christmas Day
6 Aug	Transfiguration	28 Dec	Holy Innocents

[1] Fixed feasts in the Julian Calendar fall 13 days later than the Gregorian Calendar date.

Movable Christian feasts 1997–2006

Year	Ash Wednesday	Easter	Ascension	Whit Sunday	Trinity Sunday	Sundays after Trinity	Corpus Christi	Advent
1997	12 Feb	30 Mar	8 May	18 May	25 May	26	29 May	30 Nov
1998	25 Feb	12 Apr	21 May	31 May	7 Jun	24	11 Jun	29 Nov
1999	17 Feb	4 Apr	13 May	23 May	30 May	25	3 Jun	28 Nov
2000	8 Mar	23 Apr	1 Jun	11 Jun	18 Jun	23	22 Jun	3 Dec
2001	28 Feb	15 Apr	24 May	3 Jun	10 Jun	24	14 Jun	2 Dec
2002	13 Feb	31 Mar	9 May	19 May	26 May	26	30 May	1 Dec
2003	5 Mar	20 Apr	29 May	8 Jun	15 Jun	23	19 Jun	30 Nov
2004	25 Feb	11 Apr	20 May	30 May	6 Jun	24	10 Jun	28 Nov
2005	9 Feb	27 Mar	5 May	15 May	22 May	26	26 Jun	27 Nov
2006	1 Mar	16 Apr	25 May	4 Jun	11 Jun	24	15 Jun	3 Dec

Ash Wednesday, the first day of Lent, can fall at the earliest on 4 February and at the latest on 10 March.

Palm (Passion) Sunday is the Sunday before Easter; Good Friday is the Friday before Easter; Holy Saturday (often referred to as Easter Saturday) is the Saturday before Easter; Easter Saturday, in traditional usage, is the Saturday following Easter.

Easter Day can fall at the earliest on 22 March and at the latest on 25 April. Ascension Day can fall at the earliest on 30 April and at the latest on 3 June. Whit Sunday can fall at the earliest on 10 May and at the latest on 13 June. There are not fewer than 22 and not more than 27 Sundays after Trinity. The first Sunday of Advent is the Sunday nearest to 30 November.

Saints' days

The official recognition of Saints, and the choice of a Saint's Day, varies greatly between different branches of Christianity, calendars and localities. Only major variations are included below, using the following abbreviations:

C Coptic   E Eastern   G Greek   W Western

❑ January

1 Basil (*E*), Fulgentius, Telemachus

2 Basil and Gregory of Nazianzus (*W*), Macarius of Alexandria, Seraphim of Sarov

3 Geneviève

4 Angela of Foligno

5 Simeon Stylites (*W*)

7 Cedda, Lucian of Antioch (*W*), Raymond of Penyafort

8 Atticus (*E*), Gudule, Severinus

9 Hadrian the African

10 Agatho, Marcian

12 Ailred, Benedict Biscop

13 Hilary of Poitiers

14 Kentigern

15 Macarius of Egypt, Maurus, Paul of Thebes

16 Honoratus

17 Antony of Egypt

19 Wulfstan

20 Euthymius, Fabian, Sebastian
21 Agnes, Fructuosus, Maximus (E), Meinrad
22 Timothy (G), Vincent
23 Ildefonsus
24 Babylas (W), Francis de Sales
25 Gregory of Nazianzus (E)
26 Paula, Timothy and Titus, Xenophon (E)
27 Angela Merici
28 Ephraem Syrus (E), Paulinus of Nola, Thomas Aquinas
29 Gildas
31 John Bosco, Marcella

❑ February
1 Brigid, Pionius
3 Anskar, Blaise (W), Werburga, Simeon (E)
4 Gilbert of Sempringham, Isidore of Pelusium, Phileas
5 Agatha, Avitus
6 Dorothy, Paul Miki and companions, Vedast
8 Theodore (G), Jerome Emiliani
9 Teilo
10 Scholastica
11 Benedict of Aniane, Blaise (E), Caedmon, Gregory II
12 Meletius
13 Agabus (W), Catherine dei Ricci, Priscilla (E)
14 Cyril and Methodius (W), Valentine (W)
16 Flavian (E), Pamphilus (E), Valentine (G)
18 Bernadette (France), Colman, Flavian (W), Leo I (E)
20 Wulfric
21 Peter Damian
23 Polycarp
25 Ethelbert, Tarasius, Walburga
26 Alexander (W), Porphyrius
27 Leander
28 Oswald of York

❑ March
1 David
2 Chad, Simplicius

3 Ailred
4 Casimir
6 Chrodegang
7 Perpetua and Felicity
8 Felix, John of God, Pontius
9 Frances of Rome, Gregory of Nyssa, Pacian
10 John Ogilvie, Macarius of Jerusalem, Simplicius
11 Constantine, Oengus, Sophronius
12 Gregory (the Great)
13 Nicephorus
14 Benedict (E)
15 Clement Hofbauer
17 Gertrude, Joseph of Arimathea (W), Patrick
18 Anselm of Lucca, Cyril of Jerusalem, Edward
19 Joseph
20 Cuthbert, John of Parma, Martin of Braga
21 Serapion of Thmuis
22 Catherine of Sweden, Nicholas of Flüe
23 Turibius de Mongrovejo
30 John Climacus

❑ April
1 Hugh of Grenoble, Mary of Egypt (E), Melito
2 Francis of Paola, Mary of Egypt (W)
3 Richard of Chichester
4 Isidore of Seville
5 Juliana of Liège, Vincent Ferrer
7 Hegesippus, John Baptist de la Salle
8 Agabus (E)
10 Fulbert
11 Gemma Galgani, Guthlac, Stanislaus
12 Julius I, Zeno
13 Martin I
15 Aristarchus, Pudus (E), Trophimus of Ephesus
17 Agapetus (E), Stephen Harding
18 Mme Acarie
19 Alphege, Leo IX
21 Anastasius (E), Anselm, Beuno, Januarius (E)

22	Alexander (*C*)
23	George
24	Egbert, Fidelis of Sigmaringen, Mellitus
25	Mark, Phaebadius
27	Zita
28	Peter Chanel, Vitalis and Valeria
29	Catherine of Siena, Hugh of Cluny, Peter Martyr, Robert
30	James (the Great) (*E*), Pius V

❑ May

1	Asaph, Joseph the Worker, Walburga
2	Athanasius
3	Philip and James (the Less) (*W*)
4	Gotthard
5	Hilary of Arles
7	John of Beverley
8	John (*E*), Peter of Tarantaise
10	Antoninus, Comgall, John of Avila, Simon (*E*)
11	Cyril and Methodius (*E*), Mamertus
12	Epiphanius, Nereus and Achilleus, Pancras
14	Matthias (*W*)
16	Brendan, John of Nepomuk, Simon Stock
17	Robert Bellarmine, Paschal Baylon
18	John I
19	Dunstan, Ivo, Pudens (*W*), Pudentiana (*W*)
20	Bernardino of Siena
21	Helena (*E*)
22	Rita of Cascia
23	Ivo of Chartres
24	Vincent of Lérins
25	Aldhelm, Bede, Gregory VII, Mary Magdalene de Pazzi
26	Philip Neri, Quadratus
27	Augustine of Canterbury
30	Joan of Arc

❑ June

1	Justin Martyr, Pamphilus
2	Erasmus, Marcellinus and Peter, Nicephorus (*G*), Pothinus
3	Charles Lwanga and companions, Clotilde, Kevin
4	Optatus, Petrock
5	Boniface
6	Martha (*E*), Norbert
7	Paul of Constantinople (*W*), Willibald
8	William of York
9	Columba, Cyril of Alexandria (*E*), Ephraem (*W*)
11	Barnabas, Bartholomew (*E*)
12	Leo III
13	Anthony of Padua
15	Orsisius, Vitus
17	Alban, Botulph
19	Gervasius and Protasius, Jude (*E*), Romuald
20	Alban
21	Alban of Mainz, Aloysius Gonzaga
22	John Fisher and Thomas More, Niceta, Pantaenus (*C*), Paulinus of Nola
23	Etheldreda
24	Birth of John the Baptist
25	Prosper of Aquitaine
27	Cyril of Alexandria (*W*), Ladislaus
28	Irenaeus
29	Peter and Paul
30	First Martyrs of the Church of Rome

❑ July

1	Cosmas and Damian (*E*), Oliver Plunket
3	Anatolius, Thomas
4	Andrew of Crete (*E*), Elizabeth of Portugal, Ulrich
5	Anthony Zaccaria
6	Maria Goretti
7	Palladius, Pantaenus
8	Kilian, Aquila and Prisca (*W*)
11	Benedict (*W*), Pius I
12	John Gualbert, Veronica
13	Henry II, Mildred, Silas
14	Camillus of Lellis, Deusdedit, Nicholas of the Holy Mountain (*E*)
15	Bonaventure, Jacob of Nisibis, Swithin, Vladimir
16	Eustathius, Our Lady of Mt Carmel

17 Ennodius, Leo IV, Marcellina, Margaret (E), Scillitan Martyrs
18 Arnulf, Philastrius
19 Macrina, Symmachus
20 Aurelius, Margaret (W)
21 Lawrence of Brindisi, Praxedes
22 Mary Magdalene
23 Apollinaris, Bridget of Sweden
25 Anne and Joachim (E), Christopher, James (the Great) (W)
26 Anne and Joachim (W)
27 Pantaleon
28 Innocent I, Samson, Victor I
29 Lupus, Martha (W), Olave
30 Peter Chrysologus, Silas (G)
31 Giovanni Colombini, Germanus, Joseph of Arimathea (E), Ignatius of Loyola

□ August

1   Alphonsus Liguori, Ethelwold
2   Eusebius of Vercelli, Stephen I
4   Jean-Baptiste Vianney
6   Hormisdas
7   Cajetan, Sixtus II and companions
8   Dominic
9   Matthias (G)
10 Laurence, Oswald of Northumbria
11 Clare, Susanna
13 Maximus (W), Pontian and Hippolytus, Radegunde
14 Maximilian Kolbe
15 Arnulf, Tarsicius
16 Roch, Simpliciano, Stephen of Hungary
17 Hyacinth
19 John Eudes, Sebaldus
20 Bernard, Oswin, Philibert
21 Jane Frances de Chantal, Pius X
23 Rose of Lima, Sidonius Apollinaris
24 Bartholomew (W), Ouen
25 Joseph Calasanctius, Louis IX, Menas of Constantinople
26 Blessed Dominic of the Mother of God, Zephyrinus
27 Caesarius, Monica

28 Augustine of Hippo
29 Beheading of John the Baptist, Sabina
30 Pammachius
31 Aidan, Paulinus of Trier

□ September

1   Giles, Simeon Stylites (E)
2   John the Faster (E)
3   Gregory (the Great)
4   Babylas (E), Boniface I
5   Zacharias (E)
9   Peter Claver, Sergius of Antioch
10 Finnian, Nicholas of Tolentino, Pulcheria
11 Deiniol, Ethelburga, Paphnutius
13 John Chrysostom (W)
15 Catherine of Genoa, Our Lady of Sorrows
16 Cornelius, Cyprian of Carthage, Euphemia, Ninian
17 Robert Bellarmine, Hildegard, Lambert, Satyrus
19 Januarius (W), Theodore of Tarsus
20 Agapetus or Eustace (W)
21 Matthew (W)
23 Adamnan, Linus
25 Sergius of Rostov
26 Cosmas and Damian (W), Cyprian of Antioch, John (E)
27 Frumentius (W), Vincent de Paul
28 Exuperius, Wenceslaus
29 Michael (Michaelmas Day), Gabriel and Raphael
30 Jerome, Otto

□ October

1   Remigius, Romanos, Teresa of the Child Jesus
2   Leodegar (Leger)
3   Teresa of Lisieux, Thomas de Cantilupe
4   Ammon, Francis of Assisi, Petronius
6   Bruno, Thomas (G)
9   Demetrius (W), Denis and companions, Dionysius of Paris, James (the Less) (E), John Leonardi
10 Francis Borgia, Paulinus of York
11 Atticus (E), Bruno, Nectarius

388

12 Wilfrid
13 Edward the Confessor
14 Callistus I, Cosmas Melodus (*E*)
15 Lucian of Antioch (*E*), Teresa of Avila
16 Gall, Hedwig, Lullus, Margaret Mary Alacoque
17 Ignatius of Antioch, Victor
18 Luke
19 John de Bréboeuf and Isaac Jogues and companions, Paul of the Cross, Peter of Alcántara
21 Hilarion, Ursula
22 Abercius
23 John of Capistrano
24 Anthony Claret
25 Crispin and Crispinian, Forty Martyrs of England and Wales, Gaudentius
26 Demetrius (*E*)
28 Firmilian (*E*), Simon and Jude
30 Serapion of Antioch
31 Wolfgang

❑ November
1 All Saints, Cosmas and Damian (*E*)
2 Eustace (*E*), Victorinus
3 Hubert, Malachy, Martin de Porres, Pirminius, Winifred
4 Charles Borromeo, Vitalis and Agricola
5 Elizabeth (*W*)
6 Illtyd, Leonard, Paul of Constantinople (*E*)
7 Willibrord
8 Elizabeth (*E*), Willehad
9 Simeon Metaphrastes (*E*)
10 Justus, Leo I (*W*)
11 Martin of Tours (*W*), Menas of Egypt, Theodore of Studios
12 Josaphat, Martin of Tours (*E*), Nilus the Ascetic
13 Abbo, John Chrysostom (*E*), Nicholas I
14 Dubricius, Gregory Palamas (*E*)
15 Albert the Great, Machutus
16 Edmund of Abingdon, Eucherius, Gertrude (the Great), Margaret of Scotland, Matthew (*E*)

17 Elizabeth of Hungary, Gregory Thaumaturgus, Gregory of Tours, Hugh of Lincoln
18 Odo, Romanus
19 Mechthild, Nerses
20 Edmund the Martyr
21 Gelasius
22 Cecilia
23 Amphilochius, Clement I (*W*), Columban, Felicity, Gregory of Agrigentum
25 Clement I (*E*), Mercurius, Mesrob
26 Siricius
27 Barlam and Josaphat
28 Simeon Metaphrastes
29 Cuthbert Mayne
30 Andrew, Frumentius (*G*)

❑ December
1 Eligius
2 Chromatius
3 Francis Xavier
4 Barbara, John Damascene, Osmund
5 Clement of Alexandria, Sabas
6 Nicholas
7 Ambrose
10 Miltiades
11 Damasus, Daniel
12 Jane Frances de Chantal, Spyridon (*E*), Vicelin
13 Lucy, Odilia
14 John of the Cross, Spyridon (*W*)
16 Eusebius
18 Frumentius (*C*)
20 Ignatius of Antioch (*G*)
21 Peter Canisius, Thomas
22 Anastasia (*E*), Chrysogonus (*E*)
23 John of Kanty
26 Stephen (*W*)
27 John (*W*), Fabiola, Stephen (*E*)
29 Thomas à Becket, Trophimus of Arles
31 Sylvester

Confucianism

Founded 6th-c BC in China.

Founder K'ung Fu-tse (Confucius) (c.551–c.479BC).

Sacred texts Shih Ching, Li Ching, Shu Ching, Chu'un Ch'iu, I Ching.

Beliefs The oldest school of Chinese thought, Confucianism did not begin as a religion. Confucius was concerned with the best way to behave and live in this world and was not concerned with the afterlife. He emerges as a great teacher who tried to replace the old religious observances with moral values as the basis of social and political order. He laid particular emphasis on the family as the basic unit in society and the foundation of the whole community. He believed that government was a matter of moral responsibility, not just manipulation of power.

Organization Confucianism is not an institution and has no church or clergy. However ancestor-worship and veneration of the sky have their sources in Confucian texts. Weddings and funerals follow a tradition handed down by Confucian scholars. Social life is ritualized and colour and patterns of clothes have a sacred meaning.

Divisions There are two ethical strands in Confucianism. One, associated with Confucius and Hsun Tzu (c.298–c.238BC), is conventionalistic: we ought to follow the traditional codes of behaviour for their own sake. The other, associated with Mencius (c.371–c.289BC) and medieval neo-Confucians, is intuitionistic: we ought to do as our moral natures dictate.

Major Chinese festivals

January/February	Chinese New Year
February/March	Lantern Festival
March/April	Festival of Pure Brightness
May/June	Dragon Boat Festival
July/August	Herd Boy and Weaving Maid Festival
August	All Souls' Festival
September	Mid-Autumn Festival
September/October	Double Ninth Festival
November/December	Winter Solstice

Hinduism

Founded c.1500BC by Aryan invaders of India with their Vedic religion.

Sacred texts The Vedas ('knowledge'), including the Upanishads which contains much that is esoteric and mystical. Also included are the epic poems the Ramayana and the Mahabharata. Best known of all is the Bhagavad Gita, part of the Mahabharata.

Beliefs Hinduism emphasizes the right way of living (dharma) and embraces many diverse religious beliefs and practices rather than a set of doctrines. It acknowledges many gods who are seen as manifestations of an underlying reality. Devout Hindus aim to become one with the 'absolute reality' or Brahman. Only after a completely pure life will the soul be released from the cycle of rebirth. Until then the soul will be repeatedly reborn. Samsara refers to the cycle of birth and rebirth. Karma is the law by which consequences of actions within one life are carried over into the next.

Organization There is very little formal structure. Hinduism is concerned with the realization of religious values in every part of life, yet there is a great emphasis on the performance of complex demanding rituals under the supervision of a Brahman priest and teacher. There are three categories of worship: temple, domestic and congregational. The most common ceremony is prayer (puja). Many pilgrimages take place and there is an annual cycle of festivals.

Divisions As there is no concept of orthodoxy in Hinduism, there are many different sects worshipping different gods. The three most important gods are Brahman, the primeval god, Vishnu, the preserver, and Shiva, both destroyer and creator of life. The three major living traditions are those devoted to Vishnu, Shiva and the goddess Shakti. Folk beliefs and practices exist together with sophisticated philosophical schools.

Major Hindu festivals

S = Sukla ('waxing fortnight') K = Krishna ('waning fortnight')

Chaitra	S 9	Ramanavami (Birthday of Lord Rama)
Asadha	S 2	Rathayatra (Pilgrimage of the Jagannatha Chariot at Puri)
Sravana	S 11–15	Jhulanayatra (Swinging the Lord Krishna)
Sravana	S 15	Rakshabandhana (Tying on Lucky Threads)
Bhadrapada	K 8	Janamashtami (Birthday of Lord Krishna)
Asvina	S 7–10	Durga-puja (Homage to Goddess Durga) (*Bengal*)
Asvina	S 1–10	Navaratri (Festival of Nine Nights)
Asvina	S 15	Lakshmi-puja (Homage to Goddess Lakshmi)
Asvina	K 15	Diwali, Dipavali (String of Lights)
Kartikka	S 15	Guru Nanak Jananti (Birthday of Guru Nanak)
Magha	K 5	Sarasvati-puja (Homage to Goddess Sarasvati)
Magha	K 13	Maha-sivaratri (Great Night of Lord Shiva)
Phalguna	S 14	Holi (Festival of Fire)
Phalguna	S 15	Dolayatra (Swing Festival) (*Bengal*)

Islam

Founded 7th-c AD.

Founder Mohammed (c.570–c.632).

Sacred texts The Koran, the word of God as revealed to Mohammed, and the Hadith, a collection of the prophet's sayings.

Beliefs A monotheistic religion, God is the creator of all things and holds absolute power over man. All persons should devote themselves to lives of grateful and praise-giving obedience to God as they will be judged on the Day of Resurrection. It is acknowledged that Satan often misleads humankind but those who have obeyed God or have repented of their sins will dwell in paradise. Those sinners who are unrepentant will go to hell. Muslims accept the Old Testament and acknowledge Jesus Christ as an important prophet, but they believe the perfect word of God was revealed to Mohammed. Islam imposes five pillars of faith on its followers: belief in one God and his prophet, Mohammed; salat, formal prayer preceded by ritual cleansing five times a day, facing Mecca; saum, fasting during the month of Ramadan; Hajj, pilgrimage to Mecca at least once; zakat, a religious tax on the rich to provide for the poor.

Organization There is no organized priesthood but great respect is accorded to descendants of Mohammed and holy men, scholars and teachers such as mullahs and ayatollahs. The Shari'a is the Islamic law and applies to all aspects of life, not just religious practices.

Divisions There are two main groups within Islam. The Sunni are the majority and the more orthodox. They recognize the succession from Mohammed to Abu Bakr, his father-in-law, and to the next three caliphs. The Shiites are followers of Ali, Mohammed's nephew and son-in-law. They believe in 12 imams, perfect teachers, who still guide the faithful from paradise. Shi'ah practice tends towards the ecstatic. There are many other subsects including the Sufis, the Ismailis and the Wahhabis.

Major Islamic festivals

1 Muharram	New Year's Day; starts on the day which celebrates Mohammed's departure from Mecca to Medina in AD622.
12 Rabi I	Birthday of Mohammed (Mawlid al-Nabi) AD572; celebrated throughout month of Rabi I.
27 Rajab	'Night of Ascent' (Laylat al-Miraj) of Mohammed to Heaven.
1 Ramadan	Beginning of month of fasting during daylight hours.
27 Ramadan	'Night of Power' (Laylat al-Qadr); sending down of the Koran to Mohammed.
1 Shawwal	'Feast of Breaking the Fast' (Id al-Fitr); marks the end of Ramadan.
8–13 Dhu-I-Hijja	Annual pilgrimage ceremonies at and around Mecca; month during which the great pilgrimage (Hajj) should be made.
10 Dhu-I-Hijja	Feast of the Sacrifice (Id al-Adha).

Jainism

Founded 6th-c BC in India.

Founder Vardhamana Mahavira (c.540–c.468BC).

Sacred texts Svetambara canon of scripture and Digambara texts.

Beliefs Jainism is derived from the ancient jinas ('those who overcome'). They believe that salvation consists in conquering material existence through adhering to a strict ascetic discipline, thus freeing the 'soul' from the working of karma for eternal, all-knowing bliss. Liberation requires detachment from worldly existence, an essential part of which is Ahimsa, non-injury to living beings. Jains are also strict vegetarians.

Organization Like Buddhists, the Jains are dedicated to the quest for liberation and the life of the ascetic. However, rather than congregating in monastic centres, Jain monks and nuns have developed a strong relationship with lay people. There are temple rituals resembling Hindu puja. There is also a series of lesser vows and specific religious practices that give the lay person an identifiable religious career.

Divisions There are two categories of religious and philosophical literature. The Svetambara have a canon of scripture consisting of 45 texts, including a group of 11 texts in which the sermons and dialogues of Mahavira himself are collected. The Digambara hold that the original teachings of Mahavira have been lost but that their texts preserve accurately the substance of the original message. This disagreement over scriptures has not led to fundamental doctrinal differences.

Judaism

Founded c.2000BC.

Founder Abraham (c.2000 – c.1650BC), with whom God made a covenant, and Moses (15th–13th-c BC), who gave the Israelites the law.

Sacred texts The Hebrew Bible consisting of 24 books, the most important of which are the Torah or Pentateuch — the first five books. Also the Talmud made up of the Mishna, the oral law, and the Gemara, an extensive commentary.

Beliefs A monotheistic religion, the Jews believe God is the creator of the world, delivered the Israelites out of bondage in Egypt, revealed his law to them, and chose them to be a light to all humankind. However varied their communities, Jews see themselves as members of a community whose origins lie in the patriarchal period. Ritual is very important and the family is the basic unit of ritual.

Organization Originally a theocracy, the basic institution is now the synagogue, operated by the congregation and led by a rabbi of their choice. The chief rabbis in France and Britain have authority over those who accept it; in Israel the two chief rabbis have civil authority in family law. The synagogue is the centre for community worship and study. Its main feature is the 'ark' (a cupboard) containing the handwritten scrolls of the Pentateuch. Daily life is governed by a number of practices and observances: male children are circumcised, the Sabbath is observed and food has to be correctly prepared. The most important festival is the Passover, which celebrates the liberation of the Israelites from Egypt.

Divisions Today most Jews are descendants of either the Ashkenazim or the Sephardim, each with marked cultural differences. There are also several religious branches of Judaism from ultra-liberal to ultra-conservative, reflecting different points of view regarding the binding character of the prohibitions and duties prescribed for Jews.

Major Jewish festivals

1–2 Tishri	Rosh Hashana (New Year)	15–21 Tishri	Sukkot (Feast of Tabernacles)
3 Tishri	Tzom Gedaliahu (Fast of Gedaliah)	22 Tishri	Shemini Atzeret (8th Day of the Solemn Assembly)
10 Tishri	Yom Kippur (Day of Atonement)	23 Tishri	Simchat Torah (Rejoicing of the Law)

25 Kislev to			15–22	Nisan	Pesach (Passover)
2–3 Tevet	Hanukkah (Feast of Dedication)		5	Iyar	Israel Independence Day
10 Tevet	Asara be-Tevet (Fast of 10th Tevet)		6–7	Sivan	Shavuot (Feast of Weeks)
13 Adar	Taanit Esther (Fast of Esther)		17	Tammuz	Shiva Asar be-Tammuz (Fast of 17th Tammuz)
14–15 Adar	Purim (Feast of Lots)		9	Av	Tisha be-Av (Fast of 9th Av)

Shintoism

Founded 8th-c AD in Japan.

Sacred texts Kojiki and Nihon Shoki.

Beliefs Shinto 'the teaching' or 'way of the gods', came into existence independently from Buddhism which was coming to the mainland of Japan at that time. It subsequently incorporated many features of Buddhism. Founded on the nature-worship of Japanese folk religions, it is made up of many elements; animism, veneration of nature and ancestor-worship. Its gods are known as kami and there are many ceremonies appealing to these kami for benevolent treatment and protection. Great stress is laid on the harmony between humans, their kami and nature. Moral and physical purity is a basic law. Death and other pollutions are to be avoided. Shinto is primarily concerned with life and this world and the good of the group. Followers must show devotion and sincerity but aberrations can be erased by purification procedures.

Organization As a set of prehistoric agricultural ceremonies, Shinto was never supported by a body of philosophical or moralistic literature. Shamans originally performed the ceremonies and tended the shrines, then gradually a particular tribe took over the ceremonies. In the 8th-c Shinto became political when the imperial family were ascribed divine origins and state Shintoism was established.

Divisions In the 19th-c Shinto was divided into Shrine (jinga) Shinto and Sectarian (kyoko) Shinto. Jinga became a state cult and it remained the national religion until 1945.

Major Japanese festivals

1–3 Jan	Oshogatsu (New Year)
3 Mar	Ohinamatsuri (Doll's or Girls' Festival)
5 May	Tango no Sekku (Boys' Festival)
7 Jul	Hoshi matsuri or Tanabata (Star Festival)
13–31 Jul	Obon (Buddhist All Souls)

Sikhism

Founded 15th-c in India.

Founder Guru Nanak (1469–1539).

Sacred text Adi Granth.

Beliefs Nanak preached tolerance and devotion to one God before whom everyone is equal. Sikh is the Sanskrit word for disciple. Nanak's doctrine sought a fusion of Brahmanism and Islam on the grounds that both were monotheistic. God is the true Guru and his divine word has come to humanity through the 10 historical gurus. The line ended in 1708, since when the Sikh community has been called guru.

Organization There is no priestly caste and all Sikhs are empowered to perform rituals connected with births, marriages and deaths. Sikhs worship in their own temples but they evolved distinct features like the langar, 'kitchen', a communal meal where people of any religion or caste could eat. Rest houses for travellers were also provided. The tenth guru instituted an initiation ceremony, the Khalsa. Initiates wear the Five Ks (uncut hair, steel bangle, comb, shorts, ceremonial sword) and a turban. Members of the Khalsa add the name Singh (lion) to their name and have to lead pure lives and follow a code of discipline. Sikhs generally rise before dawn, bathe and recite the japji, a morning prayer. Hindu festivals from northern India are observed.

Divisions There are several religious orders of Sikhs based either on disputes over the succession of gurus or points of ritual and tradition. The most important current issue is the number of Khalsa Sikhs cutting off their hair and beards and relapsing into Hinduism.

Taoism

Founded 600BC in China.

Founder Lao-tzu (6th-c BC).

Sacred texts Chuang-tzu, Lao-tzu (Tao-te-ching).

Beliefs Taoism is Chinese for 'the school of the tao' and the 'Taoist religion'. Tao ('the way') is central in both Confucianism and Taoism. The former stresses the tao of humanity, the latter the tao of nature, harmony with which ensures appropriate conduct. Taoist religion developed later and was probably much influenced by Buddhist beliefs. The doctrine emphasizes that good and evil action decide the fate of the soul. The Taoists believe that the sky, the earth and water are deities; that Lao-tzu is supreme master; that the disciple masters his body and puts evil spirits to flight with charms; that body and spirit are purified through meditation and by taking the pill of immortality to gain eternal life; and that the way is handed down from master to disciple. Religious Taoism incorporated ideas and images from philosophical Taoist texts, especially the Tao-te-ching but also the theory of Yin-Yang, the quest for immortality, mental and physical discipline, interior hygiene, internal alchemy, healing and exorcism, a pantheon of gods and spirits, and ideals of theocratic states. The Immortals are meant to live in the mountains far from the tumult of the world.

Organization This is similar to Buddhism in the matter of clergy and temple. The jiao is a ceremony to purify the ground. Zhon-gyual is the only important religious festival, when the hungry dead appear to the living and Taoist priests free the souls of the dead from suffering.

Divisions Religious Taoism emerged from many sects. These sects proliferated between 618 and 1126AD and were described collectively as Spirit Cloud Taoists. They form the majority of Taoist priests in Taiwan, where they are called 'Masters of Methods' or Red-headed Taoists. The more orthodox priests are called 'Tao Masters' or Black-headed Taoists.

Sacred texts of world religions

Religion and Texts

Baha'i Most Holy Book, The Seven Valleys, The Hidden Words and The Bayan

Buddhism Tripitaka, Mahayana Sutras, Milindapanha, Bardo Thodol

Christianity Old Testament: Genesis, Exodus, Leviticus, Numbers, Deuteronomy, Joshua, Judges, Ruth, 1 Samuel, 2 Samuel, 1 Kings, 2 Kings, 1 Chronicles, 2 Chronicles, Ezra, Nehemiah, Esther, Job, Psalms, Proverbs, Ecclesiastes, Song of Solomon, Isaiah, Jeremiah, Lamentations, Ezekiel, Daniel, Hosea, Joel, Amos, Obadiah, Jonah, Micah, Nahum, Habakkuk, Zephaniah, Haggai, Zechariah, Malachi. New Testament: Matthew, Mark, Luke, John, Acts of the Apostles, Romans, 1 Corinthians, 2 Corinthians, Galatians, Ephesians, Philippians, Colossians, 1 Thessalonians, 2 Thessalonians, 1 Timothy, 2 Timothy, Titus, Philemon, Hebrews, James, 1 Peter, 2 Peter, 1 John, 2 John, 3 John, Jude, Revelation. Apocrypha (Revised standard version 1957): 1 Esdras, 2 Esdras, Tobit, Judith, Additions to Esther, Wisdom of Solomon, Ecclesiasticus, Epistle of Jeremiah, Baruch, Prayer of Azariah and the Song of the Three Young Men, (History of) Susanna, Bel and the Dragon, Prayer of Manasseh, 1 Maccabees, 2 Maccabees. (The Authorized version incorporates Jeremiah into Baruch; the prayer of Azariah is simply called the Song of the Three Holy Children. The Roman Catholic Church includes Tobit, Judith, all of Esther, Maccabees 1 and 2, Wisdom of Solomon, Ecclesiasticus and Baruch in its canon.)

Confucianism Shih ching, Li ching, Shu ching, Chu'un Ch'iu, I Ching

Hinduism The Vedas (including the Upanishads), Ramayana, Mahabharata and the Bhagavad Gita

Islam The Koran, the Hadith

Jainism Svetambara canon, Digambara texts

Judaism The Hebrew Bible: Torah (Pentateuch): Genesis, Exodus, Leviticus, Numbers, Deuteronomy. Also the books of the Prophets, Psalms, Chronicles and Proverbs. The Talmud including the Mishna and Gemara. The Zohar (Book of Splendour) is a famous Cabalistic book.

Shintoism Kojiki, Nihon Shoki

Sikhism Adi Granth

Taoism Chuang-tzu, Lao-tzu (Tao-te-ching)